CISM COURSES AND LECTURES

Series Editors:

The Rectors of CISM
Sandor Kaliszky - Budapest
Mahir Sayir - Zurich
Wilhelm Schneider - Wien

The Secretary General of CISM
Giovanni Bianchi - Milan

Executive Editor
Carlo Tasso - Udine

The series presents lecture notes, monographs, edited works and
proceedings in the field of Mechanics, Engineering, Computer Science
and Applied Mathematics.
Purpose of the series is to make known in the international scientific
and technical community results obtained in some of the activities
organized by CISM, the International Centre for Mechanical Sciences.

CISM COURSES AND LECTURES

Series Editors:

The Rectors of CISM
Sandor Kaliszky - Budapest
Mahir Sayir - Zurich
Wilhelm Schneider - Wien

The Secretary General of CISM
Giovanni Bianchi - Milan

Executive Editor
Carlo Tasso - Udine

The series presents lecture notes, monographs, edited works and
proceedings in the field of Mechanics, Engineering, Computer Science
and Applied Mathematics.
Purpose of the series is to make known in the international scientific
and technical community results obtained in some of the activities
organized by CISM, the International Centre for Mechanical Sciences.

INTERNATIONAL CENTRE FOR MECHANICAL SCIENCES

COURSES AND LECTURES - No. 383

USER MODELING

PROCEEDINGS OF THE
SIXTH INTERNATIONAL CONFERENCE
UM97
CHIA LAGUNA, SARDINIA, ITALY
JUNE 2-5 1997

EDITED BY

A. JAMESON
UNIVERSITY OF SAARBRÜCKEN

C. PARIS
CSIRO AUSTRALIA

C. TASSO
UNIVERSITY OF UDINE

Springer-Verlag Wien GmbH

Le spese di stampa di questo volume sono in parte coperte da
contributi del Consiglio Nazionale delle Ricerche.

This volume contains 108 illustrations

ISBN 978-3-211-82906-6   ISBN 978-3-7091-2670-7 (eBook)
DOI 10.1007/978-3-7091-2670-7
© 1997 by Springer-Verlag Wien
Originally published by CISM, Udine in 1997.

In order to make this volume available as economically and as
rapidly as possible the authors' typescripts have been
reproduced in their original forms. This method unfortunately
has its typographical limitations but it is hoped that they in no
way distract the reader.

ISSN 1091-2789 User Modeling Inc.

Preface

User modeling researchers look for ways of enabling interactive software systems to adapt to their users—by constructing, maintaining, and exploiting *user models*, which are representations of properties of individual users. User modeling has been found to enhance the effectiveness and/or usability of software systems in a wide variety of situations.

Techniques for user modeling have been developed and evaluated by researchers in a number of fields, including artificial intelligence, education, psychology, linguistics, human-computer interaction, and information science. The biennial series of International Conferences on User Modeling provides a forum in which academic and industrial researchers from all of these fields can exchange their complementary insights on user modeling issues. The published proceedings of these conferences represent a major source of information about developments in this area.

This volume contains the papers that were presented at the Sixth International Conference on User Modeling, UM97, which was was held at Chia Laguna, Sardinia, from June 2nd through 5th, 1997.[1]

For the main technical program, 96 submissions were received from 18 countries in five continents. The reviewing of a submission was done by at least two members of the UM97 program committee. Where necessary, discussion among reviewers and/or additional reviews were arranged. Because of the large number of manuscripts that received favorable reviews, the selection criteria were stringent. Several presentations were accepted conditionally and reviewed a second time. Ultimately, 28 submissions were accepted for presentation as full papers.

This volume also includes summaries of the following contributions to UM97:

- the fifteen poster presentations, which served as a basis for the discussion of ongoing research;
- the two invited talks, by Eric Horvitz and Constantine Stephanidis, which highlighted important recent paradigms in user modeling; and
- the six presentations at the doctoral consortium, at which PhD students received feedback on their research from experienced colleagues.

All of the contributing authors participated in an editing procedure for the final manuscripts that was designed to maximize the clarity and stylistic consistency of this volume within the given time constraints.

A look at the Table of Contents will show that these contributions represent many different approaches to user modeling research, including some novel types of application. The papers and the poster summaries are organized in sections of the book according to the nature of the user modeling application that they address. The Reader's Guide points to some of the further relationships among these contributions.

---

[1] The two preceding conferences in this series, UM94 and UM96, were held in Hyannis, Massachusetts, in August 1994, and Kailua-Kona, Hawaii, in January 1996, respectively. Further information about the earlier conferences and their proceedings volumes can be found on the World Wide Web site of User Modeling, Inc.: http://um.org.

Three quite different approaches to user modeling are represented by the papers that were selected by the program committee as recipients of Kluwer Academic Publishers' Distinguished Paper award:

- *Inspectable User Models for Just-In-Time Workplace Training,* by Jason A. Collins, Jim E. Greer, Vive S. Kumar, Gordon I. McCalla, Paul Meagher, and Ray Tkatch;
- *On-Line Student Modeling for Coached Problem Solving Using Bayesian Networks* by Cristina Conati, Abigail S. Gertner, Kurt VanLehn, and Marek J. Druzdzel; and
- *Levels of Expertise and User-Adapted Formats of Instructional Presentations: A Cognitive Load Approach,* by Slava Kalyuga, Paul Chandler, and John Sweller.

In addition to the contributions that are represented in this volume, UM97 featured two tutorials:

- *User Modeling in Information Retrieval,* presented by Nicholas J. Belkin; and
- *Student Modeling: Cognitive Psychology Meets Eduction,* presented by Albert T. Corbett.

Another major part of UM97 were the six workshops, whose separate proceedings can be accessed via the Web site of User Modeling, Inc.:

- *Adaptive Systems and User Modeling on the World Wide Web,* organized by Peter Brusilovsky, Josef Fink, and Judy Kay;
- *Advances in Languages for User Modeling,* organized by Stefano A. Cerri and Vincenzo Loia;
- *Embedding User Models in Intelligent Applications,* organized by Vadim L. Stefanuk;
- *Machine Learning for User Modeling,* organized by Mathias Bauer, Wolfgang Pohl, and Geoff Webb;
- *User-Adapted Multimedia Documentation in Industry,* organized by Alessandro Mura, Pietro Carratu, and Loredana De Dominicis; and
- *User Models in the Real World,* organized by Judy Kay and Gerhard Fischer.

We trust that, because of all of the efforts mentioned above and in the Acknowledgements that follow, the present volume will long remain a valuable resource for those who are interested in user modeling. We wish you an enjoyable and profitable reading experience.

A. Jameson
C. Paris
C. Tasso

Acknowledgements

The success of the Sixth International Conference on User Modeling depended on a large number of people who deserve our warmest thanks. In particular, we would like to thank the members of the program committee for their considerable effort in reviewing the submissions and selecting the invited speakers and the winners of the Distinguished Paper award.

Nicholas J. Belkin	Eric Horvitz	Robert J. Mislevy
Béatrice Cahour	Judy Kay	Riichiro Mizoguchi
Sandra Carberry	Alfred Kobsa	Edie M. Rasmussen
Albert Corbett	Diane Litman	John Self
Fiorella de Rosis	Pattie Maes	Julita Vassileva
Oren Etzioni	Uwe Malinowski	Wolfgang Wahlster
Gerhard Fischer	Gordon McCalla	Geoff Webb
Helen M. Gigley	Michael McTear	Ingrid Zukerman
Brad Goodman	Alessandro Micarelli	

We would also like to thank the following external reviewers, who provided additional expertise in the reviewing of the submissions:

David Albrecht	Mitsuru Ikeda	Michael Pieper
James Ambach	Philippe Laredo	Alexander Repenning
Patrick Boylan	Henry Lieberman	Jörg Schreck
Stefano A. Cerri	Stefanie Lindstaedt	Filippo Sciarrone
Berardina Nadja De Carolis	Weiru Liu	Giuseppe Sindoni
Hal Eden	Alexandros Moukas	Gerry Stahl
Tsukasa Hirashima	Jonathan Ostwald	Riccardo Torlone
Jun Hong	Corrina Perrone	

Submissions to the doctoral consortium were reviewed by the following committee chaired by Berardina Nadja De Carolis and Fiorella de Rosis:

Béatrice Cahour	Frank Linton	Cécile Paris
Eric Horvitz	Diane Litman	Linda Strachan
Judy Kay	Uwe Malinowski	Julita Vassileva
Alfred Kobsa	Susanne van Mulken	Ingrid Zukerman

Significant contributions to the conference were likewise made by the workshop organizers:

Mathias Bauer	Josef Fink	Alessandro Mura
Peter Brusilovsky	Gerhard Fischer	Wolfgang Pohl
Pietro Carratú	Judy Kay	Vadim L. Stefanuk
Stefano A. Cerri	Vincenzo Loia	Geoff Webb
Loredana De Dominicis		

In addition, we extend our thanks to:

- Alessandro Micarelli for managing the local organization;
- Riccardo Scateni for maintaining the mirror Web site in Sardinia;
- Christoph G. Thomas for coordinating the workshops;
- Giorgio Brajnik for organizing the system demonstrations;
- the members of the AI Lab at the University of Saarbrücken for supporting the editing process;
- Nicholas J. Belkin and Albert T. Corbett for preparing tutorials; and
- Eric Horvitz and Constantine Stephanidis for presenting invited talks.

UM97 was organized jointly by the Department of Mathematics and Computer Science of the University of Udine, the Department of Scientific Disciplines of the University of Rome 3, the Department of Informatics of the University of Bari, and CRS4 (Center for Advanced Studies, Research and Development in Sardinia), under the auspices of User Modeling, Inc.

Generous support was provided by AI*IA, the Italian Association for Artificial Intelligence; CISM, the International Centre for Mechanical Sciences; and Kluwer Academic Publishers, who sponsored the Distinguished Paper award.

CONTENTS

INFORMATION PRESENTATION

INTERFACE ADAPTION

AUTHOR INFORMATION

Reader's Guide

There are several questions that can be asked about virtually any instance of user modeling research. One way of bringing to light the relationships among the papers and poster summaries in this volume is to compare the corresponding answers to these questions, in all cases in which the questions are applicable.

The following six tables address the following questions in turn, assuming that in each case considered, user modeling techniques are being investigated that are intended to enable some system S to adapt to each individual user U.

1. Purposes of user modeling
   In what way is S's adaptation to U intended to be beneficial to U? The organization of the contributions in the Table of Contents is likewise based on this question, but Table 1 takes advantage of the opportunity to list a given contribution more than once.
2. Content of the user model
   What sort of information about U is represented in S's user model?
3. Methods for exploiting the user model
   According to what principles or inference techniques does S decide how to adapt its behavior on the basis of the information in its user model?
4. Input data for user model construction
   On the basis of what types of evidence does S construct its user model?
5. Methods for constructing the user model
   According to what principles or inference techniques does S arrive at the hypotheses about U that are stored in the user model?
6. Empirical foundations
   What sorts of empirical data give us reason to believe that S's methods are valid and useful?

In each citation in the tables, the number given after the name(s) of the author(s) is the first page of the paper or poster summary in question

Table 1. Purposes of user modeling.

***

Help *U* to find information
Remind *U* of previous Web navigation paths (Maglio and Barrett, 5)
Recommend Web pages (Akoulchina and Ganascia, 21)
Implicitly recommend Web hyperlinks (Gori et al., 17)
Recommend potentially suitable existing solutions to a problem (e.g., airplane flights) (Linden et al., 67)
Select documents of interest to *U* (Benaki et al., 55)
Adapt hypertext links and recommendations to *U*'s previous navigation behavior (Staff, 33)
Adapt hypertext navigation mode to *U*'s knowledge (De Carolis and Pizzutilo, 37)
Filter WWW documents in accordance with *U*'s interests (Ambrosini et al., 59)

Tailor information presentation to *U*
Adapt appearance of charts to *U*'s abilities and preferences (Gutkauf et al., 159)
Choose appropriate form of presentation with text and/or diagrams (Kalyuga et al., 261)
Take into account *U*'s available working memory capacity (Schäfer and Weyrath, 377)
Adapt comparisons in text to *U*'s knowledge (Milosavljevic, 119)
Tailor arguments to *U*'s beliefs and values (Grasso, 83)
Adapt hypermedia presentations to *U*'s interests and knowledge (De Carolis and Pizzutilo, 37; Fink et al., 171)
Adapt health-education documents to individual patients (Hirst et al., 107)
Present decision-supporting information according to *U*'s personality and preferences (Paranagama et al., 79)
Adapt handling of incorrect answers to the student's preferences (Murphy and McTear, 301)

Adapt an interface to *U*
Offer Web navigation shortcuts (Maglio and Barrett, 5)
Facilitate selection of presumably relevant Web hyperlinks (Gori et al., 17)
Adapt interface features and hints to *U*'s familiarity with *S* (Brusilovsky and Schwarz, 177)
Add tailored hypermedia links that reflect past accesses (Maglio and Barrett, 5)
Translate high-level visualization preferences into concrete camera control actions (Bares and Lester, 215)
Recommend settings for technical devices (Doux et al., 359)
Recommend keyboard adaptations for users with disabilities (Trewin and Pain, 135)
Adapt a hypermedia interface to *U*'s disabilities (Fink et al., 171)
Suggest corrections of (idiosyncratic) spelling errors of dyslexic users (Spooner and Edwards, 147)
Offer a suitable next move after an unexpected, ambiguous dialog act (Stein et al., 89)
Provide special support and interface simplifications for novice users (Strachan et al., 189)

Choose suitable instructional exercises or interventions
Choose math exercises taking into account *U*'s subskill proficiencies (Beck et al., 277)
Generate medical cases of an appropriate difficulty level (Carberry and Clarke, 273)
Select suitable language exercises (Murphy and McTear, 301)
Guide *U* toward suitable instructional Web pages (Weber and Specht, 289)
Present instructional examples from *U*'s own learning history (Weber and Specht, 289)
Tailor instructional interventions to *U*'s state of knowledge (Conati et al., 231)
Take into account changes in a student's beliefs (Giangrandi and Tasso, 415)
Derive a differentiated assessment of a trainee's problem solving skills (Moinard and Joab, 255)
Support mastery learning by tracing the development of *U*'s knowledge (Corbett and Bhatnagar, 243)

Give *U* feedback about *U*'s knowledge
Provide to students feedback on their strengths and weaknesses in foreign language writing (Bull, 315)

(continued)

Table 1. (continued)

Support collaboration
   Select appropriate collaborators (or help U to do so) and facilitate communication between
   collaborators (Collins et al., 327)
   Recommend specific forms of collaboration between students (Bull and Smith, 339)

Predict U's future behavior
   Predict correct and incorrect answers of a student (Chiu et al., 347)
   Predict goals, actions, and locations of an agent in a large domain (Albrecht et al., 365)

[Other functions]
   Verify U's competence to add information to S (Akoulchina and Ganascia, 21)
   Take into account U's cooperativeness, sincerity, and credulity (Quaresma and Lopes, 101)
   Anticipate other agents' actions so as to coordinate with them (Noh and Gmytrasiewicz, 389)
   Enable U to write and debug programs using high-level concepts that U finds natural (Seta et al., 203)
   Support various types of adaptation with a general user modeling shell system (Pohl and Höhle, 403)
   Take into account factors such as U's relationship with S and the importance of U's goals. (Vassileva,
   433)

Table 2. Content of the user model.

U's preferences, interests, attitudes, and goals
   Preferences concerning possible solutions to a problem (Linden et al., 67)
   Weights of decision-relevant attributes (Paranagama et al., 79)
   Payoff matrices that underlie U's behavior (Noh and Gmytrasiewicz, 389)
   User-specific low-level parameters concerning camera control (Bares and Lester, 215)
   Preferences concerning aspects of charts (Gutkauf et al., 159)
   Preferences concerning the modality of hypermedia-presented information (Fink et al., 171)
   Preferences and attitudes concerning aspects of language learning (Murphy and McTear, 301)
   Context of current hypertext node, which reflects U's interests (Staff, 33)
   U's interests with respect to information on the WWW (Ambrosini et al., 59)
   Goals of U's Web searches (Akoulchina and Ganascia, 21)
   General goals motivating U's use of a hypermedia system (Fink et al., 171)
   Problem solving strategy currently pursued by U (Conati et al., 231)
   Attitudes concerning medical issues (Grasso, 83; Hirst et al., 107)
   Cooperativeness, sincerity, and credulity; and specific goals (Quaresma and Lopes, 101)

Specific aspects of U's knowledge and beliefs
   Knowledge concerning features of a complex interface (Brusilovsky and Schwarz, 177)
   Knowledge of particular concepts in instructional material (Weber and Specht, 289)
   A student's strengths and weaknesses in a subject area (qualitatively and quantitatively assessed) (Bull,
   315)
   A student's knowledge of particular problem-solving rules (Conati et al., 231; Corbett and Bhatnagar,
   243; Chiu et al., 347)
   Ability to perform specific steps of a task (Collins et al., 327)
   Characterization of skills at the *operational*, *tactical*, and *strategic* levels. (Moinard and Joab, 255)
   Proneness to and causes of particular language errors (Murphy and McTear, 301)
   Rules that underlie U's incorrect spelling behavior (Spooner and Edwards, 147)
   U's knowledge of domain concepts relevant to a hypermedia presentation (Milosavljevic, 119; Fink et
   al., 171)
   U's overall familiarity with the subject matter of a hypertext (De Carolis and Pizzutilo, 37)

(continued)

Table 2. (continued)

U's factual beliefs about medical issues (Grasso, 83)
Dialog-relevant factual beliefs (Quaresma and Lopes, 101)
Beliefs held during particular (underspecified) time intervals (Giangrandi and Tasso, 415)

U's proficiencies
Mastery of particular math subskills (Beck et al., 277)
Command of the declarative knowledge relevant to problem solving (Corbett and Bhatnagar, 243)
Proficiency with respect to the target language and the domain (Murphy and McTear, 301)
Level of domain expertise (Kalyuga et al., 261)
A medical student's level of diagnostic expertise (Carberry and Clarke, 273)
Rates at which U learns and forgets instructional content, respectively (Beck et al., 277)
Ability to handle particular topics individually and in collaboration (Bull and Smith, 339)
Competence in dealing with computers and with a specific hypermedia system (Fink et al., 171)
Proficiency in the task domain and in the use of S (Strachan et al., 189)
U's domain expertise and theoretical orientation (Akoulchina and Ganascia, 21)
U's familiarity with emergency situations (Schäfer and Weyrath, 377)

U's noncognitive abilities
Visual perceptual abilities; mental rotation ability (Gutkauf et al., 159)
Perceptual and motor abilities relevant to both computer use and real-world activities (Fink et al., 171)

Personal characteristics
Location, job title, etc., of potential collaborators (Collins et al., 327)
Personal characteristics recorded in U's medical record (Hirst et al., 107)
Level of education, age, etc. (De Carolis and Pizzutilo, 37; Murphy and McTear, 301)
Personality type (Paranagama et al., 79)

History of U's interaction with S
Aspects of U's keyboard use (Trewin and Pain, 135)
U's WWW navigation history (Maglio and Barrett, 5; Gori et al., 17; Weber and Specht, 289)
History of interaction with hypermedia system (Milosavljevic, 119)
History of dialog acts (Stein et al., 89)
U's use of interface features and reading of hints about them (Brusilovsky and Schwarz, 177)
U's execution of specific steps in the current task (Collins et al., 327)
Observed actions and locations of U within a large domain (Albrecht et al., 365)

[Other types of content]
Assignment to one of a set of classes of similar users of technical devices (Doux et al., 359)
Available working memory capacity, emotional state, etc. (Schäfer and Weyrath, 377)
U's higher-order beliefs about the system's payoffs and beliefs (Noh and Gmytrasiewicz, 389)
U's goal priorities, emotions, moods, and relationship with S (Vassileva, 433)
A *task ontology* that is suited to U's way of thinking (Seta et al., 203)

Table 3. Methods for exploiting the user model.

___

Decision-theoretic methods
  Quantitative evaluation of possible solutions according to *U*'s preferences (Linden et al., 67; Paranagama et al., 79)
  Recursive Modeling Method for predicting another agent's actions (Noh and Gmytrasiewicz, 389)

Logic-based techniques
  Abduction (Stein et al., 89)
  Logic programming (Quaresma and Lopes, 101)
  Various inference techniques within a modal logic framework (Pohl and Höhle, 403)

Bayesian methods
  Probabilistic prediction of rule mastery on the basis of past performance and level of declarative knowledge (Corbett and Bhatnagar, 243)
  Use of Bayesian networks to predict a student's problem solving behavior (Conati et al., 231)
  Dynamic Bayesian Networks for prediction of temporally variable actions and properties of *U* (Albrecht et al., 365; Schäfer and Weyrath, 377)

Machine learning techniques
  Use of Input-Output Agent Modeling to predict a student's responses (Chiu et al., 347)
  Use of neural networks to predict *U*'s interest in Web pages (Gori et al., 17)
  Use of K-Means classification technique to find a behavior close to the one that *U* would choose (Doux et al., 359)

Other general techniques and principles
  General techniques for the sequencing of instructional material (Brusilovsky and Schwarz, 177)
  General search techniques and heuristics (Spooner and Edwards, 147)
  Use of semantic networks to assess the relevance of documents to *U*'s interests (Ambrosini et al., 59)
  Episodic learner modeling for retrieval of suitable instructional examples (Weber and Specht, 289)
  Formalization of rhetorical techniques (Grasso, 83)
  Hypertext architecture in which context is taken into account (Staff, 33)
  Techniques for executing and tracing conceptual-level programs (Seta et al., 203)

Application-specific computational procedures
  Computations concerning potentially interesting Web pages (Akoulchina and Ganascia, 21)
  Algebraic technique for choosing suitable math exercises (Beck et al., 277)
  Quantitative criteria for determining keyboard adaptation recommendations (Trewin and Pain, 135)

Application-specific qualitative rules and procedures
  Method for processing a history of Web page visits (Maglio and Barrett, 5)
  Criteria for recommending the next instructional Web page to visit (Weber and Specht, 289)
  Rules for providing a simpler interface and more support to novice users (Strachan et al., 189)
  Rules for adapting hypermedia presentations to various properties of users (Fink et al., 171)
  Rules linking user properties with hypertext generation parameters (De Carolis and Pizzutilo, 37)
  Hypertext search techniques that take context into account (Staff, 33)
  Rules for taking into account preferences and abilities relevant to chart design (Gutkauf et al., 159)
  Provision for queries to *U*'s medical record in an authoring environment (Hirst et al., 107)
  Rules based on empirically determined relationships between domain expertise and appropriate presentation format (Kalyuga et al., 261)
  Rules for selecting comparisons to be used in text generation (Milosavljevic, 119)
  Principles for generating cases of particular difficulty levels (Carberry and Clarke, 273)
  Procedure for matching requests for help with profiles of potential collaborators (Collins et al., 327)
  Rules for recommending forms of collaboration between students (Bull and Smith, 339)

Interface techniques for communicating about the user model
  Techniques for making the student model inspectable and eliciting feedback on it (Bull, 315)
  Techniques for presenting relevant parts of a user model to potential collaborators (Collins et al., 327)

___

Table 4. Input data for user model construction.

Explicitly stated preferences, goals, etc.
Critiques of proposed solutions (Linden et al., 67; Paranagama et al., 79; Gutkauf et al., 159)
High-level visualization preferences (Bares and Lester, 215)
Interest in particular topics dealt with by documents (Benaki et al., 55)
Preferences and goals concerning hypermedia presentations (Fink et al., 171)
Explicit selection of hypertext *contexts* (Staff, 33)
Preferences and attitudes concerning aspects of language learning (Murphy and McTear, 301)

Explicitly elicited information on personal characteristics
Information about personal characteristics related to hypermedia use (Fink et al., 171)
Job title, level of education, etc. (Strachan et al., 189; Murphy and McTear, 301; Collins et al., 327)

Self-assessments
Self-assessments of domain and system competence (De Carolis and Pizzutilo, 37; Strachan et al., 189)
Self-assessments of language proficiencies and motivation (Murphy and McTear, 301)
Self-reports on the successful completion of specific subtasks (Collins et al., 327)
Self-reports on disabilities (Fink et al., 171)

Specific actions of the user
History of dialog acts (Stein et al., 89)
U's actions and locations within a large domain (Albrecht et al., 365)
U's use of interface features and reading of hints about them (Brusilovsky and Schwarz, 177)
Hypermedia pages that U has visited (Maglio and Barrett, 5; Gori et al., 17; Akoulchina and Ganascia, 21; Staff, 33; Milosavljevic, 119; Weber and Specht, 289)
U's misspellings and ultimately chosen corrections (Spooner and Edwards, 147)
Aspects of disabled users' keyboard use (Trewin and Pain, 135)
Previous handling of instructional examples by U (Weber and Specht, 289)
Dialog actions in use of a hypermedia system (Fink et al., 171)
Performance of particular tasks (Strachan et al., 189)
Choices of device settings in various environments (Doux et al., 359)
Aspects of behavior that reflect available working memory capacity (Schäfer and Weyrath, 377)

Responses to test or practice items
Responses to game-like ability tests (Gutkauf et al., 159)
Answers to test questions handled individually or in collaboration (Bull and Smith, 339)
Answers to math problems; nature of hints required before answering (Beck et al., 277)
Answers to test items in a tutoring system (Weber and Specht, 289)
Handling of previously presented medical cases (Carberry and Clarke, 273)
Performance on language test items (Murphy and McTear, 301)
Answers to test questions (Akoulchina and Ganascia, 21)
Answers to subtraction problems (Chiu et al., 347)
Observable steps in a student's problem solving (Conati et al., 231)
Performance of a student when given an opportunity to apply a given production rule (Corbett and Bhatnagar, 243)
Problem-solving actions within a training system (Moinard and Joab, 255)
Student actions or utterances that imply possession of a particular belief at a given time (Giangrandi and Tasso, 415)
Expressed interest in sample documents (Benaki et al., 55)

Other types of input
Explicit assessments of U by a human instructor (Bull, 315)
U's medical record (Hirst et al., 107)
Behavior with technical devices in various environments (Doux et al., 359)
Student's performance on tests of declarative knowledge (Corbett and Bhatnagar, 243)

Table 5. Methods for constructing the user model.

Bayesian methods

Bayesian procedure for computing probabilities that production rules are known (Corbett and Bhatnagar, 243)

Bayesian networks for inferences about unobservable aspects of a student's problem solving (Conati et al., 231)

Dynamic Bayesian networks for inferences about unobservable temporally variable properties (Schäfer and Weyrath, 377)

Machine learning techniques

Use of Input-Output Agent Modeling to derive a theory of a student's subtraction knowledge (Chiu et al., 347)

Use of neural networks to adapt the system's profile of a decision maker (Paranagama et al., 79)

Neural networks as an alternative technique for triggering stereotypes (Ambrosini et al., 59)

Use of recurrent neural networks to summarize U's Web navigation behavior (Gori et al., 17)

Use of a variant of the K-Means algorithm to classify users (Doux et al., 359)

Decision-theoretic techniques

Principled method for elicitation and interpretation of critiques of proposed solutions (Linden et al., 67)

Stereotype-based techniques

Ascription of properties associated with types of hypermedia users (Fink et al., 171)

Ascription of WWW-related interests on the basis of user stereotypes (Ambrosini et al., 59)

Derivation of initial proficiency estimates on the basis of U's overall level of advancement (Murphy and McTear, 301)

Logic-based techniques

Various inference techniques within a modal logic framework (Pohl and Höhle, 403)

Algorithms for making (nonmonotonic) inferences about beliefs held in particular time intervals (Giangrandi and Tasso, 415)

Application-specific procedures for interpreting responses to test items

Procedures for the interpretation of perceptual ability tests (Gutkauf et al., 159)

Principle for inferring knowledge of concepts that are prerequisites for known concepts (Weber and Specht, 289)

Procedure for assessing U's domain expertise on the basis of U's answers to test questions (Akoulchina and Ganascia, 21)

Calculus for updating assessments of U's subskill proficiencies (Beck et al., 277)

Computational procedures for estimating proficiencies and error-pronenesses (Murphy and McTear, 301)

Procedures for summarizing results of tests taken individually and in collaboration (Bull and Smith, 339)

Algorithm for generalizing the human instructor's assessments of U's strengths and weaknesses (Bull, 315)

Computation of declarative knowledge factor scores (Corbett and Bhatnagar, 243)

Comparison of a trainee's actions with those of an expert problem solving module (Moinard and Joab, 255)

Other application-specific computations

Updating of weights of incorrect spelling rules (Spooner and Edwards, 147)

Algorithm for updating assessments of system-related proficiency (Strachan et al., 189)

Application-specific qualitative rules

Principles for inferring knowledge on the basis of dialog acts (Fink et al., 171)

Rules for deriving low-level camera directives from visualization preferences (Bares and Lester, 215)

Table 6. Empirical foundations.

Knowledge acquisition from domain experts
Judgments of an expert surgeon concerning factors that influence the difficulty of medical cases (Carberry and Clarke, 273)
Retrospective thinking-aloud study of inferences by firemen about emergency callers (Schäfer and Weyrath, 377)

Empirical studies conducted prior to system design
Study of relationships between personality variables and decision making behavior (Paranagama et al., 79)
Observation of Web navigation behavior (Maglio and Barrett, 5)
Experiments on relationships between expertise, presentation format, and comprehension by users (Kalyuga et al., 261)
Derivation of conditional probability distributions for a Bayesian network from a database of observations (Albrecht et al., 365)
Assessment of accuracy of knowledge tracing predictions that do not take declarative knowledge into account (Corbett and Bhatnagar, 243)

Experience with real use of the system
Responses to a flight recommendation system by Web users (Linden et al., 67)

Informal responses by early users
Students' comments on an inspectable student model (Bull, 315)
Learners' responses to a commercial adaptive CALL system (Murphy and McTear, 301)
Users' responses to a conceptual-level programming environment (Seta et al., 203)

Empirical evaluations of systems
Comparative evaluation of two systems' success in analyzing students' performance on subtraction problems (Chiu et al., 347)
Comparison of the Recursive Modeling Method with simpler methods and with human performance (Noh and Gmytrasiewicz, 389)
Evaluation of a technique's performance on real and simulated data (Doux et al., 359)
Assessment of accuracy of knowledge tracing predictions that take declarative knowledge into account (Corbett and Bhatnagar, 243)
Ratings of 3D visualizations produced on the basis of stated visualization preferences (Bares and Lester, 215)
Assessment of the appropriateness of keyboard adaptation recommendations (Trewin and Pain, 135)
Study of relationships among models of spelling behavior of different dyslexic writers (Spooner and Edwards, 147)
Evaluation of use of an adaptive chart-editing system (Gutkauf et al., 159)
Study of effects of navigation support on students' motivation and the efficiency of their Web navigation (Weber and Specht, 289)
Formative evaluation of a math tutoring system (Beck et al., 277)
Rating of adaptive and nonadaptive versions of a system by real users (Strachan et al., 189)
Study of the feasability of the use of approximative inference algorithms (Conati et al., 231)
Assessment by users of the relevance of documents supplied by an information filtering system (Ambrosini et al., 59)

INFORMATION RETRIEVAL

Hypermedia Navigation

How to Build Modeling Agents to Support Web Searchers

Paul P. Maglio and Rob Barrett

IBM Almaden Research Center, San Jose, CA, USA

Abstract. In this paper, we sketch a model of what people do when they search for information on the web. From a theoretical perspective, our interest lies in the cognitive processes and internal representations that are both used in and affected by the search for information. From a practical perspective, our aim is to provide personal support for information-searching and to effectively transfer knowledge gained by one person to another. Toward these ends, we first collected behavioral data from people searching for information on the web; we next analyzed these data to learn what the searchers were doing and thinking; and we then constructed specific web agents to support searching behaviors we identified.

1 Introduction

The World Wide Web connects tens of millions of people with hundreds of millions of pages of information. The web's explosive growth, its simple means for authoring, and its simple means of access have combined to make it a place many people now rely on to find information on almost any topic. Yet people trying to use the vast resources of the web to answer particular questions often face substantial problems in locating information. For example, one question we encountered recently was, "What percentage of calories from fat do French fries contain?" We observed a person search the web for this information for more than 30 minutes before giving up. What influences a searcher's success or failure? Such questions are only now starting to be explored for the web and for other online information sources (Marchionini, 1995).

In this paper, we consider the problem of building agents to facilitate a person's search for information on the web. From a theoretical perspective, our interest lies in the cognitive processes and internal representations that are both used in and affected by the search for information. From a practical perspective, our aim is to construct personal supports for information-searching and to enable transfer of knowledge gained by one person to another. In the end, we describe mechanisms for building user models to support web searching. We rely on data gathered from observing the behavior of experienced web users searching for specific information on the web. Our observations suggest that (a) individuals repeat the same search patterns, and that they recall their searches in terms of their standard patterns—almost regardless of what they actually did; and (b) people focus on key nodes when recalling their searches, and that these structure memory for the searches. To assist searchers, we built two personal web agents: the first, to identify repeated search patterns and to suggest similar patterns for new searches; and the second, to identify key nodes in finding a piece of information and to maintain personal trails in terms of these. The agents were constructed using the Web Browser Intelligence toolkit (WBI, pronounced "WEB-ee"; see Barrett et al., 1997a). WBI provides a way to tap into the data flowing between a web browser and the web, enabling construction of agents that monitor user behavior, model user behavior, modify what the user sees, and add new user functions to the web.

This paper is organized in four parts. First, we sketch our data collection method. Second, we present data collected from several people searching the web for specific information. Third, we discuss the construction of user modeling agents to assist web searchers, outline the WBI architecture for building web agents, and detail the specific agents we constructed. Finally, we summarize our results and discuss future directions.

2 How Data Were Collected

Seven experienced web users, five males and two females, each reporting more than two year years of almost daily web use, participated in this study. They were instructed to find the answers to three questions:

1. Does the University of Western Ontario offer a Master's degree in psychology?
2. What are three drugs currently being tested to help Alzheimer's patients?
3. In how many U.S. states was Ralph Nader on the ballot for president in 1996?

These questions were chosen to represent three kinds of searches. The first one has a reasonably well defined target location: web page about the psychology program at the University of Western Ontario. In this case, it is merely a matter of finding that location. The second question is less well defined; answers might be found in recent news, in medical information, or in Alzheimer's specific sites. Moreover, a full answer might require finding several sites. The third question could be answered using U. S. election results, state by state results, federal election commission information, or Nader-specific web sites.

Questions were presented one at a time. The participant was then asked how he or she was going to obtain the information from the web, that is, to verbally provide a rough plan of attack. Next, the participant used the web to try to find the information (for up to 15 minutes). Each participant returned the following day and was presented again with the same three questions in the same order. In this case, however, the task was to first verbally recall what he or she had done the previous day in searching for the answers to each question, and then to retrace the steps by performing the same search using the web. Note that participants were not told on the first day that recall of the details of their searches would be required on the second day.

We analyzed the data by comparing each search path generated by an individual participant on the first day with the one generated on second day. In addition, we examined how the verbal reports of search plans on the first day and the verbal recall of the searches on the second day corresponded to what was actually done.

3 How People Search the Web

Each of the seven participants completed at least one of the searches on both days, but only two completed all three searches. Of the possible 21 (7 × 3) searches, 15 were completed on both days. Only three of these 15 were repeated identically on the second day. In what follows, we consider mainly the 15 completed searches. We sketch our data and analyses to argue that (a) people conceptualize their searches in terms of standard routines for searching, and (b) they remember only key nodes when recalling their searches.

3.1 Searchers Rely on Routines

Our data suggest that individuals rely on personal routines when trying to find information. For instance, some participants routinely used a particular search engine, such as AltaVista, whereas others routinely used a particular hierarchical catalog, such as Yahoo! The point is not that our searchers merely preferred to use one approach over another; rather, we believe that they *conceptualized* their search tasks in terms of their favorite routines. We believe this because it often did not matter what was actually done on the first day, our searchers remembered searching *as if* their personal routines had been followed.

More precisely, our data show that (a) each individual has a standard pattern of search behavior; and (b) when an individual deviates from the standard pattern, he or she recalls the search as fitting the standard pattern. For example, participant T usually queried the AltaVista search engine to find likely starting points. She used AltaVista in all three of her searches the first day. For the Ralph Nader question, however, T began with the Yahoo! catalog instead. It turned out that Yahoo! did not provide easy access to good candidates, and so T wound up using AltaVista in the end anyway. The next day, when asked what steps she had followed for that search, she did not mention Yahoo!, and when retracing her steps, she did not go to Yahoo! (see Figure 1). Yet at other times, T was very concerned with following as many of the first day's dead ends on the second day as she could find. In this case, T's use of Yahoo! was forgotten, presumably because Yahoo! was not her standard pattern of behavior.

To take another example, participant D recalled one of his searches as fitting his standard routine when in fact it had not. For the Ralph Nader question, D carefully retraced his first 11 steps on the second day, including several that took him down a dead end path (see Figure 2). On the second day, however, D finished his search by using AltaVista—which he stated was his standard routine, and which he used for the other two searches—though he did not use AltaVista for this search on the first day. Even D's verbal recall of the first day's search was inaccurate:

> I started at the Mercury News and I looked for election information, and it was a dead end because all of the links were not as current ... they give results and not ballot information. So then I went to Yahoo! for election information ... and then went to AltaVista to search for Ralph Nader and Green.

Thus, it was not merely that D could not find the same set of links from Yahoo! that he found the first day (see Figure 2), he remembered his search as fitting his standard routine. Unlike the case previously described for participant T, in which non-standard paths were omitted during recall, in this case participant D *added* his standard routine during recall.

All participants relied on their own standard routines, such as searching for starting points using AltaVista or using Yahoo! More importantly, on the second day, *five of the seven added a routine or deleted a non-routine pattern* in the ways we have just illustrated. Thus, because personal routines play an important role in how people remember their searches, we conjecture that such routines form the basis for how people conceptualize searching.

3.2 Searchers Rely on Waypoints

In addition to the use of personal routines, a second observation that emerged from the behavioral data is that participants recalled and relied on only a few of the sites they visited. For instance,

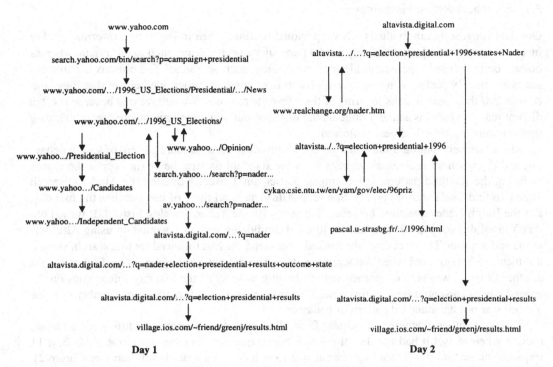

Figure 1. On the second day, participant T seemed to forget that she had used Yahoo! extensively on the first day. In this figure (and in those that follow), the nodes represent unique web pages, and the arcs represent transitions between pages.

some participants recalled mainly query terms to produce search results, one of which would often be recognized as one of the URLs that had lead to the goal. Others recalled a few of the specific URLs along the path they had followed, such as the University of Western Ontario home-page or the Alzheimer's Association home page, and set out to find these. In short, participants remembered key nodes or *waypoints* that led to the goal. Formally, we define a waypoint as a node along a search path from which there is an unbroken sequence of links on successive pages that lead to the goal node (i.e., no URLs need to be typed in or explicitly recalled). Once traversed, waypoints are *recognized* as lying along the path to the goal—even if the same path is not followed to the goal in every case. For our participants, searching on the second day often meant finding waypoints encountered on the first day, rather than finding paths found on the first day.

Consider Figure 1 again. As shown, T's search for the number of states in which Ralph Nader was on the U. S. presidential ballot ultimately relied on a specific AltaVista query: namely, one containing the keyword "results". In fact, T explicitly mentioned this during verbal recall:

> and I finally decided, oh yeah, I should just look under results or something, and then after, I went to a site that had the results, including how many states listed Ralph Nader on the ballot.

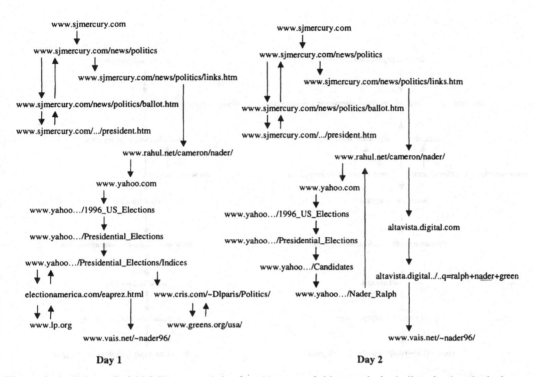

Figure 2. Participant D faithfully retraced the first 11 steps of this search, including dead ends, before switching to his usual routine (i.e., using AltaVista), even though he did not use AltaVista on the first day.

In this case, T's search depended on a waypoint created by querying AltaVista. Participant W used the same approach, recalling only the top level query used in his search for the answer to the same question:

> I went to AltaVista and looked for the California Green Party and I wandered around and eventually I found it.

For these two participants, the query terms used as part of their standard routines were most important because the answer did not lie far from the query.

In another case, T's search depended on getting to a web page at the library of the University of Western Ontario (UWO). As shown in Figure 3, T retraced her steps to a web page at UWO's library, but not to the same page she had visited the previous day. This method of retracing steps by waypoints is also evident in how T verbally recalled the search:

> ...once I got there [AltaVista] ...I just looked for anything that had ...University of Western Ontario ...and one was the library and I thought ...there's probably a link back once I get to that point ...some sort of a directory ...so I got into the library and ...I in fact did find a link that took me back ...[to] this meta level for the University of Western Ontario, and then I went down to academic units ...and under there they have psychology, and under psychology they had programs or degrees ...

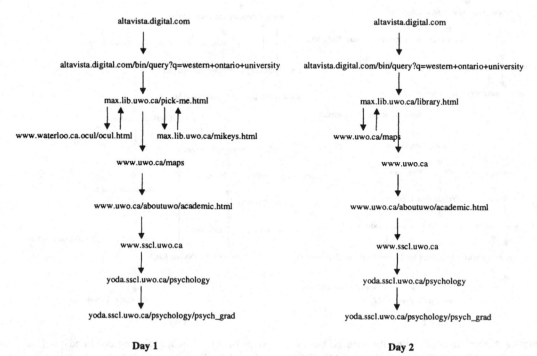

Day 1   **Day 2**

Figure 3. T's search for the psychology department at the University of Western Ontario depended on the UWO's library, but not on a specific location at the library.

This time, T recalled more than query terms, presumably because more than an AltaVista search was needed to find the answer. That is, AltaVista helped find a starting point at the University of Western Ontario, but the search proceeded independently from there.

Participant D had a similar experience finding the psychology department at UWO. As shown in Figure 4, D's waypoint was the homepage for the university, but his paths after finding this point were completely different on the two days. His verbal report suggests that finding UWO was the priority:

> I'll go to AltaVista again. I searched on University of Western Ontario ... and then take it from there.

Obviously, D believed the path would be clear once the UWO homepage was located. In a sense, the path followed the first day did not matter because some path could be found from the waypoint.

We found evidence in the behavioral data that each of the seven participants used waypoints in the ways just described. Specifically, for one of the completed searches, each participant either found a *similar* node on the second day from which the same path to the goal followed, or found the same node on the second day from which a *different* path to the goal followed. Overall, the

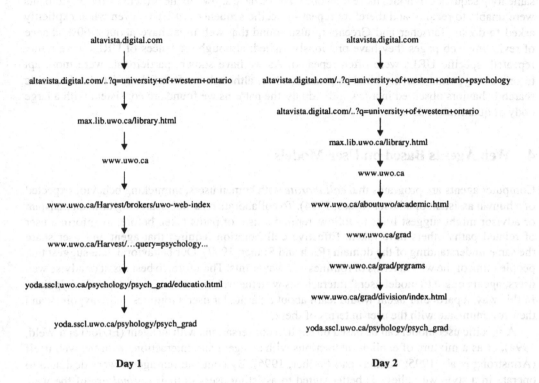

Figure 4. D's search for the psychology department at the University of Western Ontario depended on the UWO's homepage, but took different paths from there on the two days.

data suggest that memory for prior searches was structured around important nodes that led to the goal.

In summary, when searching the web, people use standard routines to find key points that are close to the desired information. To make this case, we have shown that our searchers: (a) generated only a few of the important nodes they visited when recalling their searches (both verbally and behaviorally); and (b) relied on personal routines both to find important nodes and to find specific information starting from these nodes. It follows that searchers do not fully *plan* in advance, but rely instead on heuristics (routines) and local context (waypoints) to find information (cf. Georgeff and Lansky, 1987). Put another way, searchers interleave directed and structured behavior—searching—with opportunistic and unstructured behavior—browsing—to find information (Bates, 1989; Marchionini, 1995).

3.3 Related Studies of Web Use

Our findings accord with other recent studies of how people use the web. Catledge and Pitkow (1995) and Tauscher and Greenberg (1996) analyzed several weeks worth of normal web usage gathered from dozens of individuals. Both studies found that web users do not often traverse the same long sequence of nodes more than once. As we have shown in the present study, participants were unable to recall—and therefore repeat—specific sequences of URLs even when explicitly asked to do so. Tauscher and Greenberg also found that web users have about a 60% chance of revisiting web pages they have previously visited; although sequences of URLs were rarely repeated, specific URLs were often repeated. As we have shown, participants were more apt to refind waypoints than to refind sequences. Thus, although we focused on details of specific search behaviors observed in a few individuals, the patterns we found are consistent with a large body of quantitative data.

4   Web Agents Based on User Models

Computer agents are programs that *collaborate* with human users, mimicking behavior expected of a human assistant or advisor (Maes, 1994). To collaborate on a web searching task, an assistant or advisor might suggest links to follow, remind a user of paths taken before, or inform a user of related paths others have taken. Effective collaboration requires that agent and user share the same understanding of the domain (Rich and Sidner, 1997). Our behavioral data suggest that people think of the web in terms of routines and waypoints. Therefore, to best assist or advise web users, agents ought to model users' interactions with the web in terms of routines and waypoints. In this way, a particular agent would learn about a particular user's routines and waypoints, and then communicate with the user in terms of these.

A specific user model can be based on explicit conversations with an agent (Etzioni and Weld, 1994), or as a mixture of explicit interactions with an agent and interactions with the web itself (Armstrong et al., 1995; Thomas and Fischer, 1996). By contrast, our agents were designed to operate in a style we believe is better suited to assisting users in their *normal use* of the web. That is, rather than radically changing the web experience, our aim has been to incorporate new functions without substantially altering a user's ordinary interaction (Norman, 1994). Thus, to build a user model, our web agents monitor user-web interactions implicitly (Selker, 1994), and to communicate with the user, our agents annotate retrieved web pages and respond to specific user requests (see also Barrett et al., 1997a).

In particular, we built two web agents. One identifies repeated link-following patterns and suggests similar patterns in similar contexts. The other identifies waypoints used in finding information to help visualize user trails. These agents were constructed using the WBI toolkit.

4.1   WBI Agent Architecture

WBI provides an architecture that taps into the communication stream between a user's web browser and the web itself. Using WBI, we can attach agents to this stream to observe the data flowing along the stream, or to alter the data as it flows past. Such agents can learn about the user, influence what the user sees by marking-up pages before passing them on, and provide entirely new functions through the web browser. WBI is implemented as a proxy server that can run either on the user's client workstation or on a server that many users access (and can be downloaded for Windows 95/NT or OS/2, see IBM).

In WBI, agents are defined by a set of monitors, editors, generators, and rules. A monitor is given a copy of a web request and a copy of the resulting page so that it can record user actions.

For example, a *history* agent would use monitors to record the series of URLs visited and the contents of the pages viewed. An editor is allowed to modify the resulting page before it is returned to the browser. For example, an editor might be used to add extra buttons for accessing WBI functions. A generator is used to handle web requests. For example, a generator can be used to search a user's history and return a list of pages that contain a given keyword. Rules define which specific monitors, editors, and generators should be instantiated for a given request. For example, certain editors might only want to modify HTML documents, and certain monitors might only want to observe requests made to servers in a certain domain. A more complete description of the WBI architecture can be found elsewhere (Barrett et al., 1997a, 1997b).

4.2 Shortcut Agent Identifies Repeated Patterns

As we have argued, people follow standard routines when searching for information. To support this behavior, we constructed a *shortcut* agent to extract repeated patterns from a user's history of interactions with the web. For instance, suppose a user routinely searches for documentation on the Java programming language by going to the Java home page, then to programming information, then to the reference manual. The shortcut agent identifies this pattern of repeated actions in the user's history and adds a link on the Java home page to the Java reference manual page. Thus, the user can jump directly from the Java home page to the reference manual, skipping intermediate pages (see Figure 5).

The shortcut agent relies both on a monitor that records an ordered list of all URLs visited, and on an editor to add links to web pages. When a user requests a URL, the editor scans the visited list for previous occurrences of it. All URLs that were visited within a certain neighborhood of each previous occurrence of the current URL (e.g., within 5 steps) are collected and sorted by frequency. Any such neighboring URLs that were visited more than a a certain number of times (e.g., 4) and more than a certain proportion of the time (e.g., 25%) are added to the top of the page by the shortcut editor.

4.3 Waypoint Agent Identifies Key Nodes

It seems clear users would benefit from being able to see their histories of interaction with the web—so that they can return to previously found locations, or so that they can share their histories with others, to list two examples. Our behavioral data suggest that people rely on waypoints rather than on sequences of URLs to reconstruct their searches. This implies that displaying a complete history of URLs is not only redundant but potentially confusing for users (see also Tauscher and Greenberg, 1996, and Cockburn and Jones, 1996). We built the *waypoint* agent to extract likely waypoints from a user's history of interactions with the web to enable appropriate visualization of user trails. Recall that a waypoint is a node from which there is an unbroken sequence of links on successive pages that lead to some goal. As a first pass at this, our waypoint agent partitions the user's history of interactions into segments that contain no backtracking and that are connected by a sequence of links. The user can request that the waypoint agent display his or her interaction history in terms of such node groups (see Figure 6).

The waypoint agent relies on a monitor that records each URL requested as well as hyperlinks on all pages retrieved. In addition, the waypoint agent uses a generator to construct a web page to display the user's history of interactions. To do this, the generator constructs a disconnected

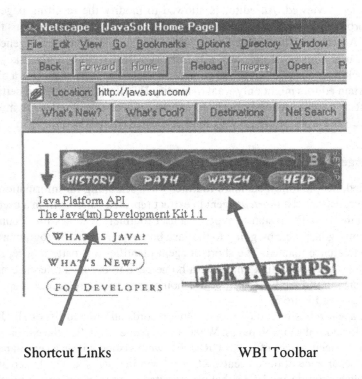

Shortcut Links   WBI Toolbar

Figure 5. The shortcut agent has added two links to the top of the JavaSoft homepage, one to the Java APIs, the other to the development kit. These links were added because the user routinely follows a path from here to the development kit page and then to the APIs page.

graph of the user's path through the web using the link information that the monitor has recorded, and removes backtracking from these each of the connected subgraphs. Discontinuities arise when there are no links connecting successive pages. Finally, this generator is invoked when the user visits a specific URL (such as `http://wbi/mytrails`), and each of the subgraphs is displayed as an ordered list of titles with duplicates removed. Note that in this preliminary version, the waypoint agent does not distinguish between important and unimportant URLs in the clusters it generates, and so does it not in fact produce specific waypoints. The clusters it produces, however, distill a user's traversal of the web into self-contained regions.

4.4   Related Work

In general, WBI's waypoint and shortcut agents are unique in that they are based on an analysis of *how people search the web*. For instance, Thomas and Fischer (1996) describe modeling agents that assist web searchers. One difference between Thomas and Fischer's BASAR system and WBI is that users explicitly configure and interact with BASAR's agents through a special interface, whereas users interact with WBI's modeling agents by simply searching the

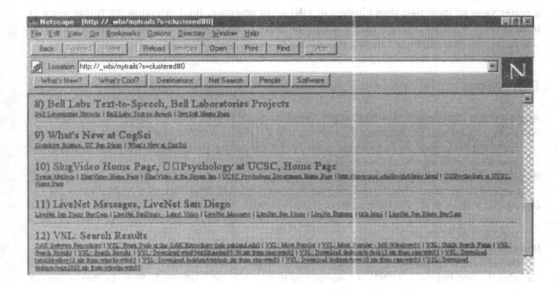

Figure 6. The waypoint agent displays a user's history of interactions with the web in terms of locally connected clusters of URLs.

web. Similarly, Armstrong et al.'s (1995) WebWatcher is a web search assistant that requires explicit user feedback to incrementally learn the key words that distinguish one topic from another. WebWatcher uses a statistical machine learning algorithm to try to partition the universe of key words. Lieberman's (1995) Letizia uses simple heuristics, such as persistence-of-interest and limited lookahead, to determine which links a user might want to follow. WBI's modeling agents differ from all of these is that WBI's agents are empirically motivated.

5 Conclusion

Using data gathered by observing experienced web users searching for specific information on the web, we argued that (a) individuals repeat the same search patterns and conceptualize their searches in terms of their standard patterns, and (b) people focus on key nodes or waypoints when recalling their searches. On the basis of these findings, we built two personal web agents to assist searchers: the shortcut agent identifies repeated search patterns and suggests similar patterns for new searches, and the waypoint agent identifies and displays nodes that go together in a user's history. Because these agents communicate with a user in terms close to the user's model of the domain, we believe these agents are well-adapted for user-web collaboration.

One direction for future work is to empirically determine whether our modeling agents make web searching easier. Do people repeat searches faster using these agents? Do they locate information more quickly in the first place? Informal observations suggest that shortcuts in fact enable users to skip steps—and therefore to save time and cut down on confusion—when repeating standard patterns of action. A second direction is to define a method to find the most important nodes in the clusters the waypoint agent generates. Do individual waypoints give users a better view of their past than clusters of URLs? In any case, final direction for future work is to determine whether a single user's waypoint history can be easily used by others. That is, do waypoints capture the most important structure of a user's trails?

References

AltaVista. AltaVista Search. Available as http://altavista.digital.com.

Armstrong, R., Freitag, D., Joachims, T., and Mitchell, T. (1995). WebWatcher: A learning apprentice for the World Wide Web. In *Proceedings of the 1995 AAAI Spring Symposium on Information Gathering from Heterogeneous, Distributed Environments*.

Barrett, R., Maglio, P. P., and Kellem, D. C. (1997a). How to personalize the web. In *Proceedings of the Conference on Human Factors in Computer Systems (CHI '97)*. New York, NY: ACM Press.

Barrett, R., Maglio, P. P., and Kellem, D. C. (1997b). WBI: A confederation of agents that personalize the web. In *Proceedings of the First International Conference on Autonomous Agents*, 496–499. New York, NY: ACM Press.

Bates, M. J. (1989). The design of browsing and berrypicking techniques for the on-line search interface. *Online Review* 13:407–431.

Catledge, L., and Pitkow, J. (1995). Characterizing browsing in the World-Wide Web. In *Proceedings of the Third International World Wide Web Conference*.

Cockburn, A., and Jones, S. (1996). Which way now? Analysing and easing inadequacies in WWW navigation. *International Journal of Human-Compter Studies* 45:105–129.

Etzioni, O., and Weld, D. (1994). A softbot-based interface to the internet. *Communications of the ACM* 37(7):72–76.

Georgeff, M., and Lansky, A. (1987). Reactive reasoning and planning. In *Proceedings of the Sixth National Conference on Artificial Intelligence*, 677–682.

IBM. Web Browser Intelligence. Available as http://www.raleigh.ibm.com/wbi/wbisoft.htm.

Lieberman, H. (1995). Letizia: An agent that assists web browsing. In *International Joint Conference on Artificial Intelligence*, 924–929.

Maes, P. (1994). Agents that reduce work and information overload. *Communications of the ACM* 37(7):31–40.

Marchionini, G. (1995). *Information Seeking in Electronic Environments*. Cambridge, England: Cambridge University Press.

Norman, D. A. (1994). How might people interact with agents. *Communications of the ACM* 37(7):68–71.

Rich, C., and Sidner, C. L. (1997). COLLAGEN: When agents collaborate with people. In *Proceedings of the First International Conference on Autonomous Agents*, 284–291. New York: ACM Press.

Selker, T. (1994). COACH: A teaching agent that learns. *Communications of the ACM* 37(7):92–99.

Tauscher, L., and Greenberg, S. (1996). How people revisit web pages: Empirical findings and implications for the design of history systems. Unpublished manuscript. University of Calgary, Department of Computer Science.

Thomas, C. G., and Fischer, G. (1996). Using agents to improve the usability and usefulness of the World-Wide Web. In *Fifth International Conference on User Modeling*, 5–12.

Yahoo! Yahoo! Available as http://www.yahoo.com.

Web-Browser Access Through Voice Input and Page Interest Prediction

Marco Gori, Marco Maggini, and Enrico Martinelli

Dipartimento di Ingegneria dell'Informazione (DII), Università di Siena, Italy

Abstract. We propose a system that supports the interaction of handicapped people with web browsers for Internet navigation using voice. This system supports the interaction by offering a voice interface for implementing a pointing device. Moreover, it minimizes the number of voice commands by making predictions about the hyperlinks that the user is likely to select next.

1 The Web Browser Control Method

The effective use of graphical interfaces is severely limited for most physically handicapped people, who find it very hard to control typical pointing devices. To provide a usable interface to people with such inabilities we conceived both a vocal device based on the simplest sounds that can be emitted clearly (vowels) and a system to aid user interaction by means of prediction of actions. The predictor aid is particularly useful since the voice input device has very limited control capabilities.

The method we are currently developing controls one of the most popular web browsers, Netscape. The decision to build a method for this particular browser is due both to the large diffusion it has and to the powerful control mechanisms it provides.

1.1 Netscape Control

The application control method tracks Netscape activity, providing the HTML page the user is reading to the prediction system. Then, depending on predictions, it generates the proper actions to aid the user interaction.

As shown in Figure 1 the control module is supposed to provide two different aid schemes.

The first aid is based on the definition of large attraction areas around the most interesting hyperlinks or on control of the pointer motion in order to cycle through the hyperlinks.

A second kind of support is provided by displaying a separate pop-up window containing the most interesting hyperlinks ordered from the highest to the lowest degree of relevance (Kühme et al., 1993). When the pointer is inside this pop-up window the control module will cause it to cycle through the possible choices.

The control module also controls other browser actions directly, such as scrolling the page.

1.2 The Page Interest Estimator

The problem is to estimate in advance the interest the user may have in following the hyperlinks contained in the page currently displayed by the browser. The module computes the estimated

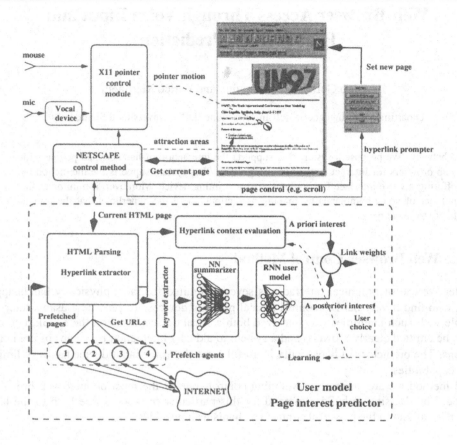

Figure 1. Scheme of the control method for Netscape.

degree of interest of each hyperlink in order to produce the hints needed by the Netscape control method. This module is based on a user model that is adapted during the interaction by observing the user decisions.

The algorithm processes the hyperlinks to evaluate both the *a priori* and the *a posteriori* user interest. The *a priori* interest is related to the likelihood for a link to be selected without knowing the exact contents of the referred page. The only available information for the user is the hyperlink context and the format of the current page. If the referred page was available, the user would be able to decide if it was actually interesting. This information is needed to decide the *a posteriori* degree of relevance.

The evaluation algorithm tries to predict both levels using a prefetching technique to obtain the referred pages (Lieberman, 1995).

The current HTML page is analyzed and its hyperlinks are extracted. The hyperlink URLs are passed to the prefetch agents that contact the remote hosts and transfer the referred pages. Each page is then parsed and its contents are extracted. The occurrence of predefined keywords in the document text is evaluated and the document signature is then computed from the vector of the keyword frequencies using a neural network.

The neural network summarizer is obtained by training a neural network to autoassociate document keyword vectors. The training phase uses a neural network having as many outputs as inputs and is performed off-line. The neural network weights are optimized in order to produce the best identity mapping between inputs and outputs on a given set of document examples (Bianchini et al., 1995). The hidden layer outputs are used as the document signature; they represent the *compressed* contents of the documents. Thus, when using the neural network as a summarizer only the input and hidden layers are needed.

A recurrent neural network (RNN) is then used to model user trajectories through hypertext pages. A path through documents is represented by trajectories in an N-dimensional space using the document signatures computed by the neural summarizer. In recurrent neural networks some of the neurons' outputs are fed back to inputs. In so doing the network computation depends both on the current input and on the network internal state that memorizes the past history of input activity (Williams and Peng, 1990).

The current RNN state represents the path followed by the user in reading documents up to the current page. When feeding the network with a document signature the network computes the user degree of interest, i.e. the probability that the page will be selected by the user. The evaluation depends both on the current trajectory (i.e. the network state) and on the user preferences (i.e. the network weights). The network is applied to the signatures of the documents prefetched by the Internet agents in order to compute the a posteriori interest of all hyperlinks.

The RNN weights are adapted on-line by comparing the actual user choice with the values produced by the network for each hyperlink.

Besides the prefetching mechanism, another evaluation algorithm has to be used in order to provide the a priori interest of each hyperlink. The hyperlink evaluation based on the current page contents may be necessary when the time needed to prefetch the referred pages is too long. The evaluation is based on both the hyperlink tag keyword and the context the hyperlink is in (i.e. text, list of hyperlinks).

The a priori and a posteriori interest degrees are combined in order to produce the final ranking for the hyperlinks needed by the control method.

References

Bianchini, M., Frasconi, P., and Gori, M. (1995). Learning in multilayered networks used as autoassociators. *IEEE Transactions on Neural Networks* 6(2):512–515.

Kühme, T., Malinowski, U., and Foley, J. D. (1993). Adaptive prompting. Technical Report GIT -GVU-93-05, Georgia Institute of Technology.

Lieberman,H. (1995). Letizia: An agent that assists web browsing. In Mellish, C. S., ed., *Proceedings of the Fourteenth International Joint Conference on Artificial Intelligence*. San Mateo, CA: Morgan Kaufmann. 924–929.

Williams, R. J., and Peng, J. (1990). An efficient gradient-based algorithm for on-line training of recurrent network trajectories. *Neural Computation* 2(4):490–501.

SATELIT-Agent: An Adaptive Interface Based on Learning Interface Agents Technology

Irina Akoulchina and Jean-Gabriel Ganascia

LAFORIA-IBP-CNRS (LIP6), University Paris-VI, Paris, France

Abstract. This article presents an adaptive interface agent for SATELIT, a system that integrates Artificial Intelligence methods and hypermedia technology. SATELIT is implemented on the Internet, represented as a set of interactive World Wide Web (WWW) pages with their own functionalities. The SATELIT learning agent was developed for adaptive interface maintenance and pursues either of two main goals, depending on the user's intentions. First, it is capable of distinguishing the profile of SATELIT experts, whose purpose is to construct a SATELIT application, and it offers a special interface to them. The second aim of SATELIT-Agent is a response to the general hypermedia problem of "getting lost in hypermedia space". With the help of a learning interface agent, SATELIT will infer an analogue of the user's search requirements and help him to achieve it, proposing good navigation routes. In this manner SATELIT-Agent functions as an active browser, interactively assisting and guiding the user.

1 Introduction

With the appearance of hypertext and hypermedia tools offering new text reading possibilities, a new information era has begun. But at the same time, a common problem about navigating and "getting lost" in the global hyper-space has become very essential. Especially now, when hypermedia use enormous information networks like the Internet, this problem is drawing more and more attention. In the Internet there is a fundamental imbalance between the extraordinary breadth of represented information and the limited amount of knowledge that manages the navigation. It is evident now that the technology responsible for the processes of management is far less efficient than the technology responsible for the information accumulation (see, e.g., Floridi, 1995). The question arises again: How to reduce the risk of user disorientation so that a naive user will not lose the right direction in the navigation process and ignore important information. To this end, different researchers have proposed various methods of adaptive hypermedia interfaces that could construct themselves according to the user's needs, knowledge, and preferred navigation strategies.

At present, all research in the field of adaptive hypermedia interfaces construction is adopting *user-centered system design*, a paradigm advocated by Norman and Draper (1986). As part of this new approach, the first direct manipulation interfaces appeared. Instead of communicating through a "linguistic" intermediary such as command languages, menus or forms, the user directly initiates tasks and monitors events. He or she can, for example, activate hypertext links, move backwards, or search for needed information. For a long time, interface designers have been opposing these two interaction paradigms, direct manipulation and indirect management. But recently a new, complementary style of interaction has been proposed: The user engages in a cooperative process in which a human and one or more *learning intelligent interface agents* both initiate communication, monitor events and perform tasks.

The objective of this new complementary interaction style is to allow a user direct manipulation and, at the same time, to offer him a new intelligent intermediary that assists him or her in indirect manipulation. With the apparition of the new learning agents conception, researchers have begun to place the emphasis of their work on learning from user activity and on developing systems based purely on user criticism. Having studied the particular user, his habits and preferences, this personal assistant, invisible to the user, interprets his directives and anticipates the next action. Thus, learning interface agents act as personalized assistants which "look over the user's shoulder" and learn the user's interests in order to act on his behalf. Agent programs differ from regular software in that an agent is (1) *autonomous*, in that it can sense the current state of its environment and act independently to make progress toward its goals; (2) *adaptive*, in that it is capable of learning and of adapting to situations, and (3) *non-restricting*, in that it does not insist and the user can always ignore the the suggestion and take a different action.

For acquiring information about the user, there are four sources of information for interface agents (see Figure 1): observation and imitation of repetitive user actions; analysis of positive and negative user feedback; learning from explicit user instructions; and multi-agent collaboration.

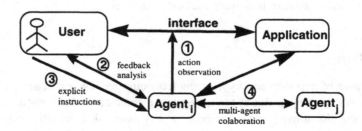

Figure 1. Four knowledge acquisition sources for learning interface agents.

The application domains for agents are strikingly varied. Agents have found employment in mail management (Maes, 1994), meeting scheduling (Mitchell et al., 1994), and information retrieval in the Internet jungle (see, e.g., Armstrong et al., 1995, or Edwards et al., 1996). They help users to learn software (Selker, 1994), handle the multimedia virtual conference (Riecken, 1994), etc. In our research group, we are developing a learning agent for an adaptive interface of the SATELIT system, which has been implemented on the Internet. With the help of this agent, SATELIT will be able to learn details about its users and consequently to distinguish among the users and among their goals.

An analysis of all possible SATELIT user profiles is given by Akoulchina and Ganascia (1996). For two main user profiles—experts and novices—our SATELIT-Agent proposes different interfaces, in accordance with their intentions. For the expert, it first verifies the user's competence level in order to permit this expert to construct some SATELIT application; later, it proposes special application development tools. The problem of expert profile distinction is very important in the Internet environment as it addresses a question of system security. For the novice, SATELIT-Agent plays the role of an intelligent assistant that learns a search goal from the user's ordinary browsing actions. In this way, our SATELIT-Agent tries to solve the problem mentioned above by reducing the risk of user disorientation in the browsing process. Let us begin by considering some original aspects of our SATELIT system and explaining why it needs an adaptive interface. We will then demonstrate in detail our use of the learning interface agent techniques for two user profiles—expert and novice.

2   Original Aspects of the SATELIT System

The SATELIT system belongs to the class of hypermedia systems that hold both textual information and knowledge about the domain. SATELIT allows the acquisition of a formalized knowledge base and the automatic indexing of Internet hypermedia documents according to the contents of this knowledge base in order to facilitate information access (see Faron and Kieu, 1995, and Faron et al., 1996, for details). In this way, our system is also capable searching for precise information, since the knowledge base structure provides an initial hypermedia network.

The application domains of SATELIT are the sciences of analysis and observation, like botany and zoology. Those domains are characterized on the one hand by a great amount of information scattered in catalogues, and on the other hand by a taxonomic organization of multimedia data. Bringing this information together on an electronic medium is a crucial task. In these domains, knowledge objects are clustered according to their similarities to make up classes, called *taxa*, organized in hierarchical structures, called *taxonomies*. The taxum description is a synthesis of the common anatomy of its instances and characteristics of these instances. An appropriate knowledge representation formalism here is the Conceptual Graphs model suggested by Sowa (1984), which allows the elaboration of structured descriptions and the subsequent indexing of multimedia documents on the basis of these descriptions. The general structure of the SATELIT architecture is shown in Figure 2.

Different types of information nodes appear in the network; they correspond, and are indexed to, different parts of the knowledge base: *taxa* nodes, *concept* nodes, *taxonomy* nodes and the *terminology* node. Taxa nodes are compound nodes, their different kinds of description being complementary: In addition to a structured description (a conceptual graph), hypertextual and graphic descriptions are associated with each taxum. A conceptual graph allows formal manipulation of a taxum description but does not account for all shades in a textual or graphic description. Concept nodes are also compound: Specialized texts and sketches clarify the meaning of concept types and references appearing in conceptual graphs describing taxa. The terminology node is composed of several hypermedia glossaries indexed to the concept types lattice. In order to handle the acquired knowledge, SATELIT offers information retrieval and object identification tools. Thus the originality of SATELIT consists in the integration of efficient hypermedia information access procedures that require reasoning on previously acquired formalized knowledge.

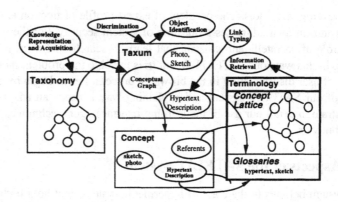

Figure 2. The SATELIT architecture.

Using the Java language, we are developing SATELIT in the Internet as a set of interactive World Wide Web (WWW) pages and special windows with their own functionality. Some Web pages contain interactive terminology glossaries, other pages contain hypertext and hypermedia information about taxa. Each taxum has its own special window holding an interactive conceptual graph. Two other windows represent a taxonomy and a concept lattice. The procedure of information retrieval is maintained in a special SATELIT window; it will be discussed below. An example of some SATELIT windows and Web pages is shown in Figure 3.

There are two main types of SATELIT user profiles, which are associated with different experience levels: an expert in one of the domains considered, whose goal is to construct an application with the help of SATELIT, and a novice who consults hypermedia using some information search strategy.

For these different user profiles, SATELIT-Agent offers different interface tools. For an expert it is necessary, first, to confirm their level of expertise and, second, to offer them concrete tools, so that they may access the object taxonomy and add new taxa, acquire new knowledge about them, and construct new conceptual graphs representing taxa, hypertexts and sketches associated to an object, as well as "active" glossaries.

For a user who consults existing hypermedia and searches for some specific information (with the help of formalized knowledge), SATELIT offers possibilities of indexing, composing search requests and consulting glossaries. But such flexibility always has the disadvantages discussed above: Users have great difficulty in formulating their search goals precisely, and they tend to get lost quickly. Our SATELIT-Agent pursues the aim of actively helping the user to find the necessary information and decreasing the risk of disorientation.

Let us consider the details of SATELIT-Agent's work for these two different user profiles.

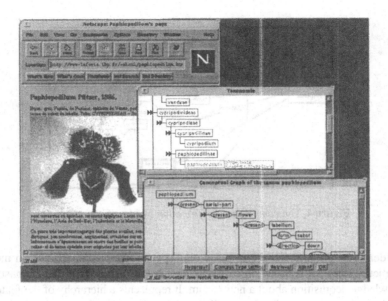

Figure 3. Several SATELIT windows and Web pages.

3 SATELIT-Agent for the Expert User Profile

As was mentioned above, the SATELIT system organizes hypermedia information available on the Internet in the form of taxonomies and adds knowledge that manages information access. In the *observation sciences*, such as botany or archaeology, taxonomic data organization is es sential. For instance, in the domain of orchideology, which we have worked with, the taxonomy makes it possible to foresee more easily the possibilities of hybridations between different orchid sorts. But the classification problem in these domains is very complicated, as there are no general methods. The results derived from the same observation set may be interpreted differently according to the "classification school" that the expert belongs to. It is therefore necessary not only to confirm an expert user profile, but also to distinguish among different schools in order to propose to them different SATELIT application development tools.

Furthermore, the expert distinction problem is crucial in the Internet environment. Only experts can access applications system construction. To permit a user to add a new taxum to the existing taxonomy or to acquire new associated knowledge, it is necessary to be assured that this user has competence in the domain under consideration. This task is closely linked with the problem of Internet security.

Just asking for user passwords is not sufficient for expert recognition. As the number of Internet users is enormous, some of them, who are experts in the domain under consideration, may wish to complete a taxonomy by adding new information or to add new knowledge into existing taxa. For the distinction of the user's expertise level, a *competence confirmation by identification* technique was developed.

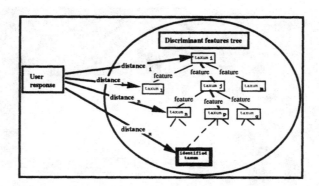

Figure 4. The *competence confirmation by identification* process.

Object identification in SATELIT is based on a special knowledge acquisition method developed by Aimeur (1994). It is based on a discriminant features tree. This tree is constructed at the time of knowledge acquisition about a new taxum. It represents a hierarchy of the features (at least one feature in each tree level). The feature distinguishes the taxum from its brothers in the taxonomy. It has one of the following forms:

1. *[concept i]* → *(composed)* → *[concept j]*, where the "composed" reference is "present", "absent" or "unidentified", or
2. *[concept i]* → *(characterized)* → *[concept j]*, where the "characterized" reference may be any of several different characteristics, such as "value", "form", "number", or "texture".

To go down this discriminant features tree, the agent asks the user questions about the presence of the concepts mentioned in each feature, or about the values of the concept's characteristics. At the end, the tree leaf holds a taxum name with the desired discriminant features. The agent asks the user to give this name and compares the response string with the real value. The agent analyses the user's response according to the fast algorithm for finding the nearest neighbor of a word in a dictionary that was proposed by Bunke (1993) and calculates the *error scores*—the values that reflect the distances between the user's response and all taxa names (see Figure 4).

If the user is wrong and the lowest error score exceeds a certain established limit, SATELIT-Agent does not confirm the expert status for this user and denies the user access to the application development SATELIT tools. If the minimal distance is the distance between the user response and the true response (*distance x* in Figure 4), the agent confirms the expert profile. The expert then has the right to: add a new taxum to an existing taxonomy; introduce new knowledge to existing conceptual graphs representing taxa; introduce new hypermedia information for taxa; and introduce new information for glossaries.

In the other case, if the smallest distance is between the false user response and one of the taxa in the taxonomy (*distances i, l* or *n* in Figure 4), the agent concludes that from the same observation feature the user constructs a different classification from the proposed one. This means that the user is an expert but belongs to a different classification school. In this case, SATELIT-Agent repeats the expert confirmation by identification process again for another discriminant features tree, as SATELIT holds in its knowledge base several taxonomies (and, thus, several discriminant features trees) for the same domain field. If this iterative process is completed successfully once, the agent finds a taxonomy that agrees with the classification school of this expert and offers him or her the SATELIT application development tools mentioned above. Otherwise, the agent allows the expert to create a new SATELIT application—a new taxonomy in the domain field under consideration—and adds it to its taxonomies base.

4 SATELIT-Agent for the Consulting User Profile

The user consulting a SATELIT application on the Internet environment searches with one or more of the following goals: to identify an object with certain known properties; to find precise SATELIT hypermedia information about a taxum; to find other information about a taxum available on the Internet; to consult the dictionary in the domain field under consideration; and to consult the catalogue of authors of the taxonomy classification. It is evident that such a search in the large and complex SATELIT knowledge bases is a very difficult process. The user always has difficulty describing his or her search goal directly and precisely. The system proposes some tools such as *Retrieval*, *Concept Lattice*, *Identification*, and *Glossary*, which help to formulate a request, but the user may easily get lost in the huge amount of concepts, references, characteristics and taxa names. Furthermore, studies (see, e.g., Fischer and Nieper-Lemke, 1989) have shown that browsing is a strategy that is preferred over analytic methods that require a formulation of well-structured queries. This means that browsing is seen as a more natural and effective process when the user is uncertain about the target description. The user prefers to repeat the browsing process iteratively, skimming the results and evaluating and refining the search goal at each step. Our approach involves inferring the users' search goals by learning their repetitive browsing actions. The aim of our SATELIT-Agent is to add an active component to the existing SATELIT and Internet browsing tools in order to anticipate the next browsing action.

We distinguish two types of agents: those who use the previously acquired domain knowledge and those who do not. The *agents without pre-acquired knowledge* have been developed for active browsing on the Internet. These agents (see, e.g., Lieberman, 1995; Armstrong et al., 1995; Edwards et al., 1996) combine machine learning techniques with information filtering methods. They track users' behaviour and attempt to anticipate their next Internet browsing actions by doing concurrent, autonomous exploration of links starting from the user's current position. The agents of this type are distinguished by the level of "browsing autonomy", the nature of the feedback from the user, and the machine learning techniques used. By contrast, the agents of the second type, who have explicit knowledge models of the particular domain, work in the environment of local systems with a limited number of users (see, e.g., Drummond, 1995). The principal idea behind SATELIT-Agent development is to combine the advantages of these two types of agents. Our agent is applied not to all Web pages but to a subset of pages that contain SATELIT hypermedia information. In addition, it is based on a precise model of SATELIT knowledge about the application field. In this way, it integrates the methods of analysis of the user's behaviour with the techniques of knowledge based systems.

Like the majority of the learning interface agents, SATELIT-Agent for the consulting user profile observes and imitates the user's regular browsing actions (the source 1 in Figure 1) and constructs the adaptive user model after inferring the user's search goal analogue. The next browsing actions predicted by SATELIT-Agent appear in the special window called "Agent suggests". The agent displays these suggestions according to their weights, as it estimates their relevance to the user. But the agent's suggestions are not obtrusive, as only the user is responsible for the choice of next browsing action. The agent gradually gains competence also by analyzing the user's feedback, i.e, positive or negative responses to proposed agent recommendations. Such criticism dependency is the second source of knowledge acquisition in the schema of Figure 1. In addition, as a third source, it is possible for the user to instruct the SATELIT agent explicitly. Thus, the user can create a hypothetical situation and show the agent what should be done.

The interface of the consulting user profile and SATELIT-Agent is presented in Figure 5.

SATELIT-Agent has to work in real-time mode and to make its suggestions while the user is browsing the system. This means that it must be *transparent* and use only the time that is available between the user's actions. In order to satisfy this aim and to reduce the time for the agent's work, the SATELIT-Agent search mechanism is composed of three main parts: an inference engine, a pattern matcher and a confidence calculator. The general architecture of SATELIT-Agent is presented in Figure 6.

The *inference engine* induces an analogue of the user's search goal from observation of their browsing actions by constructing a browsing action *pattern* and inferring a type of *matching procedure* for this pattern. Constructed patterns are held in the Working Memory. The pattern description has the form *"property = value"* and contains information about the number of the executed action, the tool used, the action type and the action's attribute type. The types of action and attribute depend on the concrete action performed by the user to the current tool. An attribute may be of one of three types: a *taxum*, a *concept*, or a *triplet* of the form "concept—relation—concept". For instance, while the user constructs a request in the *Retrieval* tool in order to find the taxa which have a staminod in the shield form, the pattern attribute has a triplet of the form "staminod—form—in shield". An attribute of the concept type is constructed, for example, when the user clicks the *stamen* link in the Web page dedicated to the *orchis* taxum (this action means that the user is searching for explication of the stamen concept in the Glossary). In this way, the Working Memory also keeps the traces of executed actions, so that the agent can reason about the entire chain of actions that led directly to the current one. Furthermore, owing to this action trace, the agent can detect patterns in the user's search, even when the user is interrupted by spurious exploratory browsing actions.

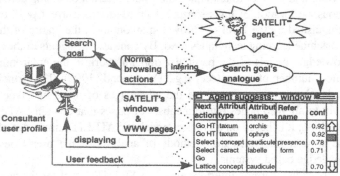

Figure 5. User-agent interface for the consulting user profile.

The general idea for reducing the duration of the agent's work is to be highly selective about which pattern properties are proposed to the pattern matcher and which matching procedure is used. Among the possible matching procedures are the following: "Find taxum name", "Find characteristics for a given concept", "Find taxum son", and "Find concept's synonyms".

The pattern matcher carries out a proposed matching procedure, finds taxa and concepts related to the properties under consideration, and estimates their relativity measures. The *relative attributes* (taxa, concepts and triplets) are those connected by a path in the Canonical Graphs, in the Concept Types Lattice or in the Taxonomy, the three main structures that represent the SATELIT knowledge base. The relativity measure, also called *importance* ($Imp(A_i)$), expresses the closeness of a relative attribute A_i to a direct attribute A (chosen by the user in an action); it ranges between 0 and 1. The importance of the direct attribute is 1. The importance equals 0 for a relative attribute that is present in the Working Memory but not connected to the current action. The importance of the relative attributes increases with lower (more specific) levels of the Canonical Graph, the Lattice, or the Taxonomy. The default importance values change gradually depending on the user's feedback. If the user does not accept an agent's advice, the importance of the proposed attribute is decreased by 0.5; otherwise the importance is increased by 0.5 and becomes equal to 1.5.

The weight W of an attribute A_i connected to an Action M is the sum of its old weights (calculated for other Actions $\{m_1,...m_k\}$ to which the attribute A_i has been connected) and the product of the frequency measure of the attribute A_i and its current importance :

$$W(A_i,M) = frequency(A_i) / n \bullet Imp(A_i) + \sum_{j=1}^{k} W(A_i, m_j) ,$$

where *frequency*(A_i) is the number of appearances of the attribute A_i and n is the number of all attributes' appearances in the Working Memory. The names of the identified related taxa, concepts and triplets and their calculated weights are added to the Working Memory; they represent statistics of the attributes considered in the browsing session.

Finally, a special engine calculates a confidence level *conf* for a suggested action M using an attribute A_i. It takes into consideration the statistics of related properties and their influence on executed actions :

$$conf(A_i, M) = \sqrt{\frac{N/A_i => M}{N}} \bullet W_{A_i}$$

where N is the number of actions executed during the given browsing session, $N/A_i => M$ is the number of times that an attribute A_i has been the cause of the appearance of the action M, and W_{A_i} is the weight of A_i calculated before. These confidences are calculated for all actions related to a given situation. After obtaining the result, SATELIT-Agent posts a list of proposed actions with related attributes and orders them according to its confidence measure. The user may choose one of the proposed actions (in this case, he gives the agent new feedback for learning), or he may ignore these suggestions and execute other browsing actions. Figure 5 gives examples of an agent's suggestion for a user who at that moment is in the *Retrieval* tool and is selecting the next action.

At the beginning of a browsing session, when the Working Memory does not have much information, the agent cannot make strong suggestions about next actions. But with time it accumu-

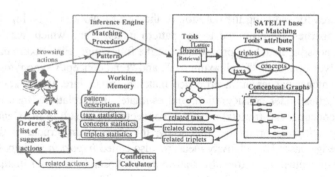

Figure 6. The SATELIT-Agent architecture (in the mode of consulting user profile interaction).

lates more knowledge and becomes better able to infer an analogue of the user's search goal. The user's actions implicitly carry information about his or her search goal, because they have been deliberately chosen to serve the user's interests. However, such freedom of choice brings some important problems that are connected with ambiguousness and noisiness of learned information. As the user has many possible choices of actions, concepts and taxa at each browsing step, the agent may either propose many equally plausible explanations for a choice or not find any explanation. Noisy information arises when the user changes his or her search goal too quickly. One way to reduce the ambiguity is to present less information at each browsing step. Our agent takes the possibility of misleading actions into account by decreasing the importance of old information. SATELIT-Agent weights properties according to their frequency of appearance; therefore, the weights of the properties that are closely related to the inferred search goal analogue will be augmented continually, whereas the weights of properties of items that are visited randomly will not.

Let us consider an example of a typical browsing process in the Orchideology domain, where the user tries to identify a plant and SATELIT-Agent attempts to infer an analogue of the search goal. The user begins by searching for information about a certain orchid with an unknown name. First, he sees a general Web page dedicated to the Orchids family and a Taxonomy tool in a special window. The user reads this page and understands that the labellum is the most informative characteristic of an orchid. He clicks on the *labellum* link and goes to the Glossary Web page that explains this notion and demonstrates some images of different labellum forms. Now it is clear to the user that his particular flower has a labellum in the *sabot* form and that it has a white color. At the moment when the user has performed his browsing action, the agent keeps its trace in the Working Memory, searches related attributes for the *labellum* concept, and calculates their weights. The first agent's suggestions are ready: It proposes using the Retrieval tool and to compose one of the three following requests: to search taxa with a labellum in strip form, with a red labellum or a with very big labellum. The user does not accept these recommendations, because he is interested in a sabot form of labellum. Nevertheless, the user decides to apply the Retrieval tool in order to find taxa satisfying the condition "labellum—form—sabot". SATELIT finds in response several relevant taxa: *Cypripedioideae*, *Cypripedium*, *Phragmopedilinae*, *Phragmopedium*, etc. (see Figure 7).

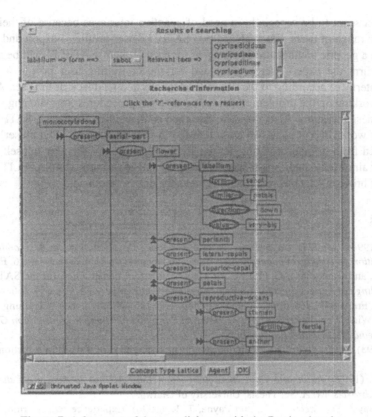

Figure 7. A fragment of the user dialogue with the Retrieval tool.

The user is perplexed: Which of these taxa should he choose? The agent tries to help him and suggests selecting the Cypripedium taxum (as this genus is the first in the list of the relevant taxa that belong to a lower level in the Taxonomy and, consequently, have maximal weights). At this point, the user accepts the recommendation, clicks on it in the Retrieval tool, and visits Cypripedium's Web page. The user sees the pictures of this genus of flowers and understands that this is not the desired plant. At the same time, the agent prepares new suggestions: to consult the Web page of Phragmopedium; to formulate the query "labellum—color—yellowish"; or to choose the "labellum—value—big" triplet in the Retrieval tool. The user accepts the first recommendation, visits the Phragmopedium page, and finds the flower he or she was trying to identify. The browsing process, which has been accelerated by the agent, is completed, and the user has received significant help.

5 Conclusion

In this paper we have presented a model of an adaptive interface for the Internet-based SATELIT system that is based on a metaphor of a new complementary interaction style that involves intelligent agents. We have demonstrated that hypermedia authoring or browsing systems on the Internet seem to be especially in need of adaptive interfaces because of their complexity and their wide range of users. We analyzed two SATELIT user profiles—expert and consulting— and presented a generic architecture of the agent for each of them. SATELIT will be able to recognize and confirm the expert user profile; and for the consulting user profile it will propose appropriate interfaces according to the observable actions and feedback of the user. At the present time we are working on the problem of designing efficient procedures for matching and for calculating relatedness measures. Also, we have designed some studies for testing SATELIT-Agent in two modes of work. In particular, we are interested in finding out how often a user's search goal can be inferred from normal browsing actions by the agent before the user himself achieved the goal. Another aim of our studies is to answer the question: How much can SATELIT-agent reduce the number of browsing actions required to achieve the user's search goal?

References

Aimeur, E. (1994). *METIS: Un système et une méthode d'explicitation de taxinomies destinés à l'identification de structures conceptuelles.* Thèse de Doctorat de l'Université Paris 6, France.

Akoulchina, I., and Ganascia, J.-G. (1996). An adaptive interface construction for the SATELIT system. In *Proceedings of Applications for Computer Systems Conference (ACS'96),* 259-266.

Armstrong, R., Freitag, D., Joachims, T., and Mitchell, T. (1995). WebWatcher: A learning apprentice for the World Wide Web. In *Proceedings of the AAAI Spring Symposium on Information Gathering from Heterogeneous, Distributed Environments,* 6-12.

Bunke, H. (1993). A fast algorithm for finding the nearest neighbor of a word in a dictionary. IAM-93-025.

Drummond, C. (1992). *Automatic Goal Extraction From User Actions to Accelerate the Browsing of Software Libraries.* M. A. Sc. Thesis, University of Ottawa.

Edwards, P., Bayer, D., Green, C. L., and Payne, T. R. (1996). Experience with learning agents which manage Internet-based information. In *Proceedings of the AAAI Spring Symposium on Machine Learning in Information Access,* 31-40.

Faron, C., and Kieu, Q. (1995). SATELIT, un outil d'explicitation de connaissances hypermedias. In *Actes des Journées d'Acquisition des Connaissances JAC'95.*

Faron, C., Akoulchina, I., and Ganascia, J.-G. (1996). Integrating knowledge in hypermedia: The system SATELIT. In *Proceedings of the CESA'96 IMACS Multiconference,* 94-98.

Fischer, G., and Nieper-Lemke, H. (1989). HELGON : Extending the retrieval by reformulation paradigm. In *Proceedings of CHI'89 Human Factors in Computing Systems,* 357-362.

Floridi, L. (1995). Internet: Which future for organized knowledge, Frankenstein or Pygmalion? *International Journal of Human-Computer Studies* 43:261-274.

Lieberman, H. (1995). Letizia: An agent that assists Web browsing, In *Proceedings of the Fourteenth International Joint Conference on Artificial Intelligence,* 924-929.

Maes, P. (1994). Agents that reduce work and information overload. *Communications of the ACM* 37(7).

Mitchell, T., Caruana, R., Freitag, D., McDermott, J., and Zabowski, D. (1994). Experience with a learning personal assistant. *Communications of the ACM* 37(7):81-91.

Norman, D. A., and Draper, S., W., eds. (1986). *User Centered System Design: New Perspectives on Human-Computer Interaction.* Hillsdale, NJ: Erlbaum.

Riecken, D. (1994). An architecture of integrated agents. *Communications of the ACM* 37(7):107-116.

Selker, T. (1994). COACH: A teaching agent that learns. *Communications of the ACM* 37(7):92-99.

Sowa, J. F. (1984). *Conceptual Structures: Information Processing in Mind and Machine.* Addison Wesley.

HyperContext: A Model for Adaptive Hypertext

Christopher Staff

Department of Computer Science and A.I., University of Malta, Malta

Abstract. HyperContext is a 3-layer model for adaptive hypertext. The model supports the use of multiple *interpretations* of objects of information. Whenever an object is accessed, HyperContext determines the *context* in which the access has taken place and presents the appropriate interpretation to the user.

1 Overview of Adaptive Hypertext

Adaptive Hypertext Systems (AHSs) generally provide capabilities for adaptive navigation, adaptive presentation, or both (Brusilovsky, 1996). *Adaptive presentation* enables the information content of objects (*nodes*) to adapt to the user's expectations or requirements. For instance, a student new to user modeling may be unfamiliar with certain terminology in a paper on the subject. An AHS may automatically expand the text to include the meanings of terms. *Adaptive navigation*, on the other hand, guides a user through a hypertext by recommending those links likely to lead to information relevant to the primary task, or by changing the destinations of links.

AHSs usually separate the information base from the adaptive *agent* (Mayfield, 1994). The agent determines the requirements of the user, and provides a "virtual view" of the underlying information base. The user of an adaptive hypertext system browses, or navigates, through a virtual hyperspace in which the underlying information is represented by a structure which dynamically changes to accommodate the needs and requirements of that user.

There are several methods used to elicit the needs and requirements of users. The adaptive agent may interact with a user model (see, e.g., Kobsa et al., to appear). Alternatively, usage patterns may be observed and subsequently generalised or specialised into search strategies (e.g., Armstrong et al., 1995, and Rabinowitz et al., 1995). Matching users with the appropriate strategy is generally performed either by evaluating a user query or by observing user access paths (i.e., recording which links in a hypertext are followed) and then offering the user "short cuts" to the information likely to be of interest (either based on prior knowledge or computed dynamically).

2 An Example of Adaptation in HyperContext

Two users, Eric and Pat, are browsing through the same HyperContext system, starting from different locations. Eric is interested in the architecture of cathedrals in South-East England, whereas Pat is searching for information about different organs in Kent. The links they follow eventually lead them to the same node, which contains general information about Canterbury Cathedral. Since the node has been accessed from different locations related to the different tasks, the way the node is linked to other objects is changed, so Eric will see links to other resources on the Cathedral's architecture, whereas Pat will be presented with links to more information about the Cathedral's organ. Users can be confident that the adaptive nature of the hypertext will assist them in their particular task; they are not encumbered by having to decide if a link will mislead.

3   The Structure of HyperContext

HyperContext is a 3-layer model which supports the use of multiple *interpretations* of objects of information to achieve adaptive hypertext (Staff, 1997). An interpretation is a description of the object in a particular *context*. A context is a tuple consisting of a parent object name and the name of the directed link connecting the parent to the other object. In the World-Wide Web (WWW), the contexts of a particular Web page would be those pages containing a link to that page and, if WWW links were named, the names of the links leading to that page.

Each HyperContext object has a context-free description called a *profile*, which is registered in the model's Object Layer. The profile consists of a set of *labels*, which are descriptive keywords or key phrases. An object interpretation is a subset of the object's profile which forms a context-sensitive description. Consequently, an interpretation consists of only those labels from the profile which describe the object in a specific context.

Interpretation and link information is maintained by the Structure Layer. One HyperContext object is linked to another by associating a label in an interpretation of the parent object with a destination object (child). The creator of the link selects those of the child's labels (from the profile) which describe the child in the new context. Once completed, the modified interpretation of the parent, the new interpretation of the child, and the context which relates them are immediately available to the user community at large. Any user, at any time, can create directed links between any objects—and justify the link creation by describing how the child is to be interpreted in the new context. Creating links within interpretations means that it is possible for a label to be linked to different children depending on the context in which the object has been accessed.

A user interacts with HyperContext through the Presentation Layer, which itself interacts with the other layers to supply the context to a link traversal, retrieve the destination object, and apply the appropriate interpretation to the retrieved object. The advantage to a user browsing through such an adaptive hypertext system is that he or she can follow a previously constructed *context path* leading to information which has already been interpreted by other users with similar needs.

The total number of links a node can have (across all contexts) can be larger than that of nodes in non-adaptive hypertext systems, because in HyperContext, irrelevant links will not exist in the chosen interpretation. Users can amend existing interpretations and create new ones, so over time the adaptive hypertext system reflects the cumulative usage of its users.

4   Information Retrieval in HyperContext

HyperContext includes three context-sensitive information retrieval methods, which assist the user in locating relevant information.

The Traditional Information Retrieval (TIR) method takes a search query, composed of one or more search terms, and returns a list of relevant HyperContext objects found from a centrally held index. A HyperContext object is considered relevant if there is an interpretation of the object which supports the criteria of the terms expressed in the query.

Information Retrieval-in-Context (IRC) also takes a user query. However, IRC assumes that the query is related to the node the user is currently visiting and searches for relevant objects that are reachable from that location. The search is constrained to relevant objects, i.e., those which are connected by a path to the interpretation of the object at which the user is currently located. Once an object that satisfies the search criteria is found, IRC can lead a user to it.

Whereas TIR and IRC are initiated by the user, Adaptive Information Discovery (AID) automatically guides the user to relevant information by assessing through observation the interests of the user. The Presentation Layer maintains a *context session*, which is a record of the interpretations of objects and the contexts in which they have been visited. A context session terminates whenever the user performs a *context switch*. A context switch occurs when the user changes the context in which the current object should be interpreted or hyper-leaps to an object. AID generates a description of the object that it calculates to be of interest to the user based on the interpretations of objects, the contexts, and the links followed during the context session. It then attempts to locate an object interpretation which satisfies the description. If it or an approximation is found, AID attempts to discover where the object is in relation to the objects in the context session. The object may already be in the context path, may be reachable from an object in the context session if the context of that object is switched, or not reachable. AID can guide the user to the relevant object or can assist the user in creating a new context path to the object.

5   Conclusion

HyperContext is a model for adaptive hypertext in which information is interpreted according to the context in which it is accessed. Users can also locate information using HyperContext's information retrieval methods. When new interpretations of information and the contexts in which they apply are created, they are immediately available for use by the user community.

References

Armstrong, R., Freitag, D., Joachims, T., and Mitchell, T. (1995). WebWatcher: A learning apprentice for the World Wide Web. In *Proceedings of the 1995 AAAI Spring Symposium on Information Gathering from Heterogeneous, Distributed Environments*, 6–12.

Brusilovsky, P. (1996). Adaptive hypermedia: An attempt to analyse and generalize. In Brusilovsky, P., Kommers, P., and Streitz, N., eds., *Multimedia, Hypermedia, and Virtual Reality: Models, Systems, and Applications*. Berlin: Springer. 288–304.

Kobsa, A., Nill, A., and Fink, J. (to appear). Adaptive hypertext and hypermedia clients of the user modeling system BGP-MS. In Maybury, M., ed., *Intelligent Multimedia Information Retrieval*. Cambridge, MA: MIT Press.

Mayfield, J. (1994). Two-level hypertext models as an underpinning for AHSs. In Brusilovsky, P., and Beaumont, I., eds., *Workshop on Adaptive Hypertext and Hypermedia*. Available from http://www.education.uts.edu.au/projects/ah/AH-94.html.

Rabinowitz, J., Mathé, N., and Chen, J. R. (1995). Adaptive HyperMan: A customizable hypertext system for reference manuals. In *Proceedings of the AAAI Fall Symposium on Artificial Intelligence Applications in Knowledge Navigation and Retrieval*, 110–115.

Staff, C. (1997). HyperContext: Using context in adaptive hypertext. In *Proceedings of the International and Interdisciplinary Conference on Modeling and Using Context '97*, 243–255.

From Discourse Plans to User-Adapted Hypermedia

Berardina De Carolis and Sebastiano Pizzutilo

Department of Informatics, University of Bari, Italy

Abstract. This summary describes how user-adapted hypermedia can be generated from discourse plans; the application domain is that of instruction manuals.

1 Introduction

Various methods can be employed to build user-adapted hypermedia (Brusilovsky, 1996). One can start from a maximally connected graph, in which several pages are associated to each node, by defining context-related pages and link selection heuristics. Alternatively, one can employ a knowledge base to generate what is needed in each context. In this paper, we discuss the potential of the discourse plan as a knowledge source in this building process. Discourse planning has proved to be an efficient method for generating user-adapted multimedia. Its application to hypermedia generation is suited to those cases in which knowledge underlying the discourse structure can contribute to making the hyperdocument understandable to the user. We claim that this is the case for educational hypermedia, and in particular for instruction manuals, which can be viewed as on-line information systems with a strong educational aspect. These manuals comprise two main components: a *description* of device elements and an *instruction set* on how to use the device. Their navigation space is not very large. Consequently, the purpose of adaptation is not to avoid informational disorientation by limiting browsing or by reducing the information detail in each page; adaptation is rather aimed at reducing the cognitive effort of learning. To this end, the following hyperdocument aspects can be adapted to the user:

Page presentation: Every page should clearly show its communicative goal and the relationships among information items it contains, through an appropriate space arrangement and media and style selection; the same presentation criteria should be applied consistently through the whole document.

Navigation: The hyperdocument should select, in every situation, the navigation path which ensures learning of all items of relevance by minimizing the number of visited pages.

Orientation: The hyperdocument should ensure that users always know in which phase of the learning process they find themselves.

2 Outline of GeNet

Our prototype hypermedia generation system (GeNet, developed in C++) employs the following knowledge sources:

- the *discourse plan* (which we call *Dplan*): a tree structure to whose nodes we associate an instructional goal, a rhetorical relation (RR), a focus and (to the leaves) an elementary

communicative act; it represents how the communicative goal is decomposed into subgoals, until communicative acts are defined, with RRs among them (Hovy, 1993; Mann and Thompson, 1988);
- a textual and/or graphical database and
- a User Model, a very simple stereotype which includes: age, educational level, experience in the application domain and in hypermedia.

In the hyperdocument (which we call *Hypm*), the instruction process is represented by a top-down refinement of the main instructional goal. Different levels of detail in *information content* are provided by varying information in each page and by restricting navigation in the document; in *page presentation*, media employed, format and space distribution of items can also be varied. Different *navigation styles* are implemented by varying: (i) the *way* the tree is explored (depth first vs. breadth first); (ii) the *flexibility* of activated paths (entire vs. partial exploration of the tree) and (iii) the *control* of exploration made by users. Various forms of *orientation support* are introduced, to favour remembering the instructional goals.

A set of rules connects attitudes in the User Model to level of detail, page presentation, navigation style and orientation support options. For example:

1. IF the user is elderly THEN employ larger characters;
2. IF the user's level of education is not high, THEN insert more details into every instruction step;
3. IF the user is at his/her first access to the hypermedia AND he/she is not assumed to know about the device, THEN select a detailed, inflexible navigation mode and introduce a high level of orientation support.

GeNet generates hyperdocuments in the HTML language, as follows:

Page content: Dplan is explored in a top-down way. Its nodes are aggregated into Hypm pages according (i) to the complexity of the subtree starting from each node and (ii) to the associated RR, so as to obtain a reasonable page complexity in each context, by avoiding breaking strong RRs (such as a Contrast or a Motivation). This aggregation algorithm is parametrized to create pages with variable information load.

Page layout: Pages have four components (Title, Head, Body and Footer), each built by means of three functions: (i) a linguistic realization λ (at present, just a template-filling), which transforms the instructional goals or the elementary communicative acts associated with Dplan nodes into sentences; (ii) a graphical transformation π, which processes images associated to Dplan leaves; (iii) a multimedia realization Φ, which combines results of λ and π as a function of the RR associated with the top node. The three functions are parametrized in order to generate different pages from the same Dplan items: sentences of varying complexity, images of different size and colour, different presentation orders and positions, different types of lists and so on.

Link introduction. Some anchors in the Body refer to device descriptions: A matching function α finds a device item name in the Body and adds a link to the address of the corresponding page. Other anchors in the Body, and buttons in the Footer, define two main navigation modes within the instructional part of the manual, which are suited to users with different domain experience: (i) A *guided tour* in which the user is solicited to explore the hyperdocument in a top-down, depth-first way by means of buttons in the Footer. A button is built using the function β that selects items in a library of semantically organized buttons and icons and associates them with pages. The button text is a function of the RR (*link annotation*), so as to support local orientation. For example, "next or previous step" in an Elaboration Process Step, "next or previous item" in a Sequence, rather than plain "next or previous" buttons. To enhance global orientation, a *connection page* can be added after exploring a subtree, to synthetize the goal of that subtree and the goal of the immediately following one; this enables users to understand what they have seen and what they are going to see next. (ii) A *free navigation* mode in which users are left free to select the path they want to follow by means of anchors in the Body. In this case, at the end of navigation, the system can examine the paths that the user did not look at, to check that these do not contain essential information.

Adaptation is obtained by linking λ, π, Φ and β parameters to user attitudes. For example, rules R1 and R2 are translated into a parameter setting in λ and Φ, R3 in the creation of a "guided tour with connection pages", and so on.

3 Comments

User-adapted educational hypermedia are usually aimed at explaining concepts, entities or topics (de Rosis et al., 1993; Boyle and Encarnacion, 1994; Milosavljevic and Dale, 1996); the descriptive part of our manuals has the same purpose. The main difference in generating the instructional part of these manuals is that instructors have strong tutorial knowledge in their minds, which the hyperdocument should respect. In our first prototype we use a preliminary definition of the way in which this knowledge adapts to the circumstances. We plan to refine the user modeling structure and the adaptation rules according to the results of a set of experiments that we are planning in cooperation with the Department of Psychology of the University of Reading.

References

Boyle, C., and Encarnacion, A. O. (1994). Metadoc, an adaptive hypertext reading system. *User Modeling and User-Adapted Interaction* 4:1–19.

Brusilovsky, P. (1996). Methods and techniques of adaptive hypermedia. *User Modeling and User-Adapted Interaction* 6(2–3): 87–128.

de Rosis, F., De Carolis, N., and Pizzutilo, S. (1993). User-tailored hypermedia explanations. In *Adjunct Proceedings of INTERCHI 93*, 169–170.

Hovy, E. H. (1993). Automated discourse generation using discourse structure relations. *Artificial Intelligence* 63:341–385.

Mann, W. C., and Thompson, S. A. (1988). Rhetorical Structure Theory, towards a functional theory of text organization. *Text* 8: 243–281.

Milosavljevic, M., and Dale, R. (1996). Text generation and user modeling on the web. In *Proceedings of the Workshop on User Modeling for Information Filtering on the WWW, 5th International Conference on User Modeling*, 2–8.

Intermediaries and Information Filtering

Users and Intermediaries in Information Retrieval: What Are They Talking About?

Tefko Saracevic[1], Amanda Spink[2], and Mei-Mei Wu[3]

[1] School of Communication, Information and Library Studies, Rutgers University,
New Brunswick, NJ, U.S.A.
[2] School of Library and Information Sciences, University of North Texas, Denton, TX, USA
[3] Department of Social Education, National Taiwan Normal University, Taipei, Taiwan, R.O.C.

Abstract. Discourse between users and intermediaries (human agents), as they interact when searching large databases, serves the function of user modeling. Selected data from a real-life study are presented, categorizing the utterances and elicitations (questions) into seven categories. The results provide an empirical picture of constructing user models through discourse and searching. A stratified interaction model is used as a theoretical model and framework.

1 Information Retrieval and User Modeling

When, at the beginning of 1950's, Calvin Mooers, one of the information science pioneers, coined the term *information retrieval* (IR) he also defined the problems addressed by the activity: (1) How to represent and organize information intellectually? (2) How to specify a search intellectually? and (3) What systems and techniques to use for those processes? (Mooers, 1951). Since Mooers' time, IR has developed in sophistication in both theory and practice. Interaction evolved to become a hallmark of modern IR. However, on a basic level, the problems defined by Mooers are still with us. It is the second of these problems, *how to search intellectually*, that directly involves user modeling. Searching is based on queries derived from users. In turn, they represent a whole set of underlying variables related to users and use. Thus, from the very outset to this day, user modeling (although not necessarily under this name) has been an integral component of IR. There is no IR without user modeling of some sort.

Effectiveness in IR concerns retrieval not of any old information but of *relevant information*. Or rather objects—texts, images, sounds, or for short *texts*—conveying potentially relevant information. The term *relevant* refers to information that pertains to the user's problem or situation at hand, involving also the user's cognitive and affective states and beliefs. Thus, by choice *relevance* became the basic underlying notion in IR, with all its attendant ambiguities as a very human notion. Not that the notions of *uncertainty,* used in expert systems and knowledge bases, or *aboutness,* used in classification and indexing systems, are any less ambiguous.

Thus, user modeling in IR has to be understood in terms of (1) the notion of relevance, and (2) the process of interaction to sharpen the likelihood of relevance. The object of user modeling in IR is to bring about retrieval of relevant texts for (a) given user(s) or use(s) through a variety of interactive processes. A number of methods for user modeling have been developed in IR, as summarized later. The most powerful method in existence so far involves mediated interaction, that is, an interaction involving a user, a human intermediary, and an IR system. The intermediary is an information professional (variously also called an information scientist, a reference or special librarian, an information broker, a searcher, an information officer, or the like) skillful in both user modeling and the subsequent searching of and retrieval from various IR systems and large databases. Intermediaries play various roles, among them to: assist in the diagnosis of the user's problem and in the (re)formulation of the question; suggest appropriate systems or databases for searching; translate the question into one or more queries and search strategies acceptable to the given system and database; conduct and modify searching; assist in the evaluation of results; provide the user with appropriate outputs; and/or counsel the user in follow-up activity. In other words, to use the AI parlance, an intermediary is a truly intelligent agent constructing, implementing, and modifying user models in all their complexity with considerable feedback.

2 Rationale and Objectives of the Study

Even since the advent of user modeling by automatic or semiautomatic means in IR, or for that matter in AI, nothing has come close to matching the extent, complexity, and success of user modeling as done by skillful professional intermediaries in direct interactive contact with users. Thus, the observation and analysis of such activities involving users and human agents is of critical importance for understanding user modeling (Belkin et al., 1987). Moreover, unlike many other user modeling efforts, it is real and it has a rich context.

Intermediaries use various empirical methods for defining user models, which are also found in other diagnostic, interviewing, and counseling activities. This is accomplished through discourse, a complex dialog that takes place between users and intermediaries (dyadic dialog), or among users, intermediaries, and systems (triadic dialog). The modes of discourse may vary: oral, written or both; face-to-face or remote; with or without relevant or not relevant texts as models of what is or is not desired (relevance feedback); etc. But the basics of discourse remain.

This brings us to the central point of the study. The problem underlying all of the theoretical, experimental, and empirical activities in user modeling revolves around the classic and most difficult question (Belkin, 1993): What it is important to know about the user in order to support the user in interaction with the IR system? The answer has not been found by a long shot either in IR or in AI. In this study, we are trying to contribute some answers to that classic question. Discourse is the way in which users are modeled in IR. We may think that even users searching without intermediaries are engaged in a discourse with themselves, the system, and/or the retrieved texts. Users talk to themselves, carry on a dialog (written or oral) with a system, and converse with outputs. But the discourse between users and intermediaries is the most observable instance of user modeling. Thus, we suggest that analysis of such discourse can and does provide for a better understanding of what is involved in user modeling. In turn, a better understanding of this process is a necessary condition for improvements.

Data for analysis were selected from a large study whose aim was to contribute to formal understanding and characterization of IR interactions from the human perspective. The objective of this paper is to characterize discourse between users and professional intermediaries in interactive IR situations, in order to derive a discourse- and interaction-based user model for IR. The following questions are asked: What topics are covered in discourse and to what extent? What type of questions are asked by users and by intermediaries? How can we model these as interactions? The study is distinguished in that it derives data from observation of real users and intermediaries, in real IR interactions and settings. It is an empirical evaluation of what we believe is a typical behavior of users and intermediaries. It is a naturalistic study, one of the largest, if not the largest of its kind.

3 Approaches to User Modeling in Information Retrieval

System-centered approaches. Many formal methods related to IR systems have been developed and tested. In the *relevance feedback* approach, users are modeled through texts that are assessed as relevant (or not relevant)—they are used to retrieve or reject similar texts or clusters of texts (Spink and Losee, 1996). In the *query expansion* approach the initial or modified query is used as a basis for user modeling. Terms and logical connectives are expanded, contracted, added, switched etc. by automatic, semi-automatic, and manual techniques (Efthimidiadis, 1996). Another method is to build into the system ways and means by which users can on their own model their problem with the system's assistance. Examples are experimental systems by Oddy (1977) and Croft and Thompson (1987), but unfortunately such systems have remained in labs. Finally, the most widely used method combines the system- and user-centered approach. Originally, it was developed by Hans Peter Luhn, the most inventive information science pioneer, under the name of Selective Dissemination of Information (SDI) (Luhn, 1961). SDI, known also under a number of other names, involves the periodic retrieval of texts from recent updates, or filtering from streams of oncoming texts, based on what Luhn called *user profiles*. A profile is a search statement expressing user interests—it is a user model. Profiles are dynamic, they can and do change, and after a time they may stabilize. Elaborate ways have been developed for arriving at changing and testing user profiles. The Text Retrieval Conference (TREC), a current very large scale international IR evaluation effort, includes a routing track, which involves tests of profile optimization and learning. Profiles in IR largely precede and outperform "intelligent" agents and knowbots in AI.

Human-centered approaches. This perspective also involves several approaches. The area is rich, thus only a few examples are given. *Question analysis* and the reference interview are methods by which user modeling is accomplished through various interview and analysis techniques; they have received considerable attention over time (see, e.g., Taylor, 1968, Harter, 1992, Radford, 1996). Users' *cognitive aspects* have also been investigated to a great extent (see, e.g., Allen, 1991). In interactive studies, user modeling is treated as an integral part of the IR process (Belkin, 1993), a stance taken here. The main point in all of these studies is that user modeling is highly dynamic.

Connections. Although they address very similar processes, there is little crossover between the studies of user modeling in IR on the one hand and AI and cognitive science on the other hand. For example, user modeling studies such as the ones in the compilation by Kobsa and Wahlster (1989) or in articles appearing in the journal *User Modeling and User-Adapted Interaction* by and large do not cite or reflect on user modeling in IR. Conversely, only a few IR user modeling studies use concepts and techniques developed in AI. Notable exceptions in IR are works by Brajnik et al. (1987), who used analytic cognitive models developed in expert systems research for user modeling in "intelligent" IR, and by Logan et al. (1994), who applied Galliers' theory of belief revision, developed in AI, for use in IR. This relative isolation is unfortunate. Wheels are widely reinvented on both sides.

4 Modeling IR Interaction

The traditional IR model, represented in two prongs, a system and user one, in reality concentrates on the system side only. Moreover, it does not reflect and incorporate interaction at all (Belkin, 1993). Thus, a number of interactive IR models have been developed, and these models, unlike the traditional model, are suitable as a context for user modeling. Ingwersen (1996) took a broad approach and suggested cognitive representations by all participants in interaction users, texts, intermediaries and systems to serve as the base for a cognitive model of IR. Belkin et al. (1995) took a more specific approach and treated IR interactions as a series of episodes or frames, each of which supports different types of interactions and tasks. Finally, Saracevic (1996a, 1996b) proposed a stratified model of IR interactions, used in this study.

Space allows for only a brief description of the stratified model. Interaction is taken as a discourse between a user and "computer" through an interface. The "computer" involves much more than hardware (hence the quotation marks). It includes, among other things, computational capacities and procedures, and information resources or content. Both users and the "computer" are decomposed into different strata (levels), comprising distinctly identifiable elements or variables affecting the process in different ways. Interaction is then treated as an interplay between different user and "computer" strata or levels realized on the *surface level* through the interface. On the user side we can model *surface, cognitive, affective,* and *situational* levels. On the "computer" side we can also model levels: *surface, engineering, processing,* and *content,* as shown in Figure 1.

Interaction is a series of dynamic interplays and adaptations between levels. As the interaction progresses things change. For instance, on the surface level a query may be changed, terms added or deleted, different tactics employed, and so on, reflecting and affecting changes at other levels. Situational and cognitive states may be re-interpreted, new texts sought, etc.

We applied the stratified model to consider other IR notions also in strata. Relevance inferences are made in connection with different strata; thus, we suggested that in IR we have a dynamic interdependent *system of relevances* (note the plural) (Saracevic, 1996b). The model was also used in a study of identification and effectiveness of sources of search terms in queries (Spink and Saracevic, 1997). We are using here the stratified model as a basis for the explication of user modeling in IR. We are suggesting that user modeling is (i) an interactive process that (ii) proceeds in a dynamic way at different levels trying (iii) to capture user's cognitive, situational, affective and possibly other elements (variables) that bear upon effectiveness of retrieval, (iv) with an influence of intermediary interface capabilities, and (v) with an interplay with "computer" levels. It is an interactive diagnostic and counseling process.

5 Data Corpus

Details are presented in a number of papers, among them those by Saracevic et al. (1990) and Spink and Saracevic (1997); thus only a sketch is presented here. Forty self-selected academic users (faculty and doctoral students) with real information problems provided one question each for online searching on DIALOG. Four professional search intermediaries were involved, each handling ten questions. Questions concerned topics in medicine, the social sciences, the physical sciences and the humanities. A mean of 3 databases were searched per question.

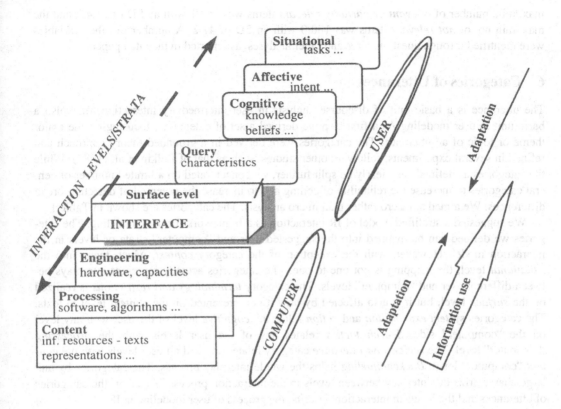

Figure 1. Elements in the stratified model of IR interaction.

Prior to the search users provided a written question statement. The interaction between users and intermediaries was videotaped during a pre-online search interview and during the actual online search. There were 46.05 hours of videotape (with a mean of 69.08 min. per question). The mean time for the pre-search interview was 13.04 min. and for online search 56.04 min. The transaction logs of searches (computer commands and responses) were also recorded. The discourse between users and intermediaries was transcribed from videos. Utterances in discourse were analyzed to develop a grounded-theory set of categories, as defined below, and then categorized accordingly. Similarly, computer commands and responses were categorized according to our own categories. The utterances in discourse from the transcripts and commands/responses from the transaction logs were synchronized with respect to time.

Users were given a printout of all items retrieved. They judged retrieved items as *relevant*, *partially relevant*, or *not relevant*. Altogether 6225 items were retrieved, of which users judged 3565 as relevant or partially relevant, and 2660 as not relevant, for a mean precision of 57%. However, there was considerable variation in retrieval from question to question: the maximum/ minimum number of *total items* retrieved was 427/13 with a standard deviation of 85.9; the max./min. number of *relevant or partially relevant* items was 348/1 with an SD of 71.43; and the max./min no. of *not relevant* items was 180/0 with an SD of 47.2. A number of other variables were identified through questionnaires and other analyses, as reported in the cited papers.

6   Categories of Utterances

The utterance is a basic unit of discourse analysis in user-intermediary interaction, thus also a basic unit in user modeling As a first step we derived a set of categories, focusing on the major theme or topic of an utterance. The categories were derived in a grounded theory approach and refined in several experiments, following other studies, such as that of Belkin et al. (1987). While the categories as defined can clearly be split further, we concentrated on a limited number of general categories to increase the reliability of coding and to increase the potential of detecting broad differences. We aimed at macro rather than micro analysis. The categories are shown in Table 1.

We suggested a stratified model of IR interaction as a framework for user modeling. The categories we defined can be mapped into the suggested user and "computer" strata or levels in the interaction model. However, with the exception of the category *context*, which maps into the *situational* level, the mapping is not one to one. The categories actually represent interplays between different user and "computer" levels. The category *terminology and restrictions* is realized on the *surface* level, but it is also affected by how it is represented on the *content* level in texts. The categories *system explanation* and *action* relate the *cognitive* level of the user with any level on the "computer" side. *Search tactics* relates any of the user levels with the *processing* "computer" level. The *review and relevance* category relates any and all user levels with the *content* "computer" level. *Backchanneling* helps the whole interplay process. The categories by and large characterize the interplay between levels in the interaction process. Together, the categories of utterances and the levels in interaction describe the process of user modeling in IR.

7   Results: Distribution of Utterances and Elicitations

Table 2 presents the number of utterances according to the defined categories, excluding the last category *extraneous* because those utterances do not contribute to user modeling. The arrangement is from the highest to the lowest number of utterances in the "Total" column.

The great variation in retrieval results, mentioned above, is mirrored in the variation in the number of utterances from question to question. The mean number of user utterances per question was 243, with a maximum/minimum of 665/62, and an SD of 126.34. The mean number of intermediary utterances was 283, with a max./min of 714/94 and an SD of 132.14. We also calculated the interaction times: The mean time per question for user utterances was 21.32 minutes (max./min. of 48.3/4.36 minutes with an SD of 644); the mean time for intermediary utterances was 47.69 minutes (max./min. of 102.5/16.3 minutes with an SD of 1251).

Let us now concentrate on the analysis of elicitations—a subset of utterances that refer to a verbal request for information by either party. They could be in a question or a non-question form, hence the term *elicitation* rather than *question*. Since elicitations reveal topics queried in interaction, they are a critical aspect in any and all user modeling. Data on elicitations, presented in Table

Table 1. Categories of utterances distinguished in the empirical study.

Category number and name	Description
1. Context	User's problem or task at hand; information seeking stage; information, if any, collected so far; expectations and other aspects underlying the question; user domain and problem knowledge; user's plans.
2. Terminology and restrictions	Elaboration on and modification of concepts, terms, keywords and descriptors; generation of terms; specification of borderlines; restrictions such as with respect to language, years; technical term spelling.
3. Systems explanations	Workings and technical aspects of system used; technical explanation of searching; characteristics of databases and documents in system; other possible information sources; obtaining texts; costs involved.
4. Search tactics and procedures	Selection and variation of terms, fields, morphology, logic in search statements; commands; selection and variation in magnitude and output sizes, formats, order; output specification; correcting mistakes.
5. Review and relevance	Review of search statements with respect to the output; evaluation of output sources or content; relevance judgments of and feedback from outputs; decisions or questions on what is wanted based on search statements or output.
6. Action	Description of an ongoing or impending activity, e.g. thesaurus lookup, output formats, printing; explanation of what is happening.
7. Backchanneling—prompts, echoes	Communication prompts, fillers, acknowledgments, formulaic expressions, etc. indicating listeners involvement, e.g. "O.K.", "Wow!", "Unhuh", "Right"; echoes and requests for repetitions e.g., "What?", "Pardon?", "Say that again"; pauses.
8. Extraneous	Utterances extraneous to the search interaction—greetings, formulaic courtesies, social comments and questions; personal matters.

3, are culled from two studies that used the same data corpus: one that studied elicitations by users alone (Wu, 1993), and another that incorporated both users' and intermediaries' elicitations (Spink et al., 1996). However, we modified somewhat the elicitation categories from those two studies to conform to our categories of utterances. Wu had 10 categories for user elicitations and Spink et al. had 15 categories for intermediary elicitations; we combined some of the more detailed categories in each that obviously fall into categories of utterances as defined above. We also eliminated extraneous elicitations, for the reason given above. Again, the categories are ordered according to the number in the "Total" column.

Table 2. Distribution of utterances in user-intermediary interaction (each percentage refers to the column in question).

Category number and name	Intermediary		User		Total	
4. Search tactics and procedures	3360	30%	1680	17%	5040	24%
7. Backchanneling—echoes	1179	10%	3179	33%	4358	21%
5. Review and relevance	1996	18%	1825	19%	3821	18%
2. Terminology and restrictions	1265	10%	904	9%	2169	10%
3. Systems explanations	1399	12%	625	6%	2024	10%
6. Action	1554	14%	399	4%	1953	9%
1. Context	565	5%	1102	11%	1667	8%
Total	11318	100%	9714	100%	21032	100%
% of Total		54%		46%		100%

Table 3. Distribution of elicitations by intermediaries and users (each percentage refers to the column in question).

Category number and name	Intermediary		User		Total	
2. Terminology and restrictions	817	55%	288	32%	1105	46%
5. Review and relevance	251	17%	107	12%	358	15%
4. Search tactics and procedures	59	4%	240	27%	299	13%
3. Systems explanations	103	7%	174	20%	277	12%
1. Context	172	12%	1	0%	173	7%
7. Backchanneling—echoes	50	3%	47	5%	97	4%
6. Action	34	2%	34	4%	68	3%
Total	1486	100%	891	100%	2377	100%
% of Total		63%		37%		100%

8 Discussion: Implications for User Modeling

Several aspects are of interest to note from the distribution of utterances (Table 2). Users talk somewhat less than intermediaries (46% vs. 54% of all utterances), but the difference is not that large. Both take about the same number of turns. If we consider that the basic object of interaction is to model users, then both parties are participating in the process almost equally.

The top category, comprising one fourth of the utterances, deals with various *search tactics and procedures*, with intermediaries in this category talking substantially more than (twice as much as) users. In other words, users get and exchange a lot of information about the immediate processes concerned with the search itself. Searching itself, with associated changes, enters into user modeling in a major way. In contrast, the bottom category, comprising only 8% of all utterances, deals with the *context* of the question and user. This was a surprise—we expected that there would be much more talk about the various things that fall under context. Neither users nor intermediaries explicate on this topic a lot. This challenges the usual assumption that user modeling largely involves modeling of context.

Interestingly, *backchanneling,* with over a fifth of the utterances, is the second largest category. These are brief utterances (even grunts) that facilitate communication, indicate active participation, provide echoing questions, and the like. They seem to play a significant role in interaction. Users made considerably more than twice as many backchanneling utterances, which may reveal characteristic features of the nature of user participation, such as a lot of confirmation, indication of understanding, and posing of brief questions. Backchanneling represents a unique human device and tactic that speeds communication and increases mutual understanding, and it seems to be important in user modeling. Maybe communication with computers is so limited and unsatisfactory because it does not involve this important human communicative element.

With fewer than a fifth of the utterances, *review and relevance* is the third highest category. Here, the utterances are almost equally divided among users and intermediaries. These utterances reflect possible changes in or confirmations of what is going on in searches, outputs, and their relations. In turn, they may suggest new and other terminology and tactics, thus they may affect considerably the subsequent utterances in other categories. Thus, review of searches and relevance assessments also play an important role in user modeling.

Utterances about *terminology and restrictions, systems explanations,* and *action* comprise the other three categories, with roughly one tenth of the utterances each. Not surprisingly, intermediaries made about three times as many utterances in categories dealing with systems explanations and action as users—after all, that is their domain. These categories indicate the importance of providing users with explanations of what is in the systems, what capabilities exist, and what is going on, as an integral part of user modeling.

Elicitations present quite a different picture than utterances overall. Close to one tenth of all utterances were elicitations. This small proportion also surprised us. Intermediaries made about three fifths of all elicitations, showing a reliance on the question-answer process for user modeling by intermediaries. However, users also had their fair share of elicitations, with some two fifths of the total, showing a similar reliance by users on understanding what is going on. Elicitations are a leading edge of interaction, triggering other actions. The question is: What kind? User modeling and elicitations go hand in hand.

As to the categories, close to half of all elicitations are about *terminology and restrictions,* with intermediaries asking about one and a half times as many terminological questions as users, probably suggesting or confirming choices. There seems to be a terminological imperative governing elicitations. This is not surprising, because queries entered into the interface for searching are terminology to start with, and terminology presents a major problem and decision making aspect in IR and in user modeling. Thus, terminology plays a major role in question-answer sequences of user modeling and predominates over other questions.

The other half of elicitations cover the other six categories. About a seventh of all elicitations are devoted to *review and relevance.* This was a surprise, for we thought that there would be more elicitations about these topics. *System explanations* and *search tactics and procedures* had a bit more than a tenth of the elicitations each. Surprisingly, only 7% of the elicitations were about *context.* Finally, *backchanneling* and *action* are at the bottom with negligible percentages. The combined elicitations related to relevance, tactics and systems explanation seem to be another major component in user modeling, while context elicitations play a smaller role.

The difference in the number of utterances from question to question was very large. So was the difference in the time spent talking by users and intermediaries. In general, intermediaries talked much longer, over two times as long as users. By far the longest time was spent by intermediaries on the category *terminology* and related aspects, the same category where they had the most elicitations. This again indicates the power of the terminological imperative in user modeling. Clearly, all questions are not equal, indicating that the nature of the question itself and all that goes with it requires user modeling of different intensity, and even different types.

What is not evident from the data as presented, but comes out clearly from a qualitative evaluation of the process, is the nature of the changes that occur during each interactive session. Utterances are here categorized with respect to their basic category, but as in a grammar they do not reflect semantics, even less pragmatics, that is they do not reflect the meaning of what is actually going on. Most evident are considerable *shifts* or *transitions* that happen as the interaction unfurls. Among these are: shifts in terminology and tactics; redefinition of the problem and refitting to the situation; illumination of some dimension of the situation; changes in rationale and expectations; changes in cognitive realization, understanding and learning, and the like. Thus, as a rule and not as an exception, a question as asked and subsequently processed is quite different at the end than at the beginning, undergoing a number of transformations in between. User models and modeling changes in the course of the interactive process. Unfortunately, in IR and elsewhere we have not as yet developed methodologies that may appropriately aggregate such changes, shifts, and transitions in interaction, and provide a sort of transitional grammar. We do not even have a good classification of these shifts. Beyond anecdotes we cannot document them well. For user modeling these shifts are crucial, critical incidents. However, intermediaries understand professionally that user modeling is an evolving transitional, shifting process, thus they direct the interaction, utterances, elicitations, decisions, suggestions etc., accordingly. User modeling in IR comprises shifts and transitions. It evolves as it goes along. It is not a static, one time deal. It does not rest on the initial query alone.

The data presented here are descriptive of the types of utterances and elicitations that go on in user-intermediary interaction. However, the data do not address the effectiveness of different elements or categories in interaction. In this analysis we have not addressed the critical questions related to effectiveness, such as: Are some interactions with different distributions of categories more effective than others in terms of retrieval of relevant texts? In terms of user utility and satisfaction ratings? Do they provide significant (positive or negative) correlation with a myriad of other variables that enter into IR? We have data that may answer some of these questions, e.g. correlations between the distribution of utterance categories in different questions with a variety of effectiveness measures and other variables. But these data await another analysis and another paper. However, even the picture we presented is useful in itself for further understanding of the content and diversity of the interactive user modeling process.

9 Conclusions

The central premise of this study is that analysis of discourse between users and intermediaries can provide a better understanding of user modeling. To do this, we have shown the distribution of categories of utterances, including elicitations, by users and intermediaries from a large corpus of interaction data, and we have discussed these categories at length as types involved in user modeling in IR. Furthermore, we have suggested a stratified IR interaction model to serve as a framework for user modeling. The categories of utterances for the most part represent interplays between user and "computer" levels in interaction. The strength of the study is that it is based on empirical, real-life evidence. It is also a unique study in many respects, particularly with respect to size. The weakness is the same as in all empirical studies: Conclusions pertain really only to the evidence at hand. That is, generalizations, while documented, should be taken as no more than hypotheses to be confirmed by further study.

Data show an extensive and dynamic interplay between users, intermediaries, and the "computer" as the third party in discourse. Many of the utterances and categories pertain to the actions or results related to the interplay with that third party. A large proportion of the utterances, in particular elicitations, were aimed at a dynamic (re)formulation of the user model, with an active involvement of "computer" levels. For instance, a lot of the utterances deal with the system itself, how users react and remodel themselves from what the system provides and how. This indicates that in user modeling there is much more going on than in the narrow perspective of user modeling encompassed by relevance feedback, query expansion, and related automatic or semi-automatic techniques in IR, or in AI. User modeling involves various interactive loops among various levels on both sides—a user model is evolving and changing as the process unfurls. We suggest that along with a system of relevances, we have a system of user models (plural) in IR involved in every interaction where users participate actively. The stratified model describes the elements in this system and categories of utterances describe the interplays between elements.

The concepts and findings elaborated here do suggest a different understanding of what is involved in user modeling in or outside of IR. We also question whether user modeling, as such a complex process, can be attempted with any degree of success by reducing it to one or just a few elements, whatever they may be. Yet this is a common approach in both IR and AI. Many approaches rest on assumptions that constitute a gross oversimplification of user modeling. Reductionism did not work elsewhere, and it does not work with user modeling either. It is not surprising then that attempts to automate user modeling have been quite limited. We are suggesting again, as we did at the outset, that detailed observation of what is actually going on in user modeling, particularly involving human agents, is a fruitful ground for further understanding of the process, which in turn is a prerequisite for any improvements and for the derivation of design criteria for automating this delightful and completely human process.

References

Allen, B. L. (1991). Cognitive research in information science. In Williams, M. ed., *Annual Review of Information Science and Technology* 26:3–37.

Belkin, N. J., Brooks, H. M. and Daniels, P. J. (1987). Knowledge elicitation using discourse analysis. *International Journal of Man-Machine Studies* 27:127–144.

Belkin, N. J. (1993). Interaction with text: Information retrieval as information seeking behavior. *Information Retrieval: 10. Von der Modellierung zur Anwendung.* Konstanz, Germany: Universitätsverlag Konstanz, 55–66.

Belkin, N. J, Cool, C., Stein, A., and Thiel, U. (1995). Cases, scripts, and information seeking strategies: On the design of interactive information retrieval systems. *Expert Systems with Applications* 9:379–395.

Brajnik, G., Guida, G., and Tasso, C. (1987). User modeling in intelligent information retrieval. *Information Processing & Management* 23:305–320.

Brajnik, G., Mizzaro, S., and Tasso, C. (1996). Evaluating user interfaces to information retrieval systems: A case study of user support. In *Proceedings of the Nineteenth Annual ACM/SIGIR Conference on Research and Development in Information Retrieval*, 128–136.

Croft, W. B., and Thompson, R. (1987). I^3R: A new approach to the design of document retrieval systems. *Journal of the American Society for Information Science* 38:389–404.

Efthimidiadis, E. N. (1996). Query expansion. In Williams, M. ed., *Annual Review of Information Science and Technology* 31:121–187.

Harter, S. P. (1992). Psychological relevance and information science. *Journal of the American Society for Information Science* 43:602–615.

Ingwersen, P. (1996). Cognitive perspectives of information retrieval interaction: Elements of a cognitive IR theory. *Journal of Documentation* 52:3–50.

Kobsa, A., and Wahlster, W., eds. (1989). *User Models in Dialog Systems*. Berlin: Springer.

Logan, B., Reece, S., and Sparck Jones, K. (1994). Modeling information retrieval agents with belief revision. In *Proceedings of the Seventeenth Annual ACM/SIGIR Conference on Research and Development in Information Retrieval*, 91–100.

Luhn, H. P. (1961). Selective dissemination of new scientific information with the aid of electronic processing equipment. *American Documentation* 12:131–138.

Mooers, C. (1951). Zatocoding applied to mechanical organization of knowledge. *American Documentation* 2:20–32.

Oddy, R. N. (1977). Information retrieval through man-machine dialogue. *Journal of Documentation* 33:1–14.

Radford, M. L. (1996). Communication theory applied to the reference encounter: An analysis of critical incidents. *The Library Quarterly* 66:123–137.

Saracevic, T. (1996a). Modeling interaction in information retrieval. In *Proceedings of the 59th Annual Meeting of the American Society of Information Science* 33:3–9.

Saracevic, T (1996b) Relevance reconsidered. In Ingewersen, P., and Pors, N. O., eds., *Information Science: Integration in Perspectives*. Copenhagen: Royal School of Librarianship. 201–218.

Saracevic, T., Mokros, H., and Su, L. (1990). Nature of interaction between users and intermediaries in online searching: A qualitative analysis. In *Proceedings of the 53rd Annual Meeting of the American Society for Information Science*, 27:47–54.

Spink, A., Goodrum, A., Robins, D., and Wu, M. M. (1996). Search intermediary elicitations during mediated online searching. In *Proceedings of the 19th Annual ACM/SIGIR Conference on Research and Development in Information Retrieval*, 120–127.

Spink, A., and Saracevic, T. (1997). Interactive information retrieval: Sources and effectiveness of search terms during mediated online searching. *Journal of the American Society for Information Science* 48. Forthcoming.

Spink, A., and Losee, R.M. (1996). Feedback in information retrieval. In Williams, M., ed., *Annual Review of Information Science and Technology* 31:33–78.

Taylor, R. S. (1968). Question negotiation and information seeking in libraries. *College & Research Libraries* 29:178–194.

Wu, M. M. (1992). *Information Interaction Dialogue: A Study of Patron Elicitation in IR Interaction*. Unpublished Ph.D. dissertation, Rutgers University, New Brunswick, NJ.

Integrating User Modeling Into Information Extraction: The UMIE Prototype

Eftihia Benaki, Vangelis A. Karkaletsis, and Constantine D. Spyropoulos[*]

Institute of Informatics & Telecommunications,
National Centre for Scientific Research (N.C.S.R.) "Demokritos", Athens, Greece

Abstract. This paper introduces user modeling into the process of information extraction. It presents the user modeling prototype (UMIE) that we developed during the research project ECRAN. UMIE takes as input information extracted from corpora and adapts it according to the user's interests in domain categories.

1 Introduction

Text-based information systems deliver to users information derived from texts. Information retrieval systems, based on the user's query, retrieve relevant documents from a relatively static set of documents. Information filtering systems examine a dynamic stream of documents and display only those which are relevant to the keywords profile of a user. Information extraction systems extract facts from documents in a domain. The extracted facts fill the pre-defined templates for the specific domain.

Today's overload of information often makes information systems ineffective. What is important is to deliver to the user information according to his needs, interests, expectations. One of the possibilities is to use user models (Allen, 1990). Regardless of the process used by the information system to deliver information, user modeling is necessary to enhance this process.

User modeling has been integrated into information retrieval (Croft and Thompson, 1986; Brajnik et al., 1990) and into information filtering systems (Brajnik and Tasso, 1994; Kay, 1995; Orwant, 1993). To our knowledge, user modeling has not been integrated so far into information extraction systems.

The objective of this work and one of ECRAN's objectives is to examine the integration of user modeling techniques in the IE process. In the context of ECRAN, we developed the UMIE prototype (Karkaletsis et al., 1996), a user modeling component that creates and stores user models and adapts the extracted information according to these models.

2 User Modeling in UMIE

In ECRAN we analysed data about the company news domain and we defined the domain and user knowledge as well as mechanisms for manipulating this knowledge.

---

[*] ECRAN (Extraction of Content: Research At Near-market) is a Language Engineering research project (LE-2110), partially supported by the EU, that aims at developing a new technology for information extraction systems in order to reach the market with those systems.

2.1 Modeling the Domain and User Knowledge

Domain. The domain knowledge consists of different domain categories, organised in a single-rooted hierarchical knowledge base. In the company news domain, for instance, such categories are "management successions", "joint ventures", "company results" and so on. Each domain category corresponds to a different template and the slots of the template define the attributes of the category. For instance, attributes of the "management successions" category are the management post, the company, the person who is vacating the post and so on. Apart from the domain knowledge base there is also a translation rules knowledge base which is used to match the user interests with the filled templates.

Stereotypes. Stereotypes are groups of users who share the same interests according to a set of criteria (Rich, 1983). A criterion in the company news domain is the department of users. A user belonging to the management department is typically interested in "management successions", "manpower planning", "joint ventures", "mergers" and so on. Stereotypes are organised in a single-rooted hierarchical knowledge base. A user does not cease to belong in a stereotype since the triggers of the stereotypes are facts that do not change. Stereotypes do not change over time.

User models. User models are stored in a database at the end of each session and retrieved at the beginning of a new one. Apart from the user's name and the stereotypes he belongs to, the user model contains the domain categories along with a rating that shows if the category is *interesting* / *not interesting* / *indifferent* for the user and a confidence factor that indicates how strongly UMIE believes this rating. *Indifferent* categories are the ones for which UMIE has little or no knowledge as to whether they are *interesting* or *not interesting*. For each category there may be some specific attribute values in which the user is interested.

2.2 Acquiring User Knowledge

UMIE initialises user models by using a set of sample documents, a few from each domain category. Each document is attached with a rating (default value = *indifferent*). The user may change the rating value to *interesting* / *not interesting*. The final document rating values are used to initialise the rating and the confidence factor for each category. To enhance the initial knowledge, the user optionally answers some questions about himself and his answers classify him under one or more stereotypes. The stereotypes that apply to him provide only *interesting* domain categories and therefore increase the confidence factor for them.

After initialising the user model, UMIE presents the user the information of the filled templates in a document-like form (canned text generation is used). These documents are classified in three different "baskets". For instance, the documents belonging in an *interesting* category C are classified in the "interesting" basket (default rating value = *interesting*). The user may change the document ratings to *not interesting* / *indifferent*. The final document rating values may increase or decrease the confidence factor for category C. The same happens with the *indifferent* and *not interesting* categories.

The user can also state explicitly his interest / indifference / disinterest in the domain categories. Explicit information increases or decreases the confidence factor of the domain categories. The user can also explicitly specify the values of one or more of the category attributes. For example, he can specify that he is interesting in management successions concerning chairmen (management post = chairman) .

Each of the sources of information (feedback to sample documents, stereotypical knowledge, feedback to resulted documents, explicit statement) changes the confidence factor with a different weight, according to its importance. Stereotypical knowledge is the least important source, while explicit statement is the most important one. A *(not) interesting* category can become *indifferent* if its confidence factor is (more) less than a certain threshold very close to 0.0. A simple function is used to update the confidence factor each time new information arrives from a source.

3   Current State and Future Work

We are currently testing UMIE with categories in the company news domain. We are using templates of "management successions" and we plan to use templates of "joint ventures" and "company results" in the near future. We are also designing a Web page for empirical tests with real users. We intend to focus our tests on the function that updates the confidence factor and on the automatic inference of some attributes values. We will also examine the integration of the domain ontology used during information extraction with the domain knowledge base exploited by UMIE.

References

Allen, R. B. (1990). User models: Theory, method, and practice. *International Journal of Man-Machine Studies* 32:511–543.

Brajnik, G., Guida, G., and Tasso, C. (1990). User modeling in expert man-machine interfaces: A case study in intelligent information retrieval. *IEEE Transactions on Systems, Man, and Cybernetics* 20:166–185.

Brajnik, G., and Tasso, C. (1994). A shell for developing non-monotonic user modeling systems. *International Journal of Human Computer Studies* 40:31–62.

Croft, B., and Thompson, R. (1986). An overview of the I³R Document Retrieval System. In *Proceedings of the Second Conference on Computer Interfaces and Interaction for Information Retrieval*.

Karkaletsis, E., Benaki, E., Spyropoulos, C., and Collier, R. (1996). D-1.3.1: Defining User Profiles and Domain Knowledge Format. *ECRAN*.

Kay, J. (1995). The um toolkit for cooperative user modeling. *User Modeling and User-Adapted Interaction* 4:146–196.

Orwant J. (1993). *Doppelgänger Goes to School: Machine Learning for User Modeling*. MSc Thesis, Massachusetts Institute of Technology.

Rich, E. (1983). Users are individuals: Individualising user models. *International Journal of Man-Machine Studies* 18:199–214.

A Hybrid Architecture for User-Adapted Information Filtering on the World Wide Web

Leonardo Ambrosini, Vincenzo Cirillo, and Alessandro Micarelli

Dipartimento di Informatica e Automazione, Università di Roma Tre, Italy

Abstract. In this paper we present an Information Filtering system of HTML/Text documents collected from the World Wide Web (WWW), based on a representation of user interests as inferred by the system through a dialogue. One of the distinguishing features of the system is the use of a hybrid approach to user modeling, in which case-based components and an artificial neural network are integrated into one coherent system. Moreover, in order to perform an accurate filtering, the system takes advantage of semantic networks and a well-structured database. The results of the first experiments with the system are very encouraging.

1 Introduction

The growth of Internet and WWW gives the end user access to a huge amount of information. Filtering information on the Web has become an increasingly relevant issue (Belkin, 1992; Kay & Kummerfeld, 1996). In this work we present a system for information filtering of documents collected from the WWW, where the selection of documents relevant for a particular user is performed on the basis of a model representing the user's interests. The whole system has two components: HUMOS (Hybrid User Modeling Subsystem) and WIFS (Web-oriented Information Filtering Subsystem). The system has been implemented in Java[TM] and it is presently being used as an intelligent interface to the search engine AltaVista[TM]. The system performs the following activities: a) it identifies the user; b) retrieves the user model, if any, or performs a preliminary interview; c) it requests input and connects to AltaVista; d) it constructs a structured representation of documents retrieved by AltaVista; e) it filters documents according to the user model; and f) it updates the user model, using the relevance feedback given by user.

2 The User Modeling Subsystem HUMOS

HUMOS uses an approach for user modeling based on *stereotypes* (Rich, 1983). A *stereotype* is a description of a prototypical user of a given class. We have proposed a case-based approach (Kolodner, 1993) for the task of automatically inferring user stereotypes. The case library contains the old cases (gathered from experts in the domain) in the form of frames, whose slots are the "user description" (a pattern constituted by the current values of the attributes for a particular user), the "active stereotype" (which can be viewed as a pointer to the Library of Stereotypes) and a procedural attachment, activated when the old case is indexed, which triggers the knowledge base of adaptation rules; these adapt the selected stereotype to the content of the user model. A problem we have noticed is that this type of classification must be made in the light of incomplete and often conflicting information. Our proposed solution (see also Micarelli and Sciarrone, 1996) consists in the use of a *function-replacing hybrid* (Goonatilake and Khebbal, 1995), where an artificial neural network implements (i.e., is functionally equivalent to) the indexing module. The procedural attachment is activated according to the selected stereotype and the actual pattern. The old cases are used as *training records* for the network. As a result, the metric of the indexing module is replaced by the *generalization* capability of the network. One advantage is that the distributed representation and reasoning of the neural network allows the system to deal with incomplete and inconsistent data and also allows the system to "gracefully degrade". Since this kind of classification problem is not, in general, *linearly separable*, a *Multi-Layer-Perceptron* (Rumelhart and McClelland, 1986) with three distinct layers has been used. The *input layer* is composed of the neurons relative to the n attributes (that are coded into numeric values) present in all the stereotypes. The *output layer* is composed of as many neurons as the number of the stereotypes. The output values correspond to the computation of a rank-ordered list of stereotypes present in the library. As for the *hidden layer* we have selected the optimal number of neurons in the context of the training procedure, where the *backpropagation* algorithm (Rumelhart and McClelland, 1986) has been used. The network has been trained with more than 1500 training records. During the training phase, we have used the *Simulated Annealing* algorithm to avoid local minima.

The proposed hybrid architecture has been tested and compared to the traditional approach to stereotype recognition via triggers (see for example Brajnik and Tasso, 1994; Kobsa and Pohl, 1995). Our system implements both approaches, permitting us to choose one or the other and thus compare results for an identical search. In the testing phase 111 new patterns were input into the system; we have considered two main parameters: a) root mean square error (*RMSE*) to express the "distance" between the values of the rank ordered list computed by the system and the expected ones; b) *accuracy*, defined as percentage of the stereotypes of those most expected by the human experts for each testing pattern, that actually appeared (at least in the second position) in the list provided by the system. The proposed hybrid architecture has proved to be more precise. In fact, with the hybrid architecture the RMSE has reached 0.0191654 and the accuracy reached 95%, whereas with the traditional triggers incorporated in the program, when activated by selecting a commutation switch, the RMSE was 0.2143423 and the accuracy 80%.

3   The Information Filtering Subsystem WIFS

Filtering is done by our proposed algorithm *MAF* (Matching Algorithm for Filtering), whose main task is to assign a *Score* to each document calculated as the similarity between its representation, the user model and the query. Besides evaluating the conventional vector product (between corresponding vectors of document, model and query), MAF properly exploits the occurrence of semantic links and terms (see below) found in the document. An important feature of MAF is the ability to identify topics composed by multiple keywords, such as "Network oriented languages". Feedback is done by our proposed algorithm *SAF* (Semantic net/DB-based Algorithm for Feedback). It asks the user a relevance value, for each viewed document: This feedback, the document representation and the query will be used to modify the user model by inserting new found topics and updating the weight of topics already in the model (see above). Thus the model evolves as the user behaviour does. The SAF will also delete any topic whose weight is below a certain threshold, so that all attributes not "refreshed" by the user will be set aside. The updated user model is sent to HUMOS to carry out the modeling process. In addition, SAF inserts new topics in the model: If the system finds a new keyword k in a document, it first uses the *Terms DataBase* (TDB) to find the semantic meaning of the item. The TDB is structured to facilitate this task and evolves dynamically. If k is in the TDB, then the model is updated by inserting k, already known by the system: this dynamically broadens the semantic aspect of the model and, with it, the inferential capabilities. If k does not have a value in the TDB, a *Semantic Network* is called, whose structure has a central node representing a potential topic of user interest and a set of satellite nodes representing keywords which co-occur in the same document. In this case the unknown keyword k is inserted as a "co-keyword" in the model and, by using the weighted semantic links present in the Semantic Network, k is connected to the model topics found in the document. This enables the system to distinguish among different meanings of a word by its context, hence dynamically widening the semantic contents of the user model. These features extend information filtering based on user modeling with the capabilities of *behaviour-based* interfaces. Rather than relying exclusively on a pre-programmed knowledge representation structure (stereotypes, rules, neural networks, etc.), the knowledge about the domain is acquired as a result of inferences from the user's information requirements.

We have carried out some experiments to evaluate user satisfaction. After each query, the user gave relevance feedback to the three most relevant documents. It thus was possible to measure the normalised average position of these documents to compare the performance of the system (rank-ordered list of the retrieved documents) with the rank-ordered list provided by AltaVista. With respect to this measure of performance, our system improves the capabilities of AltaVista (which can be rated as about 75%) up to 95%.

References

Belkin, N. J., and Croft, W.B. (1992). Information filtering and information retrieval: Two sides of the same coin? *Communications of the ACM* 35:29-38.

Brajnik, G., and Tasso, C. (1994). A shell for developing non-monotonic user modeling systems. *International Journal of Human Computer Studies* 40:31-62.

Goonatilake, S., and Khebbal, S., eds. (1995). *Intelligent Hybrid Systems*. Wiley.

Kolodner, J. (1993). *Case-Based Reasoning*. San Mateo, CA: Morgan Kaufmann.

Kay, J., and Kummerfeld, B., eds. (1996). Workshop on User Modeling for Information Filtering on the WWW. *Printings of a Workshop at the Fifth International Conference on User Modeling*.

Kobsa A., and Pohl, W. (1995). The User modeling shell system BGP-MS. *User Modeling and User-Adapted Interaction* 4:59-106.

Micarelli, A., and Sciarrone, F. (1996). A case-based toolbox for guided hypermedia navigation. In *Proceedings of the Fifth International Conference on User Modeling*, 129-136.

Rich, E. (1983). Users are individuals: individualizing user models. *International Journal of Man-Machine Studies* 18:199-214.

Rumelhart, D. E., and McClelland, J. L. eds. (1986). *Parallel Distributed Processing*. Cambridge, MA: MIT Press.

INFORMATION
PRESENTATION

Decision Support

Interactive Assessment of User Preference Models:
The Automated Travel Assistant

Greg Linden, Steve Hanks, Neal Lesh*

Department of Computer Science and Engineering,
University of Washington, Seattle, WA, U.S.A.

Abstract. This paper presents the *candidate/critique* model of interactive problem solving, in which an automated problem solver communicates *candidate solutions* to the user and the user *critiques* those solutions. The system starts with minimal information about the user's preferences, and preferences are elicited and inferred incrementally by analyzing the critiques. The system's goal is to present "good" candidates to the user, but to do so it must learn as much as possible about his preferences in order to improve its choice of candidates in subsequent iterations. This system contrasts with traditional decision-analytic and planning frameworks in which a complete model is elicited beforehand or is constructed by a human expert. The paper presents the *Automated Travel Assistant*, an implemented prototype of the model that interactively builds flight itineraries using real-time airline information. The ATA is available on the World Wide Web and has had over 4000 users between May and October 1996.

1 Introduction

Building an accurate user model is essential to decision making and decision-support tasks; a model of the user's preferences is required to make good decisions or to suggest good alternatives. Representations for preference models have been studied extensively in the literature on multi-attribute utility theory (e.g., by Keeney and Raiffa, 1976), which provides compact representations and elicitation techniques for preference models, but generally assumes that the model is built by a human expert. Problem solvers like AI planning algorithms generally assume that the complete preference model is provided as an input, but this is not a good approach to interactive problem solving in complex domains. Ahead-of-time elicitation demands a tremendous amount of information from the user, most of which will be irrelevant to solving the particular problem at hand. An alternative approach has been to infer a user model automatically over multiple interactions with the user that is used to support decision making and information filtering (e.g. Thomas and Fischer, 1996, McCalla et al., 1996, and Mukhopadhyay and Mostafa, 1996). But there is also a class of problems for which a user model must be built up quickly and without previous problem-

---

*This work was supported in part by ARPA/Rome Labs grant F30602-95-1-0024. Thanks to Oren Etzioni, Dan Weld, Adam Carlson, Marc Friedman, Keith Golden, Nicholas Kushmerick, and the anonymous reviewers for good comments and suggestions.

solving episodes, thus requiring the direct participation of the user. Consider, for example, the following interaction between a travel agent and a client:

Client:	"I want to fly from Seattle to Newark next Tuesday afternoon."
Agent:	"I've got a United flight at 3:30pm for $500 and an American flight at 12:30pm for $520."
Client:	"I can't leave before 3:00pm but I do prefer American."
Agent:	"I have another American flight through Denver at 4:00pm for $530."
Client:	"That's pretty expensive. I'd be willing to go on a later flight or another airline if it'd be much cheaper."
Agent:	"The cheapest flight is USAir at 8pm for $490."
Client:	"In that case, the American flight is fine."

Figure 1: Example dialogue between a travel agent and client.

Note that as the interaction progresses, the travel agent learns more and more about the client's preferences. The travel agent learns that the client prefers to fly on American Airlines, is somewhat price-sensitive, and has both hard and soft time constraints. Additionally, the client's preferences are rather complex and reflect complicated tradeoffs between cost of the flight, airline, and departure time. Our system aspires to this sort of interaction, where the system provides information about available options and the user provides information about the quality of those options. The system's user model—and thus the quality of the proposed options—improves over time, ultimately resulting in an option that is acceptable to the user. We consider a specific class of these models called *candidate/critique*, in which communication from the system is in the form of *candidate solutions* to the problem, and communication from the user is in the form of *critiques* of those solutions.

The main goal of the system is to present the user with an "acceptable" solution, but to do so, the *candidate critique agent* (CCA) must balance several competing needs. First, the CCA must attempt to display the optimal solution available in the dataset by suggesting optimal and near-optimal solutions based on its current model of the user's preferences. Second, the CCA must try to elicit and refine the user model. This may involve displaying "bad" candidates; the critique of a bad candidate can indicate which attributes are the most important. Third, the CCA must also describe the range of available solutions in the dataset to the user. Note, in the above interaction, that the client does not accept the optimal solution as soon as it is presented but only after he is convinced that it is the optimal solution by being told that the cheapest possible flight is $490.

In this paper, we present a general framework for building candidate/critique agents and we describe the implemented Automated Travel Assistant (ATA) system[1], a CCA for assisting users with planning airline travel that provides real, current information from the Internet Travel Network world wide web service. In a typical interaction with ATA, the user initially provides some

---

[1] Available at http://www.cs.washington.edu/homes/glinden/TravelSoftBot/ATA.html

preferences over itineraries—perhaps only the departure and destination cities and the approximate dates of travel—and the system provides several itineraries that satisfy those preferences. After examining the itineraries offered by the system, the user notes favorable or unfavorable characteristics. The system responds to the user's actions, offering new flight information, and the interaction continues until the user finds a satisfactory itinerary.

Many tasks besides making travel plans fit the candidate/critique model, such as assisting people find information on the Web, selecting merchandise, or graphical layout problems where the person is searching for the layout which best satisfies their preferences.

The contributions of this paper are an exploration of the use of candidate/critique models to elicit and refine user models, the design and implementation of a complete system for performing candidate/critique interactions in a travel domain, and four techniques that are effective in improving these interactions. These techniques are incorporating default preferences into the user model, suggesting trips that lie on the extreme spectrum of available trips (e.g. the cheapest trip), introducing variety into the suggested trips based on a definition of when one trip is *significantly different* than another, and a criterion for determining when one trip is *dominated* by another.

The rest of this paper is organized as follows. In Section 2, we give a formal problem specification and discuss the abstract candidate/critique model, then in Section 3 we describe the design of our CCA, including the four techniques mentioned above. In Section 4, we briefly describe the Automated Travel Assistant system, a prototype CCA, and discuss an extended example of how a typical interaction between a person and our system. In Section 5, we discuss related work. In Section 6, we discuss future work. We conclude and summarize in Section 7.

2   Problem Specification

In this section, we first discuss the candidate/critique model in general, define key terms and present simplifying assumptions, describe our user model, and specifying the input/output of the CCA agent.

2.1   General Architecture

We ultimately aspire to produce automated decision support systems that produce dialogues like the hypothetical interaction between travel agent and user presented in Section 1. In that case, a free-form natural-language dialogue allows solution information to be communicated concisely from the system to the user and allows arbitrary information about the user's preferences to be communicated from user to system.

Although we do not attempt to implement a natural language interface, we would still like to capture the essence of this problem-solving process. In these problems, the system has access to a large dataset and problem-solving methods unavailable to the user. The user has access to preference information not directly available to the system. The basic mode of interaction is iterative and cooperative, where the system and the user both attempt to convey only relevant knowledge. The problem is considered solved when the user is presented with a solution he considers acceptable.

A candidate/critique agent (CCA) implements this style of problem solving but restricts the way in which information is communicated between the agent and the user. The agent presents a short, carefully selected list of candidate solutions to the user. The user responds by either accepting one of these options, or by critiquing one or more of them. Critiques provide additional information about the user's actual preferences, which in turn lead to new and better candidates.

The format of both candidate solutions and critiques will depend on the details of the particular problem domain. In their most general forms, preferences can amount to an explicit total order over all candidate solutions, and critiques would be a pairwise comparison between two candidates where nothing more could be inferred about the user's preference ordering. The model is intractable and unrealistic in its full generality, however, so we present a common special case below.

We conclude this discussion of the abstract CCA model by posing the question of evaluation: what constitutes a good CCA problem solver? We consider two evaluation criteria. First, the CCA should lead the user to find an acceptable solution quickly. Second, the CCA should lead the user to find a solution that has high quality relative to the user's preferences. This second criterion might be considered controversial because it is only necessary if the user sometimes accepts a low quality solution.

2.2 Terms and Assumptions

In this section, we introduce the particular simplified model of the general CCA architecture. In this model, the domain can be described using attribute/value pairs, preferences can be described using soft constraints over these attributes, and preferences over constraint violations are additive. Problem domains are commonly defined using a predefined set of attributes $A_1, A_2, \_, A_n$, each of which takes on values from an underlying set $dom(A_i) = \{v_{i,1}, v_{i,2}, \_, v_{i,k}\}$. In this case, a *candidate solution* can be described using a tuple of the form $(v_1, v_2, \_, v_n)$. For example, in the travel domain, the dataset might describe all currently available flights and each flight might be represented by a set of attributes including the cost of the flight, airline, departure and arrival cities, and time and date of travel.

We describe the user's preferences in terms of soft constraints on the values of attributes. A *constraint* is a function $C_i(v)$: $dom(A_i) \rightarrow [0,1]$. We use the convention that $C_i(v) = 0$ means the constraint is fully satisfied and $C_i(v) = 1$ means the constraint is fully unsatisfied. Values in the open interval represent partial satisfaction of the constraint.

An assumption we make that is not inherent to the candidate/critique model, but does make the problem more tractable, is that the preferences are additive independent (Keeney and Raiffa, 1976), meaning that preferences over the individual attributes do not depend on the level at which the other attributes are achieved. For example, we would assume a person's preferences over price (e.g. the person strongly prefers cheaper flights) do not depend on whether or not the flight is a nonstop or how close to the desired arrival time it lands.[2]

2.3 User Model

The purpose of the user model is to describe a person's preferences over a set of solutions. In the most general form, the preferences can be arbitrary formulas that impose a total order over solutions. Under the assumption of additive independence, we can represent the user's preference over candidate tuples as a weighted sum of constraint functions. The user model consists of a set of constraints and a weighting indicating the importance of each constraint. Formally, the *user model*

---

[2] The actual definition of additive independence is slightly stronger, but this does not affect our analysis.

is a pair $(\{C_1..C_n\}, \{w_1,..,w_n\})$ where C_i is a constraint and w_i is the weight, a real number in $[0,1]$, of constraint C_i. A user model provides a partial ordering over all solutions. We will call this the *error* of the candidate solution, which is of the form

$$E((v_1, v_2, \_, v_n)) = \sum_{i=1}^{n} C_i(v_i)*w_i$$

Note that assuming additive independence simplifies the model specification, reducing it to n soft constraints and n weighting coefficients, and simplifies the notion of what a critique is. If the assumption holds, the quality of a candidate solution can be incorrectly computed for only one of two reasons: Either the soft constraint for one of the attributes is incorrect, or one of the attributes is weighted improperly. In our implementation in the travel domain, the user is allowed to adjust both of these model parameters directly.

A user model can either completely or partially describe a user's preferences. In our system, the user model initially describes only a few of the user's preferences. As weights are adjusted or constraints are added or updated, the user model becomes a more accurate reflection of the user's true preferences.

2.4 Candidate/Critique Interaction

In this section, we describe the interaction between a candidate/critique agent and a user and specify the input/output behavior of the CCA.

On each iteration, the CCA uses the current user model to suggest a set of annotated solutions. In our implementation, a solution is annotated if it has the best value in a particular attribute of all the candidate solutions with respect to the current user model. For example, in the travel domain, the cheapest trip of all trips considered by the system would be labeled as "cheapest". Formally, the CCA is a function from a partial user model and a set of solutions to a small set[3] of suggested solutions. The system calls the CCA with the current user model, and then presents the suggested solutions.

After a set of solutions has been suggested the user can either choose one and end the interaction, or add a new constraint, modify an existing constraint, or adjust the weighting of a constraint. This can be accomplished, as in our implementation, though the use of a graphical user interface that allows the user to critique the solutions suggested by the CCA. After the user critiques the suggested candidates, the CCA is called with the updated user model, which results in a new set of solutions being suggested.

3 CCA Design

In this section we first discuss general design principles of a CCA and then describe four general-purpose techniques for building CCA. In the process of describing these techniques, we show how we instantiated them within the travel domain.

---

[3] In our implementation, five solutions are suggested in each iteration.

3.1 Design Principles

The overall objective of the system is to help the user find an optimal solution quickly. Hypothetically, presenting the optimal solution for the user immediately would clearly lead to a short, high-quality interaction, but the CCA's user model is initially only a very rough approximation of the user's true preferences and, as such, will not typically generate the optimal solution with respect to the user's true preferences.

In general, there are two ways to generate a short, high-quality interaction: Find a solution that satisfies the user during this iteration of the interaction and present information to the user that increases the likelihood of generating a satisfactory solution in a future iteration. The former can be implemented by optimizing over preferences and requires an accurate user model. The latter involves providing information that allows the user to evaluate the solutions, understand what types of solutions are available, and express additional preferences, refining the user model.

Our technique combines both of these approaches. The system has three goals in terms of presenting solutions to the user:

- Suggest solutions that are optimal or near-optimal with respect to the user preferences.
- Inform the user of the full range of available solutions.
- Present solutions that allow the CCA to learn more about the user's preferences and update the user model.

Note that these three goals can often be in conflict. Suggesting optimal and near-optimal solutions can allow the user to end the interaction very quickly if the user model is accurate, but these solutions may not provide information about the range of options or motivate the user to provide additional preference information. Providing information about the range of available options allows the user to determine what better solutions are available and what the tradeoffs are between solutions, but these solutions are often sub-optimal. For example, in the travel domain, presenting the user with a $300 round-trip from Seattle to Chicago is meaningless unless the user has some information about the range of prices among all flights. Eliciting additional preference information may require presenting "highly critiqueable" solutions that are not optimal. In the next section, we discuss the problem of selecting solutions that satisfy these three goals.

3.2 Algorithm

In this section, we describe the CCA algorithm that uses the partial user model to suggest possible solutions to the user. We describe the CCA by first presenting a simple algorithm and then presenting a series of four improvements to this algorithm.

A straightforward CCA would simply rank all possible solutions according the stated preferences and display the top choices, selecting arbitrarily if the preferences did not provide a total order. For example, in the travel domain, if the user indicated that he wanted to a one-way flight from Seattle to Newark on January 2, this CCA would arbitrarily choose a few of the hundreds of available flights between those two cities on that day. If the user then stated a preference for cheaper flights, this CCA would display a few of the cheapest flights.

Will this approach work? As long as the user continues to state and refine constraints that reflect his true preferences, the user model will eventually converge to an accurate model of the user's preferences. Thus, the CCA will eventually suggest the solution that optimally satisfies the users preferences. However, we believe this approach would require the user to go through many unnecessary iterations with the CCA. Furthermore, a user might not state all of his preferences and may not have enough information about available solutions if he is not presented with more varied or extreme information. We have incorporated the following four improvements over the straight-forward approach described above.

Add default preferences to model. The CCA adds default preferences to the user's expressed preferences, generating a user model that is likely to reflect more accurately the user's true prefer-ences. In our implementation in the travel domain, the default preferences are currently that the user is moderately price sensitive, prefers fewer stops to more stops, and prefers to fly on as few different airlines as possible. For other attributes, if the user has not specified a preference over that attribute, he is assumed to be indifferent. Adding default preferences saves the user work by allowing him to provide fewer preferences initially. Assuming the defaults are accurate, the CCA will generate a shorter interaction since the user is not required to explicitly provide all the prefer-ences.

Exclude dominated solutions. The CCA should never suggest a solution that is *dominated* by, or strictly inferior to, another suggested solution. For example, if the user prefers cheaper flights and has expressed that he has no preference over airlines, a $49 United flight is better than a $59 Con-tinental flight that leaves at the same time (and is equal in other respects, as well). Even if the Continental flight is the second best trip, there is no need to show it to the user since he should strictly prefer the United flight. Formally, a solution S_2 is dominated by another solution S_1 if

$\forall$ constraints C_i in the user model:
$$C_i(v_{i,1}) \le C_i(v_{i,2})$$
and for some constraint C_j:
$$C_j(v_{j,1}) < C_j(v_{j,2})$$
where $v_{i,1}$ and $v_{i,2}$ are the values of the ith attribute of S_1 and S_2 respectively.

Prefer significantly different solutions. The CCA will not suggest solutions that are too similar to other suggested solutions. Formally, a solution is significantly different than another solution if

$$\sum_i w_i |v_{i,1} - v_{i,2}| \ge \delta$$

where $v_{i,1}$ and $v_{i,2}$ are the values of the attributes for the first and second solutions and w_i is a weighting of the difference for the attribute, and δ is the difference threshold.

This criterion biases the selection process in favor of variety. For example, if the system is picking two of a set of three flights, a 8am United flight, a 2pm United flight, and a 2pm Delta flight (all other attributes being equal), selecting the 8am United and 2pm Delta gives the most variety and the most information to the user. Variance in the set of solutions selected by the CCA allows the user to eliminate entire classes of solutions. For example, showing one trip in the morning and one in the afternoon is likely to elicit a user's preference over time of day, if one exists.

Suggest extrema. Extrema are solutions that optimize one attribute of the solution. For example, with air travel, the cheapest possible trip optimizes the price attribute of the trip. Extrema can elicit more information from the user about the relative weighting of their preferences and provide the user with critical information about how much a potential solution could be improved in terms of a specific attribute, given the available solutions and the current preferences. For example, if the system advises the user that the cheapest possible trip is only $20 cheaper, the user may decide that flying on their preferred airline is worth the slight increase in cost.

In our implementation, we find and present two extrema of interest, the cheapest trip and the best nonstop trip. The cheapest trip is defined as the feasible trip[4] that minimizes the price of the trip. When multiple feasible trips all have the minimal price, the one with minimal error (relative to the current user model) is selected. The best nonstop is defined as the trip of all the feasible trips consisting of all nonstop flights with minimal error.

4 Extended Example

We have implemented a CCA, the Automated Travel Assistant (ATA), in the travel domain. The system is available as a web service[5] and has had over 4000 users between May and October 1996, and has been highly regarded by the major Java applet indexing services[6]. To demonstrate the operation of the system, we provide an example of using the system to find a round-trip between the San Francisco bay area and Philadelphia.

The interaction with the system starts with the user providing a minimal amount of information. In this case, the user states that he wishes to travel between San Jose and Philadelphia, leaving any time on September 25 and returning any time on October 6.

The system converts these preferences into a user model, adding default preferences for unspecified attributes: moderate price sensitivity, preference for fewer stops, and a weak preference for flying on fewer different airlines. These preferences are common to almost all users, though the system can revise them if the user's preferences are atypical.

The system finds flights that satisfy the given preferences, groups the flights into trips, and ranks the trips using the preferences in the user model. Of the top-ranked trips, three significantly different, undominated trips[7] will be displayed along with two extrema, the cheapest trip and best non-stop trip.

ATA presents the display shown in Figure 2. In this case, no non-stop trips are available between San Jose and Philadelphia. The user is interested in seeing a non-stop trip. He's largely indifferent between flying out of San Francisco and San Jose airports. He modifies his expressed preferences accordingly, setting the value of San Francisco to be slightly lower than San Jose to express a mild preference for San Jose.

Given the additional option of leaving and arriving in San Francisco, the system was able to find non-stop trips. The first trip listed is a USAir nonstop round-trip between San Francisco and

---

[4] A *feasible trip* is any trip that at least partially satisfies all the preferences.

[5] The system is written as a Java applet and is available at the following URL:
http://www.cs.washington.edu/homes/glinden/TravelSoftBot/ATA.html

[6] Rated "Top 1% of Java applets" by the Java Applet Review Service (http://www.jars.com) and "Featured Applet" and "What's Cool" by the Gamelan service (http://www.gamelan.com).

[7] *Significantly different* and *dominated* are defined in Section 3.2.

Philadelphia. The user is happy with a non-stop out of San Francisco, but would prefer to fly on United. He adds a preference for United Airlines.

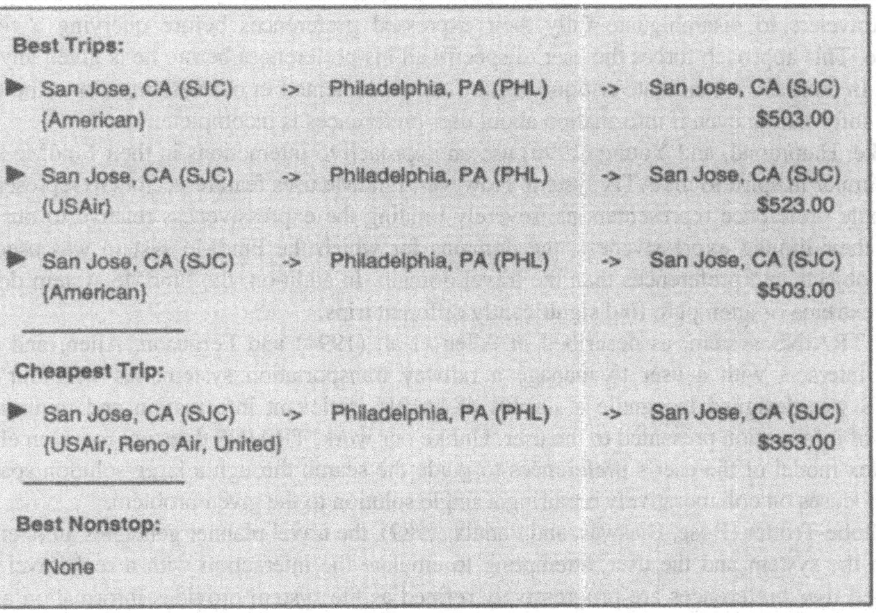

Figure 2. Trips displayed by ATA after the initial query for a round-trip from San Jose to Philadelphia leaving any time Sept. 25 and returning any time Oct. 6. Each trip can be expanded to show information about the flights of the trip and each flight can be expanded to show information about the flight legs.

The system considers this new information and offers a few United non-stops. The first trip listed is a United nonstop from San Francisco to Philadelphia round-trip leaving at 11:05am on September 25 and returning at 10:00am on October 6. The 11:05am flight of the trip leaves too early for the user. The user modifies his departure time for that flight, specifying that he is indifferent between any time 2-5pm, will leave no earlier than about 12pm and no later than about 8pm.

The system finds trips to satisfy these additional constraints, displaying a United non-stop trip with a flight leaving SFO at 2:10pm on September 25 and returning at 10:00am on October 6. Satisfied, the user ends the session.

5 Related Work

Several systems automatically infer a relatively simple user model for information filtering and classification tasks based on observation of the user (Burke, Hammond, and Young, 1996, among others), including work using neural networks to learn user models (Karunanithi and Alspector, 1996, for example). Our approach infers a more complex model, but requires direct participation of the user. On the other extreme, decision-support systems that contain hand-coded utility functions can allow more expressive representations than our system, including relaxing the assumption of additive independence, though these systems require extensive effort on the part of a human expert to build the user model.

Raskutti and Zukerman (1994) use an approach in the RADAR system where the system requires travelers to disambiguate fully their expressed preferences before querying a fictional database. This approach forces the user to specify all his preferences before he is given any information. In contrast, a candidate/critique session, as implemented in our system, allows the user to retrieve information even if information about user preferences is incomplete.

Burke, Hammond, and Young (1996) use an approach to interactions in their FindMe system that is similar in spirit to the ATA system. However, FindMe uses feature vectors to represent data and simple preference representations, severely limiting the expressiveness relative to our work. Due to their limited expressiveness, the domains for which the FindMe system was used have simpler objects and preferences than the travel domain. In addition, the FindMe system does not present extrema or attempt to find significantly different trips.

The TRAINS system, as described in Allen et al. (1994) and Ferguson, Allen, and Miller (1995), interacts with a user to manage a railway transportation system. As with our ATA, TRAINS was designed to handle a surplus of largely irrelevant information and minimize the amount of information presented to the user. Unlike our work, TRAINS does not focus on eliciting a complex model of the user's preferences to guide the search through a large solution space but instead focuses on collaboratively repairing a single solution to the given problem.

In Globe-Trotter (Bose, Biaswas, and Padala, 1989), the travel planner generates an interaction between the system and the user, attempting to emulate the interaction with a real travel agent. Expressed user preferences are progressively refined as the system provides information and the user modifies his profile. Globe-Trotter matches incomplete information about user preferences to a set of predefined cases that fully express the preferences. Huang and Miles (1995) use a similar approach. However, this approach "makes (often unwarranted) assumptions based on the user-provided information", as Cleary and Zeleznikow (1991) argue, and can direct the user toward inappropriate, rigid, predefined profiles of user preferences. Our approach makes very few assumptions about the user, instead providing the user with information about potential options while seeking more information from the user about his preferences.

Jameson et al. (1995) introduce the idea of *evaluation-oriented information provision* system (EOIP). The ATA can be viewed as an EOIP and is closest in spirit to the PRACMA system described in the paper. Both systems use multi-attribute utility theory as the underlying user model and establish a dialogue between user and system, though PRACMA may be more ambitious in that it seems to use a limited form of natural language. PRACMA, like ATA, assumes that preferences are additive independent. PRACMA models uncertainty about the user model using a probabilistic network, which requires assessing probability distributions over all model parameters. While it would be possible to adopt this approach in the ATA framework, doing so would be difficult due to the number of parameters involved and the need to discretize attribute values (e.g. the arrival time of a flight). PRACMA does not specifically address the issue of informing the user of the space of possible options and, more generally, choosing a set of alternatives that lead to quick problem solving, but the approach is not incompatible with these goals. Our ultimate goal in building CCA systems is to let the user model guide the process of *solution construction*, which is somewhat beyond the characterization of EOIP systems made in the Jameson paper, since the systems are selecting from a pre-enumerated set of candidate objects and are not interleaving the refinement of the user model with solution construction.

Siklóssy (1978) notes the need for a question-answering system to be *impertinent*, that is to ask questions or provide information not explicitly requested by the user. He uses a travel-planning domain to illustrate his main point that the system should "be impertinent if and only if there is a large, favorable *discontinuity* in the answer space for some point(s) in question space near the question." This is another way of motivating our policy of showing options that look favorable along one dimension (i.e. the policy of informing the user of extreme values), though our policy is motivated using a value-theoretic argument and is imbedded in a problem-solving system rather than one that answers questions.

Several on-line air travel planning systems currently exist that access real-time airline data, including the Internet Travel Network (http://www.itn.net), Microsoft Expedia (http://www.expedia.com), Travelocity (http://www.travelocity.com), and PCTravel (http://www.pctravel.com). These systems often provide a large list of undifferentiated information, forcing the user to sort through and find the pieces of relevant information in the sea of irrelevant data. Additionally, it is often difficult and tedious to modify the expressed preferences once flight information is retrieved from the system.

6 Future Work

As noted in Section 2.2, our implementation relies on the additive independence assumption. Although our experience has been that, in most cases, the assumption is warranted, there are some exceptions. For example, one user had a strong aversion to stopovers only if they were in Chicago. We will work toward extending the specifics of the CCA model to handle preference structures that violate the additive independence assumption at least in limited instances. The challenges here are to recognize an assumption violation during the problem-solving session itself and developing interfaces that support critiquing options given the richer preference models.

Other planned work includes (a) empirically evaluating the techniques presented in Section 3.2, (b) adding a facility for explaining the system's rankings to the user, and (c) adding knowledge that will allow the system to explore travel options and suggest flights that violate the user's expressed preferences when appropriate.

7 Conclusion

In decision-making and decision-support tasks, a model of the user's preferences is required to make good decisions or to suggest good alternatives. We explore the use of candidate/critique models to elicit and refine user modes and present a complete implementation of a CCA in the travel domain. We offer four general techniques for improving an interaction between a CCA and the user: default preferences, presenting extrema, presenting significantly different solutions, and eliminating dominated solutions.

Our implemented CCA, the Automated Travel Assistant, assists the user in finding an optimal or near-optimal trip by presenting the user with carefully selected exemplars that characterize the solution space and allowing the user to express additional or modify existing preferences. The system is available on the World Wide Web and has had over 4000 users between May and October 1996.

References

Allen, J., et al. (1995). The TRAINS Project: A case study in building a conversational planning agent. *Journal of Experimental and Theoretical AI.* 7–48.

Bose, P.K., Biswas, G., and Rao-Padala, A.M. (1989). Globe-Trotter: An intelligent flight itinerary planner. *IEEE Expert* 4(2):56–64.

Burke, R., Hammond, K., and Young, B. (1996). Knowledge-based navigation of complex information spaces. In *Proceedings of the National Conference on Artificial Intelligence (AAAI)*, 462–468.

Cleary, D., and Zeleznikow, J. (1991). L-CATA: An intelligent logic based expert travel assistant. In *Eleventh International Conference on Expert Systems and their Applications*, 111–22.

Ferguson, G., Allen, J., and Miller, B. (1996). TRAINS-95: Toward a mixed-initiative planning assistant. In *Proceedings of the Third Conference on Artificial Intelligence Planning Systems (AIPS)*, 70–77.

Huang, Y., and Miles, R. (1995). Combining case based and constraint based techniques in travel reservation systems. In *Proceedings of the Eleventh Conference on Artificial Intelligence for Applications*, 46–54.

Jameson, A., Schäfer, R., Simons, J., and Weis, T. (1995). Adaptive provision of evaluation-oriented information: Tasks and techniques. In *Proceedings of the Fourteenth International Joint Conference on Artificial Intelligence (IJCAI)*, 1886–1893.

Karunanithi, N., and Alspector, J. (1996). A feature–based user model for movie selection. In *Proceedings of the Fifth International Conference on User Modeling*, 29–34.

Keeney, R., and Raiffa, H. (1976). *Decisions With Multiple Objectives: Preferences and Value Tradeoffs.* Wiley.

McCalla, G., Searwar, F., Thomson, J., Collins, J., Sun,Y., and Zhou, B. (1996). Analogical user modelling: A case study in individualized information filtering. In *Proceedings of the Fifth International Conference on User Modeling*, 13–20.

Mukhopadhyay, S., Mostafa, J., and Palakal, M. (1996). An adaptive multi-level information filtering system. In *Proceedings of the Fifth International Conference on User Modeling*, 21–28.

Raskutti, B., and Zukerman, I. (1993). Generating queries during cooperative consultations. In *Proceedings of the 6th Australian Joint Conference on Artificial Intelligence*, 389–94.

Raskutti, B., and Zukerman, I. (1994). Acquisition of information to determine a user's plan. In *Proceedings of the European Conference on Artificial Intelligence*, 28–32.

Siklóssy, L. (1978). Impertinent question-answering systems: Justification and theory. In *Proceedings of the ACM National Conference*, 39–44.

Thomas, C., and Fischer, G. (1996). Using agents to improve the usability and usefulness of the World-Wide Web. In *Proceedings of the Fifth International Conference on User Modeling*, 5–12.

Wilson, M., and Borning, A. (1993). Hierachical constraint logic programming. *Journal of Logic Programming* 16(3–4):277–318.

Modelling the Personality of Decision Makers for Active Decision Support

Priyanka Paranagama, Frada Burstein, and David Arnott

Department of Information Systems, Monash University, Australia

Abstract. A recent research project showed that decision-makers with different personality dispositions may display distinct preferences when making decisions. This paper presents a decision support framework which attempts to provide the basis for systems that are capable of adapting to their users based on their personality preferences. The capabilities of adaptation are facilitated through the construction of profiles of decision-makers, decision situations and decision domains. An inference mechanism that utilises neural networks is employed to build these profiles. A mature system may be capable of identifying inconsistencies in an individual's decision making and providing active decision support.

1 Introduction

This paper describes how decision support system (DSS) generators may provide customised support to individuals based on their personality dispositions. A system framework for DSS generators is illustrated. The future course of this research is briefly described.

In considering differences between decision-makers it is important to define how these differences may be used in practical applications. Artificial intelligence (AI) and other user modelling research has been concerned with providing different styles to the interface and performing information filtering, while little attention has been given to achieving decision suggestions which are congruent with the style of an individual. DSS are, by definition, computer based systems that support individual decision makers. Hence, achieving personalised goals is within the scope of developing such systems. Arguably, from a decision support systems perspective, providing decision suggestions compatible with the individual is most important, as systems development efforts have to maintain a decision focus.

An important issue in the quest for understanding how the personality of decision-makers affects their decision making is the distinction between the relative effects of personality and the decision situation. Personalogism (the study of person), compared to situationism (the study of situation), is a perspective which has historically lost favour in organisational behaviour research. Much of the criticism of personalogism is attributed to assertions about the percentage contribution of personality aspects in a given decision situation.

Conclusions made about using individual factors as the basis for information system design, such as Huber's (1983) arguments, have also centered around this. However, Weiss and Adler (1984) show that these percentages can be affected by many other factors in experimental designs. They warn against discarding personality as a valid area of study in organisational behaviour and highlight the need for more research in this area. They show that a considerable body of literature in domains such as goal setting, leadership and the level of aspiration point to the influence of personality. These are all areas relevant to building DSS. The importance of *interactionism* is stressed in the study of personality in organisations. The aim of this research work is to rely more on the interaction between personality and the situation. Reliance on absolute or relative consistency may be limited to being a means of first approximation. Information maintained for individual decision-makers may be aligned with decision scenarios so that it is possible to infer situation, or domain-specific tendencies. Our attempts may be seen as a method of augmenting the familiar situation modelling approach in DSS. This approach is compatible with the basic principles of interactionism.

2   The Framework

The first stage of this research project consisted of a differential study conducted to investigate whether the personality of individuals leads to distinct decision preferences. Decision preferences are explained in terms of multi-criteria decision-making methods (Abelson and Levi, 1985). These methods include two distinct entities: *attributes* and *weights*. Attributes are the factors (variables) to be considered when making a decision. Situational factors of the decision are commonly introduced into a multi-criteria model through the measurement of attributes (criteria). Each attribute may not be equally important to an individual making a given decision. Therefore, the individual may have different preferences for the attributes. Weights are used to represent the importance of attributes. The collective set of these preferences is regarded as the *decision preference model* for that individual.

The differential study showed that individuals belonging to different personality types (based on the Myers-Briggs Type Indicator) have distinct decision preference models (Paranagama and Burstein, 1996). From the experimental data it was also observed that decision preferences of individuals can be predicted depending on their personality types. Given that there is a relationship between individual differences and decision preferences, the next stage of this project investigated how such differences can be exploited to adapt decision support systems to their users.

As such adaptation would rely on learning about the decision maker's preferences through repeated use, the greatest utility can be expected from decision support system generators rather than ad-hoc DSS. The system framework for adaptive DSS consists of a decision model, a collection of profiles and an inference mechanism (Figure 1). Profiles are maintained for each decision-maker and decision that has been supported using the system. These profiles are also aligned with decision domains and are organised in a hierarchical manner. Each profile takes the form of a decision preference model. The inference mechanism synthesises profile information and situational factors so that they can be used in the decision model. When a decision instance is to be supported using an adaptive DSS, the *inference manager* determines the most appropriate source of information by traversing the profile hierarchy. The rules for traversing are given in a *decision context selection table*. The synthesised information is provided to the decision-maker as approximations of their preferences to decision variables. The decision-maker manipulates the model components until a satisfactory decision outcome is obtained. At this stage the inference mechanism feeds the preference information provided by the decision-maker through a set of neural networks. The abstractions performed are then written back to relevant profiles. The profiles are continually improved in this manner. Thus, the system learns from each decision making instance so that better approximations can be provided for subsequent instances. The framework also consists of an active decision support component that monitors all the manipulations performed by the decision-maker. If preferences deviate from pre-defined thresholds, warnings are generated. The thresholds are based on what the system has learnt from previous decision instances.

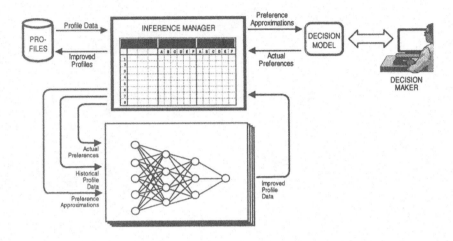

Figure 1. Inferencing with the adaptive DSS framework.

3 Conclusion and Further Research

A system based on this framework has now been completed to demonstrate the viability of the framework. As the final stage, the usefulness of such systems in supporting senior decision-makers is being investigated. This research project attempts to further understand an important determinant of human decision-making: personality. The differential study provided the basis for facilitating active decision support by adapting a system to the decision-making behaviour of individuals. Successful adaptation may lead to the desirable goal of providing intellectual support.

References

Abelson, R.P., and Levi, A. (1985). Decision-making and decision theory. In Lindzey, G., and Aronson, E., eds., *Handbook of Social Psychology*. New York: Random House, 3rd editon, volume 1. 231-309.

Huber, G. P. (1983). Cognitive style as a basis for MIS and DSS Designs: Much ado about nothing? *Management Science* 29:567-582.

Paranagama, P. C., and Burstein, F. V. (1996). A preliminary study of the relationship between the decision-makers' personality and models of their preferences. *Proceedings (Supplement) of the IFIP WG 8.3 Working Conference*. 19-38.

Weiss, H. M., and Adler, S. (1984). Personality and organisational behaviour. *Research in Organizational Behavior* 6:1-50.

Using Dialectical Argumentation for User Modelling in Decision Support Systems

Floriana Grasso*

Department of Computing and Electrical Engineering, Heriot-Watt University, Edinburgh, UK

Abstract. Often the aim of a decision support system is to give advice rather than to inform users. This work shows how linguistic theories of dialectical argumentation can provide a user modelling framework able to take account of the user's current perspectives and values, in addition to prior knowledge and goals.

1 Introduction: Generating Health Promotion Advice

User models in current adaptive information systems embody knowledge about users' goals and beliefs in order to present tailored information. It is often the case, however, that the system's aim is not only to inform users about some topics, but also to help them making decisions, or even to persuade them to undertake some actions. Argumentative skills are useful in these cases to improve both the persuasive power of system's advice and the effectiveness of system's answers to questions and/or objections about the claims it presents. This work shows how a linguistic theory of argumentation provides an appropriate user modelling framework, able to take account of the user's current *perspective(s)* as well as beliefs, and able to handle a *dialectic* rather than logic-based approach to argumentative discourse.

These strategies are implemented in a health promotion system. Most of the current systems in this domain (see Carenini et al., 1994, Binsted et al., 1995, de Rosis et al., 1995) stress the representation of informative goals. However, in a typical health promotion scenario, other types of problem can arise: users can disagree with the educator's points of view, or decide not to follow educator's advice if they are not persuaded enough. A sounder framework for generating personalised health education is needed, that considers not only addressees' prior knowledge and information needs, but also their mental attitudes and value systems.

2 User Model and Argumentation Techniques

In the generic situation modelled in this work, two opponents (O_1 and O_2) argue to defend their own theses, which can be either two complementary statements (e.g. smoking vs. not smoking) or two different, mutually exclusive claims (e.g. eating fruit vs. eating crisps at lunchtime).

Objects in the user model. The choice for the items to formalize was inspired by Perelman's (1979) work on *New Rhetoric*. A user model will contain the following items. **Facts**: statements which both O_1 and O_2 acknowledge to be true. **Presumptions**: statements which are believed

---

* This research is being supported by grant GR/K55271 from EPSRC.

by either O_1 or O_2 but not both. **Hierarchies of Perspectives**: a perspective is a *point of view* with respect to which one can judge facts and presumptions (such as *Health, Economy, Social Life, etc.*). Each participant can assign different importance to each perspective, so O_1 and O_2 will typically have two different hierarchies of them. **Values**: attribution of *importance* to a particular presumption/fact with respect to a Perspective. For instance *HasValue(O_1, SaveMoney, EconomicPersp)* means that O_1 thinks that saving money is important from the economic point of view. **Loci**: values which are acknowledged by everyone and then *HaveValue* for every perspective. For instance *Locus(Health)* means that Health has a value for both the opponents in every perspective. This expresses rules such as *the healthier a thing is, the better it is*.

Argumentation strategies and tactics. The goal of each participant is to *promote* its own statement, by letting the opponent reach a belief state where it *has value* with respect to some perspective, and where its complement *does not have value* in any higher perspective.

Let us call St_1 and St_2 the claims defended by O_1 and O_2 respectively. In order to defend its thesis, each opponent can: explicitly **promote** it, that is for instance for O_1 to find a perspective x_p so that *HasValue (O_2, St_1, x_p)*; or **denigrate** the complementary claim, that is again for O_1 to find a perspective y_p so that $\neg$*HasValue(O_2, St_2, y_p)*. The choice between the two strategies will be based on the image of the opponent's belief state and hierarchy of values.

A single move to promote a statement St will consist in finding a claim x such that: (i) the opponent can easily believe in it (because it can be derived either from facts or from the opponent's presumptions); (ii) it either leads to St (for instance it is a premise for St) or vice-versa (for instance it is a consequence of St) and (iii) the claim has value for the opponent from one particular perspective. The orator can then claim that the statement St as well should have value from the same perspective. The opposite technique will be applied to denigrate a statement.

When choosing between applying a promotion strategy for a claim or a denigration strategy for the opposite claim, or when choosing among several chains of dialectic inferences reaching the same conclusion, the following considerations hold. Appealing to a fact is more effective than appealing only to presumptions. On the other hand, appealing to a personal value is more effective than appealing only to a locus: the hypothesis is that a person is more likely to be affected by his or her own personal feelings than by something *general*, although well established.

Once a chain (then an argument) has been chosen, an orator has two different options. (i) It can communicate only its conclusion (*Eating apples is important from the economic perspective*). The intent is to encourage the opponent to draw the same conclusion. This tactic can be used when the argument is not strong enough, because assumptions were made about the opponent's model: the orator hopes that the opponent will accept the claim as it is. (ii) Alternatively, it can enter into a *question/answer* dialogue with the opponent, forcing it to accept every single step of the chain, so that it will necessarily draw the same conclusion itself (*Money is the most important thing for you, isn't it? And eating apples is cheap, isn't it? So you should eat apples at lunchtime!*). This tactic can be used when the orator is sure about the opponent's reactions: if the opponent does not accept a step in the chain, the whole argument will be weakened. It can also be used when the orator knows that another chain leading to the opposite conclusion could be more effective. It hopes to reinforce its argument by forcing the opponent to admit it.

The opponent may disagree with the claim proposed because of diverse aspects: the claim itself (*apples aren't cheap*), the attribution of a value (*saving money is not important*), the hierarchy of values (*saving money is not the most important thing for me*), or it can agree about the statement but disagree about the fact that the same does not apply for the statement's comple-ment, at least in particular circumstances (*crisps are cheap too!*). In discovering a disagreement, the opponent can: (i) just express the reason for the disagreement (leaving to the opponent the choice of the next move); (ii) go on with the previous strategy (and ignore the opponent's claim); (iii) apply a denigration strategy for the conflicting claim; (iv) search for a compromise, finding a new statement St_3 which fits into both its opponent's requirements and its own ones.

3 Conclusions

This work presented a user modelling framework to handle a dialectic rather than logic-based approach to argumentative discourse. The formalization is based on linguistic theories of ar-gumentation. The research is at an early stage: a first prototype was built which engages in a conversation with a user about some health concerned advice. The user is not for the moment allowed to express his or her counterarguments freely. The two opposite claims are chosen at the beginning of the session, and then the system both reasons about its beliefs and tries to simulate the user's behaviour: it proposes to the user the utterance corresponding to the strategy it has chosen to defend its position, and at every point where the user is supposed to intervene, a menu of possible replies is proposed, among which the user will choose the most appropriate. The formalization differs from other theoretical or applicative works in argumentation (see, among others, Loui, 1994, Karacapilidis and Gordon, 1996, Elhadad, 1995, McConachy and Zukerman, 1996) both because it is concerned with the effectiveness of arguments rather than their *sound-ness* and because, in the process of tailoring the arguments to the users, attention is paid to *not purely logical* attitudes, rather than just beliefs and knowledge. It is believed that an explicit rep-resentation of users' values and perspectives may help in handling situations where users have no definite opinions about a subject and that dialectical argumentation, being more similar to the way humans argue, can improve the effectiveness of a system's advice.

References

Binsted, K., Cawsey, A., and Jones, R. (1995). Generating personalised patient information using the medical record. In Barahona, P., et al., eds., *Proceedings of the 5th Conference on Artificial Intelligence in Medicine Europe*, volume 934 of *Lecture Notes in Artificial Intelligence*, 29–41.

Carenini, G., Mittal, V., and Moore, J. (1994). Generating patient specific interactive explanations. In *Proceedings of the 18th Symposium on Computer Applications in Medical Care*. McGraw-Hill Inc.

de Rosis, F., Grasso, F., Berry, D., and Gillie, T. (1995). Mediating hearer's and speaker's views in the generation of adaptive explanations. *Expert Systems with Applications* 8(4):429–443.

Elhadad, M. (1995). Using argumentation in text generation. *Journal of Pragmatics* 24:189–220.

Karacapilidis, N., and Gordon, T. (1996). Dialectical planning: Designing a mediating system for group decision making. In Sauer, J., Günter, A., and Hertzberg, J., eds., *Proceedings of the 10th Workshop Planen und Konfigurieren*, 205–216.

Loui, R. (1994). Argument and arbitration games. In *Working Notes of the Workshop on Computational Dialectics, 12th National Conference on Artificial Intelligence*, 72–83.

McConachy, R., and Zukerman, I. (1996). Using argument graphs to generate arguments. In Wahlster, W., ed., *Proceedings of the 12th European Conference on Artificial Intelligence*, 592–396.

Perelman, C. (1979). *The New Rhetoric and the Humanities: Essay on Rhetoric and Its Application*. Dordrecht: Reidel.

Dialog Management

Making Sense of Users' Mouse Clicks:
Abductive Reasoning and Conversational Dialogue Modeling

Adelheit Stein[1], Jon Atle Gulla[2], and Ulrich Thiel[1]

[1] GMD-IPSI, German National Research Center for Information Technology, Integrated Publication and Information Systems Institute, Darmstadt, Germany
[2] Department of Computer Science, Norwegian University of Science and Technology, Trondheim, Norway

Abstract. Intelligent information systems are expected to interpret the users' information needs semantically, taking the dialogue context into account. Whereas many research prototypes attempt to address the semantic interpretation of queries, only a few try to reason about other aspects of the user's individual dialogue behavior. This paper introduces an approach to context-dependent interpretation of ambiguous user dialogue acts in information seeking interactions. We illustrate the dialogue analysis and planning methods in the framework of the logic-based information retrieval system MIRACLE. Based on a dialogue model which describes potential developments of the interaction and recommended problem-solving steps, the abductive dialogue component (ADC) deals with unexpected user inputs which are ambiguous with respect to the intended course of action. Exploiting the dialogue history, the ADC uses abduction to generate interpretations of these inputs and thus to offer the user situation-dependent options for proceeding in the retrieval dialogue.

1 Introduction

User models are generally construed as a means to enhance a system's reactiveness to user needs. Whereas most approaches rely on the user's individual properties as the primary knowledge source, another valuable part of the user model can be provided by the user's interactive behavior. Indeed, the short-term conditions of the dialogue—for instance, what has been presented or what has gone wrong—may have a considerable impact on the results and adequateness of the interaction. Additionally, while user characteristics including extra-dialogic features like background knowledge, skills, and interests are not always available and hard to obtain, short-term individual user models built up incrementally (Rich, 1989) contain features of only the current dialogue, i.e., certain parts of the recorded dialogue history/discourse structure (see Schuster et al., 1988, for a discussion of the relationship between user models and discourse models).

However, as it seems to be a good idea to exploit knowledge acquired from the user's actual dialogue behavior, we have to face another problem: Although easily accessible via traces of dialogue sessions, these data about user actions are often too fine-grained to be helpful as they are. What we need is (1) a thorough account of what entities are to be represented in the *dialogue history* (e.g., the discourse referents/objects mentioned and, additionally, intentional structures as described by Grosz and Sidner, 1986) and (2) a way to *interpret* these data in order to infer useful strategies for improving the system's cooperative responses.

Dialogue modeling has traditionally been motivated by the assumption that interactions are not arbitrary exchanges of messages, but exhibit certain patterns that can be described by rules.

In the human-machine interaction case we can use this assumption, on the one hand, to determine a set of dialogue contributions recommended to the user in order to keep the interaction going (of course, a user might deviate from this recommended course), and, on the the other hand, to prescribe a useful machine reaction. Most dialogue models are made explicit in a declarative notation, which is sufficient for the purpose of linguistic dialogue analysis. When they are to be used for dialogue planning, the formalism has to provide some active component which allows us to compute desirable future dialogue states, or, an explanation for a given user input.

Combining the approach of discourse analysis with frame theory, we find a good example in Reichman's notion of "context spaces" (Reichman, 1985): The frame structures allow the dialogue contributions to be related to each other together with the usual inferences known in frame systems, e.g., instantiation or matching. Later on, more sophisticated structures were used to model dialogue (e.g., Grosz and Sidner, 1986), and also more ambitious inference systems were employed. The logical tradition of viewing dialogue as rational action gave rise to formal speech act theory and illocutionary logics. Computational dialogue models developed in this tradition mostly follow a plan-based approach considering the agents' beliefs or attitudes and employ reasoning techniques for plan recognition and generation (cf. Taylor et al., 1996). As it is not sufficient to reason about individual acts, soon models were devised which accounted for the context of the single acts. In the tradition of Winograd and Flores' seminal work (1986), sequences of speech acts can conveniently be modeled as paths in transition networks, where dialogue moves are associated with speech acts or tacit transitions. Thus, the reasoning can be based on individual acts and their properties, as well as on characteristics of the whole interaction.

In this paper we introduce an abduction-based approach to the recognition and interpretation of ambiguous and changing user intentions in the framework of an intelligent information retrieval (IR) system. The IR application context differs in many respects from other task-oriented dialogue systems (see LuperFoy et al., 1996, for a recent collection) and systems which are traditionally concerned with discourse and user modeling, such as natural language explanation/tutoring systems (e.g., Chu-Carroll and Carberry, 1995, Moore and Paris, 1993, and Zukerman and McConachy, 1993) and multimodal presentation planning systems (see a selection in Maybury, 1993). They tend to focus on intentional aspects at the domain level, and most dialogue systems presuppose well-defined task settings (e.g., repair of technical devices or travel planning). Information retrieval is a complex but less well-defined task, as the users' information needs are often vague, and users tend to opportunistically change their goals and retrieval strategies as the dialogue develops.

Information retrieval involves a variety of reasoning tasks, ranging from problem definition to relevance assessment—the standard tasks of formulating and processing queries being only a few in this spectrum. Although a user's relevance judgements of retrieved items are an important means for the system to increase its effectiveness (Koenemann and Belkin, 1996), the primary goal of the user is not the judgement of these objects/items as, for instance, in evaluation-oriented information provision systems (Jameson et al., 1995). Advanced IR systems provide facilities for, e.g., knowledge-based information filtering, query construction, and automatic query expansion. These facilities are, however, mostly treated as isolated extra-dialogic functions, while neglecting the fact that the quality of information retrieval is heavily dependent on the *entire retrieval interaction* (see Belkin, 1996, and Belkin et al., 1995, for detailed discussions).

In the retrieval system MIRACLE (see Section 2), various facets of the actual dialogue behavior of users are represented in a complexly structured dialogue history. Given a comprehensive dialogue model (see Section 3) which describes the potential developments of the interaction, we need an inference mechanism which allows us to exploit the richness of the model and the dialogue history. The inference mechanism we use for this purpose is abductive reasoning. To make sense of ambiguous—linguistic and non-linguistic—user inputs, the abductive dialogue component (ADC) described in Section 4 generates plausible interpretations of these inputs. What is more, depending on the current context, the ADC infers a variety of possible system reactions, which then might be weighted according to a preference measure. This allows us to derive not only just one hypothetical explanation of a user input, but all of them, and—considering individual user preferences—to offer the user plausible options for progressing in the dialogue.

2 Retrieval System MIRACLE

The multimedia retrieval system MIRACLE integrates three active components: a probabilistic multimedia indexer for texts and images, an abductive information retrieval engine (AIR), and the abductive dialogue component (ADC) presented in this paper. MIRACLE allows for semantic retrieval in large collections of multimedia documents, the current prototype interfacing a subset of Macmillan's Dictionary of Arts.[1]

Both the retrieval engine and the dialogue manager employ abductive inference to make sense of ambiguous user inputs—the retrieval engine dealing with the interpretation of user *queries* and the dialogue component with other ambiguous user acts, i.e., certain *dialogue control acts* such as "undo", rejections, requests for clarification, etc. As the dialogue component will be described in later sections, we briefly outline here MIRACLE's retrieval functionality so as to illustrate the wider application context for the dialogue planning (detailed information on the retrieval model employed and the retrieval engine can be found in Thiel et al., 1996).

Queries are entered via a query form, which allows the specification of restrictions on the attributes of objects to be retrieved. The system retrieves relevant parts of artists' biographies or other documents related to the query concepts, together with factual information from a database (see Stein et al., 1997, for a number of illustrative examples). However, the retrieval process is not confined to keyword matching but employs a concept model to establish the relationship between query concepts and access paths to the database. If a user query is ambiguous with respect to the semantic domain model, the abductive inference mechanism of the retrieval engine generates query reformulations considering the available information structures. Consider the following example: A query like "Search for artists with style *Art Deco* in country *France*" might be interpreted in several ways (depending on the actual domain model). The country attribute, for instance, could either be mapped onto the artists' nationality, place of birth/death, the location of one/most of their works of art, etc.

Abduction can be roughly characterized as a process which *generates explanations for a given observation*. Unlike deductive inference, abduction allows not only truth-preserving but also hypothetical reasoning (see Figure 1). In our context, the observation to be explained is

---

[1] The prototype provides access to an experimental database of SGML-structured full text documents (biographies of artists, period outlines, etc.), factual knowledge (including information about thousands of works of arts), and—additionally—a small sample of images (photographs of works of arts). MIRACLE is implemented in C, Smalltalk, and Prolog; it runs on system V and BSD platforms, allows multiple-user access, and can be used via World Wide Web.

Deduction		Abduction		
from: a → b	All art critics are experts.	*from:* a → b	(rule)	All artists are aesthetes.
a	David is an art critic.	b	(observation)	Oscar Wilde was an aesthete.
infer: b	David is an expert.	*infer:* a	(hypothesis)	Oscar Wilde was an artist.

Figure 1. Two inference paradigms.

the user's query (or any other ambiguous dialogue act of the user, as discussed in Section 4). In general, abduction will find *all* possible "explanations" with respect to a given set of data and a query formulation. As not all of the explanations need to be valid altogether, we refer to each explanation as a feasible hypothesis. The system presents these hypotheses to the user as *query interpretations*, and in the next step the user may select the appropriate interpretation(s) for retrieving instances from the database. Thus, the interpretations are negotiated during the dialogue (see examples in the next sections), and the user's preferences can be stored in the dialogue history and used as constraints to prevent the system from producing inappropriate query interpretations in subsequent dialogue steps.

3 Dialogue Model

To allow for mixed-initiative interaction, where user and system may actively engage in the negotiation of dialogue goals, a good dialogue system must provide both the necessary *flexibility* and dialogue *guidance*. In our system we deal with these issues by employing a dialogue model which consists of two interrelated tiers. The **COnversational Roles** (COR) model describes the interaction options available at any state of an exchange allowing for symmetric changes of initiative between the agents. **Dialogue scripts** represent prototype classes of dialogue for particular goal-directed information seeking strategies. Modeling the recommended dialogue steps/actions, scripts are used to guide the user through the various stages of a retrieval session.

3.1 Dialogue Acts and Conversational Roles (COR)

Information-seeking dialogues between an information seeker (A) and an information provider (B) are modeled with respect to the illocutionary aspects of the ongoing dialogue (Sitter and Stein, 1996). Abstracting away from the semantic content, the interpersonal functions of dialogue contributions are of central concern, as are the mutual role assignments and expectations. The agents enter commitments and try to fulfill pending commitments, or, if this is impossible, withdraw or reject them in a way that can be understood and accepted by both agents.

Figure 2 displays types and functions of some prototypical COR dialogue acts/moves, expected responses and the discretionary alternatives. After an introductory phase (meta-dialogue in state 1, where the dialogue strategy is negotiated), a retrieval dialogue may be initiated by a request for information (A: request) or by an offer to search for and then provide information

Dialogue Act Type			Follow-up Move		
Name	Transition	Condition	Expected Move	Alternative Move	Transition
A: request	1 → 2	A wants: B does a	promise (B,A,T)	reject_request (B,A,T) withdraw_request (A,B,T) subdialogue (B,A,T)	2 → 1 or 7 2 → 1 or 7
B: offer	1 → 2'	B intends: B does a	accept (A,B,T)	reject_offer (A,B,T) withdraw_offer (B,A,T) subdialogue (A,B,T)	2' → 1 or 7' 2' → 1 or 7'
B: promise	2 → 3	B intends: B does a*	inform (B,A,T)	withdraw_promise (B,A,T) subdialogue (A,B,T)	3 → 1 or 8
A: accept	2' → 3	A wants: B does a*	inform (B,A,T)	withdraw_accept (A,B,T) subdialogue (B,A,T)	3 → 1 or 8
B: inform	3 → 4	B believes: p	evaluate (A,B,T)	evaluate (A,B,T) subdialogue (A,B,T)	4 → 5
A: evaluate	4 → 1	A believes: p	request (A,B,T) offer (B,A,T)	dialogue (_,_,m) withdraw (_,_,m) subdialogue (B,A,T)	1 → 1 1 → 6
A: withdraw_request	2 → 1	A wants: [not (B does a*)]	request (A,B,T) offer (B,A,T)	dialogue (_,_,m) withdraw (_,_,m) subdialogue (B,A,T)	1 → 1 1 → 6
A: reject_offer	2 → 1	A wants: [not (B does a*)]	request (A,B,T) offer (B,A,T)	dialogue (_,_,m) withdraw (_,_,m) subdialogue (A,B,T)	1 → 1 1 → 6
B: reject_request	2 → 7	B intends: [not (B does a*)]	[END]	subdialogue (A,B,T)	
......	......	......	......	......	

A information seeker
B information provider
– A or B
T type of dialogue or move:
  m = meta; r = retrieval

A: < ... > atomic act
< ... > (_,_,T) complex move
p proposition
a action (defined here)
a* action adopted from previous move

States 1–4 are within a dialogue cycle; states 5–8 are terminal states of a dialogue or subdialogue.

Figure 2. Functions of COR dialogue acts and responses.

(B: offer), defining the conditions of action (a) and the global topic of the current dialogue cycle. Follow-up moves either comply with the inherent expectations (e.g., to answer a request or to accept an offer), indicate that the action cannot be performed (withdrawal/rejection), or postpone the decision (e.g., by initiating a subdialogue). As can be seen from their definition, the initiating moves, request and offer, and the inform move are forward directed and contribute most to the topical progression of the dialogue, whereas the other moves have a more pronounced "dialogue control function". They are backward directed in that they relate to previous acts and the conditions of action expressed there, whether in the affirmative or negative.

The COR model is internally represented as a recursive transition network (RTN). Transitions in a dialogue net are *moves* and *meta-dialogues* (between dialogue cycles). Transitions in a move net are atomic dialogue *acts*, other complex *moves*, and *subdialogues* of the same structure as the top-level dialogue (see Stein et al., 1997, for details on the networks of the current COR version). Adopting terms used in Rhetorical Structure Theory (Mann and Thompson, 1987), the act which determines the main illocutionary function of the superordinate move is viewed as its "nucleus" (e.g., A: request in the move request(A,B,T)), and the other optional elements of a move (e.g., subdialogues for clarification and additional comments) are the "satellites".

Note that the full COR model allows any move in a retrieval dialogue (except inform) to be jumped, i.e., be a tacit transition. For a given application genre, however, we might need to restrict these possibilities and disallow such jumps for certain moves and/or particular dialogue situations. The first can be done by specifying variants of networks for different types of moves and dialogues, e.g., considering the domain of discourse (meta-level vs. object-level) and the general function of moves for a dialogue cycle (task-oriented function vs. dialogue control function). The second can be done by implementing dialogue control rules (see Section 4 for examples) which are equally domain-independent but task-dependent.

The analysis of the example dialogue below shows the COR acts assigned to the single contributions and illustrates the resulting dialogue structures (see right-hand side). Using the COR model we can analyze and represent the interchange of moves and acts—including their propositional content—in a structured history. COR accounts for possible continuations in any dialogue state, but does not determine which of the possible moves should be preferred in a particular dialogue context. Therefore, we additionally combine various task-related dialogue scripts with COR to provide the necessary user guidance.

Example dialogue

S: You may (1) search DB, (2) check DB structure.	S: offer	dialogue(A,B,m)
U: chooses (1, search DB)	U: accept	
S: displays the query form	S: inform	
U: enters in free text field: "St. Peters", and in town field: "Rome"	U: request	dialogue(A,B,r)
S: Please choose an interpretation to search the DB:	S: request	subdialogue(B,A,r)
Rome be the artist's (1) place of birth, (2) of death.		
U: None is relevant.	U: reject	
S: Do you want to (1) extend your previous query	S: offer	dialogue(A,B,m)
(2) enter a completely new query		
(3) forget your query and restart session?		
U: chooses (3, restart)	U: accept	
S: OK, your last query is deleted.	S: inform	
S: You may (1) check DB structure, (2) access thesaurus.	S: offer	dialogue(A,B,m)
U: chooses (2, access thesaurus)	U: accept	
S: displays table of contents of arts thesaurus	S: inform	
U: chooses starting point for browsing	U: request	dialogue(A,B,r)
S:		

3.2 Dialogue Scripts and Strategies

Referring to a multi-dimensional classification of information seeking strategies, Belkin et al. (1995) suggested the definition of prototypical dialogue scripts for distinct strategies (e.g., either finding items by specification of search terms or by browsing in an information source). In our current system, a script is an executable representation of actions that are necessary or useful to fulfill a specified retrieval strategy or other related tasks. That is, the script contains all possible system actions and all recommended user actions at the various stages of the retrieval dialogue. A script may call other sub-scripts to deal with smaller tasks. We use a recursive transition network (RTN) formalism to represent the scripts, the transitions containing references to COR dialogue acts (see Figure 3). Preconditions decide when an act is available, and postconditions ensure that the system executes the necessary actions.

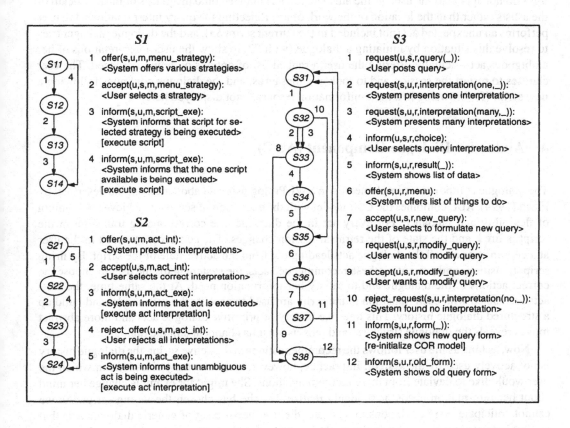

Figure 3. Structure of scripts *S1*, *S2*, and *S3*.

The three scripts displayed in Figure 3 are invoked to help construct the example dialogue given above. *S3* is the *standard script of a retrieval dialogue* in MIRACLE for the strategy: searching, with the goal of selection, by specification, in the target domain database. Note that it differs from "classical" retrieval interactions in that it is not restricted to flat query–result–evaluation cycles, but includes passages for negotiating the query interpretations generated and ways of how to proceed with retrieved items and the like. *S1* and *S2* are scripts for two different kinds of meta-dialogues: *S1* models the *introductory phase* of any retrieval session and is also called in any phase during a session in which user and system need to negotiate for a new strategy and/or script (e.g., in the fourth cycle of our example dialogue). By contrast, S2 implements the system's *strategy for dealing with unexpected user acts*, for example, when the user has selected an ambiguous function from the user interface, such as "undo" or "cancel".

In our example the user first chooses to search a database on arts and art history (which triggers *S3*) and then fills out the query form produced by MIRACLE. Looking for artists who were involved in the design of the St. Peters dome in Rome, the system-generated query interpretations do not appeal to the user, as the attribute town is mapped onto the places of birth or death of the artists rather than the location of the work of art. Rejecting the query interpretations, the user performs an unexpected act (not included in the current script *S3*), and the dialogue manager tries to resolve this situation by initiating a dialogue (with *S2*) to show the user interpretations of her ambiguous act—actually offering the user a ranked list of options on how to proceed. The user chooses to restart the session and to look at a thesaurus, and the dialogue continues following a new script (for browsing in a meta-information resource) not displayed here.

4 Abductive Dialogue Component (ADC)

The dialogue component is implemented in SWI-Prolog using an abduction engine described by Flach (1994). ADC combines the COR model with the execution of scripts to achieve a maximum of flexibility and guidance. For every act in the dialogue, the corresponding transition in the script is fired, and the state of the retrieval session changes. The acts recommended to the user at a certain state are all the dialogue acts leading out from the active state of the script. By firing script transitions and presenting these recommended acts, the system helps the user to choose the correct actions in the dialogue and to satisfy her information need. At the same time, the COR acts associated with each transition in the script are used to execute the COR model and build up a structured dialogue history. This tree-like history of primitive dialogue acts and more abstract moves reveals the dialogue structures and tells us what has happened in the dialogue[2].

Now, as long as the user follows the recommendations in the active script, the dialogue history is not actively used by the system. In practice, however, there are many situations in which the user would like to deviate from these recommendations. She might for example change her mind about her information needs or suddenly realize that she has chosen the wrong script. As we cannot anticipate these deviations in advance, the user needs a set of generic dialogue acts that at least indicate in what direction she might like to change the course of the dialogue. These acts are the dialogue acts available from the active state of the COR model, and they focus on the semantically independent functions of the acts performed.

When the user chooses an act not recommended in the script, the dialogue component uses abduction to interpret the act in light of the current dialogue context. In the following we first explain the principles of abductive reasoning and then show how the dialogue component works for a real example dialogue.

---

[2] Grote et al. (1997) and Hagen and Stein (1996) describe a similar approach, using the dialogue model to construct a complex dialogue history. However, there is no abductive dialogue planning, and the history is used to generate context-dependent (spoken) natural language help and to constrain intonation selection.

4.1   Abduction in ADC

As opposed to the situation in deductive reasoning (see Section 2), there is already a conclusion available before the abductive reasoning process is initiated. The task of the abduction engine is to find potential facts that would logically imply the conclusion at hand. The conclusion is often referred to as the *observation*, whereas the potential facts form a *hypothesis*, from which the observation can be deduced. The reasoning process depends on a *domain theory* that defines the concepts found in the observation and logical relationships between these and other concepts. Some concepts are not defined at all in the domain theory—these are called *abducibles* and are the concepts that can be included in the hypotheses explaining the observation.

In our dialogue component the unexpected act of the user is the observation, whereas the domain theory is made up of certain *dialogue control rules*. The rules map from concrete actions and properties of the dialogue history to the more vague dialogue acts found in the COR model. When an unexpected COR act is chosen by the user, the dialogue history together with the dialogue control rules constitute a context for interpreting this indetermined act. We look for a hypothesis that would imply the unexpected act according to the following logical relationship:

$$History \cup Dialogue\_rules \cup Hypothesis \Rightarrow Unexpected\_act$$

Some of the dialogue control rules are shown below. Note that these rules contain atomic acts (but *not* moves), and the logical representation used here and in the following corresponds to the prefix notation for atomic acts used in Figure 2 and the example dialogue, e.g., $request(A,\_,\_,T)$ would correspond to A: request. The concrete actions included in the hypothesis explain why the user chose that particular act in that particular context. Often there are many hypotheses that imply the unexpected user act, and each of them is referred to as an *interpretation of the act*.

1. $request(X, Y, Z, query(I)) \wedge change\_int(request(X, Y, Z, interpretations(I))) \rightarrow$
   $reject(request(X, Y, Z, interpretations(I)))$
   If the user has posted a query and wants it to be interpreted differently, she rejects the query interpretations.
2. $restart\_session \wedge \neg\ inform(X, Y, Z, result(\_)) \rightarrow reject(\_)$
   If the user wants to start again and has no results, she rejects any offers from the system.
3. $change\_act(request(Y, X, Z, query(I))) \rightarrow change\_int(request(X, Y, Z, interpretations(I)))$
   If the user would like other interpretations, she has to change the corresponding query.
4. $redo(X) \rightarrow change\_act(X)$
   If the user redoes an act, she changes the original act.
5. $extend(request(X, Y, Z, query(Q))) \rightarrow change\_act(request(X, Y, Z, query(Q)))$
   If the user extends a previous query, she changes the original query.

Looking at the dialogue control rules, we see that a reject act can be interpreted either as dissatisfaction with the previous query (Rule 1) or as a reaction against the whole script (Rule 2). The abducibles here—the predicates *redo/1*, *extend/1* and *restart_session/0*—are concrete actions that are offered the user as possible interpretations of her ambiguous dialogue act (see Figure 4).

4.2 Interpreting Ambiguous User Acts

Consider the example dialogue above, in which the user chooses to look for some information in the database. She is given a query form that she uses to submit her query about "St. Peters" and "Rome" to the retrieval system. The first three dialogue acts all stem from the execution of script *S1*, whereas the submission of the query starts a new dialogue using script *S3* as a basis. When the user later rejects the system-generated readings of the query, she does a reject act that is not anticipated in script *S3*. The act, which is available from the COR model, triggers an abduction process in which the system tries to figure out what the user would like to do now. At this moment, there is a dialogue history containing the following two acts:

$$History = \{request(u, s, r, query(1)), request(s, u, r, interpretations(1))\}.$$

The first three acts of the example dialogue are no longer available in the history because they form a complete dialogue without any incomplete subdialogues. The subsequent rejection of the user, which is stored as *reject(request(s, u, r, interpretations(1)))*, is the observation that is to be explained. The abduction engine tries to use the dialogue control rules in the reverse direction to find possible proofs for the observation. Such a proof tree is valid when all non-proven predicates are either abducibles or are confirmed by the dialogue history. In our example dialogue three interpretations of the reject act were inferred, and their corresponding proof trees are found in Figure 4. The interpretations are presented to the user executing script *S2*.

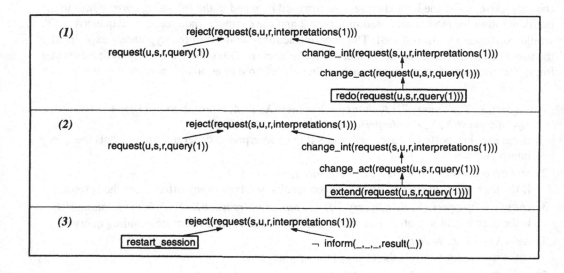

Figure 4. Three interpretations of the reject act.

In many cases dialogues are far more complex than what we saw in our example. In longer retrieval sessions, the dialogue histories grow rather large, and not all of the moves and acts in the history are relevant for the interpretation of later unexpected acts. Specifically, there are cycles of moves in the history that are more or less independent of what is happening afterwards and should not be included in later abduction processes. Another problem is that there might be some database records that have already been presented to the user, or there might be several queries in a dialogue that are dependent on each other. If the user then chooses an act that is not recommended in the active script, the abduction engine also has to reason about what to do with temporary results and queries. There will probably be more interpretations to choose among, but the abduction process itself is just as good for complex dialogue situations as for simple ones.

5 Conclusions

We have introduced an approach to dialogue planning that relies on knowledge about users which is incrementally acquired from their actual dialogue behavior. The dialogue component presented in this paper makes use of a two-tiered conversational model to construct a complex dialogue history, part of which can be used as a model of the user. Whereas the information seeking interaction is guided by dialogue scripts, the COR model together with some dialogue control rules make it possible for the user to deviate from the recommended course and change the direction of the dialogue. Employing abductive reasoning mechanisms, the dialogue component ADC interprets ambiguous user acts in light of the history, telling the user how these acts may relate to concrete functions and strategies available in the retrieval system. The dialogue history explicitly represents both the intentional structure of the discourse and knowledge about the user's preferences for particular query interpretations and retrieval strategies/scripts. Although there is no distinguished user modeling component in the MIRACLE system, the dialogue component takes over the role of adapting the system's behavior to user preferences in a certain dialogue context and suggesting to the user plausible continuations of the retrieval interaction.

Given the dialogue model and the reasoning mechanism, the major problem for the abductive dialogue component is to formulate good dialogue control rules that have the necessary generality. The rules must refer to the functionality of the given retrieval system but also take previous dialogue acts and strategies into account. Also, it might be useful to explicitly refer to other user properties in the dialogue control rules, such as to interpret things differently depending on the user's background knowledge or interests. A specific interpretation may also include an abducible that assumes certain properties of the user, and if this interpretation is selected, the assumption is found valid and used to filter the interpretations of later user acts. Future work involves the extension of our rule set and the integration of the dialogue component in a new retrieval system prototype under development at GMD-IPSI.

References

Belkin, N. J., Cool, C., Stein, A., and Thiel, U. (1995). Cases, scripts, and information seeking strategies: On the design of interactive information retrieval systems. *Expert Systems and Applications* 9(3):379–395.

Belkin, N. J. (1996). Strategies for evaluation of interactive multimedia information retrieval systems. In Ruthven, I., ed., *MIRO 95. Proceedings of the Final Workshop on Multimedia Information Retrieval*. Berlin and New York: Springer (eWiC, electronic Workshops in Computing series).

Chu-Carroll, J., and Carberry, S. (1995). Generating information-sharing subdialogues in expert–user consultation. In Mellish, C. S., ed., *Proceedings of the 14th International Joint Conference on Artificial Intelligence (IJCAI '95)*. San Mateo, CA: Morgan Kaufmann. 1243–1250.

Flach, P. (1994). *Simply Logical: Intelligent Reasoning by Example*. Chichester: John Wiley.

Grosz, B. J., and Sidner, C. L. (1986). Attention, intentions and the structure of discourse. *Computational Linguistics* 12(3):175–204.

Grote, B., Hagen, E., Stein, A., and Teich, E. (1997). Speech production in human-machine dialogue: A natural language generation perspective. In Maier, E., Mast, M., and LuperFoy, S., eds., *Dialogue Processing in Spoken Language Systems*. Heidelberg: Springer. To appear.

Hagen, E., and Stein, A. (1996). Automatic generation of a complex dialogue history. In McCalla, G., ed., *Advances in Artificial Intelligence. Proceedings of the Eleventh Biennial of the Canadian Society for Computational Studies of Intelligence (AI '96)*. Berlin and New York: Springer. 84–96.

Jameson, A., Schäfer, R., Simons, J., and Weis, T. (1995). Adaptive provision of evaluation-oriented information: Tasks and techniques. In Mellish, C. S., ed., *Proceedings of the 14th International Joint Conference on Artificial Intelligence (IJCAI '95)*. San Mateo, CA: Morgan Kaufmann. 1886–1893.

Koenemann, J., and Belkin, N. J. (1996). A case for interaction: A study of interactive information retrieval behavior and effectiveness. In Tauber, M. J., et al., eds., *Human Factors in Computing Systems: CHI '96 Conference Proceedings*. New York: ACM Press. 205–212.

LuperFoy, S., Nijholt, A., and van Zanten, G. V., eds. (1996). *Dialogue Management in Natural Language Systems. Proceedings of the Eleventh Twente Workshop on Language Technology*. Enschede, NL: Universiteit Twente.

Mann, W. C., and Thompson, S. A. (1987). Rhetorical structure theory: A theory of text organization. In Polanyi, L., ed., *The Structure of Discourse*. Norwood, NJ: Ablex. 85–96.

Maybury, M. T., ed. (1993). *Intelligent Multimedia Interfaces*. Menlo Park, CA: AAAI Press/MIT Press.

Moore, J. D., and Paris, C. L. (1993). Planning text for advisory dialogues: Capturing intentional and rhetorical information. *Computational Linguistics* 19(4):651–694.

Reichman, R. (1985). *Getting Computers to Talk Like You and Me*. Cambridge, MA: The MIT Press.

Rich, E. (1989). Stereotypes and user modeling. In Kobsa, A., and Wahlster, W., eds., *User Models in Dialogue Systems*. Berlin and New York: Springer. 35–51.

Schuster, E., Chin, D., Cohen, R., Kobsa, A., Morik, K., Sparck Jones, K., and Wahlster, W. (1988). Discussion section on the relationship between user models and dialogue models. *Computational Linguistics* 14(3):79–103.

Sitter, S., and Stein, A. (1996). Modeling information-seeking dialogues: The conversational roles (COR) model. *RIS: Review of Information Science (online journal)* 1(1). Available from http://www.inf-wiss.uni-konstanz.de/RIS/... Extended and revised version of: Modeling the Illocutionary Aspects of Information-Seeking Dialogues. *Information Processing & Management* 1992, 28(2):165-180.

Stein, A., Gulla, J. A., Müller, A., and Thiel, U. (1997). Conversational interaction for semantic access to multimedia information. In Maybury, M. T., ed., *Intelligent Multimedia Information Retrieval*. Menlo Park, CA: AAAI/The MIT Press. 399–421.

Taylor, J. A., Carletta, J., and Mellish, C. (1996). Requirements for belief models in cooperative dialogue. *User Modeling and User-Adapted Interaction* 6(1):23–68.

Thiel, U., Gulla, J. A., Müller, A., and Stein, A. (1996). Dialogue strategies for multimedia retrieval: Intertwining abductive reasoning and dialogue planning. In Ruthven, I., ed., *MIRO 95. Proceedings of the Final Workshop on Multimedia Information Retrieval*. Berlin and New York: Springer (eWiC, electronic Workshops in Computing series).

Winograd, T., and Flores, F. (1986). *Understanding Computers and Cognition*. Norwood, NJ: Ablex.

Zukerman, I., and McConachy, R. (1993). Consulting a user model to address a user's inferences during content planning. *User Modeling and User-Adapted Interaction* 3(2):155–185.

Modeling Agents in Dialogue Systems

Paulo Quaresma and José Gabriel Lopes

Departamento de Informática, Universidade Nova de Lisboa, Portugal

Abstract. In this paper we present an extended logic programming framework that allows the modeling of dialogues between agents with different levels of sincerity and credulity. An agent is modeled by a set of extended logic programming rules, and the agent's mental state is defined by the well-founded model of the extended logic program. Using this modeling process, an agent is able to participate in dialogues, updating and revising its mental state after each sentence.

1 Introduction

In order to participate in dialogues, an agent needs the capability of modeling mental states. Specifically, it is necessary to represent the agent attitudes (beliefs, intentions, and objectives), world knowledge, and temporal, reasoning and behavior rules. In this paper, we propose a logic programming framework that allows the representation of agent models. Agents are defined as logic programs that are extended with explicit negation. The semantics of the programs is given by the well-founded semantics of logic programs with explicit negation (from Alferes and Pereira, 1996). The well-founded semantics has a complete and sound top-down proof procedure with polynomial complexity, and there is an implemented prototype (Damásio et al., 1994) which allows us to obtain experimental results.

2 Logic Programming Framework

Logic programs extended with explicit negation are finite sets of rules of the form

$$H \leftarrow B_1, \ldots, B_n, not\, C_1, \ldots, not\, C_m \quad (m \geq 0, n \geq 0),$$

where H, B_1, $\ldots$, B_n, C_1,..., C_m are objective literals. An objective literal is an atom A or its explicit negation $\neg A$; *not* stands for negation by default; *not* L is a default literal. Literals are objective or default and $\neg\neg L \equiv L$.

The set of all ground objective literals of a program P designates the extended Herbrand base of P; it is represented by $\mathcal{H}(P)$. An interpretation I of an extended program P is represented by $T \cup not\, F$, where T and F are disjoint subsets of $\mathcal{H}(P)$. Objective literals of T are true in I; objective literals of F are false by default in I; objective literals of $\mathcal{H}(P) - I$ are undefined in I. Moreover, if $\neg L \in T$ then $L \in F$. An interpretation I of an extended logic program P is a partial stable model of P iff $\Phi_P(I) = I$ (see Alferes and Pereira, 1996, for the definition of the Φ operator). The well-founded model of the program P is the F-least partial stable model of P. The well-founded semantics of P is determined by the set of all partial stable models of P.

2.1 Events

As a time formalism, we use a variation of the Event Calculus (Quaresma, 1997; Missiaen, 1991) that allows events to have an identification and a duration. As a consequence, events may occur simultaneously.

The predicate $holds\_at(P, T)$ defines the properties P that are true at a specific time T; the predicate $happens(E, T_i, T_f)$ means that the event E occurred between T_i and T_f; $initiates(E, T, P)$ means that the event E initiates P at time T; $terminates(E, T, P)$ means that the event E terminates P at time T; $persists(T_i, P, T)$ means that P persists from T_i until T (at least); $succeeds(E, T_i)$ means that the event E may occur at time T_i (i.e., its preconditions are satisfied).

3 Agents' Mental States

In our proposal, agents are modeled by the well-founded model of an extended logic program representing the agents' behavior rules, rationality, action descriptions, world knowledge, and temporal formalisms. In this summary, we will analyze only kthe behavior rules for credulity and sincerity. The agent attitudes are: $bel(A, P)$, which mean that agent A believes in proposition P; $int(A, \alpha)$ meaning that agent A intends action α to be executed; $ach(A, P)$ meaning that proposition P is a goal of agent A.

Credulity and sincerity define how an agent accepts or transmits information from or to other agents. The main process defines how beliefs are transferred:

$$holds\_at(bel(A_1, P), T) \leftarrow holds\_at(bel(A_1, bel(A_2, P)), T), \qquad (1)$$
$$holds\_at(bel(A_1, credulous(A_1)), T),$$
$$holds\_at(bel(A_1, sincere(A_2)), T).$$

This rule specifies that an agent believes in a proposition if he believes that another agent believes in it, and if he believes he is credulous and that the other agent is sincere. This rule can be changed for more sceptical agents through the addition of more preconditions (e.g., a test of whether the belief contradicts previous beliefs).

4 Example: Non-Sincere Dialogue

In this section we show an example of a dialogue between two sincere and credulous agents (Astérix and the modeled agent Obélix) and a non-sincere agent (Lierix). Our agent, Obélix, has the goal of being happy, and he can execute one action to achieve his goal: to beat the Romans.

The dialogue we want to model is the following:

1. Lierix to Obélix: There are Romans at Babaorum!
2. Obélix does not believe this, because he believes Lierix is not sincere.
3. Astérix to Obélix: There are Romans at Petibonum!
4. Obélix believes this, and he may act in order to go to Petibonum and to beat the Romans.

The initial Obélix objective is to be happy $(holds\_at(ach(obelix, happy(obelix)), t_0))$. The domain-specific action is (we are using the A-language as an action description language):

$$to\_beat\_romans(obélix) \; causes \; happy(obélix) \; if \; at(obélix, Place), at(romans, Place) \qquad (2)$$

This action specifies that Obélix may beat the Romans if he is at a place where the Romans are.

In the first sentence, Lierix says to Obélix that there are Romans at Babaorum. The following facts are created from the analysis of the sentence (in the rules, *lierix* is abbreviated with *l*, *asterix* with *a*, and *obelix* with *o*):

$$happens(e_1, t_1, t_2), act(e_1, inform(l, o, at(romans, babaorum))). \qquad (3)$$

However, the information is not transferred, because Obélix believes that Lierix is not sincere (rule 1).

The second sentence, from Astérix, creates the following facts:

$$happens(e_2, t_3, t_4), act(e_2, inform(a, o, at(romans, petibonum))). \qquad (4)$$

In this situation, the belief is transferred, and Obélix starts to believe that there are Romans at Petibonum. In this situation, the planning process could identify the need to go to Petibonum as a precondition of the action of beating Romans. However, the planning process is not analyzed in this paper. (In Quaresma and Lopes, 1995, we propose an abduction procedure that allows the inference of plans.)

5 Conclusions

We have proposed an agent modeling process defined over a logic programming framework with specific semantics (the well-founded semantics of extended logic programs). This process allows the definition of behavior rules that enable us to model non-well-behaved agents.

In future work we intend to integrate this agent modeling framework in a more general architecture that allows a complete representation of dialogues.

References

Alferes, J. J., and Pereira, L. M. (1996). *Reasoning With Logic Programming*, volume 1111 of *Lecture Notes in Artificial Intelligence*. Springer.

Damásio, C., Nejdl, W., and Pereira, L. M. (1994). Revise: An extended logic progamming system for revising knowledge bases. *Proceedings of KR'94*.

Missiaen, L. (1991). *Localized Abductive Planning With the Event Calculus*. Ph.D. Dissertation, University of Leuven, Belgium.

Quaresma, P., and Lopes, J. G. (1995). Unified logic programming approach to the abduction of plans and intentions in information-seeking dialogues. *Journal of Logic Programming* 54.

Quaresma, P. (1997). *Inferência de Atitudes em Diálogos*. Ph.D. Dissertation, Faculdade de Ciências e Tecnologia da Universidade Nova de Lisboa. In Portuguese. To appear.

Natural Language Generation

Authoring and Generating Health-Education Documents That Are Tailored to the Needs of the Individual Patient

Graeme Hirst[1], Chrysanne DiMarco[2], Eduard Hovy[3], and Kimberley Parsons[2]*

[1] Department of Computer Science, University of Toronto, Canada
[2] Department of Computer Science, University of Waterloo, Canada
[3] Information Sciences Institute, University of Southern California, U.S.A.

Abstract. Health-education documents can be much more effective in achieving patient compliance if they are customized for individual readers. For this purpose, a medical record can be thought of as an extremely detailed user model of a reader of such a document. The HealthDoc project is developing methods for producing health-information and patient-education documents that are tailored to the individual personal and medical characteristics of the patients who receive them. Information from an on-line medical record or from a clinician will be used as the primary basis for deciding how best to fit the document to the patient. In this paper, we describe our research on three aspects of the project: the kinds of tailoring that are appropriate for health-education documents; the nature of a tailorable master document, and how it can be created; and the linguistic problems that arise when a tailored instance of the document is to be generated.

1 The Value of Tailored Health-Education Documents

Health-education and patient-information brochures and leaflets are used extensively in clinical settings for many purposes:

- To educate patients about a particular medical condition and its management: *Treatment choices for breast cancer: The surgery decision*; *Living with diabetes*.
- To tell them how to follow a medical regimen, prepare for a medical procedure, or manage recovery: *Getting ready for your bowel surgery*; *Instructions for patients following hysterectomy*.
- For general health education: *About smoking and pregnancy*.

* The HealthDoc project is supported by a grant from Technology Ontario, administered by the Information Technology Research Centre. Vic DiCiccio was instrumental in helping us to obtain the grant, and has been invaluable in subsequent administration. The other members of the HealthDoc project have contributed to the work described here, especially Steve Banks, Phil Edmonds, Mary Ellen Foster, Bruce Jakeway, Jon Litchfield, Daniel Marcu, Peter Vanderheyden, Leo Wanner, John Wilkinson, and Susan Williams. Victor Strecher and Sarah Kobrin kindly discussed details of their research with us. We are grateful to Dominic Covvey, Brigitte Grote, Manfred Stede, Dietmar Rösner, John Bateman, and the patient-education committees of our partner hospitals—Sunnybrook Health Sciences Centre (University of Toronto), Massachusetts General Hospital (Boston), and Peel Memorial Hospital (Brampton, Ontario)—for helpful advice, insightful discussions, and other contributions.

Recent experiments have shown that such health-education documents can be much more effective if they are customized for individual readers in accordance with their medical conditions, demographic variables, personality profile, or other relevant factors. For example, Strecher and colleagues sent unsolicited leaflets to patients of family practices on topics such as giving up smoking (Strecher et al., 1994), improving dietary behaviour (Campbell et al., 1994), or having a mammogram (Skinner, Strecher, and Hospers, 1994). Each leaflet was tailored to the recipient, taking into account such characteristics as reasons for smoking or belief in the efficacy of mammography; this information had been asked of each patient in an earlier survey. In each study, the tailored leaflets were found to have a significantly greater effect on the patients' behaviour than generic leaflets had upon the behaviour of patients in a control group.

However, in these experiments a ten-minute interview was required with each patient to elicit the information necessary for tailoring the document. This amount of effort is not, in general, practical. Nor can this problem be avoided by naïvely assuming that patients will just go Web surfing to seek out the health information that they need, volunteering their demographic or medical profiles to some on-line tailoring system.[1] On the contrary, much health education must be initiated by the clinician in response to the patient's medical situation, and the information must generally be presented on paper for the patient to refer to later. Fortunately, in such clinical situations, much of the information that is needed for tailoring health-education material is available in the patient's medical record. Indeed, a medical record can be thought of as an extremely detailed user model for (potential) readers of health-education documents.

This paper describes research undertaken in the HealthDoc project, which is developing text-generation methods for producing health-information and patient-education material that is tailored to the personal and medical characteristics of the individual patient receiving it. Information from an on-line medical record or from a clinician will be used as the primary basis for deciding how best to fit the document to the patient; but reader models derived from other sources, such as interviews or surveys, could also be used. Moreover, while the project is concentrating on the production of printed materials, much of the research will also be applicable to the creation of tailored Web pages and interactive, hypertext-like health-education systems that we and others are developing (e.g., DiMarco and Foster, 1997; Cawsey, Binsted, and Jones, 1995; Buchanan et al., 1995).

The structure of the HealthDoc system is shown in Figure 1. The major components will be described as we discuss our research in the sections that follow, concentrating on three aspects of the project: the kinds of tailoring that are appropriate for health-education documents; the nature of a tailorable master document, and how it can be created; and the linguistic problems that arise when a tailored instance of the document is to be generated. We assume the following model for use of the system:

Master documents. Each tailored brochure on a particular topic is produced from a *master document* on that topic, which has been created by a professional medical writer, using an authoring tool that we will describe in Section 4 below. The master document contains all the information, including illustrations, that might possibly be included in any individual brochure, along with *annotations* as to the conditions under which each piece of information is relevant. The nature of the master document will be described below in Section 3.1.

---

[1] For the few patients who do, companies such as MicroMass Communications Inc. have produced some tailorable health-education 'magazines'; see *http://www.micromass.com/demos.html.*

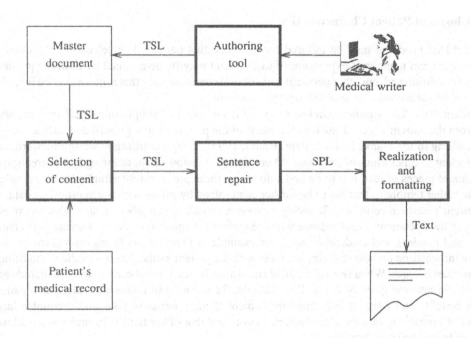

Figure 1. Generation of a tailored document by the HealthDoc system. Boxes with heavy lines represent processes, and boxes with light lines represent sources of information; the arrows represent flow of information.

Dimensions of tailoring. A HealthDoc brochure may be tailored in accordance with information about the individual patient: both the selection of content and the manner of expression of that content may be determined by the patient's medical condition and their personal and cultural characteristics (see Section 2.1 below).

HealthDoc in the clinical setting. In clinical use, HealthDoc will have access to the on-line medical records of patients. When the clinician wishes to give a patient a particular brochure from HealthDoc, she selects it from a menu of master documents, and specifies the name of the patient to whom it is to be given; in addition, she may offer, or be asked to provide, information to supplement that which the system will find in the patient's record.

HealthDoc will then generate a version of the document appropriate to that patient. It may be printed directly, or it may be generated to a file for a word processor so that the clinician may edit it as desired before it is printed. The final document will be attractively laid out and formatted, and possibly run off on pre-printed stationery.[2]

---

[2] The creation of a complete system as just described is well beyond the current scope and resources of the HealthDoc research project. We are concentrating on authoring and sentence repair, and therefore

2   Tailoring Patient-Education Material

2.1   Classes of Patient Characteristics

A HealthDoc brochure may be tailored for an individual patient. The selection of content of the brochure and manner of expression of that content may be determined by both the patient's medical condition and any other personal and cultural characteristics that might either be included in their medical record or available from the clinician.

Patient data. The simplest kind of tailoring is inclusion of simple numerical or alphabetic data from the patient's record, such as the name of the patient or of a prescribed medication—in effect, filling in the blanks in a template (Reiter, 1995). Template-filling is straightforward, and independent of other kinds of tailoring. Where we speak below about tailoring by the creation or inclusion of pieces of text, it is to be understood that these pieces might actually be not complete text but rather templates that are to be further customized by filling with the appropriate data.

Patient's medical condition. Tailoring by medical condition entails choosing what to say and not say in the document, in accordance with the patient's diagnosis, physical characteristics (such as age and gender), and medical history. For example, a brochure on living with diabetes may include information on how diabetes interacts with the patient's other known medical conditions, such as heart disease. When several medical conditions interact, the choice of what to include and exclude can become quite complex. For example, the tailoring of a brochure advising a patient on the benefits and risks of hormone-replacement therapy needs to take into account a large number of interacting factors in her medical history and that of her family. In such cases, tailored documents will be of particular utility.

Patient's culture, health beliefs, and other personal characteristics. Tailoring by patient characteristics involves the choice of both form and content. Many health communication studies have shown that the 'same' message often needs to be framed or presented in very different ways in order to be communicated most effectively and most persuasively to different people; indeed, what may be persuasive to one person can actually reduce compliance in another (Monahan, 1995). In health education, individual and cultural differences in health beliefs, perception of and attitude to risk, and level of education are among the factors that must be considered when tailoring a message to an individual (Masi, 1993,; Kreps and Kunimoto, 1994). For example, health messages that attempt to arouse high amounts of fear are effective on people with low anxiety, but less so on people with high anxiety (Hale and Dillard, 1995); similarly, anti-drug messages are more effective when matched to the individual's degree of need for sensation (Donohew, Palmgreen, and Lorch, 1994).

Characteristics that are of particular interest to us at this stage of the project include locus of control (the degree to which the patient regards herself as being 'in charge' of her health), ability or desire to read technical detail, and the degree to which appeals to authority in the presentation of information are persuasive to the patient. For more discussion, see DiMarco, et al. (1995).

---

other parts of the system—i.e., the user interface for the clinician, the software interface to the on-line medical-records system, and the module for document layout, formatting, and printing—are only simple demonstration prototypes. To avoid a commitment to any of the emerging standards for electronic medical records and the interchange of health information, we use a fictional medical database in our own idiosyncratic format. Implementation with any particular system of on-line medical records will require the adaptation of our query format to that of the system.

2.2 What's in the Medical Record?

When a medical author creates a HealthDoc text that is to be tailored in one or more of the ways described above, he or she must know what information is likely to be present in a patient's on-line medical record, or must at least make assumptions as to what information is available. (An electronic medical record may contain free text or scanned documents in addition to structured data; thus the information required might be present and yet not readily available. The extraction of information from heterogeneous electronic medical records is a research problem in itself.) And present-day systems are unlikely to offer the kinds of non-clinical information that will often be important in tailored health education, such as culture, level of education, or locus of control. We believe that as electronic *medical* records start to become electronic *health* records in the not-too-distant future, this kind of information will become more readily available. In any case, HealthDoc will query the clinician user for any characteristic of the patient that it cannot obtain from the on-line record. The medical writer is thus free to use any patient characteristic in tailoring that he or she wishes, while considering that it would be a burden on the clinician if too many characteristics cannot be found in the on-line record.

Regardless of what information a medical records system offers in principle, the information might not, in practice, be available for the particular patient in question, neither from the system nor the clinician. The writer must therefore always consider what the default action should be when some characteristic of the reader is unknown. The default could be to include selections for *all* possible values of the characteristic, or to use instead a distinct, more-generic selection; or a default value for the characteristic might be assumed. For example, in a brochure on diabetes, if it is not known whether a patient has the insulin-dependent or non–insulin-dependent form, one would probably choose to give information on both. But one would probably not include information on the interaction of diabetes with a rare or unusual medical condition unless it were known for certain that this was relevant to the particular patient.

3 Representing a Tailorable Document

3.1 Finding an Appropriate Level of Abstraction

As explained above, a master document is a specification of all the information that might be included in a brochure on a particular topic, along with annotations indicating what is to be included when. We now discuss the nature of this master document and the problems of combining selections from it.

In an AI-heavy approach, the elements of the master document would be pieces of a language-independent structure in some knowledge representation ('KR') formalism, which would be selected for content, as appropriate for the particular patient, but not form. These elements would then have to pass through some complete language-generation system that would decide how to organize and express the content, given information about the form best suited to the patient's personal characteristics. This approach is elegant and language-independent, but is not yet close to being possible, even with state-of-the-art techniques, for domains as complex as those of interest here.

On the other hand, Strecher and colleagues created the tailored texts that they used in their experiments simply by building a large set of simple snippets of text that were included or excluded as appropriate for both the content and form of a patient's brochure. This method is straightforward, but it requires that an extremely large number of bits and pieces of text be available; Strecher and colleagues found that the creation and management of the large number of text fragments involved became extremely difficult (Victor Strecher and Sarah Kobrin, personal communication).

Moreover, the assembly of such bits and pieces suffers from the obvious problem that the resulting document might not be coherent or cohesive, or at the very least, not stylistically polished. It might be thought that the snippets of text could be constructed, or alternative expressions of the same idea be written where necessary, so that all possible selections would result in a well-formed document; indeed, Strecher and colleagues attempted to do essentially this. However, they found it extremely difficult to achieve, even for their fairly simple document (Victor Strecher and Sarah Kobrin, personal communication); it would surely be quite impossible for complex documents, unless the granularity were extremely coarse, thereby increasing the number of distinct elements required. In the limit, one would not tailor the text at all, but simply store thousands of distinct documents, each pre-written for every single combination of possibilities—a situation that is quite impractical.

Our approach, therefore, is to use neither a KR formalism nor snippets of text, but an abstract, albeit language-dependent, text specification language, TSL, which we will describe in Section 3.2 below. This language expresses not only the content of the document and the conditions under which each element is to be selected for an individual patient, but also information that assists a subsequent process of generating coherent, well-polished text. Selections from this document are made for both content and form, as in the text-snippet approach, but are automatically post-edited—'*repaired*'— for form, style, and coherence. We will discuss the nature of these 'repairs' in Section 5 below. Because the repairs take place upon the abstract representation, and are guided by the additional information that it contains, the process is much simpler than would be required for revision of an assemblage of text snippets.

We regard this use of a master document as a new approach to natural language generation, in which generation from scratch is avoided. *Generation by selection and repair* uses a partially specified, pre-existing document as the starting point. The approach is discussed at greater length by DiMarco, Hirst, and Hovy (1997).

3.2 Text Specification Language

Text Specification Language, or TSL, is the language used to represent master documents in the HealthDoc system. TSL not only expresses the content of the master document but also includes annotations on each element of that content (both textual and non-textual, at all levels of document granularity), giving the circumstances under which the element is to be selected for use. TSL annotations can also provide information—coreference links and rhetorical relations—that guides the repair of the selected text. An example of a TSL representation of a sentence is shown in Figure 2.

TSL represents a sentence both in English and in the sentence plan language SPL. The latter is used by the Penman text generation system (Penman Natural Language Group, 1989,; Bateman, 1995) that is incorporated into HealthDoc (see Section 6 below).[3] An SPL expression

---

[3] TSL can actually accommodate multiple representations of a sentence. For example, our WebbeDoc project (DiMarco and Foster, 1997) uses TSL with sentences marked up in HTML.

```
(variation
 :name 'var2
 :condition '(AND high-cholesterol
                 (OR insulin-dependent non-insulin-dependent)
                 low-technical)
 :sentence-list '(sent2) )

(sentence
 :name 'sent2
 :english "High blood cholesterol levels raise the risk of heart disease."
 :focus chol1
 :coref '( (hd2 specific comp0) (lev9 generic lev8) (risk6 generic risk1) )
 :spl
 '(raise / nondirected-action
   :lex raise
   :tense present
   :actor (lev9 / abstraction
            :lex level
            :number plural
            :class-ascription (chol1 / abstraction
                                :lex blood-cholesterol)
            :property-ascription (high / quality
                                  :lex high))
   :actee (risk6 / abstraction
            :lex risk
            :determiner the
            :part-of (hd2 / abstraction
                       :lex disease
                       :determiner zero
                       :class-ascription (heart1 / object
                                           :lex heart)))))
```

Figure 2. Example of TSL representation of a sentence.

is an abstract specification of a sentence, which Penman can convert to the corresponding surface form. This permits expression of the content of the document. These basic SPL structures are augmented with information for selection and repair. An example of an annotation for selection may be seen in the slot named :condition in Figure 2; the sentence will be selected if the patient has high cholesterol, either insulin-dependent or non–insulin-dependent diabetes, and is to receive a minimum of technical detail in the document.

Other annotations are used to guide later repairs to the text. *Coreference links* join two or more references to a single object that occur in different parts of the document. A link also indicates the kind of reference: definite, indefinite, generic, or intensional, and so on. Thus, it will always be known if two different sentences refer to the same thing, and pronominalization can occur accordingly (see Section 5 below). For example, the coreference information in the :coref slot in Figure 2 indicates that hd2, representing the reference to heart disease, is a specific reference that is coreferential with comp0, which is mentioned in some other sentence. The other elements in the list represent the other two references in the sentence, i.e., to high blood cholesterol levels and to the risk of heart disease.

Rhetorical relations are cohesive relationships between sentences, such as *cause, effect, elaboration,* and so on. All such relationships between sentences in the document are recorded in the TSL, so that explicit discourse connectives can be used in the text where appropriate (see Section 5). For the example shown in Figure 2, the rhetorical relations would be listed at a higher level in the TSL and might look like this:

```
:relations '( (evidence sent1 sent2)
              (elaboration sent2 sent3) )
```

4   Authoring a Tailorable Document

Master documents may be based on the natural-language text of pre-existing health-education material, or they may be created from scratch (or some combination of the two). Either alternative requires a human and an authoring tool.

The creator of a master document would normally be a professional medical writer, who will need to understand the nature of tailored and tailorable texts, but who should not be assumed to have any special knowledge or understanding of TSL or the innards of HealthDoc. The authoring tool, therefore, should be no more difficult for the writer to use than, say, the more-sophisticated features of a typical word processor. The text is therefore written in English, and semi-automatically translated to TSL (see below). (The English source text is retained in the TSL for use in subsequent authoring sessions—for example, if the document is updated or amended.)

It is the writer's job to decide upon the basic elements of the text, the rhetorical and corefer-ential links between them, and the conditions under which each element should be included in the output. The elements of the text are typed into the authoring tool, and are marked up by the writer with links for cohesion and coreference and with conditions for inclusion. The conditions for inclusion are, of course, queries on the medical record of the patient for whom a tailored copy is to be produced.

Figure 3 shows a snapshot of the authoring tool in use (Parsons, 1997). The sample text shown is part of a section about health risks in diabetes, from a brochure about this condition. The left-hand portion of the screen, labeled *Selection Criteria,* contains a list of the patient conditions that the author is using to specify the selection of pieces of text. The right-hand portion of the screen contains a window on the text of the master document. Each box in the view contains a piece of text and the inclusion conditions for that piece of text. Groups of boxes represent mutually-exclusive pieces. The rhetorical relations between sentences are represented by arrows drawn between the related boxes. Using the mouse, the author specifies the two boxes that are related. A window containing a list of possible rhetorical relations appears; the relations are colour-coded, so when the author chooses a relation from the list, an arrow is drawn between the two boxes, its colour indicating the relation that was specified. Coreference relations are also colour-coded. Each reference to the same object or concept (e.g., heart disease) is specified by the author by highlighting the reference and clicking with the mouse. A window that contains the

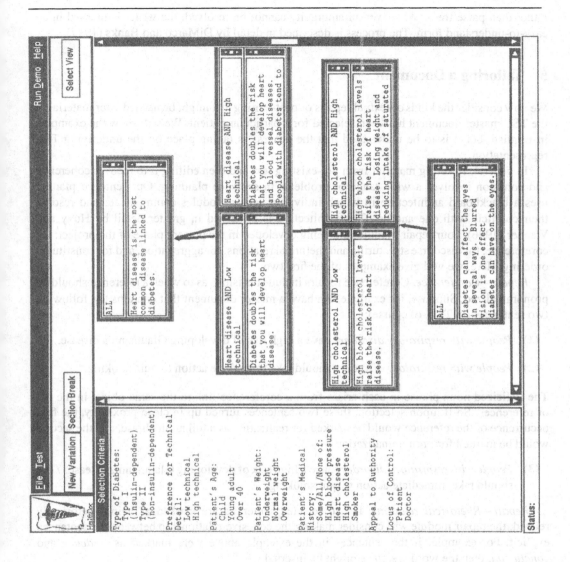

Figure 3. A screen from the authoring tool.

lists of coreference links pops up, and the author specifies the list that the current object should be added to. The reference changes colour to match those with which it is coreferential (e.g., all references to heart disease might become blue).

After the document has been written, the text is semi-automatically translated into SPL. This is essentially a process of parsing, but the resultant structures are (annotated) SPL expressions rather than parse trees. Whenever an ambiguity cannot be resolved, the writer is queried in an easy-to-understand form. The process is described in detail by DiMarco and Banks (1997).

5   Tailoring a Document

We now consider the kinds of textual repairs or post-editing that might be needed after material in the TSL master document has been selected for a particular patient. We will show the examples in English, but it is to be understood that the process is taking place on the underlying TSL representation.

In general, selecting material from pre-existing text and then editing it to recover coherence and cohesion involves a wide range of problems in sentence planning. Our sentence planner uses a blackboard architecture in which individual repair modules communicate and resolve their conflicts with one another. The architecture is described in greater detail by Hovy and Wanner (1996). Four repair modules are being developed in the present phase of the project: for coreference, for discourse structuring and rhetorical relations, for aggregation, and for constituent ordering. Here, we will give examples of the first two.

Repair—Coreference. Coreference repairs include decisions as to when a reference should be pronominalized. Suppose, for example, we have a master document that contains the following two sentences (in TSL, of course):

(1)   *People with respiratory disorders* have a high risk of developing Glaumann's disease.

(2)   *People with respiratory disorders* should take immediate action to quit smoking.

The italicized noun phrase in each arises from a coreference link to the same object in the list of references. So if, upon selection, these two sentences turned up in close proximity, the first occurrence of the reference would be marked for realization as a full noun phrase, and the second would be marked for pronominalization:

(3)   *People with respiratory disorders* have a high risk of developing Glaumann's disease. *They* should take immediate action to quit smoking.

Repair—Rhetorical relations. If two selected sentences are marked as being rhetorically related, the repair module will consider making the cohesive relationship between the sentences explicit. For example, if the sentences in the example above were marked as *evidence* and *conclusion*, then the word *therefore* might be inserted:

(4)   People with respiratory disorders have a high risk of developing Glaumann's disease. They should *therefore* take immediate action to quit smoking.

6   Realization and Formatting

The final specifications for the repaired text, represented in SPL, are passed to the realization stage, which uses KPML (Bateman, 1995), a descendant of Penman, to generate an appropriate surface form in English. A formatter then lays out the text attractively and adds headings and illustrations for final printing.

7 Conclusion

In the HealthDoc system, we are tailoring health-education and patient-information documents by using the medical record as a model of the reader that allows us to select appropriate elements from a master document encoded in TSL. A subsequent process of 'repair' ensures that the selections form a coherent, linguistically well-formed document. We have adopted a model of patient education that takes into account patient information ranging from simple medical data to complex cultural beliefs. A number of important issues for research in tailorable health-communication documents and their authoring have been raised during the first phase of the project.

The basis for tailoring health information to a given individual. Although the need for tailored health communication has been recognized, there has as yet been little research on how information may be conveyed most effectively to a known individual to motivate a change in their behaviour. (The present state of the art is represented by Kreps and Kunimoto, 1994,; and Maibach and Parrott, 1995.) In the next stage of the project, identifying critical examples of variations in text by medical condition and by culture and health beliefs will be an important task.

Authoring tailorable documents. We have not yet worked with any real-life medical writers, and hence have not tested our assumptions as to whether medical writers would be able to design tailorable documents with our authoring tool as we have conceived it—or even in principle.

Language dependence. Both the authoring tools and the processes that refine the selections from the master document are necessarily language-dependent, so at present HealthDoc is limited to English, our working language. It is hoped that in the long term it will be possible to add master documents in other languages, such as German, Spanish, and French, for which the necessary grammars and lexicons are being developed in other projects in natural language generation. Unfortunately, there is little or no applicable research in the languages—Chinese, Vietnamese, Khmer—that are the greatest problems for the hospitals with which we are collaborating.[4]

Development of the master document. Our consideration of how patient-information documents should be initially written and then tailored has led us to propose the use of a master document. However, the nature of the master document may need to be redesigned as we begin to address questions of stylistic and pragmatic tailoring, such as the incorporation of persuasive effects. The master document is a set of TSL fragments, but it lacks the information needed to do the kind of whole-scale revision that would be needed for this level of pragmatic tailoring. We expect to augment TSL with additional fields for discourse-level, semantic, and stylistic information.

References

Bateman, J.A. (1995). KPML: The KOMET–Penman multilingual linguistic resource development environment. *Proceedings, 5th European Workshop on Natural Language Generation*, Leiden, May 1995, 219–222.

---

[4] All three of our partner hospitals serve large, multi-ethnic, multicultural communities, and intercultural and multilingual communication—indeed, the practice of multicultural health care in general—is a continuing problem for them.

Buchanan, B., Moore, J.D., Forsythe, D.E., Carenini, G., Ohlsson, S., and Banks, G. (1995). An intelligent interactive system for delivering individualized information to patients. *Artificial Intelligence in Medicine*, 7:117–154.

Campbell, M.K., DeVellis, B.M., Strecher, V.J., Ammerman, A.S., DeVellis, R.F., and Sandler, R.S. (1994). Improving dietary behavior: The effectiveness of tailored messages in primary care settings. *American Journal of Public Health*, 84:783–787.

Cawsey, A., Binsted, K., and Jones, R. (1995). Personalized explanations for patient education. *Proceedings, 5th European Workshop on Natural Language Generation*, Leiden, May 1995, 59–74.

DiMarco, C. and Banks, S. (1997). Using subsumption classification on a stylistic hierarchy in the multi-stage conversion of natural language text to sentence plans. In preparation.

DiMarco, C. and Foster, M.E. (1997). The automated generation of Web documents that are tailored to the individual reader. *Proceedings, AAAI Spring Symposium on Natural Language Processing on the World Wide Web*, Stanford University, March 1997.

DiMarco, C., Hirst, G., and Hovy, E. (1997). "Rewriting is easier than writing": Generation by selection and repair in the HealthDoc project. In preparation.

DiMarco, C., Hirst, G., Wanner, L., and Wilkinson, J. (1995). HealthDoc: Customizing patient information and health education by medical condition and personal characteristics. *Workshop on Artificial Intelligence in Patient Education*, Glasgow, August 1995.

Donohew, L., Palmgreen, P., and Lorch, E.P. (1994). Attention, need for sensation, and health communication campaigns. *American Behavioral Scientist*, 38:310–322.

Hale, J.L. and Dillard, J.P. (1995). Fear appeals in health promotion campaigns: Too much, too little, or just right? In Maibach and Parrott 1995, 65–80.

Hovy, E.H. and Wanner, L. (1996). Managing sentence planning requirements. *Proceedings, ECAI-96 Workshop 'Gaps and Bridges': New Directions in Planning and Natural Language Generation*, Budapest, August 1996.

Maibach, E. and Parrott, R.L. (1995). *Designing health messages: Approaches from communication theory and public health practice*. Thousand Oaks, CA: Sage Publications.

Masi, R. (1993). Multicultural health: Principles and policies. In Masi, R., Mensah, L., and McLeod, K.A., eds., *Health and cultures: Exploring the relationships. Volume I: Policies, professional practice and education*. Oakville, Ontario: Mosaic Press, 11–22.

Monahan, J.L. (1995). Thinking positively: Using positive affect when designing health messages. In Maibach and Parrott 1995, 81–98.

Parsons, K. (1997). *An Authoring Tool for Customizable Documents*. M.Math. thesis, Department of Computer Science, University of Waterloo, forthcoming.

Penman Natural Language Group (1989). The Penman primer, The Penman user guide, and The Penman reference manual. Information Sciences Institute, University of Southern California.

Reiter, E. (1995). NLG vs. templates. *Proceedings, 5th European Workshop on Natural Language Generation*, Leiden, May 1995, 95–105.

Skinner, C.S., Strecher, V.J., and Hospers, H. (1994). Physicians' recommendations for mammography: Do tailored messages make a difference? *American Journal of Public Health*, 84:43–49.

Strecher, V.J., Kreuter, M., Den Boer, D.-J., Kobrin, S., Hospers, H.J., and Skinner C.S. (1994). The effects of computer-tailored smoking cessation messages in family practice settings. *The Journal of Family Practice*, 39:262–270.

Augmenting the User's Knowledge via Comparison

Maria Milosavljevic*

Microsoft Research Institute, Macquarie University, Sydney NSW, Australia

Abstract. The process of learning is an incremental exploration of a domain; we do not learn the concepts in a domain in an isolated manner, but instead augment our existing knowledge with new concepts. Consequently, when teaching a new concept to a student, her existing knowledge should be employed in a way which facilitates the process of learning. In describing a new concept to a hearer, it is often beneficial to compare the concept to other concepts with which the hearer is familiar. In particular, comparisons are often used in descriptions in order to reduce the cognitive load on the hearer. This paper outlines three types of comparison found in encyclopædia descriptions, and describes how a model of the user's knowledge can be employed to produce descriptions which introduce new concepts by comparison, thus grounding descriptions in the hearer's existing knowledge. The results are illustrated in the PEBA–II natural language generation system.

1 Introduction

A model of the user's knowledge is a fertile resource which can be used to improve the transfer of knowledge from a system's domain model to the user. It should not simply be used for keeping track of what the user knows in order to present only new information to her. Instead, new information should be presented in a manner which builds on her existing knowledge, allowing her to understand new concepts more effectively. A natural language generation (NLG) system can utilise a model of the user's knowledge and a record of the previous discourse in order to tailor descriptions to a particular user's knowledge. Discussions of the utility of a user model and discourse history in NLG systems are given by Paris (1987, 1993) and Moore (1989, 1995), respectively.

Comparison is an important and useful tool in language. When describing an entity to a person who is unfamiliar with that entity, an NLG system can use comparisons in order to tailor the description to the user's knowledge. In particular, it is *important* to distinguish an unfamiliar entity from other entities which are potential confusors of that entity, and it is *useful* to compare the unfamiliar entity to known concepts (see Milosavljevic, 1996).

The purpose of comparison is to aid the hearer's learning of an unfamiliar concept or to sharpen the hearer's existing knowledge of a concept. As a result, the content of a comparison— exactly which properties are used in the comparison—and the realisation of the comparison— how the comparison is expressed in a natural language—will depend crucially on the hearer's existing knowledge (if any) of the concepts appearing in that comparison. In particular, if the hearer has very limited knowledge of the concepts in a comparison, then the comparison needs to be explicit and detailed about the properties of those concepts.

* Thanks to Robert Dale, Eric Horvitz, Mike Johnson, Cécile Paris and the members of MRI for useful discussions of this work. Thanks also to the reviewers for their comments.

In Section 2 of this paper, we present an overview of PEBA–II, a natural language generation system which we use as a test–bed for our research in comparison generation. Section 3 describes the necessity for and utilisation of a model of the user's knowledge in the automatic production of comparisons, and discusses the GROUNDEDNESS and SYMMETRY of comparison. Section 4 describes the utilisation of user–specific comparisons in the descriptions produced by the PEBA–II system. Finally, Section 5 presents some conclusions and points to our future directions.

2 The PEBA–II System

PEBA–II is a natural language generation system which produces hypertext descriptions and comparisons of entities as world wide web pages.[1] An overview of the system will be given here; for more details, see Milosavljevic et al. (1996).

The architecture of the PEBA–II system, shown in Figure 1, is typical of many NLG systems, but is adapted for use as a WWW server. The system begins with a discourse goal, which at this stage can be either to describe a single entity or to compare two entities. Based on this discourse goal, the system selects a discourse plan from the plan library which can be used to satisfy the goal. We currently use two high level discourse plans which correspond to the discourse goals: identify for producing descriptions; and compare–and–contrast for producing comparisons. These discourse plans are similar to those used by McKeown (1985) but have been modified for use in a hypertext environment.

After selecting a discourse plan, the text planning component instantiates it with facts from the knowledge base. The knowledge base used by PEBA–II has been hand–constructed from encyclopædia articles of animals and consists of a taxonomic backbone of animal classes (the Linnaean taxonomy) together with the properties of each class. The user modeling component currently serves two functions: to provide two different views of the animal taxonomy for naïve and expert users; and to keep specialised information about particular users in order to modify how descriptions and comparisons are presented. The user can inform the system of her details (name, geographical location, age and those entities with which she is very familiar) using a user's preferences page.

A record of the discourse is maintained for each user, and is used in combination with the user model in order to improve the conceptual coherence of descriptions. For example, if the user has knowledge of an entity (as per the user model) or has been told about an entity (as per the discourse history), then the entity can be used by the system in later descriptions where a comparison can be made with that entity. The types of comparisons which are produced using this information will be described in Section 4.

The discourse history is also utilised to improve the textual coherence of descriptions. For example, the entity which is currently being described (the *focused entity*) can be related to the most–recently described entity in order to smooth the transition from one description to the next. This functionality provides a more natural discourse between the user and the system (see Dale and Milosavljevic, 1996, and Dale et al., 1997).

Once the text planning component has pulled together all the information about the entity (or entities) to be described in the document according to the user's knowledge, the filled discourse plan is passed to the surface realisation component. Here, the leaves of the discourse plan

---

[1] A version of PEBA–II is available on the Web at URL: http://www.mri.mq.edu.au/ltg/peba/.

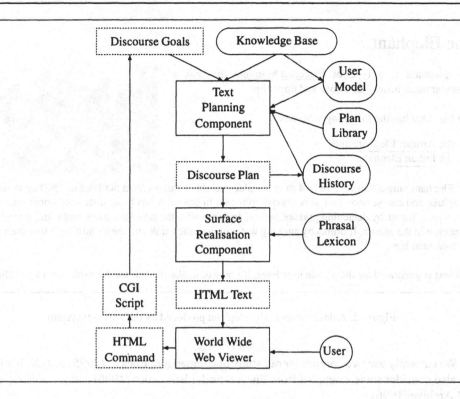

Figure 1. The PEBA–II system architecture.

are realised as natural language sentences, and HTML tags are positioned within the text to allow the user to request *follow–up* questions by selecting them (see Moore, 1989, and Dale and Milosavljevic, 1996). If a picture exists for the focused entity, the surface realisation component includes it in the hypertext page. An example description produced by PEBA–II is shown in Figure 2. When the user selects a hypertext tag (the underlined words) within the description, a new discourse goal is posted to the text planning component, and the cycle repeats.

3   Comparison and the User's Knowledge

Comparison is an important and useful tool in language. In particular, it can be used in order to: aid a hearer's understanding of a new concept by relating that concept to other known concepts (see Milosavljevic, 1996); aid the description process (see Zukerman and McConachy, 1993); and correct the user's misconceptions (see McCoy, 1989).

In this section, we first outline the comparison types we have found in encyclopædia articles (see Milosavljevic and Dale, 1996), describing their purposes and the role of the user's knowledge in the decision to produce them. We then discuss the effect of the user's knowledge on the realisation of comparisons, and in particular, the GROUNDEDNESS and SYMMETRY of comparisons.

The Elephant

The Elephant is a type of <u>Placental Mammal</u> that has a muscular trunk instead of a nose and upper lip.

The Elephant has the following subtypes:

- the <u>African Elephant</u> and
- the <u>Indian Elephant.</u>

The Elephant ranges from 2.5 m to 4 m in shoulder height. It ranges from 5000 kg to 7500 kg in weight. It has sparse and coarse body hair. It is grayish to brown in colour. It has tusks instead of upper incisors. It is a herbivore. It eats by detaching grasses, leaves, and fruit with the tip of the trunk and using it to place this vegetation in the mouth. It drinks by sucking water up into the trunk and then squirting it into the mouth. It has columnar legs.

This text is generated for the novice user level. If you would like the text for the expert user level click <u>here</u>.

Figure 2. A description of the elephant produced by the PEBA–II system.

We currently use two corpora for our study of comparison: Encarta (1995) and Grolier (1992). We also consider some examples from Encyclopædia Britannica (1996) and the Australian Animal Archive (1996).

3.1 Types and Purpose of Comparison

Comparison is useful for distinguishing or likening entities. When describing an entity to a listener, comparison can be used to perform many different functions, including: distinguishing the focused entity from potential confusors; likening the focused entity to other similar entities; illustrating a particular property of the focused entity with the same property of another known (but not necessarily similar) entity; and distinguishing the subtypes of the focused entity from each other (if they exist). These functions are achieved using the three types of comparison outlined below (see Milosavljevic and Dale, 1996, for more details of these comparison types and how they relate to other work).

Direct comparison: When a user requests a comparison of two entities, she is typically interested in knowing which properties the entities have in common and which properties distinguish them. Neither entity is more important in the comparison, and therefore it is essentially *bi–focal*. Direct comparisons are commonly found in class descriptions where they are employed to distinguish the subtypes of the class. Example (3–1) in Figure 3 is typical of the direct comparisons found in the animal corpus, where only one distinguishing property is used in order to distinguish the two subtypes of a class. Example (3–2) is a direct comparison of the two subtypes of the echidna class. In this comparison, the two subtypes are compared based on their geographical location, length, body–shape and spines.

(1) There are two kinds of camels: the dromedary, or Arabian camel, which has one hump, and the Bactrian camel, which has two humps.†

(2) Echidnas of the genus Zaglossus, the several forms of which are usually considered races of Z. bruijni of New Guinea, are 45 to 78 cm (18 to 31 inches) long and rather piglike, with short, wide–set spines. The other species, Tachyglossus aculeatus, found in many habitats across Australia and Tasmania (the latter population sometimes considered a separate species, T. setosus), is 35 to 53 cm (14 to 21 inches) long and has spines like a hedgehog's.‡

(3) Coati, also coatimundi, mammal resembling the raccoon, but with a slimmer body, a longer tail, and an elongated, flexible snout.†

(4) Cheetah, common name for a large cat, found mainly in Africa but with small populations in Iran and northwestern Afghanistan, that has a similar body weight to the leopard (50 to 60 kg/110 to 130 lb) but has a longer body, much longer legs, and a smaller head.†

(5) Goat, common name for any of eight species of cloven–hoofed, horned mammals closely related to the sheep. The two differ in that the goat's tail is shorter and the hollow horns are long and directed upward, backward, and outward, while those of the sheep are spirally twisted. The male goats have beards, unlike sheep, and differ further by the characteristic strong odor they give off in the rutting season.†

(6) They [Aye–aye] are about the size of a large cat and have long, bushy tails, a shaggy brown coat, and large ears.†

(7) Typical large kangaroos have sheeplike heads.†

(8) This echolocation system, similar to that of a bat, enables the dolphin to navigate among its companions and larger objects and to detect fish, squid, and even small shrimp.†

(9) Viscacha, South American rodent related to chinchillas. Slightly larger than chinchillas, the mountain viscachas have long, rabbitlike ears and a long squirrel–like tail. They live in rock crevices and feed during the day. The larger plains viscacha has shorter ears and a large, blunt head and resembles the paca.†

Figure 3. Some comparisons from the animal corpus. †(Encarta, 1995) ‡(Britannica, 1996)

Clarificatory comparison: A user might request a direct comparison between two entities in order to aid and/or sharpen her understanding of the concepts (or the differences between the concepts). In a similar way, an NLG system can aid the user's understanding of a concept by opportunistically using clarificatory comparison in order to relate new information to her existing knowledge: If in describing a concept x to the user, there is another concept y with which the user is familiar, and which is similar to x, then it might be useful to describe x by comparing it to y, thus allowing the user to understand x more easily. In such a clarificatory comparison, the discourse is *uni–focal*, since the *focused entity* is more central to the discourse than the *potential confusor*. Clarificatory comparisons typically occur in the initial paragraph of a description of an entity; three examples are shown in (3–3), (3–4) and (3–5).

Clarificatory comparison can be used to achieve two purposes. First, if the user is familiar with the similar entity y, then we can introduce x by comparison with y, thus allowing the user to understand x more easily. Second, if the user is not familiar with y, and y is a potential confusor of x, then the description of x might need to first distinguish x from y in order to prevent the user from confusing the two entities.

The clarificatory comparison given in example (3–5) might arguably have been utilised for the first purpose since the target audience for these texts is very likely to be familiar with the sheep, and possibly less familiar with the goat. If, however, the reader is not familiar with either the goat or the sheep, then this comparison might also achieve the purpose of ensuring she does not confuse them. It is therefore difficult to determine which purpose might have led to a clarificatory comparison in the first instance, and we can only guess as to the author's intentions or ideas about the target audience. In an NLG system, however, we can make use of a model of the hearer's knowledge in order to produce texts for either purpose.

Illustrative comparison: Comparisons are not only made between essentially similar entities as in direct and clarificatory comparison; we can also relate the focused entity to entities which are quite different, but familiar to the hearer. Illustrative comparison is a useful tool for describing a single attribute of an entity by comparing it to the same attribute of a known entity. Three example illustrative comparisons are shown in (3–6), (3–7) and (3–8). There seems to be no constraint on the types of attributes which can be used in illustrative comparisons, and in these examples, the size, head–shape and navigation–system attributes of the focused entities are illustrated.

It is important to note that in some cases, comparison might be the only effective means for describing a property. In particular, the shape of the kangaroo's head in example (3–7) might not be adequately describable in any way other than by comparison with the sheep (or another animal with a similarly–shaped head).

In order to demonstrate the domain–independence of this categorisation of comparison types, Figure 4 contains some example comparisons from other domains. Examples (4–1) and (4–2) show direct comparisons between the two types of accordion and the two sections of the Alpine mountain range respectively. The cornet is introduced by clarificatory comparison with the trumpet in example (4–3), and the mechanical watch is distinguished from the coiled spring watch in example (4–4). Finally, example (4–5) illustrates the keys of some accordions with the piano, and in example (4–6) the size of the Avebury henge is illustrated with the size of the Avebury village.

3.2 The Groundedness of Comparison

In the clarificatory comparison shown in example (3–4), the cheetah is described with reference to the similar leopard. Although the weight of the two animals is explicitly stated, the length of their bodies and legs and the size of their heads are not. In other words, the weight comparison does not rely on the user to know the value of the shared property, whereas the size comparisons leave the user to reason about the actual sizes of the entities.

The purpose of clarificatory comparison is either to distinguish the focused entity from a potential confusor, or to introduce a focused entity by comparing it to a similar entity with which the user is familiar. If the user is very familiar with the leopard then the size comparisons in (3–4) will be appropriate, since we are introducing the cheetah by comparison with a known entity. However, if the user is not familiar with the leopard, and the purpose of the comparison is to distinguish the cheetah from the leopard (within a description whose purpose is to describe

(1) The two main types of accordion are single–action and double–action. In single–action accordions, each button produces two notes, one on the push and another on the draw. In double–action accordions, each key or button produces the same note on the push as on the draw.†

(2) Structurally, the Alpine mountain system is divided into the Western and Eastern Alps by a furrow that leads from the Rhine Valley in northern Switzerland, across Splgen Pass to Lake Como in northern Italy. The Western Alps average about 1,000 m (3,300 ft) higher and are narrower and more rugged than the Eastern Alps.†

(3) The cornet has three valves, a medium–narrow conical bore, and a deep, funnel–shaped mouthpiece. In contrast, a trumpet bore is cylindrical, its mouthpiece is cup–shaped, and its tone is less mellow than the cornet's.†

(4) A mechanical watch uses a coiled spring as its power source. As in spring–powered clocks, the watch transmits the spring's energy to the hands by means of a gear train, with a balance wheel regulating the motive force.†

(5) Accordion, a hand–held musical instrument consisting of a bellows attached to two oblong frames, on which buttons and, in some types, piano–like keys are mounted.†

(6) Over 80 henge monuments are known to exist in Britain from areas as far apart as Cornwall and Orkney, but Avebury is set apart by its sheer size; it is large enough to contain the present–day village of Avebury within its bounds.†

Figure 4. Example comparisons from other domains. †(Encarta, 1995)

the cheetah), then the comparison might fail to fully achieve its purpose. The reader may be able to distinguish these entities if presented with fully–grown versions of them both at the same time, but she will not be able to recognise whether a given entity is one or the other. Therefore, if the purpose of a comparison is to enable the hearer to distinguish two entities, then those characteristics which are utilised in the comparison need to be accessible to the hearer.

The content of a comparison should therefore be a reflection of the user's knowledge of both the focused entity and the comparator; if the user is completely unfamiliar with the comparator, then each property comparison needs to be *grounded* in the user's existing knowledge. That is, the user must not be left questioning what the actual value of the attribute being compared is for either the focused entity or the comparator. On the other hand, if the user is extremely familiar with the comparator, then references to the properties of both entities can be *ungrounded*, since we can assume that the user will be able to infer more about the similarity or difference being described.

In the direct comparison shown in (3–2), two ungrounded comparisons are used: the long–beaked echidna (genus Zaglossus) is described as *piglike* assuming the user knows what a pig looks like; and the short–beaked echidna's (Tachyglossus aculeatus) spines are likened to the hedgehog's spines, assuming the user not only knows about hedgehogs, but also remembers details about their spines. It is quite likely that most readers will be familiar with the general shape of the pig, and hence should understand more about the shape of the long–beaked echidna. However, unless the reader is very familiar with the hedgehog, it is highly unlikely that she will be able to understand what the short–beaked echidna's spines are like from this description. Furthermore, if the reader has never seen an animal with spines, then it is highly unlikely that she will be able to infer what the length of *short* spines is, or determine precisely what *wide–set* means in the context of spines.

In the two illustrative comparisons in (3–6) and (3–7), the writer assumes that the reader is familiar with the size of cats and the shape of the sheep's head. These might be safe assumptions; however, if the reader is not familiar with the comparator entities, then she might be confused by these ungrounded comparisons. A grounded comparison, on the other hand, allows the author to draw the connection between the focused entity and a comparator, and also to ensure that the comparison is meaningful if the user is not familiar with the comparator.

It is possible that for some properties there is no means for grounding a comparison. For example, it is difficult to see how one might ground the comparison of the kangaroo's head in example (3–7). Furthermore, it is difficult to see any way of describing the kangaroo's head other than by making such a comparison. If the user fails to learn what the kangaroo's head is like, then she will not necessarily be disadvantaged, since the kangaroo's head–shape is not a particularly important feature of the kangaroo. In cases where the property being illustrated is an important feature of the focused entity, then the user might be disadvantaged by an ungrounded comparison.

In the description of the viscacha shown in (3–9), unless the listener is familiar with chinchillas, rabbits, squirrels and pacas, she might be left quite confused and could forget most of the description due to her lack of understanding.

It is therefore crucial that the user's knowledge be taken into account when making comparisons, and in cases where it is probable that the user is unfamiliar with a comparator, that a grounded comparison be used instead of an ungrounded comparison. This can also be extended to descriptions in general; that is, the description of a property of the focused entity needs to be understandable to the user. For example, one could imagine a situation where a particular user is more familiar with the weight of a domestic cat than with a particular measurement system such as kilograms. Even if the user is familiar with this measurement system, she might more easily understand the weight of a focused entity if it is related to the weight of other familiar entities.

3.3   The Symmetry of Comparison

In the direct comparison shown in example (3–2) values for the attributes of geography, size and spine–type are given for both the long–beaked and short–beaked echidnas. However, although the value for the shape attribute is given for the long–beaked echidna (*piglike*), no contrastive value for this attribute is given for the short–beaked echidna. Instead, this comparison assumes that the user will realise that since we are making a direct comparison of these two entities and are therefore attempting to contrast them, it would be senseless to state that the short–beaked echidna is *not* piglike.

In the clarificatory comparison shown in example (3–3), the coati's snout is described as elongated and flexible, but since this description forms part of a comparison, the reader is left questioning what the raccoon's snout is like. If the reader is familiar with the raccoon then this comparison will not be ambiguous; however, for the reader who is not familiar with the raccoon, this statement might be confusing. In particular, it is difficult to determine whether the statement is actually part of the comparison with the raccoon; the coati's snout might be elongated with respect to the raccoon's snout, the snout–size of most mammals (or some other class), or the size of its head or other body–parts. If the two entities had a similar snout, then this statement would be unnecessary within the comparison, and hence the naïve reader is left in a state of bewilderment about the raccoon and the coati.

We label comparisons which explicitly state the values for the compared attribute for both entities as *symmetrical* comparisons, and comparisons which only mention the value of the compared attribute for one of the entities as *non–symmetrical* comparisons. Non–symmetrical comparisons occur frequently in cases where the entities being compared have directly opposite values for a particular attribute. In particular, if one entity has a property which the other entity does not share (for example, a tail), or if there is no obvious method for describing the value of an attribute for one entity (such as, perhaps the shape of the short–beaked echidna), then a non–symmetrical comparison might be necessary.

If the reader is very familiar with the comparator entity, then non–symmetrical comparisons involving the focused entity might be quite appropriate. That is, if a property is ascribed to the focused entity which the user knows the comparator does not share, then the comparison will not be ambiguous for her, and she will not be given information she already knows. On the other hand, non–symmetrical comparisons involving the comparator could be ambiguous to her. In this case, and for the user who has no knowledge of the comparator, the non–symmetrical comparison might still have some meaning, but problems of ambiguity might arise.

Non–symmetrical comparisons can often be ambiguous, not only since the user might not be able to infer the property of the other entity, but also since it is often difficult to determine whether a statement is actually a comparison at all. In example (3–5), although the length of the goat's horns is described as *long*, no counterpart for the length of the sheep's horns is given. In this case, the reader might assume that the sheep's horns are *not* long, and given her knowledge of the horns of animals, she might form a misconception about the sheep's horns. On the other hand, the comparison of the presence or absence of a beard is explicitly made symmetrical in order to avoid confusion through the use of the *unlike sheep* clause.

4 Comparisons in the PEBA–II System

The PEBA–II system currently maintains a model of the user's knowledge and a record of the past discourse for each user in order to tailor descriptions to the user's knowledge. In particular, the system will attempt to compare a focused entity to another entity with which the user is assumed to be familiar.

Clarificatory comparison is used by the PEBA–II system if the focused entity has a potential confusor. In order to find the potential confusors of an entity, we require a similarity metric which determines the similarity of the focused entity and other entities in the knowledge base. We currently side–step this issue by explicitly representing the potential confusors of each entity in the knowledge base, particularly since most of the available similarity metrics are not suitable for our task. However, we are currently working on a similarity metric which is based on Tversky's (1977) feature–based metric, but which recognises the inter–relatedness of properties such as size and shape. The algorithm used by PEBA–II for selecting the content of a clarificatory comparison (or the set of properties which are compared) is described by Milosavljevic (1997).

If the user is already familiar with the potential confusor of the focused entity (based on information contained in either the user model or the most recent discourse history), then the system

The Alligator

The Alligator is a member of the <u>Crocodylidae Family</u> that has a broad, flat, rounded snout. It is similar in appearance to the related <u>Crocodile</u>. The Crocodile is a member of the Crocodylidae Family that has a narrow snout. The Crocodile is much longer than the Alligator (5.25 m vs 3.75 m). The Alligator has longer teeth on the lower jaw which cannot be seen when its mouth is closed whereas the Crocodile has one longer tooth on each side of the lower jaw which can be seen sticking up when its jaw is closed.

The Alligator has the following subtypes:

- the <u>American Alligator</u> and
- the <u>Chinese Alligator</u>.

The Alligator feeds on fish, frogs, snakes, turtles, birds, mammals, and carrion. It can survive a wide range of temperatures, and is found in more temperate regions.

This text is generated for the novice user level. If you would like the text for the expert user level click <u>here</u>.

Figure 5. A description of the alligator produced by the PEBA–II system.

will make ungrounded comparisons for quantitative attributes such as length, height, shoulder–height, tail–length, lifespan and so on. For example, the description of the alligator shown in Figure 5 contains a clarificatory comparison with the crocodile. Since this particular user was not familiar with the crocodile, the size–based comparison is grounded. For a user who is familiar with the potential confusor, this property comparison would be ungrounded with the actual values not stated.

Illustrative comparisons are used by PEBA–II when a known entity has the same or a similar value for an attribute as the focused entity (see Milosavljevic and Dale, 1996, for the algorithm used by PEBA–II for determining the best comparator). For example, the description of the platypus shown in Figure 6 contains an ungrounded comparison with the domestic cat, since this user is assumed to be very familiar with the domestic cat. This is determined based on either confirmed knowledge contained in the user model, expected knowledge from the discourse history, or assumed knowledge for the user–type (expert/naïve). On the other hand, the comparison with the rabbit is grounded,[2] since this particular user requested a description of the rabbit in the recent (but not *most* recent) discourse history. The system assumes that the user is only likely to remember specific details about the most recently described entities, and although comparisons are made with entities which have been described earlier, the comparisons are grounded to ensure the user does not become confused.

---

[2] Of course this can only really be said to be grounded if we assume that the user knows and understands what *1.55 kg* means.

The Platypus

The Platypus is a type of <u>Monotreme</u> that has short legs with webbed feet for swimming.

The Platypus is about the same length as a <u>domestic cat</u>. It ranges from 5 cm to 6 cm in nose length. It ranges from 10 cm to 15 cm in tail length. It is about the same weight as a <u>Rabbit</u> (1.55 kg). It is dark brown on its back and silvery to light brown underneath. It eats insect larvae, worms and crustaceans. It is found in Australia. It lives in and near rivers and lakes. It is active at dawn and dusk. It lives by itself. It has an average lifespan in captivity of 17 years.

This text is generated for the novice user level. If you would like the text for the expert user level click <u>here</u>.

Figure 6. A description of the platypus produced by the PEBA–II system.

In order to avoid ambiguity, all the comparisons produced by the PEBA–II system are currently symmetrical. Furthermore, the discourse is structured so that there is a clear distinction between a clarificatory comparison and the rest of the description; this is realised as a paragraph break in the hypertext description.

5 Conclusion

Comparison is a useful tool for augmenting the user's existing knowledge with new knowledge. In particular, when describing a new concept to a user, we can often make references to other concepts with which the user is familiar in order to reduce the learning difficulty and conceptualisation of the new concept. It is also important to distinguish the new concept from potential confusors in order to prevent the user from forming misconceptions.

The realisation of a comparison depends crucially on the purpose of the comparison and on the user's knowledge of both the focused entity and the comparator. If the user is very familiar with both the focused entity and the potential confusor, then the property comparisons can be both ungrounded and non–symmetrical. On the other hand, if the user is completely unfamiliar with the entities being compared, then it is important that all the property comparisons are both grounded and symmetrical in order to avoid ambiguity and to prevent the user from forming misconceptions. Since each different user will have unique knowledge of the entities in any domain, a natural language generation system must weigh up the user's existing knowledge and the complexity of any new information in order to produce a description which is the most effective for that particular user.

This research forms part of an ongoing investigation into the utility of comparisons for the efficient transfer of knowledge from the system's domain model to the user. In particular, comparison is an important and useful tool for a language production system, and we are therefore interested in determining the precise role of comparison in the description process and how the content and realisation of comparison is influenced by factors such as the user's knowledge.

References

Dale, R., and Milosavljevic, M. (1996). Authoring on demand: Natural language generation of hyperme-dia documents. In *Proceedings of the First Australian Document Computing Symposium (ADCS'96)*. Melbourne, Australia.

Dale, R., Milosavljevic, M., and Oberlander, J. (1997). The web as dialogue: The role of natural lan-guage generation in hypertext. In *Proceedings of the AAAI Spring Symposium on Natural Language Processing for the World Wide Web*, 35–43. Stanford University, California.

Encyclopædia Britannica. (1996). Copyright ©1996 Encyclopædia Britannica, Inc.

McCoy, K. F. (1995). Generating context–sensitive responses to object–related misconceptions. *Artificial Intelligence* 41:157–195.

McKeown, K. R. (1985). Discourse strategies for generating natural–language text. *Artificial Intelligence* 27:1–41.

Microsoft (R) Encarta'95 Encyclopedia. (1995). Copyright ©1994 Microsoft Corporation. Copyright ©1994 Funk and Wagnall's Corporation.

Milosavljevic, M. (1996). Introducing new concepts via comparison: A new look at user modeling in text generation. In *Proceedings of the Fifth International Conference on User Modeling, Doctoral Consortium*, 228–230.

Milosavljevic, M., and Dale, R. (1996). Strategies for comparison in encyclopædia descriptions. In *Pro-ceedings of the 8th International Workshop on Natural Language Generation*, 161–170. Sussex, UK.

Milosavljevic, M., Tulloch, A., and Dale, R. (1996). Text generation in a dynamic hypertext environment. In *Proceedings of the Nineteenth Australasian Computer Science Conference*, 417–426. Melbourne, Australia.

Milosavljevic, M. (1997). Content selection in comparison generation. In *Proceedings of the Sixth Euro-pean Workshop on Natural Language Generation*. Duisburg, Germany.

Moore, J. D. (1989). *A Reactive Approach to Explanation in Expert and Advice–Giving Systems*. Ph.D. Dissertation, University of California, Los Angeles.

Moore, J. D. (1995). *Participating in Explanatory Dialogs: Interpreting and Responding to Questions in Context*. Cambridge, MA: MIT Press.

Paris, C. L. (1987). *The Use of Explicit User Models in Text Generation: Tailoring to a User's Level of Expertise*. Ph.D. Dissertation, Columbia University.

Paris, C. L. (1993). *User Modeling in Text Generation*. London: Pinter Publishers.

The Australian A–Z Animal Archive. (1996). http://www.aaa.com.au/A_Z/Home.html

The New Grolier Multimedia Encyclopedia. (1992). ©Grolier Incorporated, ©1987–1992 Online Com-puter Systems, Inc.

Tversky, A. (1977). Features of similarity. *Psychological Review* 84:327–352.

Zukerman, I., and McConachy, R. (1993). Generating concise discourse that addresses a user's inferences. In *Proceedings of the Thirteenth International Joint Conference on Artificial Intelligence*, 1202–1207. Chambery, France.

INTERFACE ADAPTION

Tailoring to Abilities, Disabilities, and Preferences

Dynamic Modelling of Keyboard Skills: Supporting Users With Motor Disabilities

Shari Trewin* and Helen Pain

Department of Artificial Intelligence, University of Edinburgh, Scotland

Abstract. This paper describes the effective application of user modelling to the assessment of the physical ease with which a user can operate a standard QWERTY keyboard. The application is unusual in the sense that physical rather than cognitive skills are being modelled. The model examines four important skills which a user may have difficulty with, and produces an assessment of the ideal keyboard configuration for that user. This assessment can then be used to adapt the keyboard. For users with motor disabilities, such adaption can minimise or even eliminate the problems they experience. The model dynamically adapts to the current user and operates on free English text input. It has been evaluated using typing data from twenty keyboard users with disabilities and six without. The configuration recommendations made are very well matched to the users' problem areas.

1 Introduction

Computer users with motor disabilities can experience difficulties with the operation of QWERTY keyboards. If we were able to identify and model the specific difficulties of individual users, we could then use such models as the basis for recommendation of a more appropriate keyboard configuration for each user. We believe that this would make the keyboard easier to use, and reduce the number of errors occurring. This paper describes the development and evaluation of techniques for identifying and modelling keyboard difficulties. Our focus is on the modelling of physical skills, rather than on cognitive skills.

Although alternative input devices (such as switches) are available, many users with disabilities find that keyboards provide a more efficient input device. Errors that occur through physical difficulty in manipulating the keyboard are referred to here as *performance errors*. Empirical research with keyboard users with disabilities has highlighted six common classes of performance error (Trewin and Pain, 1996a). These are:

1. *Long Key Press Errors*: An alphanumeric key is unintentionally pressed for longer than the default key repeat delay. On the majority of operating systems, there is a *Repeat Keys* facility, which allows the user to control the length of time a key must be held down for before it repeats. Setting an appropriate delay, or disabling key repeats altogether, can prevent long key press errors.
2. *Dropping Errors*: The user fails to press two keys simultaneously (e.g. use of the *Shift* key). This error type is just one manifestation of difficulty in pressing down two keys at once. The *Sticky Keys* facility, when activated, causes modifier keys to latch. When pressed, they stay active until the next key has been pressed. With *Sticky Keys*, a user presses *Shift* and then 'a' to produce a capital 'A'. Use of *Sticky Keys* can eliminate dropping errors.

* The authors acknowledge the support of the University of Edinburgh in funding this research.

3. *Additional Key Errors*: A key adjacent to the intended key is activated. In the majority of such errors, both the intended and additional keys are pressed, and the key presses overlap in time. For this class of additional key errors, the *Overlap Keys* configuration facility has been proposed (Trewin and Pain, 1996b). This would inhibit one or both of the overlapping keystrokes, and may be useful for keyboard users who do not overlap keystrokes in their normal typing.

4. *Bounce Errors*: The user unintentionally presses the intended key more than once. These errors are targeted by the *Bounce Keys* facility, available on many operating systems. *Bounce Keys* introduces a delay after a key press, during which time the same key cannot be reactivated. The length of the delay can be adjusted.

5. *Missing Key Errors*: The user fails to activate their intended key, either because they missed it, or because they did not press it hard enough. No existing keyboard configuration facility can alleviate missing key errors.

6. *Remote Key Errors*: The user unintentionally activates a key remote from any key they intended to activate. This can happen if, for example, a user leans on some part of the keyboard. No existing software configuration facility can alleviate remote key errors.

While it may be possible to reduce or eliminate these errors by using specialised keyboards, current device selection methods are subjective and time consuming, involving much trial and error (Broadbent and Curran, 1992, Casali, 1995, and Smutz et al., 1994). Standard keyboard configuration facilities can be tried immediately, cost nothing, and do not restrict the user to a single machine. Often they are sufficient to allow good keyboard access.

Unfortunately, users are frequently unaware of facilities that could be used to customise their particular environment, for example setting appropriate values for the key repeat delay. Rather than flooding the user with information about what they might do, a user model can be used to focus on those facilities which are most relevant to their specific needs. Such a model can be developed from monitoring the user's typing skills, and identifying their performance errors.

As Self (1988) has pointed out, there is little point in modelling problems for which there is no solution. Consequently, our model focuses on the first four error types listed: those for which existing or proposed keyboard configuration facilities provide support.

The following section discusses established user modelling techniques, and explores why, despite its good fit with the high level goals of a user model, this domain is unsuitable for the majority of existing techniques.

2 User Modelling Techniques

The problem of choosing an appropriate configuration is in many respects a traditional user modelling problem. It fits the definition of "the knowledge and inference mechanism which differentiates the interaction across individuals", suggested by Allen (1990). The system is required to adapt to individual users whose requirements vary enormously, and it takes responsibility for ensuring successful system-user communication (see Rich, 1983, and Kass and Finin, 1988). By Rich's classification, it is individual and implicit: that is, it performs its own customisation through choosing an appropriate set of configuration options to suggest. The target users are not able to choose their own set of configuration options, hence an explicit model is of little use to them.

The model used by a configuration support application must be dynamic (as defined by Kass and Finin, 1989): it must be able to adjust to the changing requirements of users, which may vary greatly according to factors such as fatigue. It must also adapt to different users who may be using the same computer, where there may be no explicit indication of the change of user. Further requirements are that the model should be unobtrusive and general, so that users are not required to perform specific tasks in order for their keyboard skills to be assessed. Ideally assessment should take place during their normal typing, potentially allowing a large volume of typing data to be examined.

Despite the problem of interest being characterised as a traditional user modelling problem, many of the common techniques used are not suitable here. Those that rely on stereotyping (Rich, 1989) are not applicable: similar keyboard problems may stem from very different disabilities, and similar disabilities may produce very different performance errors.

Approaches using bug libraries and overlay models, such as those used in intelligent tutoring systems (see Clancey, 1987, and Brown and Burton, 1978) are also either too restrictive or inappropriate. These models capture information about how a student's skills and knowledge differ from those of an expert, and are dependent on knowing the user's task, and either identifying missing knowledge or hypothesising about the reason for any incorrect answers. Since free text is permitted, a mechanism reliant on knowing the text a user was trying to type would be too restrictive. For similar reasons, feature based modelling (Webb and Kuzmycz, 1996) is also inappropriate. A further constraint on such approaches is their assumption of consistency in the user's behaviour. Keyboard errors are highly inconsistent, in that they do not occur at every possible opportunity: not every key press will be too long, for example. It is the frequency of errors that indicates those with genuine difficulties. Even in teaching domains, this assumption can cause problems (Self, 1988). Any technique for modelling keyboard skills must deal in frequencies, rather than binary values like known/not known.

The model should also be capable of managing uncertainty over the classification of a character sequence as being correct or containing some performance error. Uncertainty arises here because the user's task is unknown. Established numerical techniques for managing uncertainty – Bayesian networks and Dempster-Schafer theory (Jameson, 1996) – are not ideal. Bayesian networks could in principle be applied, but the full power of this technique is not required, due to the small number of sources of evidence available. Similarly, the ability of Dempster-Schafer theory to combine pieces of uncertain evidence is also not required, as the information sources available are reliable. Given the simplicity of the data available, less complex (and less theoretically motivated) criteria have proved adequate for decision-making.

Because of the uncertainty in the interpretation of an input stream, the model must be tolerant of errors in the performance error recognition mechanisms. It must also be sensitive to medium term variations in the user's typing characteristics, so that the configuration can be altered as the user's requirements change. The following section outlines the approach taken.

3   Recognising Keyboard Difficulties

The model of typing abilities focuses on the four classes of performance error for which some compensatory mechanism exists or has been proposed. Investigation of these areas is carried out unobtrusively by trapping and examining keyboard events before they are passed on to the application in use.

Key Press Length	Use of Modifier Keys
Average Press Length Press Length Variation Repeat Keys: Recommended delay	Evidence of Difficulty Sticky Keys: Useful/Maybe/Not Useful

Bounce Errors	Additional Key Errors
Evidence of bounce errors Bounce Keys: Useful/Not Useful Bounce Keys: Recommended delay	No. of Errors Detected Tendency to Naturally Overlap Key Presses Overlap Keys: Useful/Not Useful

Figure 1. Outline of the user model.

The user model itself is outlined in Figure 1. It contains both general information about the user's typing characteristics and specific information about the recommended keyboard configuration for the current user. The model is dynamically updated as evidence about the current user's typing abilities is gathered. Threshold values and decay of evidence over time are used to damp out the effect of small variations in typing style, and of any errors made in the recognition of difficulties. Note that no changes are made to the actual keyboard configuration in use – the model simply makes recommendations.

Throughout the assessment of keyboard difficulties, an assumption is made that the user is typing English text, probably in a word processing application. The model uses a database storing the frequency with which a given character is followed by another given character in modern English.[1] The frequencies were calculated from the British National Corpus, which contains over 100 million words, representing many different varieties of English. (More information is available at: http:info.ox.ac.uk/bnc.) The digram information could be replaced or supplemented with similar statistics about languages other than English, or any command or programming language.

The key repeat delay chosen for the current user is based on their average key press length, and the amount by which their key presses tend to vary upwards from that average value. These calculations are limited to those keys which are rarely deliberately repeated. For example the *Backspace* key is often held down for a long period in order to delete a sequence of characters, and is excluded from the calculation. In addition, abnormally long key presses are ignored, on

---

[1] The use of digram frequencies, as opposed to a dictionary, has a number of advantages. It eliminates effects due to misspellings in other parts of a word, or words not in the dictionary, and can also handle errors involving the space bar. Digram lookup is also faster than dictionary search, and requires less memory. Speed of classification is important, since the model should not visibly affect the response time of the user's application.

the basis that they are likely to be deliberate, or caused by an event such as the user leaning on the keyboard. The recogniser chooses a value which is longer than approximately 98% of key presses. If large numbers of abnormally long key presses are observed, it is recommended that the repeat facility should be disabled.

Assessment of the user's ease of use of modifier keys is based on the observation that, in the data available, subjects who had difficulty in pressing two keys at once would often type characteristic keystroke sequences, or adopt specific strategies for avoiding multiple key presses. Recognition of difficulties in pressing multiple keys at once is based on the detection of such patterns, and these are weighted according to the strength of the evidence they provide. Indicative patterns include:

- Use of *Caps Lock* for a single key press.
- Pressing a modifier key, followed by a small letter, followed by the *Backspace* key.
- Starting a sentence with a small letter.

In the vast majority of the 163 additional key presses observed in the data available, the unintended key press overlapped in time with that of the intended key. Given this observation, all overlapping keystrokes are candidate additional key errors. Using knowledge of the keyboard layout, English digram frequencies, and the current user's typing style, each overlap is classified as deliberate, an error, or of unknown cause. In the data available, 77% of the subjects rarely or never deliberately overlapped keystrokes, so the user's typing style is an important source of information in this process. The current keyboard layout is that of a Macintosh QWERTY keyboard, but other keyboards could easily be used.

Detection of bounce errors is the most difficult of the four areas tackled by the model. Many people who make bounce errors are also capable of fast deliberate double key presses. The recogniser therefore has two challenges: to spot people who are making bounce errors, and to select a delay which will minimise deliberate key press loss, while eliminating as many bounce errors as possible.

The recogniser operates by examining all double letters and assessing their likelihood of being bounce errors. Knowledge of word processing, English and the timing of the double letter is used. For each double, an evidence value between zero and ten is calculated. The greater the value, the higher the system's confidence that a bounce error has occurred. The choice of value for the delay to be imposed is conservative, preferring to miss some bounce errors rather than eliminate deliberate double key presses.

4   Evaluation

Evaluation of the model is based on typing data gathered from an empirical study of the keyboard difficulties experienced by people with motor disabilities, described by Trewin and Pain (1996a). Twenty subjects with motor disabilities and six without were asked to type a set passage twice. The passage was approximately 100 words (547 characters) long and required 25 uses of a modifier key. The errors made were established through direct observation and video evidence, while a detailed log recorded the KeyDown and KeyUp events reported to the computer, including timings measured in *ticks* (sixtieths of a second). Macintosh computers and the ClarisWorks word processing package were used.

From this study, 44 log files were available. These were used to simulate direct computer input – reading from the file instead of the event queue.[2] When the whole log file had been read, the state of the user model was examined. For long key press errors, additional key errors and bounce errors, the accuracy of the model's configuration recommendations is assessed by examining the number of errors occurring in each typing test, and where possible comparing this with an estimate of the number of errors that would have occurred had the recommended configuration been used. For modifier key usage, a more sophisticated approach is required, to take into account the coping strategies adopted by users who find it difficult to press two keys at once. Assessment of the model in this area is based not only on error numbers, but also on the user's reported and observed ease of using both hands, and their preference (if known) for using *Sticky Keys*.

The model is text-independent, but because the evaluation data consists of many copies of the same text passage, further evaluation of the modelling techniques in real situations is necessary to increase confidence in the accuracy of the model over general English text.

The following sections describe the results achieved by these techniques in each of the four areas of keyboard difficulty where configuration may be helpful.

5 Detection of Long Key Press Errors

Long key press errors were the most common type of difficulty found in the original study, and choosing an appropriate setting for the key repeat delay is for many the single most important mechanism for improving keyboard usability.

Table 1 shows the results of the model for the twenty subjects with disabilities (1-20) and the comparison group (C1-C6). The table shows each subject's reported level of difficulty in making quick key presses, the repeat delay setting (measured in ticks) recommended by the recogniser for each of their two typing tasks (T1 and T2), the number of long key press errors that would have occurred in each task had the recommended repeat delay been in force for the whole of the time spent typing, and the average key press length.

The recommended delays ranged from 10 to 41 ticks, and the maximum number of long key press errors remaining in a single task was 17, for Subject 17, which represents a 2.8% error rate. In the original data, the maximum error rate for a default repeat delay of 16 ticks was 66.6%, for Subject 13.

Six of the subjects reported some difficulty in making short key presses, and indeed the three subjects for whom the longest repeat delays were suggested were among this group. A total of 17 subjects, including one from the comparison group (a novice computer user), were advised to use key repeat delays longer than the default.

One interesting result is that for Subject 5, who rated short key presses as 'easy'. In both her typing tasks the average key press length was 5 ticks, but the variation among key press lengths was large. She made many long key presses, particularly in the second task (fatigue may have contributed to the difference). Because the recogniser takes into account this variation, long repeat delays are advised in order to cope with the longer key presses she sometimes makes. A

---

[2] In a real situation, dynamic events rather than a log file would be used. This avoids potential misuse of logs for the assessment of typing productivity.

Table 1. Long key press recognition.

Subject	Reported Difficulty	Setting Chosen		Errors Remaining		Average Key Press
		T1	T2	T1	T2	Length
1	easy	15	18	1	0	7
2	easy	12	-	0	-	5
3	easy	21	21	4	5	9
4	easy	11	11	1	2	4
5	easy	19	30	11	13	6
6	easy	24	22	12	10	10
7	some difficulty	24	25	11	11	11
8	easy	22	-	15	-	12
9	easy	19	21	9	12	9
10	hard	38	-	5	-	17
11	easy	11	11	3	2	4
12	easy	35	32	1	0	16
13	very hard	41	-	0	-	20
14	hard	22	-	1	-	10
15	hard	21	23	2	0	10
16	easy	12	12	0	0	5
17	easy	26	-	17	-	10
18	easy	20	-	0	-	9
19	extreme	34	36	1	0	16
20	easy	24	23	1	1	10
C1	easy	19	-	0	-	8
C2	easy	11	12	0	0	5
C3	easy	11	11	0	0	4
C4	easy	12	12	0	0	5
C5	easy	10	11	0	0	4
C6	easy	13	13	0	0	5

recogniser based purely on average key press lengths would be unable to accommodate subjects with similar wide variations in their key press lengths.

The projected total number of long key press errors for all subjects using their recommended setting is 151, as opposed to the 2610 projected errors under a default key repeat delay. This represents a significantly improved individual configuration for the subjects studied.

6 Detection of Problems Pressing Two Keys at Once

The results of modelling difficulties in the use of modifier keys are summarised in Table 2. The table shows, for each subject,[3] the difficulty they reported in performing multiple key presses, the

---

[3] The comparison group are included in this analysis but excluded from the table – none had difficulty in using modifier keys, and *Sticky Keys* was not suggested or recommended for any of them. Only one dropping error occurred, and very little evidence of difficulty was gathered.

number of dropping errors they made in each typing task (T1 and T2), the final total of accumulated evidence of a need for *Sticky Keys*, the *Sticky Keys* setting recommended by the recogniser ('on', 'off' or 'maybe'), and the setting that would have been chosen for each subject in a real situation. This last value was arrived at by considering whether the subject is a predominantly one-handed typist, their reported level of difficulty, their preferred configuration, and the number of dropping errors they made.

Table 2. Modifier key difficulty recognition.

Subject	Reported Difficulty	Dropping Errors		Sticky Keys Evidence		Recommended Setting		Ideal Setting
		T1	T2	T1	T2	T1	T2	
1	impossible	0	3	47	81	on	on	on
2	easy	0	-	7	-	off	-	on
3	easy	0	1	0	0	off	off	off
4	moderate	8	6	25	19	maybe	maybe	maybe
5	hard	0	0	1	1	off	off	on
6	impossible	2	3	70	60	on	on	on
7	easy	4	0	22	4	maybe	off	maybe
8	easy	0	-	2	-	off	-	off
9	some difficulty	0	2	3	6	off	off	maybe
10	very hard	0	-	71	-	on	-	on
11	impossible	0	0	84	48	on	on	on
12	some difficulty	4	2	54	53	on	on	on
13	easy	3	-	14	-	maybe	-	maybe
14	easy	0	-	0	-	off	-	off
15	hard	11	2	36	61	on	on	on
16	easy	0	0	9	0	off	off	off
17	easy	0	-	0	-	off	-	off
18	easy	0	-	43	-	on	-	off
19	moderate	0	0	11	0	maybe	off	maybe
20	moderate	2	2	58	14	on	maybe	on

The configuration recommended agrees with the 'ideal' configuration for 22 of the 26 subjects. Of the four cases where the recogniser made a less than ideal choice, three were subjects for whom *Sticky Keys* might be useful, but for whom it was not recommended. All of these subjects were able to use modifier keys competently, but typed predominantly with one hand. The recogniser cannot detect how awkward or tiring an action may be for the user, and can only judge their actual performance.

In the remaining case, that of Subject 18, the model mistakenly recommended the use of *Sticky Keys*. This recommendation was based on the observation that Subject 18 used the *Caps Lock* key for all single capital letters. This was actually due to a lack of understanding of the keyboard, rather than difficulty with modifier key presses. Cases such as this may be common, and the possibility that the user does not understand the use of *Caps Lock* or *Shift* should be considered by any system interpreting these recommendations.

Overall, the performance of the model is good. The use of *Sticky Keys* was recommended for all those who rated modifier key presses as very hard or impossible.

7 Detection of Additional Key Errors

Additional key errors were relatively common in the data available, and usually involved two key presses which overlapped in time. Table 3 shows, for each subject, their reported ease of isolating keys to press (Reported Difficulty), whether a problem with additional key errors was found by the model (Problem Indication), and the actual numbers of additional key errors made in the tests (Additional Errors) .

Table 3. Additional key error recognition.

Subject	Reported Difficulty	Problem Indication		Additional Errors		Number Detected		Spurious Errors		Deliberate Overlaps
		T1	T2	T1	T2	T1	T2	T1	T2	
1	moderate	1	1	29	29	23	24	0	2	no
2	easy	0	0	0	-	0	-	0	-	no
3	some difficulty	0	0	5	4	2	2	0	0	yes
4	some difficulty	0	0	3	0	1	0	0	1	no
5	some difficulty	0	0	2	0	2	0	0	0	no
6	easy	0	0	0	1	0	1	0	0	no
7	some difficulty	0	0	3	0	0	0	0	0	no
8	easy	0	0	3	-	1	-	0	-	no
9	easy	0	0	2	0	2	0	0	1	a little
10	easy	0	0	3	-	2	-	0	-	no
11	easy	0	0	3	1	3	0	0	0	no
12	easy	0	0	2	0	0	0	0	0	no
13	easy	0	0	0	-	0	-	0	-	no
14	some difficulty	0	0	0	-	0	-	0	-	no
15	some difficulty	0	0	5	7	3	3	1	0	no
16	easy	0	0	1	0	0	0	0	0	no
17	easy	0	0	4	-	4	-	0	-	no
18	easy	0	0	0	-	0	-	0	-	no
19	moderate	1	0	18	11	8	3	1	2	yes
20	easy	1	1	14	9	10	8	0	0	no
C1	easy	0	-	0	-	0	-	0	-	no
C2	easy	0	0	1	0	0	0	3	2	yes
C3	easy	0	0	0	2	0	0	0	0	a little
C4	easy	0	0	1	0	1	0	1	1	a little
C5	easy	0	0	0	0	0	0	1	0	no
C6	easy	0	0	0	0	0	0	0	0	no

A problem was identified for three subjects. These were the three subjects who made the most additional key errors, including the two who reported the most difficulty. The majority of the remaining subjects did make some additional key errors, but their error rates were low.

The table also shows the number of genuine errors that were detected (Number Detected) – 63% of those present in the original data. Errors are missed most frequently for those subjects who often deliberately overlap keystrokes. These are indicated in the final column of the table (Deliberate Overlaps). For these subjects, particularly Subject 19, additional key errors are difficult to distinguish from normal typing. The error detection mechanism is conservative, in order to avoid detection of errors where none exist. Nevertheless, 16 spurious errors (Spurious Errors) were found, also shown in the table.

To allow for spurious errors, a rate of one or two errors in every 100 characters is tolerated. Error rates above this threshold will cause a problem to be flagged. For some users who make additional key errors, *OverlapKeys* may provide a useful level of support.

Table 4. Bounce error recognition.

Subject	Bounce Key Setting		Bounce Errors		Bounce Evidence	
	T1	T2	T1	T2	T1	T2
1	off	off	0	0	0.0	0.0
2	off	-	0	-	0.0	-
3	off	off	0	0	0.0	0.7
4	off	off	0	0	0.0	0.0
5	off	off	0	0	0.0	0.0
6	2	2	8	12	17.9	6.9
7	off	off	0	0	0.0	2.3
8	off	-	0	-	0.0	-
9	off	3	0	1	0.8	5.8
10	off	-	0	-	0.0	-
11	3	off	0	0	7.1	0.0
12	off	off	2	1	0.0	1.0
13	6	-	3	-	7.9	-
14	off	-	0	-	0.0	-
15	5	off	3	3	16.1	0.0
16	off	off	0	0	1.6	0.0
17	off	-	0	-	2.8	-
18	off	-	0	-	0.0	-
19	off	off	3	0	1.8	0.0
20	5	off	5	3	18.5	3.2
C1	off	-	0	-	0.9	-
C2	off	off	0	0	0.0	2.3
C3	off	off	0	0	0.0	0.0
C4	off	off	0	0	1.6	0.1
C5	off	off	0	0	1.8	0.0
C6	off	off	0	0	0.0	0.0

8   Detection of Bounce Errors

Seven subjects made up the total of 44 bounce errors. The results of bounce error detection are shown in Table 4. The use of *Bounce Keys* is recommended in six of the eleven tasks in which at least one bounce error occurred. Six bounce errors were on the *Caps Lock* key, including all three of the errors in Subject 15's second typing task. Bounce errors on *Caps Lock* cannot be detected by this mechanism, or eliminated by the use of *Bounce Keys*.

Bounce Keys is also recommended for one subject who did not make bounce errors. In this case, a high level of spurious evidence had been gathered. A longer typing test is necessary to reveal whether this evidence would decay into insignificance, or whether similar results would develop for other subjects.

The *Bounce Keys* settings chosen by the model varied between 2 and 5 ticks. Imposing these recommended delays on reactivation of keys would have eliminated 15 of the 38 bounce errors not on the *Caps Lock* key. They would also eliminate 5 deliberate key presses. It is difficult to separate deliberate key presses from bounce errors, and so the results here seem a good compromise – losing one deliberate key press for every three errors eliminated.

9   Summary

We have developed a model of a user's keyboard abilities in four important areas. In all of these areas, existing or proposed keyboard access facilities can alleviate or eliminate difficulties that a user with motor disabilities may experience. The model uses simple statistical techniques. Unlike many traditional user modelling techniques, it has no knowledge of what the user is attempting to type. The solutions are dynamic, user-specific and unobtrusive.

The accuracy of the model has been evaluated using a set of 44 recorded typing logs, made by twenty users with motor disabilities, and six without. Evaluation on dynamic typing data is in progress. If the recommendations made by the model were applied to the original logs, the chosen *Repeat Keys* settings could have reduced the number of long key press errors from 2610 to 151. Use of *Sticky Keys* where recommended could have eliminated 54 of the 56 dropping errors, and would have helped 9 of the 11 subjects who reported difficulty in using modifier keys. The use of *Overlap Keys* was suggested for all 3 subjects prone to additional key errors, and the use of *Bounce Keys* was suggested for 5 of the 7 subjects who made bounce errors. Throughout the four areas and 44 tasks, in only two cases did the model recommend the use of an unnecessary facility. One of these was due to the subject's misunderstanding of the use of modifier keys.

The model we have developed makes explicit configuration recommendations, on which a user is free to act. It does not, however, offer the user any support with understanding, finding and setting the recommended options. While simple recommendations leave the user in control, some users may be unable to alter their configuration themselves. The authors' current work is investigating the feasibility of an adaptive configuration support system incorporating this model, and the use of such a system to actively help keyboard users with motor disabilities to find and set up the keyboard configuration that best suits their needs.

References

Allen, R. (1990). User models: Theory, method and practice. *International Journal of Man-Machine Studies* 32:511–543.

Broadbent, S., and Curran, S. (1992). *The Assessment, Disability and Technology Handbook.* Oldham: North West Regional ACCESS Centre and Oldham Education Department.

Brown, J., and Burton, R. (1978). Diagnostic models for procedural bugs in basic mathematical skills. *Cognitive Science* 2:155–192.

Casali, S. (1995). A physical skills based strategy for choosing an appropriate interface method. In Edwards, A. D. N., ed., *Extra-Ordinary Human-Computer Interaction: Interfaces for Users with Disabilities.* Cambridge University Press. chapter 17, 315–341.

Clancey, W. (1987). *Knowledge-Based Tutoring: The GUIDON Program.* MIT Press.

Jameson, A. (1996). Numerical uncertainty management in user and student modeling: An overview of systems and issues. *User Modeling and User-Adapted Interaction* 5:193–251.

Kass, R., and Finin, T. (1988). A general user modelling facility. In *Proceedings of Computer Human Interaction*, 145–150. New York: ACM.

Kass, R., and Finin, T. (1989). The role of user models in cooperative interactive systems. *International Journal of Intelligent Systems* 4:81–112.

Rich, E. (1983). Users are individuals: Individualising user models. *International Journal of Man-Machine Studies* 18:199–214.

Rich, E. (1989). Stereotypes and user modeling. In Kobsa, A., and Wahlster, W., eds., *User Models in Dialog Systems.* Berlin: Springer-Verlag. 35–51.

Self, J. (1988). Bypassing the intractable problem of student modelling. In Gauthier, G., and Frasson, C., eds., *Proceedings of Intelligent Tutoring Systems '88*, 18–24.

Smutz, P., Serina, E., and Rempel, D. (1994). A system for evaluating the effect of keyboard design on force, posture, comfort and productivity. *Ergonomics* 37(10):1649–1660.

Trewin, S., and Pain, H. (1996a). Keyboard and mouse errors due to motor disabilities. DAI research paper 838, AI Dept, University of Edinburgh. Submitted for publication.

Trewin, S., and Pain, H. (1996b). On the adequacy and uptake of keyboard access facilities for people with motor disabilities. DAI research paper 839, AI Dept, University of Edinburgh. Submitted for publication.

Webb, G., and Kuzmycz, M. (1996). Feature based modelling: A methodology for producing coherent, consistent, dynamically changing models of agents' competencies. *User Modeling and User-Adapted Interaction* 5:117–150.

User Modelling for Error Recovery:
A Spelling Checker for Dyslexic Users

Roger I. W. Spooner and Alistair D. N. Edwards

Department of Computer Science, University of York, York, Great Britain

Abstract. In the pursuit of a remedy for the poor spelling of dyslexic writers, a software system has been developed which features centrally a user model of the writer's spelling error patterns. Dyslexic writers are poorly catered for by most spelling programs because of their diverse errors. In this system, Babel, a user model directs the search towards likely corrections considering the writer's common errors. Babel includes the novel idea of more complex rules which describe permutations of errors typically made by dyslexic writers. It also measures and improves the accuracy of its user model using as feedback the choices made from its list of suggestions. Samples of writing from dyslexic users have been used to show successful detection and correction of typical errors, consistent between samples by the same writer and distinct from other writers. The user model allows, for some users, more diverse errors to be corrected more effectively than in systems without individual user models.

1 Introduction

For centuries literacy has been gradually increasing in importance. One hundred years ago Morgan (1896) documented the case of a boy who seemed intelligent in conversation and reasoning but was extremely poor at reading and writing. Dyslexia is now often diagnosed in a person whose reading and writing age is at least two years behind what would be expected considering their age, education and non-linguistic intelligence.

Work on dyslexia has gathered pace recently with myriad papers on many topics including the causes and diagnosis of the condition (Ellis, 1984; Coltheart et al., 1993; Boder, 1973; Brown and Ellis, 1994; Galaburda et al., 1994) as well as more practical works on available remediation.

Research work on the association between computing and dyslexia perhaps began with neural networks modelling language dysfunctions (Harley, 1993; Hinton and Shallice, 1991). Nicolson and Fawcett (1993) proposed teaching methods to assist dyslexic children and Elkind and Shrager (1995) looked for the optimal input modality for computer usage.

While spelling correction has been of interest for many years in computer science there has been little work on applying those techniques to assist dyslexic writers. One of the reasons for this may be that the spelling patterns of individuals with dyslexia are peculiar. Thus a coventional spelling checker may not cover the kinds of errors made by such writers. In particular, many spelling correction programs cannot cope with more than one error per word. At the same time a dyslexic writer needs a spelling corrector which will suggest a small number (ideally one) of corrections, rather than a long list, which will be hard for the person to select from. The individuality of errors made by dyslexic writers implies that there is a need for the spelling checker to embody a user model of the writer, of their particular spelling patterns.

The program described in this paper, Babel (named after the communication problems of people in the Tower of Babel), addresses these problems. It can cope with multiple errors in words and embodies a model of each user's spelling patterns. This paper describes the system that has been built and some preliminary results of testing it on samples of dyslexic writing.

2   User Model Operation

Production rules are a familiar concept in computer science and artificial intelligence (see for example Young and O'Shea, 1981, Brown and Burton, 1978). A production rule takes the form: *rule* → *condition* , whereby in a situation in which the *condition* is true, the rule is said to *fire*. Some complex systems can be described by a set of such rules, known as a *production system*. At any time in some system, if its state indicates that the condition for a rule is met, then that rule may fire. That firing will change the state of the system, so that another rule may now be eligible and so on.

Young and O'Shea (1981) showed that arithmetic subtraction could be described by a production system. Furthermore, they demonstrated that common errors made by children performing subtraction sums could be modelled by adding mal-rules to the system. The rules of subtraction may be thought of as the method taught by the teacher and the mal-rules are mutations of them which are the rules as understood by the child. The child applies the mal-rule in the belief that it will lead to a correct calculation.

The rules for English spelling are more complex than those of arithmetic. Hence the approach taken here is to model the mal-rules only. That is to say that Babel does not attempt to derive correct spellings from scratch, but when a spelling error is considered, Babel attempts to identify rules which will generate the correct word from the mis-spelt one.

The rules are derived from a cognitive model. In the case of Babel, the model is that of Patterson and Shewell (1987) although the same user model architecture could be used in a different application by being based on a different model. This model (shown in Figure 1) describes the flow of information between processing units in the brain. It includes stages such as Orthographic Output Lexicon (to convert word meanings to spellings), Phoneme to Orthography Conversion (to convert sounds about to be said into spellings) and Sub-Word Level Orthographic to Phonological Conversion (to pronounce written words in parts).

The suggestion is that some (if not all) of the errors made by dyslexic people can be attributed to deviations within this model. For instance, some errors can be explained by errors in the phoneme-to-orthography conversion stage. That is to say that the user correctly spells a word which they identify wrongly; they believe it to be one which sounds similar to the correct word. An example would be mis-spelling *thought* as *fought*.

An example of a specific error is the frequent substitution of the letter *b* in place of its mirror image, *d*, due to an error in the orthographic-analysis or writing output buffer stages of the Patterson model. Another example would be the writing of a single consonant within a word in which that letter should be doubled (e.g. writing *leter* instead of *letter*). This can be traced to an error in the orthographic-output-lexicon or phoneme-to-orthography-conversion stages of the model.

The rules must describe every possible error made by the user. Specific rules such as these are the most valuable since they give the most information about the individual, but to ensure

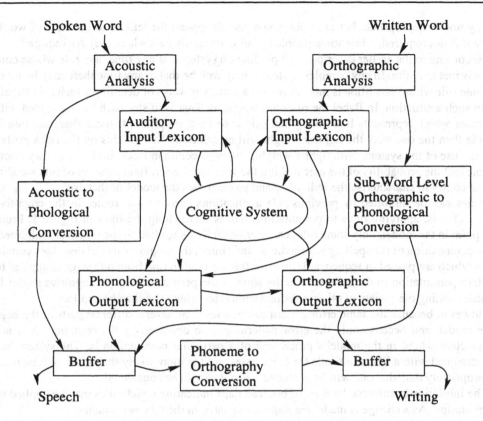

Figure 1. The universal dual route model of language production from Patterson and Shewell (1987).

complete coverage more general rules are also included. At the extreme any word can be transformed into any other word by deleting all the letters of the first word and inserting all those of second!

As far as possible the rules should represent expected fundamental errors rather than string transformations which have been observed. The derivation of the rules is not important to the user model, however. If, once executed, a rule is found to be used many times it may be possible to sub-divide it to allow the user model to gain a more detailed image of the user. This evolutionary procedure is not haphazard but systematically experimental (Mitchell and Welty, 1988, offer a good discussion of the unfortunate lack of experimentation in Computer Science).

Each rule is implemented in a routine that takes a spelling permutation (a data structure described below). The rules perform a number of preliminary tests and produce zero or more new permutations in addition to the one presented as input. A routine will be called by the user model if required. Each permutation is a data structure which contains the current letter sequence of the word it describes as well as a record of the rules used.

Rules often (but not invariably) exist in pairs, a positive and negative form. This is because, when a person is composing the spelling of a word, he or she will apply spelling rules which may or may not be appropriate. For example, some people append the letter *e* to the ends of words where it is not required, while some people fail to write trailing *e*'s where they are required.

According to the earlier description of production systems, at any time, any rule whose condition is met may fire. In any complex system it may well be that at any time there may be more than one rule whose condition is met. There are a variety of ways of deciding which rule should fire in such a situation. In Babel the rules are weighted. That is to say, each rule is tagged with a number which represents how likely that rule is to be appropriate. If more than one rule is eligible then the one with the lightest weight will be selected. The weights on the rules evolve with the use of the system, with lighter weights on more common rules. In this way they come to represent the probability of the user making the associated error. Hence the set of rule weights in time comes to characterise the individual and so embodies the model of that user.

Rules can be inhibited by previous rule applications according to routes in the cognitive model. That is, applying rules to permutations moves them along the lines in Figure 1. From each point in the model, only some rules can meaningfully be applied so the others are inhibited. In the composition of the spelling within the writer's mind, the cognitive model describes certain stages which are passed in sequence. If an error transformation rule from one stage is applied to a certain permutation in the software, the location of the permutation in the cognitive model is defined, limiting the variety of other transformation rules which can then be applied.

However, because the same error pattern can be caused by several different parts of the cognitive model, and because only the error patterns can be observed by the computer, it is not always clear where in the model's processing of a particular permutation is. The system has been designed with a liberal attitude for these cases, so it is more likely that a rule will be tried inappropriately than that one will be excluded when it should be considered.

The inhibition is enforced by a set of boolean flags indicating which rules may be applied to a permutation. As a change is made, the flags are updated in the new permutation.

2.1 Generality Score

As noted above, some rules such as wildcard operations are more general than others, and it is the more specific (less general) ones which are most informative. This is captured by a generality score, which ensures that a less general rule will be chosen where possible in preference to a more general one.

Features to be captured by the user model which are general cases of others are not a new concept, although most user models based on hand-designed cognitive architectures generally do not allow overlap between cases. Webb and Kuzmycz (1996) note which features are general cases of others and have prepared rules preventing their combination at run-time. Finlay (1990) uses automatic classification processes which do not lead to general rules.

Babel, unlike existing systems, allows the summation and comparison of a sequence of transformations on a string; it will select the transformation path with the lowest total number of general operations rather than operating on individual rules which might lead to a heuristically less desirable result.

The system produces as output a list of transformation paths which use the transformation rules to convert written to correct word spellings. In some cases several paths will exist because several different combinations of rules can achieve the same final spelling. In those cases which employ more specific rules, other permutations will exist which employ more general rules (for example where a *b* has been changed to a *d* in one permutation, another will exist which uses a generic letter substitution).

Each rule has been given a generality score by the designer. Those rules which are general cases of others (such as wildcard rules) have higher scores. Those rules which are unrelated to each other (the majority) have no predetermined relationship in their generality scores.

It is important to take care when assigning generality values, a process done at the time of creating the rule set. Only three levels of generality have been used. In normal system use, when a word's spelling has been corrected and a number of different paths all lead to the same spelling, the generality values for each rule used in each permutation are added. Only the permutations with the smallest summed value are considered further. This excludes unnecessary wildcards in corrections which will almost always appear.

2.2 Weight Adjustment

The key to the user model is the weight of each rule. When a rule is applied to a spelling permutation its weight is added to those already used; the final permutation therefore has a weight equal to the sum of the rules used in constructing it. The weights are adjusted (a lower weight is used for a more common rule) for each person to represent the errors they have been found to make. A permutation with a lighter summed weighting is more likely than a heavier one; this fact can be used in pruning the search space and in ordering suggestions to the user.

Once the system has been offered to a new user it is important to model their errors as quickly as possible. This is proposed in two stages; a short period of training in which a proficient user (such as a teacher) helps the new person to learn how to use the system and ensures that the correct transformations are chosen from the list of suggestions (i.e. that the user does not select the wrong word from the list of suggestions, which would reinforce the wrong set of rules) followed by an ongoing refinement of the model using the ordinary search with feedback from the user as to choices made.

During training, the system is simultaneously given a word as written by the author and a corrected spelling of the same word. The directed search is then applied to find a path between these two spellings. This is described further below.

In normal use of the system, a word is given to the system which then produces a list of suggestions consisting of words from the dictionary found using the most likely transformation rules. When one is selected, the rules used in that permutation are modified (the weights are reduced) and the weights for rules used in the remaining incorrect permutations are increased, so lessening their future usage.

For each correction word pair (written/correct spellings) a number of paths may exist. However, only one sequence of rules is required to account for an error, so the most appropriate single path for each error must be found. A heuristic method described below will be used to find the smallest set of rules used in the largest number of correction pairs, operating over a substantial number of corrected error words.

For those rules which have been used very rarely, the number of occurrences may not be representative of future errors. The number required to trust the rule weightings should be a constant, and the value 3 has been suggested in Webb and Kuzmycz (1996).

2.3   Path Choice Heuristic

After a number of words have been corrected, there will be a set of string pairs (written, correct) and one or more different transformation paths employing one or more rules to achieve each correction. The task then is to select the most appropriate single transformation path for each correction and to strengthen the rule weights used in that path. The other possible paths not selected are of no further interest.

For each word pair, the number of rules used in the transformation paths are counted. Any path with more than the minimum number of rule applications is discarded on the grounds that spelling errors are most likely to be simple (and it is the responsibility of the rule set designer to capture the errors with sufficient descriptive power).

This will probably leave more than one transformation path for many word pairs; these must be reduced to exactly one in all cases. The entire set of remaining paths is then searched for rules used more frequently and which are less general than others used. Where there are several rule paths which can be used to correct the same written/correct word pair and at least one uses the most common rule, the other paths for that word pair are discarded. The process is repeated with the second most common rule and so on until only one correction permutation exists for each word pair.

2.4   Directed Search

In the event of the target (correct) word being known and no transformation path having been found using the ordinary search method, this evolutionary method will be used. This means in practice that it will be used during training after meeting a new user. It disregards the rule weights which are known to have failed, and uses a simple *local search* to find a solution. The local search (Kerninghan and Lin, 1970) is a predecessor to genetic algorithms. There is much literature about these algorithms, for example Goldberg (1989). Local search was designed for graph partitioning but contains the essence of an evolutionary approach.

Starting with the written word, all rules are applied once to produce new permutations. The similarity between each permutation and the target word is found, and all but the most similar ones are deleted. The process then repeats with the remaining permutations.

The similarity between each permutation and the target word is measured using *trigrams*; clusters of three letters. The number of matching trigrams between two permutations can be counted and used as a fitness function for the search.

Trigrams are used for the similarity measure because they are quite unlike the other methods used in the system and so should perform differently (and hopefully better) for difficult cases.

2.5   Normal Use

The ordinary case of real-time spelling correction, in which the written word is known and a correction list must be produced for presentation to the user is similar to the preferred case during training. This is a novel heuristic search unlike most existing algorithms because it uses feedback from previous cases to modify the weights of the rules which will be used in future cases. It applies transformations to permutations and tests them with a simple boolean fitness function: whether the new permutation is in the dictionary of known words.

The list of permutations produced so far is searched for the one with the smallest summed weights (of the rules applied to it so far). Initially the written word is the only permutation present with no rules applied and a weight of 0. The chosen permutation then has all applicable rules applied to it, to produce new permutations with higher total weightings.

The search is stopped after several words from the dictionary have been reached, after a certain large number of permutations have been considered or the summed weights of all permutations exceed a limit, or after all allowable rules have been applied.

If other information were available such as the grammatical correctness of each word or the appropriateness of a word in the context of discourse, such information could be used to exclude some words from the list of suggestions and then re-order it. The incorporation of such grammatical information might form the basis of future work.

3 Dyslexic Writing Samples

The dyslexic writing samples are from school children aged 13–16 in schools in York, Surrey and Edinburgh, and from university students in York and Hull being assessed for dyslexia. They have varying degrees of dyslexia, although those university students who were found not to be dyslexic have been excluded in the sample.

The samples are mostly of hand writing. It is the most easily available form because many school age dyslexic pupils do not write with computers (and, indeed, do not write much at all). Hand writing may be different from typed material in a number of ways which will be tested for formally later in this research project, but it can initially be assumed to be similar in spellings to typed text. When writing by hand, some dyslexic writers attempt to shape letters ambiguously so as to have a better chance of appearing to have used the right letter. Considering the ambiguity in letter shapes, proof reading a document becomes more difficult for a dyslexic writer (who has difficulty reading anything). Unreadable words have been marked as such and are not included in further study.

To allow automated analysis of the writing samples, they have been transcribed into a machine-readable format including the intended words (as judged by a human reader) for each erroneous spelling. A total of 160Kbytes of material by more than 30 people has been transcribed from nearly 80 documents, including more than 2700 simple mis-spelt words (not multi-word errors). Efforts to obtain further samples continue, although this remains something of a problem considering how little dyslexic writers produce.

Although this may seem like a substantial sample, and is more than that collected for other projects reported in the literature (PalSpell, Wright and Newell (1991), was based on 221 sample words from 4 people), it is still not enough for a comprehensive analysis. With the best samples in this project at present, there are approximately 400 mis-spelt words per person. Since the purpose of the project is to correct the errors of individuals, the quantity of text from each person is crucial and so data collection is an ongoing process.

An on-line experiment (Spooner, 1996) has been prepared on the World Wide Web in the programming language Java, inviting users to type some sentences to dictation. This is bringing in more material with the advantage of being first-generation typed material without transcription errors. Also, the timing of keystrokes is available for inspection, and the same words have been written by each person. At the time of this writing (March 1997), only a small number of people have participated.

4   Testing and Results

The software system Babel, having been built as described above, has been tested using the corpus of sample texts. The corpus contains several documents from each of several students. On the first pass the model operates with its directed search and builds a user model for each document. The path choice heuristic is then applied to reduce the user model to a characteristic minimum of features, and then the system may be re-run in its normal search mode to attempt to correct actual errors. User models for different documents by the same author can be compared to establish consistency.

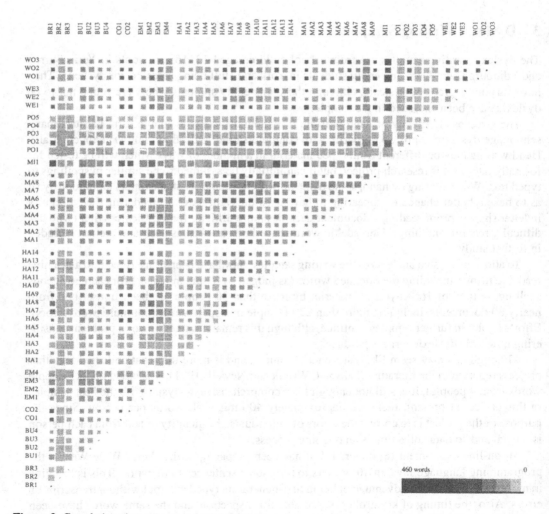

Figure 2. Correlations between user models built from documents by various authors. The ideal would be small boxes at the intersection of documents by the same author and large boxes elsewhere.

Some errors which were expected have not been made in the sample text, for example confusions between *G* and *Q* (which look similar). Other rules have proved surprisingly common, for example the consonant doubler (in which the writer misses one of a double consonant, as in *realy ← really*). This error occurs not only in the mis-application of suffices to root words, but at all positions in words. The misuse of final *e*'s occurs moderately, as expected; writers both insert and remove *e*'s from the ends of words incorrectly, omitting them slightly more often.

If the system is to achieve a signficant improvement over other spelling checkers then it must identify characteristics of each user which are notably different from those of other users. It is a hypothesis on which the rest of the work rests that a person's spelling errors contain consistencies over long time periods. This is implicitly accepted by people who work with dyslexic texts but has never before been measured.

Figure 2 shows the similarities between user models built by Babel, based only on the frequency of application of rules. A number of documents written by a number of people are compared. The size of each box indicates the strength of the correlation between the user models of the two samples; a small box indicates a good correlation. The shading of each box indicates the number of words considered in the smaller document and hence the reliability of the result; a dark box indicates many words and thus a more reliable model.

Several things can be seen from this comparison. Except in a few cases, the number of words compared is small (typically around 70). Some documents have a poor match with almost all other documents although often a better match with pieces by the same author.

The correlation is measured as a distance between two points in a multidimensional space. If each error pattern rule represents a dimension then any particular user model is a point in that space. The vector length between two points is the difference between the user models. The dimensions are first scaled so that each has the same maximum. Thus instead of one unit being one application of the transformation rule, it is proportional to the total number of applications of that rule. By this scaling, rarely used rules can still form an important part of the characterisation.

The number of documents written by each author varies simply because only the material available for research could be used. Those with more material were welcomed and those with less were not excluded. Documents with less than 25 misspelt words have been excluded.

Choosing a statistical analysis for the results has proved somewhat troublesome, and at the time of this writing a conclusion cannot be drawn with confidence. Research on this project is continuing, and will presently include a proper analysis of the results.

A preliminary analysis suggests that two authors out of the population of nine have user models for their individual documents which are more similar to each other than to those of other authors. These are shown in Figure 2 as users MA and HA.

This is weak but positive support for the suggestion that a dynamic user model can help in spelling correction for some writers' error patterns. If the user models are not significantly different from each other then there is no point having a dynamic model and one might as well use an ordinary spelling checker.

After running the software in its normal mode (instead of the directed search), it was able to correct about 80% of the error words from the dyslexic authors. Research is continuing into the nature of the errors corrected and missed, and unfortunately more detailed information is not available at this time.

5   Discussion

The user modelling system has so far not yielded convincing correlations of the type that were expected. This may be because the spelling errors are not consistent in the ways examined by this user modelling system, although they may well be consistent in other respects.

However, it is impossible to be definite about the cause of the low correlation at this point since the samples are rather small. The collection of more data, and especially of large samples from individuals, thus remains a priority. Research will also continue in investigating correlations of other sorts such as position in sentences, word types and so on. Needless to say, the collection of more data, and especially of large samples from individuals, remains a priority.

It remains likely that certain errors are typical of certain people; for example in this study one author frequently used left-right mirroring within letters, in letters within words and in words within a phrase. Other writers typically confuse *b* for either *d* or *p*.

A number of methods could be employed to improve accuracy, such as weighting suggestions by frequency, recency, or discourse domain. This will be done presently to enhance the research work, but at this stage they would obscure the underlying performance of the rules.

The system is in the process of refinement and current results are somewhat preliminary. Although the results are encouraging, it is clear that for many of the sampled writers, the rules in Babel are too general. Nevertheless, results so far suggest that the individualised spelling correction that it can provide based on its user model will provide a more valuable spelling aid to dyslexic users than general conventional spelling checkers for at least some users.

The creation of new transformation rules would help refine and improve the remaining errors although the necessary coarse phonetic transformations are not simple. The position of rule use within each word, and the choice of letter where a wildcard is used, will be incoporated into the system soon.

A number of possibilities exist for the continuation and generalisation of this work. As was mentioned earlier, it may be that the system's accuracy might be enhanced by the incorporation of natural language processing which may improve the identification of intended spellings. There are also a number of user interface questions which could be addressed once a working system has been established. For instance, how does one present information about spelling correction to a person who has difficulty reading?

This work also has wider implications in that Babel's user modelling techniques might also be applied to other "strings". Instead of letters these might for instance represent sequences of actions, where a "mis-spelling" might represent an incorrect action sequence. For instance, the sequence of actions undertaken by an aircraft pilot performing a standard task such as taking off might be encoded as a string. Any deviation from the normal sequence should be investigated further; it might represent a dangerous error.

References

Boder, E. (1973). Developmental dyslexia: a diagnostic approach based on three atypical reading-spelling patterns. *Developmental Medicine and Child Neurology* 15:663–687.

Brown, J., and Burton, R. (1978). Diagnostic models for procedural bugs in basic mathematical skills. *Cognitive Science* 2:155–192.

Brown, G. D., and Ellis, N. C. (1994). *Handbook of Spelling: Theory, Process and Intervention*. New York: John Wiley.

Coltheart, M., Curtis, B., Atkins, P., and Haller, M. (1993). Models of reading aloud: Dual-route and parallel-distributed-processing approaches. *Psychological Review* 100(4):589–608.

Elkind, J., and Shrager, J. (1995). Modeling and analysis of dyslexic writing using speech and other modalities. In Edwards, A. D., ed., *Extra-Ordinary Human-Computer Interaction: Interfaces for Users with Disabilities*. New York: Cambridge University Press.

Ellis, A. W. (1984). *Reading, Writing and Dyslexia*. London: Lawrence Erlbaum.

Finlay, J. E. (1990). *Modelling Users by Classification: An Example-Based Approach*. Ph.D. Dissertation, University of York, UK.

Galaburda, A. M., Menard, M. T., and Rosen, G. D. (1994). Evidence for aberrant auditory anatomy in developmental dyslexia. *Proceedings of the National Academy of Sciences* 91:8010–8013.

Goldberg, D. (1989). *Genetic Algorithms in Search, Optimization and Machine Learning*. Hillsdale, New Jersey: Addison-Wesley.

Harley, T. A. (1993). Connectionist approaches to language disorders. *Aphasiology* 7(3):221–249.

Hinton, G. E., and Shallice, T. (1991). Lesioning an attractor network: Investigations of acquired dyslexia. *Psychological Review* 98(1):74–95.

Kerninghan, B. W., and Lin, S. (1970). An efficient heuristic procedure for partitioning graphs. *The Bell System Technical Journal* 49:291–307.

Mitchell, J., and Welty, C. (1988). Experimentation in computer science: An empirical view. *International Journal of Man-Machine Studies* 29:613–624.

Morgan, W. (1896). A case study of congenital word blindness. *British Medical Journal* 2:1378.

Nicolson, R. I., and Fawcett, A. J. (1993). Computer based spelling remediation for dyslexic children using the selfspell environment. In Wright, S., and Groner, R., eds., *Facets of Dyslexia and Its Remediation*. Elsevier Science Publishers. 551–565.

Patterson, K., and Shewell, C. (1987). Speak and spell: Dissociations and word-class effects. In Coltheart, M., Sartori, G., and Job, R., eds., *The Cognitive Neuropsychology of Language*. London: Lawrence Erlbaum Associates. 273–294.

Spooner, R. I. (1996). On-line typing experiment. http://www.cs.york.ac.uk/dyslexia/.

Webb, G. I., and Kuzmycz, M. (1996). Feature Based Modelling: A methodology for producing coherent, consistent, dynamically changing models of agents' competencies. *User Modeling and User-Adapted Interaction* 5:117–150.

Wright, A., and Newell, A. (1991). Computer help for poor spellers. *British Journal of Educational Technology* 22(2):146–149.

Young, R. M., and O'Shea, T. (1981). Errors in children's subtraction. *Cognitive Science* 5(2):153–177.

A User-Adaptive Chart Editing System Based on User Modeling and Critiquing

Bernd Gutkauf[1], Stefanie Thies[2], and Gitta Domik[2]*

[1] C-LAB, Paderborn, Germany
[2] Department of Computer Science, Paderborn University, Germany

Abstract. Electronic publishing is being influenced by the increasing complexity and reach of information and by a rapidly growing user population. Because of these developments, average authors of electronically published documents have little expert knowledge about how to create well-designed charts. Authors are also confronted with considerable individual differences among remote recipients in culture, social life, education, psychology and physiology. In order to compensate for these differences it is necessary to integrate the interpretation and interaction abilities of individual users into future editing and presentation systems. We are developing a chart editing and presentation system which generates critiques and suggestions for authors and recipients on request. These critiques are based on individual user models and on expert knowledge in chart editing. Critiques are generated on user request depending on the state of a chart. The system helps authors to avoid commonly made mistakes. It empowers recipients to adapt chart parameters (e.g., colors, font size) to their individual abilities, disabilities and preferences.

1 Introduction

The fast dissemination of the World Wide Web (WWW) has established a large community of authors and recipients of electronically published documents. Many of these authors using electronic media are not publishing experts. They know little about human perception and interaction on computer systems. Preliminary studies (Gutkauf, 1994) have also shown significant differences among recipients in their interpretation and interaction abilities. These factors are often the source of poor quality presentations on the author's side (cyan text on green background, too small fonts, etc.) and of misinterpretation on the recipient's side. It is desirable to improve this situation

- for authors, by giving "expert" advice during the task of designing a document,
- for recipients by giving advice in adjusting certain parameters to their very individual abilities, disabilities and preferences. Sometimes it is even necessary to call the user's attention to the fact that her/his disability does not allow correct interpretation (e.g., colors are used which cannot be discriminated by a particular user)

* We would like to thank all participants in the user tests, Dr. Tauber and the senior-project group for implementing the chart editor, and the multimedia research group at C-LAB for valuable input. C-LAB is the Joint R & D Institute of Paderborn University and Siemens Nixdorf Information Systems.

An adequate way to achieve this improvement is to combine an editing system with a coopera-tive knowledge-based system (Fischer et al., 1990). The latter produces critiques by user request (for further discussion we will use the term *critiquing system* to refer to the knowledge based sys-tem). Critiques are based on

- rules which apply to expert knowledge in an application domain,
- rules which apply to individual abilities and preferences derived from a user model, and
- the current work context, i.e. the present state of the edited document.

Figure 1 illustrates that every user has a local user model containing information about indi-vidual abilities, disabilities and preferences. Authors create a document and send it to recipients, who can still adjust the document according to their user model. The distinction between authors and recipients is for mere understanding and explanation purposes only. The system is exactly the same for authors and recipients.

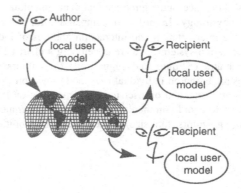

Figure 1. Author-recipient interaction. Authors use the system to create a well-designed document and send an electronic version to recipients. Recipients are given advice about adjusting documents to their individual abilities, disabilities and preferences according to the user model. The distinction between authors and recipients is for explanation purposes only. All users work with exactly the same system. Thus, information exchange is bidirectional.

Further discussion and implementation refers to the chart editing system. The main compo-nents are a chart editor (similar to Microsoft's Excel chart editor), a critiquing system, a user model, and tests to derive user abilities. We will show the overall system design, how we gather information about a user, and how we apply this information to improve chart editing and inter-pretation. We want to emphasize that similar systems can be used for other types of media (sound, animation, etc.) and other types of editors (e.g., 3D-graphics editors, slide editors).

The following scenario is intended to give a feeling of how the system works and the kind of improvements that can be achieved. Of course the functionality of the chart editing system is by far more complex than this scenario can demonstrate.

2 Scenario

The author starts the chart editor and begins with the work. In the middle of the work a new color has to be chosen. S/he starts the critiquing system and asks for advice. When finished s/he checks the work again by requesting additional critiques. The critiquing system suggests using a larger font for the y-axes. However, s/he ignores that critique and sends the chart (data plus object information) to the recipient.

The recipient loads the chart and requests critiques from the critiquing system. Before checking which colors are used the critiquing system realizes that there is no information about the user's color perception. It asks the user if s/he is willing to take a color perception test. Since the user agrees, the color perception test pops up on the screen and the user enjoys taking the game-like test. The results are stored for further use in the user model. The test results indicate that the author used some colors which can't be discriminated well by the user. The system reports this fact to the user and suggests alternative colors. The user clicks on the "Accept" button and—wow—now the chart really makes sense.

3 System Design

Major factors in designing a successful system are controllability, transparency and predictability (Höök et al., 1995). The system should also be enjoyable to the user (Rudisill et al., 1996). Special care was taken during system design to fulfill these requirements. We try to augment the user's capabilities rather than replace them. Keeping these design guidelines in mind our system was designed as shown in Figure 2. It is divided into well-defined components with particular functionality.

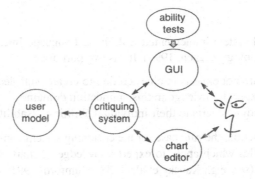

Figure 2. System Overview. The user interacts mainly with 1) the chart editor to create a chart and 2) the critiquing system (via a graphical user interface to request critiques based on expert knowledge, the user model, and the working context. Whenever it is convenient, the user can take game-like ability tests (which measure interpretation and interaction abilities) to adapt the system to individual abilities. All information about the user is stored in the user model.

3.1 User Model

The user model contains information about the interpretation and interaction abilities of a user. The abilities are derived through game-like ability tests. The user model contains also preferences of a user (e.g., suppression of known critiques, preferred colors).

3.2 Ability Tests

Ability tests are mainly based on standardized tests from cognitive psychology which were adapted to the computer. The purpose of these tests is to learn about the user's interpretation and interaction abilities (e.g., color perception, mental rotation, fine motor coordination). The tests are implemented at the motivational level of educational games in order to keep the user interested in taking the tests. More information about ability tests is presented in Section 5.

3.3 Graphical User Interface

The graphical user interface (GUI) serves two purposes. It presents the critiques (delivered by the critiquing system) in a structured and synoptic form. We adopt the approach of presenting information on several levels of detail (Fischer et al., 1990) and apply it to all information and critiques presented to the user. If the user is not sure what to do next, additional information is presented that helps to find the right decision. At the final level, links to the WWW are presented to the user. Feedback (input) from the user to the critiquing system is also provided by the GUI.

The other purpose of the GUI is to present the ability tests to the user. The critiquing system asks the user if s/he is willing to take a test. If the answer is "yes", it initiates the appropriate test. The test results are handed via the GUI and the critiquing system to the user model.

3.4 Critiquing System

This is a knowledge based system implemented with the C Language Integrated Production System (Clips: Software Technology Branch, 1995). It has two purposes:

- It helps authors who are not experts in chart editing to create well-designed charts by delivering context-based expert knowledge in this application domain.
- It helps recipients to adjust charts to their individual abilities, disabilities and preferences.

According to this distinction, the rule base for the critiquing system consists mainly of two sets of rules. First, there are rules which apply to expert knowledge in chart editing. These rules are derived from the literature (see, e.g., Kansky et al., 1988; Mumford, 1991; di Primio, 1995; Senay and Ignatius, 1994; and Zelanzy, 1986).

Second, there are rules which rely on user-specific attributes. These attributes are part of the user model and supply the critiquing system with user-specific information (e.g., a function tells the system that two colors cannot be discriminated). If the critiquing system realizes that data about the user are missing in the user model, either it suggests performing the appropriate user test or it tries to get this data through questions. Which approach is chosen depends on the information the critiquing system needs. In this way the system learns new facts about the user during a session. At the end of a session, the list of new facts is presented and the user can decide if these facts should be stored in the user model for further use.

In order not to overwhelm users with critiques and information, we coupled the critiquing system to the data structure of the chart editor. As a consequence the critiquing system produces only critiques which are relevant to the current work context (e.g., a critique about color conflicts is only given if this conflict really exists). Currently, rules for bar charts, pie charts, and scatter plots are implemented.

3.5 Chart Editor

The chart editor is used to create and view charts. It is similar to commercially available chart editors. When a user wants to request critiques s/he can press a "Critique"-button which will start the critiquing system.

The system as a whole has "user-controlled self-adaptive" behavior as defined by Dieterich et al. (1993). Adaptivity is achieved through changes in the user model. The techniques we use to initialize and update the user model can be seen in the next section.

The critiquing mechanism is initiated only by the user and critiques can be explained on user request. This is especially important for achieving transparency and predictability. It is also desirable that the system is useful and usable for novice and expert users. We are not distinguishing between novice and expert users by categorizing them but through system design. The key issue is separating the editor from the critiquing component and delivering critiques only on request. Each user can decide when to request critiques and will then be advised depending on the present working context. Using this approach, a novice user can be guided when creating a chart. An expert might request critiques only after completing the work or not at all.

4   User Modeling

Information about the user can be obtained using several techniques. We employ the following types of user modeling, which will be explained in further detail:

- explicit modeling,
- implicit modeling, and
- goal directed modeling.

4.1 Explicit User Modeling

Explicit user modeling involves filling out forms or asking questions. We perform explicit user modeling at the following times:

- the first time the user is logged onto the system. The user is asked a few questions. These questions are intended to pre-categorize the user and to initialize the user model. The user is also asked if s/he is willing to answer further questions to refine the user model. If the user is not willing to do so, a default user model will be used without further refinement.
- during each session when the user is starting to edit a new chart. The user is asked for all facts which can't be determined by the system but by querying the user (e.g., the user is asked for interpretation goals of her/his data).

4.2 Implicit User Modeling

Implicit user modeling extracts information from observation of the user's interaction with the system. Information from the user model is used to set certain parameters (after user confirmation!) in the chart. Examples are: text size, legend style, preferred colors. The user can also set these parameters manually in the chart editor. This can cause discrepancies between the user model and the actual chart (e.g., the use of a legend style different from the one usually preferred). All discrepancies between actual parameters set in a chart and information in the user model is gathered during an editing session.

At the end of the session the user gets a list containing all these discrepancies. The user can then decide for each discrepancy if s/he wants to update the user model according to this information. Although this type of user modeling causes some additional load on the user (once a session) it has proven to be very effective and was well accepted by users of the system.

4.3 Goal Directed User Modeling

Goal directed user modeling is performed to measure abilities of a user which cannot be derived by explicit and implicit user modeling. For this purpose the user is given special tasks to perform. The system observes the user when s/he is solving these tasks and records results. Using this technique we measure the interpretation and interaction performance of a user. The results depend not only on the user's abilities (e.g., color deficiency, fine motor coordination) but also on the quality of the hardware (e.g., monitor, input device) and the working environment. For our purposes we see this as an advantage of modeling the current environment as perfectly as possible rather than a lack of separation between the content of user model and a possible resource model.

5 Ability Tests

The following abilities have been investigated in more detail and are presented in this paper: color perception, gray scale perception, and mental rotation. Other implemented tests include a fine motor coordination test, a color ranking test, a color naming test, and a line recognition test. For results and implementation details of these tests, the interested reader is referred to Gutkauf (1994) and to Domik and Gutkauf (1994).

Additionally we have found several abilities that might be of influence, but have not been investigated in any detail so far: reasoning, size recognition, perceptual speed, visual versus verbal recognition, and embedded figure recognition.

The ability tests should not be an additional load on users. Users should not be afraid of being bored by the tests either. For this reason we designed the tests to be like computer games. One essential issue in keeping users motivated is immediate feedback about their performance.

5.1 Color Perception Test

Color perception is the process of distinguishing the color of points or homogeneous patches of light. It is a cognitive ability that varies among people. Accurate color perception can be influenced by a possible color deficiency (8% of men have some kind of color-defective vision due to a genetic defect—Hunt, 1987), poor quality monitors, and other factors (Gutkauf, 1994).

Since color graphics computers have become standard equipment, color coding is one of the most commonly used visualization techniques to represent data. The goal of the color perception test is to identify sets of colors a particular user cannot distinguish. A standardized test optometrists use to determine color deficiencies, the Farnsworth Hue 100 test (Higgins, 1975), has been used as a basic layout for our color perception test. In a very similar manner, the essence of our test is to sort forty pastel (low-saturation) color chips. The chips appear in one row on the screen. At the beginning of the test the color chips are randomly mixed. The user has to sort the color chips so that every chip has a minimal color difference to its neighbor. In order to use perceptually similar leaps between the forty color chips, the CIELUV color space (Foley, 1990) is used. Colors that cannot be distinguished appear out of order in the test results. We use only forty colors instead of one hundred or more to keep the user motivated to perform the test. Our results indicate that these forty colors give us enough information to eliminate colors that would cause problems for color coding.

For twenty users an error factor describing the errors in the final arrangement of the color chips was measured. User 9 and User 18 show significantly high error factors. Both users have been diagnosed as color deficient in competent optometry tests.

The error factor ec calculated for each test result is dependent on the misplacements of chips relative to their neighbors:

$$ec = abs(cc{-}cl) + abs(cr{-}cc){-}2,$$

with cc = current chip number, cl = number of left chip, and cr = number of right chip.

Figure 3 shows the error factor of each chip for User 9 and User 18 (color deficient). As a result of this test the user model contains the ranges of colors a user cannot distinguish.

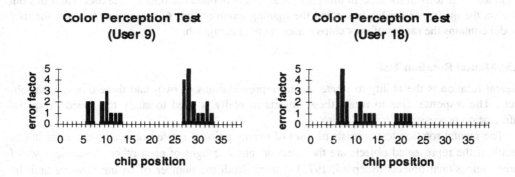

Figure 3. Results of the Color Perception Test for two color deficient users. User 9 could not discriminate colors in the yellow-green and cyan-blue range. User 18 could not discriminate colors in the yellow-green range. The four bars at chip position 19-22 (User 18) indicate that two neighbored chips (20,21) were exchanged. Such minor mistakes were not considered since results of many non color-deficient users showed this pattern.

5.2 Gray Scale Test

The gray scale test we employ is very similar to the color deficiency test. Instead of color chips forty equidistant gray patches from black to white were used. On high quality monitors almost no chips were mistaken by users. However, color monitors have often problems displaying dark gray and very light gray brightnesses. Figure 4 illustrates the test results of a user on such a monitor.

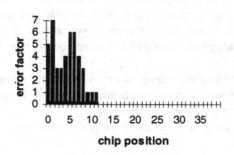

Figure 4. Typical result of the gray scale test on a poor quality monitor. The first 11 gray values cannot be distinguished. Any use of these brightnesses would result in a loss of information.

As in all other tests introduced in this paper, the results depend not only on the user's abilities but also on the quality of the hardware and the lighting environment. As a result of this test the user model contains the ranges of gray chips a user cannot distinguish.

5.3 Mental Rotation Test

Mental rotation is the ability to rotate mental representations of two- and three-dimensional objects. The response time to rotate these objects mentally is used to study the speed of spatial information processing.

The mental rotation test consists of a set of twenty pairs of rotated objects; the viewer has to decide if the represented objects are the same or mirror images of each other. A standard set of three-dimensional objects (Shepard, 1971) is used. Both the number of wrong answers and the response time are measured and recorded. From the mean response time of the user a mean decision time (time to decide whether to click on the left or right mouse button without mental rotation) is subtracted. The result is the mean mental rotation time presented in Figure 5.

A value close to zero expresses (almost) no hesitation between deciding between mirror and rotated image. The results of fifteen test users in Figure 5 are divided into four quadrants: Quadrant III shows users that are both fast and accurate in their mental rotation ability; Quadrant I shows users that are both slow and error prone.

The divisions between the quadrants are established by the mean values over all users. For users in Quadrant I, charts that encode rotation should be avoided. As a result of this test, the user model contains a classification of the user's mental rotation ability. Possible values of this classification are: good (Quadrant III), intermediate (Quadrant II and IV), poor (Quadrant I). The results of this test have not been integrated into the critiquing mechanism yet.

Results - Mental Rotation Test

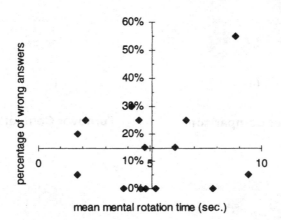

Figure 5. Results of the mental rotation test. The x-axis describes the mean mental rotation time in seconds, the y-axis the percentage of wrong answers. The divisions between the quadrants (I-IV) are determined by the mean values over all users.

6 Application Example

In order to compare the chart editing process of conventional chart editing systems and our system we performed a first test series with 18 users.

The users got several written tasks which involved visualization. The first step was to create a chart without the assistance of the critiquing system. Figure 6a shows this type of "before" picture. Then the user could request critiques and change the chart according to the critiques delivered (Figure 6b-e). The user could also ignore critiques s/he did not consider useful. For full details about the full user test series we refer the interested reader to Thies (1997). There are also statistics about: how often critiques fired, and which critiques were considered to be "important", "useful hints" and "unimportant". In this paper we will present one representative example out of the full test series.

The following task was given to the users: "A company has different product lines. This year 6000 bikes, 2000 books, 1000 computer games, and 10000 stuffed animals were sold. Compare the number of sold articles for these product lines." Figure 6 illustrates the design process for two users (the author, 6a-c, and the recipient, 6d-e) who had little experience in editing charts. User modeling was performed for both author and recipient. Picture 6a shows the initial chart the author created for the given task. After starting the critiquing system the author could inform the system that the interpretation goal was a comparison of percentages.

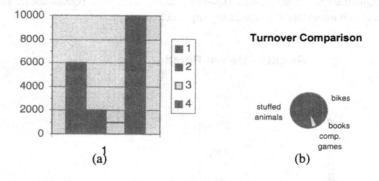

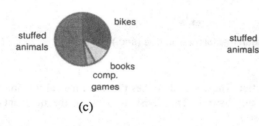

Figure 6. Example of an actually performed chart design task. Pictures a-c represent the design process at the author's side, pictures d-e the process at the recipient's side.

a: The initial chart an author (with little experience in designing charts) created for the given problem.

b: The solution after requesting and following critiques the first time.

c: The final chart created by the author after requesting critiques the second time.

d: The way the chart is displayed at the recipient's side. Notice that the gray values for "bikes" and "stuffed animals" are the same in this case due to a reduced number of displayable gray values.

e: The final chart at the recipient's side after requesting and following the critiques.

Then the following critiques (messages) were delivered:

- For a comparison of percentages, a pie chart is recommended (weight 1.0).
- Your user model indicates that you prefer direct labeling to legends (weight 0.8).
- The standard legend is used.
- The chart has no title.

At this point the user started to modify the chart as shown in 6b and then followed additional critiques:

- The colors for "bikes" and "books" cannot be easily discriminated on a black-and-white print-out (weight 0.76).
- The font for the title is small (weight 0.51).
- The font of several (5) labels is small (weight 0.5).

After applying these critiques the user stopped editing the chart 6c without considering the final critique:

- Your data have nominal character whereas you color mapping has ordinal character (weight 0.7).

Chart 6c was sent to a recipient. At the recipient's side, "bikes" and "stuffed animals" were mapped to the same gray value (6d) because the monitor could display only 16 different gray values. The critiquing system responded with the following critique:

- The colors for "bikes" and "stuffed animals" cannot be discriminated easily (weight 0.76).

The user accepted the suggestion by the system and got the final result 6e.

The results of the first test series showed the potential and limits of the system, especially in terms of the implemented rules and weighting factors. In order to be able to include new rules and change existing ones without much overhead, we are working on a compiler which generates the knowledge basis for Clips. Compiler input consists of simple forms containing rules and explanations for these rules. We are also implementing new ability tests to collect more information about the interaction and interpretation abilities of users.

7 Future Work and Conclusions

Currently the chart editor, the critiquing system, the user model and the ability tests are implemented. However, they are not well connected and they therefore cause considerable overhead for the user. We are working on minimizing this overhead through direct data exchange between the critiquing system and the chart editor. We are also investigating the possibilities of linking the critiquing system to commercially available chart and slide editors.

The results of the first test series showed the potential and limits of the system, especially in terms of the implemented rules and weighting factors. In order to be able to include new rules and change existing ones without much overhead, we are working on a compiler which generates the knowledge basis for Clips. Compiler input consists of simple forms containing rules and explanations for these rules. We are also implementing new ability tests to collect more information about the interaction and interpretation abilities of users.

Rule based visualization systems like Vista (Senay and Ignatius, 1994) and PRAVDAColor (Bergman, 1995) try to guide authors by applying rules which are applicable to average users. Our approach differs from these systems in several ways. Rules are based not only on expert knowledge in an application domain but also on knowledge about individual users—the user model. To fill the user model we perform explicit, implicit, and goal directed (special tasks) user modeling. The user's individual abilities, disabilities and preferences are recorded. Instead of sending a static picture (e.g., a GIF picture) to the recipient, all data necessary to rebuild the chart at the recipient's side are transmitted.

Since author and recipient have different user models, the critiquing system can react differently. The critiquing system can inform the recipient that the author used visual cues within a chart which are not appropriate for her/him. This approach is also applicable to other application domains where individual interpretation and interaction abilities play a critical role. One challenging example is navigation in virtual realities, where mental rotation and 3-dimensional sound perception influence the user's ability to interact with the system.

References

Bergman, L. D., Rogowitz, B. E., and Treinish L. A. (1995). A rule-based tool for assisting colormap selection. In *Proceedings of IEEE Visualization '95*, 118–125.

Dietrich, H., Malinowski, U., Kühme, T., and Schneider-Hufschmidt, M. (1993). State of the art in adaptive user interfaces. In *Adaptive User Interfaces: Principles and Practice*, Amsterdam: Elsevier Science Publishers.

di Primio, Franco (1995). *Methoden der künstlichen Intelligenz für Grafikanwendungen*. Addison-Wesley.

Domik, G. O., and Gutkauf, B. (1994). User modeling for adaptive visualization systems. In *Proceedings of IEEE Visualization '94*, 217–223.

Fischer, G., Mastaglio, T., Reeves, B., and Rieman, J. (1990). Minimalist explanations in knowledge-based systems. In *Proceedings of the 23rd Annual International Conference on Systems Sciences*.

Foley, D., and van Dam, A. (1990). *Computer Graphics*. Addison-Wesley.

Gutkauf, B. (1994). *User Modeling in Scientific Visualization*. Graduate Thesis, Department of Computer Science, University of Colorado, Boulder, CO.

Höök, K., Karlgren, J., and Wærn, A. (1995). A glass-box intelligent help interface. In *Proceedings of the First International Workshop on Intelligence and Multimodality in Multimedia Interfaces*.

Higgins, K. E. (1975). *The Logic of Color Vision Testing. A Primer*.

Hunt, R.W. (1987). *Measuring Color*. Chichester, England: Ellis Horwood.

Kansy, K., and Wißkirchen, P. (1988). *Graphiken im Bürobereich*. Springer.

Mumford, A. M. (1991). *Scientific Visualization—Techniques and Applications*. Springer.

Rudisill, M., Lewis, C., Polson, P. B., and McKay, T. D. (1996). *Human-Computer Interface Design*. San Francisco, CA: Morgan Kaufmann.

Senay, H., and Ignatius, E. (1994). A knowledge-based system for visualization design. In *IEEE Computer Graphics and Applications* 14:36–47.

Shepard, R.N., and Metzler, J. (1971). Mental rotation of three dimensional objects. *Science*, 171:701–703.

Software Technology Branch. (1995). *Clips Reference Manual*. Lyndon B. Johnson Space Center, (http://www.jsc.nasa.gov/~clips)

Thies, S. (1977). *Ein benutzeradaptives Kritiksystem für Grafiken modelliert durch eine Regelsprache*. Ph.D. Dissertation, Department of Computer Science, Paderborn University, Germany. In preparation.

Zelanzy, G. (1986). *Wie aus Zahlen Bilder werden*. Wiesbaden: Gabler Verlag.

Adaptable and Adaptive Information Access for All Users, Including the Disabled and the Elderly

Josef Fink, Alfred Kobsa, and Andreas Nill

GMD FIT, German National Research Center for Information Technology,
St. Augustin, Germany

Abstract. The tremendously increasing popularity of the World Wide Web indicates that hypermedia is going to be the leading online information medium for the years to come and will most likely be the standard gateway to the "information highway". Visitors of web sites are generally heterogeneous and have different needs, and this trend is likely even to increase in the future. The aim of the AVANTI project is to cater hypermedia information to these different needs by adapting the content and the presentation of web pages to each individual user. The special needs of elderly and handicapped users are also considered to some extent. Our experience from this research is that adaptation and user modeling techniques that have so far almost exclusively focused on adapting interactive software systems to "normal" users also prove useful for adaptation to users with special needs.

1 User Needs in a Metropolitan Information System

The aim of the AVANTI project (see the AVANTI Home Page) is to develop and evaluate a distributed system which provides hypermedia information about a metropolitan area (e.g. about places of interest, transportation, and public services) for a variety of users, including tourists, residents, travel agency clerks, elderly people, blind persons, wheelchair-bound people, and users with slight forms of dystrophy. The system is to be used at people's homes, public information kiosks and in travel agencies, each with different hardware platforms, software environments, network speeds, and environmental surroundings.

From interviews that we conducted and from literature (e.g., Zeiner et al., 1995) we determined that our users partially differ in their aims, interests, experience and abilities. Here are a few examples concerning elderly and handicapped users:

- In general, elderly users prefer cultural and historic information, while young travelers are more interested in shopping and entertainment possibilities, as well as sports events.
- For vision-impaired users, the screen display should be enlarged. For blind users, the modality of the presented information must be changed to tactile and/or audio output. Moreover, additional orientation and navigation aids (e.g., tables of contents, indices) are helpful for this user group (Kennel et al., 1995).
- For wheelchair-bound users, information concerning the accessibility of premises (e.g., the existence, location, and the dimensions of ramps and elevators, the type and width of doors) is important and should therefore be automatically provided.

- For users with slight forms of dystrophy, including many elderly persons, the graphical interface (i.e., the interaction objects and associated manipulation techniques) should be
  made less sensitive to erratic hand movements.

2   Adaptable and Adaptive System Behavior

In order to cater to different user needs, information systems can be tailored manually by the user
or system administrator, or automatically by the system based on assumptions about the user. Both
features, adaptability and adaptivity (Oppermann, 1995), will be provided by the AVANTI system:

- *Within the user interface*, special I/O devices (e.g., macro mouse, Braille display, speech
  synthesizer), visual and non-visual interface objects, and associated interaction techniques
  are integrated (cf. Savidis et al., 1995);
- *Within hypermedia pages*, the information content, information modality, information
  prominence, orientation and navigation aids, search facilities, and links to other hypermedia pages are adapted (cf. Brusilovsky, 1996).

Whereas the first group of adaptations aims at enabling and improving the overall access to information systems, the second group of adaptations aims at individualizing one specific hypermedia
system. In the remainder of this paper we will focus on adaptivity within hypermedia pages, emphasizing adaptation to elderly and certain types of handicapped users.

3   User and Usage Model

In order to provide user-oriented adaptivity, a *user model* is maintained by the AVANTI system
which contains assumptions about relevant user characteristics, including:

- *motoric and sensory abilities*, such as the user's ability to overcome physical obstacles
  (e.g. stairs, narrow passageways), to perceive visually presented information, and to select
  objects on the user interface;
- *interests and preferences*, such as the user's interest in accessibility information for premises (e.g., the availability of ramps and elevators), detailed information about the history of
  points of interests, or preferences for certain presentation modalities (e.g., graphics, video);
- *domain knowledge* with respect to the contents of the information system;
- *competence* in handling computers and the AVANTI system.

Different methods for acquiring assumptions about the user have been discussed in the literature
(Chin, 1993). In AVANTI, assumptions are based on the following sources of information:

- An initial interview allows for the acquisition of primary assumptions about the user and is
  therefore a valuable source of information for initially assigning the user to certain user
  subgroups (see the 'stereotypes' below).
- Certain dialog actions performed by the user can be exploited for the acquisition of primary
  assumptions. For instance, if the user requests an explanation for a technical term then it
  can be assumed that he or she is not familiar with it (Kobsa et al., 1994).

- Based on primary assumptions about the user and additional information about the application domain, the system can draw inferences in order to acquire further assumptions about the user. For instance, if the user more than once requests detailed information on the history of some church, he or she can be assumed to be interested in churches, and similar detailed information will henceforth automatically be provided.
- Stereotypes contain assumptions about interesting characteristics of user subgroups (e.g., tourists, blind users). They can be applied to a user if certain preconditions are met.

A subcomponent of the user model, the *usage model*, additionally contains a record of the user's interaction with the system as well as information about the location and environmental surroundings of the user's terminal, its technical abilities, and the network quality.

4 Discussion

Computer access for the handicapped has been a research issue for many years. Considerable efforts have been put into making software systems usable by people for whom they were not originally designed (e.g. access to graphical user interfaces for visually or manually impaired users), and into developing databases with dedicated information for the handicapped (e.g., information on wheelchair accessibility of public transportation, or verbal descriptions of paintings in museums) to supplement existing data collections that lack this essential information for people with special needs. These solutions are mostly restricted to fairly small classes of handicapped users and are therefore usually quite expensive due to the small number of potential customers. It seems, however, that techniques from the area of user-adapted interaction can be extended in such a way that they permit to some extent the tailoring of generic interactive software systems to all users, including many handicapped and elderly people. This approach not only is theoretically more satisfactory but may also be economically more viable than isolated dedicated solutions.

References

AVANTI Home Page. Available at http://www.gmd.de/fit/hci/projects/avanti.

Brusilovsky, P. (1996). Methods and techniques of adaptive hypermedia. *User Modeling and User-Adapted Interaction* 6:87–129.

Chin, D. N. (1993). Acquiring user models. *Artificial Intelligence Review* 7:185–197.

Kennel, A., Perrochon, L., and Darvishi, A. (1996). WAB: World-Wide Web access for blind and visually impaired computer users. New technologies in the education of the visually handicapped. *ACM SIGCAPH Bulletin* 55:10–15.

Kobsa, A., Müller, D., and Nill, A. (1994). KN-AHS: An adaptive hypertext client of the user modeling system BGP-MS. In *Proceedings of the Fourth International Conference on User Modeling*, 99–105.

Oppermann, R. (1995). *Adaptive User Support: Ergonomic Design of Manually and Automatically Adaptable Software*. Hillsdale, NJ: Erlbaum.

Savidis, A., and Stephanidis, C. (1995). Developing dual user interfaces for integrating blind and sighted users: The Homer UIMS. In *Proceedings of the CHI'95 Conference on Human Factors in Computing Systems*, 106–113.

Zeiner, M., Harrer, B., and Bengsch, L. (1995). *Städtetourismus in Deutschland*. Deutscher Fremdenverkehrsverband, Bonn.

Provision of Help

User as Student: Towards an Adaptive Interface for Advanced Web-Based Applications

Peter Brusilovsky[1] and Elmar Schwarz[2]

[1] Human-Computer Interaction Institute, Carnegie Mellon University, Pittsburgh, PA, U.S.A.
[2] Department of Psychology, Carnegie Mellon University, Pittsburgh, PA, U.S.A.

Abstract. This paper discusses the problems of developing adaptive self-explaining interfaces for advanced World-Wide Web (WWW) applications. Two kinds of adaptation are considered: incremental learning and incremental interfaces. The key problem for these kinds of adaptation is to decide which interface features should be explained or enabled next. We analyze possible ways to implement incremental learning and incremental interfaces on the WWW and suggest a "user as student" approach. With this approach, the order of learning or enabling of interface features is determined by adaptive sequencing, a popular intelligent tutoring technology, which is based on the pedagogical model of the interface and user knowledge about it. We describe in detail how this approach was implemented in the InterBook system, a shell for developing Web-based adaptive electronic textbooks.

1 Introduction

Current advanced World Wide Web-based applications are more than networks of static hypertext pages. They offer a rather complex interface with a number of different windows, subwindows (frames), forms, and buttons. What is often missing is adaptivity and adaptability. Users of these applications with different abilities, Web experience, knowledge, and background get the same pages in the same context. The class of users who need adaptivity really urgently comprises millions of Web newcomers. These users, who have almost no Web experience (and often no general computer experience), just cannot deal with complex interfaces of advanced Web-based applications. The problem of how to help novice users of advanced WWW applications is the first one that has to be solved on the way to adaptive Web-based systems, and this paper is centered around this problem.

A good example of advanced Web-based applications is found in *interbooks*. These are adaptive electronic textbooks (AET) that are developed with InterBook, a tool for the authoring and delivery of Web-based AETs (see http://www.contrib.andrew.cmu.edu/plb/InterBook.html; and Brusilovsky et al., 1996). AETs served on the Web by InterBook have a powerful and complicated interface. InterBook uses several separate windows, further subdivided into frames, to provide the user with useful tools, orientation support, navigation support, and other interface features that are known to be useful from the research literature (Figure 1). InterBook is being used to develop AETs for courses offered at Carnegie Mellon University. Communicating with people involved in teaching various courses, we have found that the InterBook interface is too complex for many users. Some interface features, such as the separate table of contents, were misunderstood. Such helpful features of InterBook as the search interface or prerequisite help have never been used.

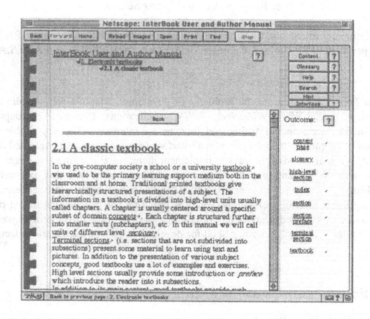

Figure 1. This picture shows a complex interface of InterBook. All features are switched on. The complexity of the interface often confuses novices. At the top right corner you can find the "Hint" and the "Interface" button, which are used for interface customization.

We think that InterBook provides a good case for investigating the problem of novice users working with complicated interfaces on the Web. The WWW context adds new dimensions to this classic problem of human-computer interaction. Generally speaking, there is a whole tree of computer-supported solutions (not mutually exclusive) for this problem. Either the user has to adapt to the complex interface by learning it, or the system has to adapt to the user's level of knowledge and skills. In turn, an interface could be learned in advance (comprehensively) using some kind of on-line tutorial; or at work (incrementally) using some kind of on-line help. Experimental research shows that some users prefer the comprehensive and others the incremental way of learning (Fischer, 1988; van der Veer, 1990). On-line help could be static (i.e., non-adaptive) or adaptive.

We have already tried two non-adaptive options within this taxonomy in InterBook. From the very beginning, InterBook was available together with the "InterBook manual", a combination of on-line tutorial and on-line help. Unfortunately, very few users have ever tried to read this manual. Either users are too eager to start real work as soon as possible in the WWW context, or the reading of the Web-based manual was a complicated task in itself. This paper presents our efforts to investigate two adaptive options: incremental learning with adaptive help; and an adaptive interface.

2 A Review of Relevant Work

2.1 Adaptive Help Systems for Incremental Learning

The problem of incremental learning of complex interfaces has traditionally been addressed by the research on adaptive help systems (more often called *intelligent help systems*, IHSs). The goal of intelligent help systems is to provide personalized help to a user working with a complex interface by diagnosing errors and suboptimal user behavior, identifying missing pieces of knowledge about the interface, and providing on-demand incremental learning to extend the user's knowledge (for a review see Breuker, 1990; Wasson and Akselsen, 1992).

The area of intelligent help systems has been well investigated. The first wave of research on intelligent help was initiated when UNIX systems, with their complicated interface, were distributed widely in universities and came to the workplaces of many computer-naive users. Due to this fact, almost all early research on intelligent help systems was focused on UNIX and its utilities (Breuker, 1990; Jones et al., 1988; Matthews and Nolan, 1985; Nessen, 1989; Wilensky et al., 1984; Wolz et al., 1989). The appearance of "friendly" WIMP interfaces created a pause in IHS research, but in just a few years even these interfaces had reached the level of complexity where intelligent help is really important. The current second wave of research on IHSs investigates useful ways of providing intelligent help in modern application systems (Encarnação, 1995; Fox et al., 1993). Probably, a third wave will be created by advanced WWW applications.

Traditionally, IHSs are divided into two classes: *active* and *passive* help systems. In a passive help system, it is the user who initiates the next help session by asking for help. An active help system initiates the help session itself. "Passive-active" and "static-adaptive" are two different dimensions of classification. A well-known example of active but non-adaptive help is "did you know" (DYK) help, which offers users random pieces of knowledge (called *hints*) during their work. A number of modern applications (like Microsoft Word) usually suggest DYK help at the beginning of a session.

Adaptive passive help systems support incremental learning by suggesting the next piece of knowledge to be learned by the user when help is requested. The main problem for these systems is how to decide what to say. The suggested piece of knowledge has to be both new and relevant to the user's current goal (otherwise the user will not be interested in learning it!). To determine what is new and relevant, IHSs track the user's goals and the user's knowledge about the interface. This information about the user is stored in the user model (Chin, 1989; Nessen, 1989; Winkels, 1990). The user model is often initialized through a short interview with a user and then kept updated through automatic user modeling. IHS researchers have investigated a number of effective techniques of automatic user modeling. Most of them are variants of two basic technologies which were tried in the very first IHS projects (Matthews and Nolan, 1985; Zissos and Witten, 1985): (1) tracking the user's actions to understand which commands and concepts are known to the user and which are not and (2) using task models to deduce the goal of the user. The first technology is reasonably simple—the system just records all used commands and parameters, assuming that "used means known". The second technology is much more complicated; it is based on plan recognition (Goodman and Litman, 1992) and advanced domain knowledge representation in a "goal-plan-action" tree or some other form of task model (Hoppe, 1993). To identify missing pieces of knowledge, the system (1) infers the user's goal from an observed sequence of commands, (2) tries to find a more efficient sequence of commands to achieve this goal, (3) identifies knowledge elements required to build this more efficient sequence but not required to make the original (less efficient) sequence. Presumably, the lack of this knowledge prevented the user from applying the more efficient sequence. These knowledge elements are declared to be unknown (unless they were recorded as known on the basis of the simpler technology) and become the best candidates for knowledge extension on demand.

Adaptive active help systems make all decisions that adaptive passive help systems make plus one more decision: when to interrupt the user's work and suggest help. The problem of when to interrupt is older than IHSs themselves. This problem is known in the area of intelligent tutoring systems (ITSs) as the problem of *coaching* (Burton and Brown, 1979), and here IHSs apply the ideas developed by earlier ITSs (Breuker, 1988; Fischer, 1988). The secret of good coaching is not to interrupt the user's work in each situation when the user makes an error or demonstrated suboptimal behavior and the system has something to say about it. A good coach will interrupt the user only if the work situation is relevant for correcting the user or suggesting a new piece of knowledge. Usually, a set of heuristic rules (mostly domain-dependent) is used to determine whether the situation is relevant.

2.2 Adaptive Interfaces

Interface adaptation to users with different levels of knowledge about interface features is not a mainstream direction of research on adaptive interfaces (Dieterich et al., 1993). The only relevant technology developed so far is that of incremental interfaces. The idea of incremental interfaces is the following one: A novice user starts with some subset of a complex interface, and then more advanced interface features are enabled incrementally as soon as the user needs them and is ready to use them. Incremental interfaces were developed for two intelligent learning environments: ITEM/IP (Brusilovsky, 1993) and ELM-PE (Brusilovsky et al., 1995). Both systems have no model of user knowledge about interface features and use a model of user knowledge on the subject being learned (a programming language) to decide which interface features to enable. For example, if a particular LISP function becomes known to the user of ELM-PE, the button for this function in an adaptive structure editor is enabled.

3   User as Student: Applying Adaptive Sequencing Technology

3.1   The Architecture and the Problem of Sequencing

The work discussed above on adaptive help systems and adaptive interfaces suggests a clear way of implementing both incremental learning and an incremental interface. Two decision-making mechanisms have to be implemented. The "what" mechanism has to decide which unknown interface features the user could and would like to learn next. With incremental learning, these features will be introduced and explained to the user. With the incremental interface, these features will be enabled (and probably explained). The "when" mechanism has to decide whether a particular moment of time is appropriate one at which to interrupt the user and introduce the next set of new features. The work discussed above shows that the "when" mechanism does not pose a real problem. First, it is always possible to implement a simple "when" mechanism on the basis of a small set of domain-dependent heuristics or just to use the non-adaptive DYK style. Second, the mechanism is used only in active help systems. The key problem is the "what" mechanism, or sequencing mechanism. It is used for both passive and active help, and it is where the main "intelligence" of an adaptive interface is.

The work discussed above shows several ways of implementing an adaptive sequencing mechanism. However, we have found that existing experience cannot be applied directly in the Web context because current Web-based interfaces are different. What we call an "interface" in a Web-based application is not a conventional interface. For example, what looks like a button is nothing more than an iconized hyperlink. In essence, a Web-based interface supports hypertext navigation with some amount of form-filling. The problem is that watching what the user is doing in hypermedia provides insufficient information for user modeling (Brusilovsky, 1996). Most known plan-recognition-based techniques of automatic user modeling can hardly be applied in this area. The only information about the user's actions which the system can record is the user's path through the hyperspace and the time spent on each node. The bandwidth of this channel is much lower than in UNIX-like command-based interfaces (Breuker, 1990; Jones et al., 1988; Wolz et al., 1989), action-based interfaces (Encarnação, 1995; Fox et al., 1993) or natural language interfaces (Wilensky et al., 1984).

3.2 Our Solution: The User-as-Student Metaphor

Our solution to the problem of novice users working with complicated interfaces on the Web is to apply the known technologies of incremental interfaces and incremental learning but to use a different sequencing mechanism. Rather then using sequencing based on plan recognition, which is not very suitable for current Web-based interfaces, we use sequencing based on the internal logic of the domain which is represented in a domain model. Domain-model-based sequencing is a classic technology of intelligent tutoring systems (Polson and Richardson, 1988). The heart of this technology is a domain model represented as a network of domain concepts (a concept in ITS is an elementary piece of knowledge). Links between concepts represent the logic of the domain: various semantic relationships between concepts, such as *is-a*, *part-of*, or *prerequisite*. The domain model is used in parallel with an overlay student model of domain knowledge which stores separately the student's level of understanding of each domain model concept. Using domain and student models, an ITS could perform concept sequencing, i.e., build a dynamic personalized sequence of concepts to be learned based on the internal logic of the domain and the student's knowledge. Most advanced ITSs could also perform learning unit sequencing or task sequencing, where a learning unit is an educational task of any kind: an explanation, a test, an example, a problem, etc. (Barr et al., 1976; Brusilovsky, 1992; Capell and Dannenberg, 1993; Vassileva, 1990).

Our idea is to treat a user as a student and an interface as a domain to be learned. Driven by this metaphor, we suggest (1) using an ITS-like domain and student knowledge representation, with each interface feature treated as a domain concept and each hint as a learning unit; (2) applying a well-developed task sequencing technology to build a sequence of interface features to be learned or enabled and a sequence of hints to be presented. We think that this way is a good alternative solution to the sequencing problem for Web-based interfaces in general. Some additional benefits of this solution for InterBook are that this adaptive educational system already has a formalism for domain modeling, student modeling and indexing and that it has some already implemented sequencing mechanisms. In the following sections, we describe briefly the original domain-independent sequencing mechanism implemented in InterBook and explain in detail how we have used this mechanism to implement incremental learning and an incremental interface.

4   An Adaptable and Adaptive Interface in InterBook

As an advanced WWW-application, the InterBook system provides a suitable basis for implementing our ideas. The InterBook system is described in more detail elsewhere (Brusilovsky et al., 1996). Here we provide the minimal description that is required to understand how the incremental interface and the adaptive on-line documentation inherited the adaptation techniques that are already used for adaptive hypermedia in general.

4.1   Adaptive Electronic Textbooks and Techniques

The keys to adaptivity in InterBook are the domain model and the overlay student model. The domain model is a set of concepts that describe the educational domain. All pages of InterBook-based hypertext books can be indexed with domain model concepts by the course author. For each page, an author can provide a list of related concepts, which describe the educational contents in terms of the domain model. Each concept in the index has different roles, being either an outcome concept or a prerequisite of the page. A concept is an outcome concept of a page if this page presents the piece of knowledge designated by the concept. A concept is a prerequisite concept if a user has to know this concept to understand the content of the page. The overlay model keeps track of the individual student's knowledge by assigning to each concept from the domain model scores for reading pages about these concepts and solving tests or problems. It is updated whenever a student reads a related page or solves a test or problem that deals with the particular concept. Indexing is a relatively simple but powerful mechanism, because it provides the system with knowledge about the content of its pages: The system knows which concepts are presented in each section and which concepts have to be learned before starting to learn each section.

Sequencing is one of the applications of the student model in InterBook. The goal of sequencing is to determine the next page that should be learned by the student. This is done in three steps. First, the system computes overall scores for the supposed state of knowledge for each concept. On the basis of these scores, the system can decide whether a concept is already well-learned or should still be the subject of further teaching operations. Second, the system decides for all pages, on the basis of the computed knowledge scores, which pages contain suggested teaching operations or which have missing prerequisites. The results of the second step are used for adaptive annotation of links: Links to concepts and sections of different educational states are annotated by different icons (Figure 1). Third, the system selects the most optimal page from among all available pages that introduce unknown concepts and that are missing no prerequisites. For this purpose, all pages are assigned a certain priority for presentation that is based upon a default value and modified according to the supposed state of knowledge of the required and introduced concepts.

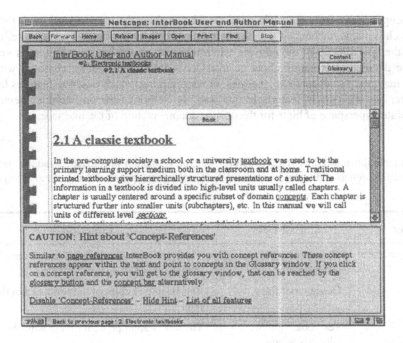

Figure 2. A simplified interface of InterBook that meets the purposes of novices. Disabled features are introduced incrementally with hints. The hint displayed here introduces "Concept References" (Table 1).

4.2 Incremental Interface Learning

According to our original idea of looking at the interface as a domain to be learned, we have created a domain model for the interface. A concept in this model is either an *atomic* interface feature that could be disabled or enabled independently (like "glossary button") or a more high-level interface-related concept (like "concept-based navigation"). Our interface model has more than fifty interface features. This model is dynamically extendible, since it relies on similar domain-independent mechanisms which are implemented for the electronic textbooks themselves. The interface concepts do not differ from other InterBook concepts that are created by authors of various InterBook-based electronic textbooks. In fact, we have re-indexed the InterBook manual, which is an electronic textbook itself, with a set of interface concepts to integrate the common adaptive electronic textbook with the adaptive interface documentation. In InterBook, incremental learning and interface documentation are implemented with hints (Figure 2). A hint is a textual explanation of one or more interface features (Table 1). Unlike common instructional information, interface documentation has to provide more than "know that" and "know how" aspects of concepts, which explain the location and nature as well as the functionality of the interface features. Interface documentation in an adaptable and adaptive context also has to introduce the user to the "know why" aspect of an interface feature, which explains why the user should switch on and use a certain feature. A hint is presented to the user at the bottom of the corresponding InterBook window, in which the introduced feature is located. Hints appear in separate frames, which are scrollable independently from the main window. This enables the user to work with the original window, which remains unchanged without being disturbed by the hints. Furthermore, this technique binds the hint directly to the relevant window, in which the interface feature is visible. To provide more detailed information about an interface feature, hints can be authored with hyperlinks, which may point to deeper explanations, or related hints, which describe features that might enhance or replace the current feature. In this way, the author of the on-line documentation can create a separate hyperspace of hints for the on-line documentation of the interface.

Table 1. This table illustrates the overall structure of a hint. It implements didactic relations and the documentation itself as well as additional information for event-driven appearance and adaptive sequencing.

Slot	Example	Function
prerequisites	Concepts, concept bar	These concepts or interface features must be known before the hint is presented.
outcome	Concept hot-links	This feature or concept in introduced in this hint.
windows	Textbook window, Glossary window	The hint is appropriate for these windows.
features	Concept hot-links, concept bar	These features are relevant to the hint, because the user might want to switch them on or off, when he or she learns about new features and functionalities.
title	Hint about "Glossary window"	The title of the hint by which it can be identified by system and user.
documentation	"You have just opened the glossary window..."	The text describing new interface features and their functionality.
appearance	"Current page contains a hot-link to a concept"	Rule that describes when a hint should be presented.
priority	10	The default priority by which the hint is chosen by the sequencing algorithm.

Hints can be presented in both active and passive modes. Active mode means that hints can appear when a particular window is updated if the sequencing mechanism suggests its presentation. Passive mode means that at any time the user can request a hint himself or herself by using the button "Hint" (Figure 1). This causes the system to present the next most relevant hint. The decision which hint to present is made by the sequencing mechanism. The user can override system's selection by using the "Interface" button, which will bring up a list of all available features. Each feature in this list has attached links, which point to the most relevant hint.

The incremental interface is driven by a simple sequencing mechanism, which chooses a hint if all prerequisites are already known and new outcome concepts are introduced. If the rule that determines the occurrence of a hint applies, the hint will be selected based upon its priority (see Table 1), since several hints might apply in the same situation.

The sequencing mechanism has to made two decisions. The first decision is *what* kind of information the user might be interested in. This decision is made by the general sequencing mechanism based on outcome and prerequisites that is used in InterBook. The second even more important decision, *when* to present this information, is made by simple rules, which enable event-driven occurrence of hints. These rules are implemented by LISP-functions, which are called with an identifier of the contents of the relevant window and the user model. Further, these rules have full access to information about the contents of the window the identifier refers to. This information can be taken into account for the computation of these rules.

An important piece of information for the *when* decision, is the window or interface element a feature might appear in. For instance, features which are specific to the table of contents will be presented only in the contents window. This basic mechanism has been made generic and is explicitly encoded into the structure of a hint (Table 1).

4.3 The Incremental Interface

The incremental interface is linked to incremental learning in that both are integrated into the structure of the hints (see Table 1). Each hint is indexed not only by concepts of the interface domain but also by interface features which are relevant to the hint. For example, when a new feature is introduced, this feature is listed in this slot. Currently, the incremental interface is an option. If the incremental interface is disabled, a hint simply draws the user's attention to new interface features and describes them, leaving the choice to enable them to the user. If the incremental interface is active, the hint also triggers the state of the features that the hint explains. These features are enabled in an InterBook window simultaneously with a display of the hint about them in the bottom frame of this window (Figure 2).

In active or passive mode, users always have the opportunity to enable and disable certain interface features. The features relevant to a hint are listed as links at the bottom of each hint, and their settings can be altered by using those links. Changes in the settings will appear immediately in the assigned window. In this way, the student can systematically explore the look of the interface with and without certain features enabled. Once the user has chosen his settings and deselected the hint, he or she is still able to modify the current settings using the interface button. Selecting this button, the user is provided with a list of all features that are relevant to the current window. Each feature is attached to a link that alters the setting as well as to a link to a relevant hint.

4.4 Default Settings and Stereotyped User Models

In an adaptable and adaptive interface, the user model is divided into two parts: One part tracks users' knowledge about concepts in the overlay model, and another one the current settings for the interface. To meet each user's need from the very beginning, InterBook provides a mechanism for loading both a default overlay model and some default interface settings. The course author has the opportunity to encode both into the subscription page of the system, in which the user has to register him- or herself. During that registration, the user can choose his or her individual level of experience with advanced Web-based applications. Each selection is associated with a stereotype, i.e., a set of domain concepts and default settings, that will be loaded when the user subscribes (Figure 3).

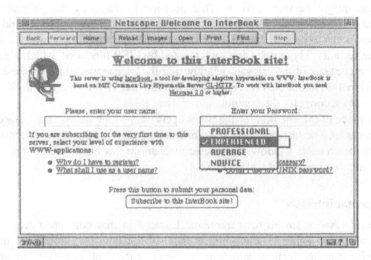

Figure 3. The user must register to allow InterBook to provide individual support. During that dialog, the user can choose his or her individual level of experience with Web-based applications. This selection is associated with default interface settings and the user model.

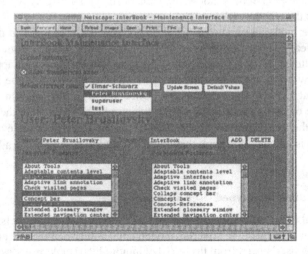

Figure 4. Through the maintenance interface of InterBook, instructors can change the current interface settings of individual students.

A second way of changing the user's interface setting from the side of the course author is provided by a maintenance interface. This interface allows the maintainer of the server to alter each student's setting at any moment via the WWW. Each interface setting can be either enabled or disabled—or even marked as being forbidden for certain students, if the teacher dislikes certain interface features of InterBook (Figure 4).

5 Conclusion

This paper is centered around the problem of novice users working with complex interfaces of advanced Web-based applications. It investigates two possible adaptive ways to help these users: incremental learning and an incremental interface. An analysis of existing relevant research shows that the key problem to be solved is how to build an adaptive sequence of interface features to introduce or to enable. Classic plan-recognition-based sequencing mechanisms are not very suitable in the WWW context. The main theoretical contribution of the paper is the suggestion to use a domain-logic-driven sequencing mechanism which is known in the area of intelligent tutoring systems. The slogan is to treat a user as a student and an interface as a domain to be learned. It implies that we use an ITS-like knowledge representation with an interface feature treated as a domain concept and a hint as a learning unit and to apply task sequencing technology developed in the area of ITS. The practical contribution of the paper is an implementation of domain-logic-driven sequencing of hints in InterBook, a shell for developing adaptive electronic textbooks on the WWW. InterBook is an intelligent educational system and it has an embedded sequencing mechanism which was originally applied for course sequencing. In the second part of the paper we described briefly the original domain-independent sequencing mechanism implemented in Inter-Book and explained in detail how we have re-used this mechanism to implement incremental learning and an incremental interface. We think that InterBook provides a good model for other researchers working on adaptive interfaces for Web-based applications.

References

Barr, A., Beard, M., and Atkinson, R. C. (1976). The computer as tutorial laboratory: The Stanford BIP project. *International Journal of Man-Machine Studies* 8:567-596.

Breuker, J. (1988). Coaching in help systems. In Self, J., ed., *Artificial Intelligence and Human Learning: Intelligent Computer-Aided Instruction*. London: Chapman and Hall. 310-337.

Breuker, J. (1990). *EUROHELP: Developing Intelligent Help Systems*. Final Report on the P280 ESPRIT Project EUROHELP. Copenhagen: EC.

Brusilovsky, P. (1993). Student as user: Towards an adaptive interface for an intelligent learning environment. In Brna, P., Ohlsson, S., and Pain, H., eds., *Proceedings of AI-ED'93, World Conference on Artificial Intelligence in Education*. AACE. 386-393.

Brusilovsky, P. (1996). Methods and techniques of adaptive hypermedia. *User Modeling and User-Adapted Interaction* 6:87-129.

Brusilovsky, P., Schwarz, E., and Weber, G. (1996). A tool for developing adaptive electronic textbooks on WWW. In Maurer, H., ed., *Proceedings of WebNet'96, World Conference of the Web Society*. AACE. 64-69.

Brusilovsky, P., Specht, M., and Weber, G. (1995). Towards adaptive learning environments. In Huber-Wäschle, F., Schauer, H., and Widmayer P., eds., *Herausforderungen eines globalen Informationsverbundes für die Informatik: GISI 95*. Berlin: Springer. 322-329.

Brusilovsky, P. L. (1992). A framework for intelligent knowledge sequencing and task sequencing. In Frasson C., Gauthier G., and McCalla, G. I. (eds.), *Intelligent Tutoring Systems: Proceedings of Second International Conference, ITS'92.* Berlin: Springer-Verlag. 499-506.

Burton, R. R., and Brown, J. S. (1979). An investigation of computer coaching for informal learning activities. *International Journal of Man-Machine Studies* 11:5-24.

Capell, P. and Dannenberg, R. B. (1993). Instructional design and intelligent tutoring: Theory and the precision of design. *Journal of Artificial Intelligence in Education* 4:95-121.

Chin, D. N. (1989). KNOME: Modeling what the user knows in UC. In Kobsa, A., and Wahlster, W., eds., *User Models in Dialog Systems.* Berlin: Springer. 74-107

Dieterich, H., Malinowski, U., Kühme, T., and Schneider-Hufschmidt, M. (1993). State of the art in adaptive user interfaces. In Schneider-Hufschmidt, M., Kühme, T., and Malinowski, U., eds., *Adaptive User Interfaces: Principles and Practice.* Amsterdam: North-Holland. 13-48

Encarnação, L. M. (1995). Adaptivity in graphical user interfaces: An experimental framework. *Computers and Graphics* 19:873-884.

Fischer, G. (1988). Enhancing incremental learning process with knowledge-based systems. In Mandl, H., and Lesgold, A., eds., *Learning Issues for Intelligent Tutoring Systems.* New York: Springer. 138-163.

Fox, T., Grunst, G., and Quast, K.-J. (1993). *HyPlan–A context-sensitive hypermedia help system.* Available as Report 743, GMD, St. Augustin, Germany.

Goodman, B. A., and Litman, D. J. (1992). On the interaction between plan recognition and intelligent interfaces. *User Modeling and User-Adapted Interaction* 2:83-115.

Hoppe, H. U. (1993). Intelligent user support based on task models. In Schneider-Hufschmidt, M., Kühme, T., and Malinowski, U., eds., *Adaptive User Interfaces: Principles and Practice.* Amsterdam: North-Holland. 167-181.

Jones, J., Millington, M., and Ross, P. (1988). Understanding user behavior in command-driven systems. In Self, J., ed., *Artificial Intelligence and Human Learning: Intelligent Computer-Aided Instruction.* London: Chapman and Hall. 226-235.

Matthews, M. M., and Nolan, T. (1985). Levi: A prototype active assistance interface. *Proceedings of USENIX Association Summer Conference,* 437-454.

Nessen, E. (1989). SC-UM: User modelling in the SINIX consultant. *Applied Artificial Intelligence* 3:33-44.

Polson, M. C., and Richardson, J. J., eds. (1988). *Foundations of Intelligent Tutoring Systems.* Hillsdale, NJ: Erlbaum.

van der Veer, G. C. (1990). *Human-Computer Interaction. Learning, Individual Differences and Design Recomendations.* Amsterdam: Vrije Universiteit.

Vassileva, J. (1990). An architecture and methodology for creating a domain-independent, plan-based intelligent tutoring system. *Educational and Training Technology International* 27:386-397.

Wasson, B. and Akselsen, S. (1992). An overview of on-line assistance: From on-line documentation to intelligent help and training. The *Knowledge Engeneering Review* 7.

Wilensky, R., Arens, Y., and Chin, D. (1984). Talking to UNIX in English: An overview of an on-line UNIX consultant. *Communications of the ACM* 27:574-593.

Winkels, R. G. F. (1990). *User Modelling in Help Systems.* Berlin: Springer. 184-193.

Wolz, U., McKeown, K. R., and Kaiser, G. E. (1989). Automated tutoring in interactive environments: A task-centered approach. *Machine Mediated Learning* 3:53-79.

Zissos, A. J. and Witten, I. H. (1985). User modelling for a computer coach: A case study. *International Journal of Man-Machine Studies* 23:729-750.

Pragmatic User Modelling in a Commercial Software System

Linda Strachan[1], John Anderson[1], Murray Sneesby[1,2], and Mark Evans[1,2]*

[1] Department of Computer Science, University of Manitoba, Canada
[2] Emerging Information Systems Inc., Winnipeg, Manitoba, Canada

Abstract. While user modelling has become a mature field with demonstrable research systems of great power, comparatively little progress has been made in the development of user modelling components for commercial software systems. The development of minimalist user modelling components, simplified to provide just enough assistance to a user through a pragmatic adaptive user interface, is seen by many as an important step toward this goal. This paper describes the development, implementation, and empirical evaluation of a minimalist user modelling component for TIMS, a complex commercial software system for financial management. The experimental results demonstrate that a minimalist user modelling component does improve the subjective measure of user satisfaction. Important issues and considerations for the development of user modelling components for commercial software systems are also discussed.

1 Introduction: Pragmatic User Modelling

Modern software systems are complex, and they often support a wide variety of tasks and diverse groups of users with differing problems and needs. This has led to an increased focus on the user in commercial software development and an increasing research focus on user modelling and user-adapted interaction.

User modelling as a field has become more mature in recent years, to the point where research systems show great promise and demonstrate the feasibility of user modelling techniques such as stereotyping and the separation of user knowledge into a user model database (see Kobsa, 1993, and McTear, 1993, for overviews). However, it is also being recognized that in spite of the demonstrated capabilities of many research systems, comparatively little progress has been made in taking advantage of individualized interactions in commercial software systems. This lack of progress, like the lack of emphasis on empirical studies, is considered to be one of the most important concerns in modern user modelling research (McTear, 1993).

Part of the reason for the lack of commercial deployment of user modelling systems is the fact that there are important considerations in commercial software systems that are largely ignored in research systems. The most obvious consideration is the performance overhead that must be incurred when a user modelling system is included. Also important are the time and expense that are involved in including a user modelling component, in comparison to the often unproven advantages which the added expense may bring. Other less obvious factors include the design changes

---

* Special thanks to the EISI team who developed the original TIMS system and provided support for this research.

that may be necessary for the inclusion of a user modelling component and the very real costs of training and support in an environment where a system's interaction is not necessarily consistent between one user and the next.

Despite the many details of design, implementation, maintenance, and support overhead, there is a much broader reason for the lack of commercial user modelling systems that has been speculated upon in the literature. Many of the approaches embodied in research systems are too complex or impractical for use in commercial software systems (Kobsa, 1993, McTear, 1993, Oppermann, 1994, McCalla et al., 1996). The identification of this shortcoming has prompted researchers to create pragmatic user modelling architectures and techniques, simplified from theoretically-motivated approaches. From a commercial standpoint, this "good enough" user modelling involves the inclusion of a minimalist user modelling component that has some of the major advantages demonstrated by large research systems, with minimal cost and commercial disruption.

While the application of minimalist user modelling techniques to commercial systems shows promise, many questions remain. Many involve the efficacy and cost-benefit ratio of a minimalist user modelling component. Can a relatively small number of user-specific adaptations help to support the user in navigating a complex computer application? Can these adaptations be employed practically in a commercial system? What balance is needed between sophistication and cost of a user modelling system and the practical considerations of commercial software development? There are also many practical issues that must be addressed in supporting user modelling in ongoing commercial software development.

This paper describes the design, implementation, and empirical evaluation of a pragmatic user modelling component for the Tax and Investment Management Strategizer, or TIMS, a complex commercial financial planning software system. The addition of this component is intended to address the needs of novice users while minimizing the impact on expert users. The paper presents an analysis of the domain, a description of the functionality of the user modelling component, and the description and results of an empirical study designed to identify the impact of this component on user satisfaction levels.

2   Tax and Investment Management Strategizer (TIMS)

The Tax and Investment Management Strategizer (TIMS) is a sophisticated commercial software system for financial planning that was developed by Emerging Information Systems, Inc. (EISI) of Winnipeg, Canada. TIMS allows a financial planner to analyze the financial status of a client and to demonstrate and evaluate various financial planning strategies in order to improve the client's financial situation. The system's objectives are to maximize the effectiveness of expert planners and to increase the effectiveness of non-experts in the application of financial planning strategies. The latter will enable individuals with limited training in financial planning to employ both simple and more complex financial planning strategies.

TIMS uses a desktop metaphor and operates with datasets known as *situations*, which represent the financial situation of a client at a particular time. A TIMS user creates a situation through a series of data entry dialogs, and the system creates a graphical display of the client's financial situation in a window known as the Situation Window. The financial planner can then implement and evaluate numerous financial planning strategies to produce alternative situations.

Much of the user's interaction with TIMS is performed through system components known as *Strategies*. Strategies implement financial planning techniques that human planners suggest to their clients or those that clients already have in place to properly reflect their overall financial picture. Nineteen different strategies are implemented in the current version of TIMS, including a variety of savings strategies, debt reduction strategies, and asset redemption strategies. Strategies are intended to provide an intuitive method of implementing financial planning tasks, to free users from excessively detailed input. Strategies can be invoked at a high level in order to automatically contribute their expertise by defining various low-level transactions (e.g. buying, selling) that will then be automatically carried out over a specific period of time, or upon a specific date or event. The financial planner can also insert the appropriate transactions at a more detailed level of input. Strategies serve to insulate the novice. By invoking the Strategy at a high level, novice users need not be exposed to an excessive level of detail.

TIMS also provides three unique *Assistants*, which are knowledge-based components that provide intelligent support for system interaction. Assistants provide an even higher level of interaction, allowing the automatic analysis of situations and the generation of recommendations for system tasks. For example, novice TIMS users are encouraged to use the *Planning Assistant* for the analysis of tentative strategies and for final plan creation. The Planning Assistant analyzes aspects of each situation and displays the analysis and the customized recommendations in a window. The user can implement recommended Strategies in the Planning Assistant, and also has access to a menu of Data Entry dialogs to directly make changes to the client's data, Strategies used, and other Assistants provided by TIMS. TIMS also provides intelligent *Cash Flow* and *Strategy Assistants* that perform analogous functions for their particular aspects of the system. The Cash Flow Assistant provides a complete analysis of a client's cash flow for any given year and allows the financial planner to make changes to the client's current situation and view the results, while the Strategy Assistant is designed to help the user easily select and apply multiple financial planning Strategies. Assistants require direction from the user to implement Strategies because the final decision rests with the planners. Financial planning is very subjective and the system would not be accepted if it was too intrusive.

Like other systems functioning in complex domains, TIMS must support a diverse range of users along two major dimensions. While many financial planners still have little computer expertise, some are sophisticated computer users with little or no need of lengthy demonstrations and extensive explanation facilities. Just as importantly, however, many TIMS users are expert financial planners with extensive knowledge of the domain, and use TIMS mainly for convenience. Others will have only limited financial planning skills and will rely on TIMS to fill in gaps in their own knowledge. Even among expert financial planners, the extent of their knowledge of the domain will vary from area to area. For example, an expert in life insurance might have little or no knowledge of leveraged investments.

A study conducted on the first commercial version of TIMS, released in 1995, confirmed the power and sophistication of the system, but identified concerns with the complexity of the system and the impact of this on novice users. These concerns, along with the breadth of user experience that must be supported and the goals of TIMS itself, led to the decision to begin developing an adaptive user interface for TIMS. The use of a minimalist user modelling component to implement this adaptive user interface arose from commercial concerns and the issues described in Section 1.

These were, essentially, a desire to bring to the system the benefits of user-adapted interaction with a minimum of cost and commercial disruption.

3 Supporting User-Adapted Interaction in TIMS

In the initial stages of developing a user modelling component for TIMS, it was decided to focus on the necessary adaptations for novice users. This was primarily because TIMS was originally developed in collaboration with high-end expert financial planners and had already been structured to reflect the organization of material that was helpful to them. A focus on novices, however, does not eliminate expert users from consideration. The usability of the software must not be limited by the adaptations that are necessary to support novices.

A number of areas where novice support could be increased in TIMS via a minimalist user modelling component were identified through interactions with users during the testing of the initial release of the system. These adaptations were implemented in several stages and resulted in the development of Personalized-TIMS (P-TIMS), an adaptive version of the TIMS system. The foundation of P-TIMS is the user modelling component illustrated in Figure 1.

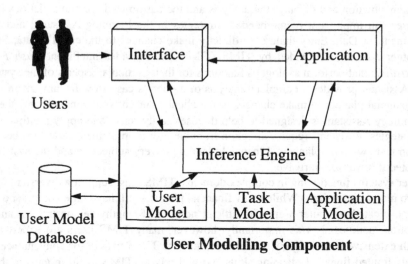

Figure 1. The user modelling component architecture of Personalized-TIMS.

The architecture consists of a long-term user model (also stored in a user model database); a task model containing descriptions of a subset of tasks in the system (such as rankings of the complexity of Strategies and Assistants); and an application model containing information about the relationships between a subset of the tasks in the system (such as information on Strategies or combinations of Strategies that are equivalent to one another). The inference engine contains simple rules about the relationships between these three models and the possible adaptations that can be performed on the application and the interface.

Each P-TIMS user has their own unique user model, which is initially based on a set of stereotypes triggered by their job title (chosen from a menu of generic job titles) and a self-assessment of Windows experience and previous TIMS experience. Each of the two experience categories is divided into Novice, Intermediate, and Expert levels. Because of the two-dimensional diversity of TIMS users described in Section 2, a decision was made to have four stereotypes within P-TIMS: Novice TIMS users (NTIMS), Novice Financial Planners (NFP), Experienced TIMS users (ETIMS), and Experienced Financial Planners (EFP). These four categories were chosen as a reasonable representation of the TIMS user population in order to keep the number of stereotypes to a minimum. The combination of the appropriate Financial Planning and TIMS experience stereotypes results in a basic user model containing settings specific to the various adaptations that are supported by the user modelling component. The user model also contains information about the user's interaction with each of the TIMS Strategies and Assistants (allowing a simple interaction history to be available to the user and to indicate the Strategies and Assistant demonstrations that have been previously viewed).

In an effort to make the user model visible and modifiable by the user, the user model attributes are accessible to the user through the Preferences dialog shown in Figure 2. Thus, while the most significant updating of the user model occurs during the initialization phase of the system, the user can also update his or her own user model at any time. Other modifications occur when the tasks represented in the task model are used. Reclassification of a user in the initialization phase, however, is done only once per day in order to minimize potential problems with users repeatedly entering and exiting the program during initial experimentation (see Figure 3).

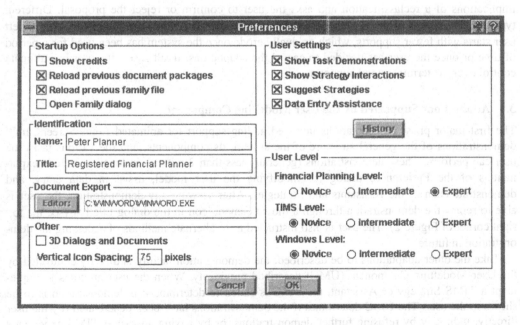

Figure 2. Preferences dialog for Personalized-TIMS.

If the date has changed do the following:

    If the user has been away too long (currently 30 days)
        Downgrade TIMS experience level by 1 category
    If the user has the used the system long enough since the last update (currently 10 sessions)
        Upgrade TIMS experience level by 1 category
    Examine all Strategies/functions used recently (within the last 5 sessions) by the user
        If more than 2 are more complex than the user complexity level then
            Increase user complexity level by 1
        If all are less complex then
            Decrease user complexity level by 1
        Update financial planning expertise
    Update counter fields

Figure 3. The basic algorithm for update of the user model in the initialization phase.

Over time, the adaptive system gradually diminishes into the original, non-adaptive system. Because the user modelling component is focusing on the support of novice users through the system, support is terminated with the user's permission once a user has achieved a minimum level of proficiency and has used the system for a predetermined period of time. Once the system determines that the user should be re-classified, a proposal is presented to the user that explains the implications of a reclassification and asks the user to confirm or reject the proposal. Different types of adaptations in the system have different termination points. The intermediate or expert user starts with fewer supports, which gradually erode once the system has been used for a period of time or once the user has decided to cancel the adaptations. In all cases, the user has ultimate control over the termination of supports.

3.1 Adaptations Supported by the User Modelling Component

The first major phase of adaptations involved adding support for animated Lotus ScreenCam™ demonstrations of the general structure of the system, its components, and the various tasks the user can perform. These demonstrations (generally less than 2 minutes in length[1]) include explanations of the Preferences dialog for modifying the user model, assist in data entry, and demonstrate each of the Assistants and Strategies. After viewing any demonstration, the user is able to replay the demonstration through a movie camera icon in the dialog title bar (see the top right corner of Figure 2). The user is also instructed as to alternate methods of accessing the demonstration in future.

Like the other adaptations to be described, the demonstration facility is directly controlled by the User Modelling Component (UMC) described previously. When the user attempts to implement a TIMS Strategy or Assistant, the UMC is called to determine if a demonstration is to be shown to the user. The UMC determines if the demonstrations have been deactivated (by the user directly, indirectly by refusing further demonstrations, or by having an expert TIMS experience

---

[1] Pilot testing revealed that the maximum user attention span for the demonstrations was about 2 minutes.

level). If the option is determined to be active, the user is asked if he or she would like to view a demonstration of that particular component. If the user refuses a particular demonstration, a second dialog is presented which allows the user to discontinue all prompting regarding demonstrations. This deactivates the Show Task Demonstrations checkbox in the Preferences dialog, but a user is free to reactivate it again if desired (see Figure 2). These adaptations benefit the novice user most during the first few sessions, and conversely, require the greatest amount of input from the user in the first few sessions. The ultimate ability of the user to refuse further demonstrations at any time minimizes the level of intrusion of this series of adaptations.

While demonstrations of Strategies are certainly helpful to novices, some Strategies are more difficult to employ than others, and may also interact in ways that are not always obvious. The second set of implemented adaptations were designed to recommend simpler alternatives to complex actions in the system, as well as to point out interactions.

These adaptations rely heavily on the task and application models maintained in the UMC. All of the Strategies and the more difficult system functions are represented in the task model and include a numeric complexity rating. A complexity rating is also maintained as part of the user model (initially set by the triggered financial planning stereotype), and when a complex procedure is invoked, this rating is compared with the complexity rating of the task in the task model. The application model contains a mapping between complex tasks and low-level tasks (or sequences of low-level tasks), and will be checked for equivalent Strategies if the user's rating is lower than the complexity rating of the task they have selected. The user may choose to disregard any suggestions, and may also choose to deactivate subsequent suggestions at any time. Similarly, Strategy interactions are recorded in the application model, and when the UMC recognizes the interaction the user is informed of the potential difficulty. Like other adaptations, interaction detection can be deactivated and later reactivated if necessary.

Like other components of the user model, the user's complexity rating evolves over time as a result of the user's interaction history with the system. The basic algorithm for updating the user complexity level was seen in the initialization routine in Figure 3. The user complexity level is increased by 1 if the user has invoked at least two functions or Strategies that have a complexity rating higher than the current user complexity rating, and is decreased by 1 if the user has not recently (within the last five uniquely dated sessions) used any functions or Strategies that are at least as complex as the user complexity rating.

The third phase of implemented adaptations is intended to address concerns with the initial data entry process. Like many other systems, TIMS gathers data through a series of dialogs that flow in a logical sequence, and again like many other systems, it is possible to accidentally terminate the series of dialogs by hitting the wrong button on the dialog. This was addressed through the user modelling component by prompting the novice user and allowing him or her to safely return to the data entry loop if it was abnormally terminated. This warning was displayed only if the dialog was accessed as part of the initial data entry process, not if it was accessed individually. The use of this warning dialog to reduce accidental exits is directly linked to the user model, so that it would not be displayed for experienced TIMS users.

The second difficulty that was consistently reported by novice users was uncertainty during navigation through the complex process of data entry, financial situation analysis, and the production of a final printed financial plan. This was dealt with by recognizing that the ultimate goal of the user is the creation of a printed financial plan for a client. Printed financial plans are generated using Document Packages that accept data from the system and export it in the form of a Rich Text Format file that can be used by any modern word processing program. Each document package requires specific information in order to be used. For example, the default document package, Retirement Plan, requires two situations: the current financial situation and an improved situation created by applying financial planning strategies to the first situation. Because the user is performing tasks to satisfy the requirements of a document package, the user modelling component assists in advising on the next logical step by maintaining these requirements explicitly. At each step, the UMC examines the currently active document package and its outstanding requirements, and a dialog is displayed which asks the user if he or she wishes to follow what the UMC determines to be the next logical step. These adaptations are targeted directly at novice users. Experienced users will not receive any of the modifications unless they explicitly turn on the option themselves. In terms of user comments, this was by far the most useful adaptation.

On an informal basis, the adaptations and the minimalist user modelling component described in this section have all proven to be useful. A study was conducted in order to more rigorously examine the effect of these adaptations on user satisfaction. The nature and results of this investigation are described in the next section.

4 Empirical Evaluation

The purpose of this experiment was to investigate the impact of an adaptive user interface on user satisfaction levels. It was hypothesized that complex computer programs with user models produce increased levels of user satisfaction over programs with no such user models. More specifically, it was hypothesized that the TIMS program with a user model (P-TIMS) would produce increased levels of user satisfaction for novice users over a TIMS program with no user model.

Participants. Forty-four participants were selected from a pool of 3,500 employees of a large Canadian financial services company that had adopted the TIMS program as their financial planning software. Ages ranged from 27–64, with a mean of 43.6 years. Of the 44 participants, 5 were female, and 39 were male. All participants had relatively high levels of education and moderate amounts of previous computer experience. Minimal previous experience with the TIMS system was reported by 32% of the participants, while the majority (68%) reported no previous experience. All participants were judged by the experimenters to be novice TIMS users.

Questionnaire. An instrument to measure user satisfaction was chosen on the basis of its established reliability and validity (Wong and Rengger, 1990). The Questionnaire of User Interface Satisfaction (QUIS), developed by the Human-Computer Interaction Laboratory at the University of Maryland, was designed to evaluate a user's subjective satisfaction with the human-computer interface of an interactive computer system (Chin et al., 1988; see also Shneiderman, 1992, chap. 13). QUIS was also selected because it continues to be updated and refined as the focus of a long-term research project at the University of Maryland and has documented user interface evaluations in various industrial and academic environments (QUIS, 1997). Participants were given a modified short version of the Questionnaire for User Interface Satisfaction (QUIS) v5. The twenty-one item questionnaire is arranged in a hierarchical format and contains: 1) a demographic questionnaire, 2) six scales that measure overall reaction ratings of the system, and 3) four measures of specific interface factors: screen factors, terminology and system feedback, learning factors, and system capabilities.

Procedure. Two programs were compared, the original TIMS system and an adaptive TIMS system (P-TIMS). Participants were assigned to one of four groups. One TIMS group and one P-TIMS group started the first component of the experiment on Day 1, and the second TIMS and P-TIMS groups started on Day 2. Day 1 participants returned to complete the experiment on Day 3; Day 2 participants returned on Day 4. The design produces a main effect for program, a main effect for day, and a program-day interaction.

All participants chosen for this experiment took part in a three hour TIMS training program as the first component of the experiment. This training program is based on the TIMS introductory training manual.

Each participant returned 2 days later for a half-day session to perform the second component of the experiment. Each individual was given a data worksheet containing sample family financial data and a set of instructions to assist them in performing certain tasks. The worksheet detailed tasks reflecting typical system usage that the participants needed to perform to re-familiarize themselves with the TIMS system. For the group with the adaptive systems, it gave them an opportunity to experience the customization of their system. Each participant filled out an anonymous questionnaire following the completion of the worksheet.

Results. A 2×2 between-subjects multivariate analysis of variance (MANOVA) was performed on six dependent variables: the overall impression of the system (IMPRESSION), the subjective satisfaction (SATISFACTION), whether the system was dull or stimulating (STIMULATION), ease of use (EASE OF USE), whether the system was ineffective or powerful (POWER), and whether the system was rigid or flexible (FLEXIBILITY). Independent variables were Program (TIMS and P-TIMS) and Day (Day 1 and Day 2). Table 1 shows the means and standard deviations for all four groups.

Table 1. Means (and standard deviations) for the six dependent variables broken down into four groups.

Dependent variable	TIMS		P-TIMS	
	Day 1[a]	Day 2[b]	Day 1[c]	Day 2[d]
Impression	7.3 (1.3)	6.9 (1.2)	7.0 (1.2)	6.6 (1.3)
Satisfaction	6.4 (2.1)	5.7 (1.1)	6.1 (1.8)	6.7 (1.0)
Stimulation	7.4 (1.4)	6.5 (1.2)	7.6 (1.0)	7.2 (1.2)
Ease of Use	6.2 (2.1)	4.8 (1.8)	4.9 (1.8)	5.2 (1.8)
Power	7.9 (0.8)	6.9 (1.1)	8.2 (0.9)	7.9 (1.0)
Flexibility	7.4 (1.3)	6.3 (1.3)	7.0 (1.3)	6.8 (1.1)

Note. Maximum score = 9. [a]$n = 11$. [b]$n = 11$. [c]$n = 10$. [d]$n = 12$.

SPSS* MANOVA was used for the analyses. All cases contained a complete set of data, resulting in a total n of 44. There were no univariate or multivariate within-cell outliers. The assumptions underlying MANOVA were tested and found to be satisfied.

Wilks' criterion for the combined DVs was significant for Program, $F(6, 35) = 2.73$, $p < .05$, but not for Day, $F(6, 35) = 1.73$, $p > .05$, or for the overall Program and Day interaction, $F(6, 35) = 0.99$, $p > .05$. Because the omnibus MANOVA shows a significant main effect for the Program variable, it is appropriate to further investigate the nature of the relationships among the IVs and DVs.

Univariate analyses were done for each variable by Program, Day, and the interaction between Program and Day. POWER was the only significant variable ($p < .05$), both for Program and Day but not for the interaction effect.

Discussion. In this experiment, we were interested in whether the means of the six overall reaction factors measured by QUIS, representing various aspects of subjective user satisfaction, differed as a function of the program used and the day that the experiment was performed on. Are there differences in the way that the user perceives each system in aspects such as overall user satisfaction, ease-of-use, power or flexibility? Also, are there differences between groups that performed the experiment on different days?

P-TIMS users rated the factor of POWER significantly higher than the TIMS users. This was the only factor that showed a significant difference with a confidence level of 95%. Based on the informal comments by the participants in the experiment, the POWER factor represented the impression that the system was more powerful because it could perform tasks for them (it was more helpful) and that it made it easier for them to see the capabilities of the system. While it would be more gratifying for the system with the user modelling component to show a higher rating for each of the six factors, the amount of adaptation was minimal, therefore a smaller effect was expected.

5 Conclusions

There are very clear advantages for the use of a simple user modelling architecture such as this in complex systems like TIMS. Issues that are critical in large, complex user modelling systems can be minimized or ignored in a simple system. For example, there is no need for a conflict resolution scheme, which would be absolutely necessary in a more complex approach. Here, users are assigned a single stereotype chosen from a very small set of potential candidates. This stereotype is not revoked, but is simply updated as new information is presented. Similarly, neither sophisticated learning mechanisms nor uncertainty management schemes are necessary in a simplistic scheme such as this. User models contain only a minimal set of user attributes, and each attribute always contains an inherent risk that it may be inaccurate due to its generality. Very basic learning about users is possible by monitoring user actions and gathering user information from the users themselves. This information is primarily composed of the tasks performed, the number of demonstrations viewed, and the user's direct modifications of the user model. As described earlier, the user model is refined on the basis of this interaction history and the number of days the system has been used.

The most serious drawback of a simple user modelling mechanism over a more complex one is the potential for misjudging users due to the generality of the attributes recorded. Such errors have only a minimal effect on an individual user in this system. Consider the two most extreme examples: incorrectly categorizing a complete novice (a new TIMS user with limited financial planning skills) as an expert user, and vice versa. In the former category, the user would experience system interactions similar to using a system with no user modelling component. Nothing would be gained through having an adaptive system, but nothing would be lost. As the user interacted with the system over time, the user complexity attribute in the user model would decrease and the necessary support would be available. In the opposite situation, the user might take a week of system use to reach his or her true level. However, the user models are accessible and can be modified by users, so the impact of an initially inaccurate user model is low.

The accessibility of the user model to the user is an important component of this approach and of minimalist user modelling in general. Previous research on adaptive systems suggests that user control over the user modelling component is important for user acceptance (Krogsæter and Thomas, 1994; Krogsæter et al., 1994). Oppermann (1994) proposes several methods of achieving user control, from direct control of the activation and deactivation of individual adaptations and the definition of specific parameters for adaptation, to offering adaptations in the form of proposals and informing the user of the effects of adaptation modifications. The mechanisms of user control detailed throughout this paper are directly implemented from Oppermann's methods.

In addition to the quantitative results detailed in the previous section, this work has also demonstrated that there are many practical considerations that must be made when performing applied research in the commercial arena (Strachan, 1997). Beyond the many obvious logistical issues (e.g. convincing managers the research will be useful to them financially and scheduling research to coincide with corporate training schedules), there are many logistical problems that might not be anticipated. For example, when attempting to compare an adaptive and a non-adaptive commercial system during ongoing development, the adaptive system must be synchronized with the latest release in order for any test of preference to be valid. There are two reasons for this: to ensure that the differences that are detected are based solely on adaptations, and to avoid training new users on an older version of the software and returning those users to their working environment with a newer version.

The nature of the user modelling component itself is dictated by practical concerns. The adaptations that are chosen for a commercial system, for example, must reflect concerns that real users have with an existing system. It is easy to make these types of decisions in isolation and to judge proposed changes based on one's intuition. It takes much more time and effort to actually observe users in realistic situations and to note the questions and concerns they have. In our case, formal one-day TIMS training programs presented excellent opportunities to monitor hundreds of first-time users of the system as they became acquainted with TIMS.

For the next step in this research, the focus of the adaptations will expand to include the implementation of adaptations designed specifically for different user types and groups. Examples of these are restrictions of system functionality and the simplification of the system to the point where it simply performs the functions that are necessary for the performance of the user's tasks. Experienced TIMS users will be solicited for suggestions.

Some unanticipated problems occurred in the empirical testing. We had expected the overall level of computer familiarization of the users to be higher than what we experienced. As a result, the reactions to P-TIMS were very much also reactions to TIMS as well. During the experiment, users barely had time to digest the unmodified TIMS system and then they were asked to judge the adaptations. Many users were unfamiliar with Windows, their new hardware, and the new software including Microsoft® Office and TIMS. It is not surprising that the ease-of-use reaction parameter was not that high. One user commented, "I feel just like I am learning to drive a Ferrari!". Making small changes to simplify a single program is not going to help a user who is feeling that overwhelmed.

The empirical component of this work has re-emphasized, to us, the importance of the user in all aspects of the system development life cycle. We have certainly learned that assumptions made in the development environment need to be confirmed with actual users in their work environment. Introducing formal statistical analysis to this procedure was interesting because it caused us to be more cautious about over-interpreting positive results that may have occurred by chance. At the same time, we found that the informal results gathered as anecdotal stories and comments helped us to gain a better understanding of the users and their environment.

References

Chin, J. P., Diehl, V., and Norman, K. (1988). Development of an instrument measuring user satisfaction of the human-computer interface. In *CHI'88 Conference Proceedings: Human Factors in Computing Systems*. New York: Association for Computing Machinery. 213-218. Available from: http://lap.umd.edu/lapfolder/papers/cdn.html

Kobsa, A. (1993). User modeling: Recent work, prospects and hazards. In Schneider-Hufschmidt, M., Kuhme, T., and Malinowski, U., eds., *Adaptive User Interfaces: Principles and Practice*. Amsterdam: Elsevier Science Publishers B.V. 111-128.

Krogsæter, M., Oppermann, R., and Thomas, C. (1994). A user interface integrating adaptability and adaptivity. In Oppermann, R., ed., *Adaptive User Support: Ergonomic Design of Manually and Automatically Adaptable Software*. Hillsdale, NJ: Lawrence Erlbaum Associates. 97-125.

Krogsæter, M., and Thomas, C. (1994). Adaptivity: System-initiated individualization. In Oppermann, R. ed., *Adaptive User Support: Ergonomic Design of Manually and Automatically Adaptable Software*. Hillsdale, NJ: Lawrence Erlbaum Associates. 67-96.

McCalla, G., Searwar, F., Thomson, J., Collins, J., Sun, Y., and Zhou, B. (1996). Analogical user modelling: A case study in individualized information filtering. In *Proceedings of UM'96, the Fifth International Conference on User Modeling*, 13-20.

McTear, M. (1993). User modelling for adaptive computer systems: A survey of recent developments. *Artificial Intelligence Review* 7:157-184.

Oppermann, R. (1994). Introduction. In Oppermann, R., ed., *Adaptive User Support: Ergonomic Design of Manually and Automatically Adaptable Software*. Hillsdale, NJ: Lawrence Erlbaum Associates. 3-12.

QUIS (1997). Available from: http://www.lap.umd.edu/QUISFolder/quisHome.html

Shneiderman, B. (1992). *Designing the User Interface: Strategies for Effective Human-Computer Interaction*. Reading, MA: Addison-Wesley, 2nd edition.

Strachan, L. (1997). *Pragmatic User Modelling for Complex Knowledge-Based Systems*. Ph.D. Dissertation, Department of Computer Science, University of Manitoba (forthcoming).

Wong, G., and Rengger, R. (1990). *The validity of questionnaires designed to measure user-satisfaction of computer systems*. National Physical Laboratory Report DITC 169/90, Teddington, Middlesex, UK.

High-Level Programming and Control

Capturing a Conceptual Model for End-User Programming: Task Ontology As a Static User Model

Kazuhisa Seta[1], Mitsuru Ikeda[1], Osamu Kakusho[2], and Riichiro Mizoguchi[1]

[1] Institute of Scientific and Industrial Research, Osaka University, Japan
[2] Faculty of Economics and Information Science, Hyogo University, Japan

Abstract. To realize a human friendly conceptual level programming environment, it is very important to build a static user model based on the analysis of what concepts are most important for end-users when performing the task and which concepts of a problem solving specification could be out of their awareness. We have investigated a task ontology for building the static user model. Putting task ontology on the basis of a Conceptual LEvel Programming Environment, CLEPE, provides three major advantages: 1. It provides human-friendly primitives in terms of which users can easily describe their own problem solving process (descriptiveness, readability). 2. The systems with the ask ontology can simulate the problem solving process at an abstract level in terms of conceptual level primitives (conceptual level operationality). 3. It provides the ontology author with an environment for building a task ontology so that he/she can build a consistent and useful ontology.

1 Introduction

In practice, it is really hard to develop an automatic problem solving system that can cope with the variety of problems we expect to be solved by computer systems. The main reason is that the knowledge needed for solving the problems varies considerably depending on the properties of the problems. This implies that we should realize the well-known fact, sometimes ignored, that users have more knowledge than computers. From this point of view, the importance of user-centric systems (DeBellis, 1996) is now widely recognized by many researchers.

An end-user programming environment, as an incarnation of the philosophy, provides end-users with a variety of functional components which stand for the concepts appearing in the target task and allows them to build their own problem solving models in terms of those components. In such an environment, end-users can easily describe their knowledge by using the components.

To realize an end-user programming environment, the environment should 1. adaptively evolve according to changes in requirements and changes in the target world that it deals with (Fischer, 1996); 2. have a framework for explicitly representing the computational semantics of the components provided for end-users; 3. have a framework for end-users to easily and smoothly externalize the problem solving knowledge in their mind in computer-readable form; and 4. have the capability to interpret the description and generate the runnable problem solving model with both rigid computational semantics and high cognitive fidelity.

Our research on task ontology concerns all of the above requirements for end-user programming environments. In principle, task ontology is a systematic definition of the concepts appearing in the end-users' understanding of problem solving. In this sense, it can be viewed as a static model of the end-users.

We expect that, in terms of ontology, the environment will be able to capture the end-users' conceptual model of problem solving on the level of abstraction and provide them with useful programming guidance.

Our research project aims at developing a task ontology (static user model) embedded in the environment which satisfies all of the four requirements above. In this paper, however, we will concentrate on the last two, 3 and 4, from the viewpoint of user modeling.

2   CLEPE: An Environment for End-User Programming

The Conceptual LEvel Programming Environment (CLEPE) that we have been developing has two aspects. One is an environment for the ontology author to build a task ontology as a static user model and the other is one for the end-users to describe problem solving knowledge based on the task ontology. What functionality the environment should present to ontology authors is also an important issue. Because of space limitations, however, we omit this topic. In the following discussions, we assume that a task ontology as a static user model has already been built in the environment by the ontology author, and we focus on the issues concerning the availability of the static user model from the viewpoint of its use.

The target tasks of CLEPE are rather routine tasks, such as scheduling and salary calculation. Currently, we have been investigating a variety of scheduling tasks, whose goal is to find an assignment of scheduling recipients to scheduling resources that satisfies given constraints, e.g., to assign nurses to all the jobs (night duty, semi-night duty, day duty) taking fairness into consideration.

In CLEPE, end-users describe their own problem solving knowledge in a diagrammatic representation with a constrained set of natural language sentences. Then they can verify the system's interpretation of the description using the conceptual level execution functionality of CLEPE. The

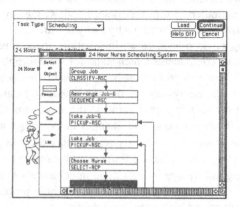

Figure 1. A screen image of CLEPE.

continuity from the diagrammatic representation to conceptual computational semantics is one of the key features of CLEPE, which originated in our precedent project MULTIS (Tijerino and Mizoguchi, 1993).

To realize such an environment in which the end-users can 1. describe their own problem solving processes using the concepts of which they are most conscious, 2. understand the execution result of the model on an appropriate level of abstraction and 3. debug it at the conceptual level, it is necessary to analyze 1. what concepts are most important for the end-users when performing the task, 2. which concepts of problem solving specification might be out of their awareness and 3. what kind of troubles end-users would face in the environment and what their causes might be.

2.1 Design Principle

It is quite a time-consuming task for the end-users to describe their own problem solving processes with reasonable precision. To lighten the load of the end-users, it is important for a task ontology to reflect their common perception of problem solving. On the other hand, from the computer's standpoint, the description of the problem solving should be rigid enough to specify the computational semantics. We could say that this conflict is a common problem of program
ming languages for end-users. The key to the problem is to shift task ontology close to the end-users and to embody the function to fill the gap between end-users and computers. Let's look at the typical situation. The structure of the problem solving process is roughly divided into control structure and data structure. In general, we can expect that the control structure of the problem solving knowledge in the end-users' mind has something in common with the control structure in the externalized description of it. On the other hand, the conceptual structure of the domain world perceived by the end-users could be different from the data structure appearing in the description, because they are not aware of the operational concepts needed for problem solving. So CLEPE allows the end-users to describe their own problem solving control structures in terms of domain activities and domain objects which are familiar to them.

The key features of CLEPE can be summarized as follows: 1. The end-users can describe their own problem solving processes in terms of human friendly primitives. 2. The end-users can observe the task execution process and debug their own description at the conceptual level. 3. The continuity from the user's description of problem solving to computational semantics is maintained.

2.2 Framework for Describing Problem Solving

Figure 1 shows an image of the interface for end-users. The network in the figure is called a Generic Process Network (GPN). GPN represents the end-users' problem solving knowledge in terms of lexical level task ontology (to be explained later in Section 3). Each node of the GPN, called a *generic process*, is separated into two parts. The upper part represents a domain process in terms of natural language, and the lower is a generic process which is a lexical level task ontology translation of the upper part. Each generic process is a combination of a verb and a noun:

$$\text{Generic Process (GP)} = \text{Generic Verb} + \text{Generic Noun}$$

Figure 1 shows a GPN for a 24-hour nurse allocation task. A node represents a generic process and a link represents the control flow of problem solving. The goal of the task is to allocate the nurses to the jobs under some constraints. In the top node in Figure 1, for example, "Grouping the Jobs" is a domain process and "Classify Scheduling-Resource (RSC)" is the corresponding generic process.

In the following, with the abstract scenario, we describe how CLEPE supports the end-users' work. The scenario is roughly divided into three phases.

Phase 1: Description of problem solving knowledge (by end-users). In this phase, the work of an end-user is to specify his/her own problem and then to compose a GPN to solve it. First, the end-user is asked to fill in some fields in the visual workplace for a problem specification. Then, to lighten their initial load, CLEPE retrieves a set of similar task cases from the GPN library based on the specification and shows them to end-users (Tijerino and Mizoguchi, 1993). End-users can refer to or reuse them to describe their own problem solving knowledge.

During the composition of a GPN, an end-user inputs the domain process in the upper field of a GPN node and then translates it into the generic process in the lower field. In this phase, lexical level task ontology plays an important role in providing vocabulary for the description of generic processes. The end-user selects the appropriate terms from the vocabulary shown in the lexical level task ontology browser and composes the generic process sentences.

It is important that lexical level task ontology be acceptable to both end-users and the environment, because its role is to lay the foundation for them to share the syntax and the semantics of the common language (GPN) to represent problem solving knowledge. Thus, from the viewpoint of user modeling, we could say the lexical level task ontology should be designed by taking the linguistic properties of the end-users' problem solving description into consideration. On the other hand, from the viewpoint of the end-user programming environment, the interpretation mechanism to clarify the semantics of the end-user's description should be available. In CLEPE, the semantics of GPN is explicitly represented as a conceptual level execution model based on conceptual level task ontology. In the following phase, CLEPE interprets the end-user's GPN and generates the corresponding conceptual execution model.

Phase 2: Making up for the incompleteness of a problem solving description (cooperative work of an end-user and CLEPE). To provide a human-friendly environment for describing problem solving knowledge, computers need to be as close as possible to humans so that they can easily make up the incompleteness in a problem solving description, if it exists. Let us take an example of the incompleteness in a problem solving description.

The lack of the human's awareness of the objects to which a process applies is a source of the incompleteness. When end-users put a generic verb into a generic process, input objects and output objects should be bound into the input port and the output port of the generic process, respectively. However the bindings cannot always be specified by an end-user explicitly. For example, in the case of a check process to check the termination condition of the loop for a sequential scan of a set, input/output objects are often omitted in the description, because the condition is quite obvious to an end-user: "until the set is exhausted". This is a typical example of the lack of a human's awareness of problem solving. They know it but don't write it explicitly. The respect for a user's awareness of problem solving is a key to the end-user friendliness of CLEPE.

To make up for the incompleteness, CLEPE analyzes the GPN and tries to reconstruct the object flow intended by the end-user. The mechanism is called *object flow analysis* (Seta et al., 1996). In this phase, CLEPE generates the object flow model (shown in Figure 2 in Section 4). Conceptual level ontology (an explanation will appear in Section 3) plays an important role in this phase. It specifies the meaning of task concepts. Based on the meaning, CLEPE checks the consistency of object flow models, for example, the consistency of changes of objects through the object flow. Once inconsistency or incompleteness of a problem solving description is identified, CLEPE tries to make up for it based on the conceptual level ontology by interacting with the end-user.

Phase 3: Conceptual level execution (by CLEPE). Once a GPN has been built by an end-user, CLEPE interprets it on the assumption that the user completely agrees with the static user model. However, there might be a gap between the interpretation and the end-user's intention, because the agreement is only partial. In such a case, we have no choice but to expect the end-user to revise the GPN. To support the user's work, CLEPE provides the functionality of conceptual level execution of a GPN.

The advantages of conceptual level execution are the following: 1. The end-user can recognize the difference between the meaning intended by him/her and the system's interpretation. 2. The end-user and the system can reach an agreement on the problem solving description more explicitly. Conceptual level ontology plays an important role in the conceptual level execution. It specifies the meaning of activities and objects and provides the framework for representing the changes of objects which are caused by activities. In this phase, the system can explain the role of each process in the task flow and the history of changes of each object. The explanation is generated based on the conceptual level execution model built by object flow analysis in Phase 2. For example, CLEPE explains that the role of the assign process (shaded in Figure 1) is to generate an assignment which consists of a picked-up job and the nurse selected for the job in each iteration of the loop. In Sections 4 and 5, we will discuss the conceptual level execution in more detail.

3 Task Ontology as a Static User Model

From now on, we focus on the role of task ontology as a static user model embedded in the end-user programming environment. The aim of user modeling research, in general, is to enable smooth communication between humans and computers. The approach to this goal can be roughly divided into two phases: static analysis and dynamic adaptation. Static analysis is the process of analyzing the end-user's epistemological conceptual structure of problem solving prior to the environment design. The goal of dynamic adaptation is to change the conceptual structure embedded into the environment and to become well suited to the individual properties of end-users when it is in operation. It seems that most attention has been paid to the latter phase in the area of user modeling without any particular reason. However, in the domain of programming, it is very difficult to dynamically capture the individual properties of a programmer as a dynamic user model because the programming task is too complex. Thus, a static user model, instead, is expected to play a more important role than a dynamic one. We believe that the environment becomes more supportive for end-users by integrating a well-defined task ontology as a static user model, because it can capture their intentions adequately with the aid of the ontology. Furthermore, we believe the integration makes dynamic user modeling easier, because it lays the foundation for analyzing and representing individual properties of programming behavior. This is the underlying philosophy of our research.

Task ontology is a systematic definition of conceptual structure to represent the end-user's awareness of various kinds of problem solving activities. It serves as a kind of meta-definition of a problem solving description language, GPN in our case. In this sense, it plays a role similar to that of the Meta Object Protocol (MOP) for the CLOS language. By using MOP, one can adjust the computational semantics of CLOS to his/her own objectives. Task ontology, on the other hand, specifies the conceptual meaning of the concepts appearing in GPNs. This means that the epistemic fidelity of GPN depends largely on how deeply we can capture the end-user's conceptual structure of problem solving in a task ontology. Once the task ontology is embedded in the environment, it provides some functions for the end-users; those are consistency checking of a GPN, conceptual level execution of it, and its compilation in the runnable computer program. The guidance presented to the end-users based on the functions can be appreciated by them when the task ontology is designed well enough to capture the end-user's conceptual structure of problem solving. By integrating task ontology into the environment, three major advantages mentioned in Section 2.1—descriptiveness/readability, conceptual level operationality, and symbol level operationality—can be realized.

A task ontology is composed of two layers. The top layer is called *lexical level ontology* and the bottom layer is called *conceptual level ontology*. Lexical level ontology specifies the language in terms of which end-users externalize their own knowledge of the target task, while conceptual level ontology is an ontology which represents the knowledge in their minds. All the concepts of lexical level ontology are organized into word classes, such as, *generic verb, generic noun, generic adjective*, etc. In the conceptual level ontology, the concepts to represent the end-user's perception of problem solving are organized into generic concept classes such as *activity, object, status*, and so on. Intuitively generic verb, generic noun, and generic adjective in the lexical world correspond to activity, object, and status in the conceptual world, respectively.

End-users can describe their problem solving knowledge using the words defined in the lexical level ontology and the system can interpret end-users' intentions in the description based on conceptual level ontology.

Generally an ontology is composed of two parts: taxonomy and axioms. Taxonomy is an ordered system of concepts, and axioms are established rules, principles, or laws relating the concepts.

4 Advantages of a Conceptual Model of Problem Solving

Task ontology consists of a variety of axioms which play the important role of realizing most of the functions of CLEPE. Because of space limitations, here we will take up some of the axioms needed for conceptual level execution and show an example of a conceptual problem solving model and its advantages.

Conceptual level execution is a function which provides the trace information on the execution process of a GPN on the appropriate level of abstraction. The function reduces the load of the end-users' work while they are debugging the GPN. In general, an end-user using a conventional programming environment often feels uncomfortable, because the level of abstraction of the trace information such as real data is too low to allow them to match it against their understanding of the problem solving. On the other hand, conceptual level execution provides end-users with conceptual level information which can be easily mapped onto their understanding of the intended behavior of the GPN. In the following, we introduce the concept of *problem solving causality*, which plays an important role for generating appropriate information about the behavior of a GPN.

The information provided by the conceptual level execution mainly concerns how objects and the relations among them change during problem solving. An idea of a *version* of objects is introduced as a source of the information. A change of version represents when and how the change of an object or relation happened. Furthermore, changes of version are propagated over the model; for example, a change in a part of an object is propagated to the whole object. It reflects how end-users recognize the changes in objects in the domain world. An important point here is that all of the changes that happen in the domain world should not be reported to end-users, because too much information would bother them. Instead, the report should include only the information really useful for the end-user to grasp the problem solving behavior clearly. Problem solving causality is a set of axioms needed to realize this summarization function. Here, we show (1) *part-whole causality* and (2) *loop-invariant generate causality* as examples. Figure 2 shows an object flow model (partially) and a domain model corresponding to it. The lexical level model (GPN) depicted in the Figure 2 is a simplified version of the one in Figure 1.

In the object flow model, all the effects of an activity at each step of the GPN are represented. In the domain model which corresponds to the given task flow model, changes in domain objects caused by the activities and the changes of relations among the objects are also represented in terms of versions.

In Figure 2, we discuss the relation between task flow and changes in domain world objects, taking the part-whole causal relation as an example. Let's focus on the causal relation between the *update* process in the k-th iteration of the loop and the *select* process (which selects a nurse with minimum load from a set of nurses) in the $(k+1)$th iteration. When the update process updates the load data of the nurse who is assigned to a job in the assign process in the k-th iteration, we can say the version of the nurse changes. In addition to this, the set of nurses including the nurse also changes its status. This is an example where the change in a part is propagated to the whole through the *component-of* relations among objects specified in the domain world. However, whether this propagation should be reported to end-users or not is a matter for argument concerning problem solving causality. Problem solving causality answers the question based on whether the change is important or not from the problem solving viewpoint. In this case, it is important, because the change in the set of nurses guarantees the correctness of the input to the *select* process in the succeeding iteration. Thus, when the *select* process is executed in the $(k+1)$th iteration of the loop, conceptual level execution shows end-users that the input object of the *select* process is identical to the one in the k-th iteration and that the load data of all of its members are appropriately updated by the update process in the k-th iteration. By representing the changes in objects caused by task execution in terms of versions of the domain objects, it is possible for CLEPE to explain the behavior of problem solving at arbitrary times using appropriate expressions. For example, CLEPE explains the roles of the *select* process at every loop iteration as follows: "The *select* process, in each the loop iteration, selects a nurse with minimum load from the set of the nurses, whose loads were adequately updated by the update process in the last iteration of the loop."

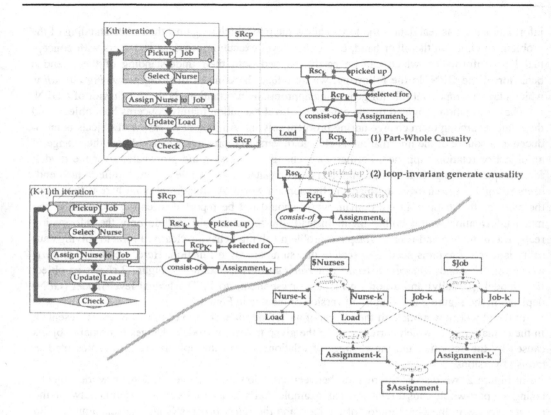

Figure 2. Examples of problem solving causality.

Another example is the one we call *loop-invariant generate* causality. In preparation, let us consider the life of a relation among objects. In Figure 2, we can see two types of relations, that is, loop-temporal relations and permanent relations. The "Picked_up" binary relation for Job-K is an example of a loop-temporal relation. This fact becomes evident when the pickup process outputs Job-K in the *k*-th iteration of the loop and disappears when the iteration is completed. The same thing is true for the "Selected for" relation for Nurse-k.

The life span of the "Picked_up" relation in the Pickup-Check loop structure is specified by the axiom of the task ontology. The version maintenance function of CLEPE sets up the life span of each instance of the relation based on the axiom. In case of the "Selected_for" relation, it becomes more complex. In the axiom related to the *select* process, there is no specification for the life span of the relation. Instead, the general axiom of task ontology says "If a conceptual entity depends tightly on the other conceptual entities, their life spans should be same." Following this principle, "Selected_for (Nurse-k, Picked_up(Job-K))" should disappear at the same time that "Picked_up(Job-K)" disappears, because Nurse-k is Selected_for "Picked_up(Job-K)". Here, however, we should notice that the generic relations, Picked_up(*) and Selected_for(*,*), form an *invariant structure* through the iteration of the loop.

On the other hand, the "consist-of" relation among Assignment, Job and Nurse is an example of a permanent relation. There are two kinds of permanencies in our task ontology; *problem solv-*

ing permanency and *problem permanency*. The former means that a conceptual entity remains throughout problem solving but disappears upon completion. The latter means that an entity never disappears if it is needed to represent the results of problem solving, as with the "consist-of" relation in our example.

The life of each conceptual entity appearing in problem solving processes is maintained by the version management mechanism of CLEPE. The problem solving causality is specified in terms of the relations among the version changes of the conceptual entities.

Loop-invariant generate causality is specified as follows: "If a portion of the problem solving model generates permanent conceptual entities from loop-invariant ones, there may exist *loop-invariant generate causality*". In our case, the causal relation extracted by the causality is this: "The assign process generates an Assignment which consists of Picked-up Job and Nurse Selected for the Job in each iteration of the loop." Assignment is added to the Assignment-set which is the solution to the given problem.

As we have seen in the above two examples, the problem solving causality can extract a meaningful set of relations from the large number of relations in the problem solving model. Without it, end-users would be bored with verbose reports about insignificant relations.

5 Capturing the Problem Solving Model

Problem solving causality is built into the task ontology as a general relation among problem solving processes and objects. As we can see in the examples of the previous section, by using the problem solving causality, the dynamics of problem solving processes are presented to end-users not only as the time series of computational operations but also as meaningful causal relations among the changes in objects which keep the correspondence between problem solving processes and domain concepts. The presentation should be acceptable to end-users because it appropriately reflects the epistemic properties of their understanding of the problem solving process. Thus, we could say that problem solving causality is one of the most important parts of task ontology as a user model.

Problem solving causality is a set of causal relations among the parts of a problem solving model. Once the object flow model corresponding to the given GPN is identified, CLEPE tries to find out the causal relations underlying the problem solving model based on the ontology of problem solving causality and then to build a conceptual level execution model. When CLEPE provides end-users with the trace information of conceptual level execution, the problem solving causality plays an important role as a basic agreement among end-users and CLEPE to share the common understanding of the problem solving process. The major role of the causality, in general, is to assign a meaningful role to the objects from the problem solving viewpoint.

In general, the causal relations underlying a problem solving model are quite complicated and entangled. If one tries to draw the figure to show the causal relations of a certain problem solving model, one will find that they are too complicated to draw on one plane. Thus, it is quite difficult for end-users to describe the causal relations explicitly by themselves, even if the relations are obvious for them. So, in order for end-users and CLEPE to share the common understanding of the problem solving model, we cannot expect end-users to express their intentions by themselves as input to CLEPE. Instead, CLEPE accepts a rather simple description of the problem solving process, such as GPNs, and then reconstructs the object flow model and reveals the causal relations underlying it based on task ontology. In practice, of course, the reconstruction task is not an easy one even with the aid of a task ontology. To overcome the difficulty, CLEPE interacts with end-users to reveal end-users' real intentions concerning the GPN. Nevertheless, if there still remains some gap between end-users' intentions and CLEPE's understanding, CLEPE provides end-users with the conceptual level execution function and expects them to adapt (debug) their problem solving description to the task ontology by themselves. In this sense, we believe that the conceptual level execution function, together with the reconstruction function of problem solving causality, is an indispensable one for an end-user programming environment.

As we discussed in the previous section, it is desirable that the problem solving causality be presented to the end-user in domain-oriented manner, because end-users prefer domain-oriented representations to task-oriented ones in general. To cope with the domain-oriented property of end-users' awareness of problem solving, the task-oriented representation of the causality, which is specified in the task ontology, needs to be translated into a domain-oriented representation. To embody such a hybrid representation, we introduced a task-domain binding (TD-binding) mechanism which acts as glue for integrating the domain concepts into the task context. For example, in Figure 1, we can say that the nurse of a domain concept is integrated into the task context and assigned the role of a scheduling recipient (RCP). In this case, TD-binding binds the domain concept, *nurse*, and the task concept, *RCP*, together, and serves either the meaning of nurse or the one of RCP in compliance with requests.

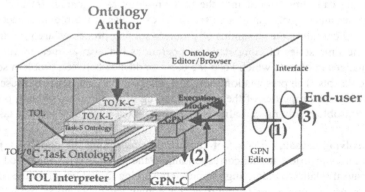

Figure 3. Overview of CLEPE. (TOL: Task ontology representation language. TO/K-L: Lexical level ontology. TO/K-C: Conceptual level ontology. GPN-C: GPN compiler, which translates a GPN into a conceptual level execution model.)

Figure 3 shows an overview of the conceptual level programming environment CLEPE. The processes represented by arrows marked with (1), (2), and (3) are the end-user's work of describing the GPN, object flow model construction, and conceptual level execution respectively. All the processes are supported based on task ontology, for example, lexical level task ontology specifies the syntax of the GPN description in (1), and conceptual level task ontology and TD-binding specify meaning of the object flow model in (2). In (3), as we discussed thus far, problem solving causality plays important role.

6 Concluding Remarks

In general, the design of an end-user programming environment depends largely on the goal of the end-users' task. For example, the goal of KIDSIM end-users is to learn new concepts by observing the behavior produced by the programs that they have written (Cypher and Smith, 1995). In an application of KIDSIM, for example, schoolchildren are expected to learn both elementary physics and programming concepts by observing the physical phenomena simulated by their own programs. Direct manipulation techniques and programming by demonstration (PBD) act as the key technologies of KidSim to help learners to understand the relation between their programs and observed behavior. The educational goal of a KidSim application and the target concepts of learning are implicitly embedded into the application by the authors. Then the learners are expected to find out the concepts, which are carefully hidden in the microworld, by themselves through trial-and-error experiments. This is a form of discovery learning. Therefore, the implicitness of the application author's educational intention is beneficial from the educational viewpoint. On the other hand, where the end-user's goal is simply software development, as with CLEPE, the implicitness is rather undesirable, because the conceptual structure of the target task, task ontology in our case, is hopefully shared by ontology authors and end-users, as we have discussed in this paper. Thus, we could say that the explicitness of the task ontology as a static user model is the distinctive feature of CLEPE compared to KidSim.

The DODE (Domain Oriented Design Environment) architecture developed by G. Fischer and the TOVE (TOronto Virtual Enterprise) project are closely related to our research.

The DODE project (Fischer, 1996) has developed a human friendly framework in which a wide variety of domain concepts can be integrated, for example, network design, voice dialog design, kitchen design, and so on.

The advantages of their research include the following: (1) To facilitate software development, they realize the collaborative environment based on the analysis of all of the stakeholders' activities. (2) They propose a theory, called SER (Seeding, Evolutionary growth and Reseeding), to capture the software evolution process explicitly. End-users can adjust their own workbench designed on the basis of the theory to dynamic change of the environment, e.g., software requirements, evolution of the domain, and so on.

In our research, the framework corresponding to this theory is called "ontology swapping". In the framework, an end-user can select a task-type-specific ontology (Seta et al., 1996) from a task ontology library. A task-type is a kind of categorization of tasks, for example, the scheduling task-type, the book-keeping task-type, the demand analysis task-type and so on. As shown in Figure 3, task-type specific (Task-S) ontology is placed at the top of ontology hierarchy and specifies the descriptive primitives provided for end-users. By swapping the ontology, the end-user programming environment can be adjusted for the end-users' target task.

The TOVE (Fox et al., 1993) ontology and ours share a similar goal in the sense that both approaches aim at formulating the conceptual meaning of a variety of types of activities in the target world as ontologies. The TOVE project has built a practical ontology of enterprise activities and developed a framework which can answer a variety of questions about dynamic aspects of the activities based on it. The difference between TOVE and our research is that TOVE provides an environment in which end-users can directly manipulate the rather complex data model (corresponding to our conceptual level execution model) based on the ontology, while CLEPE respects human friendliness and adopts the simple description scheme (GPN) which reflects the end-users' awareness of problem solving. In addition, CLEPE also provides the conceptual level execution function based on task ontology to promote ontological agreement between end-users and CLEPE.

From the viewpoint of transferability of the architecture, most of the functional modules of CLEPE are basically independent of the task domain. A task-type-specific ontology as a static user model is transferable over the domains of the same task-type, e.g., the scheduling task-type-specific ontology can act as a static user model for the 24-hour nurse allocation problem, the vehicle allocation problem, and so on. Only the workplace is not transferable in any sense, because it tightly depends on a certain task-type. As we have discussed, the "ontology swapping" mechanism is a key technique for enhancing the flexibility of the architecture. In the CLEPE project, we have a plan to integrate a wide variety of task-type-specific ontologies into a task ontology library to enhance the flexibility of CLEPE.

To verify the utility of task ontology from the viewpoint of user modeling, we asked thirteen scheduling experts to compose GPNs to represent their problem solving knowledge for their own real world scheduling problems. After some trial-and-error, all of them completed their description. And we got an entirely favorable response from them. After the development of CLEPE is completed, we will perform a more careful empirical study to evaluate the utility of the whole architecture.

References

Cypher, A., and Smith, D. C. (1995). KidSim: End user programming of simulations. In *Proceedings of Computer Human Interaction '95,* 27-34.

DeBellis, M. (1995). User-centric software engineering. *IEEE Expert* 10:34-41.

Fisher, G. (1996). Seeding, evolutionary growth and reseeding: Constructing, capturing and evolving knowledge in domain-oriented environment. In *Domain Knowledge for Interface System Design.* London: Chapman & Hall. 1-16

Fox, M. S., Chionglo, J., and Fadel, F. (1993). A common-sense model of the enterprise. In *Proceedings of the Industrial Engineering Research Conference.*

Seta, K., Ikeda, M., Kakusho, O., and Mizoguchi, R. (1996). Design of a conceptual level programming environment based on task ontology, In *Proceedings of Successes and Failures of Knowledge Based Systems in Real World Applications,* 11-20.

Steels, L. (1990). Components of expertise. *AI Magazine* 11(2):28-49.

Tijerino, A. Y., and Mizoguchi, R. (1993). MULTIS II : Enabling end-users to design problem-solving engines via two-level task ontologies, In *Proceedings of the European Knowledge Acquisition Workshop '93,* 340-359.

Yost G., Klinker, G., Linster, M., Marques, D., and McDermott, J. (1994). The SBF Framework,1989-1994: From applications to workplaces, In *Proceedings of the European Knowledge Acquisition Workshop '94,* 318-339.

Cinematographic User Models for Automated Realtime Camera Control in Dynamic 3D Environments

William H. Bares and James C. Lester*

Multimedia Laboratory, Department of Computer Science,
North Carolina State University, Raleigh, NC U.S.A.

Abstract. Advances in 3D graphics technology have accelerated the construction of dynamic 3D environments. Despite their promise for scientific and educational applications, much of this potential has gone unrealized because runtime camera control software lacks user-sensitivity. Current environments rely on sequences of viewpoints that directly require the user's control or are based primarily on actions and geometry of the scene. Because of the complexity of rapidly changing environments, users typically cannot manipulate objects in environments while simultaneously issuing camera control commands. To address these issues, we have developed UCAM, a realtime camera planner that employs cinematographic user models to render customized visualizations of dynamic 3D environments. After interviewing users to determine their preferred directorial style and pacing, UCAM examines the resulting cinematographic user model to plan camera sequences whose shot vantage points and cutting rates are tailored to the user in realtime. Evaluations of UCAM in a dynamic 3D testbed are encouraging.

1 Introduction

Dynamic 3D environments hold great promise for a broad range of educational and scientific applications. By enabling users to participate in immersive experiences as they learn about complex systems or perform complicated tasks, 3D environments can help students and scientists achieve greater levels of performance. Fortunately, recent advances in graphics hardware have created significant opportunities for making dynamic 3D environments available on a broad scale. With the proliferation of inexpensive graphics accelerators, dynamic 3D environments can soon become an indispensable, cost-effective means of delivering customized instruction and visualizations in domains as diverse as molecular biology, computer engineering, and medicine. By enabling users to view complex processes and interact with objects in 3D animations in realtime, dynamic 3D environments can significantly increase the effectiveness of knowledge-based learning environments and scientific visualization systems.

Effective realtime camera control is critical to the successful deployment of dynamic 3D environments. In dynamic 3D environments, virtual cameras track the objects of interest to depict the most salient aspects of complicated scenes. Two approaches have been proposed for camera control. Some systems require users to directly control low-level camera positioning and

---

* Support for this work was provided by the IntelliMedia Initiative of North Carolina State University and donations from Novell, Inc.

orientation parameters, while others automatically control camera movement without considering users' visualization preferences. The first approach is problematic when users must perform complex tasks while simultaneously issuing camera control commands, a particularly acute problem in highly dynamic environments. Although the second approach frees users from camera control, it fails to consider their individual visualization preferences.

Dynamic 3D environments must accommodate a broad range of users. Each individual brings his or her own idiosyncratic visualization preferences for experiencing a particular 3D environment. While some users prefer informative styles, others prefer visualizations with a dramatic flair. Some users may be unfamiliar with a task that involves unusually complex visualizations; these situations call for slower camera pacing, gradual transitions, and an informational visualization style. Moreover, users that are intimately familiar with a particular aspect of a task may prefer a faster camera pace and rapid transitions.

Given the broad range of students and scientists who will interact with dynamic 3D environments, user-sensitive automated camera control is quickly becoming essential. However, user-sensitive camera control poses a difficult challenge: determining the positions and directions of virtual cameras in realtime is enormously difficult because shots must clearly depict the portion of the scene most relevant to the user while at the same time taking into account his or her visualization preferences. These functionalities call for a user modeling approach to representing users' visualization preferences and to performing customized realtime camera planning. While a growing body of work considers user modeling for multimedia presentation systems (André et al., 1993, McKeown et al., 1992, Roth et al., 1991, van Mulken, 1996) the problem of user modeling for camera control in dynamic 3D environments has not been addressed: current environments rely on sequences of viewpoints that directly require the user's control or are based primarily on actions and geometry of the scene (Butz, 1997, Christianson et al., 1996, Drucker and Zeltzer, 1995, Karp and Feiner, 1993, Mackinlay et al., 1990, Ware and Osborn, 1990).

To address these problems, we have developed the *cinematographic user modeling* framework for user-sensitive realtime camera control in dynamic 3D environments. This domain-independent framework has been implemented in UCAM,[1] a user-sensitive realtime camera planner. After constructing an expressive representation of users' visualization preferences, UCAM creates customized immersive experiences by exploiting its cinematographic user model to plan camera positions, view directions, and camera movement in response to users' manipulations of objects in 3D environments. UCAM has been evaluated in a 3D environment with subjects from both technical and art backgrounds. Subjects interacted with UCAM to perform two families of tasks: a visualization task in which they specified their cinematographic preferences to create a 3D visualizations of long sequences of actions, and a navigation task in which they maneuvered a virtual vehicle through a cityscape. The results of this evaluation are encouraging and demonstrate that user-sensitive automated realtime camera control significantly improves users' interactions with dynamic 3D environments.

2   Customized Camera Planning in 3D Environments

Realtime camera planning in dynamic 3D environments entails selecting camera positions and view directions in response to changes to objects in the environment that are caused by users'

---

[1] User-Customized Automated Montage

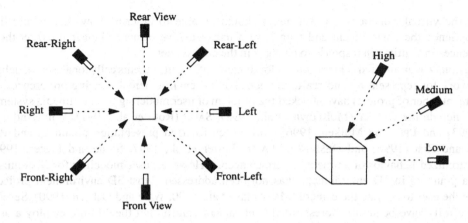

Figure 1. Camera viewing angles and elevations for 3D environments.

manipulations or a simulation. A virtual camera must track the objects by executing cuts,[2] pans, and zooms (pull-ins and pull-outs) to make on-the-fly decisions about camera viewing angles, distances, and elevations. Planning camera shots and camera positions while preserving continuity requires solving precisely the same set of problems that are faced by cinematographers, with the additional constraint that they must be solved in realtime.

In dynamic 3D environments, camera planners must continually make decisions about shot types and camera positions. *Shot types* are characterized by several dimensions, including the size of the subject as it appears in the frame and the relative position of the camera to the subject. For example, the subject occupies all of the frame for a close-up shot. In a long shot, the subject occupies a small portion of the frame. Different shot types are more useful in particular situations. Long shots are preferred for depicting wide-ranging action or showing relative size or position of subjects. Close-up shots are useful for emphasizing detail and for focusing on a single subject (Millerson, 1994). Camera *positions* are defined by the viewing angle and elevation relative to the subject (Figure 1). For example, the camera can be placed directly in front of the subject or to the right of the subject; it can be placed slightly below the subject and gaze up towards it to exaggerate its size, or high above the subject gazing downwards. High and far shots present more information about the scene but tend to be less interesting (Mascelli, 1965). Preserving continuity during transitions such as cuts, panning, and tracking is critical. However, it is also difficult because camera planners must maintain the viewer's interest with a variety of shots without introducing jarring visual discontinuities (Mascelli, 1965).

Given the complexities of camera planning, users performing tasks in 3D environments should be able to delegate the myriad micro-level camera planning decisions to an automated camera planner in order to focus their attention on their own tasks. For example, a biologist observing the effects of a T-cell's traversal of the lymph system should not be forced to continually make decisions about how to adjust the virtual camera's elevation, orientation, and zoom level, when to make cuts, and how to pan left and right. Rather than making a series of incremental, ongoing modifications to the virtual camera, perhaps even by specifying 3D motion spline paths along

---

[2] A *cut* is an instantaneous change from one shot to another without an intervening transition.

which the virtual camera will travel, users should be able to describe how they would like to experience the environment and then have a user-sensitive camera planner interpret these preferences in realtime in response to changes in the environment.

Customized automated camera control for dynamic 3D environments calls for a user modeling framework for representing and reasoning about users' environmental viewing preferences. A growing number of projects have attacked the problem of user modeling for multimedia systems. These include the COMET (McKeown et al., 1992), SAGE (Roth et al., 1991), WIP (André et al., 1993) and PPP (van Mulken, 1996) work on customized presentation planning, and PPP André and Rist (1996) and DESIGN-A-PLANT (Lester et al., 1997, Stone and Lester, 1996) for customized behavior of animated interface agents. However, user modeling for customized camera planning in 3D environments has not been addressed. Most 3D environment projects require the user to operate the camera (Mackinlay et al., 1990, Ware and Osborn, 1990). Several recent efforts have begun to address intelligent camera control, but they do not employ a user model to represent users' visualization preferences. CAMDROID (Drucker and Zeltzer, 1995) allows the user to design a network of camera modules and constraints but has no user model. The VIRTUAL CINEMATOGRAPHER (Christianson et al., 1996) and ESPLANADE (Karp and Feiner, 1993) employ film idioms to successfully maintain camera shot sequences that are consistent with film conventions, but they cannot customize animations since no user model is maintained. CATHI (Butz, 1997), which is part of the PPP project (André and Rist, 1996) permits users to state visualization preferences such as the use of spotlights, depth of field, and animation duration, as well as animation preferences that include two cinematic styles. However, the cinematic styles are specified by the choice of one of two grammars of film rules rather than more fine grained user modeling of individual cinematic attributes such as camera pacing, viewpoint style, and transition style.

3   Cinematographic User Modeling

To address the problem of customized realtime camera control for dynamic 3D environments, we have developed the domain-independent *cinematographic user modeling* framework and implemented it in UCAM, a realtime cinematographic user modeling system (Figure 2). By constructing cinematographic user models and creating a camera planner that exploits the models to select camera shots and enact camera transitions, UCAM creates interactive viewing experiences that are highly customized to individual users' preferences in realtime. Cinematographic user models enable users—including users with no cinematographic expertise—to become "directors" of their experiences through a two step process:

1. **User Model Construction:** To accommodate the majority of users' lack of familiarity with cinematography, it is critical that a "director studio" provide them with a tool that is simple yet expressive. As users describe their visualization preferences for how they wish to interactively experience a 3D environment, UCAM constructs a cinematographic user model. Represented in a *Cinematographic Specification Language* (CSL), cinematographic user models consist of probabilistic micro-level camera planning directives including specifications for shot type selection, camera orientation, minimum shot durations, and angular difference thresholds for cut/pan decisions.

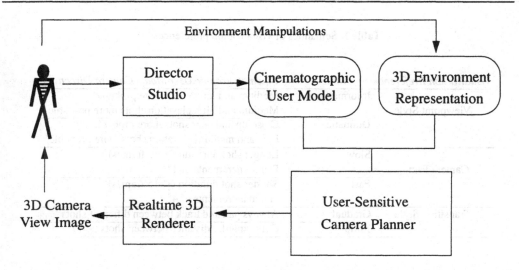

Figure 2. The UCAM architecture.

2. **Customized Realtime Camera Planning:** A camera planner interprets these models to plan camera positions, view directions, and camera transitions in realtime. As users navigate through an environment (perhaps traversing an expansive complex landscape) and manipulates objects in the scene, the planner computes executable directives for *shot type* (e.g., close-up, long), *viewing angle* (e.g., front-left), *viewing elevation*, *transitions* (cut, tracking, panning), *shot duration*, and *panning* and *tracking speeds* in realtime to frame objects of interest as they move about.

These directives are then passed to the renderer, which composes the next frame depicting the 3D environment. The net effect of viewing these rapidly rendered frames is a seamless immersive experience that is customized for users' visualization preferences.[3] UCAM also permits users to modify their visualization preferences at any time.

3.1 Constructing Cinematographic User Models

In interacting with a customized camera planning system, it is critical that users can easily express their visualization preferences without being overwhelmed by an enormous number of selections. UCAM therefore provides a menu-based "director studio" with which users classify their visualization preferences along three dimensions: viewpoint style, camera pacing, and transition style as shown in the first two columns of Table 1.

Specific viewpoint styles can be achieved with different shot types and elevations, which together bring about a specific cinematographic impact (Mascelli, 1965). Users can select either an informational or a dramatic viewpoint. Specifying an *informational* viewpoint style will produce a visualization that is more clear and informative by employing more medium and long shots, as well as more medium and high elevation shots. Specifying a *dramatic* viewpoint style

---

[3] UCAM completes the planning-rendering cycle every 1/8 of a second on a PC.

Table 1. Semantics of visualization preferences

Visualization Preference	Value	Cinematographic User Model Camera Directives
Viewpoint Style	Informational	Medium and long shots more probable
		Medium and high elevation shots more probable
	Dramatic	Close-up and near shots more probable
		Low and medium elevation shots more probable
Camera Pacing	Slow	Longer shot duration ($\geq$ 35 frames)
		Pan in increments of $1°$
	Fast	Shorter shot duration ($\leq$ 15 frames)
		Pan in increments of $4°$
Transition Style	Gradual	Always pan and track between different shots
	Jump	Cut if angular distance between shots > $60°$

will produce an experience that is more dramatic by having the camera planner prefer close-up and near shots and low and medium elevation shots.

Users may also state pacing and transition preferences. *Slow* pacing will produce an interactive experience that is perceived as slower by increasing shot durations and reducing the speed of tracking and panning shots. *Fast* pacing will produce an experience that seems more intense by decreasing shot durations and increasing tracking and panning speeds. Preferences for transition styles can be either gradual or jumping. A *gradual* transition preference will achieve a more relaxed experience by causing the camera planner to opt for panning and tracking between shots, while a *jump* transition preference will produce a more staccato experience by causing the camera planner to cut from shot to shot. Users can state their preferences for these dimensions in any order.

The director studio builds a cinematographic user model by mapping high-level visualization preferences to low-level camera planning directives expressed in the probabilistic CSL. The semantics of the user's visualization preferences are summarized in the third column of Table 1. To illustrate, suppose a user expresses her preferences for a dramatic viewpoint style, fast pace, and jump transitions. The director studio creates a cinematographic user model with a 30% probability for close-ups, 40% for near shots, 20% for medium shots, and 10% for far shots. It selects camera elevation probabilities of 50% for low, 50% for medium, and 0% for high. It chooses a minimum shot duration of 15 frames, a panning/tracking rate of $4°$ per unit time, and a minimum cut angle of $60°$.[4] All of these factors will be considered by the camera planner in making shot modification determination decisions, shot selection decisions, and camera transition decisions at each instant of the visualization.

3.2 User-Sensitive Realtime Camera Planning

UCAM's camera planner exploits the visualization directives represented by cinematographic user models to create customized experiences for users interacting with 3D environments. As a

---

[4] Specific probabilities and cut angle values in the implementation were developed empirically to reflect the semantics of Table 1.

```
        loop
                3DEnvironment ← update-environment
                if user modifies visualization preferences then
                        CinematicUserModel ← construct-UM (VisualizationPrefs)
                if NumFrames < MinimumShotDuration then
                        (* no change to CamShot but move camera to track object *)
                        CamPosition ← select-new-position (3DEnvironment, null-transition)
                else {
                        CamShot ← select-new-shot (CinematicUserModel, 3DEnvironment)
                        NumFrames ← 0
                        if AngleToNewShot < MinimumCutAngle then
                                CamTransition ← pan to new position
                        else
                                CamTransition ← cut to new position
                        CamPosition ← select-new-position (3DEnvironment, CamTransition)}
                NumFrames ← NumFrames + 1
                NewFrame ← render (3DEnvironment, CamShot, CamPosition)
        until user exits visualization
```

Figure 3. Realtime user-sensitive camera planning.

user manipulates objects in an environment, the camera planner considers his or her preferred viewpoint style, pacing, and transition style to make continuous runtime decisions about camera positioning. A visualization begins with the user expressing his or her preferences through the director studio interface, which are used to construct a cinematographic user model. After initializing the camera shot and position to display the *primary object of interest*, e.g., for a physiologist this might be a particular molecule she wishes to track, the camera planner then performs the user-sensitive camera control algorithm shown in Figure 3. The planning-rendering loop begins with an update to the 3D environment model. This update may stem from either the user's manipulation of objects in the environment, a new state of a simulation, or both. The camera planner then makes three sets of decisions on each iteration of the loop to support the user's visualization preferences:

- *Shot modification determination:* The camera planner determines when a new shot should be selected based on the camera pace preference.
- *Camera shot selection:* If it has been determined that a new shot should be planned, the camera planner composes the new shot based on the viewpoint style preference.
- *Camera transition selection:* If a new shot will be presented, the camera planner determines whether to pan from the current shot to the new shot or whether to cut directly to the new shot based on the transition style preference.

When users state their preference for a faster or slower pace, UCAM changes shots more or less frequently. This is accomplished by the user model stipulating either a smaller or larger *MinimumShotDuration*.[5] Even if the camera planner opts to maintain the current distance, angle,

---

[5] In UCAM, the *MinimumShotDuration* for a *slow* pace is 35 frames and for a *fast* pace is 15 frames.

and elevation relative to the primary object, movement of the object in the environment may require it to modify the camera position. For example, if a red blood cell in a cardiovascular environment moves from one ventricle of the heart to another, the camera must track it.

User-sensitive camera shot selection decisions are made when the camera planner has determined that a new shot should be planned. UCAM composes new shots by selecting a new camera-subject distance (zooming in or out) and/or changing the camera's elevation. Because variability is of paramount importance in maintaining the user's interest, in most applications it is critical that a camera planner *not* employ a fixed sequence of shots. UCAM therefore employs a probabilistic shot selection algorithm that exploits probabilities on camera directives stipulated by the user model. Recall that more dramatic visualizations are produced with more frequent use of close-ups, near shots, and shots that are of lower elevation (Mascelli, 1965), while the converse holds for more informational visualizations. For variety, UCAM also varies the camera's view angle by selecting from one of the eight possible angles.[6] Together, these probabilistic decisions produce camera positions and orientations that reflect the user's viewpoint style preferences.

When UCAM selects a new shot, it enacts a transition that will achieve the user's visualization preferences. This decision is made by considering (1) camera transition directives specified in the user model and (2) the relative positions of the camera's current location/orientation with respect to the location/orientation it must travel to in order to make the new shot. Users who prefer gradual transitions will experience smoother visualizations through camera panning and tracking, while users who prefer jump transitions experience the environment with more frequent cutting from one shot to another. However, because of continuity concerns, jump transitions are often inappropriate: jumping from one shot to another shot which is only slightly different produces a very jarring effect (Mascelli, 1965). UCAM therefore compares the angular difference between the current and new shots with the *MinCutAngle* represented in the user model to make its decisions. If a user prefers jump transitions, the *MinCutAngle* threshold will be 60°, while the *MinCutAngle* for users preferring gradual transitions is ∞. The effect of these thresholds is as follows: for users who prefer gradual transitions, the camera will always transition with a combination of panning and tracking; for users who prefer jump transitions, a cut will be selected only if the angular difference exceeds the *MinCutAngle*.

Once the new shot is selected, UCAM computes the new coordinates for the camera. To accomplish this, it transforms the camera position from coordinates in the local coordinate system anchored at the object of interest to coordinates in the global XYZ coordinate system. The planning-rendering loop is completed by rendering the current scene in the environment from the new camera position. UCAM executes the body of the algorithm for each frame to produce a continuous interactive visualization as the user manipulates objects in the environment.

---

[6] To permit a cleaner evaluation, the version of UCAM employed in the evaluation described below assigns equal probabilities to each of the eight possible view angles. However, UCAM also has a sophisticated *occlusion avoidance system* that modifies the viewing angle to eliminate occlusions of the primary object by objects that come between the virtual camera and the primary object. As the user moves through the dynamic environment, the camera planner invokes the occlusion avoidance system to obtain an obstruction-free view of the primary object. The occlusion avoidance system was disabled during the evaluation.

4 An Implemented User-Sensitive Camera Planner

UCAM is a full-scale realtime implementation of the cinematographic user modeling framework.[7] To investigate UCAM's behavior, we constructed a navigable 3D environment testbed, CARPARK. In the CARPARK environment, users drive a sports car through a scenic maze of rectangular city blocks populated by tree-lined parks. On their journey they can pass other cars as they make their ways towards an enormous stop sign.

Suppose a user (User 1) prefers to experience his navigation of CARPARK at a slow pace that is less dramatic and with gradual transitions. As the user steers his car through the city, stopping and turning as he sees fit, UCAM creates a customized experience whose visualizations are tailored to his preferences. Incremental screen shots along his tour are shown in the left column of Figure 4. For the initial shot, UCAM depicts the car from a front-left angle at a high elevation and far viewing distance (a). In (b), the camera keeps the same front-left viewing angle, but gradually zooms to a medium distance shot. In (c), the camera has panned and tracked to a rear-right view to show the car rounding the corner. For the final shot in (d), the camera gradually pans and tracks around the car until it reaches the rear-left viewing angle as the driver brings the car to a halt.

Suppose that another user (User 2) prefers to experience her navigation of CARPARK at a faster pace that is more dramatic and includes jump transitions. For purposes of comparison, suppose that User 2 issues precisely the same navigation commands at precisely the same locations and with precisely the same timing as User 1.[8] The resulting experience is much more dramatic and seems much faster (Figure 4, right column). UCAM chooses more close-up-to-the-action views and sometimes sweeps in low to the ground to increase the sense of excitement. The initial shot in (a) shows the car from a front-left angle at low elevation and at a medium viewing distance. UCAM then cuts directly to the near front-left shot in (b), where the driver's car has just passed a parked car. As the driver's car rounds the corner, UCAM instructs the camera to zoom in for a close-up view from a front-left viewing angle and medium elevation. To transition from the shot in (b) to the shot in (c), although User 2 prefers jump transitions, UCAM employs a gradual zoom in and pan because the angular difference between the shot in (b) and the shot in (c) is too small for a cut without a jarring effect. For the final shot (d), the camera cuts to a low view of the car arriving at the stop sign.

5 Evaluation

To gauge the effectiveness of the cinematographic user modeling framework for creating customized visualization experiences in dynamic 3D environments, an empirical evaluation was conducted. The evaluation was designed to determine if (1) cinematographic user modeling could accurately represent users' preferences by producing visualizations that met their expectations, and (2) the resulting visualizations were clear and/or visually appealing.

---

[7] UCAM is implemented in C++ and employs the OpenGL graphics library for 3D rendering. It runs at 8 frames/second with 16 bits/pixel color on a Pentium 133 Mhz PC equipped with a 2D video board and 32 megabytes of memory. It consists of approximately 14,000 lines of code.

[8] Because CARPARK writes out a navigation script of a user's interactions, it is possible to replay a navigation and experience it with different visualization preferences.

User 1   User 2

{ informational, slow, gradual }   { dramatic, fast, jump }

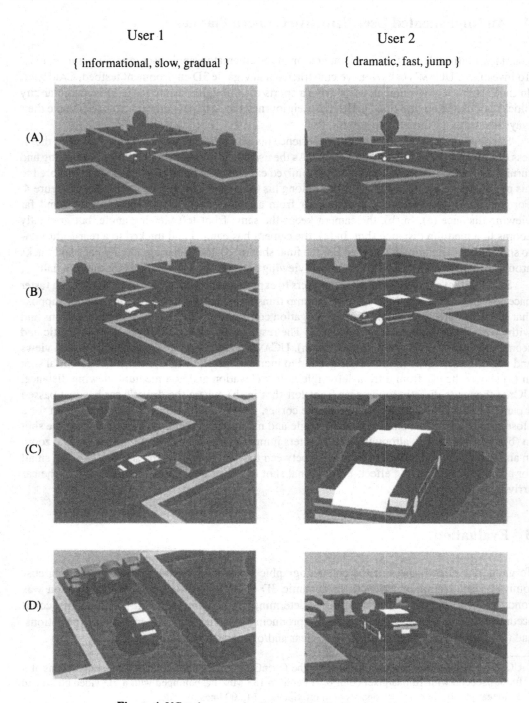

Figure 4. UCAM's customized tours of the CARPARK testbed.

The subjects of the study were 10 skilled computer users, all of whom were familiar with 3D computer animation and multimedia applications. To obtain a broad spectrum of responses, subjects were chosen from both artistic and technical backgrounds. Of the 10 subjects, 6 were graphic designers and 4 were computer scientists. Subjects interacted with two different versions of the CARPARK testbed. In the first version, users interacted with UCAM's director studio interface; in the second, they interacted with a direct camera control interface that presents a large number of options for specifying the same low-level camera control parameters automatically controlled by UCAM.

Subjects were given two sets of tasks to perform. In the first set of tasks, they were asked to serve as the director for a 3D movie, which was generated from a navigation script of the CARPARK testbed environment. They interacted with UCAM to specify two different sets of visualization preferences and observe the effects of these preferences as UCAM created the customized visualizations. They then repeated this process with the direct camera control interface. For their second set of tasks, users navigated through the CARPARK environment in realtime.

Results of the evaluation suggest that cinematic user modeling is an effective means for achieving customized camera control of dynamic 3D environments in realtime. Specific findings include the following: The dramatic viewpoint style was rated more interesting in 8 of the 11 times it was selected but found more difficult to follow in 6 of the 11. The informative viewpoint style was found easier to follow 7 of the 9 times when it was selected. The jump transition style was rated more interesting 6 of 9 times but was rated more difficult to follow in 5 of 9. The gradual transition style was found easier to follow 7 of the 10 of times it was selected. The slow camera pace was found easier to follow 5 of the 7 times it was selected, but was judged less interesting, while the fast camera pace was found to be more interesting 12 of 13 times and easy to follow 8 of 13 times.

The cinematographic user modeling approach was preferred by 8 of 10 for the 3D movie viewing directing task over the direct camera control. With the direct control, subjects reported being distracted by having to pay more attention to the camera controls. For the 3D navigation task, half of the subjects preferred cinematographic user modeling. Given the extreme simplicity of the CARPARK task, it is interesting to note that 8 of the 10 subjects (including those preferring direct control) reported being distracted by having to attend to both the camera control and the navigation in the direct control version.

Overall, the cinematographic user model system produced the expected visual result in 70 percent of the trials. Situations in which expectations were not met are attributable to the animation speed not being fast enough, the lack of establishing shots, and "line crossing" problems, i.e., the sudden apparent reversal of an object's direction of motion. Soon-to-be-released 3D graphic accelerators will provide a solution to the first concern by delivering an order-of-magnitude greater speed. As a result of the evaluation, UCAM has been extended to address the second and third concerns. In short, cinematographic user modeling enabled users to quickly specify their visualization preferences, it accurately modeled their preferences, and it permitted them to focus their attention on the task at hand.

6   Conclusion

Dynamic 3D environments offer great potential for a broad range of educational and scientific visualization tasks. We have proposed the cinematographic user modeling framework for dynamically customizing 3D environment experiences to users' visualization preferences. By considering these preferences, it plans camera positioning and orientation in realtime as users interact with objects in 3D environments. An empirical evaluation of an implemented domain-independent cinematographic user modeling system suggests that the approach can accurately model users' visualization preferences. This work represents a promising first step toward creating adaptive 3D environments. Perhaps the greatest challenge ahead lies in extending cinematographic user models to account for context-sensitivity to users' tasks. We will be investigating these issues in our future research.

References

André, E., and Rist, T. (1996). Coping with temporal constraints in multimedia presentation planning. In *Proceedings of the Thirteenth National Conference on Artificial Intelligence*, 142–147.

André, E., Finkler, W., Graf, W., Rist, T., Schauder, A., and Wahlster, W. (1993). WIP: The automatic synthesis of multi-modal presentations. In Maybury, M. T., ed., *Intelligent Multimedia Interfaces*. AAAI Press. chapter 3.

Butz, A. (1997). Anymation with CATHI. To appear in *Proceedings of the Innovative Applications of Artificial Intelligence Conference*.

Christianson, D. B., Anderson, S. E., He, L.-W., Salesin, D. H., Weld, D. S., and Cohen, M. F. (1996). Declarative camera control for automatic cinematography. In *Proceedings of the Thirteenth National Conference on Artificial Intelligence*, 148–155.

Drucker, S., and Zeltzer, D. (1995). CamDroid: A system for implementing intelligent camera control. In *Proceedings of the 1995 Symposium on Interactive 3D Graphics*, 139–144.

Karp, P., and Feiner, S. (1993). Automated presentation planning of animation using task decomposition with heuristic reasoning. In *Proceedings of Graphics Interface '93*, 118–127.

Lester, J. C., FitzGerald, P. J., and Stone, B. A. (1997). The pedagogical design studio: Exploiting artifact-based task models for constructivist learning. In *Proceedings of the Third International Conference on Intelligent User Interfaces*, 155–162.

Mackinlay, J., Card, S., and Robertson, G. (1990). Rapid controlled movement through a virtual 3D workspace. In *Proceedings of ACM SIGGRAPH '90*, 171–176.

Mascelli, J. (1965). *The Five C's of Cinematography*. Cine/Grafic Publications, Hollywood.

McKeown, K. R., Feiner, S. K., Robin, J., Seligmann, D., and Tanenblatt, M. (1992). Generating cross-references for multimedia explanation. In *Proceedings of the Tenth National Conference on Artificial Intelligence*, 9–15.

Millerson, G. (1994). *Video Camera Techniques*. Focal Press, Oxford, England.

Roth, S. F., Mattis, J., and Mesnard, X. (1991). Graphics and natural language as components of automatic explanation. In Sullivan, J. W., and Tyler, S. W., eds., *Intelligent User Interfaces*. New York: Addison-Wesley. 207–239.

Stone, B. A., and Lester, J. C. (1996). Dynamically sequencing an animated pedagogical agent. In *Proceedings of the Thirteenth National Conference on Artificial Intelligence*, 424–431.

van Mulken, S. (1996). Reasoning about the user's decoding of presentations in an intelligent multimedia presentation system. In *Proceedings of the Fifth International Conference on User Modeling*, 67–74.

Ware, C., and Osborn, S. (1990). Exploration and virtual camera control in virtual three dimensional environments. In *1990 Symposium on Interactive 3D Graphics*, 175–184.

INSTRUCTION AND TRAINING

Knowledge and Skill Diagnosis

On-Line Student Modeling for Coached Problem Solving Using Bayesian Networks

Cristina Conati[1], Abigail S. Gertner[2], Kurt VanLehn[1,2], and Marek J. Druzdzel[1,3]⋆

[1] Intelligent Systems Program, University of Pittsburgh, PA, U.S.A.
[2] Learning Research and Development Center, University of Pittsburgh, PA, U.S.A.
[3] Department of Information Science, University of Pittsburgh, PA, U.S.A.

Abstract. This paper describes the student modeling component of ANDES, an Intelligent Tutoring System for Newtonian physics. ANDES' student model uses a Bayesian network to do long-term knowledge assessment, plan recognition and prediction of students' actions during problem solving. The network is updated in real time, using an approximate anytime algorithm based on stochastic sampling, as a student solves problems with ANDES. The information in the student model is used by ANDES' Help system to tailor its support when the student reaches impasses in the problem solving process. In this paper, we describe the knowledge structures represented in the student model and discuss the implementation of the Bayesian network assessor. We also present a preliminary evaluation of the time performance of stochastic sampling algorithms to update the network.

1 Introduction

ANDES is an Intelligent Tutoring System that teaches Newtonian physics via *coached problem solving* (VanLehn, 1996), a method of teaching cognitive skills in which the tutor and the student collaborate to solve problems. In coached problem solving, the initiative in the student-tutor interaction changes according to the progress being made. As long as the student proceeds along a correct solution, the tutor merely indicates agreement with each step. When the student stumbles on a certain part of the problem, the tutor helps the student overcome the impasse by providing tailored hints that lead the student back to the correct solution path. In this setting, the critical problem for the tutor is to interpret the student's actions and the line of reasoning that the student is following. To perform this task the tutor needs a student model that performs plan recognition (Charniak and Goldman, 1993; Genesereth, 1982; Huber et al., 1994; Pynadath and Wellman, 1995).

Inferring an agent's plan from a partial sequence of observable actions is a task that involves inherent uncertainty since often the same observable actions can belong to different plans. In coached problem solving, two additional sources of uncertainty increase the difficulty of the plan recognition task. Firstly, coached problem solving often involves interactions in which most of

---

⋆ This research is supported by AFOSR under grant number F49620-96-1-0180, by ONR's Cognitive Science Division under grant N00014-96-1-0260 and by DARPA's Computer Aided Education and Training Initiative under grant N66001-95-C-8367. In addition, Dr. Druzdzel was supported by the National Science Foundation under Faculty Early Career Development (CAREER) Program, grant IRI–9624629. We would like to thank Zhendong Niu and Yan Lin for programming support.

the important reasoning is hidden from the coach's view. This is especially true when the coach decides to reduce the level of guidance in the problem solving process by no longer requiring the student to explicitly show the problem solving steps that can be performed mentally. Secondly, there is additional uncertainty regarding the student's level of understanding of the domain theory and, therefore, the kind of knowledge that she can bring to bear in generating solution plans.

This paper describes a framework for student modeling in Intelligent Tutoring Systems that takes into account both the uncertainty about the student's plans and the uncertainty about her knowledge state. The framework uses a Bayesian network (Pearl, 1988) to represent and update the student model on-line, *during* problem solving. The student model is constructed by the Assessor module of ANDES and it is used to tailor ANDES' coaching to the problem solving performance of each individual student.

2   The ANDES Student Modeling Framework

ANDES' student model represents a significant contribution to research in probabilistic user modeling for three reasons.

First, the model uses a probabilistic framework to perform three kinds of assessment: (1) *plan recognition*, inferring the most likely strategy among possible alternatives the student is following, (2) *prediction* of students' goals and actions, and (3) *long-term assessment* of the student's domain knowledge. None of the existing systems that perform probabilistic user modeling seem to combine all three of these functions (Jameson, 1996). ANDES' Assessor evolves from POLA (Conati and VanLehn, 1996a, 1996b), our first attempt at a student model for coached problem solving. Unlike POLA, which exploited only the diagnostic capabilities of its Bayesian network, the Assessor also provides predictions about the inferences that the student may have made but not yet expressed via actual solution steps, and the inferences that may cause problems. These predictions will provide ANDES with more principled information to generate effective coached problem solving than the heuristics used by POLA.

Second, this model performs plan recognition by integrating in a principled way knowledge about the student's behavior and mental state with knowledge about the available plans. While substantial research has been devoted to using probabilistic reasoning frameworks to deal with the inherent uncertainty of the plan recognition task (Carberry, 1990; Charniak and Goldman, 1993; Huber et al., 1994; Pynadath and Wellman, 1995), none of it encompasses applications where much uncertainty concerns the knowledge that the user has to generate the plans.

If the assumption that the planning agent has complete and correct knowledge is reasonable in many plan recognition applications, it is certainly not realistic for plan recognition in an Intelligent Tutoring System, whose primary goal is to improve the incorrect and incomplete knowledge of the student. Nonetheless, the few existing systems that perform plan recognition for intelligent tutoring systems rely on a library of available plans, without taking into consideration the student's degree of mastery in the target domain (Genesereth, 1982; Kohen and Greer, 1993; Ross and Lewis, 1988). The model-tracing tutors of Anderson et al. (1995) assess both a student's mastery of the domain and the solution that the student is following during problem solving, but they do not integrate the two kinds of assessment. They apply probabilistic methods only for knowledge assessment and reduce the complexity of plan recognition by restricting the number of acceptable solutions the student can follow and by asking the student when there is still some ambiguity.

Third, the student model will be used in real-time to tailor the coaching of students' problem solving. Bayesian networks have been used for the off-line assessment of student's domain knowledge from problem solving performance (Collins et al., 1996; Gitomer et al., 1995; Martin and VanLehn, 1995; Mislevy, 1995; Petrushin and Sinitsa, 1993), but none of these systems uses the information in the Bayesian student model to guide a real-time tutorial dialogue. One reason for this may be that belief updating in Bayesian networks is in the worst case NP-Hard, and this intractability often manifests itself when the application calls for large and complex models, as is the case with Intelligent Tutoring Systems.

In ANDES, the computational complexity of the network evaluation is definitely an issue. Our networks are fine-grained models of the complex reasoning involved in physics problem solving and can contain from 200 nodes for a simple problem to 1000 nodes for a complex one. Moreover, since ANDES will be part of the curriculum of the introductory physics course at the United States Naval Academy, its response time will be a decisive factor for the success of the innovation that ANDES represents for the classical curriculum. We are devoting great effort to obtain acceptable performances from our student model by using approximate anytime algorithms based on stochastic sampling.

3   The ANDES Tutoring System

The ANDES project is a joint collaboration between the University of Pittsburgh and the Naval Academy involving about 10 researchers and programmers. Beginning in 1998, ANDES will be used by approximately 200 students per semester in the introductory physics class at the United States Naval Academy. ANDES is implemented in Allegro Common Lisp and Microsoft Visual C++ on a Pentium PC running Windows 95.

ANDES has a modular architecture comprising, besides the Assessor, a graphical Workbench with which the student solves physics problems, an Action Interpreter that provides immediate feedback to student actions, and a Help System.[1] ANDES' Help System comprises three separate modules responsible for Procedural, Conceptual, and Meta Help (VanLehn, 1996). The probabilities calculated by the Assessor will be used by the Help modules, both to *diagnose* which concepts the student needs more detailed tutoring on, and to *predict* what hints are most relevant to the student's current strategy. The knowledge assessment capabilities of the Assessor can be used to select appropriate problems for the student, and can also serve as an additional assessment tool for the teacher.

4   Probabilistic Assessment in ANDES

4.1   The Solution Graph Representation

One of the issues that must be considered when using Bayesian networks for plan recognition is where the network and its parameters come from. Designing the network by hand for each plan recognition task requires a considerable knowledge engineering effort and it is an unacceptable

---

[1] All modules except the Help System have already been implemented. The Help System will be implemented in the next version of ANDES.

option in a system like ANDES, where teachers should be able to easily extend and modify the set of physics problems available to students.

In POLA we solved this problem by adopting the approach, introduced by Huber et al. (1994) and Martin and VanLehn (1995), of automatically constructing its Bayesian networks from the output of a problem solver that generated all the acceptable solutions and solution plans to a problem. Similarly, the solution graph structure used by ANDES' Assessor is generated prior to run time by a rule-based physics problem solver. The rules are being developed in collaboration with three physics professors from the Naval Academy, who are the domain experts for the ANDES project.

Since the output of the problem solver will be used to model the student's activity and make tutoring decisions, it is important to choose an appropriate grain size for its knowledge representation. We have based ANDES' problem-solving rules on the representation used by Cascade (VanLehn et al., 1992), a computational model of knowledge acquisition developed from an analysis of protocols of students studying worked example problems. This analysis results in a rather fine grain size which, as we will discuss in Section 4.4, can produce large models that pose a real challenge for current Bayesian network updating algorithms. However, we argue that such a fine-grained representation is necessary for making the kinds of tutoring decisions ANDES will make.

Both POLA's and ANDES' problem solvers contain knowledge about the qualitative and quantitative reasoning necessary to solve complex physics problems. However, while POLA's problem solver generates plain sequences of solution steps (Conati and VanLehn, 1996a), AN-DES' problem solver has explicit knowledge about the abstract planning steps that an expert might use to solve problems, and about which ANDES will tutor students. Thus, it produces a hierarchical dependency network including, in addition to all acceptable solutions to the problem in terms of qualitative propositions and equations, the abstract plans for how to generate those solutions. This network is called the *problem solution graph*, and is the starting point for the construction of the Assessor module's Bayesian network.

The Problem Solver starts with a set of propositions describing the situation, and a goal statement that identifies the sought quantity for the problem. It begins by iteratively applying rules from its rule set, generating sub-goals and intermediate propositions. When it reaches an equation, it determines what quantities in the equation are still unknown and forms new sub-goals to find the values of those quantities, so that it will be possible to solve for the sought quantity when all the sub-goals have been achieved.

For example, consider the problem statement shown in Figure 1A. The problem solver starts with the top-level goal of finding the value of the normal force N_{at}. From this, it forms the sub-goal of using Newton's second law to find this value. Next, it generates three sub-goals corresponding to the three high level steps specified in the procedure to apply Newton's second law $(\Sigma(F_i) = m * a)$: (1) choose a body/bodies to which to apply the law, (2) identify all the forces on the body, (3) write the component equations for $\Sigma(F_i) = m * a$. The resulting plan is a partially ordered network of goals and sub-goals leading from the top-level goal to a set of equations that are sufficient to solve for the sought quantity.

Figure 1B shows a section of the solution graph for the problem in Figure 1A involving the application of Newton's second law to find the value of the normal force. In the following section we use this example to show how the solution graph is converted into a Bayesian network by the

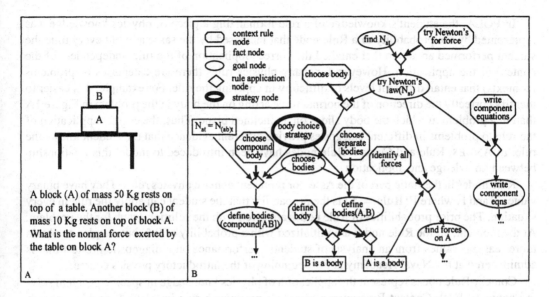

A block (A) of mass 50 Kg rests on top of a table. Another block (B) of mass 10 Kg rests on top of block A. What is the normal force exerted by the table on block A?

Figure 1. A physics problem and corresponding solution graph segment.

Assessor module, and describe the different types of nodes in the network and the relationships between them.

4.2 The Assessor's Bayesian Network

The Assessor Bayesian network consists of two parts, one static and one dynamic. The static part is built when the ANDES domain knowledge is defined and is maintained across problems. The dynamic part is automatically generated when the student selects a new problem and is discarded when the problem is solved. The following sections will describe the semantics and the structure of the nodes in the static and in the dynamic network.

As far as the parameterization of the network is concerned, we mainly rely on canonical interactions, known as Noisy/Leaky-OR and Noisy/Leaky-AND (Henrion, 1989), to automatically specify the conditional probabilities in the network. These canonical interactions are good approximations of the probabilistic relationships in the network and provide a fundamental advantage: they reduce logarithmically the number of conditional probabilities required to specify the interaction between a node and its parents by requiring only a single parameter that represents the noise or the leak in the canonical interaction. At the moment the parameters in the canonical interactions, along with the prior probabilities in the network, derive from our rough estimates. We plan to refine them based on the judgment of the domain experts in the ANDES project.

The static part of the Assessor. The static part of the Assessor consists of Rule nodes and Context-Rule nodes. We use these two kinds of nodes to model what it means for a student to know a piece of physics knowledge. Our definition is that a student knows a rule when she is able to apply it correctly whenever it is required to solve a problem, i.e. in all possible contexts.

In POLA, the student's knowledge of a rule formalizing a piece of physics knowledge was represented by the probability of a Rule node that increased by the same amount every time the student performed an action that entailed the correct application of the rule, independent of the context of the application. However, for many physics rules there are categories of problems (contexts) that entail different levels of difficulty in applying the rule. For example, it is easier to identify correctly the direction of the normal force acting on the body in the problem in Figure 1A than in a problem in which the body slides on an inclined plane. Thus, the correct application of the rule to problems in different categories provide different evidence that the student knows the rule. In ANDES, Rule and Context-Rule nodes have been introduced to model this relationship between knowledge and application.

Rule nodes in the static part of the Assessor represent generic physics rules. They have binary values T and F, where $P(\text{Rule} = T)$ is the probability that the student can apply the rule in every situation. The prior probabilities of Rule nodes are given with the solution graph for the problem. At the moment, all the Rule nodes are initialized with a probability of 0.5, but we plan to obtain more realistic values from an analysis of students' performance on a diagnostic pre-test that is administered at the Naval Academy at the beginning of the introductory physics course.

Context-Rule nodes represent the application of physics knowledge in specific problem solving contexts. Each Context-Rule corresponds to a production rule in ANDES' problem solver. Context-Rules are shown in Figure 1B as the octagonal nodes. For each Rule node the Assessor contains as many Context-Rule nodes as there are contexts defined for that rule. Context-Rule nodes have binary values T and F, where $P(\text{Context-Rule} = T)$ is the probability that the student knows how to apply the rule to every problem in the corresponding context. Each Context-Rule node has only one parent, the Rule node representing the corresponding rule.

$P(\text{Context-Rule}_N = T|\text{Rule} = T)$ is always equal to 1, since by definition $P(\text{Rule} = T)$ means that the student can apply the rule in any context. $P(\text{Context-Rule}_N = T|\text{Rule} = F)$ represents the probability that the student can apply the general rule in the corresponding context even if she cannot apply it in all contexts. This probability implicitly defines the level of difficulty of a context for the application of a rule—the easier the context, the higher this conditional probability.

As we will illustrate in Section 4.3, the marginal probabilities of Rules and Context-Rules will carry over from one problem to the next, encoding the long-term knowledge assessment for each student that has been solving problems with Andes.

The structure of the static part of the student model entails two *independence* assumptions. The first assumption is that Rule nodes are independent of each other, the second is that Context-Rule nodes are conditionally independent given Rule nodes. These assumptions simplify the modeling task and reduce the computational complexity of belief updating. However, they do not always hold in the physics domain, and we are planning to work with the domain experts to model correctly the existing dependencies.

The dynamic part of the Assessor. The dynamic part of the Assessor contains Context-Rule nodes and four additional types of nodes: Fact, Goal, Rule-Application and Strategy nodes. All the nodes are read into the network from the solution graph for the current problem at the beginning of problem solving. The structure of the solution graph already encodes the causal structure of the problem solutions and therefore is maintained in the Bayesian network. For example, a segment of the Bayesian network created for the problem in Figure 1A corresponds exactly to the solution graph segment in Figure 1B.

Fact and Goal nodes. Fact and Goal nodes look the same from the point of view of the Bayesian network. They both represent information that is derived while solving a problem by applying rules from the knowledge base. The difference between Goal and Fact nodes is in their meaning to the help system: The probability of Goal nodes will be used to construct hints focused on the qualitative analysis of the problem and on the planning of the solution, while the probabilities of Fact nodes will be used to provide more specific hints on the actual solution steps.

Goal and Fact nodes have binary values T and F. $P(\text{Fact} = T)$ is the probability that the student knows that fact. $P(\text{Goal} = T)$ is the probability that the student has been pursuing that goal. A weakness of the current representation of Goal nodes is that the probability $P(\text{Goal} = T)$ does not specify whether the student has simply established the goal during the problem solving process or she has also accomplished it. The distinction between established and accomplished goals is crucial for the help system since the student may need help in reaching a goal that she has established but not on a goal that she has already accomplished. At the moment we use a separate procedure to detect the goals that have already been accomplished when the Help System needs to intervene.

Goal and Fact nodes have as many parents as there are ways to derive them. The conditional probabilities between Fact and Goal nodes and their parents are described by a Leaky-OR relationship (Pearl, 1988). This models the fact that a Fact or Goal node is true if the student performed at least one of the inferences that derive it, but it can also be true when none of these inferences happened because the student may use an alternative way to generate the result, such as guessing or drawing an analogy to another problem's solution.

Strategy nodes. Strategy nodes represent points where the student can choose among alternative plans to solve a problem. Strategy nodes are the only non-binary nodes in the network: they have as many values as there are alternative strategies. The children of Strategy nodes are the Rule-Application nodes that represent the implementation of the different strategies. In Figure 1B, for example, the strategy node *body choice strategy* points to the two application nodes representing respectively the decisions to choose block A and block B as separate bodies and to choose as a body the compound of the two blocks.

The values of a Strategy node are mutually exclusive strategies which represent the fact that, at each solution step, the student is following exactly one of the represented strategies. Thus, evidence for one strategy decreases the probability of the others. Like Rule nodes, strategy nodes have no parents in the solution graph.

Rule-Application nodes. Rule-Application nodes connect Context-Rule, Strategy, Fact and Goal nodes to new derived Fact and Goal nodes. Rule-Application nodes have values T and F. $P(\text{Rule-Application} = T)$ represents the probability that the student has applied the corresponding Context-Rule to the facts and goals representing its preconditions to derive the facts and goals representing its conclusions.

The parents of each Rule-Application node include exactly one Context-Rule, some number of Fact and/or Goal nodes, and optionally one Strategy node. The probabilistic relationship

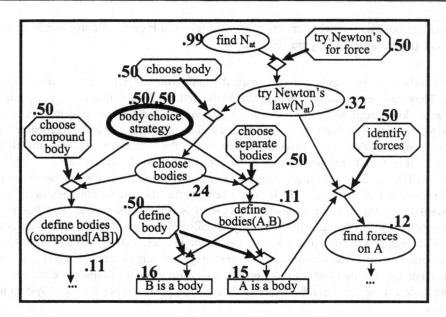

Figure 2. The network before observing A-is-a-body.

between the Rule-Application node and its parents is a Noisy-AND. The noise in the AND relationship models the probability that the student will not apply the rule even if all the preconditions are known.

4.3 Example of Propagation of Evidence in the Assessor

Suppose that a student is trying to solve the problem in Figure 1A and that her first action is to select Block A as the body. In response to this action the fact node *A-is-a-body* is clamped to T. Figure 2 shows the probabilities in the network before the action. Note that the *a priori* probability of Fact and Goal nodes is rather low, especially when the evidence is far from the givens in the network, because of the large number of inferences which must be made in conjunction in order to derive the corresponding facts and goals.

After the first action, evidence propagates upward increasing the probability of its parent nodes *define-body* and *define-bodies-(A,B)*, as shown in Figure 3. The upward propagation also increases slightly the probability of the value *separate-bodies* of the Strategy node *body-choice-strategy*, represented in Figure 3 by the right number of the pair associated to the strategy node. The changes in the probabilities of nodes that are ancestors of the observed action represent the model's assessment of what knowledge the student has brought to bear to generate the action. The fact that such changes are quite modest is due to the leak in the Leaky-OR relation between the observed Fact node and its parent Application node. Given the current low probability of the Application node the leak absorbs most of the evidence provided by the student's action. In general the influence of the leaks in the network will decrease as the student performs more correct actions.

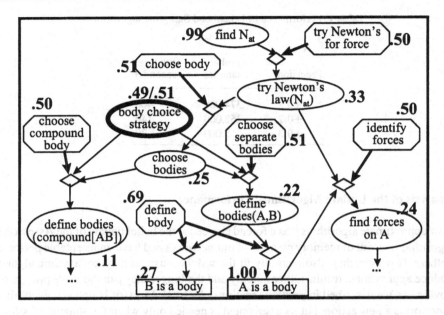

Figure 3. The network after observing A-is-a-body.

At this point, downward propagation changes the probabilities of yet to be observed nodes, thus predicting what inferences the student is likely to make. In particular, the relationship enforced by the Strategy node *body-choice-strategy* on its children will slightly diminish the probability of the Goal node *define-bodies(AB)*. Moreover, the increased probability of the Goal node *define-bodies(A,B)* will propagate downward to increase the probability of the Fact node *B-is-a-body* while the increased probability of the Fact node *A-is-a-body* will slightly increase the probability of the Goal node *find-Forces-on(A)*, as shown in Figure 3.

If the student asks for help after having selected block A as a body, the Help System separates the nodes that are ancestors of the performed actions from the nodes that can be directly or indirectly derived from the performed actions. The Goal and Fact nodes in the latter group represent the set of inferences that the student has not yet expressed as actions, and from which the Help System can choose to suggest to the student how to proceed. The probabilities of these nodes will aid the Help System in deciding what particular inference to choose.

Once the student has completed a problem, the dynamic part of the Bayesian network is eliminated and the probabilities assessed for the Context-Rules that were included in the solution graph for the problem are propagated in the static part of the network. Upward propagation in the static network will modify the probability of Rule nodes, generating long-term assessment of the student physics knowledge. Downward propagation from Rule nodes to Context-Rule nodes not involved in the last solved problem generates predictions of how easy it will be for the student to apply the corresponding rules in different contexts.

Table 1. Performance of Likelihood Sampling algorithm.

Precision	Number of samples	Run time (seconds)
±0.1	1,374,000	400
±0.2	362,000	140
±0.3	5,000	30

4.4 Analysis of the Update Algorithms' Performance

The use of approximate algorithms was a forced choice for the belief update of the Assessor, since exact algorithms run out of memory on most of our networks and have unacceptable performance on the others. However, they also naturally fit the task because, as they are anytime algorithms, they produce approximate results rather quickly and the longer they run the more precise results they provide. As we described in previous sections, ANDES' Assessor is updated every time the student performs a new action, but its assessment is needed only when the student asks for help. The Bayesian network is updated in a background thread, so the student can go on working on the Workbench without any awareness that the network calculation is happening, until she invokes the Help System. Only then the student may have to wait until the results of the belief updating algorithm are precise enough for the Help system to generate a reliable response.

We have tested the time taken by two different stochastic sampling algorithms, Logic Sampling and Likelihood Sampling (Cousins et al., 1993), to bring the probability of every node in a representative network within a small threshold precision. The network we tested had to be small enough to also run an exact evaluation algorithm to produce the exact posterior probabilities for comparison. The network was generated from a very simple problem and had 110 nodes. Stochastic sampling algorithms typically do not perform well on networks with unlikely evidence, as our networks often are, and we found that the Likelihood Sampling algorithm was the only one with acceptable performances on our test network.

Table 1 shows the number of samples and running time it took Likelihood Sampling to get all nodes in the network within a precision of ±0.1, ±0.2, and ±0.3, compared with the probabilities calculated by the exact algorithm, when all actions that form the problem solutions have been observed.

The running time of stochastic algorithms increases approximately linearly with the number of nodes. Therefore, given the results in Table 1, Likelihood Sampling would take several minutes to update to high precision our largest networks, which are up to ten times larger than our test network. On the other hand, we have observed that the students who have used ANDES so far usually pause for a while before asking for help and the Assessor has some time to run the updating algorithm. Besides, when Likelihood Sampling reaches the 0.2 precision for all the nodes 98% of the nodes are already within 0.1 precision, and when it reaches the 0.3 precision 98% of the nodes are already within 0.2 and 66% of the nodes are within 0.1 precision. Therefore, it may be the case that we won't need dramatically better updating time in order for the Assessor to reach acceptable performances. While we intend to continue to work on improving the speed of the Assessor's belief updating, we also plan to run pilot subjects to measure the average waiting time before a help request, and to evaluate what precision thresholds will allow for adequate assessment.

5   Conclusions and Future Work

The Bayesian student modeling framework presented in this paper contributes to research on probabilistic user modeling in a number of ways. First, it uses a probabilistic framework to perform three kinds of assessment: plan recognition, prediction of students' goals and actions, and long-term assessment of the student's domain knowledge. Second, it performs plan recognition by integrating in a principled way knowledge about the student's behavior and mental state with knowledge about the available plans. Third, it represents a substantial effort toward obtaining acceptable real time performance in the evaluation of very complex Bayesian networks (ranging from 200 to 1000 nodes) to be used for the on-line tailoring of the dialogue with the student.

In this paper we have described in detail the structure of the Bayesian network and how it is automatically constructed from the output of a problem solver that generates all of the acceptable abstract solution plans and actions sequences to solve a problem. We have also presented a preliminary evaluation of the performance of the Assessor's update algorithms on a representative network.

A number of issues remain to be addressed for the ANDES Assessor. The first is to improve the performance of belief updating. We are currently exploring the possibility of applying methods based on relevance and focused reasoning (Druzdzel and Suermondt, 1994; Lin and Druzdzel, 1997), which we believe will lead to a significant speedup of our algorithms. Second, the knowledge base used by the problem solver will be further developed. In particular, we plan to add incorrect rules corresponding to common physics misconceptions. Third, we will work with our domain experts to refine the parameters in the Bayesian networks and to model dependencies among physics rules. Fourth, we will explore how to make the Assessor able to take into account student actions that do not correspond to a correct entry in the solution graph, such as erroneous entries and deletion of previous entries.

More issues could be addressed to refine the accuracy of the student model, such as how to explicitly represent time in the Bayesian network to take into consideration the temporal sequencing of the student actions and changes in the students' knowledge due to forgetting. On the other hand, as Self (1988) points out, the complexity of a student model should always be calibrated against the accuracy of its predictions. We believe that it is important to continuously verify the adequacy of the model as we develop it, through formative evaluations with the intended users of the system. ANDES' Assessor will be incrementally modified and improved as we gain insight from these evaluations.

References

Anderson, J., Corbett, A., Koedinger, K., and Pelletier, R. (1995). Cognitive tutors: Lessons learned. *The Journal of the Learning Sciences* 4(2):167–207.

Carberry, S. (1990). Incorporating default inferences into plan recognition. In *Proceedings of the 8th National Conference on Artificial Intelligence*, 471–478.

Charniak, E., and Goldman, R. (1993). A Bayesian model of plan recognition. *Artificial Intelligence* 64(1):53–79.

Collins, J. A., Greer, J. E., and Huang, S. X. (1996). Adaptive assessment using granularity hierarchies and Bayesian nets. In Frasson, C., Gauthier, G., and Lesgold, A., eds., *Proceedings of the 3rd International Conference on Intelligent Tutoring Systems ITS '96*. Berlin: Springer. 569–577.

Conati, C., and VanLehn, K. (1996a). POLA: a student modeling framework for Probabilistic On-Line Assessment of problem solving performance. In *Proceedings of the 5th International Conference on User Modeling*, 75–82.

Conati, C., and VanLehn, K. (1996b). Probabilistic plan recognition for cognitive apprenticeship. In *Proceedings of the 18th Annual Conference of the Cognitive Science Society*, 403–408.

Cousins, S., Chen, W., and Frisse, M. (1993). A tutorial introduction to stochastic simulation algorithms for belief networks. *Artificial Intelligence in Medicine* 5:315–340.

Druzdzel, M. J., and Suermondt, H. J. (1994). Relevance in probabilistic models: "Backyards" in a "small world". In *Working notes of the AAAI-1994 Fall Symposium Series: Relevance*, 60–63.

Genesereth, M. (1982). The role of plans in intelligent teaching systems. In Sleeman, D., and Brown, J. S., eds., *Intelligent Tutoring Systems*. New York: Academic Press. 137–156.

Gitomer, D., Steinberg, H., S., L., and Mislevy, R. J. (1995). 'Diagnostic assessment of troubleshooting skill in an intelligent tutoring system. In Nichols, P., Chipman, S., and Brennan, R., L., eds., *Cognitively Diagnostic Assessment*. Hillsdale, NJ: Erlbaum.

Henrion, M. (1989). Some practical issues in constructing belief networks. In Kanal, L. N., Levitt, T. S., and Lemmer, J. F., eds., *Proceedings of the 3rd Conference on Uncertainty in Artificial Intelligence*, 161–173. Elsevier Science Publishers.

Huber, M., Durfee, E., and Wellman, M. (1994). The automated mapping of plans for plan recognition. In *Proceedings of the 10th Conference on Uncertainty in Artificial Intelligence*, 344–351.

Jameson, A. (1996). Numerical uncertainty management in user and student modeling: An overview of systems and issues. *User Modeling and User-Adapted Interaction* 5(3-4):193–251.

Kohen, G., and Greer, J. (1993). Recognizing plans in instructional systems using granularity. In *Proceedings of the 4th International Conference on User Modeling*, 133–138.

Lin, Y., and Druzdzel, M. J. (1997). Computational advantages of relevance reasoning in Bayesian belief networks. In *Proceedings of the 13th Conference on Uncertainty in Artificial Intelligence*. To appear.

Martin, J., and VanLehn, K. (1995). A Bayesian approach to cognitive assessment. In Nichols, P., Chipman, S., and Brennan, R. L., eds., *Cognitively Diagnostic Assessment*. Hillsdale, NJ: Erlbaum.

Mislevy, R. J. (1995). Probability-based inference in cognitive diagnosis. In Nichols, P., Chipman, S., and Brennan, R., L., eds., *Cognitively Diagnostic Assessment*. Hillsdale, NJ: Erlbaum.

Pearl, J. (1988). *Probabilistic Reasoning in Intelligent Systems: Networks of Plausible inference*. Los Altos, CA: Morgan Kaufmann.

Petrushin, V. A., and Sinitsa, K. M. (1993). Using probabilistic reasoning techniques for learner modeling. In *Proceedings of the 1993 World Conference on AI and Education*, 426–432.

Pynadath, D. V., and Wellman, M. P. (1995). Accounting for context in plan recognition, with application to traffic monitoring. In *Proceedings of the 11h Conference on Uncertainty in Artificial Intelligence*, 472–481.

Ross, P., and Lewis, J. (1988). Plan recognition for intelligent tutoring systems. In Ercoli, P., and Lewis, R., eds., *Artificial Intelligence Tools in Education*. Amsterdam: Elsevier Science Publishers. 29–37.

Self, J. (1988). Bypassing the intractable problem of student modeling. In *Proceedings of Intelligent Tutoring Systems '88*, 18–24.

VanLehn, K., Jones, R. M., and Chi, M. T. H. (1992). A model of the self-explanation effect. *The Journal of the Learning Sciences* 2(1):1–59.

VanLehn, K. (1996). Conceptual and meta learning during coached problem solving. In Frasson, C., Gauthier, G., and Lesgold, A., eds., *Proceedings of the 3rd International Conference on Intelligent Tutoring Systems ITS '96*. Berlin: Springer. 29–47.

Student Modeling in the ACT Programming Tutor: Adjusting a Procedural Learning Model With Declarative Knowledge

Albert T. Corbett and Akshat Bhatnagar[*]

Human Computer Interaction Institute, Carnegie Mellon University, Pittsburgh, PA, U.S.A.

Abstract. This paper describes a successful effort to increase the predictive validity of student modeling in the ACT Programming Tutor (APT). APT is an intelligent tutor constructed around a cognitive model of programming knowledge. As the student works, the tutor estimates the student's growing knowledge of the component production rules in a process called *knowledge tracing*. Knowledge tracing employs a simple two-state learning model and Bayesian updates and has proven quite accurate in predicting student posttest performance, although with a small systematic tendency to overestimate test performance. This paper describes a simple three-state model in which the student may acquire non-ideal programming rules that do not transfer to the test environment. A series of short tests assess students' declarative knowledge and these assessments are used to adjust knowledge tracing in the tutor. The resulting model eliminates over-prediction of posttest performance and more accurately predicts individual differences among students.

Mastery learning holds out the promise that virtually all students can master a domain if the domain knowledge is analyzed into a hierarchy of component knowledge units and if learning is structured so that students master prerequisites before moving to higher level knowledge (Bloom, 1968; Carroll, 1963; Keller, 1968). Meta-analyses confirm that mastery learning yields higher achievement levels (Kulik et al., 1990), but achievement gains in conventional mastery learning fall short of early expectations (Resnick, 1977; Slavin, 1987).

The ACT Programming Tutor (APT) is an intelligent tutoring system that employs a detailed cognitive model of programming knowledge in an attempt to achieve mastery learning. Our goal in the tutor is to monitor the student's growing procedural knowledge in the course of problem solving, provide sufficient learning opportunities for mastery and accurately predict students test performance. This paper describes an important step forward in this modeling process: By incorporating an independent measure of students' prerequisite declarative knowledge we substantially improve the predictive validity of the modeling process.

In this paper we briefly describe the learning environment, the cognitive model, the learning and performance assumptions that underlie knowledge tracing, and the empirical validity of knowledge tracing. We describe a battery of declarative knowledge assessments we have developed and describe the improved predictive accuracy that is achieved by incorporating them into the model.

---

[*] This research was supported by the Office of Naval Research grant N00014-95-1-0847. We thank Dana Heath and Michele Mellott for assistance in data collection.

1   The ACT Programming Tutor

APT is a problem solving environment in which students learn to write short programs in Lisp, Pascal or Prolog. Each of these three modules is constructed around a language-specific cognitive model of the knowledge the student is acquiring. The cognitive model enables the tutor to trace the student's solution path through a complex problem solving space, providing feedback on problem solving actions and, if requested, advice on steps that achieve problem solving goals. This process, which we call *model tracing,* has been shown to speed learning by as much as a factor of three and to increase achievement levels relative to those of students working on their own (Anderson et al., 1995).

Figure 1 displays the ACT Programming Tutor Lisp Module midway through an exercise. The student has previously read text presented in the window at the lower right and is completing a sequence of corresponding exercises. The problem description appears in the upper left window and the student's solution appears in the code window immediately below. The student selects operator templates and types constants and identifiers in the user action window in the middle right. In this figure the student has encoded the operator *defun,* which is used to define a new operator, and has entered the operator name, declared input variables and begun coding the body of the definition. The three angle-bracket symbols in the figure, <EXPR1>, <PROCESS1> and <EXPR0>, are placeholders which the student will either replace with additional Lisp code or delete. Communications from the tutor appear in the Hint window in the lower left. In this figure the student has asked for a hint on how to proceed.

The tutor also tracks the student's growing procedural knowledge across problems in a process we call *knowledge tracing,* which is the focus of this paper. In *knowledge tracing,* the student is represented as an overlay of the ideal model (Goldstein, 1982). The Skill Meter in the upper right corner of Figure 1 depicts the tutor's model of the student's knowledge state. Each entry in the Skill Meter represents a production rule in the cognitive model of programming knowledge. The shading represents the probability that the student knows the rule and a check mark indicates that the student has mastered the rule.

1.1   The Cognitive Model

The tutors reflect the ACT-R theory of skill knowledge (Anderson, 1993). This theory assumes a fundamental distinction between declarative knowledge and procedural knowledge. Declarative knowledge is factual or experiential. For example, the following sentence and example in the Lisp text would be encoded declaratively:

The Lisp function *car* takes a list and returns the first element.

For example, *(car '(a b c d))* returns *a.*

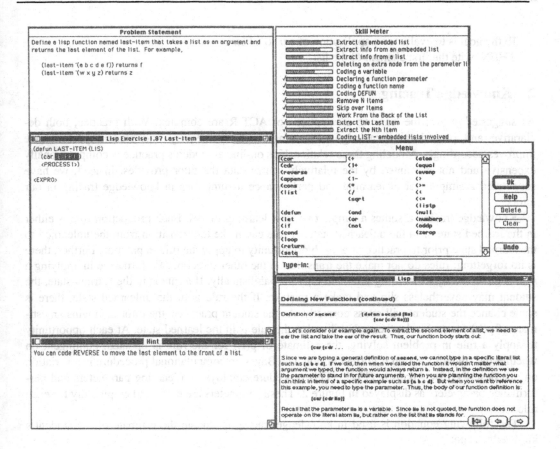

Figure 1. The APT Lisp Tutor interface.

Procedural knowledge, in contrast, is goal-oriented and mediates problem-solving behavior. ACT-R assumes that skill knowledge is encoded initially in declarative form through experiences such as reading and that domain-specific procedural knowledge results from problem solving. With practice, declarative and procedural knowledge are strengthened so that performance grows more rapid and reliable. Like many cognitive theories, ACT-R assumes that procedural knowledge can be represented as a set of independent production rules that associate problem states and problem-solving goals with actions and consequent state changes. The following two goal-oriented productions can be derived from the declarative example above through practice in writing function calls and evaluating function calls respectively:

IF the goal is to code an expression that returns the first element of a list.
THEN code the operator *car* and set a goal to code the list as its argument.

IF the goal is to evaluate an application of *car* to a list,
THEN write the first element of the list.

2 Knowledge Tracing

As suggested above, the learning assumptions of ACT-R are complex. With practice, both declarative and procedural knowledge are strengthened in memory and student performance
improves accordingly. Modeling these relationships on-line as students practice is computationally
expensive and not warranted by the relatively sparse data the tutor provides. Instead, we have
substituted a simpler set of learning and performance assumptions in knowledge tracing in our
tutors.

Knowledge tracing assumes a simple two-state learning model. Each production rule is either
in the learned state or in the unlearned state. A rule can make the transition from the unlearned to
the learned state prior to practice or at each opportunity to apply the rule in practice. Further, there
is no forgetting; rules do not make the transition in the other direction. Performance in applying a
rule is governed by its learning state, but only probabilistically. If a rule is in the learned state, the
student may nevertheless slip and make a mistake. If the rule is in the unlearned state, there is
some chance the student will guess correctly. As the student practices, the tutor maintains an estimate of p(L) for each rule, the probability that the rule is in the learned state. At each opportunity
to apply a rule in problem solving, the estimate of p(L) for the rule is updated, contingent on
whether the student's action is correct or not. The Bayesian computational procedure is a variation
on one described by Atkinson (1972). This procedure employs two learning parameters and performance parameters as displayed in Figure 2. These parameters are estimated empirically for each
rule.

The following equation is used in knowledge tracing to update the estimate of the student's
knowledge state:

$$p(L_n) = p(L_{n-1}| \text{ evidence}) + (1 - p(L_{n-1}| \text{ evidence})) * p(T) \qquad (1)$$

The probability that a rule is in the learned state following the nth opportunity to apply the rule,
$p(L_n)$, is the sum of two probabilities: (1) the posterior probability that the ideal rule was already
in the learned state contingent on the evidence (whether or not the nth action is correct) and (2) the
probability that the rule will make the transition to the learned state if it is not already there. We
use a Bayesian inference scheme to estimate the posterior probability that the rule is already in the
learned state $p(L_{n-1}| \text{ evidence})$. Following Atkinson (1972) the probability $p(T)$ of a transition
from the unlearned to the learned state during procedural practice is independent of whether the
student applies the rule correctly or incorrectly.

Individual differences among students are also incorporated into the model in the form of four
weights, one for each of the four parameter types, wL_0, wT, wG and wS. When the model is adjusted for a student, each of the four probability parameters for each rule is converted to odds form
$(p/(1-p))$, it is multiplied by the corresponding subject-specific weight, and the resulting odds are
converted back to a probability. A best fitting set of weights for each subject is generated with a

curve-fitting program for research purposes. In the tutor, these weights are estimated dynamically by means of regression equations based on raw error rates.

Knowledge tracing is employed in the tutor to implement mastery learning. In each section of the tutor curriculum the student reads an accompanying text that introduces a set of coding rules. The tutor follows with a set of exercises that provide practice on the rules. The student continues practicing exercises in a section until reaching a criterion knowledge probability for each rule in the set. That mastery criterion in the tutor is a knowledge probability of 0.975.

$p(L_0)$	Initial Learning	The probability that a rule is in the learned state prior to the first opportunity to apply the rule
$p(T)$	Acquisition	The probability that a rule will move from the unlearned to the learned state at each opportunity to apply the rule
$p(G)$	Guess	The probability that a student will guess correctly if a rule is in the unlearned state
$p(S)$	Slip	The probability that a student will slip (make a mistake) if a rule is in the learned state

Figure 2. The learning and performance parameters in knowledge tracing.

2.1 Empirical Evaluation of Knowledge Tracing

Knowledge tracing has been shown to be an effective learning tool. Students perform better on tests with knowledge tracing and remediation than in a condition in which students work through a fixed set of required problems in the tutor (Anderson et al., 1989; Corbett and Anderson, 1995a). While the most capable students may require no additional remedial problems to perform well in the tutor and on tests, other students may complete three or four times the number of required problems in remediation.

In addition, we have completed two assessments of the predictive validity of knowledge tracing (Corbett and Anderson, 1995b). The two studies had similar outcomes; the results of the second study are displayed in Table 1. As can be seen, knowledge tracing is reasonably accurate at predicting average performance on tests and moderately sensitive to individual differences. The correlation between actual and expected performance is marginally reliable for the second test and reliable and quite strong for the third test. The tests are cumulative. In the third test in this study, 56% of students in the knowledge tracing condition achieved test scores of about 90% correct or better, compared to 24% in a comparison condition in which students completed a minimum set of required problems.

Overestimating students' test performance. A consistent result in these two studies is that the knowledge tracing process tends to overestimate student performance. In Table 1 performance is overestimated by an average of about 8%. It is important to understand the nature of this overestimation in progressing toward our goal of enabling all students to reach mastery. There are at least two possible explanations for the model's overestimation: retention and transfer.

Table 1. Actual and expected proportion of exercises completed correctly across students in each of the three tests (Corbett and Anderson, 1995b).

	Mean Proportion Correct		
	Actual	Expected	Correlation[a]
Test 1	0.88	0.94	0.24
Test 2	0.81	0.89	0.36
Test 3	0.81	0.86	0.66

[a] Correlation between actual and expected proportion correct across students.

Since the tests in these studies are cumulative, the first possibility is that students fail to meet the tutor's expectations because they are forgetting material from earlier curriculum sections. The first test follows the first curriculum section, the second test follows the fourth curriculum section and the third test follows the fifth curriculum section. By the time they take the second and third tests, students may have forgotten material from the first few sections.

The second possibility is that students are acquiring suboptimal rules in the tutor environment that are sufficient to perform adequately in that environment but do not fully generalize to the test environment. For example, students may acquire rules that are sufficient when domain knowledge is partitioned into curriculum sections as in the tutor but insufficient when the partitioning is eliminated in the cumulative tests. Students may even acquire rules that hinge on specifics of the tutor interface, e.g., "use the operator that is not yet checked off in the skill meter". Students who have not adequately learned prerequisite declarative knowledge will be most vulnerable to forming such suboptimal rules. In a recent study we collected data on students' declarative knowledge that enable us to examine this possibility.

3 Declarative Knowledge Measures

As described earlier, students read text in each curriculum section before completing programming problems. We recently administered a series of tests to students that were designed to assess students' knowledge of the factual material in the text and their ability to reason with that knowledge in problem solving. One or two tests were administered after students read the text and before they completed tutor exercises in each of the first five Lisp curriculum sections. These tests tapped students': (1) factual knowledge of Lisp operators, (2) factual knowledge of list structure, (3) ability to evaluate Lisp code (at two points in the curriculum) and (4) judgments of programming problem similarity (again at two points). A factor analysis performed on these tests revealed two underlying factors, as shown in Table 2. We proposed that Factor 2 reflects declarative knowledge of the text, since tests of basic Lisp operators and list structure load heavily on this factor, and that Factor 1 reflects students' ability to bring declarative knowledge to bear appropriately in problem solving, because of the heavy loading of students' problem similarity ratings. (See Corbett and Knapp, 1996, for more details on the declarative measures and the factor analysis.) The correlations displayed in Table 3 are consistent with this analysis. In this table we have correlated students' scores on the two declarative knowledge factors with their best fitting individual difference weights for the two learning parameters in the tutor's procedural learning model. These best fitting individual difference weights essentially reflect students' error rates in completing tutor exercises. As can be seen, scores on the Factual Knowledge Factor are highly correlated with $\ln(wL_0)$, a measure of how well the student has acquired rules prior to the first practice opportunities. In contrast, the Reasoning Factor scores are highly correlated with $\ln(wT)$, a measure of how readily students acquire rules in the course of procedural practice. In this report we employ these declarative knowledge factors to evaluate the knowledge tracing and improve predictions of test performance.

4 The Study

Sixteen students in this study worked through the first five curriculum sections in the APT Lisp curriculum. This curriculum introduces two data structures, *atoms* and *lists*, and introduces *function calls*. The first section introduces three extractor functions, *car*, *cdr* and *reverse*. The second and third sections introduce three constructor functions, *append*, *cons* and *list*. The fourth section introduces extractor algorithms—nested function calls that apply successive extractor functions to extract components of lists. In the fifth section extractors and extractor algorithms are embedded as arguments to constructor function calls. These five curriculum sections contain 30 required tutor exercises.

Table 2. Loadings of six declarative knowledge measures on two factors that emerge in a factor analysis (Corbett and Knapp, 1996).

Declarative Test	Factor 1 Reasoning	Factor 2 Factual Knowledge
Lisp Operator Facts		0.85
List Structure Facts		0.77
Extractor Evaluation 1	0.49	0.54
Extractor Evaluation 2	0.54	0.56
Problem Similarity 1	0.75	
Problem Similarity 2	0.88	

Table 3. Correlation of factor scores and individual weights across students in the study (Corbett and Knapp, 1996).

Parameter weight		Factor 1 Reasoning	Factor 2 Factual Knowledge
$\ln(wL_0)$	(learning prior to problem solving)	0.20	0.65
$\ln(wT)$	(learning during problem solving)	0.52	0.34

In each curriculum section, students read text describing Lisp, completed one or two sets of questions on the text as described above, then completed a set of required programming exercises that covered the rules being introduced. Students then completed remedial exercises as needed to bring all production rules in the section to a mastery criterion (knowledge probability > .975). Finally, students completed cumulative programming tests following the first, fourth and fifth sections. These tests contained 6, 12 and 18 programming exercises, respectively. The cumulative test exercises were similar to the tutor exercises and the test interface was identical to the tutor interface, except that students could freely edit their code and received no tutorial assistance.

4.1 Results

Table 4 displays students' actual performance on the three tests in the study and the tutor's predictions of test performance on the basis of the knowledge tracing model. The correlation of actual and expected performance across students is reliable only for the third test, $r = 0.57$, $t(14) = 2.58$, $p < .05$. As can be seen, the model slightly overpredicts student performance for the more difficult second and third tests, as in earlier studies.

Test performance overestimation and forgetting. If the systematic tendency to overestimate quiz performance reflected forgetting between learning and test, we would expect the discrepancy between actual and expected scores to be monotonically related to the curriculum section number. We would expect the model's overestimation to increase as the interval between learning and test increases, so the overestimation should be greatest for the first curriculum section on each test. The model's overestimation should then systematically decrease on each test as we move forward through the curriculum sections. Table 5 displays actual and expected performance for problems grouped by curriculum section in Tests 2 and 3. As can be seen, the overprediction is smallest, rather than largest, for the first curriculum section, and it peaks in Curriculum Section 3, which contains the most challenging constructor problems. Consequently, forgetting is not a compelling explanation of the model's overestimation of test performance.

Table 4. Actual and expected proportion of exercises completed correctly in three tests.

	Mean proportion correct		
	Actual	Expected	Correlation[a]
Test 1	0.98	0.97	-0.28
Test 2	0.90	0.93	0.34
Test 3	0.85	0.90	0.57

[a] Correlation between actual and expected proportion correct across students.

Table 5. Actual and expected proportion correct as a function of tutor curriculum section.

Curriculum section	Test 2			Test 3		
	Actual	Expected	A–E[a]	Actual	Expected	A–E[a]
1	0.91	0.93	-0.02	0.89	0.93	-0.04
2	0.79	0.90	-0.11	0.76	0.90	-0.14
3	0.65	0.91	-0.26	0.65	0.89	-0.24
4	0.79	0.84	-0.05	0.76	0.90	-0.14
5	-	-	-	0.63	0.73	-0.10

[a] Actual minus expected scores.

Test performance overestimation and declarative knowledge. Table 6 displays the correlations between students' scores on the declarative knowledge factors derived from the battery of six declarative knowledge tests and (1) students' actual performance on the test and (2) the model's overestimation of students' test performance based on the knowledge tracing model. Not surprisingly, both declarative knowledge factors are strongly correlated with students' actual performance on both tests. All four of these correlations are statistically significant. More interestingly, students' declarative knowledge is correlated with the extent to which the tutor's knowledge tracing model of procedural learning overestimates their performance on the test. In particular, the tutor's overestimation of performance is strongly related to students' basic factual knowledge, although not to their ability to reason about knowledge in the problem solving context. The lower a student's factor score on basic factual knowledge, the more the tutor overestimates how well the student will perform on the test. Both of these correlations are statistically significant: For Test 2: $r = -0.63$, $t(14) = 3.06$, $p < .01$; for Test 3: $r = -0.64$, $t(14) = 3.14$, $p < .01$.

Table 6. The correlations of students' scores on the two declarative knowledge factors with their actual performance on Tests 2 and 3 and with the model's overestimation of their performance on these two tests.

	Test 2		Test 3	
Factor	Actual Performance	Model Overestimate	Actual Performance	Model Overestimate
Reasoning in Problem Solving	0.48	−0.11	0.54	−0.13
Factual Knowledge	0.67	−0.63	0.61	−0.64

5 Integrating Declarative Knowledge into Knowledge Tracing

We implemented a simple three-state model of learning to obtain an initial quantitative estimate of the impact of individual differences in factual knowledge on knowledge tracing. As in the existing model we assume that the student may learn no rule, or may learn an "ideal" rule that is sufficient for both tutor and test performance. The third possibility in this model is that the student may learn a suboptimal rule that is sufficient for the tutor but not in the test environment. Such a suboptimal rule will be indistinguishable from an ideal rule in modeling the student's tutor performance and be indistinguishable from no rule in predicting test performance. To predict test performance for student s in applying rule r on the test in this model, we simply adjusted the tutor's estimate that the student has learned the ideal rule, $p(L_{sr})$, with an additive term proportional to the student's Factual Knowledge factor score, FK_s. We assumed this proportion was constant across subjects and rules, so the probability that student s had learned an ideal version of rule r that would successfully generalize to the quiz became $p(L_{sr}) + (0.12 * FK_s)$.

We used this model to recompute predictions of students' test performance as displayed in Table 7. Given the correlations in Table 6, this model is certain to improve the quality of fit and, as can be seen in the table, (1) the tendency to overestimate test performance is essentially eliminated and (2) the model is now more sensitive to individual differences. The 0.81 correlation between actual and expected performance for Test 3 is reliably greater than the corresponding correlation of the earlier model (0.57 in Table 4), and this difference is marginally significant, $t(13) = 2.145$, $p < .06$. The difference between the 0.55 correlation for Test 2 in the new model and the earlier model (0.34 in Table 4) does not reach significance, however, $t(14) = 1.29$. These results suggest that incorporating factual knowledge can substantially improve the predictive validity of knowledge tracing, although it should be noted that these results represent an upper bound on the contribution of factual knowledge, since we are refitting the existing data with a best fitting estimate of the factual knowledge constant.

Table 7. Actual and expected proportion of exercises completed correctly across students in Tests 2 and 3 when declarative knowledge is integrated into the knowledge tracing model.

	Mean Proportion Correct		
	Actual	Expected	Correlation[a]
Test 2	0.90	0.91	0.55
Test 3	0.85	0.85	0.81

[a] Correlation between actual and expected proportion correct across students.

6 Discussion

The slight but consistent tendency of the knowledge tracing model to overestimate student performance on tests is shown not to reflect student forgetting but rather to be predicted by the quality of students' declarative knowledge. The lower a student's score on a basic declarative knowledge factor, the greater the tendency of the tutor to overestimate the student's performance. A simple assumption that integrates declarative knowledge into the knowledge tracing model of procedural learning eliminates the model's tendency to overestimate test performance and enhances the model's sensitivity to individual differences in test scores.

The most important implication of these results concerns the path to mastery learning for all students: While knowledge tracing-based remediation in the tutor successfully raises test scores, additional problem solving of exactly the same type in the tutor will probably not yield the achievement gains sufficient for all students to reach mastery. Note that if the model's overestimation had reflected forgetting, then more practice of the same type would be just what we might prescribe. But if a student learns suboptimal rules in the tutor that capitalize on accidental characteristics of the tutor curriculum and/or interface and are more or less sufficient for success in the tutor, then there is no guarantee that additional practice of the same type will affect the rules. Instead, we need to develop interventions before and/or during tutor practice to help students form more suitable rules.

Important tasks remain before these results can be translated into effective practice. First, we need to develop measures of declarative knowledge that can be dynamically incorporated into knowledge tracing to model the student's cognitive state during the learning process. Second, we need to develop effective interventions to improve prerequisite declarative knowledge and to scaffold the use of that knowledge in problem solving. Nevertheless, the results of this study bring us an important step closer to the goal of realizing the promise of mastery learning for all students.

References

Anderson, J. R., (1993). *Rules of the Mind*. Hillsdale, NJ: Lawrence Erlbaum.

Anderson, J. R., Conrad F. G., and Corbett, A. T. (1989). Skill acquisition and the LISP Tutor. *Cognitive Science*, 13:467–505.

Anderson, J. R., Corbett, A. T., Koedinger, K. R., and Pelletier, R. (1995). Cognitive tutors: Lessons learned. *Journal of the Learning Sciences* 4:167–207.

Atkinson, R. C., (1972). Optimizing the learning of a second-language vocabulary. *Journal of Experimental Psychology* 96:124–129.

Bloom, B. S, (1968). Learning for mastery. In *Evaluation Comment, 1.* Los Angeles: UCLA Center for the Study of Evaluation of Instructional Programs.

Carroll, J. B. (1963). A model of school learning. *Teachers College Record* 64:723–733.

Corbett, A. T., and Anderson, J. R., and O'Brien, A. T. (1995). Student modeling in the ACT Programming Tutor. In Nichols, P., Chipman, S., and Brennan, B., eds., *Cognitively Diagnostic Assessment.* Hillsdale, NJ: Erlbaum.

Corbett, A. T., and Anderson, J. R. (1995a). Knowledge decomposition and subgoal reification in the ACT Programming Tutor. *Artificial Intelligence and Education 1995: The Proceedings of AI-ED 95.* Charlottesville, VA: AACE.

Corbett, A. T., and Anderson, J. R. (1995b). Knowledge tracing: Modeling the acquisition of procedural knowledge. *User Modeling and User-Adapted Interaction* 4:253–278.

Corbett, A. T., and Knapp, S., (1996). Plan scaffolding: Impact on the process and product of learning. In Frasson, C., Gauthier, G., and Lesgold, A., eds., *Intelligent Tutoring Systems: Third International Conference, ITS '96.* New York: Springer.

Goldstein, I. P., (1982). The genetic graph: A representation for the evolution of procedural knowledge. In Sleeman, D., and Brown, J.S., eds., *Intelligent Tutoring Systems.* New York: Academic.

Keller, F. S. (1968) "Good-bye teacher...." *Journal of Applied Behavioral Analysis* 1:79–89.

Kulik, C. C., Kulik, J. A., and Bangert-Drowns, R. L. (1990). Effectiveness of mastery learning programs: A meta- analysis. *Review of Educational Research* 60:265–299.

Resnick, L. B. (1977). Assuming that everyone can learn everything, will some learn less? *School Review* 85:445–452.

Slavin, R. E., (1987). Mastery learning reconsidered. *Review of Educational Research* 57:175–213.

Dynamic Assessment for Operator Training

Claudine Moinard and Michelle Joab

LIP-6, Université Paris 6, France

Abstract. This paper describes the assessment of operator training in a real working context in the system DIAPASON. Not only are the trainee's results assessed but his working method is also considered critically. In DIAPASON, the trainee is assessed in terms of a norm that the instructors wish to use, which means comparing the trainee's results with a reference solution built by a solver. This solver is dynamic, it can be parametrized and it is coupled with a simulator of the device. The Evaluator guides the solver to monitor the trainee during the solving process, even if an error is made, and the assessment is built step by step as the trainee solves the problem.

1 Introduction

This paper presents the trainee assessment component specially designed for DIAPASON, a training system based on simulation. DIAPASON is to be used by telecontrol operators responsible for the management of French medium voltage power systems. A human instructor monitors the trainee who is using DIAPASON. A simulation scenario stages a real case for the trainee to deal with. As in the real working context, the trainee has to react with a telecontrol interface which centralizes all the remote signals sent by the components of the power system and telecontrols some of the components. The task of the trainee is to diagnose the fault and, more importantly, repair the installation as quickly as possible so as to restore supply to the customers. He will do his job better if he understands the type and is able to judge the seriousness of the incidents that occur.

The trainee finds himself in a problem solving situation and, without interruption, solves a problem. DIAPASON monitors what the trainee does but has no influence over him. Like every life-size problem, the building of a valuable assessment component presents a lot of difficulties. The only data DIAPASON has about the trainee are the actions he takes. Moreover, in the case of error DIAPASON does not correct the trainee, but carries on the assessment.

The trainee is assessed in terms of both efficiency and methods, with respect to a norm of the activity that the instructors wish to promote. The aim of this norm is to standardize the behavior of the agents, especially in matters of safety.

This article presents the four main characteristics of the DIAPASON Evaluator. The assessment is dynamic and takes into account the changes to the device. It is incremental, since an isolated action carried out by the trainee is not always significant. Furthermore, the Evaluator determines a relevant sequence of trainee actions so as to identify the reasoning steps. The assessment is continuous and the Evaluator is able to monitor the trainee even if an error has been made. Finally, the assessment is produced in "real time": The results follow the actions of the trainee with only a marginal delay.

2 Assessment Perspectives

The assessment of a trainee operator is mainly a question of a critical analysis of his activities. The activities are analyzed on three levels: operational, tactical and strategic. The *operational level* concerns the *execution of procedures*. At this level, errors take the form of actions that are forgotten, useless, unnecessary, repeated or carried out at the wrong moment. The *tactical level* concerns the *choice of procedures* to be implemented in order to reach a given aim. The *strategic level* concerns more global strategic problem solving choices, such as the analysis of the situation, the definition of the goals to be reached and related plans. Only errors connected to the operational level can be detected directly from the actions of the trainee. Errors at the other levels can only be detected after a sequence of actions has been interpreted.

At the operational level, what is assessed is the efficiency of the solution. The priority for an operator in the case of a power cut is to repair the system. The repair is assessed by checking to see if supply has been restored to all of he unaffected sections of the system. *At the tactical level*, assessment must see whether the solution to the problem respects the norms of that activity, since the trainee must repair the device and at the same time respect the safety standards. *At the strategic level*, assessment must measure the quality of the solution. It must see whether the strategic choices and problem solving methods adopted by the trainee are appropriate to the case in hand.

What interactive learning environment designers usually try to do is to characterize the trainee at the most abstract levels of activity. SHERLOCK assesses both the trainee's ability to decompose a problem into sub-problems and the appropriateness of the methods chosen to reach a particular goal (Lesgold et al., 1991). SAFARI assesses the forgotten and incomplete tasks and the way they are sequenced (Pachet et al., 1996). IMTS, a fault diagnosis learning environment, assesses the tests performed on the device by the trainee. IMTS only assesses the learner's tactical level (Towne and Munro, 1988). CARDIAC TUTOR, a real time training system, assesses the operational level of the activity by characterizing the actions which are missing, are unnecessary or have been carried out at the wrong time in the significant sequences of actions (Eliot and Woolf, 1995). DIAPASON assesses the trainee on the three levels of activity: operational, tactical and strategic.

3 Designing the Assessment

The assessment is based on the analysis of user results and on comparison between his solution and an expert reference structured according to the different levels of reasoning: operational, tactical and strategic.

In order to obtain this reference, a problem solver called DIAGRAL progressively and dynamically produces the appropriate solution (Moinard, 1996). DIAGRAL has been parametrized so as to monitor the user after a strategic or tactical error. The trainee's decisions, which greatly modify the state of the device and thus the series of repair actions to be performed, are imposed on the solver. In this way, throughout the problem solving process the solver's execution context is adapted to that of the user.

Expert world is the name given to the set of components which are used to build the reference, DIAGRAL and the power system simulator, while *user world* is the set of components making up the trainee's training environment, the telecontrol interface and the user simulator. The fact that there are two distinct worlds and simulation processes enables the user and DIAGRAL to function autonomously. Each one solves the problem on their own instantiation of the simulator that has been initialized by the Starter. Each one transmits the successive steps of their problem solving to the Evaluator.

The Evaluator guides DIAGRAL and modifies the execution context of the solver to adapt it to that of the user. In order to recognize the strategic or tactical choices made by the user, it analyzes the sequence of actions. Then it communicates the choices thus identified to DIAGRAL, which adopts the choice that has been imposed.

4 Appraisal

Building a reference based on a method and not just on the results raises certain difficulties which have been overcome in the framework of the control of a real time device. The dynamic functioning of the power system means that it is impossible to build solutions to the problem in advance. For this reason DIAGRAL, the solver, is dynamic and adapts its reasoning to the current state of the context. The reference solution is built progressively and guided by the user's solving process. The guidance of the solver by the evaluator means that it is possible to monitor the user even if an error has been made. However, if the trainee's behavior is erratic, this guidance technique cannot be used.

The detection of errors at the operational level is completed by an interpretation at the tactical level; a link is established between an error and a repair procedure or a telecontrol rule that has not been used correctly. However, it is not always possible to interpret an error.

The sofware engineering approach adopted here can be reused in another training systems. It requires only a dynamic solver that can be parametrized and that is coupled with a simulator of the device.

From the ergonomic point of view, our results are interesting in that they offer a great diversity of assessment and cover the different levels of activity. Based on a norm of the activity, the assessment results help the instructors dealing with the training system.

References

Eliot, C., and Woolf, B. (1995). An adaptive student centered curriculum for an intelligent training system. *User Modeling and User-Adapted interaction* 5:67–86.

Lesgold, A., Lajoie, S., Bunzo, M., and Eggan, G. (1991). SHERLOCK: A coached practice environment for an electronics troubleshooting job. In Larkin, J., and Chabay, R., eds., *Computer Assisted Instruction and Intelligent Tutoring Systems: Shared Issues and Complementary Approaches*. Hillsdale, NJ: Erlbaum. 201–238.

Moinard, C. (1996). *Evaluation dynamique d'un opérateur pour un système d'entraînement à la conduite d'un dispositif industriel*. Thèse de doctorat de l'Université Paris 6, France. Available as Rapport Interne 96–13, LAFORIA-IBP.

Pachet, F., Djamen, J. Y., Frasson, C., and Kaltenbach, M. (1996). Production de conseils pertinents exploitant les relations de composition et de précédence dans un arbre de tâches. *Sciences et Techniques Educatives* 3:43–75.

Towne, D. M., and Munro, A. (1988). The intelligent maintenance system. In Psotka, J., Massey L. D., and Mutter, S. A. eds., *Intelligent Tutoring Systems: Lessons Learned*. Hillsdale, NJ: Erlbaum. 479–530.

Tailoring to Learner Proficiency

Levels of Expertise and User-Adapted Formats of Instructional Presentations: A Cognitive Load Approach

Slava Kalyuga, Paul Chandler, and John Sweller*

School of Education Studies, University of New South Wales, Sydney, Australia

Abstract. This paper investigates interactions between user expertise and formats of instructional presentations. A cognitive load approach assumes that information presentation should be structured to eliminate any avoidable load on working memory. The level of learner expertise is a major factor determining intelligibility of information for a user. A diagram might not be intelligible in isolation for less experienced users and so require additional textual explanations. Physical integration (e.g., using spatial grouping or colour coding) of the text and diagram can reduce split attention and an unnecessary working memory load. The same diagram may be understandable for more experienced users. Eliminating redundancy may be the best way to reduce cognitive load in this situation. A series of experiments using instructions in elementary electrical engineering demonstrated the alterations in optimal instructional designs with the development of user expertise.

1 Introduction

An instructional message presented to users on a computer screen usually consists of multiple sources of information (e.g., diagrams, charts, illustrations or a variety of concepts embedded in text). The way this information is structured by designers can have substantial effects on the learnability of material. This paper investigates consequences of users' differing levels of expertise on optimal formats of instructional presentations from a cognitive load perspective.

We have known for some time that processing of information occurs within a limited working memory (Miller, 1956). Only a few items or elements of information can be handled in working memory at any time. Too many elements may overwhelm working memory decreasing the effectiveness of a presentation. An element is anything that has been learned and is handled as a single entity in working memory. Thus a simple algebraic expression (e.g. $a/b = ac/bc$), for a person familiar with basic algebra, will be processed as a single element easily handled by working memory. However, without this experience the formula will appear as a collection of individual symbols that may be much more difficult for limited working memory to process. It must be noted that while the number of elements that can be processed by working memory is limited, the amount of information that can be processed has no known limits because

---

* The work reported in this paper was supported by grants from the Australian Research Council and Australian National Training Authority. The authors wish to thank Bryan Jones, Richard Winter and the training team from Email Ltd for their ongoing collaboration and support

theoretically, any entity incorporating any amount of information can be handled as a single element. Thus a large amount of information may be processed by working memory while dealing with no more than two or three elements.

An unlimited number of elements can be held in long-term memory in the form of hierarchically organised schemas. A schema is defined as a cognitive construct that permits us to treat multiple elements of information as a single element categorised according to the manner in which it will be used. Schemas are stored in long-term memory and can be transferred to working memory as elements to be processed. Because there may be no limit to the size of these schemas, they permit the processing of the information-rich elements in working memory referred to above.

Automation similarly reduces working memory load. Schemas are stored in long-term memory with varying degrees of automaticity. If a schema can be brought into working memory in automated form, it will make limited demands on working memory resources, leaving more resources to, for example, search for a possible problem solution.

Cognitive load theory, incorporating this architecture, has been used to design a variety of instructional presentations both in computer- and paper-based forms (see, e.g., Sweller, 1994, for a recent summary). Most information can be presented in several ways and in the past most instructional design has proceeded without explicit consideration of the limitations of working memory. In contrast, cognitive load theory places a primary emphasis on limited working memory. The theory assumes that information presented to learners and the activities required of them should be structured to eliminate any avoidable load on working memory and to maximise schema acquisition. Two techniques are of relevance to the experiments of this paper.

The split-attention effect. Many instructional presentations include multiple sources of information directed to users for whom one or more sources of information are unintelligible in isolation. Understanding can be derived only by mentally integrating the various sources of information. A geometric proof consisting of a diagram and associated statements provides an example. Neither the diagram nor the statements are likely to be intelligible unless they are mentally integrated. The act of mental integration is cognitively demanding and required purely because of the traditional manner in which geometric proofs or examples are presented. If, rather than using a split-source format with the diagram and statements presented in two discrete, separated modules, the two sources of information are physically integrated, the need for mental integration is reduced. This might be expected to reduce an unnecessary working memory load, freeing resources for schema acquisition and automation. A comparison between split-source and integrated formats has indicated superiority of the integrated format, demonstrating the split-attention effect (see Chandler and Sweller, 1992; 1996).

The redundancy effect. Rather than having multiple sources of information that are unintelligible in isolation, an instructional presentation also can consist of several sources of information, each of which is self-contained and can be understood in its own right. To the extent that the sources of information cover the same area, they are redundant. A diagram associated with text that merely redescribes the diagram is an example. Findings indicate that eliminating redundancy is the best way to reduce cognitive load. When dealing with a diagram and redundant text that describes the diagram, the text should be eliminated rather than integrated with the diagram, because requiring learners to process the text imposes an unnecessary cognitive load. The redundancy effect is demonstrated when performance obtained in a condition in which redundant material is eliminated proves to be superior to a condition including this material (Chandler and Sweller, 1991, 1996; Sweller and Chandler, 1994).

Whether a source of information is intelligible in isolation depends only partly on the nature of the information. It also will depend on the level of expertise of the learner and as Ericsson and Charness (1994) indicate, differences in expertise provide the largest and most reliable differences in performance among individuals. For example, if an electrical circuit diagram is presented to learners who have not yet acquired schemas that deal with typical combinations of interacting electrical elements, it is likely to be unintelligible by itself. Learners at this level of expertise require the text to understand how basic elements interact in achieving the circuit's function. For these learners, both the diagram and the text are essential, and so they will only understand the material once they have mentally integrated both sources of information. Cognitive load theory suggests that learning will be facilitated by physically integrating the two sources of information thus reducing the need for mental integration. Fragments of text can be integrated into a diagram in close proximity to corresponding components of the diagram. Arrows directed from the text to the corresponding elements of the diagram could be used to make the search process easier for learners.

In contrast, for more expert learners who have sufficient knowledge of different types of circuits, the text might be redundant because of previously acquired schemas. They still require the diagram to provide them with information concerning this particular, novel circuit. They may prefer to ignore the text but may have difficulty doing so when the text is integrated into the diagram. It should be possible to demonstrate the redundancy effect using learners at this level because the best instructional format with the lowest cognitive load for these learners may be a diagram-alone format.

Three experiments tested these hypotheses. The first experiment used inexperienced learners and was expected to demonstrate the split-attention effect. The second and third experiments were designed to investigate the alterations in ideal instructional designs with the development of expertise.

2   Experiment 1

2.1   Method

The experiment was designed to compare three instructional formats (integrated-diagram-and-text, separate-diagram-and-text, and diagram-only), using participants who had no formal electrical training. The participants were 26 first-year trade apprentices and trainees without any specialised training in electrical circuits and wiring. All of them had just commenced their first-year trade course.

All participants were tested individually. There were two areas of instruction, one relating to electrical switching for a bell and light circuit and a second with information for a water pump circuit. For each area, the experiment consisted of the instruction and test phases. During the instruction phase, learners were asked to study an instructional material at their own pace. After each participant had finished studying the circuit, they were asked to estimate how easy or difficult a circuit was to understand on a seven point scale, ranging from 1 (extremely easy) to 7 (extremely difficult). The results were interpreted as a measure of the subjective mental load associated with learning the materials (see Paas and Van Merrienboer, 1993).

Each test consisted of three parts. Part 1 was a reproduction task which asked participants to diagrammatically reproduce the circuit. For each circuit, a mark was allocated for each correctly drawn element (e.g., start button) in its correct position. Part 2 of each test consisted of test questions relating to each circuit (the circuit diagram was available during this part of the test). The circuit questions concerned about the operation of the circuit (e.g., "Which switches are closed when the bell and light are operating?"), as well as troubleshooting tasks where participants were presented with a textual description of a hypothetical problem in the circuit (e.g., After releasing the start button the bell and light stop working) and were required to suggest a possible cause for the proposed problem. Part 3 of each test consisted of fault finding exercises. A faulty diagram of a circuit was presented to participants. They were required to identify each fault in the circuit and propose a solution for the fault. Responses were assessed by the number of correctly identified faults with appropriate solutions.

2.2 Results and Discussion

The results from Experiment 1 are illustrated in Figure 1. Analysis of variance indicated a marginal difference between groups in time to process the instructions, $F(2, 23) = 3.08$, MSe = 3111.0, $p = .065$ for the Bell & Light materials, and a significant effect, $F(2, 23) = 12.49$, MSe = 3276.0, for the Water Pump materials (the .05 level of significance is used throughout this paper). Newman-Keuls tests indicated the instruction time for the diagram-only group was significantly lower than the separate-diagram-and-text for the Bell & Light test and significantly lower than both the integrated-diagram-and-text and separate-diagram-and-text groups for the Water Pump test.

The results from the subjective ratings of mental load indicated significant differences between the groups for both sets of instructional materials: $F(2, 23) = 5.22$, MSe = .59, for the Bell & Light circuit, and $F(2, 23) = 3.54$, MSe = .65, for the Water Pump circuit. Newman-Keuls tests indicated that the integrated-diagram-and-text format was perceived to be significantly lower in mental load than the diagram-only format for both sets of instructions and significantly lower than the separate-diagram-and-text groups for the Bell & Light test.

There was no significant difference between groups for the reproduction tasks of both sets of materials. There was, however, significant differences between the groups for the circuit questions for both sets of instruction: $F(2, 23) = 8.16$, MSe = 2.32, for the Bell & Light materials, $F(2, 23) = 5.83$, MSe = 6.40, for the Water Pump materials. Newman-Keuls tests indicated that the integrated-diagram-and-text group significantly outperformed both the remaining groups for the Bell & Light test, and the diagram-only group for the Water Pump materials. Results also indicated that the separate-diagram-and-text group scored significantly higher then the diagram-only group for the water pump test questions.

There were significant differences between the groups on the fault-finding task: $F(2, 23) = 11.75$, MSe = .635, for the Bell & Light task, and $F(2, 23) = 10.64$, MSe = .98, for the Water Pump task. Newman-Keuls tests indicated that the integrated-diagram-and-text group identified significantly more faults and solutions than the diagram-only group for the Bell and Light fault finding task. There also was a significant difference favouring the separate-diagram-and-text group over the diagram-only group for the Bell & Light test. For the Water Pump test, the integrated-diagram-and-text group was significantly better than both the remaining groups.

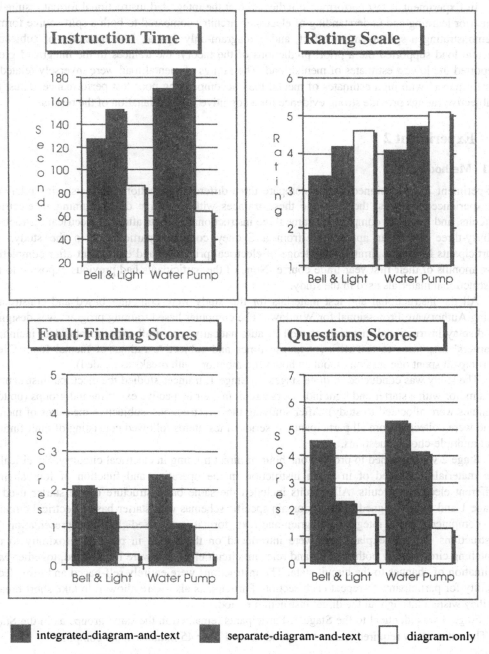

Figure 1. Charts of means for the data of Experiment 1.

In Experiment 1, test performance indicated that the integrated instructional format resulted in superior learning and understanding of electrical circuitry compared to both a split-source format, demonstrating a split-attention effect, and a diagram-only format. The measures of subjective mental load supported the a priori predictions of the theory: the trainees in the integrated group reported the lowest estimates of mental load. The ratings of mental load were inversely related to performance, with high estimates of mental load accompanying poor test performance. Thus, the subjective ratings provide strong evidence for a cognitive load explanation of the results.

3   Experiment 2

3.1 Method

Experiment 2 was designed to first compare three different instructional formats using relatively inexperienced trainees, then provide these trainees with extensive direct training in electrical circuits, and finally to compare the same three instructional formats after the electrical instruction. Thirty-three first year apprentices from a Sydney company participated in the study. All participants had some limited knowledge of electrical principles and equipment after completing two months of their first year trade course. None of the participants had previous exposure to the instructional materials used in the study.

All the instructional and test materials for this study were computer based and constructed using Authorware Professional for Windows. The computer based training program was designed to display instructional materials as well as automatically record all experimental data including learners' responses to test items, response times and subjective ratings of mental load. Every participant spent one session (about an hour) at a monitor (with breaks as needed).

The study was conducted in three stages. In Stage 1, trainees studied the electrical instructions of a motor with a starter and light indicators circuit in their respective experimental groups (up to 5 minutes were allocated to study). After studying these instructions, subjective measures of mental load were collected from all participants. A series of test items followed consisting of fault finding and multiple-choice questions.

Stage 2 was designed to provide one hour of direct training in electrical circuitry. Specifically, the materials consisted of in depth instruction in the operation and function of four slightly different electrical circuits. All circuits included the same basic structure of the starter used in Stage 1 and were designed to build domain specific schemas with starter based electrical circuits. A computer based integrated-diagram-and-text format was used for the presentation of instructions. As text explanations were introduced on the screen in physical proximity to the matching circuit entity both the text and relevant circuit element/s were highlighted, together with animation of changes to the circuit state. The instructions were entirely self-paced and provided a facility for participants to repeat each section. Participants also were allowed to take short breaks as they wished throughout the direct instruction period.

Stage 3 was identical to the Stage 1. Participants remained in the same groups as in the Stage 1. The entire study required learners to spend about 1 hour 45 minutes at the computer.

3.2 Results and Discussion

A series of three (instructional format) by two (pre and post training) ANOVA with repeated measures on the second factor were conducted. The variables under analysis were instruction time, subjective ratings of mental load, and test performance scores on fault finding and multiple-choice tasks.

Since the main purpose of this experiment was to study the dynamics of change in expertise, we were primarily interested in the interaction effect between groups and pre/post training. The interaction data of all the 3×2 ANOVA showed significant interactions for the fault-finding task, $F(2, 30) = 4.23$, MSe $= .85$, and for the multiple-choice items $F(2, 30) = 5.03$, MSe $= .38$. No significant interactions were obtained for the instruction time and subjective ratings of mental load. Interaction contrasts were carried out to isolate the source of significant interaction effect between the pre and post training. For the integrated-diagram-and-text and diagram-only groups results showed significant effects on the fault-finding task, $F(1, 30) = 4.76$, MSe $= .85$, and multiple-choice items, $F(1, 30) = 6.34$, MSe $= .38$. For the separate-diagram-and-text and diagram-only groups results showed significant effects on the fault-finding task, $F(1, 30) = 7.57$, MSe $= .85$, and multiple-choice items, $F(1, 30) = 8.45$, MSe $= .38$. For the integrated-diagram-and-text and separate-diagram-and-text groups all the contrasts were non-significant.

The significance of the interaction effects for a number of analysed variables suggests that the most efficient mode of instruction depends on the level of expertise of learners. As the level of expertise was raised in a specific instructional domain (i.e., basic starter based electrical circuits), the more effective format of instruction switched from integrated-diagram-and-text to the diagram-only format. In accordance with the prediction, as expertise increased, progress in performance of the diagram-only group was superior to both other groups.

4 Experiment 3

4.1 Method

The results of Experiment 2 indicated that participants still might not have reached a level of expertise where the textual explanations accompanying the diagrams become fully redundant. Experiment 3 was designed to use more intensive training in electrical circuitry to develop a level of expertise where text based commentaries become unnecessary. Experiment 3 was conducted about one month after Experiment 2. All the learners who participated in this experiment had participated previously in Experiment 2. In Experiment 3 they were divided into two rather than three groups: diagram-only and integrated-diagram-and-text groups. Fifteen participants were allocated to each of two groups. Those who previously had been in the integrated-diagram-and-text or diagram-only groups remained in the same groups. Participants from the separate-diagram-and-text group in Experiment 2 were randomly allocated to these two groups. By the time this study was conducted, all participants had received formal training in elementary electrical engineering as well as direct training in electrical circuits provided in Experiment 2.

As in Experiment 2, this study was entirely computer based. The experiment involved two stages. During Stage 1, all participants received additional direct training in electrical circuitry using materials which involved only starter based circuits. The training materials were in multimedia form, with text based explanations of circuits being replaced by auditory commentaries. The auditory information was coordinated with the circuit diagrams by providing screen based animations and highlights of the appropriate elements of the circuits. This training format has been shown to be an effective method of information delivery (see Mayer and Anderson, 1992). The training materials were self-paced and included a facility where sections could be repeated, as well as interactive exercises (multiple-choice questions, dragging elements of circuits to their proper locations, etc.) with hints and immediate feedback. This training period lasted for about one hour.

In Stage 2, participants were placed into their instructional format groups. They were asked to study instructional material with an electrical circuit slightly different from those studied during the training phase (Stage 1) but based on the same basic starter circuit structure. The instructional materials were presented in two formats for the two different groups, and learners studied them at their own pace but with a maximum of 5 min.

After the instructional phase, all learners were asked to rate the perceived mental load and then attempt a common test consisting of a fault-finding task and five multiple-choice questions relating to the operation and function of the circuit.

4.2 Results and Discussion

The results from Experiment 3 are illustrated in Figure 2. In order to take into account preexisting differences in learners' performance, analysis of covariance was applied to the data. The averaged scores of the Stage 3 in the Experiment 2 were used as a covariate in the analysis of covariance. Results revealed significant differences between instructional formats, $F(1, 27) = 4.83$, MSe = 1801.8 for the time to process the instructions; $F(1, 27) = 4.24$, MSe = 2.01 for the rating of subjective load; $F(1, 27) = 6.82$, MSe = 2.23, for the fault-finding test; and $F(1, 27) = 5.88$, MSe = .55 for the multiple-choice scores, with significant effects favouring the diagram-only group.

The findings of Experiment 3 provided considerable support for our hypothesis. When learners become experienced in a particular domain certain information that was previously essential for understanding becomes redundant and may impede further learning if processed. Collectively, the findings of Experiments 1 through 3 provide evidence that the "expertise" of the learner influences the efficiency of an instructional presentation with trainees benefiting from different formats at different levels of experience in a domain.

5 General Discussion

Together, the findings of this paper provide strong evidence that the efficiency of a design is in part due to the expertise of the user, with users gaining optimal benefits from different formats at different levels of expertise. Intelligibility of information presentation cannot be determined without reference to the learners for whom the information is intended. A module of information might be unintelligible to novices and thus require additional material with which it must be integrated. Physical integration should reduce cognitive load and enhance learning. The same module, presented to more experienced learners, may be both intelligible in isolation and also informative in that learners can acquire knowledge from it. Additional information is not needed because learners may have acquired schemas that easily and automatically allow inferences to be made. Those inferences cover the additional material that otherwise must be provided for less experienced learners to permit understanding. If such material is provided for more experienced learners, it is redundant and processing it may unnecessarily increase cognitive load. These learners may be assisted by the elimination, rather than the integration, of the additional material.

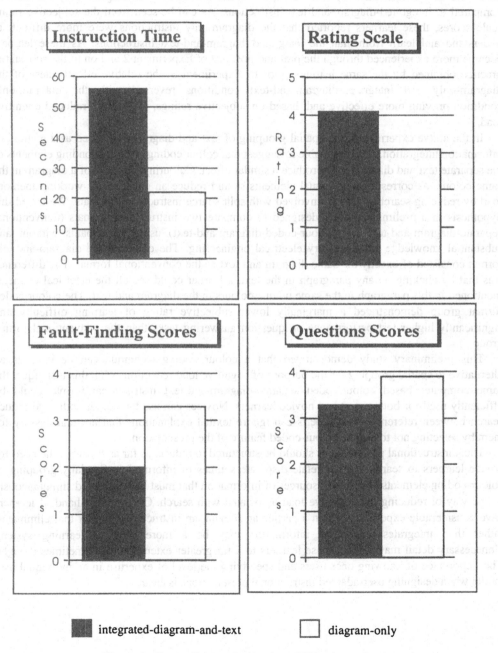

Figure 2. Charts of means for the data of Experiment 3.

The three experiments of this paper demonstrated the alterations in ideal instructional designs with the development of expertise. The cumulative nature of the results from the three experiments may be illustrated in Figure 3. The diagrams on the left side of the figure indicate that performance of the novices (Experiment 1) was very poor when presented with diagram-only instructions compared to integrated-diagram-and-text instructions. As can be seen from the subjective rating scale scores, these learners reported that the diagram-only instructions were more difficult to understand and learn from than the integrated-diagram-and-text instructions. As these learners became more experienced through the pre- and post-test of Experiment 2 and on to the substantial practice obtained by the same learners prior to Experiment 3, the relative effectiveness of the diagram-only and integrated-diagram-and-text conditions reversed with the diagram-only condition proving more effective and, based on subjective ratings, imposing a reduced cognitive load.

In the above experiments, the spatial grouping of text and diagrams was used as a method of information integration. It is reasonable to suggest that colour coding of corresponding elements of the separate text and diagram may produce a similar effect. Colouring elements of a diagram in the same colours as corresponding textual elements should reduce an unnecessary working memory load by reducing search processes involved with split source instructional formats. We tested this hypothesis in a preliminary study designed to compare two instructional formats (conventional separate-diagram-and-text and colour-coded-diagram-and-text) using participants without any substantial knowledge in elementary electrical engineering. The colour-coded-diagram-and-text format consisted of exactly the same diagram and text as the conventional format. The difference was that by clicking on any paragraph in the text, a learner could see all the electrical elements mentioned in this paragraph in the same unique colours in the diagram and text. The colour coded format group demonstrated a marginally lower subjective rating of learning difficulty and significantly higher test performance on question answering tasks than the conventional format group.

This preliminary study demonstrated that a colour coding technique can be used as an alternative to spatial grouping for the purpose of cognitive load reduction. With this technique, the same computer based colour-coded separate-diagram-and-text instructional format could be efficiently used for both expert and novice learners. Novices can use the colour coding to reduce search between referents while experts can ignore textual explanations that are unnecessary for them by selecting not to use the colour-coded feature of the presentation.

Thus, instructional presentations should be structured to reduce, as far as possible, the need for novice learners to search for and relate disparate sources of information. Spatially grouping or colour-coding elements of different sources of information that must be considered simultaneously is one way of reducing the cognitive load associated with search. On the other hand, if learners have considerable experience within a particular domain, an instructional format that eliminates, rather than integrates, redundant information may be a more efficient learning system. Unnecessary detail may distract these learners to a far greater extent than is sometimes thought. The importance of knowing ones users and specifying the level of expertise in an individual user model when designing user-adapted instructional presentations is clear.

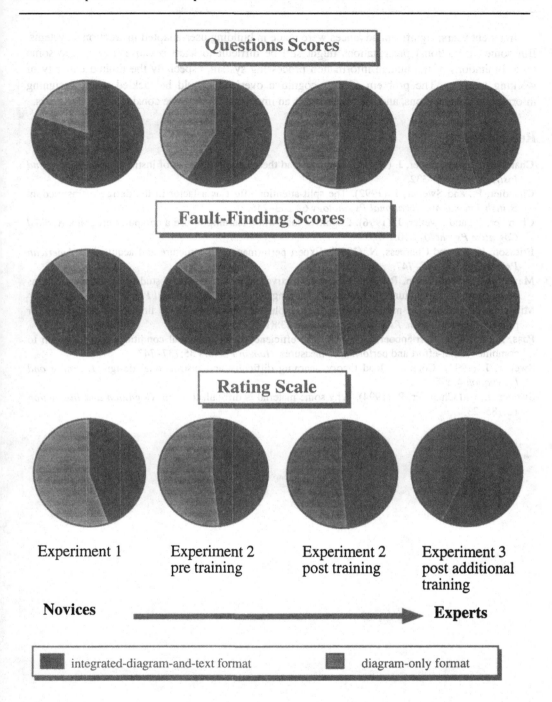

Figure 3. Relative performance indicators (comparative relations between corresponding means) on the integrated-diagram-and-text and diagram-only formats with increasing expertise.

In recent years, significant advances were made in building user-adapted instructional systems. But some instructional presentations might still be difficult to learn because they ignore some basic limitations of the human information processing system, especially the limited capacity of working memory. The problem of user cognitive overload should be tackled when designing information presentations, and user expertise is an important factor to be considered by designers.

References

Chandler, P., and Sweller, J. (1991). Cognitive load theory and the format of instruction. *Cognition and Instruction* 8:293–332.

Chandler, P., and Sweller, J. (1992). The split-attention effect as a factor in the design of instruction. *British Journal of Educational Psychology* 62:233–246.

Chandler, P., and Sweller, J. (1996). Cognitive load while learning to use a computer program. *Applied Cognitive Psychology* 10:1–20.

Ericsson, K. A., and Charness, N. (1994). Expert performance: Its structure and acquisition. *American Psychologist* 49:725–747.

Mayer, R., and Anderson, R. (1992). The instructive animation: Helping students build connections between words and pictures in multimedia learning. *Journal of Educational Psychology* 84:444–452.

Miller, G. A. (1956). The magical number seven, plus or minus two: Some limits on our capacity for processing information. *Psychological Review* 63:81–97.

Paas, F., and Van Merrienboer, J. (1993). The efficiency of instructional conditions: An approach to combine mental-effort and performance measures. *Human Factors* 35:737–743.

Sweller, J. (1994). Cognitive load theory, learning difficulty and instructional design. *Learning and Instruction* 4:295–312.

Sweller, J., and Chandler, P. (1994). Why some material is difficult to learn. *Cognition and Instruction* 12:185–233.

Generating Clinical Exercises of Varying Difficulty

Sandra Carberry[1] and John R. Clarke M.D.[2*]

[1] Department of Computer Science, University of Delaware, Newark, Delaware USA
[2] Allegheny Univ. of the Health Sciences, Philadelphia, PA USA

Abstract. This paper outlines a system, TraumaCASE, for automatically generating realistic cases of the appropriate level of difficulty based on a model of the user's current level of expertise. Such cases could be used for instructional purposes by a training module or for computer-based exams by a quality assurance module.

1 Automatic Case Generation

We have implemented a system, TraumaCASE, for generating realistic medical cases in the domain of emergency center trauma care. Such cases could be used for instructional purposes by a training module or for computer-based practice and exams by a quality assurance module. Among other benefits, this would eliminate the need to collect and pre-store a library of cases and would greatly reduce the likelihood that a selected case replicates one used previously, while ensuring that the generated cases are at the appropriate level of difficulty.

TraumaCASE selects an intended overall diagnosis, such as a tension pneumothorax, and then generates a medical case consisting of a set of initial signs and symptoms, along with symptoms that can be elicited through appropriate bedside questions and results of appropriate diagnostic procedures and tests. TraumaCASE utilizes the extensive knowledge base of the TraumAID decision-support system (Webber et al., 1992). It extracts the TraumAID goal-setting rules that post a goal of investigating the intended diagnosis, and chains backward on the TraumAID goal-setting and evidential rules to identify symptoms and findings that would lead the physician to *consider* this diagnosis; these are entered into the case being generated. TraumaCASE then extracts the TraumAID goal-procedure mapping rule that specifies (in order of preference) the typical means for ruling out the intended diagnosis, selects an appropriate procedure from among those given in the mapping rule, and chains on TraumAID's mapping rules to identify the actions comprising the procedure and the test results that might be produced by those actions. Finally, TraumaCASE extracts the TraumAID rule whose conclusion is the intended diagnosis and chains backwards on the TraumAID evidential rules to identify symptoms, findings, and test results that warrant the diagnosis being made. Since the system will only pursue an inference chain if the test results encountered during chaining are possible results of actions that have already been entered into the case, TraumaCASE's prior selection of an appropriate procedure and its constituent actions restricts the generated case to test results typically obtained in the given situation and thus prevents the system from generating an unrealistic case. As the system explores a path, it keeps track of the features already entered into the case and backtracks if a particular selection of rules would result in inconsistent features.

---
* This work was supported by the National Library of Medicine under grant R01-LM-05764-01.

2   Generating Cases of Different Levels of Difficulty

One of the co-authors of this paper is a trauma surgeon on the faculty of a medical school. We have identified features of medical cases that make them more complex or that require greater expertise, and we have captured these features in TraumaCASE. To generate cases requiring a low level of expertise, TraumaCASE can limit itself to common isolated problems that any third year medical student should be capable of handling. We have augmented the TraumAID knowledge base with a list of such low-level diagnoses and these comprise Level-1 cases. The case becomes more difficult if it includes two unrelated problems of different urgency with which the physician must deal. Such cases require that the user not only diagnose both independent problems but also that he be able to address their different priorities; these cases comprise Level-2 in our system.

For some diagnoses, if the user pursues appropriate treatment and attends to the appropriate follow-up, the user will find that the problem is actually a more serious version of the original diagnosis. Such cases require greater expertise since they require attention to followup procedures and consideration of their findings. These cases comprise Level-3 in our system. Level-4 cases are generated by selecting from among diagnoses that are less common but which a surgical resident would be expected to handle. However, if the diagnosis is suggested by some other previously diagnosed problem, then the case is part of Level-5, as discussed in the next paragraph.

One significant factor that appears to correlate with the difficulty of a case is the number of additional diagnoses that must be considered. Since the TraumAID rules specify the requisite conditions both for posting a goal of considering a particular diagnosis and for concluding that the problem is present in the patient, they can be used to establish features of the generated case that control the amount of inferencing required to handle the case. The greater the amount of inferencing required, the more difficult the case becomes. Cases that require extended inferencing comprise Level-5 in our system. Level-5 cases differ significantly from Level-3 cases; in Level-3 cases, the appropriate followup actions performed in treating the original diagnosis will produce findings indicating the more serious version of the problem, whereas in Level-5 cases the original diagnosis along with other symptoms suggest consideration of a different problem that must be confirmed by further tests and inferencing.

Within each level, cases vary in difficulty depending on whether the usual methods of diagnosing and treating the case are applicable and whether they have the expected results. This is captured in TraumaCASE. When TraumaCASE is asked to generate a relatively difficult Level-i case, it can examine the TraumAID goal-procedure mapping rules and establish conditions that make the procedure of choice inappropriate or unavailable. While the need to select an alternative procedure or attend to failure of a procedure does not radically change the level of difficulty of a generated case, it does affect its complexity with respect to other cases at that level.

3   Conclusion

Most simulations of medical cases, such as that described in (Parker and Miller 1989), rely on randomly selecting manifestations of a disease, with the manifestation's probability of inclusion in the case determined by its frequency of occurrence. These methods of generation do not permit flexibility in generating cases of varying degrees of difficulty or facilitate incremental case generation. Fontaine et al. (1994) use backward chaining on a knowledge base of rules as part of an "authoring module" for creating cases that will be presented to a student. However, the focus of their work was on assisting a human instructor in creating cases and assuring that the resultant case was consistent. Although their system has the ability to make random assignments of possible symptoms and test results, it cannot differentiate between normal and abnormal cases nor can it regulate the difficulty of the generated case. Thus it still must rely on a human instructor both to specify the desired disease or diagnosis captured by the case and to sift through all of the cases that might be generated and select those that are appropriate for the student. Eliot and Woolf (1995) developed a somewhat different approach to producing simulated cases. Their system works in the domain of cardiac resuscitation, and a simulation consists of a series of transitions between states of cardiac arrest or arrhythmias. While their system uses the probabilities of state transitions to guide the simulation, it also includes a mechanism that biases the system to enter states that provide an opportunity to teach high priority topics. However, the kind of case they produce differs from ours in that the generated case is a series of patient state transitions rather than a set of consistent symptoms, findings, actions, and test results for making a particular diagnosis.

Level of expertise has been taken into account by researchers addressing other problems. For example, Paris (1988) developed a system that switched between a process trace and a constituency schema to generate explanations tailored to the local domain expertise of the listener. Other work on level of expertise includes that of Mittal and Paris (1993) and Chin (1988).

This paper has briefly described TraumaCASE, a system for automatically generating medical cases of the appropriate level of difficulty by reasoning with the declarative knowledge base of an existing decision support system. By automatically generating tailored cases, our system exploits the knowledge already encoded in an existing knowledge base, eliminates the need to maintain a library of pre-stored cases, and can produce cases that are appropriate for the particular user and application. While our system is implemented in the domain of trauma care, we believe that our approach demonstrates the feasibility of automatically generating realistic cases of different levels of difficulty and that similar techniques can be applied to other decision support systems with declarative knowledge bases of rules. In the future, TraumaCASE will be extended to *incremental* tailored case generation.

References

Chin, D. N. (1988). Exploiting user expertise in answer expression. In *Proceedings of the Seventh National Conference on Artificial Intelligence*, 756–760.

Eliot, C., and Woolf, B. (1995). An adaptive student centered curriculum for an intelligent training system. *User Modeling and User-Adapted Interaction* 5(1):67–86.

Fontaine, D., LeBeux, P., Riou, C., and Jacquelinet, C. (1994). An intelligent computer-assisted instruction system for clinical case teaching. *Methods of Information in Medicine* 433–445.

Mittal, V., and Paris, C. (1993). Generating natural language descriptions with examples: Differences between introductory and advanced texts. In *Proceedings of the Eleventh AAAI*, 271–276.

Paris, C. L. (1988). Tailoring object descriptions to a user's level of expertise. *Computational Linguistics* 14(3):64–78.

Parker, R., and Miller, R. (1989). Creation of realistic appearing simulated patient cases using internist-1/qmr knowledge base and interrelationship properties of manifestations. *Methods of Information in Medicine* 28(4):346–351.

Webber, B. L., Rymon, R., and Clarke, J. R. (1992). Flexible support for trauma management through goal-directed reasoning and planning. *Artificial Intelligence in Medicine* 4:145–163.

Using the Student Model to Control Problem Difficulty

Joseph Beck, Mia Stern, and Beverly Park Woolf*

Department of Computer Science, University of Massachusetts, Amherst, MA, U.S.A.

Abstract. We have created a student model which dynamically collects information about a student's problem solving ability, acquisition of new topics and retention of earlier topics. This information is provided to the tutor and used to generate new problems at the appropriate level of difficulty and to provide customized hints and help. Formative evaluation of the tutor with 20 students provides evidence that the student model constructs problems at the correct level of difficulty. The problem generation technique is extensible for use in other problem-based domains. This paper describes the design and implementation of the student model and illustrates how the tutor adjusts the difficulty of a problem based on the student model.

1 Introduction

One-on-one human tutoring is much more effective than traditional classroom instruction (Bloom, 1984). We are building systems with the goal of emulating techniques that human tutors use, which can result in comparable learning gains (Shute et al., 1989). In order to do this, the tutor must maintain a representation of the student's knowledge and abilities as well as a set of teaching strategies. The student model keeps track of a student's *proficiency* on topics within the domain. Additionally, our model incorporates general factors of a student's ability, such as acquisition and retention. The model is then used for topic selection, problem generation, and hint selection. In this paper, we focus on the type of model we have implemented and how it is used to control the problem specifications. We also discuss the formative evaluation we have performed that provides preliminary evidence for the effectiveness of the student model.

The remainder of the paper is structured as follows. Section 2 discusses the domain. Section 3 describes the student model and section 4 discusses how the model is used for generating a problem. Section 5 describes how the student model is updated. Section 6 discusses the evaluation of the system. Section 7 concludes the paper.

2 The Domain

A developmental mathematics tutor, MFD (mixed numbers, fractions, and decimals), has been built and tested for fifth and sixth graders. The domain for the tutor is addition, subtraction, multiplication, and division of whole numbers, fractions, mixed numbers, and decimals. All of the problems in the tutor are presented as word problems. Because the system is being used by fifth and sixth graders, we present the problems using a compelling metaphor: endangered

* This work is supported through the National Science Foundation, under contract HRD-95555737. Any opinions, findings, and conclusions or recommendations expressed in this material are those of the authors and do not necessarily reflect the views of the National Science Foundation.

species. Students learn about, for example, the mating habits and the food requirements of various endangered animals, while solving mathematical word problems that deal with these issues.

Each type of problem in the domain is considered a *topic*. There are 14 topics in the tutor (there is no multiplication and division of mixed numbers). Each topic has an associated list of *pretopics*, which are themselves topics. These pretopics must be understood by a student before a problem of the topic can be given. For example, before a student can add mixed numbers, he must know how to add fractions and how to add whole numbers.

In addition to these pretopics, each topic has associated *subskills*, which are steps in the problem solving process for a given topic. For example, to add fractions, a student must find the least common multiple (LCM), convert the fractions to equivalent forms using that LCM, add the numerators, simplify the result, and convert the result to a proper form.[1]

3   The Student Model

The student model contains topic information and material to encode acquisition and retention.

The student model in MFD records a *proficiency* for each topic within the domain. However, unlike many student models (e.g. Anderson and Reiser, 1985, and Eliot, 1996) , ours does not use a simple number for the proficiency. A simple number, such as 0.4 (on a 0 to 1 scale) does not provide information about the context of the student's performance. Is the proficiency 0.4 because the student has just started on the topic, but is doing well? Or is the student having difficulty and his proficiency used to be higher? For these reasons, we use a history based model, so that the tutor can track the student's performance over time. This history is used in selection of high-level teaching strategies such as whether the student needs remediation or if he has forgotten a topic and needs a review.

However, even with a history model, simple numbers are too restrictive, since the tutor cannot express any degree of confidence in the proficiency. A 0.4 proficiency usually means the tutor is 100% sure that the proficiency is correct. However, this is very unlikely, since there is a significant probability that the student model is not completely accurate (Eliot, 1996). Furthermore, a single number does not provide sufficient information. A 0.4 usually means either that the student knows 40% of the material or that he has a 40% chance of knowing the material completely. Which of these choices is often left unspecified, and in any event it is often beneficial for the tutor to know both pieces of information.

When deciding what type of student model to use in MFD, we were not specifically interested in low-level representation issues associated with student models. We were not concerned if the system's beliefs were generated using methods such as Bayesian networks or the Dempster-Shafer theory of evidence. Rather, we were more interested in how to use the model to alter interactions with students. Additionally, we are investigating how to use general characteristics of students, in addition to their performance on each topic.

For these reasons, we have decided to use a simple scheme for representing uncertainty on each topic: *belief vectors*. This representation is based on the "fuzzy" distributions first used in Sherlock II (Katz et al., 1993) and also used in (Gurer et al., 1995). Each vector contains seven points, with the values summing to 1. The value at each point indicate the approximate probability

---

[1] Not all subskills will apply for a given problem. A problem such as $\frac{1}{4} + \frac{1}{4}$ will not require finding an LCM, converting to equivalent fractions, or making the result proper.

that the student is at that level of knowledge. The lowest value for the vector is (1 0 0 0 0 0 0) and the highest value is (0 0 0 0 0 0 1). A vector of (0.14 0.28 0.4 0.18 0 0 0) means the tutor believes there is approximately a 14% chance the student is at level 1, a 28% chance he is at level 2, a 40% chance he is at level 3, and an 18% chance he is at level 4. There is no chance he is above level 4. Furthermore, maintaining a list of these vectors enables the tutor to evaluate the student in the context of his past work.

This representation has some drawbacks. First, it does not actually use probability theory, but is updated via heuristics. Therefore, the values in the vector are only approximate. Second, there is no formal understanding of how this mechanism works, so it must be validated empirically. The difficulty of deriving precise estimates via experiments led (Katz et al., 1993) to consider switching to a mechanism like Bayesian networks for future implementations of Sherlock. Finally, it is difficult to relate this mechanism to other, more formal theories of representing uncertainty.

We chose to use this representation as it is easy to work with and to quickly modify as the need arises. Given that we are exploring the effect of adding new, general factors to the student model, and that this ad hoc solution appears to work adequately, it suffices for our purposes. When we develop a better understanding of how to use general factors to update our model, and how to use our model to construct problems, we will use more established frameworks.

While this vector representation gives us more information about a student's ability, we are currently collapsing the vector to a single number for the tutor to use in its calculations. To determine the value of the vector, we use a weighted calculation. Each item in the vector is multiplied by its index, and these values are summed. For example, the value of the vector (0.14 0.28 0.4 0.18 0 0 0) is 2.62.[2] This value is used as the student's proficiency in a particular topic. In the future, we will analyze the vector itself rather than calculating a single number.

3.1 Acquisition and Retention

In addition to the student model storing information on each topic within the domain, we also maintain general factors concerning the student, specifically acquisition and retention. Prior research indicates that examining general factors such as acquisition and retention can be beneficial for student modeling. Work with the LISP tutor (Anderson, 1993) and with Stat Lady (Shute, 1995) indicates that general factors are predictive of overall learning and allow for a more accurate response to the idiosyncrasies of the student.

Acquisition records how well students learn new topics. When a new topic is introduced, the tutor views how the student performs on the first few problems. If the student performs well on these problems, then he is acquiring skills quickly, and his acquisition factor will reflect this. However, if a student requires many problems on a given topic before he illustrates that he understands it, his acquisition will be lower.

Retention measures how well a student remembers the material over time. This factor is updated when the student is presented with a problem on a topic that he has not seen for a given period of time. If he answers the problem correctly without requiring any hints, then he has retained the knowledge, so his retention factor will be high. On the other hand, if he needed many hints to answer the problem, and previously he did not, then his retention is poor.

---

[2] $1 * 0.14 + 2 * 0.28 + 3 * 0.4 + 4 * 0.18$

4   Using the Student Model

As we have described previously (Stern et al., 1996), the student model is used to select the topic, generate the problem, and provide appropriate feedback. To select the topic, the proficiencies of all topics are examined, as well as the student's acquisition and retention factors. The tutor first examines topics on which the student may need remediation or may have forgotten. If no such topics exist it then selects among those that are not mastered by the student, but that he is ready to attempt.

Hints in MFD have *levels* indicating how much information they provide to the student. If the student needs a hint while solving the problem, the tutor finds a hint of the appropriate level on the skill that the student probably performed incorrectly. Within this domain, the tutor cannot be certain about which step was performed incorrectly. A set of heuristics is used to determine where the student made a mistake, and if two or more skills may be at fault, the one that must be performed earliest in the problem solving process is tagged as the likely culprit.

In the remainder of this section, we discuss how the student model is used to generate the problem for the student.

4.1   Problem Difficulty

One of the main goals of an intelligent tutoring system is to tailor instruction to the needs of each student. MFD provides problems that are at the correct level of challenge and difficulty for the student through the algorithm described in Section 4.2.

The general philosophy is that the more subskills required to solve a problem, the harder the problem. For example, when adding fractions, a problem such as $\frac{1}{3} + \frac{1}{3}$ requires few subskills, whereas $\frac{2}{3} + \frac{5}{8}$ requires many. Table 1 shows the subskills required for some sample problems.

Table 1. Three sample add-fractions problems.

	Find LCM	Equivalent Fractions	Add Numerators	Simplify	Make Proper
$\frac{1}{3} + \frac{1}{3}$	no	no	yes	no	no
$\frac{1}{3} + \frac{1}{4}$	yes	yes	yes	no	no
$\frac{2}{3} + \frac{5}{8}$	yes	yes	yes	yes	yes

Additionally, the topic itself may put certain constraints on the problem which affect its difficulty. For example, students conceptually have an easier time adding fractions that start in simplified form. Therefore these topic constraints must be taken into account when determining problem difficulty.

Given this philosophy, the goal of the tutor in generating problems is to determine how many and which subskills are needed when solving the problem, as well as which topic constraints should be used. For each problem generated, the tutor dynamically makes these decisions, and produces a problem to fit the chosen criteria.

How many subskills? As we have noted, the more subskills required in solving a problem, the harder the problem. The question is, therefore, one of determining how many subskills should be used on each problem.

In MFD, the number of subskills needed is based on two factors: topic ability and acquisition. If the student is doing well on the topic itself, then he should be challenged, and thus the problems should be more difficult. In addition to overly simple problems being an inefficient use of time, there is evidence (Kashihara et al., 1994) that for learning to occur students must be challenged mentally. On the other hand, if the student has been performing poorly on this topic, then the problems should be easier, with fewer subskills involved.

However, a student's acquisition factor should also play a role in problem difficulty. If his acquisition factor is high, then he should also be challenged, since he is able to learn the new material quickly. So even if the topic ability is low, when a student starts a new topic, the problems should not be the simplest possible.

Which subskills? The topic's proficiency affects how many subskills are needed to solve the problem. Just as with topic selection, we want students to practice those skills that they have not mastered. Therefore, the system picks which subskills the student must use based on his ability on each subskill.

To decide which subskills will be used in solving the problem, each skill is given a *priority*, which is a function of its proficiency. The lower the proficiency, the higher the priority; the higher the proficiency, the lower the priority.

Furthermore, even the subskills have levels of difficulty. For example, finding the LCM of two numbers that are multiples is much easier than finding the LCM of two numbers that are not multiples. When choosing the level of difficulty of the subskill, its proficiency is used. The higher the proficiency, the higher the level of difficulty.

It may be the case that two subskills suggest different properties for the problem. For example, the "find LCM" skill may suggest that the denominators are not multiples, but the "equivalent fraction" skill indicates that the denominators be multiples. When this occurs, the one with the lower proficiency is given the higher priority.

4.2   The Algorithm

To determine which subskills should be used for the current problem, a line is dynamically constructed on an x-y coordinate system before a problem is presented. The x-axis represents the student's ability at individual skills and the y-axis is the probability that those skills will be required to solve the problem.

The y-coordinate for the line is determined by the student's proficiency on the current topic. The slope is a function of the student's acquisition factor, and is always negative. The general equation for the line is:

$$y = f(\text{acquisition})x + g(\text{topic ability}) \tag{1}$$

The priorities for all the subskills are the x-coordinates that are plugged into the equation. For topic constraints, the topic proficiency is used as the x-coordinate. Each subskill's and constraint's y-coordinate is calculated based on the line and its x- coordinate. The higher the proficiency, the higher the x-value, and thus the lower the probability the skill will be selected.

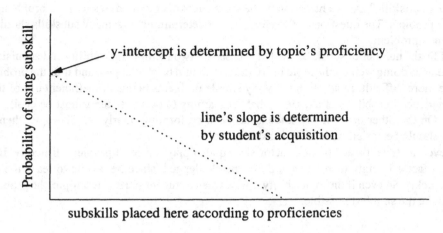

<p style="text-align:center">

Figure 1. Basic structure of problem construction.

Next a random number is generated, and if the number is less than the y-coordinate, the skill or constraint is chosen as a candidate to be used for generating the problem. The randomness is to provide for challenge and/or review. Some subskills for which the student is not ready may be chosen, and some subskills the student has mastered may also be chosen. Also, the randomness helps control for potential inaccuracies in the student model.

Once the subskills and constraints have been chosen, their levels of difficulty must be decided upon. This is determined by looking at the proficiency of the skill. If it is very low, then the easy version is selected. If it is high, the hard version is selected. Otherwise, the medium version is chosen.[3]

At this point, the problem itself can be generated. Generic problems for the chosen topic are generated, and each one is evaluated for its "goodness". This goodness factor is determined by examining how many of the chosen subskills must be applied in solving this problem, as well as how many of the topic constraints apply. Each subskill or constraint that applies contributes its priority to the goodness value. When a problem's goodness is greater than 80% of the maximum goodness,[4] then that problem is selected to be given to the student.

4.3 An Example

First consider Figure 1; this demonstrates graphically the main components of the model. The slope is a function of acquisition, the y-intercept is based on the topic's proficiency, and the subskills are arranged according to their proficiencies on the x-axis. For simplicity, this example assumes that subskills only have two levels of difficulty, and students' abilities are represented as *Excellent (1), Good (0.75), OK (0.5), Fair (0.25),* or *Poor (0)*. The example will be constructed for a student working on a problem that requires adding fractions, and who has the following set of abilities:

---

[3] We are omitting the details of the thresholds for easy, medium, and hard versions.
[4] When all subskills chosen apply and the problem satisfies all constraints.

- *Add Fraction*: Good
- *Simplify Fraction*: Good
- *Make Proper*: Fair

- *Find LCM*: Poor
- *Equivalent Fractions*: OK
- *Acquisition*: Good

Determining features of the line. The first step is to transform the problem's topic's (Add Fraction) proficiency into a y-intercept. Currently MFD simply uses the proficiency, with a maximum score corresponding to a y-intercept of 1 and a minimum score corresponding to a 0. In this case, the y-intercept will be 0.75.

Similarly, the line's slope is determined by the acquisition factor, which is a number between 0 and 1. In this case the acquisition is 0.75. However, for this model the desired slope is negative. Therefore this number is changed as follows:

$$\text{slope} = \frac{-0.5}{\text{acquisition}} \tag{2}$$

So, in this case the slope is $\frac{-0.5}{.75}$ = -0.67. This simple mathematical formulation was tried as a first approximation. If more complexity is needed to account for users' behavior there is no reason a more complex mechanism cannot be substituted in the future.

The y-intercept and slope have been computed, and the equation for the resulting line can be written as:

$$y = -0.67x + 0.75 \tag{3}$$

The y-value is the probability that the subskill will be required to solve the problem. All that remains now is to determine where each subskill is placed on the x-axis. To determine where to place a skill on the x-axis, the system simply uses its proficiency. Since the line that maps x-coordinates to probabilities has a negative slope, a subskill with a large x-value has a small chance of being used. Therefore, the tutor generates problems that require the use of subskills on which the student is not proficient.

Selecting subskills to use. Now the subskills to be used must be chosen. To determine which subskills to use, the system simply calculates the y-value of equation 3 using the proficiency as the x-value in each case. Table 2 shows the result of these steps: based on the subskills' proficiency, its priority and probability of use are calculated.

Table 2. Information about subskills from example.

	Proficiency	P(using subskill)	Priority
Simplify Fraction	0.75	0.25	0.25
Make Proper	0.25	0.58	0.75
Find LCM	0.00	0.75	1.00
Equivalent Fractions	0.50	0.42	0.50

At this stage in the algorithm, randomness is used to decide which subskills will be required of the student in order to solve this problem. For this example, assume the tutor wants to build a problem that will require the student to make the problem's answer proper and to find equivalent fractions, but the student will not have to simplify the result or find a least common multiple (i.e. the result will already be simplified, and both operands have the same denominator).

There is a contradiction between not having to find an LCM and requiring the student to make use of equivalent fractions. Rather than encode this knowledge explicitly, problems are generated and their usefulness is evaluated based on the summed priority of the subskills with which the problem agrees. Priority is the importance of requiring the student to use a subskill in the course of solving the problem, and is computed by calculating $(1 - proficiency)$. Therefore it is possible for a skill that has a high priority to be ignored if several others "vote" in the opposite direction. The tutor generates several problems and picks the one with the highest value. Table 3 provides examples of problem goodness. The first problem matches for Simplify Fraction, Make Proper, and Equivalent Fractions, while the second problem only matches for Find LCM. Thus the first problem has a goodness of 1.50, while the second has a goodness of 1.

5 Updating the Student Model

Once the student solves a problem correctly, the student model must be updated. This is accomplished by examining the hints the student needed to be able to solve the problem, the student's current ability at the topic, and his acquisition and retention factors. The mechanism is similar to that used in (Gurer et al., 1995):

$$\text{Upgrade rule: } p_i = p_i - p_i c + p_{i-1} c \qquad (4)$$

$$\text{Downgrade rule: } p_i = p_i - p_i c + p_{i+1} c \qquad (5)$$

where c is a constant that controls the rate of updating, and p_i is the value of slot i in the "belief vector" (Section 3.1).

Table 3. Value computation for sample problems.

	Priority	Desired?	$\frac{2}{3} + \frac{1}{2}$	$\frac{1}{4} + \frac{1}{4}$
Simplify Fraction	0.25	No	Match	-
Make Proper	0.75	Yes	Match	-
Find LCM	1.00	No	-	Match
Equivalent Fractions	0.50	Yes	Match	-
Problem goodness			1.50	1.00

This formula is used to update the beliefs at each slot in the vector. If a student gets an item correct, the upgrade rule is used; an incorrect response results in the downgrade rule being applied. The result of this is to shift the belief distribution either upwards towards mastery (the student probably knows the material) or downwards.

We have extended this model in two ways. First, instead of simply shifting the entire belief distribution upwards or downwards, it is shifted towards the student's most likely level of ability. Second, instead of using a constant term c, MFD uses parameters that vary as a function of the student's acquisition and retention.

5.1 Changing the Update Parameter

Rather than using a simple constant to update the vector values, MFD calculates a parameter based on the student's acquisition and retention factors. The rationale for this is the relation between how quickly values move towards the "right" of the vector and how quickly the student learns, while how quickly the student moves to the "left" is primarily a function of how likely some of the information is forgotten. If a student has been learning material quickly, his proficiency at a skill should increase more quickly than if he generally required much practice to master a skill.

5.2 Target for Updating Values

Rather than simply shifting the distribution one way or the other, the system moves the belief distribution towards what it infers the student's level of ability to be. The mechanism for computing this is similar to that described in (Stern et al., 1996): The system tracks the levels of the hints presented to the student. A hint's "level" refers to how much information it provides the student. A low-level hint may be a simple prompt such as "Recheck your work" while a high-level hint might say "The answer is 21."

The current implementation first considers the highest level hint the student needed to solve the problem, and then takes its complement[5]. The update rules given previously are used with a slight modification: For vector indices less than the hint level, the upgrade rule is used, while for indices above the hint level the downgrade rule is used.

As a result of the two changes described, the update rule takes the form:

$$\text{For } i \text{ less than the hint level: } p_i = p_i - p_i A + p_{i-1} A \qquad (6)$$

$$\text{For } i \text{ greater than the hint level: } p_i = p_i - p_i B + p_{i+1} B \qquad (7)$$

where A is a function of the acquisition factor, and B is a function of the retention factor. For example, assuming A and B are both 0.5:

$T_0 = (0.14\ 0.14\ 0.14\ 0.14\ 0.14\ 0.14\ 0.14)$; default proficiency
$T_1 = (0.07\ 0.14\ 0.14\ 0.14\ 0.14\ \mathbf{0.28}\ 0.07)$; after a level "2" hint is presented
$T_2 = (0.04\ \mathbf{0.25}\ 0.14\ 0.14\ 0.21\ 0.18\ 0.04)$; after a level "6" hint is presented
$T_3 = (0.02\ 0.14\ 0.19\ 0.14\ \mathbf{0.37}\ 0.11\ 0.02)$; after a level "3" hint is presented

The bold items indicate the most likely level of skill based on the hint given.

This sequence results in the system being able to reason that there is little chance the student knows nothing (or everything) about the domain while it is most likely his level of ability corresponds to "5". Adding this information to the update rule is justified, because of the level of the hint the student requires is closely related to his degree of proficiency (Shute, 1995).

---

[5] This is done by taking (8 − hint level) and is performed simply as a notational convenience

6   Formative Evaluation

In order to test the usefulness of the modeling techniques described, the MFD system was tested on 20 fifth graders with an average age of 10.5 years (one subject's data were discounted due to a learning disability). As this system was used on a limited basis (3 to 4 hours per student), learning gains compared to a traditional class were not the focus of the evaluation. Rather we were interested in how the subjects perceived the level of problem difficulty and the amount of help they required at the beginning of their work with the tutor, and at the end of their time with it.

If the system is adjusting problem difficulty correctly, students will almost certainly need some help from the tutor; otherwise it is probably not being assertive enough at providing difficult problems. Of course, if too much help is required, it is possible that students are having considerable difficulty and may be getting frustrated with the system.

An analysis was performed of how much help students needed as their interactions with the system progressed. For the first third of the problems students required about 0.01 hints per problem, for the medium third 0.17 hints per problem, and for the final third 1.1 hints per problem. The final number of hints per problem seems slightly high, but the first two numbers are extremely low. A reasonable conclusion is that problems should be more difficult initially, but the system was somewhat too aggressive in providing difficult problems (either through overestimating their abilities or simply constructing problems that are too difficult for a given ability).

Table 4. Student responses about problem difficulty.

Student's belief	Beginning	End
Too easy	53%	11%
Too hard	11%	58%
Just right	37%	32%

However, as Table 4 shows, examining qualitative data gathered from questionnaires gives a different perspective. Many students thought the initial problems were too easy; however for others the problems were at the right level of difficulty or too hard. Initial problems are heavily based on the default student model, which attempts to capture the "average" student. Based on student responses, it has done a good job at this. However a mechanism for quickly moving the default values towards a student's actual ability is needed. Previous researchers (Shute, 1995) have used methods such as pretests to initialize the default student model. We would prefer a more integrated mechanism that would automatically update the tutor's representation of a student's ability more quickly when the tutor's estimate is uncertain (e.g. when the student first starts working with the tutor). Alternately, if a few common types of users can be distinguished, stereotypes (Kay, 1994) can be used to provide superior default reasoning about users.

Additionally, students thought the later problems were more difficult than the analysis of hints required indicated. Students claimed the problems were too difficult, but the number of hints they required wasn't that high (we were trying to have problems that required one hint per problem). It is possible that students are underestimating their abilities as they are not needing too much help on later problems. In future studies, we will examine both the number of hints required and qualitative feedback from students in order to evaluate the system.

Students were generally enthusiastic about using the system. On a scale of 1 (don't want to work with the system again) to 7 (would like to work with the system very much) students gave the tutor a 5.5. Similarly, when asked how much of an effect the system had on their mathematics skills students reported that it had a positive effect (5.5 out of 7). An interesting item is that initially boys and girls rated problems at the same level of difficulty, but by the end the girls rated problems as being more difficult than the boys did (6.1 to 4.7). This difference was statistically significant, and troublesome as one of the system's goals is to help increase girls' confidence in their mathematics abilities. Additionally, this indicates that a tutor using gender as a variable is better able to customize its interactions to fit the user. However, this is a rather sensitive issue and altering instruction in this manner may not be appropriate. This remains a difficult balancing act between providing difficult problems vs. not allowing students to become frustrated or discouraged.

7   Conclusions and Future Work

With little extra effort, it is possible to collect additional information about how the student is currently performing and how his performance is changing over time. These data can be used to directly affect teaching strategy selection and problem generation. We have derived an algorithm, based on our model of problem difficulty, that uses the student model to adjust the characteristics, and thus the difficulty, of problems such that they are appropriate for the student's abilities. This mechanism is clearly applicable to other domains involving mathematics. With alteration, it can also be applied to areas that have procedural skills in which the steps to be performed can be considered to be subskills. For example, medical training has problems that can be categorized by topics and has distinct substeps that must be performed.

We are also interested in constructing general factors that provide an overall summary of a student's progress. While our metrics are not as accurate as those derived for Stat Lady (Shute, 1995), which used a lengthy test to derive one general factor, the factors here are easily obtainable and have a clear fit into the tutor's model of the student. Furthermore, all systems must make some assumptions about what constants to use. Rather than assuming one number will work for every student, MFD uses what data it has to get a better approximation. So even if the estimates of acquisition and retention are not precise, they are better than just using the same default value for each student.

Future research goals include finding better methods of computing general factors about the student to build a more accurate model. Additionally, finding a better use for the vector based model rather than collapsing it to a simple number is a priority. We are also investigating more formal approaches to probabilistic student models. To address these issues, the system is being tested in several local fifth grade classrooms for one month in the Spring of 1997.

References

Anderson, J. (1993). *Rules of the Mind*. Hillsdale, NJ: Lawrence Erlbaum Associates.

Anderson, J., and Reiser, B. (1985). The LISP tutor. *Byte* 10(4):159–175.

Bloom, B. (1984). The 2 sigma problem: The search for methods of group instruction as effective as one-to-one tutoring. *Educational Researcher* 13:3–16.

Eliot, C. (1996). *An Intelligent Tutoring System Based Upon Adaptive Simulation*. Ph.D. Dissertation, University of Massachusetts.

Gurer, D., desJardins, M., and Schlager, M. (1995). Representing a student's learning states and transitions. Presented at the 1995 American Association of Artificial Intelligence Spring Symposium on Representing Mental States and Mechanisms.

Kashihara, A., Sugano, A., Matsumura, K., Hirashima, T., and Toyoda, J. (1994). A cognitive load application approach to tutoring. In *Proceedings of the Fourth International Conference on User Modeling*, 163–168.

Katz, S., Lesgold, A., Eggan, G., and Gordin, M. (1993). Modelling the student in Sherlock II. *Journal of Artificial Intelligence in Education* 3(4):495–518.

Kay, J. (1994). Lies, damned lies and stereotypes: Pragmatic approximation of users. In *Proceedings of the Fourth International Conference on User Modeling*, 175–184.

Shute, V. (1995). Smart evaluation: Cognitive diagnosis, mastery learning and remediation. In *Artificial Intelligence in Education: Proceedings of AI-ED 95*, 123–130.

Shute, V., Glaser, R., and Raghaven, K. (1989). Inference and discovery in an exploratory laboratory. In Ackerman, P., Sterberg, R., and Glaser, R., eds., *Learning and Individual Differences*, 279–326.

Stern, M., Beck, J., and Woolf, B. (1996). Adaptation of problem presentation and feedback in an intelligent mathematics tutor. In *Proceedings of Intelligent Tutoring Systems*, 605–613.

User Modeling and Adaptive Navigation Support in WWW-Based Tutoring Systems

Gerhard Weber and Marcus Specht*

Department of Psychology, University of Trier, Germany

Abstract. Most learning systems and electronic textbooks accessible via the WWW up to now lack the capabilities of individualized help and adapted learning support that are the emergent features of on-site intelligent tutoring systems. This paper discusses the problems of developing interactive and adaptive learning systems on the WWW. We introduce ELM-ART II, an intelligent interactive textbook to support learning programming in LISP. ELM-ART II demonstrates how interactivity and adaptivity can be implemented in WWW-based tutoring systems. The knowledge-based component of the system uses a combination of an overlay model and an episodic user model. It also supports adaptive navigation as individualized diagnosis and help on problem solving tasks. Adaptive navigation support is achieved by annotating links. Additionally, the system selects the next best step in the curriculum on demand. Results of an empirical study show different effects of these techniques on different types of users during the first lessons of the programming course.

1 Introduction

Originally, the WWW was used to retrieve information from all over the world. Very soon, however, it became clear that the WWW will be able to allow for extended interactivity. With the increased utilization of the interactive features of the WWW a lot of learning systems emerged that introduce users into various domains. The number of learning courses is exploding, and one can see a lot of interesting features that emerge with the improved capabilities of new WWW browsers. Up to now, however, most of these systems have been in an experimental stage. They provide only limited support to users who are not familiar with the new domain. And there are only few systems that adapt to a particular user as on-site tutoring systems do.

In this paper, we first discuss why student modeling is necessary in an individualized WWW-based tutoring system and what the goals of student modeling are. Then we introduce ELM-ART II, an adaptive, knowledge-based tutoring system on the WWW that supports learning programming in LISP. We show how the goals of individual student modeling are accomplished in this system and, finally, we report on the first results of an empirical study of different types of adaptive navigation support.

---

*This work is supported by a grant from the "Stiftung Rheinland-Pfalz für Innovation" to the first author.

2   Goals of Student Modeling in WWW-Based Tutoring Systems

The two main features in intelligent tutoring systems (ITS) are curriculum sequencing and interactive problem solving support. These features differentiate intelligent learning systems from traditional computer-assisted instruction in that they incorporate intelligent techniques that skilled human teachers use in teaching classes or in coaching individual learners. Most intelligent learning systems are used in the classroom and, therefore, do not necessarily need to include all these intelligent features. Many systems concentrate on diagnosing solutions to exercises only (e.g., Johnson, 1986; Soloway et al., 1983; Vanneste, 1994) or support all stages of problem solving during work on exercises and problem solving tasks (e.g., Anderson et al., 1995; Weber and Möllenberg, 1995). WWW-based learning systems, however, can be used outside the classroom. In such a distance learning situation, no teacher is directly available who can help during learning and who can adapt the number and nature of new concepts presented to the learner's current knowledge state. Therefore, the learning system has to play the role of the teacher as far as possible. The system has to build up an individual user model for every user to be able to adapt the curriculum to the user, to help him or her navigate through the course, and to support working on exercises and problem solving individually.

2.1 Curriculum Sequencing and Adaptive Guidance

Curriculum sequencing describes the order in which new knowledge units and skills to be learned and corresponding teaching operations (e.g., presenting examples and demonstrations, asking questions, providing exercises and tests, solving problems) are presented to a particular learner. In textbooks, the traditional learning medium, the curriculum is predefined by the author of the textbook. The same holds for most texts delivered via the WWW. The curriculum is predefined by the author of the text or by the developer of the system. That is, authors provide an optimal learning path for an assumed average learner. This is a well-established strategy in the writing of textbooks.

In the case of electronic textbooks, however, the situation is totally different. Electronic textbooks are usually presented in the form of a hypertext that allows for random surfing through the text space. In order not to get lost in this hyperspace, some guidance by the system may be helpful. WWW-browsers only annotate visited links but are not able to give any hint as to what pages will be suitable to be visited next. Another situation arises when the learner is not a complete beginner in the new domain to be learned but already possesses some (possibly incomplete and incorrect) knowledge of the topics to be learned. In this case, it is a waste of time for the learner to read all of the pages of the canonical curriculum and to work at corresponding problems and tests that the learner is already familiar with.

In both situations, information contained in an individual user model can be used by the learning system to adapt the presentation of pages to the particular user. A simple type of a user model like an overlay model (Carr and Goldstein, 1977) may be well suited to represent all the necessary knowledge for individualized curriculum sequencing and adaptive guidance in the hypertext. In its simplest form, the user model contains information on whether an item of the knowledge base is learned, it is not completely learned, or its status is unknown. Examples of systems using such knowledge are BIP (Barr et al., 1976), ITEM-IP (Brusilovsky, 1992) and HyperTutor (Pérez et al., 1995a). A more elaborate user model can differentiate between more detailed knowledge states. It is important to distinguish between pages describing new knowledge that were only visited and pages where learners successfully performed some tests or problem solving tasks. Additionally, depending on results from tests and exercises, the system can decide whether some prerequisite knowledge must be known to the learner though he or she did not work at these knowledge items before.

In WWW-based learning systems, maintaining an individual user model and observing and diagnosing the learner's knowledge state is much more complicated. Only a few systems exist that use at least rudimentary types of individualized curriculum sequencing and adaptive hypertext guidance (e.g., Brusilovsky et al., 1996b; Kay and Kummerfeld, 1994; Lin et al., 1996; Schwarz et al., 1996). More advanced techniques of knowledge-based navigation support are described in KBNS (Eklund, in press) and in HyperTutor (Pérez et al., 1995b). In this paper we describe an alternative approach that is used in ELM-ART II.

2.2 Individual Help and Problem Solving Support

Knowledge-based learning systems support learners while they are working on exercises and during problem solving. There are two main techniques used. On the one hand, a lot of systems exist that provide intelligent diagnosis of complete solutions to exercises and problem solving tasks. In the domain of learning programming, several well-known systems exist that offer this type of problem solving support—e.g., MENO II (Soloway et al., 1983), PROUST (Johnson, 1986), CAMUS II (Vanneste et al., 1993), and ELM-PE (Weber and Möllenberg, 1995). On the other side, systems based on the *model tracing* approach (Anderson et al., 1995) provide continuous interactive problem solving support during working at exercises.

The currently most advanced systems are the model tracing tutors based on the ACT theory (Anderson, 1993) and the programming tutors ELM-PE and ELM-ART based on the ELM model (Weber, 1996). In the ACT-based model tracing tutors, the system observes the learner during the solving of a problem and gives advice when the solution path will result in an error. This type of tutoring is well suited for on-site tutoring systems. Up to now, however, such direct observing of single problem solving steps cannot be performed on-line in WWW-based tutoring systems because the delay caused by the correspondence with the server would be too long. In the future, this problem may be solved by creating intelligent on-site agents based on JAVA applets.

The ELM-based systems follow an episodic learner modeling approach. Episodic learner modeling is well suited for diagnosing complete and incomplete solutions to problems and giving individualized help. Moreover, examples that best fit the current learning situation can be chosen on the basis of the individual episodic learner model (Burow and Weber, 1996). The diagnosis in ELM-PE does not follow the problem solving process directly but is performed only on demand. Therefore, this approach meets the needs of the client-server communication employed in WWW-based learning systems.

3 ELM-ART II

3.1 The History of Developing ELM-ART II

The WWW-based introductory LISP course ELM-ART (ELM Adaptive Remote Tutor) is based on ELM-PE (Weber and Möllenberg, 1995), an on-site intelligent learning environment that supports example-based programming, intelligent analysis of problem solutions, and advanced testing and debugging facilities. The intelligent features of ELM-PE are based on the ELM model

(Weber, 1996). For several years, ELM-PE was used in introductory LISP courses at the University of Trier. The course materials were presented to students in regular classes (completed with printed materials) as well as to single students working on their own with the printed materials only. Students used ELM-PE to practice the new knowledge by working on exercises. In this way, they were able to acquire the necessary programming skills.

ELM-PE was limited by the platform dependent implementation of the user interface and the large size of the application. Both limitations hindered a wider distribution and usage of the system. So, we decided to build a WWW-based version of ELM-PE that can be used both in intranets and in the Internet. The first step was to translate the texts of the printed materials into WWW-readable form (html files), dividing it into small subsections and text pages that are associated with concepts to be learned. These concepts were related to each other by describing the concepts' prerequisites and outcomes, building up a conceptual network. All interactions of the learner with ELM-ART were recorded in an individual learner model. For each page visited, the corresponding unit of the conceptual network was marked correspondingly. When presenting text pages in the WWW browser, links shown in section and subsection pages and in the overview were annotated corresponding to a simple traffic lights metaphor referring to information from the individual learner model (Schwarz et al., 1996). A red ball in front of the link indicated that the corresponding section or text page was not ready to be learned because necessary prerequisites were not met. A green ball indicated that this page or section was ready and recommended to be learned and a yellow ball indicated that this link was ready to be visited but not especially recommended by the system.

ELM-ART enabled direct interactivity by providing live examples and intelligent diagnoses of problem solutions. All examples of function calls could be evaluated. When the learner clicked on such a live example link, the evaluation of the function call was shown in an evaluator window similar to a listener in ordinary LISP environments. Users could type solutions to a programming problem into an editable window and then send it to the server. Evaluation and diagnosis of problem solutions were performed the same way as in ELM-PE. Therefore, the same feedback messages that had proven to be useful in ELM-PE could be sent back to the learner.

The approach of converting printed textbooks to electronic textbooks used in ELM-ART has been developed further in INTERBOOK (Brusilovsky et al., 1996b), an authoring tool for creating electronic textbooks with adaptive annotation of links. However, from our first experiences with using ELM-ART we understood that printed textbooks are not suitable for being transformed to hypertext pages in electronic textbooks in a one-to-one manner. Textbooks are usually written in sequential order so that single pages cannot be read easily when they are accessed from any page within the course. Additionally, the simple adaptive annotation technique used in ELM-ART had to be improved. Users should get more information on the state of different concepts that they had already visited and learned or had to learn. And, perhaps most importantly, inferring the knowledge state of a particular user from only visiting (and possibly reading) a new page is not appropriate (as correctly pointed out by Eklund, in press). These objections and shortcomings were the motivation for building ELM-ART II, a new version of ELM-ART we describe in the following sections.

3.2 The Electronic Textbook and Adaptive Guidance

Knowledge representation. ELM-ART II represents knowledge about units to be learned with the electronic textbook in terms of a conceptual network (Brusilovsky et al., 1996a). Units are organized hierarchically into lessons, sections, subsections, and terminal pages. Terminal pages can introduce new concepts or offer problems to be solved. Each unit is an object containing slots for the text to be presented with the corresponding page and for information that can be used to relate units and concepts to each other. Static slots store information on prerequisite concepts, related concepts, and outcomes of the unit (they are the concepts that the system assumes to be known when the user worked on that unit successfully). Units for terminal pages have a tests slot that may contain the description of a group of test items the learner has to perform. When test items have been solved successfully the system can infer that the user possesses the knowledge about the concepts explained in this unit. Problem pages have a slot for storing a description of a programming problem.

Dynamic slots are stored with the individual learner model that is built up for each user. This user model is updated automatically during each interaction with ELM-ART. For each page visited during the course, the corresponding unit is marked as visited in the user model. Moreover, when the test items in a testgroup or a programming problem are solved correctly, the outcome concepts of this unit are marked as known and an inference process is started. In the inference process, all concepts that are prerequisites to this unit (and recursively all prerequisites to these units) are marked as inferred. Information from the dynamic slots in the user model are used to annotate links individually and to guide the learner optimally through the course.

Testgroups. Testgroups are collections of test items that are associated with page units. Single test items may belong to different testgroups. In ELM-ART II, four different types of test items are supported: yes-no test items, forced-choice test items, multiple-choice test items, and free-form test items. In yes-no test items users simply have to answer yes-no questions by clicking the "yes" or the "no" button. In forced-choice test items, users have to answer a question by selecting one of the alternative answers and in multiple-choice test items users have to answer a question by selecting all correct answers provided by the system. In free-form test items, users can type an answer to the question asked freely into a form. Each testgroup has parameters that determine how many single test items are presented to the learner. The *group-length* parameter determines how many test items are presented on a single page. The *min-problems-solved* parameter defines the minimal number of test items that have to be solved correctly within the testgroup. The *max-errors* parameter determines how many errors maximally are allowed in the test items that were presented on a single page. These parameters can be set for each testgroup.

Test items from a testgroup are presented as long as not enough test items have been answered correctly. A fixed number of test items are presented simultaneously on one page. The system gives feedback on the number of errors in the test items presented on the last page and presents all erroneous test items with both the users' answers and the correct answers. Additionally, an explanation is given why the answer provided by the system is the correct one. These explanations are stored separately with each test item. Correctly solved test items from the current testgroup can be accessed via an icon on that page. They are displayed in a new window showing the correct answers as well as the reason why this answer was correct. Users are called on to solve more test items as long as not enough test items have been solved correctly and not too many incorrect answers have been submitted with the last test items. In the individual user model, all test items that are solved correctly for a particular testgroup are stored in a dynamic slot. When enough test items are solved correctly without making too many errors, the outcome concepts of the corresponding unit are marked as solved and the inference process is started. In the current version of ELM-ART II, the values of the *min-problems-solved* parameter vary between 4 and 10 depending on the difficulty of the tests and, in most cases, the *max-errors* parameter is set to 1. That is, after solving at least a number of *min-problems-solved* test items correctly, in the next group of test items shown on a page one error is allowed.

In the LISP course, tests play a twofold role. On the one hand, tests are used to check whether the user possesses the correct declarative knowledge. This is especially useful in the beginning of the course when a lot of new concepts (data types and function definitions) are introduced. On the other hand, tests can be used in evaluation tasks to check whether users are able to evaluate LISP expressions correctly. Skills used in evaluation are the inverse skills to generating function calls and function definitions. Evaluation skills are needed to decide whether programs work correctly and to find errors in programming code. Program creation skills are practiced in special tasks. They are supported by the episodic learner model approach described in Section 3.3.

Visual adaptive annotation of links. ELM-ART II uses an extension of the traffic lights metaphor to annotate links visually (see Figure 1). On the top of each terminal page (below the navigation button line) all links belonging to the same subsection are shown with the links annotated corresponding to their current state. Green, red, yellow, and orange balls are used to annotate the links (additionally, the texts of the links are outlined in different styles to aid color-blind users).

A *green* ball means that this page is ready and suggested to be visited and the concepts taught on this page are ready to be learned. That is, all prerequisites to this concept have been learned already or are inferred to be known.

A *red* ball means that this page is not ready to be visited. In this case, at least one of the prerequisite concepts is not known to the learner (that is, the system cannot infer from successfully solved tests and programming problems that the user will possess the required knowledge). However, the user is allowed to visit this page and in the case that he or she solves the corresponding test or programming problem correctly, the system infers backwards that all the necessary prerequisites are known. This is a very strong assumption in diagnosing the user's knowledge state and will be changed through the use of fuzzy or probabilistic models in the future.

A *yellow* ball has different meanings depending on the type of page this link points to. In the case of a terminal page with a test or a problem page, the yellow ball means that the test or the problem have been solved correctly. In the case of any other terminal page, the yellow ball indicates that this page has been visited already. In the case of a lesson, section, or subsection link the yellow ball means that all subordinated pages have been learned or visited.

An *orange* ball has different meanings, too. In the case of a terminal page, an orange ball means the system infers from other successfully learned pages that the content of this page will be known to the learner (as described above). In the case of a lesson, section, or subsection link an orange ball means that this page has been visited already but not all subordinated pages have been visited or worked at successfully.

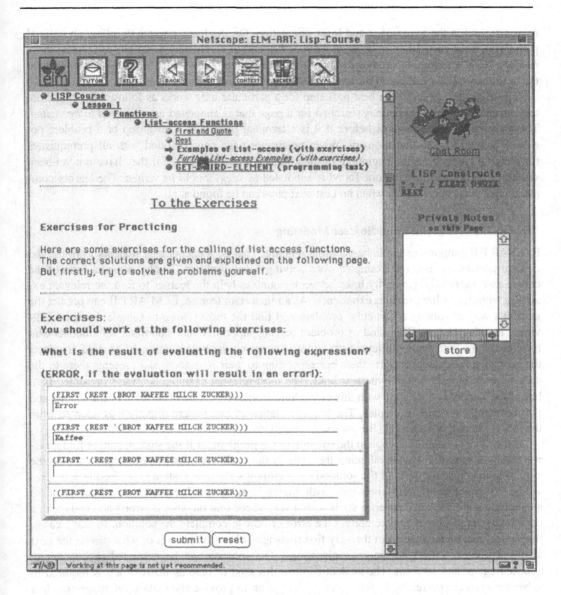

Figure 1. Example of a text page with free-form test items and adaptive annotation of links.

In browsers supporting JavaScript, the different meanings of a state of a link are explained in the status line at the bottom of the window when the cursor is located over the link (Figure 1).

Individual Curriculum Sequencing. While adaptive annotation of links is a powerful technique to aid users when navigating through the pages of the course, some users may be confused about what the best next step should be to continue with the course. This may happen when the learner moves around in the hyperspace and loses orientation. Or, the learner wants to follow an optimal path through the curriculum in order to learn as fast and as completely as possible. To meet these needs, a NEXT button in the navigation bar of the text pages allows the user to ask the system for the best next step depending on the current knowledge state of the particular user.

The algorithm to select the best next step for a particular user works as follows: Starting from the current page, the next page is searched for a page that is annotated as *suggested to be visited*. This may be the same page as before if it is a terminal page with a testgroup or a problem not solved correctly up to that moment. When no further page can be found with all prerequisites fulfilled, all pages from the beginning of the course are checked to see if they have not yet been visited or solved and the first one found is annotated as *suggested to be visited*. The learner completes the course successfully when no best next page can be found at all.

3.3 On-Line Help and Episodic User Modeling

ELM-ART II supports example-based programming. That is, it encourages students to re-use the code of previously analyzed examples when solving a new problem. The hypermedia form of the course and, especially, similarity links between examples help the learner to find the relevant examples from his or her previous experience. As an important feature, ELM-ART II can predict the student's way of solving a particular problem and find the most relevant example from the individual learning history. This kind of problem solving support is very important for students who have problems with finding relevant examples. Answering the help request, ELM-ART II selects the most helpful examples, sorts them corresponding to their relevance, and presents them to the student as an ordered list of hypertext links. The most relevant example is always presented first, but, if the student is not happy with this example for some reason, he or she can try the second and the following suggested examples. The implementation of this feature directly was adopted from the recent version of ELM-PE (Burow and Weber, 1996).

If the student failed to complete the solution to the problem, or if the student cannot find an error that was reported when evaluating the code in the evaluator window, he or she can ask the system to diagnose the code of the solution in its current state. The system gives feedback by providing a sequence of help messages with increasingly detailed explanation of an error or suboptimal solution. The sequence starts with a very vague hint on what is wrong and ends with a code-level suggestion of how to correct the error or how to complete the solution. In many cases, the student can understand from the very first messages where the error is or what can be the next step and does not need any more explanations. The solution can be corrected or completed, checked again, and so forth. The student can use this kind of help as many times as required to solve the problem correctly. In this context, the option to provide the code-level suggestion is a very important feature of ELM-ART II as a distance learning system. It ensures that all students will ultimately solve the problem without the assistance of a human teacher.

Both the individual presentation of example programs and the diagnosis of program code are based on the episodic learner model (ELM, Weber, 1996). ELM is a type of user or learner model that stores knowledge about the user (learner) in terms of a collection of episodes. In the sense of case-based learning, such episodes can be viewed as cases (Kolodner, 1993). To construct the learner model, the code produced by a learner is analyzed in terms of the domain knowledge on the one hand and a task description on the other hand. This cognitive diagnosis results in a derivation tree of concepts and rules the learner might have used to solve the problem. These concepts and rules are instantiations of units from the knowledge base. The episodic learner model is made up of these instantiations.

In ELM only examples from the course materials are pre-analyzed and the resulting explanation structures are stored in the individual case-based learner model. Elements from the explanation structures are stored with respect to their corresponding concepts from the domain knowledge base, so cases are distributed in terms of instances of concepts. These individual cases—or parts of them—can be used for two different purposes. On the one hand, episodic instances can be used during further analyses as shortcuts if the actual code and plan match corresponding patterns in episodic instances. On the other hand, cases can be used by the analogical component to show up similar examples and problems for reminding purposes.

4   An Experimental Study on Annotation and Curriculum Sequencing

With the introduction of the new version ELM-ART II, we started an accompanying empirical study to look at the effects of combining the new adaptive annotation technique used in ELM-ART II with the guidance offered by the NEXT button. Therefore, two treatments with two levels each were investigated simultaneously. The first treatment contrasts the adaptive annotation of links as described above with simply annotating links as visited (yellow ball) and not visited (orange ball). This second type of annotation used in the control group is comparable to the usual annotation performed by WWW browsers annotate links that have already been visited and that are cached. The second treatment contrasts providing a NEXT best step button with a version without this navigation button.

Each user starting to work with ELM-ART II is assigned randomly to one of the four treatment conditions. In an introductory questionnaire, users are asked whether they are familiar with programming languages and whether they already know LISP. In this experimental study, only data from subjects that do not know LISP are being used. Subjects come from an introductory LISP course held at the Psychology Department at the University of Trier. Additionally, users from all over the world can login to the LISP course.

A first hypothesis postulates that both the visual adaptive annotation of links and individual curriculum sequencing with the NEXT button will motivate users to proceed with learning. Many people from outside of our university visit ELM-ART II to see how such an introductory interactive programming course works via WWW. So, a good measure of the stimulative nature of link annotation and individual curriculum sequencing is the number of pages with tests and problems users solved correctly before they stopped working with ELM-ART II. In this first investigation, 33 subjects working with ELM-ART II, who visited more than the first five pages (that is, they had more than a first glance at the course), and without any experience in LISP did not finish the third lesson. Fourteen of these 33 subjects had no previous experience in any programming language at all, whereas 19 subjects were familiar with at least one other programming language. Results are shown in Table 1.

Table 1A shows a significant effect of individual curriculum sequencing by a specific NEXT button on subjects who had no previous experiences in any programming language. Subjects who could use such a button worked on about 10 pages more than subjects without such a button ($MS = 401.5$, $F(1,10) = 5.71$, $p < .05$). There was no effect of link annotation on how long complete beginners tried to learn with ELM-ART II. Unlike the programming beginners, subjects who were

Table 1. Mean number of pages with tests and problems that users (who did not finish the third lesson) solved correctly until they stopped working with ELM-ART II. A) Users with no previous programming language. B) Users with at least one previous programming language.

A)	Adaptive Annotation		
	With	Without	
NEXT button	21.0 ($N = 4$)	25.0 ($N = 3$)	22.7 ($N = 7$)
No NEXT button	13.8 ($N = 5$)	9.5 ($N = 2$)	12.6 ($N = 7$)
	17.0 ($N = 9$)	18.8 ($N = 5$)	17.7 ($N = 14$)

B)	Adaptive Annotation		
	With	Without	
NEXT button	23.5 ($N = 6$)	14.0 ($N = 3$)	20.3 ($N = 9$)
No NEXT button	22.4 ($N = 5$)	12.6 ($N = 5$)	17.5 ($N = 10$)
	23.0 ($N = 11$)	13.1 ($N = 8$)	18.8 ($N = 19$)

familiar with at least one other programming language (Table 1B) visited tendentially more pages and solved more exercises and problems when working with adaptive link annotation, though the effect is not quite statistically significant in our small sample (23.0 vs. 13.1 pages, $MS = 413.9$, $F(1,15) = 2.96, p = 0.11$).

These results can be easily interpreted when one looks at the navigation behavior of the complete beginners more closely. All but one of the beginners had no experience in using a WWW browser. That is, these subjects profited from being guided directly by the system when using the NEXT button. Without such a button, they had to navigate through the course materials on their own. Learning to navigate through a hypertext in addition to learning the programming language may have been too difficult. So individual adaptive guidance by the system is especially helpful for the complete beginners. Most subjects who were familiar with at least one other programming language were familiar with Web browsers. They were more pleased with the link annotation and stayed longer with the learning system when links were annotated adaptively.

A second hypothesis postulates that the number of navigation steps is reduced by both adaptive navigation support and individual curriculum sequencing with the NEXT button. Both techniques should have an additive effect on the navigation process. Fourteen subjects finished the first lesson of the introductory LISP course in ELM-ART II. The number of navigation steps used with and without link annotation and with and without the NEXT button are shown in Table 2. Differences in the average numbers of navigation steps are not significant with this small number of subjects, and the data seem to support the hypothesis only partially. Subjects that are individually guided by using a NEXT button needed fewer steps to finish the first lesson than subjects without such an option (71.9 vs. 98.6 steps, respectively). The adaptive link annotation does not seem to have any systematic effect on the number of navigation steps. These very small effects observed from the first lesson fade away during the following lessons. That is, only in the beginning does individual guidance by the system help learners to follow an optimal path through the curriculum. Later on,

Table 2. Mean number of navigation steps needed in the first lesson.

	Adaptive Annotation		
	With	Without	
NEXT button	66.6 (N = 7)	81.3 (N = 4)	71.9 (N = 11)
No NEXT button	103.4 (N = 9)	87.8 (N = 4)	98.6 (N = 13)
	87.3 (N = 16)	84.5 (N = 8)	86.4 (N = 24)

all subjects understand the simple hierarchical architecture of the programming course and most of them follow the best learning path without any guidance.

These results do not mean that adaptive link annotation and adaptive curriculum sequencing are not as important as expected. As could be shown in the data above, these techniques are especially useful in the starting phase when users, especially beginners, are often frustrated. And, these techniques will presumably be helpful to advanced users that already posses some of the to-be-learned knowledge. In this case, a system that is able to adapt to the particular user will be helpful in navigating him or her around all the pages that the system infers to be known. However, this has to be shown in a another advantage study.

5 Conclusion

The system ELM-ART II described in this paper is an example of how an ITS can be implemented on the WWW. It integrates the features of electronic textbooks, learning environments, and intelligent tutoring systems. User modeling techniques like simple overlay models or more elaborated episodic learner models are well suited to allow for adaptive guidance and to individualized help and problem solving support in WWW-based learning systems. Perhaps the WWW can help ITS to move from laboratories (where most of these "intelligent" system are used due to the enormous requirements in computing power and capacity) to classrooms and to permanent availability in distance learning.

ELM-ART–II is implemented with the programmable WWW-server CL-HTTP (URL: http://www.ai.mit.edu/projects/iiip/doc/cl-http/home-page.html). ELM-ART II can be accessed with the following URL: http://www.psychologie.uni-trier.de:8000/elmart.

References

Anderson, J. R. (1993). *Rules of the Mind*. Hillsdale, NJ: Lawrence Erlbaum Associates.

Anderson, J. R., Corbett, A. T., Koedinger, K. R., and Pelletier, R. (1995). Cognitive tutors: Lessons learned. *The Journal of the Learning Sciences* 4:167–207.

Barr, A., Beard, M., and Atkinson, R. C. (1976). The computer as a tutorial laboratory: The Stanford BIP project. *International Journal of Man-Machine Studies* 8:567–596.

Brusilovsky, P. (1992). Intelligent tutor, environment, and manual for introductory programming. *Educational and Training Technology International* 29:26–34.

300 G. Weber and M. Specht

Brusilovsky, P., Schwarz, E., and Weber, G. (1996a). ELM-ART: An intelligent tutoring system on World Wide Web. In Frasson, C., Gauthier, G., and Lesgold, A., eds., *Proceedings of the Third International Conference on Intelligent Tutoring Systems, ITS-96*. Berlin: Springer. 261–269.

Brusilovsky, P., Schwarz, E., and Weber, G. (1996b). A tool for developing adaptive electronic textbooks on WWW. *Proceedings of WebNet'96, World Conference on the Web Society*. Charlottesville: AACE. 64–69.

Burow, R., and Weber, G. (1996). Example explanation in learning environments. In Frasson, C., Gauthier, G., and Lesgold, A., eds., *Intelligent Tutoring Systems—Proceedings of the Third International Conference, ITS '96*. Berlin: Springer. 457–465.

Carr, B., and Goldstein, I. (1977). *Overlays: A theory of modelling for computer aided instruction* (AI Memo 406). Cambridge, MA: Massachusetts Institute of Technology, AI Laboratory.

Eklund, J. (in press). Knowledge-based navigation support in hypermedia courseware using WEST. *Australian Educational Computing* 11.

Johnson, W. L. (1986). *Intention-Based Diagnosis of Novice Programming Errors*. London: Pitman.

Kay, J., and Kummerfeld, R. J. (1994). An individualised course for the C programming language. *Proceedings of the Second International WWW Conference "Mosaic and the Web"*.

Kolodner, J. L. (1993). *Case-Based Reasoning*. San Mateo, CA: Morgan Kaufmann.

Lin, F., Danielson, R., and Herrgott, S. (1996). Adaptive interaction through WWW. In Carlson, P., and Makedon, F., eds., *Proceedings of ED-TELEKOM 96—World Conference on Educational Telecommunications*. Charlottesville, VA: AACE. 173–178.

Pérez, T., Gutiérrez, J., and Lopistéguy, P. (1995a). An adaptive hypermedia system. In Greer, J., ed., *Proceedings of AI-ED'95, 7th World Conference on Artificial Intelligence in Education*. Washington, DC: AACE. 351–358.

Pérez, T., Lopistéguy, P., Gutiérrez, J., and Usandizaga, I. (1995b). HyperTutor: From hypermedia to intelligent adaptive hypermedia. In Maurer, H., ed., *Proceedings of ED-MEDIA'95, World Conference on Educational Multimedia and Hypermedia*. Graz, Austria: AACE. 529–534.

Schwarz, E., Brusilovsky, P., and Weber, G. (1996). World-wide intelligent textbooks. In Carlson, P., and Makedon, F., eds., *Proceedings of ED-TELEKOM 96—World Conference on Educational Telecommunications*. Charlottesville, VA: AACE. 302–307.

Soloway, E., Rubin, E., Woolf, B., Johnson, W. L., and Bonar, J. (1983). MENO II: An AI-based programming tutor. *Journal of Computer-Based Instruction* 10:20–34.

Vanneste, K., Bertels, K., and De Decker, B. (1993). The use of semantic augmentation within a student program analyser. *Proceedings of the Seventh International PEG Conference*. 250–260.

Vanneste, P. (1994). *The Use of Reverse Engineering in Novice Program Analysis*. Ph.D. Dissertation, Katholieke Universiteit Leuven, Belgium.

Weber, G. (1996). Episodic learner modeling. *Cognitive Science* 20:195–236.

Weber, G., and Möllenberg, A. (1995). ELM programming environment: A tutoring system for LISP beginners. In Wender, K. F., Schmalhofer, F., and Böcker, H.-D., eds., *Cognition and Computer Programming*. Norwood, NJ: Ablex Publishing Corporation. 373–408.

Learner Modelling for Intelligent CALL

Maureen Murphy* and Michael McTear

School of Information and Software Engineering, University of Ulster, N. Ireland

Abstract. The demand for software for Computer-Assisted Language Learning (CALL) is increasing considerably. However a drawback of most, if not all, of the currently available CALL software is that it cannot provide very helpful feedback to the learner. The aim of this project was to work towards providing a more adequate and user-oriented interface for CALL. The project focused on the design of an application called CASTLE which takes into account the strengths, weaknesses, preferences and level of proficiency of each individual student when tutoring. This was accomplished by developing a module that provides detailed linguistic analysis of the learner's response to the exercises of the program, a module that creates a dynamic model of the learner, and a module that controls the system's reactions to the learner's input and the structure of the materials offered to the learner.

1 Introduction

Computer-Assisted Language Learning (CALL) systems are becoming increasingly popular within the educational, training and business worlds. They have many advantages, for example, giving learners more independence from classrooms and allowing them the option to work on their material at any time of the day. Once implemented, it can be expected that the cost for CALL systems is considerably lower than for classroom teaching, and when used in conjunction with traditional classroom study, students can study more independently, leaving the teacher more time to concentrate on aspects of language teaching unsuitable for the computer, such as pronunciation and work on spoken dialogue. There are many CALL packages commercially available with excellent GUIs, multimedia features and well designed tutorial sessions. However, invariably, these packages fall short when it comes to providing the learner with individualised teaching and flexible feedback, necessary features if true learning is to take place. As a result, CALL systems are often perceived by learners and teachers as dumb and inflexible, which is demotivating for the learner and restricts the independent use of CALL systems considerably.

If CALL applications are to be used more widely, and with more confidence, they need to be able to provide this support for individual learners, with course materials as well as the system's reactions to the learner's input being adapted to the individual learner's level of proficiency, preferred learning strategies, and other aspects such as their knowledge of other languages. Such adaptivity is made possible through the use of a Learner Model which stores characteristics of the learner relevant to the system's tutoring strategies.

---

*This work has been funded under the EU's Telematics Applications of Common Interest—Language Engineering LE1-1615.

This paper is concerned with the specification and design of a Learner Modelling component for a CALL system called CASTLE. CASTLE has been developed as part of the RECALL[1] project, which has sought to investigate the current market and future direction of CALL software.

2 Requirements Specification

In spite of the general observation that it would be advantageous if CALL systems were able to adapt to the needs and levels of proficiency of individual learners, it is difficult to obtain specific requirements relating to adaptivity and individualisation from users of CALL systems. This is due to the fact that such enhancements have not yet been provided in commercially available systems and, as a result, users have difficulty in visualising exactly what form such adaptivity and individualisation should take. The RECALL team adopted 3 approaches for gathering the requirements for the Learner Modelling component:

1. requirements elicited in previous market studies and reported in project deliverables;
2. requirements identified in a literature review;
3. requirements gathered as a result of a questionnaire distributed to language tutors.

On the basis of these sources, a set of 25 requirements for CALL systems in general, and for adaptivity and individualisation specifically, were gathered. These included requirements for flexibility, individualised learning activity, practice in specific areas of a language where the system has identified that the learner is weak, and adaptivity to the individual learner.

3 Functional Architecture and Design

The Learner Module is one of the components of a functional architecture which has been developed to provide the required CASTLE functionality. The system components and the functional relations between them are illustrated in Figure 1.

3.1 CASTLE Scenario

Through discussions with language teachers it became apparent that an eclectic approach is often used in contemporary language teaching. This approach embraces the traditional grammatical approach in combination with the more functional communicative approach (Thume, 1992). Consequently, in order to model the adept language tutor as closely as possible, CASTLE provides a range of communicative role-play scenarios which are supported by a grammatically based remedial tutoring facility. Learners are able to type *almost* free input to questions posed by the system. Input is restricted according to a set of allowable words, but the learner may enter a range of sentence structures using a number of different interaction modes. Thus, CASTLE allows the user to practice building (syntactically) correct sentences while mastering typical conversational situations. When the learner encounters problems, CASTLE guides her through a set of grammatically-based remedial exercises which underline the basic formal structures of the language.

---

[1] RECALL: Repairing Errors in Computer Aided Language Learning.

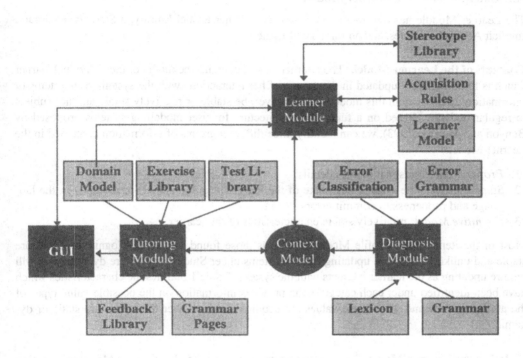

Figure 1. CASTLE architecture.

The *Context Model* is a central repository for storing all relevant data about the current state of the system, i.e., it holds all the information essential for the current session to operate. This includes the learner model information such the current learner's preferred feedback media and the exercise and item definitions of the current exercise, and the cause of the learner's error, as identified by the Diagnosis Module.

The *Diagnosis Module* checks the learner input for correctness and provides a detailed linguistic error description in the case of erroneous input. The learner input is analysed by means of a chart parser operating on a grammar, an error grammar and a lexicon. In order to describe the error in some detail, the error description is based on a hierarchy of error classes.

The two main functions of the *Tutoring Module* are to tailor the language exercises for each learner and to determine when to intercede in the lesson, using the tutoring approaches, strategies and techniques incorporated into the system. The Tutoring Module contains an explicit representation of the grammatical and linguistic concepts within the domain and how they are related, a full set of exercises, a feedback library which stores canned feedback text and a series of adaptive templates, and a full set of grammar pages which are available to the learner on demand.

3.2 Components of the Learner Module

The Learner Module has four main components: a Learner Model Library, a Stereotype Library, Implicit Acquisition Rules, and an Inference Engine.

Contents of the Learner Model. The Learner Model contains the model of the individual learner which is to be regularly updated in the course of her interactions with the system. Some items of information carried within this model will, however, be stable or relatively stable and not subject to regular updating. Based on a functional architecture for user modelling systems proposed by Benyon and Murray (1993), we can identify three different groups of information contained in the Learner Model:

1. *Profile Model:* personal learner details;
2. *Student Model:* the system's estimate of the learner's (grammatical) proficiency in the language and proneness to commit errors;
3. *Cognitive Model:* relatively stable characteristics of the learner.

Most of the items in the Profile Model as well as those found within the Cognitive Model are stable and unlikely to require updating, whereas items under Student Model are dynamic and will require updating as the learner interacts with the system. Table 1 outlines the characteristics which have been identified under each category and provides information on the possible value types of the attributes, how and when these values are acquired, and whether the values are static or dynamic.

Updating the Learner Model. In order to update the Learner Model, Context Model information is passed and analysed in the Learner Module. This information includes the error classes, the potential causes of errors which have occurred for each item, the response strategies which were selected by the Tutoring Module and the level of help that was sought by the learner.

The explicit Domain Model (handled by the Tutoring Module) is a major source of data for the update mechanisms found within the Acquisition Rules knowledge source. This model was based on three popular commercial language courses and refined by members of the RECALL pedagogic team. The curriculum upon which CASTLE was based is divided into a number of partitions: e.g. Present Simple; Past Simple; Present Continuous; Present Perfect. These partitions have an implicit ordering which indicates that Partition 1 is normally taught before Partition 2, etc. Within each partition there are a number of lower level sections, each of which is made up of grammatical and linguistic items.

Within a partition the different sections may be taught in any order, or there may be an ordering defined by the tutor. It was also found that there was a *precondition* relationship present among many of the grammatical and linguistic items which indicated that mastery of one item was dependent on mastery of other items within the language. Thus, there are two primary relation types within the Domain Model: *precondition* and *temporal* (i.e. taught before).

Table 1. Characteristics of the Learner Model.

Type	Item	Description	How acquired	When acquired	Modified by
Profile	Name	Free text	User input	First	User
	Native language	Free text	User Input	First	User
	Level of qualifications	None, primary, secondary, under-graduate, post-graduate			
	[Background language and proficiency][2]	Free text and 1 (Poor), 2 (Fair), 3 (Good), 4 (Very Good), 5 (Fluent)	User input	First	User
	Motivation	Business/ study/ recreation	User input	First	User
	Initial target language proficiency	0 (None), 1 (Poor), 2 (Fair), 3 (Good), 4 (Very Good)	User input	First	User
	Time elapsed	Time	Calculated	Each session	System
Student Model	[Domain topic and proficiency]	Entry from domain model and proficiency score	Stereotype/ inferred	Continuous	System
	[Error and proneness to commit this error]	Entry from hierarchy of Error Classes and system estimate of proneness	Inferred	Continuous	System
	[Likely cause]	Estimate of likely causes of errors	Diagnosis Module	Continuous	System
Cognitive Model	Preferred feed-back media	Sound, graphics, natural language, animation	User input	Continuous	User and system
	Preferred exercise types	Gap-filling, MCQ, Image Descriptions, Comprehension	User input	First	User and system
	Interest in Grammar	Yes / no	User input/ stereotype	First	User and system
	Usage of polite Form	Yes / no	User input	First	User

---

[2] Items surrounded by [ ] indicate that there may be zero or multiple entries for these items in the resulting Learner Model. For instance, a Learner may know multiple background languages which have associated proficiency values.

–

The precondition relation denotes the fact that in order to know a topic, the learner must know underlying, supporting topics. The temporal relation is looser in that it indicates that one topic should be taught *before* another. Thus the temporal relation is defined between the partitions while the precondition relation holds between the topics in each of these partitions.

Figure 2 illustrates a portion of the Domain Model used within CASTLE. The precondition relationships are drawn between nodes whilst the temporal relationships defined by the partitions are colour coded. To illustrate, mastery of topic 'do+does' (2c: topic c within section 2) depends upon mastery of (simpler) topics 'verbs - positive sentences' (2b) and 'to - do verbs' (1a).

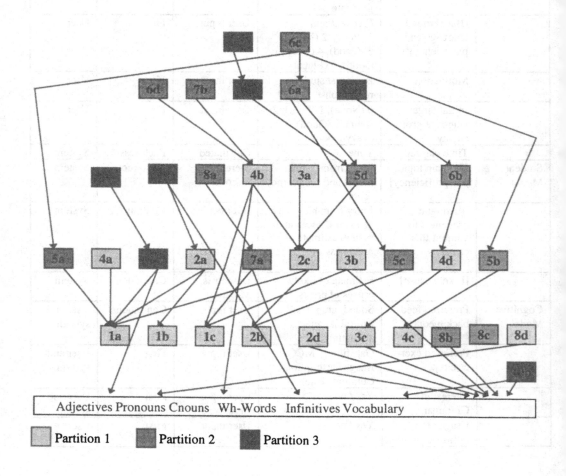

Figure 2. Grammar Domain Model.

Assigning the Initial Proficiencies. The Domain Model is used by the Stereotype Library at the start of the learner's first interaction with the system. Based on a simple test the learner is assigned to one of the four stereotype groups defined within CASTLE (novice, beginner, intermediate, advanced). The primary information held within the stereotypes is the list of grammar and linguistic items or topics which language tutors believe that members of this stereotype should be familiar with. To illustrate, the proficiencies of the novice language learner (who typically has a *poor* knowledge of the language) is defined as follows:

> *stereotype_topics(Language, Stereotype, Proficiency,Topics).*
>
> e.g.,   stereotype_topics(english, novice, 1,[2a, 2b, 3c, ...]).
>
> stereotype_topics(english, novice, 2,[1a, 1b, 1c,....]).,

where Proficiency is either 0,1,2,3,4 and Topics is a list of lists of topic numbers which have this initial Proficiency value. The Inference Engine asserts the relevant proficiency facts for maureen, a novice, into the database using the following predicate:

> *learners_achievement(User, Language, Topic, Proficiency,Source).*
>
> e.g.,   learners_achievement(maureen, english, 2b, 1, stereotype).
>
> learners_achievement(maureen, english, 1a, 1, stereotype).

with the Source argument always set to *stereotype*.

Updating the Proficiencies. This default topic information is updated during each interaction as the learner answers the questions or items within the exercises. The learner is given a score based on how well she answers the questions, and also how many times she uses the built-in help facility provided by the Tutoring Module. There are three levels of (individualised) help available for each user input, ordered so that more and more help is given until Level 3, when the answer is offered. The best result, from the user's point of view, is that she should provide a syntactically correct input, without any need to make use of the hint facility.

If the learner is able to pose a syntactically correct answer on the first attempt, the proficiency values for the underlying grammatical constructs which were used are updated positively. If, however, she enters a syntactically incorrect sentence, the Diagnosis Module must analyse the input and return an error description. This error description contains the general cause of the error (e.g. over-generalisation or interference) and the category of the error. These categories map to topics in the Student Model (see Table 1). The Context Module records the number of attempts the learner has made and the number of levels of hint she has had to use in order to answer the question correctly. The Implicit Acquisition Rules source holds a series of general update rules which are used to update the proficiency values for the topics based on the level of help which is provided to the learner. For example,

```
update_topic(Topic):-
        learners_achievement(User, Language, Topic, 2, stereotype),
        level_help(User, Language, Topic, 3),
        retract(learners_achievement(User, Language, Topic, _,_)),
        assert(learners_achievement(User, Language, Topic, 1, inferred)).
```

As the learner enters more input within the communicative scenario, the Student Model records the number of errors which has been made per category. When the learner makes three errors of the same category the Tutoring Module recommends a remedial exercise which tutors on the domain topic associated with the error category. The remedial exercises are much more directed than the conversational or communicative free input found within the role-playing scenario. In order to select suitable remedial exercises the Tutoring Module must identify which prerequisite topics may need to be introduced/ re-introduced in order that the learner can master the topic which is causing problems. The first step is to identify the prerequisite topics, and in turn the proficiencies associated with each of these pre-requisites in the Learner Model. The Student Module ranks the pre-requisites based on the proficiency values and the sources of this information. The Source argument provides an implicit belief in the accuracy of the value. Thus, the Tutoring Module would prefer a topic which has a *tested* Source argument over one which has an *inferred* value as CASTLE is more confident in the former value being true.

Within the remedial exercise the Context Module again records the average level of help which is provided to the learner when answering the exercise questions. This value is used to update the proficiency value for the remedial topic(s).

Domain topics do not need to be explicitly taught and tested in order to achieve a proficiency level. The Implicit Acquisition Rules holds a series of rules which are able to infer proficiency levels of topics which are related to topics which have been tested. This is achieved by using the precondition relation defined between topics. For instance, if a complex topic has been tested and is related to a number of prerequisite (and simpler) topics in the Domain Model, the system assumes that the learner probably knows these simple concepts, and updates the *Proficiency* argument and *Source* argument accordingly if the Source argument is set to *stereotype*.

The Learner Module also maintains an account of the learner's proneness to commit errors. A number of error types have been identified in work for the RECALL Diagnosis Module. The problem that arises for the Learner Module is that of estimating a user's proneness to commit errors of each of these types. A reliable index of a user's liability to commit an error of type E is given by comparing the number of times E has been committed in the course of the session with the total number of questions answered or sentences entered, if the exercises require composition of full sentences. Suppose, for instance, that a learner has to input answers to 10 individual questions. If it happens that she commits 15 errors of type E it is clear that her error-proneness with regard to E is very high; if she had committed only two, the proneness would have been low. Since a user's error-proneness for a given error type E is measured by her committing that error a given number of times in a set of exercises, it is represented as a percentage figure, calculated as follows:

*Proneness = (No. of errors / No. of questions) * 100.*

The learner's proneness to commit errors is expressed as a number of *error_proneness* facts. For example,

error_proneness(maureen,english,word_order,30).

The Learner Model also maintains a representation of the learner's overall proficiency in the language. The *overall-proficiency* takes the form of a percentage measure, calculated from a cumulative total of the learner's proficiency scores in all the topics that she has completed. This estimate is used primarily by the learner during runtime when she asks for an overview of the system's estimate of her knowledge of the target language.

4 Learner Module Interactions

From the Learner Module's perspective there are four main processes in the operation of CASTLE:

1. selection of exercises;
2. interpretation and diagnosis of the learner's input;
3. system's response to the input;
4. updating the Learner Model (as described previously).

The Learner Module is involved in all four processes, and continuously interacts with the central Context Model in order to accept, validate, assimilate and update the Learner Model information.

4.1 Selection of Topics

There are two cases which need to be accommodated in the selection of exercises at the beginning of a session. The first case occurs when the learner indicates that she has not used CASTLE before and the second case corresponds to the learner's use of the system at later sessions. In the latter case the learner enters a unique identifier which is passed to the Learner Module. The appropriate Learner Model is retrieved from the Learner Models knowledge source. The Learner Module provides the GUI with a summary of what topics have been covered to date in the curriculum and how well the learner is performing within the curriculum. The learner has either the option of selecting from all the available topics and scenarios within the curriculum or have CASTLE select appropriate topics based on the contents of the Learner Model. These topics are subsequently used to select a suitable communicative scenario.

If the learner selects a topic, the Tutoring Module may advise that:

1. the choice is appropriate;
2. the choice is inappropriate because it is beyond the learner's current proficiency;
3. the choice is inappropriate because it is below the learner's current proficiency, i.e. too elementary given the standard already attained.

The Tutoring Module determines which of these three cases applies by consulting the Learner Model information in the Context Model. If the choice is appropriate no further action is necessary. If it is inappropriate i.e. 2 or 3 above, a message will be displayed to the user, informing her of the inappropriateness of the choice and a suggestion of an alternative which is more in line with her current proficiency.

4.2 Interpretation and Diagnosis of the Learner's Input

When the learner types in an answer to a question (item) the input is passed to the Tutoring Module and subsequently to the Context Model. If there is a set of anticipated correct and incorrect answers tagged to a question, the learner's answer is checked against these. If the input does not match with these answers it is passed through the spell checker. These three activities obviously do not involve any learner information. If the input is not recognised at this stage it is sent to the Diagnosis Module for a full linguistic analysis. Rather than exhaustively searching the Error Grammar knowledge base, the Diagnosis Module requests learner information from the Context Model in order to prune the search. This information includes the learner's background knowledge (for the selection of possible interference errors); the proneness to commit certain errors and the causes of errors which have already been made. Having found a hypothesis, or set of hypotheses to explain the error, the Diagnosis Module passes back the hypothesis(es) in the form of an error classification and a cause to the Context Model. At the end of an exercise the Learner Module retrieves relevant information from the learner model area within the Context Model to update the long-term Learner Model using the Acquisition Rules knowledge source.

4.3 Response to the Learner's Input

If the learner's answer to a question is correct, no Learner Model information is required as a simple affirmation of the correctness of the response is given to the learner. However the Context Model will note that the learner answered the question correctly. If, however, the learner's input is incorrect the Tutoring Module needs to select an appropriate response from the Feedback Library. In the case where the Diagnosis Module has sent multiple hypotheses for the cause of the error, the Tutoring Module may also have to select the most likely cause/error before selecting a response. This may involve presenting a similar or simpler exercise to clarify where the learner may have gone wrong. For the selection of a response the Tutoring Module needs to ascertain the type of response the learner prefers, the response strategies which have already been adopted and the amount of help that has been sought on previous occasions.

5 Related Work

It is clear that the primary goal of a learner modelling component is to develop a consistent and theoretically sound model which can be used to evaluate each learner's language proficiency. McCoy et al. (1996) present an interesting architecture which involves the following Input/Feedback Cycle:

1. The user enters a portion of text.
2. The Error Identification component tags all errors (one sentence at a time).
   - A syntactic parse is carried out. If more than one parse is found then the 'best' is selected (through a scoring mechanism).
   - If a syntactic mal-rule is used in the parse then the sentence and the mal-rule annotation (indicating the type of error which has been made) is passed to the Response Generator.
3. The Response Generator processes this data with information from the Learner Model and the History Model to decide which errors to correct in detail and how they should be corrected.
4. The Response Generator selects an appropriate teaching strategy.
5. The Learner can enter corrections and have them rechecked when the Response Generator responds.

This process depends on a categorisation of errors as mal-rules for the diagnosis of learner errors and on a model of language acquisition to support the Response Generator in the selection of an appropriate teaching strategy. McCoy et al. (1996) propose a framework called SLALOM (Steps of Language Acquisition in a Layered Organisational Model) to represent the acquisition sequence of target rules. SLALOM divides language into a set of feature hierarchies (such as morphology, types of noun phrases, types of relative clauses) according to their relationship and complexity. Features of similar complexity are grouped together into layers representing stereotypical levels of language ability. These layers allow the system to make inferences. A similar hierarchy has been used in the CASTLE system for the diagnosis and treatment of the learner's errors.

A simpler type of representation is to be found in the VP^2 system, where the user's knowledge of a language is represented simply as a grammar of that language (Schuster and Finin, 1986). The sole purpose of VP^2 is to account for transfer of language structures from a speaker's native language to the target language, so this is adequate: a more comprehensive CALL system requires much more. The use of overlays involves viewing the user's current state of knowledge as a subset of that of the system (or domain model). This may be an important part of a complete student model but since it allows no representation of the student's mistakes and misconceptions, its diagnostic value seems to be minimal. Value-attribute pairs have been widely used, e.g. in GRUNDY (Rich, 1983) and also in Mr. Collins (Bull et al., 1995), to indicate those characteristics (preferences in the one case, proficiency in the other) which the user is believed to have, the value assigned to them and the confidence the system has in the rating of values for the various attributes.

Bull et al. (1995) recommend two further types of information which could be stored in the Learner Model in addition to mal-rules and the student's knowledge of other languages. These are:

1. the learning strategies which are employed by the learner (studying prior to exercises, guessing, questioning etc.);
2. the learner's confidence in her performance, which can be expressed through the assignment of belief measures.

The discussion of the student model within this system is based on belief measures, where the learner assigns a (modifiable) belief measure based on their assessment of performance and the system assigns a belief measure based on the learner's average result of the last five attempts to use a grammatical rule. Concerning the acquisition of information, Bull et al. (1995) see their model as being acquired explicitly through asking the learner to explain her choice of a (wrong) answer when the system itself is unable to choose between two or more alternative explanations— when, for example, it is unclear whether there was a confusion of two grammatical rules or a transfer of a rule from another language. Also included in this system is the idea that the learner model should be available for inspection by the learner, thereby eliminating grounds for worry about confidentiality and perhaps enabling the model itself to function as a learning resource. Whilst it was acknowledged that Bull's approach was theoretically interesting, the RECALL team adopted a more pragmatic approach to modelling. Rather than having dual measures of the learner's proficiency in the language, the system maintains an estimate of the learner's proficiency which the learner may view, and indeed modify at any time. In addition, if there are any ambiguities regarding the source of the error, the Tutoring Module may decide to present the learner with a more restricted remedial exercise with a different interaction mode which should eliminate some of the potential causes—e.g. a multiple choice question rather than free text should eliminate attentional errors. The Tutoring Module will also on occasion admit to the learner that it is unable to identify the source of the error but is happy to carry on nonetheless, rather than initiating a complex sub-dialogue between system and learner to get to the source of the problem.

6 Conclusion

CASTLE employs simple, yet effective learner modelling techniques to provide a level of adaptivity which has not been present in commercial CALL products to date. Initial reaction from the evaluation study has been positive although it is acknowledged that the facilities provided by the HTML-based GUI are rather limited. In addition, the interactions between the Prolog-based Learning and Tutoring Modules, the C-based Diagnosis Module and the HTML interface are not ideal. Future work will concentrate on liasing with language tutors to refine the learner modelling update mechanisms, incorporating more multimedia features and investigating how CASTLE can be delivered in a distributed client-server architecture.

References

Benyon, D., and Murray, D. (1993). Applying user modeling to human-computer interaction design. *Artificial Intelligence Review* 6:43–69.

Bull, S., Pain, H., and Brna, P. (1995). Mr. Collins: A collaboratively constructed, inspectable student model for intelligent computer assisted language learning. *Instructional Science* 23:65–87.

Laurillard, D. (1992). Principles for computer-based software design for language learning. *Computer Assisted Language Learning* 4(3):141–152.

Merrill, D. C., Reiser, B. J., Ranney, M., and Trafton, J. G. (1992). Effective tutoring techniques: A comparison of human tutors and intelligent tutoring systems. *The Journal of the Learning Sciences* 2(3):277–305.

McCoy, K., Pennington, C. A., and Suri, L. Z. (1996). English error correction: A syntactic user model based on principled "mal-rule" scoring. In *Proceedings of the Fifth International Conference on User Modeling*, 59–66.

Rich, E. (1983). Users are individuals: Individualizing user models. *International Journal of Man-Machine Studies* 18:199–214.

Thume, K. H. (1992). *Studien zur Entwicklung und Effektivität von computergestütztem Frendsprachenerwerb*. Regensburg: Roderer.

Schuster, E., and Finin, T. (1986). VP^2: The role of user modelling in correcting errors in second language learning. In Cohn, A. G., and Thomas, J. R., eds., *Artificial Intelligence and Its Applications*. 197–209.

Feedback and Support for Collaboration

See Yourself Write:
A Simple Student Model to Make Students Think

Susan Bull

The Language Centre, University of Brighton, UK

Abstract. This paper introduces *See Yourself Write*, a system with two components: (1) a template for tutors to provide feedback to their students on their foreign language writing, and (2) an inspectable student model which is automatically constructed for each student, based on the feedback given by the teacher. The student model holds feedback given to students across several assignments, and provides an individual evaluation of their performance. The model is designed to be viewed by the students to prompt them to reflect on and use the feedback received.

1 Introduction

How much notice of feedback do students take? The answer depends partly on the particular learning situation. However, even when there is a course requirement that work must be resubmitted with tutor (or other) feedback taken into account, it still occurs that in *subsequent* assignments students do not always look back to their earlier difficulties and recurring problems and, indeed, their strengths.

One way to capture feedback and to cross-relate it for ease of comparison by learners is to incorporate it into an inspectable student model. Student models are usually hidden from the learner who is being modelled, and are used by a computational educational system to adapt the interaction in some way to suit the individual's needs. However, *viewable* student models have also been created, where learners are able to see the representations of their knowledge or level that are held in the system. For example, Corbett and Anderson's (1995) skill meter in the ACT Programming Tutor displays current performance levels as a simple indicator to the student of how well s/he is progressing. Cook and Kay's (1994) um, an inspectable user model for the sam text editor, has educational benefits such as alerting users to the size of the domain, and easing the selection of what to learn within the domain. An important use of an inspectable student model is suggested by Self (1988), use as a *promoter of reflection*. This is also one of the reasons offered by Paiva et al. (1995) for externalising the contents of the learner model, and one of the main benefits claimed for the Mr. Collins collaborative student model (Bull and Pain, 1995; Bull and Smith, 1995).

The above student models, although open to student viewing, are nevertheless conventional in the sense that they exist for use within computationally based educational systems (or at least, systems with educational potential as one of their aims). This is a somewhat different scenario from that of the learner model to be described in this paper. It is still expected that use of the inspectable student model presented here will lead to improvement in the student's work, but this work is not necessarily computer-based, and the student model is not updated at the same time as the work is being undertaken. It is updated after completion of each assignment, with a focus on student use of the information to aid future performance, rather than system interpretation of the representations towards some desirable form of adaptation. Because of this perspective of *a student model for the student*, the likelihood of learner disinterest in their own model as described by Barnard and Sandberg (1996) is smaller. Indeed, it has been shown that if confronted directly with representations about their performance and misconceptions, students will often want to interact with this information (Bull and Pain, 1995). It is on this curiosity and student desire to make sure that their student model is right that we build here.

This paper presents *See Yourself Write*, a system comprising two parts: a template through which the teacher gives students feedback on each writing assignment they complete, and an individual student model which is automatically created from the feedback provided by the teacher, and which is built up over time. The student model of *See Yourself Write* is inspectable, to promote learner reflection and to encourage learners to use the feedback received from their tutors in their future assignments. The domain is writing in a foreign language, as this is an ideal open-ended domain in which to illustrate the benefits of an approach to student modelling which is not restricted by the limitations of the ability of a system to infer the contents of a student model from some kind of student input. Further, because there is a range of aspects of feedback which may be relevant to writing assignments it is possible to demonstrate a student model which holds a variety of information types. *See Yourself Write* differs from other computational writing environments containing a learner model (such as LICE: Bowerman, 1992), because the aims differ. Since the *See Yourself Write* model is constructed from teacher feedback, the writer is not constrained in any way during his/her writing as happens, for example, in LICE. The inferencing which takes place in the construction of the model occurs away from the learner. Because the student model aims to help students think about, and take control of their learning, the qualitative textual descriptions produced by the teacher are also an important component of the model. The term *student model* is therefore broader in this context than is customary, including both system evaluation and teacher feedback, and encompassing also what some may prefer to term texplanation". However, since this explanation is concerned with system justification of the contents of the model, and is accessed through the model, it is considered here to be part of the student model; see also Bull and Pain, 1995; Cook and Kay, 1994.) Similarly, the qualitative examples and explanations provided by the teacher which are not interpreted by the system are intended to supplement and clarify to the learner the quantitative information inferred in the model.

2 Feedback on Writing

There have been some examinations of what students do with feedback on their foreign language writing. Cohen (1987) finds that it is often the (self-rated) poorer learners who pay little or no attention to teacher feedback. In Cohen's study a very common strategy for dealing with feedback for all learner types was to make a mental note of the comments received. This result was repeated in a later study (Cohen and Cavalcanti, 1990). Another finding of the latter study was that learners claimed not to know how to handle a high proportion of the feedback received (ranging from 21% to 81% of the comments received by individuals).

Important to the question of what students do with feedback is the issue of how useful the feedback is perceived to be, and its effectiveness in leading to improved long-term performance. Grabe and Kaplan (1996) state: "responding to students' writing can greatly influence student attitudes to writing and their motivation for future learning". Cohen and Calvacanti (1990) found that there are sometimes discrepancies between the kind of feedback students desire and the feedback actually offered. Fathman and Whalley (1990) found in their study that feedback on grammar errors had a greater positive influence on subsequent rewriting than did feedback on content (though the effect here was also positive). It might therefore be useful to offer feedback on a range of issues until more is known about this.[1] Another example showed that students would have liked some information about what they were doing well, in addition to the more negative comments received (Cohen and Calvacanti, 1990).

What does this suggest for *See Yourself Write*? Clearly it will be useful to consider how to induce learners to take more account of their feedback. Consideration must also be given to ways to ensure that feedback is neither too vague nor ambiguous, and that it is actually beneficial. It should also encourage the provision of positive feedback. The following sections describe the architecture of *See Yourself Write*, and address the need for useful, usable feedback, and for attention to be given to this feedback by its recipients.

3 See Yourself Write

Writers have varied approaches to writing; therefore *See Yourself Write* is not an attempt to prescribe any particular feature(s) of the writing process, as is sometimes found (see, e.g., Salomon, 1993, for a system aimed at making young composition writers plan). *See Yourself Write* is designed for older writers, and tries to make learners more aware of why they are doing well in some aspects of their writing, and why they may be having difficulties in others.

See Yourself Write has been designed initially for students writing language assignments as part of a foreign language course. Any foreign language may be the target language, and a variety of writing tasks can be used (e.g. descriptive essay, translation, factual reports), since there are a number of aspects of writing which are common and important across different types of written document. The categories currently used in the template and student model are: content coverage, structure, argumentation, style, vocabulary, spelling, grammar and punctuation. These will not all be relevant in all cases, for example content coverage will be less of an issue in translation than in a literature review. But style, for example, will tend to have importance in both. There is also a non-specified component enabling feedback to be given on a more general level about the assignment, and also to enable feedback on areas not falling into the above categories.

The aim of the *See Yourself Write* student model differs from that of more conventional learner models in that it is not intended as a source of information for a computational educational system, but rather as a source of information *for the student*. It reflects to students feedback on their own work, and information about how they are progressing and about their overall performance. Information in the student model is both qualitative and quantitative. Its main purpose is to promote learner reflection on completed assignments in such a way as to lead students to use this feedback to improve subsequent work. Thus, *See Yourself Write* is in part a vehicle through which a simple student model may be constructed by an expert teacher, without the teachers themselves needing to analyse each student's current work with respect to that learner's previous work. The teacher provides feedback manually, in a similar form to the way in which s/he would normally give feed-

---

[1] In addition to helping students, *See Yourself Write* could itself be used to collect this type of information for research into this question.

back, and the creation of the student model is automatic: It is drawn from each of the pieces of feedback for a particular student which have been produced to date by the teacher.

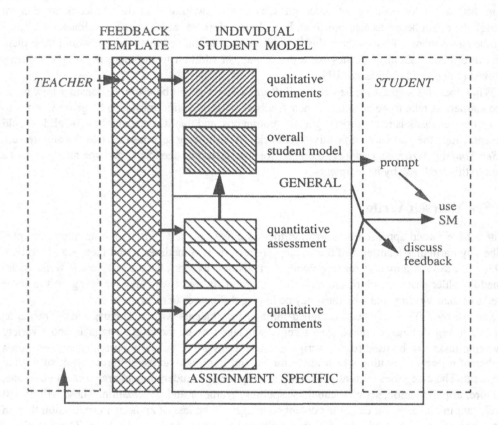

Figure 1. The architecture of *See Yourself Write*.

Figure 1 illustrates the structure of *See Yourself Write*. The expert teacher provides his/her usual feedback through a template created for the particular domain and task requirements (here, writing in a foreign language). Once the feedback has been entered into the template to the teacher's satisfaction, s/he sends it to the separate student model, where qualitative information is placed in the appropriate areas for student retrieval, and quantitative information is similarly distributed for ease of viewing. In addition, the quantitative feedback is evaluated by the system to provide a more general overview student model to be used by the student in conjunction with feedback on individual assignments.

The student model part of *See Yourself Write*, as stated above, is constructed from the teacher's feedback. The qualitative components of the student model are illustrated in Figure 1 by: //// (the closer diagonal lines depict overall or more general representations, while those with greater spacing show representations relating to a specific assignment). Quantitative representations are illustrated by the opposite pattern: \\\\ (again with spacing between lines indicating the generality of the representation). Figure 1 therefore illustrates a case where so far three writing assignments have been completed by this student, both qualitative and quantitative evaluations having been provided by the teacher for each piece of work (hence the three sections to the qualitative and quantitative spaces depicted in the assignment-specific section of the student model). The quantitative component of the assignment-specific representations is used by the system on student request, to construct the representations for the quantitative overview student model in the general section. In this space there also exists a qualitative overview, drawn from general comments submitted by the teacher separate from any one particular assignment. The thicker arrows leading from the template to the student model, and within the model—between the assignment-specific and general quantitative information—portray automatic creation of representations. The thinner arrows illustrate manual feedback produced by the teacher (via the template), and interactions of the learner with the student model. These aspects are under the control of the teacher and the student, respectively, though advice is available for students and teachers in the form of short user manuals. This information is later also to be incorporated directly into *See Yourself Write* in two help systems.

4 The Teacher's Template

Information is input by the teacher via edit fields in the template. *Quantitative information*, which is used by the system to determine the overall student model, is obtained through selections from alternatives offered by the system. This is to ensure that information is provided in a form which is usable by the system. Quantitative information is at present limited to a choice between (usually) three options to describe the performance of a student in different areas (e.g., for content coverage: "good", "okay", "superficial"; for punctuation: "good", "okay", "weak", etc.) In a later version, this aspect will be amendable by the teacher to allow as many choices as appropriate for the kind of marking scheme used.

An advantage of this approach is that it encourages teachers to give positive comments in addition to feedback on areas of difficulty, since the options available range from good to weak (or similar options). The existence of explicit pre-defined categories also encourages teachers to provide information on a variety of areas. This allows a more complete student model to be created.

Qualitative information can be input into each category in whatever textual format the tutor wishes. This information is not usable by the system in its modelling of the student, but it is important for explaining problems to the student, or acknowledging what s/he has done well; for giving examples of correct versions of problematic points, etc., i.e. aspects of writing where it is hard for a computational system to provide accurate and useful feedback. The possibility of providing qualitative feedback in distinct categories has similar advantages as for quantitative descriptions: positive comments; different areas of feedback, and so on.

5 The Inspectable Student Model

Each student receives their own individualised student model, divided into sections to represent progression over time (T1–T3 in Figure 2 below). Figure 2 is an example based on the current implementation, using Malay as the target language.

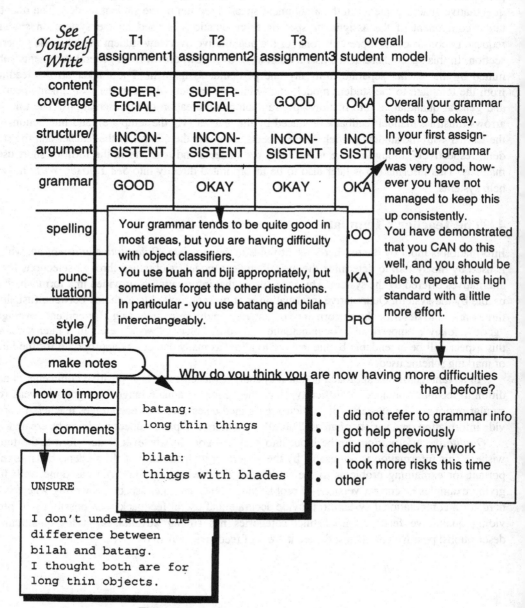

Figure 2. Examples from a student model.

In this illustration three assignments have been completed so far. The examples come from part of the information in the student model on grammar. Excerpts from other areas may look very different. The plain boxes portray information in the student model (entered by the teacher, or constructed by the system). The shadowed boxes are the student's notes to him/herself and comments to the tutor. The student may open and close boxes to access and add information as s/he wishes.

In the current version of *See Yourself Write* the generalisation algorithms performed on teacher feedback on individual assignments, which enable system construction of the underlying representations for the overall student model, are quite simple. The system averages the teacher's quantitative feedback for each category across each assignment completed, to calculate the values for the overall model. For example, if three assignments have been written, and the teacher has awarded "superficial" in the category "content coverage" for Assignments 1 and 2, and "good" for Assignment 3, the system will assign the description "okay" as the summary description for this part of the overview student model. Although all assignments for a student are taken into account by the system, greater weight is given to later ones. This is achieved by assessing assignment category values in pairs: Assignment 1 with Assignment 2, then the combined result of Assignments 1 and 2 with Assignment 3, and so on. For example:

Situation after first assignment:
category X of Assignment 1   → category X of Overall Student Model 1

Situation after second assignment:
category X of Assignment 1   → category X of Overall Student Model 2
category X of Assignment 2

Situation after third assignment:
category X of Overall Student Model 2   → category X of Overall Student Model 3
category X of Assignment 3

Qualitative information in the overall sytem model (shown in Figure 2 for grammar) is based on system selection of the appropriate template (which depends on consistency of performance in a category across assignments; whether performance is improving, etc.). The details are filled out according to each of the category evaluations of successive assignments. In the example in Figure 2, the system has selected a template which acknowledges that a student *can* write correctly according to the target language grammar but recognises that this has not been done consistently. Its choice of template for this category is based on the rule:

IF student started well AND IF performance decreased THEN choose template "good-decreasing".

The essential features of the template "good-decreasing" are acknowledgement of:

good start; decreasing performance; demonstrated ability; potential future good performance.

The details are derived from the teacher evaluations of the category in individual assignments.

A conventional student model might describe the information in Figure 2 in a way able to represent the points in Figure 3. A traditional student model will often not keep a separate record of information gathered in earlier interactions over a longer period, but will rely on overall representations such as the one in Figure 3. This may be sufficient in a model working towards collecting information for use for system adaptation, but it is of less direct use when aiming to make learners think about why they are achieving the results they are given. It is the students who should be doing the thinking, not the system. Differences are also found in the level of detail of qualitative descriptions, achievable through using real teacher feedback.

grammar: level	consistency	problems	improvement
okay	varied: decreasing	obj. classifiers: okay - buah probability high okay - biji probability high okay - batang probability low (ref bilah) okay - bilah probability low (ref batang)	possible / likely

Figure 3. Information in a "conventional" student model.

The student's consultation with the individualised student model of *See Yourself Write* is aimed at promoting reflection through scrutinising the contents of the model, and using this information in the composition of future work. All aspects of the student model are inspectable: qualitative and quantitative information, and assignment-specific and general information. In addition to the transparency of the student model, reflection is encouraged by two further means: system prompts about why the student believes this particular pattern of development of his/her work over time has occurred (see Figure 2), and the possibility of explicitly disagreeing with the contents of the model and relating this disagreement to the teacher for comment or further evaluation (comments: Figure 2). Students' willingness to dispute the contents of their student model to the computational learning environment has been suggested (Bull and Pain, 1995), as has the possibility of them defending themselves against a human assessor in a similar context (Pain et al., 1996). This kind of interaction requires justification and explanation by the student of his/her viewpoint, thereby taking advantage of self-explanation: Although students using *See Yourself Write* are here really intending to explain their perspectives to another person (the teacher), the articulation of their views in a manner which is clear enough to be understood by, and submitted to the teacher, is likely to make any problems also clearer to the students themselves—indeed, possibly to the extent that they no longer wish or need to consult their teacher over representations about which they are unsure, or even with which they initially disagreed. Therefore, as well as a facility to request further clarification, this is also a disguised attempt to promote self-explanation and reflection. It also overcomes the problem of getting students to self-explain in a realistic manner. They perceive the task as that of obtaining external assistance, and while this is still available if required, the very process of demanding it may result in the help originally sought becoming unnecessary.

Figure 2 showed how the student receives an overview of the way in which their performance on different aspects of the writing task has developed over time.[2] For example, reading left to right it can be seen that although the initial coverage of content area was weak, the student in this example has subsequently improved. The overall assessment in the final column reflects this, though it remains a little cautious since the leap was so dramatic.

Students may click on individual evaluations to obtain more detailed qualitative comments from their teacher (as shown in Figure 2 for grammar in the second assignment).[3] An overall summary for each aspect of writing, as calculated by the system, can be obtained by clicking on "options" in the final summary column as shown here for grammar.[4] This should help learners identify which areas need more work. Suggestions are also available about how easy it might be for a particular student to improve a particular aspect of their writing. Prompts (determined from the overall student model) can also be requested. These are designed to help writers work out what it is about their approaches to the task that makes them successful or unsuccessful in the different aspects of the task, and to consider how they might improve. They are also encouraged to think about the reasons for improvement over time, or to consider why their level may have decreased. Responses to the prompts are recorded for later consultation.

Clicking on the assignment numbers reveals any general comments given on that assignment. There are three further buttons: "make notes", "how to improve" and "comments", and a fourth located over the *See Yourself Write* title.

Clicking on "how to improve" displays all the information gained from all the prompts aimed at provoking metacognition which were activated (see above). This is in the form of a student's responses to questions about how they could improve their performance, and what they have already done which has led to success.

Clicking on "comments" results in a system request for information about whether the student in general agrees or disagrees with the contents of the model, or whether there are aspects about which s/he is unsure. After responding to this request, if appropriate an edit field appears where the writer may explain any disagreements, etc. As explained previously, this facility is aimed primarily at assisting the learner to resolve his/her own difficulties through reflection on problems, this occurring through the need to defend themselves by stating their standpoint explicitly. However, if no such resolution occurs, the learner's description can still be passed to the teacher for further feedback. This is important because teachers do not always identify grammatical misconceptions correctly (Chambers, 1994). Furthermore, the writer may have deliberately strayed from the standard format in order to achieve a particular specific effect (e.g. in the structuring of their document). Students can here also request clarification of any feedback they are not sure how to handle, or may request elaboration or comment on areas not represented in the feedback. In the example in Figure 2, from the student's notes it can be seen that since writing a comment to the teacher about the difference between the uses of *batang* and *bilah*, s/he has realised the distinction (and will now no longer need to ask the teacher for clarification).

---

[2] The student model appears initially to the writer in a form similar to that of the main background area in Figure 2. The textual descriptions in Figure 2 have been reduced in size and detail, to allow several examples to be included legibly in the one diagram.

[3] Teachers are also requested to list areas of difficulty so that the system and students can easily compare points (e.g. tense, affixation, etc.).

[4] For convenience of illustration the description has been shortened.

The writer may write notes on any of the information contained in the student model by clicking on "make notes". Students are thereby encouraged to interact with their feedback. They may write, or copy and paste information into the notes field in order that they may later easily locate points to which they wish to refer when writing their next document. Because of this noting facility students are likely to make more than just a mental note,[5] and are also more likely to consult this information when attempting a new assignment. The student's notes may be printed.

By clicking on *"See Yourself Write"*, writers obtain an area into which they may type any corrections or explanations that the tutor has requested. This is an additional way in which writers can be encouraged to take account of their feedback: when this facility is used, since the request will have come from the teacher, there is some expectation on the part of both the student and the teacher that the student will take account of what has been said, and provide a response. This response will be available to the teacher when s/he updates the student model after receiving the next assignment.

6 A Student-Teacher Interaction

Detailed evaluative results are not yet available. However, initial indications (from a questionnaire survey) suggest that most students will find *See Yourself Write* useful. (Two thirds of respondents answered "useful" or "very useful".) Those who were not enthusiastic stated that they would prefer to discuss their feedback face-to-face with the teacher. However, it should be noted that *See Yourself Write* is designed to be used in place of written feedback produced in the more usual linear form. There was no reduction in the time available for individual face-to-face contact between the tutor and students.

The following comment illustrates the views of learners who found the system useful:

"The feedback on assignments highlighted my weaknesses. I knew where they were but without the feedback I would never have investigated them further or have tried to correct them."

In order to illustrate the way in which *See Yourself Write* has been used to date, the following is an extract from a student-teacher interaction about the student's essay in French, on the subject of Tourism and the Environment.

A. *Teacher feedback:* STRUCTURE/ARGUMENT: INCONSISTENT
A number of illogicalities:
  1. Surely to make your point, you need to argue that expansion of tourism has led to excessive development of transport systems?
  2. What is the relevance of whaling to tourism? Are you seriously suggesting that tourists' appetite for whale-meat has endangered the species?

Student response:
  1. Yes, but it also works the other way around in that transport systems have allowed tourism to spread to more remote parts of the world.
  2. Yes, I suppose I have been a bit over the top! But if whale meat wasn't considered a delicacy in certain countries it's doubtful they would have to be killed at all.

---

[5] Sometimes this can be sufficient, but often it is not.

Teacher response:
1. Yes, that's fine. But in your essay you've first said that transport has developed, then further suggested that tourism was the cause of people wanting to travel - rather than the means of travelling (i.e. transport) leading to more tourism. The organisation of your ideas is confusing.
2. But you need to integrate this point more explicitly into the topic of the essay, which was tourism and the environment.

B. *Teacher feedback:* GRAMMAR: GOOD

Generally good, but please give correct preposition after: "il est nécessaire"; "il est important"; "penser"; "beaucoup".

Student response:

il est nécessaire + de, il est important + de; penser + à; beaucoup + de

In the above interaction the student was eager to provide information on her point of view if this appeared to conflict with the feedback she received (see A1, where she challenged the teacher's interpretation of her point). In response the teacher explained that although there was no problem with what the student had intended to say, this was not, in fact, what she had claimed in her essay. This interaction clarified to the teacher what was actually intended, and to the student that it was not the content of her argument that was at fault, but that the organisation of the argument was misleading. Without this interaction with feedback it is less likely that the misunderstanding would have been uncovered. The teacher also requested corrections where she felt these necessary. Since such requests are perceived as a task for the student to complete within *See Yourself Write*, she responds (B).

As stated above, the extent to which students interact with *See Yourself Write* varies. Some did very little (though not less than they would have done had the feedback been in another form), and some worked intensively with their feedback, and gave detailed reactions to the information in *See Yourself Write*. It is encouraging to note that some would discuss the feedback in depth through the *See Yourself Write* system, in a way which did not occur when feedback was given in a more conventional form.

7 Summary and Conclusion

See Yourself Write is aimed at helping learners to reflect on their performance, and to think about how they might improve their work by:

- viewing and interacting with a student model based on teacher feedback;
- making it easy for students to access useful comments on earlier work when composing a new piece of work;
- being prompted to explain how they could improve, or to give reasons to explain their improvement/deterioration, etc.;
- being encouraged to take advantage of self-explanation of difficulties by disguising this as a request for outside assistance.

The domain is one in which it is difficult to get useful feedback computationally. *See Yourself Write* combines the use of teacher feedback—provided in a way which suits the teacher—and the advantages of an inspectable student model, to promote reflection. The facility for learners to disagree with the model also enables teachers to become aware of their mis-diagnoses. The system-generated component is necessarily quite simple as this enables tutors to give the kind of feedback they consider most useful. However, the inclusion of system-generated representations in *See Yourself Write* allows the system to be more than a "giver of feedback" without requiring additional analyses from teachers. It also encourages teachers to provide feedback on a range of aspects of the task, positive as well as more critical. Although the quantitative representations forming the more usual aspects of the student model are limited, the qualitative components can be as detailed as the teacher wishes.

Remaining questions under investigation include: Is a more fine-grained quantitative analysis desirable? Would a more graphically oriented interface be useful? Should some of the free information provided by teachers be analysed, or would this be too restrictive?

References

Barnard, Y. F., and Sandberg, J. A. C. (1996). Self-explanations, do we get them from our students? In *Proceedings of European Conference on Artificial Intelligence and Education*, 115–121.

Bowerman, C. (1992). Writing and the computer: An intelligent tutoring systems solution. *Computers and Education* 18(1–3):77–83.

Bull, S., and Pain, H. (1995). 'Did I say what I think I said, and do you agree with me?': Inspecting and questioning the student model. In *Proceedings of the World Conference on Artificial Intelligence in Education*, 501–508.

Bull, S., and Smith, M. (1995). Using targeted negotiation to support students' learning. In *Proceedings of the International Conference on Computers in Education*, 173–181.

Chambers, F. (1994). Learners' accounts of their errors in a foreign language: An exploratory study. In Blue, G., ed, *CLE Working Papers 3*. University of Southampton. 56–70.

Cohen, A. D. (1987). Student processing of feedback on their compositions. In Wenden, A., and Rubin, J., eds, *Learner Strategies in Language Learning*. London: Prentice-Hall. 57–69.

Cohen, A. D., and Calvacanti, M. C. (1990). Feedback on compositions: Teacher and student verbal reports. In Kroll, B., eds., *Second Language Writing, Research Insights for the Classroom*. Cambridge: Cambridge University Press. 155–177.

Cook, R., and Kay, J. (1994). The justified user model: A viewable, explained user model. In *Proceedings of the Fourth International Conference on User Modeling*, 145–150.

Corbett, A. T., and Anderson, J. (1995). Knowledge tracing: Modeling the acquisition of procedural knowledge. *User Modeling and User-Adapted Interaction* 4:253–278.

Fathman, A. K., and Whalley, E. (1990). Teacher response to student writing: Focus on form versus content. In Kroll, B., ed., *Second language writing, research insights for the classroom*. Cambridge: Cambridge University Press. 178–190.

Grabe, W., and Kaplan, R. B. (1996). *Theory and Practice of Writing*. London: Addison-Wesley.

Pain, H., Bull, S., and Brna, P. (1996). A student model 'for its own sake'. In *Proceedings of the European Conference on Artificial Intelligence and Education*, 191–198.

Paiva, A., Self, J. and Hartley, R. (1995). Externalising learner models. In *Proceedings of World Conference on Artificial Intelligence in Education*, 509–516.

Salomon, G. (1993). On the nature of pedagogic computer tools: The case of the Writing Partner. In Lajoie, S. P., and Derry, S. J., eds, *Computers as Cognitive Tools*. Hillsdale, NJ: Erlbaum. 179–196.

Self, J. (1988). Bypassing the intractable problem of student modelling. *Proceedings of ITS'88*, 18–24.

Inspectable User Models for Just-In-Time Workplace Training

Jason A. Collins[1], Jim E. Greer[1], Vive S. Kumar[1], Gordon I. McCalla[1],
Paul Meagher[1], and Ray Tkatch[2]*

[1] Department of Computer Science, University of Saskatchewan,
Saskatoon, Saskatchewan, Canada
[2] Regional Psychiatric Centre (Prairies), Correctional Services Canada,
Saskatoon, Saskatchewan, Canada

Abstract. Workplace training is most effective when the training happens just in time as part of a worker's regular job activities. We are developing a just-in-time training system called PHelpS (Peer Help System) which can select peer helpers with whom the worker can interact. User modelling is central in the PHelpS system. For each worker, a user model is kept containing several kinds of information about the worker, in particular a knowledge profile of how well they can carry out various specific tasks. These user models permit the system to select a knowledgeable, available, and appropriate set of helpers if a worker signals that he or she needs help in carrying out a particular task. Many interesting user modelling issues arise in this work, most importantly employing the same user model in multiple ways, making the user models inspectable by a variety of users, doing knowledge-based matching and retrieval, and maintaining the accuracy of the user model over time. There are several social issues that this research has also exposed.

1 Introduction

Workplace training can be very effective in situations where the training happens as part of a worker's regular job activities. This *just-in-time workplace training* occurs on the job, in the context of an authentic task, and as part of the normal daily activity of the worker. The lessons learned during such training can be directly incorporated by the worker into an evolving understanding of the task, and hence recalled and used effectively when needed.

We are developing a just-in-time training system called PHelpS (Peer Help System) for helping workers in the Correctional Services of Canada (CSC) (i.e. Canada's prison system) interact with a mission-critical on-line database and management information system (called OMS) containing information about all criminal offenders in Canada. Dozens of different tasks are carried out by workers at CSC using OMS. PHelpS provides two main kinds of training when a worker

---

* This research was carried out under the auspices of the Canadian Telelearning Network of Centres of Excellence, project 6.2.4. We would like to acknowledge the funding provided to this research by the Telelearning Network of Centres of Excellence, by the Natural Sciences and Engineering Research Council of Canada, and by the University of Saskatchewan scholarship fund. We would also like to thank the Correctional Services of Canada, in particular the Regional Psychiatric Centre in Saskatoon, for supporting this project, and the workers in the RPC for giving so freely of their time and energy to help us understand their working environment. Finally, we would like to acknowledge Sherman Huang and Meg Mendoza of the Alberta Research Council in Calgary who are working with us on PHelpS, producing the case-based help component.

has a problem in carrying out a task. First, PHelpS can select peer helpers with whom the worker can interact to better understand the task, and second, PHelpS can make available previous help sessions as *cases* to be learned from.

Why peer help? Modern organizations are interested in a wider distribution of expertise throughout the organization. It is risky to have too much organizational knowledge in the heads of a few key people who then become indispensable to the organization. It is considered desirable to encourage as many workers as possible to become as broadly knowledgeable as possible so that there is flexibility in deploying workers to a variety of tasks and so that corporate knowledge is not lost when workers move on. As Constant et al. (1996) and others have pointed out, it is important in organizations to encourage among peers the development of both strong ties (where help is sought from known peers) and weak ties (where help is sought from strangers). Peer helpers can contribute to the widespread distribution of knowledge in the workplace in two ways. First, peer helpers can assist workers because of their awareness of the day-to-day issues that affect their peers and the misconceptions, difficulties and frustrations that their peers might face. Second, acting as a peer helper reinforces learning and reifies task knowledge (in the manner of reciprocal teaching, Palincsar and Brown, 1984). With peer help, everyone in the organization becomes involved in training, which gives workers a sense of involvement and ownership in their organization, while facilitating teamwork and team-building.

Why is user modelling crucial to peer help? It is necessary to provide some kind of computer support to encourage peer help in a large organization where fellow workers might be widely distributed and may not know one another. A user model can be the basis for (i) having the system select a set of knowledgeable, available, and appropriate set of helpers if a worker signals that he or she needs help in carrying out a particular task; (ii) having the worker choose among these potential helpers by inspecting the helpers' user models; (iii) having the chosen helper understand the worker's state of knowledge about the task before agreeing to embark on a subsequent help session; and (iv) facilitating better communication between the worker needing help and the helper as the help session proceeds. In all of these cases, the user model is used either by the system for support in locating a good helper, or by the humans *in the loop* (peer helper and worker needing help) who may consult each other's user model to facilitate communication. Many interesting user modelling issues arise in peer help systems because the same user model is utilized in multiple ways (by human and machine); the user models are inspectable by a variety of users; and there are significant challenges in performing constraint-based matching/retrieval and in maintaining the accuracy of user models over time.

2   Peer Help in PHelpS

The Peer Help System (PHelpS) is being developed to deliver a type of just-in-time training to users of OMS by providing help in the context of completing real tasks. The fundamental structure underlying PHelpS is the *task hierarchy*. Associated with each task commonly undertaken in OMS is a hierarchical set of steps. A fragment of a typical task (the Escorted Temporary Absence (ETA) task) is illustrated in Figure 1. The ETA task consists of a set of procedures and processes by which an offender may be granted an escorted temporary absence from the correctional facility (for example, to attend a funeral of a family member). There are approximately 80 distinct steps associated with this ETA task, some online and many involving individual or committee assessments and approvals. The task may span several days and possibly more than one correctional worker may be responsible for guiding the task through to a successful conclusion (either non-approval of the ETA or approval and detailed arrangements for the ETA). While policies and procedures for tasks like the ETA task exist within Corrections Canada, there was no existing detailed official task-hierarchy for any task when our research began. Our first steps involved doing task analyses of various tasks (in the sense of Shepherd, 1995) and constructing task hierarchies. Next we developed a facility called the *PHelpS Personal Assistant* (shown in Figure 1) which enables workers to use task hierarchies as checklists in recording steps completed within their tasks. The task–based approach has proven effective in other domains (e.g., Vassileva's hypermedia office document system, Vassileva, 1996).

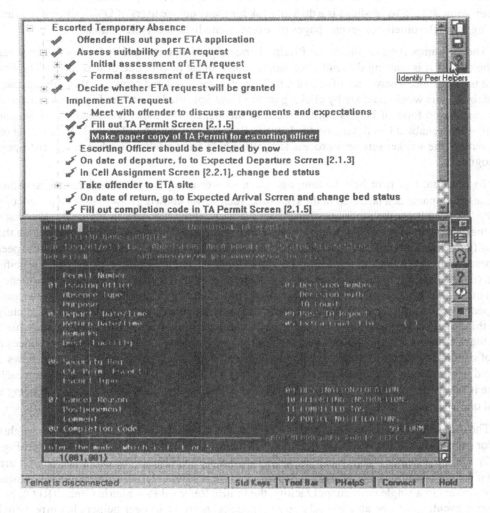

Figure 1. Personal Assistant: the Escorted Temporary Absence (ETA) task hierarchy.

Task hierarchies provide a terse description of steps that must be carried out and the recommended sequence for achieving them. Some of these steps involve the completion of forms in OMS or consultation using information contained in OMS. For example, about half of the steps in the complete ETA task involve using OMS forms. Workers completing a task with the PHelpS Personal Assistant can utilize the task hierarchy as a checklist to record the subtasks that have been achieved. Task steps can be opened to a finer grain size, or left at a coarse grain size, depending on how much detail the worker needs to see in carrying out the task. The worker can actually check off the tasks undertaken (see the check marks in Figure 1) as a reminder of where he or she is in undertaking the task. The task checklist also is hyper-linked to OMS so that clicking on a task step can take the user to the appropriate OMS screen (see the *lightning arrows* in Figure 1). For example, the checklist item in Figure 1 containing the caption *Fill out TA Permit Screen* is hyper-linked to the relevant OMS screen *[2.1.5]*. Finding the proper OMS screen without such hyper-links is a difficult task for many novice users of OMS, since it requires keying through sometimes several pages of textual menu lists of cryptic options.

The most important feature of our PHelpS Personal Assistant is the Help facility. When a step in the checklist is causing difficulty, the worker can request help in one of two forms. The first form is electronic, where a set of relevant help cases is retrieved and browsing through the cases is enabled (this would be done by clicking on the Case Specific Help tab in Figure 2). However, this case-based form of help is not the focus of this paper. The focus is instead on the second form of help enabled by clicking on the Identify Peer Helpers button in Figure 1. By clicking on this button, the worker sets up a process for getting help from a fellow worker in a peer-to-peer dialogue.

To illustrate this peer help feature, assume a worker using the PHelpS Personal Assistant reaches an impasse at a task step in the ETA task, such as not knowing how to make a paper copy of the TA Permit for the escorting officer (see the highlighted task step in Figure 1). He or she can mark the step as problematic (the ? annotation) and request a peer helper (by clicking on the Identify Peer Helpers button). PHelpS consults a knowledge base to locate a set of potential peer helpers within the organization who: (i) are knowledgeable about the problem area of the specific task, (ii) are available to provide help in the time frame required, (iii) have not been overburdened with other help requests in the recent past and (iv) have other characteristics critical to a successful peer help session, for example they speak the same language as the worker (approximately one third of CSC workers speak French as a first language, the rest English). The help request and these criteria form the inputs to a constraint solver embedded in PHelpS, which produces a set of candidate helpers ranked according to their suitability on these criteria. Figure 2 shows a ranked list of helpers resulting from a help request made in Figure 1 (the number preceding each name is the weight the constraint solver has given to indicate the likelihood of the match being a good one).

The user selects his or her preferred helper from the candidate list (perhaps using the weights and/or other information about potential peer helpers available in the Helper Profile; see Figure 2). Once the helper is selected, a helper-helpee dialogue is begun. The candidate helpers are drawn from a large pool. In our current experiments we are limited to drawing potential helpers from workers in a single correctional facility, the Prairie Regional Psychiatric Centre (RPC), but we hope eventually to be able to scale up to a national network of peer helpers in correctional institutions throughout Canada.

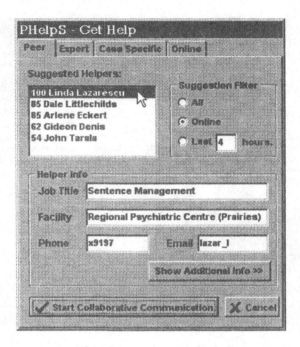

Figure 2. Peer helper suggestions.

The key to intelligently generating a reasonable candidate list involves maintaining knowledge profiles for every potential helper. The knowledge profiles are organized according to the tasks that need to be achieved within the organization. Thus, for each task hierarchy and each user, a hierarchically structured knowledge profile is constructed and annotated with the simple annotations *can help* or *can't help* attached to each task item. This knowledge profile along with other information about each potential peer helper (language spoken, rank in CSC, current availability, etc.) together constitute the user model of each peer helper. The process of creating and then maintaining these user models is discussed in more detail in Section 3.

The user models in PHelpS are inspectable by a variety of users (as in Paiva et al., 1995, and Bull et al., 1995). Inspectability is used in two places: (i) for the worker to inspect his or her own user model; and (ii) for the worker to inspect the user model of any potential peer helper. Figure 3 illustrates the form by which users can inspect and maintain their own user model. Each step in each task can be annotated with a star or an **X** indicating that the worker feels he or she *can help* or *can't help* on the step. Similarly, a worker needing peer help who wants more information about a potential peer helper can do so by clicking on the Show Additional Info button (see Figure 2). When this button is clicked the worker can see information from the user model of a potential helper. Not all information will be shown; for example, only the knowledge profile for the current task will be displayed, not the knowledge profiles of all tasks in the user model. In this way, a potential helper's level of expertise can be determined before that helper is contacted.

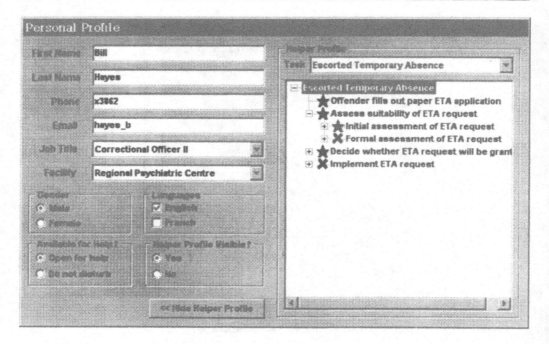

Figure 3. Inspecting a user model.

Once a peer helper is selected, a dialogue between the helper and the worker needing help ensues. This dialogue is initiated by the person needing help, and can happen off-line (e.g., by telephone or personal visit) or on-line, depending on urgency and the predilections of the two people involved. Within our current PHelpS prototype, an on-line dialogue between worker and peer helper is a database mediated talk session with some facilities for knowledge sharing which we call *PHelpS Talk*. (Our next prototypes will utilize more sophisticated collaborative work tools such as Microsoft's NetMeeting.)

The knowledge sharing facilities implemented in PHelpS Talk are related to the same check-list / knowledge profile task hierarchies used in peer helper identification. That is, the helper is provided with the marked-up checklist of the worker seeking help. In this way, the current help context is easily communicated. The helper can decide where help is needed and how many steps have been completed. In addition, in the same way the worker needing help can browse a version of the helper's user model before contacting him or her, the helper can also inspect a version of the user model of the worker seeking help. The helper may browse this model and determine the level of knowledge of the worker (in terms of the worker's annotations of *can help* and *can't help* for the task at hand) to adjust explanations appropriately. That is, a helper would provide a different kind of advice to a novice totally unfamiliar with the task than he or she would provide to a very experienced worker.

The dialogue exchanged through PHelpS Talk is trapped for each case and becomes fodder for the case-based help facility. While this paper does not discuss the case-based help in PHelpS, suffice it to say that capturing and indexing help cases is well supported by the task-hierarchy knowledge representation underlying PHelpS. Unfortunately, in situations where PHelpS Talk is passed over in favour of telephone communications or personal visits, no such knowledge capture can easily be made.

A PHelpS prototype is currently completed and is deployed in the Regional Psychiatric Centre. A variety of data is being collected and is being analyzed with respect to the effectiveness of PHelpS in supporting collaborative work. Preliminary analysis indicates that PHelpS is easy to use and that the task hierarchies are useful in helping workers organize their activities, but wider spread deployment within RPC is required in order to determine the effectiveness of PHelpS in choosing a helper and supporting the collaboration.

3   The Role of User Modelling in PHelpS

As can be seen from the above section, user modelling is at the heart of PHelpS. In this section, more details about the PHelpS approach to user modelling are presented. Each user model contains information ranging from the task-specific (e.g., the knowledge profiles showing the tasks the peer helper can perform and the level of capability in carrying out each coarse and fine-grained step in these tasks, etc.) to the very general (e.g., the peer helper's age, gender, position in CSC, linguistic fluency, current login status; the number of times the peer helper has provided help; etc.). Information in the user model changes over time, ranging from fine-grained temporal intervals (e.g., minutes or hours for login status, or to carry out a particular task step), through longer periods (e.g., days or weeks for learning a new task, months or years for changing position in CSC, etc.). The user model is thus multi-dimensional along two principle axes: temporal and task-relatedness. The task-relatedness dimension is explicitly hierarchical, following the natural topography of the various task hierarchies (see Figure 1). The temporal dimension is implicit, according to what particular information is in the knowledge profile at any given time. PHelpS thus must concern itself not only with initially stocking the user model for each peer helper, but also with maintaining the accuracy of the user model over time.

Initial knowledge acquisition of the user models is done through the filling in of a questionnaire by workers who wish to be on the peer helper roster. User model maintenance is not particularly difficult for general purpose time varying information such as login status or number of times the peer helper has dispensed help, since this information can be gleaned by the system merely by tracking logins and counting help sessions. It is more difficult, however, for changes in task-specific information to be tracked. As with initial knowledge acquisition, such tracking is the primary responsibility of the peer helpers themselves.

Nevertheless, the PHelpS approach does support such task-specific knowledge maintenance in two ways. First, as they themselves carry out various tasks, peer helpers are encouraged by PHelpS to check off task steps (see Section 2) as they proceed step-by-step through the task. Marking these checklists not only reifies the task steps in the mind of the peer helper, a useful reinforcement activity for just-in-time training on that task, but also can provide a sort of *temporal extension* of the peer helper's user model, recording the current state of his or her problem solving. The second support provided by PHelpS for peer helpers to keep their knowledge profiles up-to-date is a by-product of the peer help session itself. Since peer helpers and those being helped can inspect each others' knowledge profiles in order to better understand each other and to facilitate communication, the mutual interaction that ensues can clarify inaccuracies in the profiles of both parties.

As can be seen there is a major responsibility for PHelpS users to carry out profile mainte-nance activities. This, in fact, is how we "solve" the problems of user model maintenance that usually prove so difficult in many user and student modelling applications (Huang et al., 1991). We are not the first to suggest that users should help maintain their own user models (see Paiva et al., 1994), but in order for this to work, the context must be right for them to do so. The widespread use of PHelpS in an organization should encourage workers to ensure that the accu-racy of their own user models is maintained. They should want to keep an up-to-date record of their capabilities on various tasks (i) so that when they need help it can be targeted appropriately to take into account their strengths and weaknesses; and (ii) so that when others contact them for help, they will only be contacted on topics about which they know something. In short, an inaccurate user model will cost a worker time both when seeking help and when being sought for help.

If the user model maintenance proves to be more problematic than we hope, there are some natural extensions that can be carried out to help in maintaining the knowledge profiles. If users prove unwilling to check off their task steps at a fine grain size, but are willing to do so at a coarse grain size, then it would be possible to *infer* that the fine grained steps are known if the coarse grained ones are. If the users prove unwilling to check off any task steps at all as they carry out tasks, the hyper-links from the task hierarchies to the OMS system can be traversed in reverse to update a task hierarchy by inference from particular activities carried out in OMS. This may require the use of recognition and diagnosis methodologies from artificial intelligence. Sometimes these methodologies seem far removed from easy applicability, but, in this domain, the task-specificity of the activities carried out in OMS should allow the reasonable adaptation of methodologies like granularity-based recognition (as in SCENT, McCalla and Greer, 1994) and model/knowledge tracing (as in the LISP Tutor, Corbett and Anderson, 1995) which are explicitly designed for task-specific, real world domains.

In addition to being multi-dimensional, the user models in PHelpS are also multi-purpose. Their principal purpose is to help find an appropriate set of peer helpers for anybody needing help on a particular task. The primary requirement to be met in the choice of an appropriate helper is to find a peer who knows the task, and in particular the task step on which the person needs help. Secondary requirements are that this person be available in the time frame in which help is required, and that the person not have been asked to help others *too much* in the recent past. The primary requirement is fulfilled through use of an algorithm that matches the current task hierarchy checklist of the worker needing help with the knowledge profiles of potential peer helpers. The matching function currently operates as a constraint solver which considers the subtask (step) where help is requested, the sibling subtasks, the subsequent subtasks, and the higher-level parent subtasks. For these subtasks, a set of best candidate helpers is computed based on their ability to help, and the function returns a list of all those helpers who exceed a certain threshold. In Hoppe's terms (Hoppe, 1995), peers are chosen using a "complementarity criterion", i.e., a peer of high competence is chosen to help. Note, that unlike in Hoppe's learning domain, in our workplace environment choosing peers based on a "competitiveness criterion" is unlikely to be very effective. In future research, we may investigate incorporating information taken from the longer term knowledge profile of the person needing help (not just the checklist). The list returned from the profile matching function is further pruned by removing peer helpers who are not available or who have been overused, according to the secondary requirements above.

The remaining list of potential peer helpers is then presented to the person needing help, as in Figure 2.

This is where a second purpose of the user models becomes important: having the person needing help scan through the knowledge profiles of the potential peer helpers in order to choose somebody who has the specific combination of qualities that they prefer. These qualities may involve the peer helper having a particular pattern of task knowledge, or perhaps may involve some of the less task-specific characteristics, such as having the same gender, being of approximately the same age, or being in a similar position (same job title or same union). The literature on collaborative work and collaborative learning suggests that such characteristics are often important in facilitating effective collaboration (Dillenbourg et al., 1995). However, regardless of these statistical trends, we believe it is important to leave it to the worker needing help to decide if these are important to him or her in the current context.

The third purpose for the user models is the dual of the second purpose, namely giving the peer helper who has been contacted the ability to look at the knowledge profile of the worker needing help (as well as the task hierarchy checklist that represents that worker's current state of task completion). The peer helper has the right to refuse to help. But, if he or she does decide to help, the worker's profile (and task hierarchy checklist) and the helper's profile can form the basis for mutual understanding between the two parties. In particular, during their discussions the peer collaborators can adjust the level of their conversation to take into account differences in knowledge between the two, can point to various parts of the task hierarchies in their respective profiles, and can use the verbal descriptors in the task hierarchies as a shared vocabulary.

The power of the user modelling system in PHelpS comes from five main sources, and will need a sixth source if PHelpS is going to actually be used long term in CSC. First, the models are inspectable in the sense of Bull et al. (1995) and Paiva et al. (1995). Such inspectability is not only crucial (see the three purposes above), but is also easily achieved. The linguistic terms used in the models to describe task steps and general knowledge are familiar to the peer collaborators, since they share a common work environment with common procedures, policies, and purposes. The models are graphically displayed, and easily visualized.

The second source of power is the task-orientation of the user models. Since they model authentic and well-defined tasks in a real world environment, the usual ambiguity and complexity bedevilling the application of user modelling techniques in, say, dialogue (Kobsa and Wahlster, 1989) and intelligent tutoring (Self, 1990, and Greer and McCalla, 1994) do not appear. Such task-orientation is often crucial in achieving success, even in these domains (Grosz and Sidner, 1986, and Vassileva, 1996). It is key here, as well.

The third source of power is that the user models, in particular knowledge profiles, are represented at multiple levels of detail, allowing the models to be viewed at a coarse grain size, or to be opened to more specific levels. This facilitates the ease with which a person looking through a knowledge profile (or checklist) can access the relevant information at the level appropriate to him or her. Having many levels of detail is also useful to user model maintenance and could prove to be important to the profile matching algorithm. Granularity is an important feature in other user modelling systems (Greer and McCalla, 1994) meant for use in noisy, real world environments.

A fourth source of power of the user models is the ease with which they can be updated and maintained by the users (CSC workers). This, in fact, is critical to the long term success of the PHelpS system. It is extremely easy for a user to check off the current task's hierarchy as the task steps are completed. The inspectability and multiple levels of granularity also make it fairly easy for a user to keep his or her peer helper profile up to date. As mentioned above, the incorporation of various AI diagnosis and inference techniques may enhance the ease of updating.

A fifth source of power in the user modelling done in PHelpS is that there is an explicit role for humans in all aspects of the user modelling. The inspectability, task-orientation, multiple levels of detail, and ease of updating, make it possible for humans to use and maintain the user models. It is also natural for them to do so, both when they seek help and when they provide help. With the humans users so naturally in the loop, the user modelling can happen robustly and effectively. The humans can step in when the models fail to capture reality, but the models can augment human capabilities as well, forming a powerful synergy that benefits both the model and the human.

The above five sources of power for user modelling are already incorporated to some degree into the PHelpS design. However, there is still a sixth source of power that will be necessary once PHelpS is actually fully deployed: the acceptance of these user models by the users. That is, the users (CSC workers) will have to allow information about them to be made available to their peers, or even possibly to their superiors. The issue of privacy versus inspectability of user models is a very delicate one. Inspectable user models can be readily twisted into data for performance reviews and worker accountability, raising fears ranging from those associated with monitoring day to day work activities, through to worries about the models being misused to penalize workers who have exposed their weaknesses through their knowledge profiles. Unfortunately, until we have more experience with the prototype deployed in the Regional Psychiatric Centre of CSC, we will not really begin to know how these privacy issues shake out. However, in our preliminary study of attitudes we are encouraged that these obstacles will be overcome. The workers in the organization are accustomed to the monitoring of their activities while using OMS, since accountability for accessing sensitive information about convicted criminals (particularly high-profile offenders) is part of the workplace culture. Nevertheless, we are concerned about the workers' acceptance of inspectable user models and we are sensitive to the privacy-usefulness tradeoff.

4 Conclusion

Our work on PHelpS makes contributions to user modelling research in a number of ways. First, while traditionally researchers have sought principled and completely automated techniques for user and student modelling, in contrast we suggest in this research that user modelling can be done in a minimalist way, with the user in the loop to make sure that the model accurately reflects the user's capabilities and to constrain the system when it fails to act reasonably. Second, while user modelling is clearly useful in a wide variety of applications, there is a shortage of applications discussed in the literature where user modelling both plays a central role and can be achieved in a real world of use. PHelpS, on the other hand, is a system that can be deployed widely with the potential to have a major effect in a real workplace. Third, user and student modelling is often conceived as enhancing the individualization of the user-computer interaction. In our research, user modelling is done to enhance user-user interaction, that is to foster collaboration among peers. Fourth, in many user modelling applications, especially student modelling in intelligent tutoring systems, the system is assumed to be in control, in fact often has to be in control in order for the modelling to be done. In our research, the user is in full control. Finally, our research on PHelpS is not at all restricted to the Corrections Canada domain. The methodologies developed here are generally applicable. They are transferrable to any domain where there is a strong task structure and where users are naturally using a computer system.

References

Bull, S., Brna, P., and Pain, H. (1995). Extending the scope of the student model. *User Modeling and User-Adapted Interaction* 5:45–65.

Constant, D., Sproull, L., and Kiesler, S. (1996). The kindness of strangers: The usefulness of electronic weak ties for technical advice. *Organization Science* 7(2):119–135.

Corbett, A. T., and Anderson, J. R. (1995). Knowledge tracing: Modeling the acquisition of procedural knowledge. *User Modeling and User-Adapted Interaction* 4:253–278.

Dillenbourg, P., Baker, M., Blaye, A., and O'Malley, C. (1995). The evolution of research on collaborative learning. In Reimann, P., and Spada, H., eds., *Learning in Humans and Machines*. London: Elsevier.

Greer, J. E., and McCalla, G. I. (1994). *Student Modelling*. Berlin: Springer-Verlag.

Grosz, B. J., and Sidner, C. L. (1986). Attention, intentions, and the structure of discourse. *Journal of Computational Linguistics* 175–204.

Hoppe, H. U. (1995). The use of multiple student modeling to parameterize group learning. In *Artificial Intelligence in Education: Proceedings of AI-ED 95, AACE*, 234–241.

Huang, X., McCalla, G. I., Greer, J. E., and Neufeld, E. (1991). Revising deductive knowledge and stereo-typical knowledge in a student model. *User Modeling and User-Adapted Interaction* 1(1):87–115.

Kobsa, A., and Wahlster, W. (1989). *User Models in Dialog Systems*. Berlin: Springer-Verlag.

McCalla, G. I., and Greer, J. E. (1994). Granularity-based reasoning and belief revision in student models. In *Student Modelling*. 39–62.

Paiva, A., Self, J., and Hartley, R. (1994). On the dynamics of learner models. In *Proceedings of the 11th European Conference on Artificial Intelligence*, 163–167.

Paiva, A., Self, J., and Hartley, R. (1995). Externalising learner models. In *Artificial Intelligence in Education: Proceedings of AI-ED 95, AACE*, 509–516.

Palincsar, A. S., and Brown, A. L. (1984). Reciprocal teaching of comprehension-fostering and comprehension-monitoring activities. *Cognition and Instruction* 1(2):117–175.

Self, J. A. (1990). Bypassing the intractable problem of student modelling. In Frasson, C., and Gauthier, G., eds., *Intelligent Tutoring Systems*. Norwood, NJ: Ablex. 107–123.

Shepherd, A. (1995). Task analysis. In Monk, A. F., and Gilbert, G. N., eds., *Perspectives on HCI: Diverse Approaches*. London: Academic Press. 145–174.

Vassileva, J. (1996). A task-centered approach for user modeling in a hypermedia office documentation system. *User Modeling and User-Adapted Interaction* 6:185–223.

A Pair of Student Models to Encourage Collaboration

Susan Bull[1] and Matt Smith[2]

[1] The Language Centre, University of Brighton, UK
[2] School of Computing Science, Middlesex University, UK

Abstract. PairSM is a domain-independent system aimed at helping pairs of students to organise their revision for an approaching test. PairSM contains two individual student models which are compared by the system to enable it to suggest ways in which two students may work together effectively. It can recommend collaborative learning, peer tutoring or individual learning, depending on the comparative contents of the models. The aim is to encourage students to experience the benefits of peer interaction.

1 Introduction to PairSM

The two student models of pairSM are initially based on the results of a multiple choice pre-test entered by the tutor. The models are updated by subsequent tests. PairSM contains heuristics for recommending the kind of preparation which may be useful for the learners, by comparing the contents of the two student models, and the manner in which the learners have acquired further knowledge. An overview of the student models is given in Figure 1.

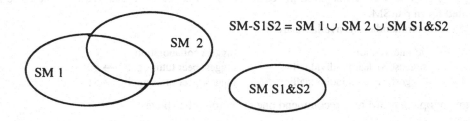

$$SM\text{-}S1S2 = SM\ 1 \cup SM\ 2 \cup SM\ S1\&S2$$

Figure 1. The two student models of pairSM.

SM 1 represents the concepts known by Student 1, and SM 2, those known by Student 2. The intersection of SM 1 and SM 2 represents shared knowledge. SM S1&S2 represents knowledge that the two students can display when working together, but that they cannot produce individually. This is similar to Vygotsky's *zone of proximal development* (Vygotsky, 1978). SM-S1S2 is the union of SM 1, SM 2 and SM S1&S2. SM-S1S2 represents knowledge that the pair can display when working together, resulting from one or both knowing the concepts individually, or from interaction between the two learners.

Simplified descriptions of the possible situations for each of the individual students are:

$(X \subset SM\ 1) \wedge (X \not\subset SM\ 2)$ X is known by Student 1 and X is not known by Student 2,
$(X \not\subset SM\ 1) \wedge (X \subset SM\ 2)$, $(X \subset SM\ 1) \wedge (X \subset SM\ 2)$, $(X \not\subset SM\ 1) \wedge (X \not\subset SM\ 2)$.

When also considering whether S1 and S2 can solve a problem or know something when working together, these are expanded to:

$(X \subset SM\ 1) \wedge (X \not\subset SM\ 2) \wedge (X \subset SM\text{-}S1S2)$, $(X \not\subset SM\ 1) \wedge (X \subset SM\ 2) \wedge (X \subset SM\text{-}S1S2)$,
$(X \subset SM\ 1) \wedge (X \subset SM\ 2) \wedge (X \subset SM\text{-}S1S2)$, $(X \not\subset SM\ 1) \wedge (X \not\subset SM\ 2) \wedge (X \subset SM\text{-}S1S2)$,
$(X \not\subset SM\ 1) \wedge (X \not\subset SM\ 2) \wedge (X \not\subset SM\text{-}S1S2)$.

There are two cases:

$\subset$ is a subset of *"is known by"*; $\not\subset$ is not a subset of *"is not known by"*.

However, in reality the situation is more complicated. For example, in the case of $(X \subset SM\ 1) \wedge (X \not\subset SM\ 2)$, if there were 5 test questions to determine this state, SM 1 might represent 4 or 5 answers correct, and SM 2 only 0 or 1. What happens in other cases? We therefore introduce the following to represent such intermediate states, e.g.:

$(X\ ??\!\subset SM\ 1) \wedge (X \not\subset SM\ 2)$ *Some of X is known by Student 1, X is not known by Student 2*

$(X\ ?\!\subset SM\ 1) \wedge (X\ ??\!\subset SM\ 2)$ *Most of X is known by Student 1, some of X is known by Student 2*

$(X \not\subset SM\ 1) \wedge (X\ ??\!\subset SM\ 2) \wedge (X\ ?\!\subset SM\text{-}S1S2)$.

We now have two further ways to represent these imprecise situations:

$??\!\subset$ *"is partially known by"*; $?\!\subset$ "is known to a fair extent by".

Further situations are possible—where a student may actually do worse when working with a partner, e.g.: $(X \not\subset SM\ 1) \wedge (X\ ?\!\subset SM\ 2) \wedge (X\ ??\!\subset SM\text{-}S1S2)$. However, this can be overcome through the provision of feedback on the correctness of responses. These cases are therefore not accounted for in pairSM.

The six recommendations available are:

no intervention	suggest collaboration
suggest S1 learn individually	suggest peer tutoring S1 $\rightarrow$ S2
suggest S2 learn individually	suggest peer tutoring S2 $\rightarrow$ S1

For a given topic pairSM may recommend one or more of the above.

2   Using PairSM

Imagine pairSM is being used to help students to prepare for a test on Catalan grammar. The following five areas are to be included in the test: articles, plurals, possessive adjectives, use of the verbs *ésser* and *estar*, and irregular verb declensions. The teacher composes a simple test consisting of example questions from the above areas, and submits these to the pre-test section of pairSM (see Figure 2). The teacher will enter as many questions on each topic as s/he feels are necessary to determine whether the students know the content sufficiently well.

Some areas will be less suitable for collaborative learning or peer tutoring. In the Catalan example, declension of irregular verbs relies more on rote learning than do the distinctions between when to use *ésser* or *estar*. Therefore the *ésser/estar* domain will have a different suitability rating from irregular verbs. PairSM can then balance the contents of the models against the suitability of each topic for peer interaction when making recommendations. Students take the pre-test individually. The questions appear as in Figure 3.

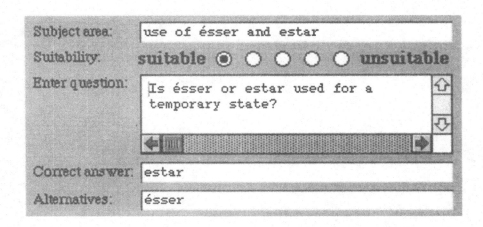

Figure 2. Creating a test.

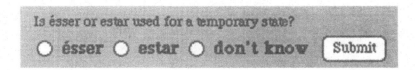

Figure 3. The test.

Once the students have each completed the pre-test, the system is able to consider where help is needed most, and whether the students can usefully collaborate or tutor each other. Students can later return to pairSM to take another test. This first occurs separately, and if the students wish to take advantage of all of the possible representations for SM-S1S2 (i.e., also including SM S1&S2) they retake the same test in a situation where they can communicate. The system is then able to compare the results of the collaboratively taken test with the identical, but individually taken version, before making its next recommendations.

In addition to the test questions, students are now also asked each time to indicate whether during their preparation they worked alone for that topic, worked collaboratively, were tutored, or did some tutoring. This helps the system to evaluate the effectiveness of the different types of preparation, for the particular students. For example, the case of: $(X \ ??\subset SM \ 1) \wedge (X \not\subset SM \ 2) \wedge (X \subset SM\text{-}S1S2) \wedge pairSM \ recommendation = collaboration \wedge approach \ used = collaboration$ indicates that for these students the recommendation of collaboration was useful.

Reference

Vygotsky, L. S. (1978). *Mind in Society: The Development of Higher Psychological Processes.* Cambridge, MA: Harvard University Press.

GENERAL TECHNIQUES AND PERSPECTIVES

Machine Learning Techniques

A Comparison of First-Order and Zeroth-Order Induction for Input-Output Agent Modelling

Bark Cheung Chiu, Geoffrey I. Webb, and Mark Kuzmycz*

School of Computing and Mathematics, Deakin University, Australia

Abstract. Most student modelling systems seek to develop a model of the internal operation of the cognitive system. In contrast, Input-Output Agent Modelling (IOAM) models an agent in terms of relationships between the inputs and outputs of the cognitive system. Previous IOAM systems have demonstrated high predictive accuracy in the domain of elementary subtraction. These systems use zeroth-order induction. Many of the predicates used, however, represent relations. This suggests that first-order induction might perform well in this domain. This paper reports a study in which zeroth-order and first-order induction engines were used to build models of student subtraction skills. Comparative evaluation shows that zeroth-order induction performs better than first-order in detecting regularities indicating misconceptions while first-order induction leads zeroth-order in detecting regularities indicating correct concepts and inducing a more comprehensible student model. This suggests there exists a trade-off between these factors and that there is still scope for improvement.

1 Introduction

Most previous approaches to producing student models have employed process models. These seek to model the internal cognition of a student's cognitive system (Anderson et al., 1985:Anderson et al., 1990; Baffes and Mooney, 1996; Brown and VanLehn, 1980; Brown and Burton, 1978; Corbett and Anderson, 1992; Giangrandi and Tasso, 1995; Goldstein, 1979; Hoppe, 1994; Ikeda et al., 1993; Langley and Ohlsson, 1984; Langley et al., 1990; Martin and VanLehn, 1995; Ohlsson and Langley, 1985; Sleeman, 1982; Sleeman et al., 1991; Young and O'Shea, 1981). In contrast, Input-Output Agent Modelling (IOAM) models an agent in terms of the relationships between the inputs and outputs of the cognitive system. This approach treats the operation of the cognitive system as a black box. This black box model can describe the capabilities of the system, but does not seek to capture the system's internal mechanisms.

Previous IOAM approaches include Feature Based Modelling (Webb and Kuzmycz, 1996), Relational Based Modelling (Kuzmycz, 1995) and C4.5-IOAM (Webb et al., 1997). These have demonstrated high predictive accuracy in the domain of elementary subtraction. The induction engines employed by FBM and RBM were specifically designed for the purpose, while the one used by C4.5-IOAM is C4.5 (Quinlan, 1993), a well-known and general-purpose learning algo-

* We thank Ross Quinlan for providing ftp access to the FFOIL program. Thanks to Zijian Zheng for his helpful suggestions and comments.

rithm. They are zeroth-order learners in the sense that they learn theories from attribute-value examples. The student model produced by both FBM and RBM is a set of classification rules (called associations) whereas C4.5-IOAM generates a set of decision trees. A comparative evaluation between C4.5-IOAM and FBM has been made in the domain of simple subtraction problems (Webb et al., submitted). It shows that the use of C4.5 increases the number of predictions made without significantly altering the accuracy of those predictions.

That study raised three questions. First, the student model induced by the induction engines mentioned above is either a set of associations or decision trees. These can be difficult for people, such as an ITS (Intelligent Tutoring System) administrator, to comprehend. Second, these induction systems make use of domain features in the form of attribute-value data only. Many of the predicates used, however, represent relations. For example, the context feature $M < S$ represents a relation between the minuend and the subtrahend. In view of this, it is plausible that the use of relational learning might produce the relevant aspects of a model more directly and hence might provide better performance or produce a more comprehensible student model. Finally, there is expert knowledge about the subtraction problems that has not been used in the above systems. Like overlay models (Burton and Brown, 1976; Carbonell, 1970) which cover expert knowledge, a comprehensible model which can represent both expert knowledge and misconceptions could benefit the work of student performance assessment. We believed the employment of a first-order induction engine such as FOIL (Quinlan, 1990) could solve the above problems when considering that it can make use of background knowledge and learn concepts in the form of a first order logic program from a set of training relations.

The primary objective of this study is to evaluate and compare the relative effectiveness, within the IOAM context, of zeroth-order and first-order induction. The use of zeroth-order and first-order inductive learning in student modelling have been studied separately (for example, Gilmore and Self, 1988; Desmoulins and Van Labeke, 1996). However, there has not been a comparative study of these two types of learning systems on a single subject domain. This paper presents a study in which a zeroth-order learner, C4.5, and a first-order learner, FFOIL (Quinlan, 1996), were used as induction engines in a student modelling system and elementary subtraction was used as the subject domain. There are a number of reasons for choosing C4.5 and FFOIL to conduct this study. Among the state-of-the-art machine learning alternatives, both C4.5 and FOIL are readily available and have been adopted by many researchers as references for evaluating other induction techniques. FFOIL, as an extension of FOIL, is designed to learn functional relations. It can learn more quickly than FOIL. In addition, FFOIL does not require negative examples in the training set. Both C4.5 and FFOIL have been developed in C by the same author. They share many similarities in their program architectures. This may be expected to minimise the number of extraneous differences between the systems that might otherwise confound attempts at systematic comparison of zeroth and first order techniques.

2 Experimental Design

This study was inspired by FBM (Webb and Kuzmycz, 1996), from which the techniques of manipulating context and action features of the problem domain were adopted in this experiment. This section first gives an overview of how FBM works; then it describes how to build two subtraction modellers, C4.5-IOAM and FFOIL-IOAM, for this experiment. Finally, it explains how the test data was collected and used.

2.1 An Overview of Feature Based Modelling

Feature Based Modelling (FBM) is an IOAM approach based on attribute-value machine learning techniques. It has been used to produce models of student's competencies in various domains. This subsection provides an overview of the approach and the way in which it has been applied to the domain of elementary subtraction. FBM requires prior identification of relevant context and action features. Context features describe the problems with which a student is faced. Action features describe aspects of a student's actions for a particular problem. The student model produced by FBM consists of a set of associations. An association is a relationship between a set of context features and a single action feature.

The subtraction domain used by FBM was limited to 3-digit subtraction problems and the answers were confined to positive values. The context features describe the column and the context in which that column appears. Such features might include symbolic indications that the subtrahend is smaller than the minuend in the current column and that the subtrahend is greater than the minuend in the column to the right. The action features describe properties of the student's answer for a single column. These might include symbolic indications that the result equals zero and that the result equals the value of subtracting the subtrahend from the minuend.

FBM manipulates a n-digit subtraction problem by treating it as n separate column problems. Each column is described by a set of context features. The problem-answer unit might be described by more than one association. Each such association links a set of context features to a specific action feature. After learning from training examples, FBM builds a set of these associations as a model of the student's problem solving competency. When a new test problem with the specified context features is applied as input, a subset of associations might be triggered. The action features for these associations can be used to predict the student's actions. Some action features will, in the context of a concrete subtraction problem, predict a specific digit for the student's response. For example, the action feature *Result = Minuend − Subtrahend* predicts that the response will be equal to the minuend minus the subtrahend. If there is no conflict among these specific predictions, a prediction of that digit will be made. Otherwise, the system makes no prediction for that problem unit.

2.2 C4.5-IOAM

The C4.5-IOAM subtraction modeller was implemented by employing the same procedures as in FBM except that C4.5 was used as the induction engine. C4.5 was originally designed to classify examples into one of mutually exclusive classes. However, the action features used by FBM are not mutually exclusive. For example, the action feature *Result = zero* may coexist with the action feature *Result = minuend − subtrahend* when the minuend and subtrahend are equal, and the student's answer exhibits these features. To solve this problem, a set of decision trees is required; each one of the trees represents a relation of a context feature vector and an action feature. There were 11 decision trees to be built. They corresponded to the action features used in the FBM study (Webb and Kuzmycz 1996):

Result = M–S,	Result = M–S–1,	Result = 10+M–S,	Result = 10+M–S–1,
Result = M,	Result = S,	Result = zero,	Result = M–S–2,
Result = 10+M–S–2,	Result = S–M,	Result = correct,	

where M and S stand for Minuend and Subtrahend respectively. The context features of a unit problem were described by 12 attributes. They are listed below with their meanings, where N stands for Not Available.

- M_is_0: {T,F},   the Minuend digit is zero.
- S_is_0: {T,F},   the Subtrahend digit is zero.
- S_is_9: {T,F},   the Subtrahend digit is nine.
- S_is_BK: {T,F},   the Subtrahend is left blank.
- M_vs_S: {G,L,E},   the Minuend is greater than, less than, or equal to the Subtrahend.
- $M\_L\_is\_0$: {T,F,N},   the Minuend digit in the column to the left is zero.
- $M\_L\_is\_1$: {T,F,N},   the Minuend digit in the column to the left is one.
- $M\_R\_is\_0$: {T,F,N},   the Minuend digit in the column to the right is zero.
- $S\_R\_is\_9$: {T,F,N},   the Subtrahend digit in the column to the right is nine.
- M_S_R: {G,L,E,N}, similar to M_vs_S, but it describes the column to the right.
- M_S_2R: {G,L,E,N}, similar to M_vs_S, but it describes two columns to the right.
- $Column$:   {L,I,R},   the current column is left-most, inner or right-most.

Let $a = action(t, p)$ denote the action feature that decision tree t selects for task p. Let $d = digit(a, p)$ be the digit specified by a and p, or '?' if $a = no\_action$. For any tree t and task p, let $prediction(t, p) = d$. The operation of this system can be described as follows.

Training stage:

1. Examples of a student's three-column subtraction performance are presented to the system.
2. The examples are processed to identify appropriate context and action features in a form suited for input to C4.5.
3. C4.5 is used to infer a decision tree t_i for each action feature exhibited by the student's answer.

Testing stage: New subtraction problems are presented to the system. For each such problem p,

1. the set of decision trees is consulted and confined to n decision trees $t_1 .... t_n$ such that $prediction(t_i, p) = d, d \in \{0, 1, ..., 9\}$;
2. if $n > 0 \land \forall ij:(1 \le i \le n \land 1 \le j \le n \land i \ne j) \rightarrow prediction(t_i, p) = prediction(t_j, p)$
   then
            prediction := $prediction(t_1, p)$
   else
            prediction := ? (indicating no prediction).

2.3 FFOIL-IOAM

An FFOIL-IOAM subtraction modeller was implemented by replacing the induction engine of C4.5-IOAM with FFOIL. The input data was processed to generate input tuples for FFOIL. There were three design issues to be considered:

- How to determine the target function to be learnt?
- What arguments should be used for the target function?
- What background relations were required?

The single digit subtraction function *subtract(Min, Sub, Ans)* and the background relation *dec(X, Y)*, denoting that X is greater than Y by one, provided a starting point. Yet these permitted only theories for the correct single column subtraction. In order to have theories that cover both students' correct and incorrect concepts, extra arguments were required to describe other problem contexts that might influence a student's answer. In C4.5-IOAM, there were 12 attributes involved to describe a unit problem. However, the problem context described by *M_is_0, S_is_0* and *S_is_9* used in C4.5-IOAM and the relations between the minuend and the subtrahend such as $M > S$ can be automatically defined in FFOIL-IOAM when there is a background relation called *gt(X, Y)* (X is greater than Y) and the arguments *Min* and *Sub* are bound to the corresponding values. The attributes *M_S_R* and *M_S_2R* used in C4.5-IOAM were considered factors that might influence a student's attention of whether a borrow should have been incurred from the column(s) to the right. Instead of using two arguments to represent these factors, a boolean argument called *Borrow* was adopted. This was found to have similar effect and with lower computational overheads. It was also found that the employment of an argument for describing the minuend in the column to the left caused no significant improvement in predictive performance. After considering these factors it appeared that five arguments, *Min, Sub, MRis0, SRis9* and *Borrow*, were sufficient to describe the problem context. The function to be learned is *subtract(Min, Sub, MRis0, SRis9, Borrow, Ans)*. An example of a training tuple is *subtract(9, 7, Mr! = 0, Sr = 9, T, 1)*. It can be interpreted as: under the problem context where *Minuend digit = 9, Subtrahend digit = 7, Minuend digit in the column to the right ≠ 0, Subtrahend digit in the column to the right = 9*, and *there should be a borrow incurred from the column to the right*, the student's answer is 1.

FFOIL only accepts extensionally defined background relations. That means all background relations have to be defined by sets of ground facts. The background knowledge for this system consists of eight relations. Two of them are simple numeric relations: *dec(X, Y)* and *gt(X, Y)*. The reasons of choosing them have been mentioned above. They could be regarded as auxiliary descriptive vocabularies to express novel answers from the students.

Relations *M–S_miss1(Min, Sub, Borrow, Ans)* and *10+M–S_miss1(Min, Sub, Borrow, Ans)* were used to describe common errors in column subtraction problems. The remaining relations, *M–S(Min, Sub, Borrow, Ans), M–S–1(Min, Sub, Borrow, Ans), 10+M–S(Min, Sub, Borrow, Ans)* and *10+M–S–1(Min, Sub, Borrow, Ans)*, were used to represent expert knowledge. The ground facts for each relation have been designed to exhibit the following corresponding properties:

M–S_miss1(Min, Sub, T, Ans):	Min ≥ Sub, Ans = Min–Sub,	e.g. (7,1,T,6).
10+M–S_miss1(Min, Sub, T, Ans):	Sub > Min, Ans = 10+Min–Sub,	e.g. (1,4,T,7).
M–S(Min, Sub, F, Ans):	Min ≥ Sub, Ans = Min–Sub,	e.g. (7,1,F,6).
M–S–1(Min, Sub, T, Ans):	Min > Sub, Ans = Min–Sub–1,	e.g. (7,1,T,5).

$10+M–S(Min, Sub, F, Ans)$:   Sub > Min, Ans = 10+Min–Sub,   e.g. (1,4,F,7).
$10+M–S–1(Min, Sub, T, Ans)$:   Sub ≥ Min, Ans = 10+ Min–Sub–1,   e.g. (1,4,T,6).

If a student solves all the problems correctly, we expect the system will generate the following theory to model the student:

subtract(Min, Sub, MRis0, SRis9, Borrow, Ans) :- M–S(Min, Sub, Borrow, Ans), !.   [expert-rule: 1a]
subtract(Min, Sub, MRis0, SRis9, Borrow, Ans) :- 10+M–S(Min, Sub, Borrow, Ans),!.   [expert-rule: 1b]
subtract(Min, Sub, MRis0, SRis9, Borrow, Ans) :- M–S–1(Min, Sub, Borrow, Ans),!.   [expert-rule: 2a]
subtract(Min, Sub, MRis0, SRis9, Borrow, Ans) :- 10+M–S–1(Min, Sub, Borrow, Ans).   [expert-rule: 2b]

Note that the *Borrow* in predicates *M–S( )* and *10+M–S( )* is always bound to *F* while it is always bound to *T* in predicates *M–S–1( )* and *10+M–S–1( )*. Also the ground facts for each relation have built-in relations (> or ≥) between the *Min* and *Sub*,[1] The above theory can be interpreted as:

> if no borrow is incurred →
> > if (Minuend ≥ Subtrahend)
> > > then result := (Minuend – Subtrahend)   [expert-rule: 1a]
> > > else result := (10 + Minuend – Subtrahend);   [expert-rule: 1b]
> > if a borrow is incurred →
> > > if (Minuend > Subtrahend)
> > > > then result := (Minuend – Subtrahend – 1)   [expert-rule: 2a]
> > > > else result := (10 + Minuend – Subtrahend – 1).   [expert-rule: 2b]

FFOIL-IOAM learns the concepts directly from the relations of problem context and the student answer. It can predict the digit directly from a set of context features. The input-output of the target relation is represented as:

$$f(c_1, ...c_5) \rightarrow [0, 1, 2...9, ?],$$

where c_i is a constant and '?', representing unknown, is generated by FFOIL when no inferred clause covers a case and a default clause is disabled. Let $d = f(c_1, ..., c_5)$ denote the functional value that satisfies the relation $subtract(c_1, ..., c_5, d)$ for a task p described by c_i. The operation of this system can be described as follows.

Training stage:

1. Examples of a student's three-column subtraction performance are presented to the system.
2. The examples are processed to identify appropriate context features in the form suited for input to FFOIL.
3. FFOIL is used to infer a functional logic program based on the positive examples and the background knowledge.

Testing stage: New subtraction problems are presented to the system. For each such problem p,
    prediction$(p) = d, d \in \{0, 1, ..., 9, ?\}$.

---

[1] Considering the search overheads, we added built-in relations to the ground facts. Otherwise a clause like M–S(Min,Sub,Borrow,Ans), gt(Min,Sub), Borrow = F,! would impose a higher computational cost as a trade-off for readability. Renaming *M–S( ) and 10+M–S–1( )* with do_M–S_M>S__borrow0( ) and do_10+M–S–1_S≥ M_borrow1( ) on FFOIL's output, for example, might improve readability as well.

2.4 Experimental Data

These two systems were applied to the subtraction data collected by Webb and Kuzmycz (1996). 73 nine- to ten-year-old primary school students were divided into two treatments, Random group (36 subjects) and Error Repeat group (37 subjects). These subjects were administered five rounds of tests. Each test consisted of 40 three-column subtraction problems. Successive tests were all administrated at weekly intervals. In both Tests 1 and 5, a set of subtraction problems was randomly generated and presented to all subjects. For Tests 2 to 4, the experimental data were collected as follows:

- For the Random group, a new set of randomly generated problems was presented to the subjects.
- For the Error Repeat group, all problems from the last problem sheet for which the subject made an error were copied to the new problem set. Mixing new randomly generated problems to make a total of 40, the new set of problems was presented to the subjects.

For each student, four turns (Turns 2 to 5) of model testing were processed. A modelling system used all data from prior rounds to build a student model and used the current round data to test the current student model. That means the system started at Turn 2 where Round 2 data was used as testing data against a student model which was built based on Round 1 data. At the fifth turn, the Round 5 data was used as testing data against a student model which was built from the data compiled over the previous four rounds.

3 Results

There were a total of 30,474 student answers, of which 3,630 were incorrect answers. The C4.5-IOAM system made 28,700 predictions, of which 26,507 (92%) were correct. Of the system's 1,999 predictions that a subject would provide an incorrect digit for a column, 1,347 (67%) were accurate, predicting the exact digit provided. The FFOIL-IOAM system made 26,560 predictions, of which 24,448 (92%) were correct. Of the system's 1,977 predictions that a subject would provide an incorrect digit for a column, 1,087 (55%) were accurate, predicting the exact digit provided. These results are summarised in Table 1.

Table 1. Overall prediction performance of two subtraction modellers.

	C4.5-IOAM	FFOIL-IOAM
Number of predictions made	28,700	26,560
Prediction rate	94%	87%
Number of predictions that were correct	26,507	24,448
Prediction accuracy	92%	92%
Number of error predictions made	1,999	1,977
Prediction rate	55%	54%
Number of error predictions that were correct	1,347	1,087
Error prediction accuracy	67%	55%

Two-tailed binomial sign tests were used to evaluate the statistical significance of the observed differences. Table 2 summarises the analysis of the 264 test sheets[2] examined where the number in the column $A > B$ represents the number of cases where A outperforms B.

Table 2. Observed differences in performance of two subtraction modellers.

Performance	C4.5-IOAM > FFOIL-IOAM	FFOIL-IOAM > C4.5-IOAM	p
More predictions made	196	61	< 0.001
Higher accuracy	163	86	< 0.001
More error predictions made	59	143	< 0.001
Higher accuracy (error prediction)	52	22	0.001

Further analyses of those results by turn reveals how the size of a training set affects the systems' performance. Figure 1 shows the prediction rate of each system. C4.5-IOAM increases the number of predictions made in Turn 3 and then levels off, while FFOIL-IOAM drops its prediction rate in Turn 3 and raises it in Turn 5 (two-tailed binomial sign tests comparing the systems turn by turn: $p = 1.000, p < 0.001, p < 0.001, p < 0.001$, respectively).

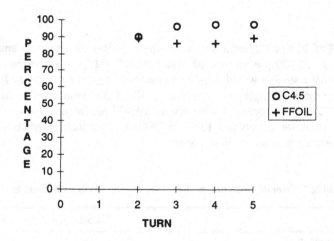

Figure 1. Prediction rates of C4.5-IOAM and FFOIL-IOAM from Turns 2 to 5.

---

[2] Model testing started from Turn 2. Only 52 subjects completed five rounds of tests, giving 208 (52×4) test sheets. The remaining subjects contributed 56 test sheets, giving a grand total of 264.

Figure 2 shows the proportion of the predictions that were correct. As can been seen, C4.5-IOAM shows a steady, if modest gain, in predictive accuracy while FFOIL starts from a lower base point from Turn 2, but then regains the same ground. Two-tailed binomial tests fail to reveal a significant advantage to either system in the last two turns ($p = 0.000$, $p = 0.046$, $p = 0.885$, $p = 0.470$, respectively).

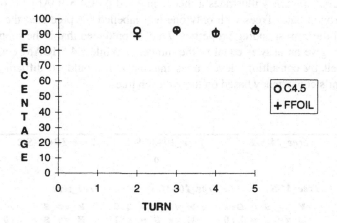

Figure 2. Proportion of predictions that were correct.

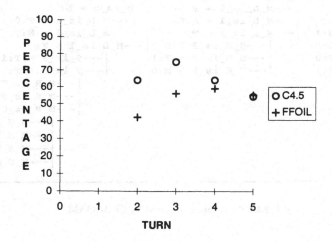

Figure 3. Proportion of predictions of an error that were correct.

Figure 3 shows, of the systems' predictions that the student would commit an error, the proportion for which the prediction was correct. As can be seen, in this respect of error prediction accuracy, C4.5 is higher than FFOIL in Turns 2 and 3 but there is no significant difference between them in the last two turns, under two-tailed binomial sign tests ($p = 0.022$, $p = 0.035$, $p = 0.629$, $p = 0.791$, respectively).

Regarding the inferred theories generated by the two systems, C4.5-IOAM always generated eleven decision trees. Figure 4 illustrates a theory inferred by C4.5-IOAM for one subject based on a set of first round data. Trees with only one leaf labelled '0' predicted the subject's answer would not exhibit the corresponding properties. Tree_M predicted that if the subtrahend was zero, the subject would give an answer equal to the minuend. While C4.5-IOAM could predict a student's answer well by consulting eleven trees internally, it would be difficult for a human to conclude a student's competency based on these eleven trees.

```
Tree_M-S-1        Tree_M-S-2        Tree_10+M-S-1       Tree_10+M-S-2

     0                 0                  0                   0


  Tree_M           Tree_M-S           Tree_10+M-S         Tree_zero

S_is_0 = F:0     M_vs_S = G:1       M_vs_S = G:0        M_vs_S = G:0
S_is_0 = T:1     M_vs_S = L:0       M_vs_S = L:1        M_vs_S = L:0
                 M_vs_S = E:1       M_vs_S = E:0        M_vs_S = E:1


 Tree_correct         Tree_S               Tree_S-M

M_S_R = G:1       M_is_0 = T:0         M_vs_S = G:0
M_S_R = L:0       M_is_0 = F:          M_vs_S = E:1
M_S_R = N:1       |---M_L_is_1 = F:0   M_vs_S = L:
M_S_R = E:        |---M_L_is_1 = N:0   |---M_L_is_1 = T:0
|---M_S_2R = G:1  |---M_L_is_1 = T:    |---M_L_is_1 = N:0
|---M_S_2R = L:0  |---S_R_is_9 F:0     |---M_L_is_1 = F:
|---M_S_2R = E:0  |---S_R_is_9 = T:1   |---S_is_9 = T:1
|---M_S_2R = N:1  |---S_R_is_9 = N:0   |---S_is_9 = F:
                                       |---M_R_is_0 = T:0
                                       |---M_R_is_0 = N:0
                                       |---M_R_is_0 = F:
                                       |---M_S_R = G:1
                                       |---M_S_R = L:0
                                       |---M_S_R = E:0
                                       |---M_S_R = N:0
```

Figure 4. A theory inferred by C4.5-IOAM.

The following is the output[3] generated by FFOIL for the subject mentioned above:

---

[3] FFOIL generated capital letters, A,B,C,... etc., to represent arguments within the relations. In this paper, they were replaced by meaningful names for better comprehension.

subtract(Min,Sub,MRis0,SRis9,Borrow,Ans):- M–S(Min,Sub,Borrow,Ans), Min<>9,!. (1)

subtract(Min,Sub,MRis0,SRis9,Borrow,Ans):- M–S_miss1(Min,Sub,Borrow,Ans),

not(10+M–S–1(Ans,Min,Borrow,Min)),!. (2)

subtract(Min,Sub,MRis0,SRis9,Borrow,Ans):- 10+M–S(Min,Sub,Borrow,Ans), M–S(Ans,Min,Borrow,G),

not(dec(G,Min)), not(dec(Sub,Ans)),!. (3)

subtract(Min,Sub,MRis0,SRis9,Borrow,Ans):- 10+M–S_miss1(Min,Sub,Borrow,Ans),!. (4)

subtract(Min,Sub,MRis0,SRis9,Borrow,Ans):- M–S(Min,Sub,Borrow,Ans), not(dec(Sub,Ans)),!. (5)

subtract(Min,Sub,MRis0,SRis9,Borrow,Ans):- M–S(Sub,Min,Borrow,Ans), M–S(Ans,Min,Borrow,G),not(gt(Min,G)),!. (6)

subtract(Min,Sub,MRis0,SRis9,Borrow,Ans):- 10+M–S(Min,Sub,Borrow,Ans), not(dec(Ans,Min)). (7)

4 Conclusions

In this paper, we described an empirical evaluation of two induction engines, C4.5 and FFOIL, for building student models. The results of, within the IOAM context, using C4.5 and FFOIL as alternative induction engines suggest that the use of C4.5 leads to a greater number of predictions and a higher accuracy of error prediction. FFOIL suffers when the size of the example set is small. Note that the proportion of students that committed errors was between 10 and 13 percent only. This may explain why FFOIL performed poorly when predicting student errors.

Our experiment shows the importance of background knowledge applying to a relational learning system when the set of training examples is incomplete. The performance of FFOIL-IOAM in this experiment has been tuned through experimental exploration of alternative sets of background knowledge. This contrasts with the C4.5-IOAM system that uses the original FBM attributes, with respect to which there has been very little attempt at optimisation. However, there is still scope for the current set of background knowledge used by FFOIL-IOAM to be improved.

Regarding the comprehensibility of inferred theories, the theory representation generated by FFOIL-IOAM is not a perfect one, but is more straightforward to comprehend. A first-order learning algorithm, such as FFOIL, could provide potential benefits for analysing the students' misconceptions but it requires a large set of training examples and imposes higher computational cost. A zeroth-order learner, like C4.5, can produce models that are more accurate, and is fast at learning theories, but the induced theories can be difficult for a human to comprehend.

References

Anderson, J. R., Boyle, C. F., and Reiser, B. J. (1985). Intelligent tutoring systems. *Science* 228:456–462.

Anderson, J. R., Boyle, C. F., Corbett, A. T., and Lewis, M. W. (1990). Cognitive modelling and intelligent tutoring. *Artificial Intelligence* 42:7–49.

Baffes, P., and Mooney, R. (1996). Refinement-based student modelling and automated bug library construction. *Journal of Artificial Intelligence in Education* 7(1):75–117.

Brown, J. S., and VanLehn, K. (1980). Repair theory: A generative theory of bugs in procedural skills. *Cognitive Science* 4:379–426.

Brown, J. S., and Burton, R. R. (1978). Diagnostic models for procedural bugs in basic mathematical skills. *Cognitive Science* 2:155–192.

Burton, R. R, and Brown, J. S. (1976). A tutoring and student modelling paradigm for gaming environments. *Computer Science and Education. ACM SIGCSE Bulletin*, 8(1):236–246.

Carbonell, J. R. (1970). AI in CAI: An artificial intelligence approach to computer-assisted instruction. *IEEE Transactions on Man-Machine Systems* 11(4):190–202.

Corbett, A. T., and Anderson, J. R. (1992). Student modelling and mastery learning in a computer-based programming tutor. In Frasson, C., Gauthier, G., and McCalla, G. I., eds., *Intelligent Tutoring Systems*. Berlin: Springer-Verlag. 413–420.

Desmoulins, C., and Van Labeke, N. (1996). Towards student modelling in geometry with inductive logic programming. In Brna, P., Paiva, A., and Self, J., eds., *Proceedings of the European Conference on Artificial Intelligence in Education*. Manuscript submitted for publication.

Giangrandi, P., and Tasso, C. (1995). Truth maintenance techniques for modelling students' behaviour. *Journal of Artificial Intelligence in Education* 6(2/3):153–202.

Gilmore, D., and Self, J. (1988). The application of machine learning to intelligent tutoring systems. In Self, J., ed., *Artificial Intelligence and Human Learning: Intelligent Computer-Aided Instruction*. London: Chapman and Hall. 179–196.

Goldstein, I. P. (1979). The genetic graph: A representation for the evolution of procedural knowledge. *International Journal of Man-machine Studies* 11:51–77.

Hoppe, H. U. (1994). Deductive error diagnosis and inductive error generalization for intelligent tutoring systems. *Journal of Artificial Intelligence in Education* 5(1):27–49.

Ikeda, M., Kono, Y., and Mizoguchi, R. (1993). Nonmonotonic model inference: A formalization of student modelling. In *Proceedings of the Thirteenth International Joint Conference on Artificial Intelligence: IJCAI'93*, 467–473.

Kuzmycz, M. (1994). A dynamic vocabulary for student modelling. In *Proceedings of the Fourth International Conference on User Modeling*, 185–190.

Langley, P., and Ohlsson, S. (1984). Automated cognitive modeling. In *Proceedings of the National Conference on Artificial Intelligence*, 193–197.

Langley, P., Wogulis, J., and Ohlsson, S. (1990). Rules and principles in cognitive diagnosis. In *Diagnostic Monitoring of Skill and Knowledge Acquisition*. Hillsdale, NJ: Erlbaum. 217–250.

Martin, J., and VanLehn, K. (1995). Student assessment using Bayesian nets. *International Journal of Human-Computer Studies* 42:575–591.

Ohlsson, S., and Langley, P. (1985). *Identifying solution paths in cognitive diagnosis*. Technical Report CMU-RI-TR-85-2, Carnegie-Mellon University, Pittsburgh, PA.

Quinlan, J. R. (1990). Learning logical definition from relations. *Machine Learning* 5:239–266.

Quinlan, J. R. (1993). *C4.5: Programs for Machine Learning*. San Mateo, CA: Morgan Kaufmann.

Quinlan, J. R. (1996). Learning first-order definitions of functions. *Journal of Artificial Intelligence Research* 5:139–161.

Sleeman, D. (1982). Assessing aspects of competence in basic algebra. In Sleeman, D. H., and Brown, J. S., eds., *Intelligent Tutoring Systems*. London: Academic Press. 185–199.

Sleeman, D., Ward, R. D., Kelly, E., Martinak, R., and Moore, J. (1991). An overview of recent studies with Pixie. In Goodyear, P., ed., *Teaching Knowledge and Intelligent Tutoring*. Norwood, NJ: Ablex. 173–185.

Webb, G. I., Chiu, B., and Kuzmycz, M. (1997). A comparative evaluation of the use of C4.5 and Feature Based Modelling as induction engines for Input/Output Agent Modelling. Manuscript submitted for publication.

Webb, G. I., and Kuzmycz, M. (1996). Feature Based Modelling: A methodology for producing coherent, dynamically changing models of agents' competencies. *User Modeling and User-Adapted Interaction* 5(2):117–150.

Young, R., and O'Shea, T. (1981). Errors in children's subtraction. *Cognitive Science* 5:153–177.

Symbolic Data Analysis With the K-Means Algorithm for User Profiling

Anne-Claude Doux[1]*, Jean-Philippe Laurent[1], and Jean-Pierre Nadal[2]

[1] Laboratoires d'Electronique Philips S.A.S., France
[2] Laboratoire de Physique Statistique, Ecole Normale Superieure, Paris, France

Abstract. We propose to simplify human-machine interaction by automating device settings that are normally made manually. We present here a classification scheme of user behaviours based on an adaptation of the K-means algorithm to symbolic data representing user behaviours. This classification enables a system to derive prototypical behaviours and to control device settings automatically.

1 Introduction

The general framework is the following: Some users, or agents, are involved in a particular task or activity, such as watching TV, where they are to set the parameters of a system according to their preferences. The chosen *actions* usually depend on external conditions, to be referred to as the *environment* (e.g., room lighting for TV picture contrast and brightness setting). Our goal is to characterize each user *behaviour* (set of pairs {environment, action}) in order to automatically generate the action which best matches the one the user would have chosen in a given environment, even if the user is not yet known.

We may presume that users will most often accept settings sufficiently close to those they would have chosen. Therefore, it should be possible to classify user behaviours, so that each user could be satisfied with the actions defined by one of the corresponding prototypes. We introduce a new method for performing behaviour classification, by means of a new generalization of the standard K-means algorithm to complex data. Our classification scheme rests on applications to real and simulated data for which we developed prototypes.

2 The Data: Symbolic Profiles of Users

Data are collected from dedicated experiments during which users are asked to give their preferences in various environmental conditions.

1. Real data set: Characteristics of 9 environments were specified. A panel of 120 users participated in the experiments, which gave rise to 38,000 observations, out of which 11 typical actions were extracted.
2. Simulated data set: Our set of simulated data, with a known underlying structure, includes 300 users. As for real data, it deals with 9 environments and 11 actions.

---

* We thank E. Diday and his colleagues from the LISE-CEREMADE group (University Paris-Dauphine) for fruitful discussions on data analysis.

We have to cope with different kinds of problems inherent to real data. Data are incomplete (many users are observed in only some of the predefined environments) and inconsistent (returning to the same environment, many users gave different preferences). From problems encountered with real users in a real application and thanks to symbolic data analysis (Diday, 1993), we build symbolic objects representing user behaviours (Polaillon et al., 1996). A user u is characterized by the set of probability rules (one per environment he had access to), which give the empirical probability that he chooses one action in a given environment.

3 Methodology of Classification With K-Means on Symbolic Objects

In order to define prototypical behaviours, so that any user is close to one of these, we propose classifying the user behaviours into K classes and computing K typical behaviours. We need an unsupervised algorithm (Duda and Hart, 1973) which can handle symbolic data, generate a representative for each class, provide the best intrinsic K, and have the ability to generalize to unknown users too (Jain and Dubes, 1988). We thus choose to adapt the K-means algorithm for these symbolic objects.

3.1 Two Main Adaptations of the K-Means Algorithm

We propose a training criterion $\mathcal{E}$ which favours homogeneous and compact classes to improve the assignment of the users and therefore to improve the quality of the partition. We perform its optimization with the K-means algorithm (Doux et al., 1996).

   We then define and compute three kinds of representatives u_k^* for each K: the *center of gravity*, which is theorically the best choice; the *paragon* (i.e., the real recorded user who is nearest to the middle of the considered class), since in some applications this realistic behaviour is required; the *horde representative* (i.e., a hybrid user with real parts of behaviours belonging to different users of the class), which represents an intermediate solution between the two previous ones. In our real application, the horde is much better than the paragon representative (see Figure 1). In fact, because of missing data, some users cannot be compared with the paragon. This problem, however, does not occur with the simulated data, and all representatives then remain acceptable. It is therefore better to choose the paragon in that case, because it is a strong and realistic behaviour.

3.2 Methodology to Validate the Partition

To check the partition's ability to generalize—that is, to match unknown user behaviours—we split the population into training and test sets. The training set is classified and provides a final partition with a number K of classes. Each user u of the corresponding test set is then assigned to a class. We finally define a generalization criterion $\mathcal{E}_g$ (Doux et al., 1996) to measure the quality of an unknown user assignment.

3.3 Intrinsic Data Structure: The Best Number of Classes

Without knowledge of the intrinsic data structure, we have to find the best K, which is linked to the ability to generalize. The F-maximum criterion (Milligan and Cooper, 1985) provides the best

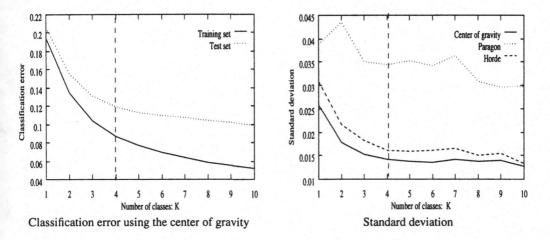

Classification error using the center of gravity   Standard deviation

Figure 1. Results on the real data set obtained by averaging over 100 random samples of the population (test, training), for each number of classes.

K on the well-structured data but fails on our real data. In our method, the standard deviation of the generalization criterion $\mathcal{E}_g$ decreases when the number of classes increases. But in fact, when reaching the optimal K, $\mathcal{E}_g$ significantly decreases and then stabilizes with the addition of more classes. With the simulated data, we find the same K as computed by the F-maximum criterion. With the real data, our method still leads to a good partition (4 or 5 classes, see Figure 1). Since our application calls for the use of as few classes as possible, the 4-class partition is chosen.

4   Conclusion

The next step of this study is to investigate further the assignment scheme for new users when very little is known about them. Assessment of user dissatisfaction also remains a question. Furthermore, we can make profiles dynamically evolve. Some work is underway to improve the assignment of users through the symbolic interpretation of classes.

References

Diday, E. (1993). An introduction to symbolic data analysis. In *Proceedings of the 4th International Conference of the Federation of Classification Societies*. Paris. Springer Verlag.

Doux, A. C., Laurent, J. P., Nadal, J. P., and Diday, E. (1996). User profiling: Dynamic clustering on symbolic objects. Manuscript submitted for publication.

Duda, R. O., and Hart, P. E. (1973). *Pattern Classification and Scene Analysis*. NJ : Wiley.

Jain, A. K., and Dubes, R. C. (1988). *Algorithms for Clustering Data*. NJ : Prentice Hall.

Milligan, G. W., and Cooper, H. C. (1985). An examination of procedures for determining the number of clusters in a data set. *Psychometrika* 50:159-179.

Polaillon, G., Getter-Summa, M., Pardoux, C., and Laurent, J. P. (1996). Approche numérique symbolique pour le codage et la classification des comportements d'utilisateurs. In *Proceedings of the 28th Days of Statistics*, 608-611.

Probabilistic Techniques

Towards a Bayesian Model for Keyhole Plan Recognition in Large Domains

David W. Albrecht, Ingrid Zukerman, Ann E. Nicholson, and Ariel Bud*

Department of Computer Science, Monash University, Australia

Abstract. We present an approach to keyhole plan recognition which uses a Dynamic Belief Network to represent features of the domain that are needed to identify users' plans and goals. The structure of this network was determined from analysis of the domain. The conditional probability distributions are learned during a training phase, which dynamically builds these probabilities from observations of user behaviour. This approach allows the use of incomplete, sparse and noisy data during both training and testing. We present experimental results of the application of our system to a Multi-User Dungeon adventure game with thousands of possible actions and positions. These results show a high degree of predictive accuracy and indicate that this approach will work in other domains with similar features.

1 Introduction

To date, research in plan recognition has focused on three main areas: (1) inferring plans during cooperative interactions, (2) understanding stories, and (3) recognising the plans of an agent who is unaware that his/her plans are being inferred (Raskutti, 1993). In the first two areas, the plan recognition process is *intended*, since a user/writer is attempting to convey his/her plan to the system. In addition, during cooperative interactions, a plan recognition system can interrogate the user when confronted with ambiguous or incomplete information (e.g., Allen and Perrault, 1980, Litman and Allen, 1987, Raskutti and Zukerman, 1991). The third area is called *keyhole* plan recognition because the information available to the plan recogniser is gleaned from non-interactive and often incomplete observations of a user (as though one was looking into a room through a keyhole). In the past, the use of hand-crafted plan libraries in systems that perform keyhole plan recognition imposed heavy restrictions on the size of their application domain, and hence on their usefulness. However, recently several researchers have applied machine learning techniques to the acquisition of plan libraries in an effort to overcome this problem (Lesh and Etzioni, 1995, Forbes et al., 1995)(Section 2).

The mechanism described in this paper is part of this trend. Our approach to keyhole plan recognition uses a Dynamic Belief Network (DBN) to represent features of the domain needed to identify users' plans and goals. Our current domain is the "Shattered Worlds" Multi-User Dungeon (MUD), an adventure game which resembles the real world in its complexity and size (Section 3). The MUD is a text-based virtual reality game where players compete for limited

* This research was supported in part by grant A49600323 from the Australian Research Council. The authors are indebted to Michael McGaughey for writing the data collection programs for the MUD and for his assistance during the initial stages of this project.

resources in an attempt to achieve various goals. The MUD has over 4,700 locations, over 7,200 actions, and 20 different quests (goals). The objective of the plan recognition mechanism is to determine, as early as possible, which quest a player is attempting, and to predict which action a player will perform in the next move and which location a player will go to next. To achieve this, the system must first learn which actions and positions or sequences of actions and positions tend to lead to a particular quest. This information is obtained from previous instances of completed quests during a training phase and modelled by means of a DBN (Section 4). During the testing phase, the DBN is used to predict a player's quest, next action and next location. To this effect, every time a player performs an action, the system updates the probability that the player is trying to achieve each of the quests, perform each of the actions and move to each of the locations. The empirical results obtained by our system using this method are described in Section 5. Section 6 discusses ideas for future work and presents concluding remarks.

2   Related Work

In recent times there has been a shift from systems that rely heavily on hand coded domain knowledge for plan recognition towards systems that apply machine learning techniques to automatically acquire domain knowledge. This has allowed a shift in domain size, whereby later systems deal with hundreds of actions in realistic domains.

The systems described by Cañamero et al. (1992) and Wærn and Stenborg (1995) rely on domain knowledge. Cañamero et al. use an abstraction/specialisation plan hierarchy to perform plan recognition from noisy input representing sequences of observations of an evolving situation in traffic monitoring. Wærn and Stenborg use a hierarchy of actions in conjunction with "compiled" plans in order to anticipate a user's intentions in domains where users exhibit reactive rather than plan-based behaviour, e.g., news reading. They perform simple probabilistic calculations to match a user's actions in a particular time window to those in the domain plans.

The system described by Bauer (1996) uses a plan hierarchy to represent the actions in the domain, but it applies decision trees (Quinlan, 1983) to obtain probabilities of different domain plans in the context of a user's actions. It then uses the Dempster-Shafer theory of evidential reasoning to assess hypotheses regarding a user's plans in context. Carberry (1990) also applies the Dempster-Shafer theory, using threshold plausibility and different levels of belief to distinguish among competing hypotheses.

The plan recognition mechanism described in Lesh and Etzioni (1995) works on a graph which represents the relations between the actions and possible goals of the domain. The system iteratively applies pruning rules which remove from the graph goals that are not in any consistent plan. In later work, they automatically construct a virtual plan library using primitive actions and the predicates of goals (Lesh and Etzioni, 1996). Two important differences between our system and Lesh and Etzioni's are: (1) they assume that any action performed by a user pertains to one of the goals in their virtual library, while our mechanism admits extraneous actions; and (2) at present, the user's goals in our system (MUD quests) are well specified, while Lesh and Etzioni admit arbitrary goals. In the future, we intend to extend our mechanism to domains with such goals, e.g., the WWW and Unix.

Charniak and Goldman (1993) use Bayesian networks[1] for plan recognition in the framework of story understanding. They dynamically generate a Bayesian network from a sequence of

---

[1] See Section 4.1 for more details about Bayesian networks.

observations by applying rules which use plan knowledge to instantiate the network. The incorporation of prior probabilities into this network supports the selection of plausible explanations of observed actions. Pynadath and Wellman (1995) and Forbes et al. (1995) use Bayesian networks for plan recognition in traffic monitoring. Pynadath and Wellman use a Bayesian network composed of loosely connected sub-networks, where each sub-network captures an intermediate structure based on one of the following factors: the context in which a plan was generated, the mental state and planning process of the agent, and the consequences of the agent's actions in the world. They apply the mechanism described by Huber et al. (1994) to map planning actions to a Bayesian network. Forbes et al. use Dynamic Bayesian Networks, emphasising issues that pertain to sensor noise or failure, and to uncertainty about the behaviour of other vehicles and about the effects of drivers' actions. Finally, Russell et al. (1995) use a gradient-descent algorithm to learn the conditional probability tables for Bayesian networks with hidden variables, i.e., variables whose values are not observable.[2]

The mechanism described in this paper resembles most closely the system described by Forbes et al. (1995), but there are several important differences: (1) we infer a user's longer term goals, i.e., quests, in addition to the locations and actions inferred by Forbes et al.; (2) our data was collected prior to the undertaking of this project, hence we have had no choice in the view of the world that we are modelling, rather than being allowed to select the observations we wish to make; (3) we observe the world only from the perspective of a single user (without information about the effect of other agents' actions on the world); and (4) we have no information regarding the quality of our observations, while they have information about sensor uncertainty and hence are able to model it.

3 The Domain

The domain of our implementation is the "Shattered Worlds" Multi-User Dungeon (MUD), which is a text-based virtual reality game where players compete for limited resources in an attempt to achieve various goals. As stated in Section 1, the MUD has over 4,700 locations, more than 7,200 actions, and 20 different quests (goals). The plan recognition problem is further exacerbated by the presence of spelling mistakes, newly defined commands and abbreviations for commands. The MUD also has reactive agents controlled by the system (non-player characters), and contains a number of items which may be acquired and used by characters in order to achieve some effect within the game. Despite the fact that the MUD is a game, only a minority of the players log-in to play. Many users log-in with other goals, such as socialising with other players, crashing the MUD, or engaging in socially aberrant behaviour. However, at this stage of our project, we are only interested in recognising one type of goal, namely quests. Examples of the simplest quests in the MUD are the "Teddy-bear rescue", which involves locating and retrieving a teddy bear lost by a non-player character called Jane, and "Wood chop", where a player must chop wood in the market place, after first acquiring an axe and eating food to obtain enough energy to carry out the wood-chopping task. More complex quests may involve solving non-trivial puzzles, interacting with various non-player characters, e.g., monsters, shopkeepers or mercenaries, or achieving a number of sub-goals, e.g., obtaining potions. Players usually know which quest or quests they wish to achieve, but they don't always know which actions are required to complete a quest. In addition, they often engage in activities that are not related to the completion

---

[2] A survey of research on learning belief networks is given by Heckerman (1995).

Table 1. Sample data for the Avatar quest.

Action No.	Time	Player	Location	Action
1	773335156	spillage	room/city/inn	ENTERS
12	773335264	spillage	players/paladin/room/trading_post	buy
17	773335291	spillage	players/paladin/room/western_gate	bribe
28	773335343	spillage	players/paladin/room/abby/guardhouse	kill
37	773335435	spillage	players/paladin/room/abby/stores	search
40	773335451	spillage	players/paladin/room/shrine/Billy	worship
54	773335558	spillage	players/paladin/room/brooksmith	give
60	773335593	spillage	players/paladin/room/shrine/Dredd	avenger
62	773335596	spillage	players/paladin/room/abby/chamber	Avatar quest

of a specific quest, such as chatting with other players or fighting with MUD agents. As a result, players typically perform between 25 and 500 actions until they complete a quest, even though only a fraction of these actions may actually be required to achieve a quest.

Analysis of the MUD yields the following features:[3] (1) it is not possible to obtain a perspicuous representation of the domain (for example in the MUD there is a vast number of actions whose effects and preconditions are not fully known); (2) there may be more than one way to achieve a goal; (3) some sequences of actions may lead to more than one eventual goal; (4) some actions leading to a goal may need to be performed in sequence, while other actions are order-independent; (5) users may interleave the actions performed to achieve two or more goals or may perform actions that are not related to any domain goal (e.g., socialising); (6) the states of the system are only partially observable; (7) the plan inference mechanism obtains information mainly from a user's keyboard commands, i.e., the mechanism has limited information about the user's knowledge and ability; and (8) the outcome of the actions is uncertain, i.e., the performance of an action is not a sufficient condition for the achievement of the action's intended effect (e.g., due to the presence of other agents who affect the states of the system).

The MUD software collects the actions performed by each player and the quest instance each player completed. In the current implementation, each data point is composed of: (1) a time stamp, (2) the name of the player, (3) the number of the login session, (4) the location where the action was executed, and (5) the name of the action. A DBN is then constructed on the basis of the collected data as described in Section 4. Table 1 illustrates some of the 62 actions performed by a player to achieve the Avatar quest (the number of the login session is not shown).[4] Without domain knowledge, it is extremely difficult to determine by inspection which of these actions (if any) are necessary to complete the quest, the order of the necessary actions, or whether an action had the intended

4 The Model

In this section we identify the interesting domain variables. We show how to represent their dependencies, and how they change over time using a belief network representation.

---

[3] Other domains which we intend to investigate, viz WWW and Unix, have most of these features.

[4] At present, the MUD software does not record keyboard commands regarding an agent's movements on the horizontal plane, i.e., North, South, East and West. In addition, only the first word of each command is considered during training and testing.

4.1 Belief Networks

Belief (or Bayesian) networks (Pearl, 1988) have become a popular representation for reasoning under uncertainty, as they integrate a graphical representation of causal relationships with a sound Bayesian foundation. Belief networks are directed acyclic graphs where nodes correspond to random variables. The relationship between any set of state variables can be specified by a joint probability distribution. The nodes in the network are connected by directed arcs, which may be thought of as causal or influence links; a node is influenced by its parents. The connections also specify independence assumptions between nodes, which allow the joint probability distribution of all the state variables to be specified by exponentially fewer probability values than the full joint distribution. A *conditional probability distribution* (CPD) is associated with each node. The CPD gives the probability of each node value for all combinations of the values of its parent nodes.

The probability distribution for a node with no predecessors is its prior distribution. Given these priors and the CPDs, we can compute posterior probability distributions for all the nodes in a network, which represent *beliefs* about the values of these nodes. Observation of specific values for nodes is called *evidence*. Beliefs are updated by re-computing the posterior probability distributions given the evidence.

Belief networks have been used in various applications which initially were static, i.e., the nodes and links do not change over time. These applications involve determining the structure of the network; supplying the prior probabilities for root nodes and conditional probabilities for other nodes; adding or retracting evidence about nodes; and repeating the belief updating algorithm for each change in evidence. More recently, researchers have used belief networks in *dynamic* domains, where the world changes and the focus is on reasoning over time (Dean and Wellman, 1991, Dagum et al., 1992, Nicholson and Brady, 1994). Such dynamic applications include the automated vehicle control (Forbes et al., 1995) and traffic plan recognition (Pynadath and Wellman, 1995) described in Section 2. In such applications the network grows over time, as the state of each domain variable at different times is represented by a *series* of nodes. Typically, for these dynamic networks, the connections over time are Markovian, and a temporal 'window' is imposed to constrain the state space to some extent. Such networks provide a more compact representation than the equivalent Hidden Markov Model (Russell et al., 1995).

4.2 Network Nodes and Structure

Based on the data we have for our domain, the domain variables, which are represented as nodes in the belief network, are as follows:

Action (A): This variable represents the possible actions a player may take in the MUD, which we take to be the first string of non-blank characters entered by a user, plus the special `other` action, which includes all previously unseen actions. For the results given in this paper, the state space size, $|A|$, is 7259.

Location (L): This variable represents the possible locations of a player, plus the special `other` location, which includes all previously unseen locations. For the results given in this paper, the state space size, $|L|$, is 4722.[5]

---

[5] Future work includes using the hierarchical structure of the location data (Section 6).

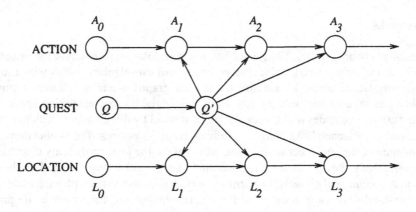

Figure 1. Dynamic Belief Network for the MUD.

Quest (Q): This variable represents the 22 different quests a player may undertake, including the other quest, which includes all previously unseen quests, and the null quest. The variable representing the previous quest achieved is set to null if the user has just started a session.

A simple dynamic belief network structure for the domain is shown in Figure 1. This network is not a pure dynamic belief network; the changes in the action and location over time are represented, but it is assumed that a player's current quest does not change. Our model makes minimal assumptions about the dependencies between the domain variables. The action and location variables, A_i and L_i, at the ith time step depend on the current quest being undertaken and the previous action and location, respectively.[6] The current quest, Q', depends on the previous quest, Q.

4.3 Probabilities and Belief Updating

The CPDs are constructed from the collected MUD data as follows. The data is pre-processed to take the following form:

Previous Quest	Current Quest	Current Action	Current Location	Next Action	Next Location
null	teddy	scream	room/sewer/sewer20	u	room/city/alley1

A frequency count is maintained for each entry in the CPD that is observed. In order to account for the possible actions, locations and quests that do not occur in the training data, we adjust the frequencies so that the resulting CPD includes some probability that the other value may occur. This adjustment consists of adding a small number that corresponds to Good's *flattening constant* (Good, 1965) or Heckerman's *fractional updating* (Heckerman, 1995). A factor of 0.5 was used for the results obtained in this paper (Wallace and Freeman, 1987). The frequencies are then converted into the CPD.

Once the DBN is constructed, new data from a user is added to the network as evidence, and belief updating is performed to give predictions for that user's next action and location, and to

---

[6] In Section 6 we describe future work with variations of this simple model.

> 1. Receive initial data: `PreviousQuest, NullAction, NullLocation`.
> 2. Add data as evidence for nodes Q, A_0 and L_0.
> 3. Perform belief updating on nodes Q', A_1 and L_1.
> 4. Loop from $n = 1$ until quest is achieved
>   4.1 Receive new data: `Action, Location`.
>   4.2 Add data as evidence for nodes A_n and L_n.
>   4.3 Perform belief updating on nodes Q', A_{n+1} and L_{n+1}.
>   4.4 $n = n + 1$.

Figure 2. Belief updating algorithm.

update the belief as to the current quest being undertaken. The evidence nodes for the domain at time-step $n + 1$ are: the last completed quest, Q, the previous actions, $A_0, \ldots, A_n$, and the previous locations, $L_0, \ldots, L_n$. The belief updating algorithm is given in Figure 2.

Belief propagation for singly-connected networks can be done efficiently using a message passing algorithm (Pearl, 1988). When networks are multiply-connected (i.e., when there is a loop in the underlying undirected graph), simple belief propagation is not possible; informally, this is because we can no longer be sure that evidence has not already been counted at a node having arrived via another route. In such cases, inference algorithms based on clustering, conditioning or stochastic simulation may be used. Although there are underlying loops in the network structure shown in Figure 1, further analysis of the structure, together with the location of the evidence nodes, identifies d-separations (Pearl, 1988), indicating that certain nodes are conditionally independent. Using these independence relations, we simplify the belief update equations for the first time step:[7]

$$\Pr(L_1 = l_1 | q, a_0, l_0) = \sum_{q'} \Pr(L_1 = l_1 | l_0, q') \Pr(q' | q),$$
$$\Pr(A_1 = a_1 | q, a_0, l_0) = \sum_{q'} \Pr(A_1 = a_1 | a_0, q') \Pr(q' | q),$$
$$\Pr(Q' = q' | q, a_0, l_0) = \Pr(Q' = q' | q).$$

For step $n + 1$ we have

$$\Pr(L_{n+1} = l_{n+1} | q, a_0, l_0, \ldots, a_n, l_n) = \sum_{q'} \Pr(L_{n+1} = l_{n+1} | l_n, q') \Pr(q' | q, a_0, l_0, \ldots, a_n, l_n),$$
$$\Pr(A_{n+1} = a_{n+1} | q, a_0, l_0, \ldots, a_n, l_n) = \sum_{q'} \Pr(A_{n+1} = a_{n+1} | a_n, q') \Pr(q' | q, a_0, l_0, \ldots, a_n, l_n),$$
$$\Pr(Q' = q' | q, a_0, l_0, \ldots, a_{n+1}, l_{n+1})$$
$$= \alpha \Pr(l_{n+1} | l_n, q') \Pr(a_{n+1} | a_n, q') \Pr(Q' = q' | q, a_0, l_0, \ldots, a_n, l_n),$$

where α is a normalizing factor.

5 Experimental Results

Methodology. A *run* is a sequence of action-location pairs, beginning either after a player enters the MUD or after a player completes a previous quest, and ending when a new quest is achieved. A certain percentage of the 4,981 runs in our corpus, chosen randomly, is used for training, and the remaining runs are used for testing.[8] All results presented in this section are for 80% training and 20% testing, except where otherwise indicated. During each test run, we used the belief updating algorithm shown in Figure 2.

---

[7] Details on the simplification of these formulae are given by Albrecht et al. (1997).

[8] During the testing phase, a value which was not seen in the training data gets classified as `other`. A prediction of `other` is always considered incorrect.

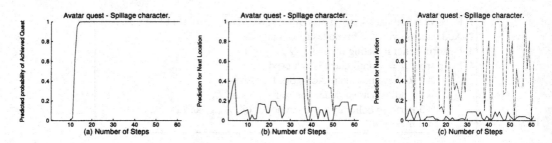

Figure 3. Predictions for `spillage` (80% training): (a) quest, (b) location, and (c) action. In (b) and (c), the solid lines represent the probability of next action/location, and the dashed lines the ratio of this probability to the probability of the most likely action/location prediction.

A single run. The output for the sample test run where the character `spillage` achieves the `Avatar` quest (Table 1) is shown in the graphs in Figure 3(a)-(c). The x-axes for these graphs show the number of time steps in the DBN, which correspond to the number of actions performed by the user. The y-axes show the current beliefs for the user's current quest (Q'), next location (L_{n+1}), and next action (A_{n+1}), respectively.

Figure 3(a) shows that initially the system predicts a nearly zero probability that the `Avatar` quest is being attempted. This reflects the prior probability that the `Avatar` quest follows the `null` quest; the CPD entry for $\Pr(Q' = \mathtt{Avatar}|Q = \mathtt{null})$ is 0.04985. The predicted probability begins to rise after about 10 steps, becoming close to 1 around step 15, and remaining there until the quest is completed in step 62. The shape of this graph is typical of the more successful output runs. Less successful runs take longer for the prediction to increase (Figure 4(a,d)), exhibit more fluctuations (Figure 4(b,c,f)), and a small percentage of the runs fail to predict the quest being attempted (Figure 4(e)).

The absolute probabilities for the next-location and next-action predictions (bottom curve of the graphs in Figure 3(b,c)) are not as high as those for the next-quest prediction. This is to be expected in light of the large number of possible actions and locations. However, the quantities of interest are the ratios of the predicted probabilities of the actual location and action to the maximum predicted probabilities of any location and action, respectively. These ratios are represented by the top curve of the graphs in Figure 3(b,c)). From these curves it is quite clear that for the vast majority of the `Avatar` quest, the locations visited by the player are those predicted by our model with the highest probability. Our action predictions are less successful than our location predictions. Nonetheless, in a substantial part of the quest our model assigns the maximum probability to the action that is actually performed by the player.

Ranking of candidate quests. The system maintains beliefs about each quest the user may attempt. We rank these beliefs and report on the ranking of the actual quest the user achieves in a given run.

Figure 5(a) shows the percentage of runs where the actual quest was predicted in the top N quests, where $N = 1$ to 3. In order to compare across runs where the number of steps (actions recorded) varies, the x-axis is the percentage of actions taken to complete a quest. The y-axis is the percentage of runs. We assess the quality of these results by comparing them to the first-

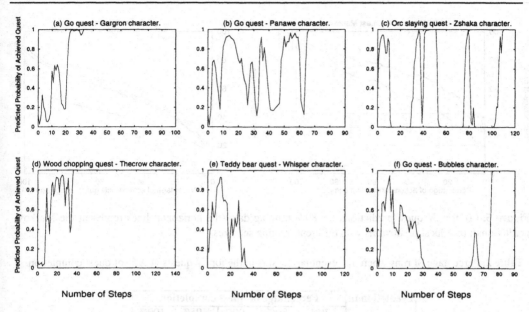

Figure 4. Typical quest prediction curves based on 80% training.

order Markov prediction obtained using only the previous quest; the horizontal lines in the graph show the prediction based purely on the frequency with which the actual quest was achieved given the previous quest. As N increases, the percentage of runs is higher, since $N = i + 1$ subsumes $N = i$. For each value of N, the predictions made by our model quickly rise above the Markov prediction, and continue to improve as quest completion progresses. Table 2 shows the percentage of correctly predicted quests at different stages prior to quest completion. For instance, when 80% of a quest has been completed, we are correctly predicting the quest being attempted in 74.84% of the runs; this quest is in the top two predicted quests in 81.41% of the runs, and in the top three predicted quests in 84.13% of the runs.

Varying the size of the training set. The final experimental results show the effect of varying the size of the training set on the predictive power of our DBN model. Figure 5(b) shows the effect of training with 5%, 20% and 80% of the data. As expected, 5% training produces the worst results. As the size of the training set increases, the predictions improve. Note that the results do not change substantially between a training set comprising 20% of the data and one comprising 80%.

6 Discussion and Future Work

We have described a Dynamic Bayesian Network which predicts a user's next location, action and quest based on a training corpus. The structure of the network itself is fairly simple, but the number of possible values of each node makes its training and evaluation a computationally complex task. As indicated in Section 2, we do not learn the structure of the network. This aspect

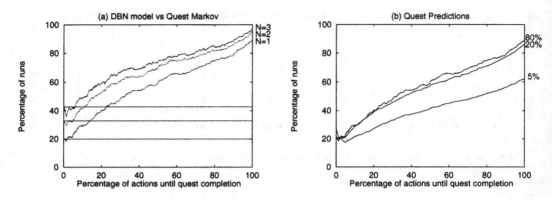

Figure 5. (a) Top N quest predictions for 80% training data (the horizontal lines represent the Markov predictions); (b) Quest predictions with different training set sizes.

Table 2. Percentage of runs where the eventual quest is in the top N quests at $X\%$ of quest completion.

Prediction in	Percentage of quest completion				
	70%	80%	90%	95%	100%
top quest	69.07	74.84	78.69	83.65	89.10
top 2 quests	77.56	81.41	85.74	89.26	95.35
top 3 quests	81.25	84.13	88.30	91.99	96.63

of our approach is domain dependent. However, our approach is sufficiently general to support additional domains, such as the WWW and Unix, which have similar features to those of the MUD.

An important feature of our model is that, due to its probabilistic training, its predictions are based on actions that are *normally* performed to achieve a goal, rather than on actions that necessarily advance a user towards the achievement of a goal. This means that actions that are necessary to achieve a goal, and are therefore performed by a large number of users, have a large effect on the predictions. However, the performance of a few extraneous actions does not preclude the correct prediction of a user's goal.

As seen in the previous section, the results obtained with this network are encouraging. However, these results were obtained under certain user-related and domain-related simplifying assumptions. Examples of the former are: all users complete a quest, all users have similar profiles, and all users attempt one quest at a time. Among the latter we have: the domain has certain independence relations, and only certain types of data are available. In the future we intend to extend our mechanism so that it can handle the relaxation of these assumptions.

The first two assumptions will be relaxed simultaneously by including non-quest runs into our observations, and using a classification mechanism to build user profiles which reflect the kinds of activities performed by different types of users. A Dynamic Belief Network which incorporates a user's class will then be built and trained from this data. The plan recognition task will involve the identification of a user's profile on the basis of his/her current actions, and the prediction of the actions, locations and objectives of this user in the context of the identified profile. The relaxation of the third assumption requires the extension of our mechanism so that it can handle conjunctive goals.

In order to relax the first domain-related assumption, we intend to investigate higher order models and networks with different connectivity; e.g., in the current model, actions and locations are only connected through quests (Figure 1). Establishing a link from L_i to A_i would reflect the influence of a location on the possible actions that can be performed in it, but at the same time increase the complexity of the belief updating process. In addition, we intend to consider the hierarchical structure of the location data, i.e., the fact that certain locations are part of the market place, others are part of the inn, etc. The consideration of this factor makes our model more domain dependent. However, this drawback may be offset by an increased accuracy in next-location predictions.

Finally, in order to relax the second domain-related assumption, we have recently started collecting additional data to those originally provided at the beginning of this research, e.g., horizontal movements and health and wealth of the players. The availability of these data will allow us to develop more detailed models, and to test them against the baseline results obtained with our current model.

References

Albrecht, D.W., Nicholson, A.E., Zukerman, I., and Bud, A. (1997). A Bayesian model for plan recognition in large, complex domains. Technical report, Department of Computer Science, Monash University, Victoria, Australia.

Allen, J.F., and Perrault, C. (1980). Analyzing intention in utterances. *Artificial Intelligence* 15:143–178.

Bauer, M. (1996). Acquisition of user preferences for plan recognition. In *UM96 – Proceedings of the Fifth International Conference on User Modeling*, 105–112.

Cañamero, D., Delannoy, J., and Kodratoff, Y. (1992). Building explanations in a plan recognition system for decision support. In *ECAI92 Workshop on Improving the Use of Knowledge-Based Systems with Explanations*, 35–45.

Carberry, S. (1990). Incorporating default inferences into plan recognition. In *AAAI90 – Proceedings of the Eight National Conference on Artificial Intelligence*, 471–478.

Charniak, E., and Goldman, R.P. (1993). A Bayesian model of plan recognition. *Artificial Intelligence* 64(1):50–56.

Dagum, P., Galper, A., and Horvitz, E. (1992). Dynamic network models for forecasting. In *UAI92 – Proceedings of the Eighth Conference on Uncertainty in Artificial Intelligence*, 41–48.

Dean, T., and Wellman, M. P. (1991). *Planning and Control*. San Mateo, California: Morgan Kaufmann.

Forbes, J., Huang, T., Kanazawa, K., and Russell, S. (1995). The BATmobile: Towards a Bayesian automated taxi. In *IJCAI95 – Proceedings of the Fourteenth International Joint Conference on Artificial Intelligence*, 1878–1885.

Good, I.J. (1965). *The estimation of probabilities: An essay on modern Bayesian methods*. Research Monograph No. 30. MIT Press, Cambridge, Massachusetts.

Heckerman, D. (1995). A tutorial on learning Bayesian networks. Technical Report MSR-TR-95-06, Microsoft Research.

Huber, M.J., Durfee, E.H., and Wellman, M.P. (1994). The automated mapping of plans for plan recognition. In *Proceedings of the Tenth Conference on Uncertainty in Artificial Intelligence*, 344–350.

Lesh, N., and Etzioni, O. (1995). A sound and fast goal recognizer. In *IJCAI95 – Proceedings of the Fourteenth International Joint Conference on Artificial Intelligence*, 1704–1710.

Lesh, N., and Etzioni, O. (1996). Scaling up plan recognition using version spaces and virtual plan libraries. Technical report, Department of Computer Science and Engineering, University of Washington, Seattle, Washington.

Litman, D., and Allen, J.F. (1987). A plan recognition model for subdialogues in conversation. *Cognitive Science* 11:163–200.

Nicholson, A.E., and Brady, J.M. (1994). Dynamic belief networks for discrete monitoring. *IEEE Transactions on Systems, Man and Cybernetics* 24(11):1593-1610.

Pearl, J. (1988). *Probabilistic Reasoning in Intelligent Systems*. San Mateo, California: Morgan Kaufmann.

Pynadath, D., and Wellman, M. (1995). Accounting for context in plan recognition with application to traffic monitoring. In *Proceedings of the Eleventh Conference on Uncertainty in Artificial Intelligence*, 472–481.

Quinlan, J.R. (1983). Inferno: A cautious approach to uncertain inference. *The Computer Journal* 26:255–69.

Raskutti, B. (1993). *Handling Uncertainty during Plan Recognition for Response Generation*. PhD thesis, Monash University, Victoria, Australia.

Raskutti, B., and Zukerman, I. (1991). Generation and selection of likely interpretations during plan recognition. *User Modeling and User Adapted Interaction* 1(4):323–353.

Russell, S., Binder, J., Koller, D., and Kanazawa, K. (1995). Local learning in probabilistic networks with hidden variables. In *IJCAI95 – Proceedings of the Fourteenth International Joint Conference on Artificial Intelligence*, 1146–1152.

Wærn, A., and Stenborg, O. (1995). Recognizing the plans of a replanning user. In *Proceedings of the IJCAI-95 Workshop on The Next Generation of Plan Recognition Systems: Challenges for and Insight from Related Areas of AI*, 113–118.

Wallace, C., and Freeman, P. (1987). Estimation and inference by compact coding. *Journal of the Royal Statistical Society (Series B)* 49:240–252.

Assessing Temporally Variable User Properties
With Dynamic Bayesian Networks

Ralph Schäfer and Thomas Weyrath*

Department of Computer Science, University of Saarbrücken, Germany

Abstract. Bayesian networks have been successfully applied to the assessment of user properties which remain unchanged during a session. However, many properties of a person vary over time, thus raising new questions of network modeling. In this paper we characterize different types of dependencies that occur in networks that deal with the modeling of temporally variable user properties. We show how existing techniques of applying dynamic probabilistic networks can be adapted for the task of modeling the dependencies in dynamic Bayesian networks. We illustrate the proposed techniques using examples of emergency calls to the fire department of the city of Saarbrücken. The fire department officers are experienced in dealing with emergency calls from callers whose available working memory capacity is temporarily limited. We develop a model which reconstructs the officers' assessments of a caller's working memory capacity.

1 Introduction

Bayesian networks (cf. Pearl, 1988) are able to handle uncertainty in an elegant way and have already been successfully used in user modeling (cf. Jameson, 1996b). They are mostly applied to the assessment of a user's properties which remain unchanged during a session. However, user properties often vary with time, e.g., in student learning situations or in cases where short-term cognitive states have to be assessed. Schum (1987) points out several problems arising due to the temporal change of such situations, e.g., the same evidence can have different meanings at different time points.

The following issue is therefore of general interest: How can temporally variable user properties be estimated with Bayesian networks?

Modeling temporally variable properties demands the creation of adequate and tractable dynamic Bayesian networks (DBNs). We identify and categorize the dependencies to be modeled, e.g., dependencies between temporally variable and temporally invariable properties. We describe how dynamic probabilistic networks (including dynamic Bayesian networks) have been applied to related problems and show how to adapt the solutions to our problems. We propose some general schemes for modeling the dependencies and discuss their assets and drawbacks.

There are many other approaches for representing temporal relationships within a probabilistic framework. For example, Conati and VanLehn (1996) solve a student modeling task by building

* The preparation of this article was supported by the German Science Foundation in its special Collaborative Program on Resource-Adaptive Cognitive Processes (SFB 378), project B2, READY. We wish to thank Anthony Jameson, Anselm Blocher, Susanne van Mulken, and the two anonymous reviewers for valuable suggestions on earlier versions of this paper.

a Bayesian network incrementally. In this way the network represents the current state of the user. This approach lacks an explicit representation of time. Cooper et al. (1988) use a probabilistic approach for diagnosing diseases. The temporal dependencies are represented directly in the conditional probabilities. This approach already contains many ideas used in DBNs, but the distinction between different types of variables is not clear, e.g., between variables evolving over time and non-evolving variables.

We show how the proposed techniques are used in the dialog system READY (Resource-Adaptive Dialog System, Wahlster et al., 1995). READY has to help a person P during an emergency. To minimize P's cognitive load, READY adapts its dialog behavior among other things to P's available working memory capacity (AWMC), which strongly varies over time. [1] Estimating P's AWMC involves uncertainty, because it cannot be directly observed.

We will show how to construct a DBN for assessing P's AWMC which is based on the results of an empirical study. We interviewed firemen at the Saarbrücken fire department who are experienced in dealing with emergency calls from people whose AWMC is temporarily limited. The DBN reconstructs the inferences of the firemen.

In the next section, we will describe the scenario of our example domain and identify the occurring dependencies. Then we will show how to model the dependencies in a DBN.

2   Dependencies in the Example Domain

People who place emergency calls to the fire department are usually anxious and distracted. Therefore their AWMC is temporarily limited. The task of a fire brigade officer is to gather details about the incident as fast as possible in order to react properly.

In an empirical study an emergency call dialog was played to the officers of a fire department who served as subjects. At particular times the tape was stopped and questions were asked about the dialog. By retrospective thinking-aloud (cf. Ericsson and Simon, 1993) the subject's assessments of the caller's properties were acquired. Based on these assessments, we identified the dependencies in the domain (cf. Jameson, 1996a) which are partly depicted in Figure 1. In order to make the explanations in the following sections more clear, we use a very simple model, i.e., we have not used the sophisticated models developed in cognitive psychology.

External causes allow us to infer *internal causes* for a limitation of P's AWMC: The larger P's AMOUNT OF EXPERIENCE WITH EMERGENCIES and the smaller the SIZE OF EMERGENCY, the more probable it is that P has the ABILITY TO HANDLE THE SITUATION. The less P has the ABILITY TO HANDLE THE SITUATION, the more probable it is that there will be a higher level of ANXIETY.

On the basis of the internal causes, P's AVAILABLE WORKING MEMORY CAPACITY (AWMC) can be assessed. ANXIETY causes a temporary limitation of P's AWMC (cf. also Calvo and Eysenck, 1996). The same is true of INTOXICATION. The higher the DIFFICULTY OF A QUESTION and the lower P's AWMC, the greater is the probability of a bad QUALITY OF THE ANSWER (which constitutes *observable evidence*) of P to the question. BREATHING NOISE suggests a high level of ANXIETY. If the LOCATION OF THE CALL IS A BAR (indicated by the BACKGROUND NOISE OF A BAR) then there is a high probability that P is in a state of INTOXICATION, which is also indicated by a POOR ARTICULATION.

---

[1] The cognitive load of a user also has to be taken into account when presenting instructions or explanations (cf. Kashihara et al., 1995). Similarly, Horvitz and Barry (1995) point out that the cognitive load of a user has to be considered when displaying information for monitoring complex systems.

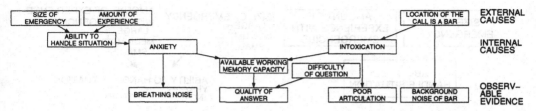

Figure 1. Dependencies in our domain (an arrow from A to B indicates that A influences B).

There are two types of user properties: *Static user properties* remain unchanged during the dialog, e.g., $\mathcal{P}$'s INTOXICATION.[2] *Temporally variable user properties* change over time, e.g., $\mathcal{P}$'s AWMC and ANXIETY. Perhaps $\mathcal{P}$ will calm down, i.e., $\mathcal{P}$'s ANXIETY will decrease. Or, the emergency may get worse and $\mathcal{P}$ may become more anxious. $\mathcal{P}$'s AWMC will also vary. It is possible that $\mathcal{P}$ is temporarily occupied with other things which also require working memory capacity.

It is very hard to predict how $\mathcal{P}$'s ANXIETY and AWMC will change over time. Observable evidence must be interpreted in order to obtain an accurate estimate.

In the following sections we will show how the described dependencies can be modeled by DBNs. Because of space limitations, we have to limit the presentation of the network to the most important parts.

3   User Modeling With Bayesian Networks

3.1   Static Bayesian Networks

A *Bayesian network* (BN) is a kind of probabilistic network (cf. Pearl, 1988).[3] A BN is a directed acyclic graph. Its *nodes* represent *random variables* consisting of a set of mutually exclusive and exhaustive propositions, called *hypotheses.* For each hypothesis the probability of being true is maintained. All these probabilities represent a *probability distribution*, called the *belief* of a node. The *links* between the nodes represent the dependencies between the propositions. Such a dependency is expressed by a *conditional probability table* (CPT).

For the *root nodes, a priori probabilities* must be defined. The belief of a node that is not a root node can be predicted from the beliefs of its *parent nodes. Observed evidence* for a node can be *interpreted* and used to recalculate its belief. Then the beliefs of its parent nodes are recalculated. This is repeated unless a node is a root node.[4]

Defining a BN implies tradeoffs, e.g., with respect to the granularity of the representation. The more fine-grained the representation, i.e, the more hypotheses the variables have, the more detailed but also the more costly the inferences will be.

After defining a BN it would be useful to *validate* the network, e.g., examine whether the inferences of the BN are comparable to the inferences of a domain expert. A *sensitivity analysis* (cf., e.g., Russell and Norvig, 1995, section 16.7) reveals the robustness of the inferences.

---

[2] Of course, this property remains unchanged only during a short period of time, e.g., during a phone call.
[3] Neapolitan (1990) and Charniak (1991) also provide introductions to Bayesian networks.
[4] This account is simplified. If there are nodes in the network which are connected via two or more paths, the network is *multiply connected* and requires more costly inference algorithms (cf. Pearl, 1988).

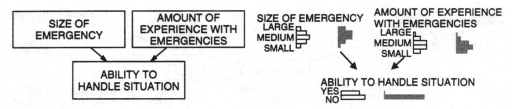

Figure 2. Static BN for processing of one observation.

Figure 2 shows a BN for estimating P's AMOUNT OF EXPERIENCE WITH EMERGENCIES.[5] The left-hand side of Figure 2 depicts the qualitative dependencies. They correspond to the upper left of Figure 1 in Section 2. The right-hand side of Figure 2 shows histograms depicting the belief of the nodes. The white histograms show the estimate in the beginning: SIZE OF EMERGENCY is estimated as most probably medium. P's AMOUNT OF EXPERIENCE WITH EMERGENCIES is regarded as most probably medium or slightly below medium. It is predicted that P will probably not have the ABILITY TO HANDLE THE SITUATION. Now assume we *observe* that P does not have the ABILITY TO HANDLE THE SITUATION (dark-shaded histogram). By interpreting this evidence, we conclude that P probably has a smaller AMOUNT OF EXPERIENCE and that the SIZE OF EMERGENCY is larger than we initially assumed (see dark-shaded histograms).

If we could observe P in a number of emergencies, we would be able to estimate P's AMOUNT OF EXPERIENCE with more certainty. Figure 3 shows a simple model. In our example in Figure 3 we observe that P fails to handle two situations. Therefore P's AMOUNT OF EXPERIENCE is assessed as quite small. The white histograms show the BN in the beginning and the grey ones after the interpretation of P's failure to handle Situation 1 (the dark-shaded ones in Situation 2).

If a static BN is defined in advance, there is a drawback. If the observations were interpreted one after the other, the interpretation of a new observation would lead to a reinterpretation of past observations, e.g., in Figure 3 the interpretation of P's inability to handle Situation 2 leads to a reinterpretation of the SIZE OF EMERGENCY 1. Such reinterpretations are not always useful. In our example we are interested only in assessing P's AMOUNT OF EXPERIENCE. In the next section we will show how to avoid the drawback by using DBNs.

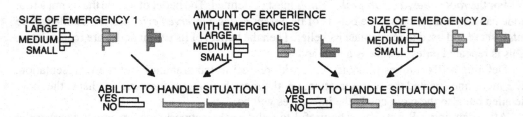

Figure 3. Static BN for processing of two observations.

---

[5] If these BNs were to be used for more than illustrative purposes, we would have to clearly define the meaning of variables like SIZE OF EMERGENCY. Spetzler and von Holstein (1975) propose a simple test: A clairvoyant should be able to predict the variable without requesting clarification of the meaning of the variable and its possible values.

3.2 Dynamic Bayesian Networks

A *dynamic Bayesian network* (DBN) is a kind of a *dynamic probabilistic network* (DPN). DPNs (cf. Dagum et al., 1992; Kjærulff, 1992; Nicholson and Brady, 1992; Tawfik and Neufeld, 1994) are networks which are able to model stochastic temporal processes.[6] For example, Dagum et al. (1992) used a dynamic network to forecast U.S. car sales in Japan. A typical application is locating a vehicle (cf., e.g., Nicholson and Brady, 1994; Forbes et al., 1995).

Typically, a *time slice* represents a snapshot of the temporal process. Usually there is a time slice representing the present (t), the past ($t - 1$) and if needed one for the future ($t + 1$).[7] The CPTs representing the dependencies between the time slices define the *state evolution model*. The objects represented by *dynamic nodes* evolve over time. *Static nodes* represent unchanging objects. We call nodes which exist in only one time slice *temporary nodes*. Usually the CPTs and the structure of the subnetwork remain the same within a time slice. However, Dagum et al. (1992) point out that unmodeled exogenous forces could lead to a deterioration of the model and require an update of the CPTs or possibly of the structure of the network.[8]

With *rollup* the DBN can be simplified: The subnetwork for slice $t - 1$ is removed after the subnetwork for slice t is established. Usually the dynamic nodes in t become root nodes and have to be assigned prior probabilities: The prior probabilities of a dynamic node D in t are defined as the belief of D in t before removing the subnetwork (cf., e.g., Russell and Norvig, 1995, section 17.5). Kjærulff (1992) generalizes this by combining several time slices to a *window of time slices*, i.e., the "present" is represented by a number of time slices. There are also *backward smoothing slices*, i.e., rollup is delayed. Similarly, there is also a number of *forecasting slices*.

In a DBN there are three types of dependencies: between dynamic and temporary nodes, between dynamic and dynamic nodes, and between static and dynamic nodes. In the following sections we will propose general schemes for modeling these dependencies and discuss the assets and drawbacks of the schemes.

Dependencies between dynamic and temporary nodes. In the simplest case, the child node of a dynamic node D is a temporary node T, e.g., an evidence node. For example, $\mathcal{P}$'s ANXIETY (D) is the cause of BREATHING NOISE (T). The dependency can be modeled adequately by the model $\mathcal{M}1$ depicted in Figure 4. Analogous modeling is employed by, e.g., Forbes et al. (1995). We will illustrate our model using the following example.

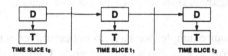

Figure 4. $\mathcal{M}1$: Modeling the dependency between a dynamic node D and a temporary node T.

---

[6] Instead of *dynamic networks*, some authors use the term *temporal networks*.

[7] The terms $t, t - 1$, and $t + 1$ represent relative descriptions of time slices, whereas t_1 or t_2 refer to absolute time slices, e.g., if the current time slice t is t_0, then slice $t + 1$ will be slice t_1.

[8] In some cases the probabilities are time-dependent (cf. Tawfik and Neufeld, 1994). Horvitz and Barry (1995) give an example in the domain of the space shuttle. If there is a propellant failure during burn, the probability that the engine will be damaged is higher the longer the burn continues.

Example 1: At the beginning of a phone call there is a lot of breathing noise. Subsequently it decreases, indicating that $\mathcal{P}$ is calming down.

Figure 5 shows a network for Example 1. For didactical reasons, we simplify the dependencies by assuming that node ANXIETY has no parents. Every time slice covers the same period. In time slice t_0 there is a lot of breathing noise, whereas in t_1 and t_2 there is little. The left-hand histograms in each time slice show the beliefs of the nodes before the interpretation of evidence, the right-hand ones after interpretation. We have to consider that $\mathcal{P}$'s ANXIETY evolves over time. In the example, $\mathcal{P}$ is very anxious during t_0. We can further deduce that $\mathcal{P}$ will probably calm down slightly from t_0 to t_1. This can be seen by comparing the dark-shaded histograms of ANXIETY in t_0 to the white ones in t_1. In Figure 5 $\mathcal{P}$'s ANXIETY in t_2 is regarded as probably low.

Figure 5. DBN according to the model $\mathcal{M}1$ for handling Example 1.

In Section 3.1, Figure 3 depicts a static BN for dealing with multiple observations which makes useless reinterpretations. To avoid this drawback Heckerman (1993) proposes a temporal definition of causal independence. Dynamic nodes are introduced in order to collect independent influences of several causes on an effect node. Jensen (1995a,1995b) also employs this idea.

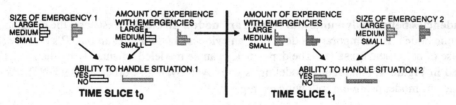

Figure 6. DBN for processing of observations.

If we apply this idea to our example, we have to collect the effects of the observations on $\mathcal{P}$'s AMOUNT OF EXPERIENCE, now modeled as a dynamic node. Figure 6 depicts the corresponding DBN. The dependency between AMOUNT OF EXPERIENCE in $t-1$ and AMOUNT OF EXPERIENCE in t is defined in a way that the belief of these two nodes is the same. By applying rollup (not shown in Figure 6) at most two time slices exist at a given moment. In this way interpretation of an unlimited number of observations can be done very efficiently.

Dependencies between dynamic nodes. Sometimes a dynamic node D2 has another dynamic node D1 as a parent node. For example, $\mathcal{P}$'s AWMC (D2) depends on $\mathcal{P}$'s ANXIETY (D1). Both AWMC and ANXIETY evolve over time.

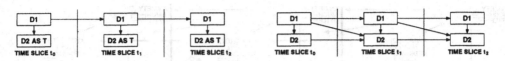

Figure 7. $\mathcal{M}2.1$ (left) and $\mathcal{M}2.2$ (right): Modeling the dependency between dynamic nodes D1 and D2. In $\mathcal{M}2.1$ dynamic node D2 is simplified as a temporary node T (D2 AS T).

In a simple modeling we can adapt the model $\mathcal{M}1$. D2, which is a child of dynamic node D1, is represented in a simplified way, *not* as a dynamic but as a temporary node T (see the model $\mathcal{M}2.1$ as depicted by the left-hand scheme in Figure 7). In each time slice a new instance of T is created by a prediction. There is no link between T in $t-1$ and T in t. T in $t-1$ influences T in t solely via their common parent nodes (D1 in $t-1$ and D1 in t). The prediction of T in t based on D1 in t will be less accurate than when it is additionally based on the estimate of T in the time slice before. We will illustrate the model with the following example, which is based on Example 1.

Example 2: At the beginning of a phone call there is a lot of breathing noise. Subsequently it decreases, indicating that $\mathcal{P}$ is calming down. In addition, $\mathcal{P}$ is asked three simple questions which $\mathcal{P}$ answers with very poor quality.

For didactical reasons we simplify the dependencies by not taking other causes for a reduction of $\mathcal{P}$'s AWMC than ANXIETY into account. In Figure 8 we show the results for Example 2 of a DBN modeled according to $\mathcal{M}2.1$. For reasons of space, DIFFICULTY OF QUESTION is not shown in Figure 8 and the following figures. In t_0 a lot of BREATHING NOISE indicates a lot of ANXIETY. Because of this and $\mathcal{P}$'s bad answer, $\mathcal{P}$'s AWMC is estimated as quite low in t_0 (see dark-shaded histogram). In t_1 AWMC has to be repredicted because it is represented as a temporary node. As can be seen by the white histogram in t_1 for AWMC, the result of the prediction is less accurate than the result obtained in slice t_0. In t_2, the little BREATHING NOISE indicates that $\mathcal{P}$ is calming down; therefore $\mathcal{P}$'s ANXIETY is estimated as lower in t_2 than in t_1 (see dark-shaded histograms). This leads to the questionable result that despite the poor answers there is a trend in ascribing approximately the same AWMC to $\mathcal{P}$ in t_2 as in t_1. (Strictly speaking there is even a slight increase.) This can be seen by comparison of the dark-shaded histograms of AWMC which indicate the state of the node after the interpretation of the bad answer. This is because AWMC depends solely on ANXIETY here and $\mathcal{P}$'s ANXIETY is estimated as probably low because of the limited BREATHING NOISE.

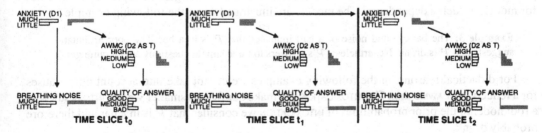

Figure 8. DBN according to the model $\mathcal{M}2.1$ for handling Example 2.

In the model $\mathcal{M}2.2$ (depicted by the right-hand scheme in Figure 7) there is no such loss of information, because D2 is appropriately modeled as a dynamic node. The effects of D1 in $t-1$

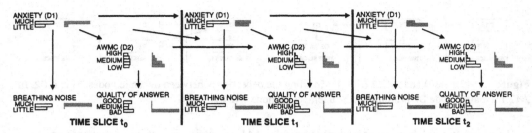

Figure 9. DBN according to the model $\mathcal{M}2.2$ for handling Example 2.

have been already considered in node D2 in $t - 1$. Node D1 in t also incorporates the cause of these effects. It is important that the effects of D1 to D2 are not counted twice. Therefore, D2 in t is linked to D1 in $t - 1$ and D1 in t. When defining the CPT for this dependency, D1 in both t and $t - 1$ can be taken into account. Considering D1 in $t - 1$ is important because D2 in $t - 1$ was already influenced by D1 in $t - 1$.

For example, in our domain we expect the AWMC in t to be roughly the same as that in $t - 1$, if ANXIETY remains unchanged. If $\mathcal{P}$ calms down, we expect AWMC to increase and vice versa. In addition, if $\mathcal{P}$ is very anxious, we are more careful in ascribing a high AWMC to $\mathcal{P}$. In Figure 9 we show how Example 2 is handled by the model $\mathcal{M}2.2$. In this case no loss of information occurs; $\mathcal{P}$'s AWMC is estimated consistently as probably low. This seems more reasonable than the results obtained by the DBN modeled according to $\mathcal{M}2.1$.

Interpretation and prediction are more costly in $\mathcal{M}2.2$ than in $\mathcal{M}2.1$. In addition, $\mathcal{M}2.2$ is harder to model: The CPT for defining the dependency between D2 in t and its parents D1 in t, D1 in $t - 1$, and D2 in $t - 1$ necessary for $\mathcal{M}2.2$ requires more values than the CPT of the dependency between T and D1 for $\mathcal{M}2.1$. If we were interested only in estimating $\mathcal{P}$'s ANXIETY we would adopt Provan's (1993) proposal of trading accuracy against efficiency and prefer $\mathcal{M}2.1$. As can be seen in our example DBNs (see Figure 8 and Figure 9), there is nearly no difference in the estimate of $\mathcal{P}$'s ANXIETY. Our goal is to estimate $\mathcal{P}$'s AWMC; therefore we prefer $\mathcal{M}2.2$.

Dependencies between dynamic and static nodes. Sometimes a dynamic node D has a static parent node S, e.g., the parent node of AWMC (D) is INTOXICATION (S). Figure 10 depicts three schemes for modeling such a dependency. The models are illustrated using the following example:

> **Example 3:** The background noise of a call indicates that $\mathcal{P}$ is in a bar. The poor articulation suggests that $\mathcal{P}$ is drunk. Nevertheless, $\mathcal{P}$'s answers to three simple questions are all quite good.

For didactical reasons, in the following examples we do not take into account other causes for a reduction of AWMC than $\mathcal{P}$'s INTOXICATION. To make our figures smaller we use INTOXICATION as a root node. In the prior probabilities of INTOXICATION we consider that $\mathcal{P}$ is in a bar and therefore probably drunk.

Jensen (1995a) proposes the incorporation of the effects of the static node S in the dynamic child node D. In this way the dynamic node D represents all of the information and the resulting network is quite simple. This idea is adopted in the model $\mathcal{M}3.1$, which is depicted in the left-hand scheme of Figure 10. Problems arise because of two points:

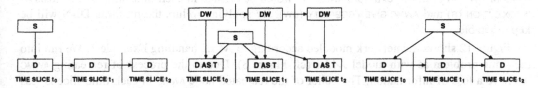

Figure 10. $M3.1$ (left), $M3.2$ (middle), $M3.3$ (right): Modeling dependency between a dynamic node D and a static node S. Dynamic node DW in $M3.2$ allows simplification of D as temporary node T (D AS T).

1. Node D must be able to represent the effects caused by S. For example, in Jensen's (1995a) wheat domain the effects of SOW DATE can be represented in the DEVELOPMENT STAGE. The DEVELOPMENT STAGE depends only on its predecessor in the previous time slice. In our domain this would not be proper, because P's AWMC in t depends on P's AWMC in $t-1$ and on P's INTOXICATION in t. If P is drunk, we will be more careful in ascribing a high AWMC to P.

2. Often, static node S is initially not known with certainty; there is only a vague estimate. This estimate will be refined during the session, e.g., imagine that not until t_2 does it become clear whether P is drunk or not. There would be a problem if we had made a rollup in t_1: Nodes of time slice t_0 would be removed. The new evidence which refined the assessment of P's INTOXICATION can no longer influence AWMC in t_2 because these nodes are no longer linked. Without rollup, the network would grow until there were so many time slices (and nodes) that it would become intractable. However, this problem can be solved by trading accuracy for efficiency: Rollup has to be delayed until the influence of S on the current time slice becomes negligible.

In Figure 11 a DBN is depicted modeled according to $M3.1$ dealing with Example 3. The result is questionable. Although P is assessed as drunk, P's AWMC is assumed to be medium up to slightly above medium (in t_3): Our network "forgot" (in t_1) that P is drunk and the (slightly below) good quality of P's answers is therefore interpreted too optimistically.

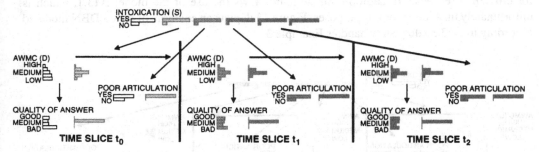

Figure 11. DBN according to the model $M3.1$ for handling Example 3.

The model $M3.2$ depicted in the middle of Figure 10 allows the static node to be refined during the session and to also have a direct impact on the estimate of P's AWMC in each time slice. In order to keep the model tractable, $M3.2$ adopts Provan's (1993) proposal of trading accuracy for efficiency: D is represented as a temporary node T which will be created anew in each time slice (cf. $M2.1$). DW represents the properties of D *without* the influence of S. T is created on the basis of DW and S. In our example AWMC (T) would be created in each time slice on the basis of INTOXICATION (S) and AWMC GIVEN SOBRIETY (DW). By applying rollup, the resulting DBN will be kept tractable.

Figure 12 shows the network modeled according to $\mathcal{M}3.2$ handling Example 3. We run into the same problem as with model $\mathcal{M}2.1$ (cf. Figure 8). Due to the process of recreating AWMC we have a loss of information. The belief of the recreated node AWMC in each time slice is less accurate than that obtained in the time slice before. This can be seen by comparing, e.g., the right-hand histogram of AWMC in time slice t_0 and the left-hand one in time slice t_1.

It is acceptable if the loss of information does not concern an important node. In our case, we are very interested in $\mathcal{P}$'s AWMC and therefore such a modeling is not acceptable.

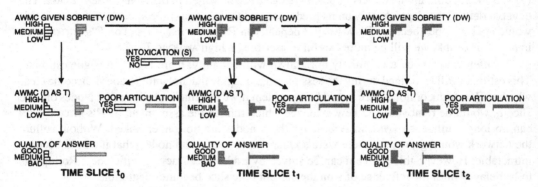

Figure 12. DBN according to the model $\mathcal{M}3.2$ for handling Example 3.

$\mathcal{M}3.3$ (cf. right-hand scheme in Figure 10) models S as static node and D as dynamic one. Such a structure is employed by Jensen (1995b) as a first model. Jensen (1995b) rejects this model for efficiency reasons.[9] In addition, his domain allows the use of the model $\mathcal{M}3.1$, which is unfortunately unsuitable for our purposes. Figure 13 depicts an example of how a DBN modeled according to $\mathcal{M}3.3$ adequately handles Example 3.

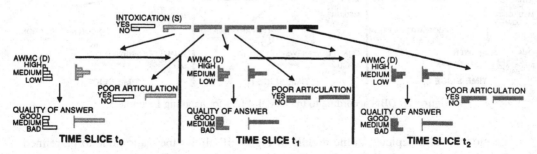

Figure 13. DBN according to the model $\mathcal{M}3.3$ for handling Example 3.

---

[9] There are nodes which are connected by two or more paths, i.e., the resulting network is multiply connected and requires costly inference algorithms.

In our examples, $\mathcal{M}3.2$ yields a similar result after the interpretation of the observable evidence of the rather good answers. If there were no such evidence $\mathcal{P}$'s AWMC would inadequately be assessed as low. This can be seen by comparison of the left-hand histograms of AWMC in time slice t_1 to time slice t_2. This is the reason why we prefer $\mathcal{M}3.3$ for modeling our domain.

For solving the problem of efficiency we again propose the trading of accuracy for efficiency. We therefore propose the use of rollups, but we delay their application so as to ensure that their effect is negligible.[10]

A variant of the model $\mathcal{M}3.3$ can be created by using the proposition made by Heckerman (1993). The static node is modeled as a dynamic one. The resulting model would be like $\mathcal{M}2.2$. This could perhaps be useful in simplifying the implementation: There would be no static nodes needing special handling when rollup is applied.

A theoretical possibility of a dynamic node as the parent of a static node still remains. That means that the proposition represented by the static node remains unchanged while its cause underlies continuous change. We doubt that there are examples of such dependencies.

4 Conclusions

In this paper we have characterized different types of dependencies that occur in networks that deal with the modeling of temporally variable user properties. We provided some general schemes which can be used to model these dependencies in a Bayesian network. The schemes were defined using existing techniques of applying dynamic probabilistic networks. We illustrated the proposed techniques with examples concerning emergency calls to the Saarbrücken fire department.

For the selection of a scheme, the dependencies among the variables of interest in the domain are the most important factors to consider. This is because the alternatives that we provided for keeping the networks tractable—by trading accuracy for efficiency—are not applicable in all domains.

References

Calvo, M. G., and Eysenck, M. W. (1996). Phonological working memory and reading in test anxiety. *Memory* 4:289–305.

Charniak, E. (1991). Bayesian networks without tears. *AI Magazine* 12(4):50–63.

Conati, C., and VanLehn, K. (1996). POLA: A student modeling framework for Probabilistic On-Line Assessment of problem solving performance. In Carberry, S., and Zukerman, I., eds., *Proceedings of the 5th International Conference on User Modeling*. Boston, MA: User Modeling, Inc. 75–82.

Cooper, G. F., Horvitz, E. J., and Heckerman, D. E. (1988). A method for temporal probabilistic reasoning. Technical report, Knowledge Systems Laboratory, Medical Computer Science, Stanford University. Revised April 1989.

Dagum, P., Galper, A., and Horvitz, E. (1992). Dynamic network models for forecasting. In Dubois, D., Wellman, M. P., D'Ambrosio, B., and Smets, P., eds., *Proceedings of the 8th Conference on Uncertainty in Artificial Intelligence*, 41–48. San Mateo: Morgan Kaufmann.

Ericsson, K. A., and Simon, H. A. (1993). *Protocol Analysis: Verbal Reports as Data*. Cambridge, MA: MIT Press, Rev. edition.

---

[10] A rollup is not trivial with a BN as defined by $\mathcal{M}3.3$. For reasons of space, we cannot explain the details.

Forbes, J., Huang, T., Kanazawa, K., and Russell, S. (1995). The BATmobile: Towards a Bayesian Automated Taxi. In Mellish, C. S., ed., *Proceedings of the 14th International Joint Conference on Artificial Intelligence*. San Mateo, CA: Morgan Kaufmann. 1878–1885.

Heckerman, D. (1993). Causal independence for knowledge acquisition and inference. In Heckerman, D., and Mamdani, A., eds., *Proceedings of the 9th Conference on Uncertainty in Artificial Intelligence*, 122–127. Morgan Kaufmann.

Horvitz, E., and Barry, M. (1995). Display of information for time-critical decision making. In Besnard, P., and Hanks, S., eds., *Proceedings of the 11th Conference on Uncertainty in Artificial Intelligence*. San Francisco: Morgan Kaufmann. 296–305. .

Jameson, A. (1996a). Inferenzen über das Arbeitsgedächtnis eines Dialogpartners. In Kluwe, R. H., and May, M., eds., *Proceedings der 2. Fachtagung der Gesellschaft für Kognitionswissenschaft*. Hamburg: Federal Armed Forces University. 59–61.

Jameson, A. (1996b). Numerical uncertainty management in user and student modeling: An overview of systems and issues. *User Modeling and User-Adapted Interaction* 5:193–251. .

Jensen, A. L. (1995a). *A probabilistic model based support system for mildew management in winter wheat*. Ph.D. Dissertation, Aalborg University.

Jensen, A. L. (1995b). Quantification experience of a DSS for mildew management in winter wheat. In Druzdzel, M. J., van der Gaag, L. C., Henrion, M., and Jensen, F. V., eds., *IJCAI-95 Workshop on Building Probabilistic Networks: Where do the Numbers Come From*, 22–31.

Kashihara, A., Hirashima, T., and Toyoda, J. (1995). A cognitive load application in tutoring. *User Modeling and User-Adapted Interaction* 4:279–303.

Kjærulff, U. (1992). A computational scheme for reasoning in dynamic probabilistic networks. In Dubois, D., Wellman, M. P., D'Ambrosio, B., and Smets, P., eds., *Proceedings of the 8th Conference on Uncertainty in Artificial Intelligence*, 121–129. San Mateo: Morgan Kaufmann.

Neapolitan, R. E. (1990). *Probabilistic Reasoning in Expert Systems: Theory and Algorithms*. New York: Wiley.

Nicholson, A. E., and Brady, J. M. (1992). The data association problem when monitoring robot vehicles using dynamic belief networks. In Neumann, B., ed., *Proceedings of the 10th European Conference on Artificial Intelligence*, 689–693.

Nicholson, A. E., and Brady, J. M. (1994). Dynamic belief networks for discrete monitoring. *IEEE Transactions on Systems, Man, and Cybernetics* 24(11):1593–1610.

Pearl, J. (1988). *Probabilistic Reasoning in Intelligent Systems: Networks of Plausible Inference*. San Mateo, CA: Morgan Kaufmann.

Provan, G. M. (1993). Tradeoffs in constructing and evaluating temporal influence diagrams. In Heckerman, D., and Mamdani, A., eds., *Proceedings of the 9th Conference on Uncertainty in Artificial Intelligence*, 40–47. San Mateo: Morgan Kaufmann.

Russell, S. J., and Norvig, P. (1995). *Artificial Intelligence: A Modern Approach*. Englewood Cliffs, NJ: Prentice-Hall.

Schum, D. A. (1987). *Evidence and Inference for the Intelligence Analyst*, volume I. Landam, MD: University Press of America.

Spetzler, C. S., and von Holstein, C.-A. S. S. (1975). Probability encoding in decision analysis. *Management Science* 22(3):340–358.

Tawfik, A. Y., and Neufeld, E. (1994). Temporal Bayesian networks. In Goodwin, S. D., and Hamilton, H. J., eds., *Proceedings of the TIME-94 – International Workshop on Temporal Representation and Reasoning*.

Wahlster, W., Jameson, A., Ndiaye, A., Schäfer, R., and Weis, T. (1995). Ressourcenadaptive Dialogführung: Ein interdisziplinärer Forschungsansatz. *Künstliche Intelligenz* 9(6):17–21. .

Agent Modeling in Antiair Defense

Sanguk Noh and Piotr J. Gmytrasiewicz*

Department of Computer Science and Engineering,
University of Texas at Arlington, U.S.A.

Abstract. This research addresses rational decision making and coordination among antiair units whose mission is to defend a specified territory from a number of attacking missiles. The automated units have to decide which missiles to attempt to intercept, given the characteristics of the threat, and given the other units' anticipated actions, in their attempt to minimize the expected overall damages to the defended territory. Thus, an automated defense unit needs to model the other agents, either human or automated, that control the other defense batteries. For the purpose of this case study, we assume that the units cannot communicate among themselves, say, due to an imposed radio silence. We use the Recursive Modeling Method (RMM), which enables an agent to select his rational action by examining the expected utility of his alternative behaviors, and to coordinate with other agents by modeling their decision making in a distributed multiagent environment. We describe how decision making using RMM is applied to the antiair defense domain and show experimental results that compare the performance of coordinating teams consisting of RMM agents, human agents, and mixed RMM and human teams.

1 Introduction

This paper describes rational decision making and rational coordination among the antiair defense units facing a missile attack. The task of automated defense units is to defend a specified territory and to coordinate their attempts to intercept the attacking missiles, given the characteristics of the threat, and given what they can expect of the other defense units.

To achieve the primary task successfully, an automated defense unit needs to *model* the other agents, either human or automated, that control the other defense batteries. We adopt an approach to modeling other agents as rational utility maximizers,[1] as defined in the field of decision theory. Our approach to this coordinated decision making problem is based on the assumption that the task of each of the defense units is to minimize the overall damages to the attacked territory. Under a realistic threat situation, friendly defense units cannot expect to have an advanced knowledge of the character of the incoming attack. It is, therefore, crucial that each of the defense units make a decision as to which incoming threat to intercept with an available interceptor by

* This research has been sponsored by the Office of Naval Research Artificial Intelligence Program under contract N00014-95-1-0775, and by a research initiation grant from the CSE Department of the University of Texas at Arlington.

[1] This approach has been advocated and used extensively in the areas of modern economic analysis to, for example, model and predict consumer and customer behavior. However, it has begun to be widely used in AI applications only recently (Jameson et al., 1995, and Poh and Horvitz, 1996), even though formal notions of rationality contributed to AI early on.

analyzing all potential threats acquired from the radar. In such cases, *coordination* requires an agent to recognize the current status, and to model the actions of the other agents to decide on his own next behavior. Since in any realistic combat situation the integrity of the defense team cannot be guaranteed, and even the very existence of the other friendly units cannot be counted on, relying on pre-established coordination protocols can be suboptimal or even dangerous. Therefore, our approach is that each unit is to independently decide on and execute his action, and that coordination among the units is to emerge on the fly as the result of the units' individual rational actions.

We begin by formulating antiair defense as a decision-theoretic problem from the point of view of an individual defense unit. As we mentioned, the objective is to *minimize damage*. Since the classical notion of a symbolic goal doesn't provide a sufficient basis for choice of action in uncertain situations (Wellman and Doyle, 1991), we need the attributes quantifying the quality of choices in the design of decision making procedures. First, each attacking missile has its threat value. We compute the missile's threat considering such attributes as the altitude of the missile and the size of its warhead. Further, the defense units should consider the probability with which their interceptors would be effective against each of the hostile missiles. Based on these attributes combined, each unit has to determine the optimal action from his probabilistic decision model.

For the purpose of coordinated decision making in a multiagent environment, our research uses the Recursive Modeling Method (RMM), previously reported in Gmytrasiewicz and Durfee (1995) and Gmytrasiewicz (1996). RMM enables an agent to model the other agents and to rationally coordinate with them even if no protocol or overall plan can be established explicitly in advance. Using RMM as a decision making tool, an agent rationally selects his action under uncertainty guided by the principle of *expected utility maximization*. We expect RMM to be appropriate to the antiair defense domain, since, as we mentioned, the coordinating units have to be able to react to threats in previously unforeseen circumstances. These can include the changing nature of the attack, other defense units being shot at and possibly incapacitated, communication lines broken down, sudden need for complete radio silence, and so on. In these unexpected conditions, relying on a globally consistent view of the situation, achieved by communication or by pre-established protocols, is unrealistic or likely to lock the agents into suboptimal forms of behavior. Further, by being competent decision makers and able to rationally model the action of other agents, RMM agents can effectively interact with human-controlled units, in spite of a lack of a predetermined protocol that a human would have to learn and follow.

2 Antiair Defense Environment

Let us consider a situation depicted in Figure 1. This scenario has six incoming missiles and two defending units in a 20 by 20 grid world. Each of the defense units independently decides to launch interceptors against the incoming missiles in the absence of communication. The incoming missiles keep going straight top-down and attack the overall ground site on which the units are located.

2.1 Attribute Analysis

One of the major problems encountered in connection with decision making process is how to model preferences and utilities. For the purpose of formalizing the decision making problem of

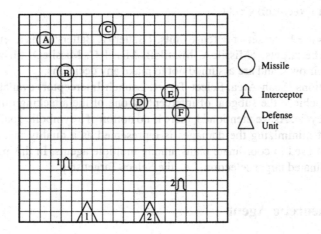

Figure 1. The antiair defense scenario.

minimizing damages, we first consider the attributes that influence the units' decision making. Each missile has its intrinsic threat value. In our model, threat is evaluated by considering the altitude of a missile and its warhead size. Intuitively, a defense battery should give priority to the missile which is closer to the ground and bigger than the others. An explosion of a missile close to the ground results in a more powerful blast, which increases the damage. Further, the measure of damage is proportional to the size of a missile's warhead. We calculate the missile threat, T, using the following formula:

$$T_n = W_n/A_n, \tag{1}$$

where

- W_n: the warhead size of missile n;
- A_n: the altitude of missile n.

A factor that does not enter into the missile threat calculation, but one that should be considered when an intercept decision is made, is the probability that an interceptor would be successful against a given missile. This probability is assumed to depend on the angle between a missile's direction of motion and the battery's line of sight. This probability is maximized when this angle is 0, as follows:

$$P(H_{ij}) = e^{-\mu \gamma_{ij}}, \tag{2}$$

where

- γ_{ij}: the angle between battery i's line of sight and missile j's direction of motion. Thus, $\gamma_{ij} = \tan^{-1} \alpha - \tan^{-1} \beta$ such that $0 \leq \gamma_{ij} \leq 90$;
- α: the slope of the missile j's direction of motion;
- β: the slope of the line of sight with which battery i aims at missile j;
- μ: an interceptor-specific constant (assumed here to be 0.01).

We will use the values of missile threat and the hit probability to develop the decision-theoretic assessment of the agent's alternative plans of action in an antiair defense environment.

2.2 Planning and Execution Cycle

In the domain in Figure 1, the set of defense units, {Battery1, Battery2}, is a set of planning and executing agents. The targets, {MissileA, MissileB, MissileC, MissileD, MissileE, MissileF}, have no plans of their own, and are assumed not to make any decisions.

The ordered actions (Scan-Area, Select-Target, Launch-Interceptor) available to agents are repeatedly used to achieve the subgoal of intercepting one of the attacking missiles during the overall plan-action cycle. As we mentioned, there is no notion of a symbolic goal in this planning. Instead, the goal of minimizing the damages is represented as a quality measure assigned to plans, which is then used to coordinate plans among multiple agents. In this paper, we address the rationally coordinated target selection, i.e., the Select-Target step.

3 Decision-Theoretic Agent

To be rational in decision-theoretic sense, the agents follow the principle of maximum expected utility (PMEU) (Russell and Norvig, 1995, chap. 14). In this section, we will show how PMEU can be implemented in the antiair defense domain using the Recursive Modeling Method (RMM). RMM (Gmytrasiewicz and Durfee, 1995, and Gmytrasiewicz, 1996) will be used to model the other agent, and to select the most appropriate missile to intercept by a given defense battery.[2]

3.1 An Example Scenario

Our approach is to take the agent-oriented perspective. In the example scenario (Figure 1), we view the decision making through the eyes of an individual defense unit, Battery1, and his radar-acquired data.[3] Figure 2 depicts the information acquired in the example scenario by Battery1 for the missiles A through F. In Figure 1, the left top corner of the screen is (0,0), x is pointing

Input Data		Attributes	
Missile (warhead, position)		**T**	
A: 470, (3,3)		T_A : 27.65	T_D : 33.64
B: 410, (5,6)		T_B : 29.29	T_E : 35.00
C: 350, (9,2)		T_C : 19.44	T_F : 45.00
D: 370, (12,9)	Equations		
E: 420, (15,8)	(1) & (2)	**P(H)**	
F: 450, (16,10)	$\longrightarrow$	$P(H_{1A})$: 0.88	$P(H_{2A})$: 0.74
		$P(H_{1B})$: 0.92	$P(H_{2B})$: 0.74
Battery (position)		$P(H_{1C})$: 0.94	$P(H_{2C})$: 0.88
Battery1: (7,20)		$P(H_{1D})$: 0.78	$P(H_{2D})$: 0.95
Battery2: (13,20)		$P(H_{1E})$: 0.71	$P(H_{2E})$: 0.91
		$P(H_{1F})$: 0.66	$P(H_{2F})$: 0.85

Figure 2. Radar data acquired by Battery1 for the missiles A through F and the derived attributes.

---

[2] For the demonstration of the antiair defense domain, refer to the Web page at http://dali.uta.edu/Air.html.
[3] Battery2 acquires the information about the environment from his point of view. Battery1 and Battery2 maintain their knowledge bases independently.

right, and y is pointing down. Applying formulas (1) and (2) to the acquired data, Battery1 can compute the relevant attributes of altitude, warhead size, and the angle γ that determines the hit probability. Battery1 also generates the expected hit probabilities for Battery2, assuming his hypothetical intercepting actions. The results are summarized in Figure 2.

3.2   Generation of the Payoff Matrix

Commonly, a decision problem is represented by a version of belief network (Pearl, 1988), called an influence diagram, which sometimes can be constructed dynamically. Poh and Horvitz (1996) use an influence diagram that includes a decision variable, with values ranging over the possible decisions; chance variables, which represent the uncertainty of the domain; and a utility node. In our work, we rely on the payoff matrix representation used in game theory. Payoff matrices, while different from influence diagrams, can be seen to faithfully summarize the information contained in them by listing the expected payoffs (obtained from the utility node) of possible decisions, depending on the parameters describing the domain (chance nodes).

The expected payoffs, corresponding to batteries' attempting to intercept the respective missiles, can be expressed as a combination of the threat of the missiles and the probability of their interception. For example, if Battery1 is faced with n missiles at some state, and he targets a missile j, the resulting threat will be reduced by the missile threat T_j multiplied by the probability of successful interception $P(H_{1j})$. If both batteries target missiles at the same time, the reduction of threat, and therefore the total payoff, is equal to the sum of the threats that each of them removes.

3.3   Modeling Other Agents: Recursive Model Structure

In order to solve his decision making problem, described by the payoff matrix generated as above, Battery1 needs to hypothesize the likely actions of Battery2. In the Recursive Modeling Method, the actions of the other rational agents are anticipated using a model of their decision making situation. We assume the following scenario: As shown in Figure 1, missiles A, B, C are coming toward Battery1 and missiles D, E, F toward Battery2. And the altitudes of missiles D, E, F are lower than those of missiles A, B, C. In this case, we allowed for uncertainty: Battery1 is uncertain whether Battery2 has any short range interceptors left, and whether he has been incapacitated by enemy fire. If Battery2 has only long range interceptors, he will be unable to attack any of the missiles D, E, or F, and can only attempt to shoot down one of A, B, or C.

From Battery1's point of view, therefore, Battery2's decision making situation could be modeled as one of three cases: Battery2 has both short and long range interceptors; Battery2 has only long range interceptors; or Battery2 has been damaged or incapacitated, in which case there is no information as to what action he would undertake. If Battery2 has only long range missiles it can only intercept the distant targets (A, B and C), even though it is faced with closer targets with larger threat value. Thus, there are three alternative models that Battery1 can use to model Battery2's decision making; one model has a fully developed payoff matrix with six alternative interception attempts corresponding to threats A through F, another has a payoff matrix with only three targets, and the third one contains no information about Battery2's action. We call the last model the *No-info* model. In RMM, each of the alternative models is assigned a probability indicating the likelihood of its correctness. Figure 3 is the Battery1's model structure of depth two for the example scenario.[4]

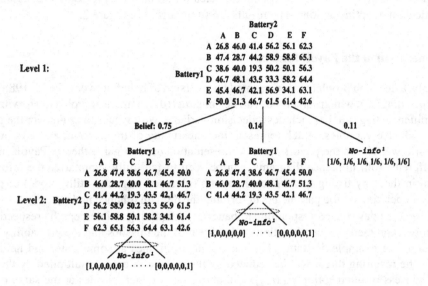

Figure 3. The recursive model structure for Battery1.

Thus, in the recursive model structure, Level 1 represents the way that Battery1 observes the situation to make his own decision, shown as Battery1's payoff matrix. Level 2 depicts the models Battery1 has of Battery2's situation. The recursive modeling could continue into deeper levels, but in this case we assumed that Battery1 has no further information. In other words, we are examining the reasoning of Battery1 in the particular case, when equipped with a finite amount of information about Battery2. To represent the fact that no further information is available, the recursive model structure terminates on the second level with two *No-info* models.

In general, the *No-info* models have to differentiate further among knowledge limitations of the different agents involved. For example, the situation in which Battery1 does not have any information about how he is modeled by Battery2 is different from the situation in which Battery1 knows that Battery2 has no information about Battery1. The right-most *No-info[1]* model in Figure 3 represents the fact that Battery1 has no information as to what Battery2 will do if he is incapacitated. The other two *No-info[1]* models on the bottom of Figure 3 represent the fact that Battery1 has no information as to how Battery2 models Battery1, if Battery2 is not incapacitated.

Since the modeling structures, such as one in Figure 3, express the optimal choices in the agents' decision making situations recursively depending on the choices of the other agents, one can use dynamic programming to solve them in a bottom-up fashion. We elaborate on the solution

---

[4] We do not elaborate on the important issues of learning and belief revision here. Thus, we analyze decision making given a pre-existing state of knowledge, but we do not detail how the models of the other agents were obtained. For our current work on learning and model formation see Kellogg and Gmytrasiewicz (1996).

procedure in more detail in Gmytrasiewicz (1996), in which we have also outlined an analytical method of dealing with the *No-info* models. For the purpose of this case study, however, we have designed and implemented a numerical method of solving the *No-info* models using logical sampling (Russell and Norvig, 1995), according to the algorithm below.

Let $A_i = \{a_i^1, a_i^2, \ldots, a_i^n\}$ be the set of actions available to agent i. Let $P_i = [p_i^1, p_i^2, \ldots, p_i^n]$ be the probability distribution over the available actions, i.e., the conjecture as to agent i's action. The conjecture, P_i, is calculated based on frequencies, $F_i = (f_i^1, f_i^2, \ldots, f_i^n)$, with which each action turns out to be optimal, as follows:

> **Procedure** No-info-PDF
> **Input** the payoff matrix M_i of agent i.
> **Output** the probability distribution, P_i, over the actions of agent i.
> **begin**
> $\quad F_i \leftarrow (0, 0, \ldots, 0)$
> $\quad N \leftarrow 0 \quad$ // the total number of probability distributions.
> $\quad$ **for** each probability distribution, P_N, in the set of sampled probability
> $\quad\quad$ distributions comprising the *No-Info* model,
> $\quad\quad$ Multiply probability distribution P_N by M_i.
> $\quad\quad$ Select an action a_i^k which has the maximum expected utility.
> $\quad\quad f_i^k \leftarrow f_i^k + 1$
> $\quad\quad N \leftarrow N + 1$
> $\quad$ **end for**
> $\quad P_i \leftarrow [f_i^1/N, f_i^2/N, \ldots, f_i^n/N]$
> $\quad$ **return** P_i
> **end**

The dynamic programming bottom-up solution starts at Level 2. Using the sampling algorithm, with the sampling density of 0.1, on the second level of the recursive model structure, reveals that, if Battery2 has both short and long range interceptors, the probability distribution over Battery2's actions becomes $[0.00, 0.00, 0.00, 0.12, 0.10, 0.78]$ for interception of missiles A through F, respectively. Thus, if Battery2 has all of the ammunition, it will most likely attempt to intercept one of the closer threatening missiles. Similarly, the sampling No-info-PDF procedure invoked for the case of Battery2 lacking short range interceptors results in a $[0.37, 0.58, 0.05, 0.00, 0.00, 0.00]$ distribution over Battery2's limited actions of intercepting the missiles A through F, respectively. Thus, if Battery2 has no short range ammunition, it would be irrational for it to attempt to intercept any of the closer threats.

The above distributions over the models of Battery2 are given the weight corresponding to the probability of the model they resulted from, and are combined with the third *No-info*[1] model: $(0.75 \times [0.00, 0.00, 0.00, 0.12, 0.10, 0.78] + 0.14 \times [0.37, 0.58, 0.05, 0.00, 0.00, 0.00] + 0.11 \times [1/6, 1/6, 1/6, 1/6, 1/6, 1/6]) = [0.07, 0.07, 0.04, 0.11, 0.10, 0.61]$. The resulting distribution is Battery1's overall expectation of Battery2's actions, given the uncertainty as to Battery2's available ammunition.

Propagating these results into Level 1, the combined probability distribution describing Battery2's actions is used to compute the expected utilities of Battery1's alternative behaviors as follows:

U_A: $0.07 \times 26.8 + 0.07 \times 46.0 + 0.04 \times 41.4 + 0.11 \times 56.2 + 0.10 \times 56.1 + 0.61 \times 62.3 = 56.55$

U_B: $0.07 \times 47.4 + 0.07 \times 28.7 + 0.04 \times 44.2 + 0.11 \times 58.9 + 0.10 \times 58.8 + 0.61 \times 65.1 = 59.17$
U_C: $0.07 \times 38.6 + 0.07 \times 40.0 + 0.04 \times 19.3 + 0.11 \times 50.2 + 0.10 \times 50.1 + 0.61 \times 56.3 = 51.15$
U_D: $0.07 \times 46.7 + 0.07 \times 48.1 + 0.04 \times 43.5 + 0.11 \times 33.3 + 0.10 \times 58.2 + 0.61 \times 64.4 = 57.14$
U_E: $0.07 \times 45.4 + 0.07 \times 46.7 + 0.04 \times 42.1 + 0.11 \times 56.9 + 0.10 \times 34.1 + 0.61 \times 63.1 = 56.29$
U_F: $0.07 \times 50.0 + 0.07 \times 51.3 + 0.04 \times 46.7 + 0.11 \times 61.5 + 0.10 \times 61.4 + 0.61 \times 42.6 = 47.85$

Thus, if Battery1 is rational, he will attempt to maximize his own expected utility and prefer to intercept MissileB first, given that he expects it most likely (with probability 75%) that Battery2 has short range interceptors, and will select MissileF simultaneously. According to the planning and execution cycle, the interceptor will be launched toward the selected missile, and the decision making process will be repeated until there are no missile threats, or until Battery1 runs out of interceptors.

4   Experimental Results

The antiair defense simulator is written in Common Lisp and built on top of the MICE simulator (Durfee and Montgomery, 1989), running on a LINUX platform. In the experiment we ran, each of two defense units could launch three interceptors, and were faced with an attack by six incoming missiles. We put all of the trials under the following conditions. First, the initial positions of missiles were randomly generated and it was assumed that each missile must occupy a distinct position. Second, the size of each missile was constant during the experiment and the warhead sizes were comparable. In this experiment, the warhead sizes were $470, 410, 350, 370, 420, 450$ for missiles A through F, respectively. Third, in the recursive model structure (Figure 3), both batteries were assumed to have short and long range interceptors with the belief 0.8 or to be incapacitated with the belief 0.2. Fourth, the performance assessments of agents with different policies were compared using the same threat situation. Further, each interceptor could intercept only one missile, and it was moving twice as fast as the incoming missile. Finally, although there was no communication between agents, each agent could see which threat was shot at by the other agent and use this information to make the next decision.

Our experiment was aimed at determining the quality of modeling and coordination achieved by the RMM agents in a team, when paired with human agents, and when compared to other strategies. To evaluate the quality of the agents' performance, the results were expressed in terms of (1) the number of selected targets, i.e., targets the defense units attempted to intercept, and (2) the total expected damage to friendly forces after all six interceptors were launched. The total expected damage is defined as a sum of the residual warhead sizes of the attacking missiles. Thus, if a missile was targeted for interception, then it contributed $(1 - P(H)) \times W$ to the total damage. If a missile was not targeted, it contributed all of its warhead size value to the damage.

The target selection strategies are as follows:
- RMM: selection by RMM.
- Human:[5] selection by human.

---

[5] We should remark that our human subjects were simply CSE and EE graduate students who were informed about the criteria for target selection. We would expect that antiair specialists, equipped with a modern defense doctrine, could perform substantially better than our subjects. However, the defense doctrine remains classified, and was not available to us at this point.

- Independent, no modeling: selection of arg $\max_j\{P(H_{ij}) \times T_j\}$ for agent i.
- Random: selection randomly generated.

The random agents were included to provide the worst base-line case of the system performance in our experiment. The performance achieved by independent agents was included to show what coordination can be expected when agents maximize but do not model each other. It turned out that the ways that human agents choose a missile were different and sometimes quite arbitrary. For example, some of our human subjects shot only the 3 missiles coming to their own side by dividing the grid world into left and right sides. They sometimes had difficulties in splitting the screen when the missiles were clustered at the center area, which led to much duplicated effort. Others tended to choose missiles with the largest missile size. Still others tried to consider the multiplication of the missile size and the hit probability, but did not model the other agent appropriately.

4.1 Performance Assessments

We experimented with the above policies to understand the agent interactions in two groups: the agent teams with the same policy and the mixed agent teams with different policies.

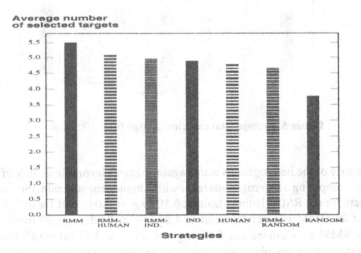

Figure 4. Average number of selected targets (over 100 runs).

As shown in Figures 4 and 5, we found that the all-RMM team outperformed the human and independent teams. The average number of selected targets by RMM after 100 trials is 5.49 ($\sigma_{\bar{x}}[6]= 0.05$), compared to 4.89 ($\sigma_{\bar{x}} = 0.08$) for the independent team and 4.77 ($\sigma_{\bar{x}} = 0.06$) for the all-human team. Further, the RMM-controlled coordinated defense resulted in the total expected damage of 488.0 ($\sigma_{\bar{x}} = 23.4$), which is much less than that of independent team (732.0, $\sigma_{\bar{x}} = 37.1$) and that of the all-human team (772.0, $\sigma_{\bar{x}} = 36.3$).

---

[6] $\sigma_{\bar{x}}$ denotes the standard error of the mean.

The human performance is very similar to the performance of independent agents. The most obvious reason for this is that humans tend to depend on their intuitive strategies for coordination, and, in this case, found it hard to engage in deeper, normative, decision-theoretic reasoning. The common reason for the lower score of human teams was the choice of the greatest threat simultaneously–they made redundant efforts to attack the same missile. This, again, suggests that human agents attempted to minimize their expected damage but did not model the decision making of the other human very well, while RMM agents were rationally optimizing given what they expected of the other agent. The performance of the RMM team was not perfect, however, since the agents were equipped with limited and uncertain knowledge of each other.

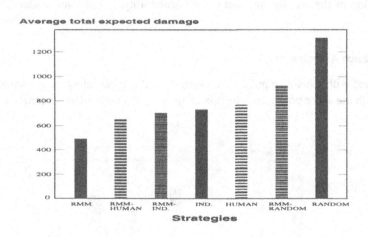

Figure 5. Average total expected damage (over 100 runs).

The performance of the heterogenous teams again suggests favorable quality of coordination of RMM agents. Comparing a heterogenous team with a homogeneous team, the average number of selected targets for the RMM-Human team is 5.10 ($\sigma_{\bar{x}} = 0.04$), and for the all-human team it is 4.77; that of the RMM-Independent team is 4.98 ($\sigma_{\bar{x}} = 0.03$) vs. 4.89 for the Independent team; that of the RMM-Random team is 4.66 ($\sigma_{\bar{x}} = 0.06$), and 3.77 for the all-Random team.

In order to test whether the observed differences among the target selection strategies were not due to chance, we used Analysis of Variance (ANOVA) technique with a 0.01 significance level. Here, all-human team and RMM-Human team were left out, because of relatively small number of participating human subjects.[7] In the experiment in which the number of selected targets was measured (Figure 4), the value 4.12 obtained for f exceeded $f_{0.01,4,\infty} = 3.32$. Therefore, we can conclude that the differences among the five target selection strategies are not due to chance with the probability 99%. This result holds also for the experiment in which the total expected damage was measured. To test the significance of the observed superiority of

---

[7] In our preliminary experiment, there are 4 pairs of all-human team and RMM-Human team. The results for humans are only suggestive and couldn't be evaluated statistically due to small number of human participants. We will conduct more exhaustive experiments during our future work.

coordination achieved by the RMM agents vs. the other strategies, the one-sided, matched-pairs t tests were performed. The result shows that the RMM team was better than any other team with the probability of 99% (0.01 level of significance).

The above results show that the recursive modeling allows RMM agents to improve the performance of target selection when paired with any other agent. A particularly promising facet of these results is that the recursive model structure (Figure 3) seems to be a robust mechanism for modeling and coordination with the human subjects, and not only among RMM agents.

5   Related Work

The approaches related to the modeling and coordination in the multiagent environment are in the area of multiagent plan recognition and plan coordination. In work on plan recognition (Rao and Murray, 1994, and Tambe and Rosenbloom, 1996), the objective is to enable an agent to model or recognize the other agents through observation to anticipate the other agents' future action, given prior knowledge about these agents. In these approaches, an agent usually compares a pre-calculated plan, or a protocol, with the on-going situation, and then chooses his next action accordingly. The process of mental-state recognition (Rao and Murray, 1994) assumes the correct and complete knowledge of the plans of the other agents, and it does not represent uncertainty that might be present in real-world domains. As Tambe and Rosenbloom (1996) pointed out, ambiguities may persist when an agent must infer unobserved actions and intentions.

Multiagent coordination without communication has been dealt with in Sen and Sekaran (1996) and Mor et al. (1996). Sen and Sekaran (1996) used a particular reinforcement learning methodology and concentrated on the learning classifier systems where agents share no problem-solving knowledge. However, the reinforcement learning method needs a super-agent for the external reward and requires numerous training cases to converge on the desirable entries. Mor et al. (1996) handled the opponent's modeling in the complexity of polynomial time, based on game-theoretic techniques. They used a deterministic finite automaton to represent an agent's strategy during a learning process leading to equilibrium.

6   Conclusion and Further Research

This paper presented a case study in modeling and coordination in the multiagent distributed environment of antiair defense. This investigation implies that RMM can be applied to high-level tactical decision making for minimizing overall damage. It turned out that it was relatively simple to quantify the missile threats and the hit probability to generate fairly realistic payoff matrices. Based on threat evaluation, we implemented the RMM agents to model the other agents and to follow the principle of maximum expected utility. We anticipate that the approach presented will also be applicable to other decision problems that require modeling and coordination.

The most promising conclusion of our case study seems to be the high quality of the co-ordinated decision making achieved by the RMM agents. This, in turn, suggests that modeling other agents, including humans, as rational decision-makers is a promising and viable approach to achieving plan recognition and coordination. Also, the relatively high quality achieved by the mixed human/RMM team shows how a nested decision-theoretic modeling can enable human-machine coordination without pre-established protocols that the human would have to learn and follow during the interaction.

In other experiment, we also implemented RMM in the predator-prey pursuit environment. There, the payoff matrices the agents used were 5-dimensional. The quality of coordination among the RMM agents for this domain is slightly inferior to that of human agents (http:// dali.uta.edu/Pursuit.html). Further, we applied Bayesian learning (Kellogg and Gmytrasiewicz, 1996) for belief update to the antiair defense domain, as well as the pursuit domain. In our future research we will investigate a communication method between agents using KQML and investigate the value of decision-model refinement (Poh and Horvitz, 1993).

References

Durfee, E. H., and Montgomery, T. A. (1989). MICE: A flexible testbed for intelligent coordination experiments. In *Proceedings of the 1989 Distributed AI Workshop*, 25–40.

Gmytrasiewicz, P. J., and Durfee, E. H. (1995). A rigorous, operational formalization of recursive modeling. In *Proceedings of the First International Conference on Multi-Agent Systems*, 125–132. Menlo Park: AAAI Press/The MIT Press.

Gmytrasiewicz, P. J. (1996). On reasoning about other agents. In Wooldridge, M., Müller, J. P., and Tambe, M., eds., *Intelligent Agents II: Agent Theories, Architectures, and Languages*, 143–155. Berlin: Springer.

Jameson, A., Schäfer, R., Simons, J., and Weis, T. (1995). Adaptive provision of evaluation-oriented information: Tasks and techniques. In *Proceedings of the 14th International Joint Conference on Artificial Intelligence*, 1886–1893. San Mateo, CA: Morgan Kaufmann.

Kellogg, T., and Gmytrasiewicz, P. J. (1996). Bayesian belief update in multi-agent systems. In preparation.

Mor, Y., Goldman, C. V., and Rosenschein, J. S. (1996). Learn your opponent's strategy (in polynomial time)! In Weiß, G., and Sen, S., eds., *Adaptation and Learning in Multi-Agent Systems — IJCAI'95 Workshop, Lecture Notes in Artificial Intelligence*. New York: Springer. 164–176.

Pearl, J. (1988). *Probabilistic Reasoning in Intelligent Systems: Networks of Plausible Inference*. San Mateo, CA: Morgan Kaufman.

Poh, K. L., and Horvitz, E. J. (1993). Reasoning about the value of decision-model refinement: Methods and application. In *Proceedings of the Ninth Conference on Uncertainty in Artificial Intelligence*, 174–182. San Mateo, CA: Morgan Kaufmann.

Poh, K. L., and Horvitz, E. J. (1996). A graph-theoretic analysis of information value. In *Proceedings of the Twelfth Conference on Uncertainty in Artificial Intelligence*. San Mateo, CA: Morgan Kaufmann.

Rao, A. S., and Murray, G. (1994). Multi-agent mental-state recognition and its application to air-combat modelling. In *Proceedings of the 13th International Distributed Artificial Intelligence Workshop*, 283–304.

Russell, S. J., and Norvig, P. (1995). *Artificial Intelligence: A Modern Approach*. Englewood Cliffs, New Jersey: Prentice-Hall.

Sen, S., and Sekaran, M. (1996). Multiagent coordination with learning classifier systems. In Weiß, G., and Sen, S., eds., *Adaptation and Learning in Multi-Agent Systems — IJCAI'95 Workshop, Lecture Notes in Artificial Intelligence*. New York: Springer. 218–233.

Tambe, M., and Rosenbloom, P. S. (1996). Architectures for agents that track other agents in multi-agent worlds. In Wooldridge, M., Müller, J. P., and Tambe, M., eds., *Intelligent Agents II: Agent Theories, Architectures, and Languages*, 156–170. Berlin: Springer.

Wellman, M. P., and Doyle, J. (1991). Preferential semantics for goals. In *Proceedings of the Ninth National Conference on Artificial Intelligence*, 698–703.

Logic-Based Methods

Mechanisms for Flexible Representation and Use of Knowledge in User Modeling Shell Systems

Wolfgang Pohl and Jörg Höhle*

GMD FIT, Human-Computer Interaction Research Department, St. Augustin, Germany

Abstract. In many user modeling systems, assumptions about the user and other user modeling knowledge are represented in a knowledge base and used for individualized behavior of applications. Hence, user modeling shell systems need to support both representation and use of knowledge. Ideally, a shell provides powerful techniques for applications with sophisticated needs but is also flexible enough to be suitable for applications with specialized, less complex requirements. This paper describes two mechanisms that were developed for increasing the flexibility of user modeling shell systems: the AsTRa (Assumption Type Representation) framework for powerful and flexible logic-based representation of user modeling knowledge; and domain-based user modeling, which allows modularization and sharing of user modeling knowledge bases particularly in centralized user modeling scenarios. Both mechanisms have been implemented in the user modeling shell BGP-MS.

1 Introduction

For almost ten years, user modeling shell or tool systems have been built in order to support developers of personalized applications. They offer generic implementations of user modeling techniques that can be exploited for the special purposes of an application. Core elements of any user modeling system and hence of any user modeling shell are mechanisms that permit the representation and use of assumptions about the user and of other user modeling knowledge. In addition, the resulting user modeling knowledge bases (short: UMKBs) must be managed and made available to applications.

In the user modeling literature, a wide range of methods has been proposed for representing user modeling knowledge and for using it via knowledge base access and reasoning. This diversity implies that no user modeling shell system will be able to satisfy the needs of all adaptive applications. Nevertheless it is a challenge for shell systems to suit as many applications as possible. On principle, this can be achieved by providing powerful mechanisms that support a wide range of user modeling needs. However, for systems within this range that do not make use of the full power provided, unnecessary overhead is caused. So, more advantageous are powerful mechanisms, which are flexible in the sense that they can be tailored to better fit the specific requirements of each application.

In this paper, we present mechanisms for flexible knowledge representation and use in user modeling shell systems. First, the AsTRa (Assumption Type Representation) framework for representation and reasoning within UMKBs is introduced. It integrates the partition approach and

* This work was supported by the German Science Foundation (grant no. Ko 1044/4). Parts of it were done while the authors were at the University of Essen. We thank the anonymous reviewers for their fruitful remarks and Anthony Jameson for his help in preparing the final manuscript.

the modal logic approach of representing information about *assumption types*, i.e. different kinds of assumptions about the user and of other user modeling knowledge. Second, a mechanism for managing user modeling knowledge for several applications and user models of several users in a centralized user modeling scenario is presented. Its fundamental notion is the domain of user modeling knowledge, and it permits developers to modularize user modeling knowledge and applications to share assumptions about their users. Both the AsTRa framework and *domain-based user modeling* have been implemented in the shell system BGP-MS.

In the next section, we will show how knowledge is represented and used in user modeling shells that were described in the literature, focusing on representation of assumption types and domains, maintenance of multiple users and applications, and reasoning possibilities and interfaces for knowledge use. In particular, the previous state of development of BGP-MS, as described by Kobsa and Pohl (1995), is summarized and discussed. The AsTRa framework, which is presented in the subsequent section, was developed as a formalization of the partition-based representation and reasoning facilities of BGP-MS in order to give them a formal semantics. Through the corresponding abstraction process, new possibilities for making BGP-MS more flexible were discovered. In Section 4, domain-based user modeling is described. The paper concludes with a summary and perspectives for future work.

2   Representation and Use of Knowledge in User Modeling Shell Systems

2.1   Representation, Reasoning, and Knowledge Base Access

User modeling shell systems can be divided roughly into two categories. These are mainly determined by the knowledge representation approach employed, which is closely related to mechanisms for knowledge use. In the first category—which comprises GUMS (Finin, 1989), UMT (Brajnik and Tasso, 1994), and TAGUS (Paiva and Self, 1995)—symbolic, logic-oriented formalisms are offered for representing user modeling knowledge. In GUMS, there is a Prolog-like formalism, which supports default reasoning. In UMT, information about the user is represented as attribute-value pairs. TAGUS offers almost full predicate calculus for expressing assumptions about the user.

In GUMS and TAGUS, special predicates can be used to distinguish between assumptions of different types. In examples given by Finin (1989) for GUMS, the predicate "knows" is used to express assumptions about user knowledge. In TAGUS, predicates like "b" and "characteristic" can be employed for assumptions about user beliefs and for (mostly fixed) characteristics of the user, respectively. While special predicates allow distinctions within a representation formalism, UMT and TAGUS make further distinctions beyond the formalism level: In both systems, inference rules are represented separately from genuine user model entries. Hence, these rules are viewed as meta-level knowledge that the user modeling system can use for determining implicit assumptions about the user.

In all logic-oriented systems, user modeling knowledge can be used via "tell and ask" command interfaces for adding knowledge and asking queries. "Tell" commands may invoke forward reasoning (UMT), while "ask" commands may invoke backward reasoning (GUMS, TAGUS). All systems deal with the problem of user model dynamics by applying logic-oriented techniques like default reasoning (GUMS) or truth maintenance systems (UMT, TAGUS).

In contrast to logic-oriented shells, both um (Kay, 1995) and Doppelgänger (Orwant, 1995) take the evidence for a user model entry as a central element of user modeling knowledge. Both systems provide quite simple representation formalisms for expressing assumptions about the user. Each assumption, however, is combined with evidence information, i.e., an evidence value and evidence sources. This representation approach is closely related to the way user modeling knowledge is used: Not UMKB contents are the main objects of manipulation, but their associated evidence information. In um, each assumption about the user (including evidence) is represented in an attribute-value structure named "component". A query to um about the value of a component is answered by resolving possibly conflicting evidence information of the component. Information is added to a um user model by adding evidence information to components. um inference rules are processed in a forward reasoning manner to add further evidence information. As in most logic-oriented shells, these rules are viewed as inference rules of the system.

In Doppelgänger, evidence information (which is split into numeric strength and confidence values) cannot be manipulated directly. Sensors, which may be hardware or software systems, report observations about user behavior to Doppelgänger. The system processes this input using statistical and machine learning algorithms to yield assumptions about the user plus strength and confidence values. User model contents can be retrieved using a matching mechanism.

In both um and Doppelgänger, assumption types are distinguished by mechanisms which, unlike the special predicates of GUMS and TAGUS, are not part of a symbolic representation formalism. In um, each component can be labeled as "preference", "knowledge", "belief", or as "arbitrary" information. In Doppelgänger, an orthogonal approach is taken: Information about the user is aggregated into lists like "preferences", "times" (of user activities), or "biographical data". These lists are themselves contained in so-called *submodels*, which partly reflect the applicability domain of user model contents. Example submodels are "news" (assumptions about news reading behavior) and "primary" (basic information about the user that is not likely to change).

2.2 Maintaining Multiple Applications and Users

In case of um, UMT, and TAGUS, maintenance of multiple users and/or multiple applications is not possible or not discussed in detail. Finin (1989) describes such maintenance mechanisms for GUMS. GUMS can store the data of multiple applications and, for each application, user models of a number of users. However, GUMS can not handle multiple applications concurrently. Exactly one application instance with one user can communicate with GUMS, which selects the appropriate user model.

Doppelgänger is the first user modeling *server*, which can be employed as a central user modeling system in a networked computing scenario. It communicates with a range of sensors for obtaining information about the user and can be accessed by multiple applications via network connections. For every user, one coherent model is maintained, which is shared by all applications. The model is stored permanently in a number of files, with each file storing one submodel. Every application instance can access every submodel, but the interest in thematic submodels like "news" may depend on the kind of application.

2.3 BGP-MS

BGP-MS (as described by Kobsa and Pohl, 1995) is a logic-oriented system, but it has its own special way of handling assumption types. Following the partition approach to belief modeling

(Cohen, 1978, Kobsa, 1985), BGP-MS divides a UMKB into partial knowledge bases, called *views*, which are represented by partitions that are organized into an inheritance hierarchy. Each view stores assumptions of one specific type about the user; typical view names are SBUB (System Believes User Believes), SBUW (analogous, with W for "wants"), and SBMBUB (MB stands for "mutually believed"). In addition, most applications of BGP-MS make use of the view SB for maintaining system domain knowledge within the user modeling system. Stereotypes are also modeled with partitions: For each stereotype there is one partition, the contents of which are inherited into view SBUB, if the stereotype is applicable to the current user.

View contents can be represented using SB-ONE, a KL-ONE-like formalism for terminological knowledge, and first-order predicate calculus (FOPC). So a content of a BGP-MS UMKB is an expression of either SB-ONE or FOPC, which is stored in one partition and hence is part of one or more views. Kobsa (1992) observed that, since SB-ONE expressions can be translated into FOPC, all view contents correspond to FOPC formulas. Hence, all BGP-MS UMKB contents can be expressed as modal logic formulas: A sequence of modal operators indicates a view, and a subsequent FOPC-expression stands for the view content. For example: An SB-ONE ISA-relation between the concepts "laserjet" and "laserprinter" that is contained in SBUB corresponds to the modal formula "$\Box_{(B,S)}\Box_{(B,U)} \forall x \, \text{laserjet}(x) \rightarrow \text{laserprinter}(x)$", where $\Box_{(m,a)}$ is a modal operator with modality m and agent a.

Modal logic is a powerful representation formalism that exceeds the possibilities of view representation. In particular, negative assumptions about the user—assumptions about what the user does *not* believe, want, etc.—and system inference rules that refer to several views can be formulated. Therefore, facilities for modal logic representation and reasoning were developed for BGP-MS that also consider view contents (Pohl, 1996). Since all UMKB contents can be expressed as modal formulas, modal logic was chosen as a uniform language for referring to UMKB contents in the "tell and ask" interface of BGP-MS. For a modal expression, BGP-MS decides if it can be represented as view content or not, and whether SB-ONE or FOPC is applicable, thus pursuing a *top-down* approach to user model representation and use. However, experiences with applications showed that often only parts of the representation facilities of BGP-MS are employed. So, a *bottom-up* approach, which allows applications to address appropriate mechanisms directly, might give applications more flexible access to and control over representation facilities.

Flexibility was also lacking with respect to maintenance of user modeling knowledge bases for applications. On the one hand, BGP-MS is typically used as a separate process and communicates with an application via an inter-process message interface. So technically BGP-MS is not part of an application, which makes it suitable for building centralized user modeling systems. On the other hand, a BGP-MS UMKB is filled with application-specific data and then used by one application only. Information sharing between different applications is not possible. Moreover, multiple users and applications are not supported by BGP-MS.

3   Flexibility Within Knowledge Bases: Assumption Type Representation

This section describes the AsTRa framework. It was originally intended as a formalisation of the representation and reasoning facilities of BGP-MS. However, the abstraction process led to a more flexible approach to representing and using user modeling knowledge which is grounded on logic-based mechanisms.

3.1 Basic Mechanisms

The *assumption type* is the central notion of the AsTRa framework. An assumption type is a partial knowledge base that is supposed to contain all assumptions of one kind within a UMKB. An entry in an assumption type knowledge base (an *assumption content*) is represented in one of a set of content formalisms. That is, an AsTRa UMKB contains AsTRa expressions *AT:ac*; such an expression denotes an assumption content *ac*, which is expressed in the language $\mathcal{L}_F$ of a content formalism F and is stored in KB_{AT}, the knowledge base of assumption type AT.

In the partition approach and in other work on belief modeling (like Taylor et al., 1996), a quite standard way of labeling different kinds of knowledge is used, which we will adopt and extend for general user modeling purposes: An assumption type label is a sequence of agent/modality pairs, $a_1 m_1 \ldots a_n m_n$. Possible agents a_i are S (the system) and U (the user), and standard modalities m_i are B (belief) and W (wants/goals). Together with B, the special agent M can be used to express mutual belief. Developers of user modeling systems can define further modalities, e.g. I for "interest", which can be used with agents S and U. All assumption type labels start with the pair SB. This is to stress that user model contents are system assumptions which are not claimed to hold objectively in the world. Examples for possible assumption types are SB, SBUB, SBUW, SBUPref (if Pref is a defined modality), SBMB, SBMBUW, etc.

The AsTRa framework also permits the representation of stereotypes (Rich, 1979). However, stereotypes do not constitute distinct assumption types. If a user is identified as member of a user group, the stereotypical assumptions about this group become part of the system assumptions about the user. Hence they belong to assumption types like SBUB, SBUW, etc., depending on whether they make a statement about potential beliefs, goals or other attitudes of group members. An AsTRa implementation should provide means for dynamically adding and removing stereotype contents to and from the knowledge bases of appropriate assumption types.

For knowledge use, the AsTRa framework provides two basic knowledge base access functions, **tell** and **ask**, thus satisfying the minimal requirement for knowledge representation formalisms (Russell and Norvig, 1995). Typically, such access functions receive two arguments: a knowledge base K and an expression ϕ. In the AsTRa framework, knowledge use additionally depends on the *level of reasoning*, which becomes a third parameter. Then, a call to **tell** schematically looks like **tell**(L, K, ϕ), where L is the reasoning level, K is an AsTRa UMKB, and ϕ is an AsTRa expression. A call to **ask** is analogous.

In the AsTRa framework as described so far, knowledge use must rely on the facilities that are provided by content formalisms. On principle, quite arbitrary formalisms are possible for assumption content representation. However, there is one main requirement: An AsTRa content formalism F must implement four knowledge base access functions:

tell$_F(K, \phi)$ adds the F-expression ϕ into the knowledge base K, perhaps after consistency checking. In addition, forward reasoning may add further, implicit knowledge to K.
ask$_F(K, \phi)$ determines if ϕ logically follows from K or not.
store$_F(K, \phi)$ simply adds ϕ to K.
fetch$_F(K, \phi)$ determines if ϕ is explicitly contained in K.

Normally, **tell**$_F$ and **ask**$_F$ consider only F-expressions, but AsTRa implementations may provide hybrid reasoning capabilities that use expressions of more than one formalism.

With the above functions at hand, we can define two AsTRa reasoning levels. At Level 0, there is no reasoning at all. At Level 1, reasoning takes place within assumption type knowledge bases. Formally, **tell** and **ask** are defined to handle AsTRa expressions AT:ac by invoking access functions of the applicable content formalism $F(ac)$ on KB_{AT} and ac:

- **tell**$(0, \text{UMKB}, AT\text{:}ac) := \textbf{store}_{F(ac)}(\text{KB}_{AT}, ac)$
  ask$(0, \text{UMKB}, AT\text{:}ac) := \textbf{fetch}_{F(ac)}(\text{KB}_{AT}, ac)$
- **tell**$(1, \text{UMKB}, AT\text{:}ac) := \textbf{tell}_{F(ac)}(\text{KB}_{AT}, ac)$
  ask$(1, \text{UMKB}, AT\text{:}ac) := \textbf{ask}_{F(ac)}(\text{KB}_{AT}, ac)$

3.2 Extended AsTRa: Adding Modal Logic Representation and Reasoning

For BGP-MS, a relationship between user model contents within views and modal logic expressions had been pointed out (see Section 2.3). In the AsTRa framework, this observation is put on a firm foundation. Given that certain conditions hold for content formalisms, a formal equivalence of AsTRa and a restricted modal logic can be proven. On this foundation, the AsTRa framework can naturally be extended with modal logic representation and reasoning mechanisms. Thus, a third level of reasoning becomes available in an *extended* AsTRa system.

A syntactical relationship between AT:ac expressions and modal logic expressions is fairly obvious: An assumption type label $AT = a_1 m_1 \ldots a_n m_n$ corresponds to a sequence of modal operators with modality and agent indices, $\mathcal{M}(AT) := \Box_{(m_1, a_1)} \ldots \Box_{(m_n, a_n)}$. Then, given that assumption contents can be transferred to FOPC, an AsTRa expression AT:ac corresponds to a modal expression $\mathcal{M}(AT)\, ac$. The multi-modal multi-agent logic, which exactly comprises such expressions, is called *assumption logic* (AL).

AsTRa requires that all expressions of a content formalism F can be translated to first-order logic. We call such formalisms *logic-based* if they additionally satisfy a second requirement: Their reasoning behavior must be sound w.r.t. FOPC entailment. Ideally it is also complete, i.e.:

$$\textbf{ask}_F(\text{KB}_{AT}, ac) = \textbf{true} \iff \text{KB}_{AT} \models ac \tag{1}$$

AL is a normal modal logic, so that the standard axioms hold for any operator $\Box_{(m,a)}$ in AL:

$$\Box_{(m,a)} \Phi \wedge \Box_{(m,a)}(\Phi \to \Psi) \to \Box_{(m,a)} \Psi \text{ (modal modus ponens)} \tag{2}$$

$$\Phi \to \Box_{(m,a)} \Phi \text{ (necessitation rule)} \tag{3}$$

AsTRa and AL are semantically equivalent if the following holds (let UMKB_{AL} be the UMKB reformulated as a set of AL formulas, and let $\vdash_{AL}$ be the derivability relation of AL):

$$\textbf{ask}(1, \text{UMKB}, AT\text{:}ac) = \textbf{true} \iff \text{UMKB}_{AL} \vdash_{AL} \mathcal{M}(AT)\, ac$$

This proposition can be proven if content formalisms satisfy proposition (1). Then, within assumption type knowledge bases modus ponens is applicable and tautologies of FOPC hold. These properties correspond to modal modus ponens (2) and the necessitation rule (3), respectively. Note that these conditions are not always desirable for user modeling; AsTRa implementations may decide to abandon them.

Given the syntactic and semantic relationships between AsTRa and the restricted modal logic AL, it is natural to extend AsTRa with representation and reasoning mechanisms for the corresponding unrestricted logic (called AL^+). In AL^+, both negative assumptions and system inference rules that express relationships between assumption types can be represented. For instance, the following formula states that the expression printed_on(userdoc,lw_plus) is not mutually believed:

$$\Box_{(B,S)} \neg\Box_{(B,M)} \text{ printed\_on}(userdoc, lw\_plus) \tag{4}$$

A rule for inferring a belief assumption (SBUB) from a goal assumption (SBUW) is

$$\forall doc, p \left[\Box_{(B,S)}\Box_{(W,U)} \text{ printed\_on}(doc, p) \rightarrow \Box_{(B,S)}\Box_{(B,U)} \text{ printable\_on}(doc, p)\right] \tag{5}$$

General relationships between assumption types may be expressed by modal formula schemes:

$$\left(\Box_{(B,S)}\Box_{(W,U)} \Phi \wedge \Box_{(B,S)}\Box_{(B,U)} (\Phi \rightarrow \Psi)\right) \rightarrow \Box_{(B,S)}\Box_{(W,U)} \Psi \tag{6}$$

(Φ and Ψ being formula variables) represents the (system) rule that users want any implication of their immediate goals if they know the implication relation.

Since both basic AsTRa expressions and extended UMKB contents can be represented as modal expressions, extended AsTRa representation and reasoning could be completely based on modal logic. However, with modal logic only, the possibility of flexibly using different formalisms for assumption contents and different reasoning levels would be abolished. This is especially disadvantageous if most parts of the UMKB can be represented within assumption types. Therefore, an extended AsTRa implementation keeps assumption types and contents. In addition, it implements modal reasoning functions **modal-tell**$(\text{UMKB}_{AL+}, \phi)$ and **modal-ask**$(\text{UMKB}_{AL+}, \phi)$, both receiving an AL^+ reformulation of the UMKB and an AL^+ expression ϕ as arguments. Then, AL^+ reasoning can be offered on a separate reasoning level, namely Level 2:

– **tell**$(2, \text{UMKB}, AT{:}ac) := \textbf{modal-tell}(\text{UMKB}_{AL+}, \mathcal{M}(AT)\,ac)$
  ask$(2, \text{UMKB}, AT{:}ac) := \textbf{modal-ask}(\text{UMKB}_{AL+}, \mathcal{M}(AT)\,ac)$

Thus, full expressive power becomes available, but the flexibility of AsTRa is not sacrificed. In order to make its internal mechanisms transparent to the user model developer, an extended AsTRa implementation may admit AL^+ as a uniform interface language for UMKB contents. This requires that simple AL expressions of the form $\mathcal{M}(AT)\,ac$ can be detected and, if desired, can be handled like their corresponding basic AsTRa expressions $AT{:}ac$.

3.3 BGP-MS Is an AsTRa Implementation

Since AsTRa was originally intended to be a formalization of the representation and reasoning mechanisms of BGP-MS, it is not surprising that BGP-MS fits into the framework:

1. Assumption types correspond to views in BGP-MS, which are organized in partition hierarchies with inheritance. Thus, BGP-MS exceeds the AsTRa framework (but does not violate its specification) in allowing inheritance relationships between assumption types.
2. SB-ONE and FOPC are available as content formalisms. They both satisfy the AsTRa conditions: First, they offer access functions **tell**, **ask**, **store**, and **fetch**, so that AsTRa knowledge base access at levels 0 and 1 can be realized; second, they are logic-based, i.e. their expressions can be translated into FOPC, and reasoning is sound w.r.t. first-order logic. FOPC reasoning is hybrid; i.e., it considers SB-ONE structures within views.

3. AL^+ representation and reasoning was realized (Pohl, 1996), so that BGP-MS is an extended AsTRa system offering knowledge base access on all three AsTRa reasoning levels.

However, the AsTRa framework is more than just the result of a formalization exercise. On the theoretical side, it provides a semantics in terms of modal logic for the representation and reasoning facilities of BGP-MS. This formal characterization is also a solid ground for modal logic reasoning in BGP-MS. E.g., specific reasoning mechanisms involving negative assumptions are currently being developed, which are derived from the modal logic semantics (cf. Pohl, 1997). On the practical side, the development of AsTRa led to several important changes to BGP-MS. These changes increase the degree of flexibility in BGP-MS significantly:

1. BGP-MS offers a standard set of modalities, B and W. An application developer is allowed to add further modalities to this set, according to application needs. So a wide range of assumption types is possible.
2. Following AsTRa, stereotypical assumptions about one user group may belong to different assumption types: BGP-MS implements stereotypes as sets of partitions. Each stereotype partition is associated with one view. If a stereotype applies to a user, all its partitions are linked to the appropriate view partitions.
3. The inner representation levels of BGP-MS, views and view contents, can be addressed directly. Specific languages $\mathcal{L}_{\text{SB-ONE}}$ and $\mathcal{L}_{\text{FOPC}}$ are available for formulating assumption contents ac in AsTRa expressions $AT{:}ac$. So the user model developer can better control how BGP-MS processes user modeling knowledge. However, the developer can still choose to employ modal logic as unique interface format for UMKB contents and let BGP-MS determine appropriate processing mechanisms.
4. BGP-MS offers a choice of three reasoning levels for knowledge base access: no reasoning, reasoning within views, and full modal logic reasoning.

Figure 1 shows a simple BGP-MS UMKB that could be used for modeling the user with respect to printing documents. The UMKB consists of four assumption types that involve modalities B and I (for "interest"). In addition, there are two stereotypes, NOVICE and EXPERT. EXPERT has only one stereotype partition, which is associated with the view SBUB, while NOVICE has two partitions, which are associated with SBUB and SBUI, respectively. The NOVICE stereotype is active, so that SBUB and SBUI inherit the contents of the NOVICE partitions. Hence, the SBUB view contains an SB-ONE structure corresponding to the $\mathcal{L}_{\text{SB-ONE}}$ expression (isa laserjet laserprinter) by stereotype inheritance and an FOPC formula corresponding to the $\mathcal{L}_{\text{FOPC}}$ expression laserjet(thunder). We present three queries to this UMKB (labelled "printing") to illustrate AsTRa reasoning (with basic mechanisms only) as implemented in BGP-MS.

1. **ask**$(0, \text{printing}, \text{SBUB}{:}(\text{isa laserjet laserprinter}))$ returns **true**, since an ISA relation between the concepts "laserjet" and "laserprinter" is explicitly contained in the view SBUB.
2. **ask**$(0, \text{printing}, \text{SBUB}{:}\text{laserprinter(thunder)})$ returns **false**, since in SBUB, the FOPC formula "laserprinter(thunder)" is not explicitly contained.
3. **ask**$(1, \text{printing}, \text{SBUB}{:}\text{laserprinter(thunder)})$ returns **true**, since FOPC reasoning (invoked via **ask**$_{\text{FOPC}}$) can infer the query expression using FOPC and SB-ONE contents of SBUB.

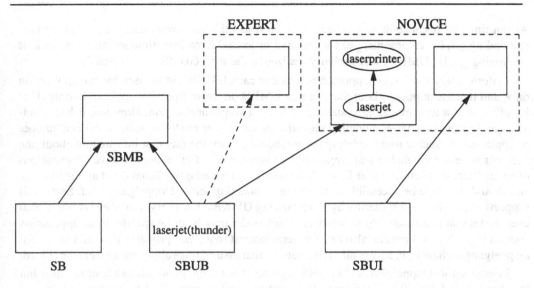

Figure 1. A simple UMKB in BGP-MS.

4 Flexibility Beyond Knowledge Bases: Domain-Based User Modeling

So far, we have discussed methods for representing knowledge in a UMKB and using it by accessing the UMKB. However, establishing flexible representation and UMKB access facilities is not sufficient for supporting the user modeling process in realistic adaptive applications. In addition, UMKBs (i.e., user models) need to be managed for developers and applications. This section describes a flexible approach to UMKB management in user modeling shell systems.

Typically, UMKBs are used during two phases of the user modeling process:

development time: User-independent user modeling knowledge is engineered for an application into a UMKB. In BGP-MS, assumption types and possible stereotypes are defined, system knowledge may be entered into assumption type SB, and system inference rules can be defined. Together with other user modeling data like dialog act types or interview definitions (cf. Kobsa and Pohl, 1995), a UMKB is maintained in a so-called *environment*, which can be saved in a file.

run time: A running application communicates with its user modeling system, reporting observations about the user and querying the current user model, which is maintained in a UMKB together with development time knowledge. In the currently distributed version of BGP-MS, an application accesses a development time environment, which is loaded from the file system. Messages from the application lead to user-specific entries into this environment.

Hence, there are mainly two kinds of UMKBs. A development time UMKB contains knowledge that is user-independent, but specific to an application A. A run time UMKB, which is accessed by an instance of A with a user U, contains both application data of A and the individual user model of U. In BGP-MS, such (A, U) UMKBs could be realized by employing user-specific copies of development time environments. These copies would be called (A, U) environments.

At run time, an instance of an application A must identify its current user U, so that the corresponding (A, U) environment can be created or loaded from long-time storage. The idea of employing (A, U) UMKBs was similarly realized in the shell GUMS (cf. Section 2).

Unfortunately, the (A, U) approach means that each UMKB can be used by one application only, and that assumptions about the user in a UMKB originate from one application only. This is sufficient if a user modeling system is built for a single application. However, it has disadvantages in centralized user modeling scenarios, where a user modeling system serves a number of applications. Such a user modeling server should exploit the fact that information about one user might be contributed to and employed by instances of different applications. Observations of an application A_i about a user U_r could be relevant to the adaptive behavior of application A_k and should therefore be accessible to it. The user modeling server Doppelgänger (cf. Section 2) supports such information sharing by modularizing UMKBs. For every user, there is one global user model that is divided into submodels. A submodel may be quite specific to an application domain (e.g., "news") but can also be of general interest (e.g., the "primary" data of a user). All Doppelgänger clients can access all submodels, so that assumptions about the user can be shared.

In contrast to Doppelgänger, BGP-MS represents not only assumptions about the user but also background data like system domain knowledge and stereotypes. So simply dividing user information into submodels is not appropriate. However, a similar idea has been employed for BGP-MS. Taken precisely, it is not *application* data that is set up at development time, but rather application *domain* data. Therefore, the (A, U) environments, which were suggested above as containers for run time UMKBs, should better be regarded as (D, U) environments that store the assumptions about a user U concerning a domain D together with other domain-specific data. There is no reason to constrain an application A_i to one domain only; user modeling data could be modularized into several domains $D_1, \ldots, D_n$. Vice versa, there is no reason to constrain a domain to be used by one application only. Another application A_k could make use of one or more domains from A_i and other applications, in addition to defining its own domains. If a domain D_y is shared by two applications, the corresponding (D_y, U) environments will be shared by their instances (cf. Figure 2).

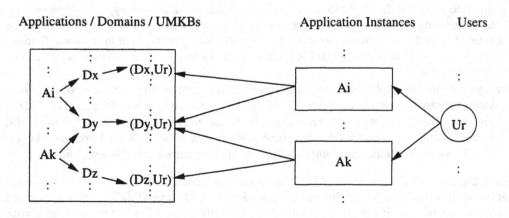

Figure 2. Applications, domains, application instances and users.

For a more illustrative example, imagine two applications "Adaptex" (a text processor) and "IntelliDraw" (a drawing tool), which both employ a centralized BGP-MS instance for user modeling. They make use of the domains "text-processing" and "vector-graphics", respectively, and share the domain "printing". Assume further that the user "WP" starts an instance of each of these applications. Using "IntelliDraw", he is observed to know the concept "PostScript", which leads to an entry of a corresponding SB-ONE concept into view SBUB in the "(printing,WP)" environment. When "WP" needs assistance in printing a document from "Adaptex", also the "(printing,WP)" environment is accessed, so that "WP" within "Adaptex" can also be assumed to know the concept "PostScript".

In sum, a new approach to managing user modeling knowledge on the UMKB level has been developed for BGP-MS, namely *domain-based user modeling*. Its main advantage is that user modeling knowledge needed by one application can be modularized and that this knowledge and the corresponding user model contents can be shared by other applications. In contrast to the approach of Doppelgänger, domain-based user modeling supports "knowledge-based user modeling" that makes use of domain-specific background knowledge.

Domain-based user modeling was developed and implemented in BGP-MS in order to realize server capabilities. At the same time, the communication interface of BGP-MS was also changed. Previously, BGP-MS could be accessed via a proprietary inter-process communication system from applications running on the same computer. Now BGP-MS offers a message interface based on KQML (Finin et al., 1994), the proposed standard communication language for knowledge-based agents. A KQML implementation is employed that permits communication with BGP-MS across the Internet. Due to domain-based user modeling, BGP-MS employs an extended syntax of KQML: First, some administrative message types ("performatives" in KQML terms) were added that allow registration of application instances and users. Second, additional parameters for domain and user information were introduced in standard performatives like "tell"; these parameters must be used to address the appropriate (D, U) environment. Currently, the European project AVANTI (Fink et al., 1997) uses BGP-MS in its distributed user modeling servers, which are the core elements of an adaptive World-Wide Web information system.

5   Summary and Future Work

In this paper, we presented mechanisms that are designed for employment in user modeling shell systems for (1) flexible representation and use of user modeling knowledge and (2) flexible management of UMKBs. The AsTRa knowledge representation framework was introduced. It basically allows expressions of logic-based formalisms to be maintained within partial knowledge bases that represent one type of assumption about the user (or other user modeling knowledge). These basic mechanisms can be related formally to modal logic and hence be extended with modal representation and reasoning. The AsTRa framework offers a rich and flexible choice of representation and reasoning possibilities. By allowing developers to define inference rules declaratively instead of providing fixed inference procedures, experiments with alternatives are possible. Flexibility is also gained with domain-based user modeling. This approach proposes an organization of user modeling knowledge and hence also of user models according to knowledge domains. An application may use one domain only or modularize its user modeling knowledge into several domains. In centralized user modeling systems that serve more than one application, sharing of domains and user models is possible.

Both AsTRa and domain-based user modeling have been implemented in the user modeling shell BGP-MS. Consequently, BGP-MS provides more powerful and more flexible features concerning knowledge representation and use than other shell systems (cf. Section 2). However, BGP-MS lags behind other shells with respect to the important aspect of handling the dynamics of user modeling knowledge. Other shell systems either use truth maintenance techniques in combination with logic-based representation or maintain changing evidence information. In principle, both approaches can be imagined as extensions to the core capabilities of the AsTRa framework. Since the framework focuses on logic-based mechanisms, truth maintenance techniques seem to be a natural add-on. But it would also be possible to assign evidence values to AsTRa UMKB contents. As in other evidence-oriented systems, they would originate from acquisition processes (i.e., also from logic-based reasoning), and could be retrieved from the user model. The integration of evidence information into BGP-MS is planned as future work.

References

Brajnik, G., and Tasso, C. (1994). A shell for developing non-monotonic user modeling systems. *International Journal of Human-Computer Studies* 40:31–62.

Cohen, P. R. (1978). On knowing what to say: Planning speech acts. Technical Report 118, Department of Computer Science, University of Toronto, Canada.

Finin, T., Fritzson, R., McKay, D., and McEntire, R. (1994). KQML as an agent communication language. In *Third International Conference on Knowledge and Information Management*, 456–463. New York, NY: ACM Press.

Finin, T. W. (1989). GUMS: A general user modeling shell. In Kobsa, A., and Wahlster, W., eds., *User Models in Dialog Systems*. Berlin, Heidelberg: Springer. 411–430.

Fink, J., Kobsa, A., and Nill, A. (1997). Adaptable and adaptive information access for all users, including the disabled and the elderly. In this volume.

Kay, J. (1995). The um toolkit for reusable, long term user models. *User Modeling and User-Adapted Interaction* 4(3):149–196.

Kobsa, A., and Pohl, W. (1995). The user modeling shell system BGP-MS. *User Modeling and User-Adapted Interaction* 4(2):59–106.

Kobsa, A. (1985). *Benutzermodellierung in Dialogsystemen*. Berlin, Heidelberg: Springer-Verlag.

Kobsa, A. (1992). Towards inferences in BGP-MS: Combining modal logic and partition hierarchies for user modeling. In *Proceedings of the Third International Workshop on User Modeling*, 35–41.

Orwant, J. (1995). Heterogeneous learning in the Doppelgänger user modeling system. *User Modeling and User-Adapted Interaction* 4(2):107–130.

Paiva, A., and Self, J. (1995). TAGUS—A user and learner modeling workbench. *User Modeling and User-Adapted Interaction* 4(3):197–226.

Pohl, W. (1996). Combining partitions and modal logic for user modeling. In Gabbay, D. M., and Ohlbach, H. J., eds., *Practical Reasoning: Proceedings of the International Conference on Formal and Applied Practical Reasoning*, 480–494. Berlin, Heidelberg: Springer.

Pohl, W. (1997). *Logic-Based Representation and Inference for User Modeling Shell Systems*. Ph.D. Dissertation, University of Essen. Forthcoming.

Rich, E. (1979). User modeling via stereotypes. *Cognitive Science* 3:329–354.

Russell, S., and Norvig, P. (1995). *Artificial Intelligence: A Modern Approach*. Upper Saddle River, NJ: Prentice-Hall.

Taylor, J. A., Carletta, J., and Mellish, C. (1996). Requirements for belief models in cooperative dialogue. *User Modeling and User-Adapted Interaction* 6(1):23–68.

Managing Temporal Knowledge in Student Modeling

Paolo Giangrandi and Carlo Tasso

Department of Mathematics and Computer Science, University of Udine, Italy

Abstract. Changes in the user's knowledge represent an important factor to be considered, particularly in the dialogue between a tutoring system and a student. In previous work we have proposed a representation formalism for describing the status and the evolution over time of a temporal student model. The specific goal of this paper is to show what algorithms can be used to manage such a temporal student model. The use of temporal constraints allows a system to cope with uncertainty and incompleteness in the information available about the student's knowledge through the description of temporal information on different levels of precision. Furthermore, nonmonotonic inferences are exploited in order to extend the temporal information available about the student's knowledge. Finally, by introducing suitable temporal constraints into the student model, we handle in a uniform and elegant way the problem of the existence of possible contradictions in the student's knowledge.

1 Introduction

A *student model* (Greer and McCalla, 1994) describes the knowledge of the student in a specific subject domain and it is used for designing appropriate tutorial and remedial actions that are tailored to him. Many intelligent tutoring systems are based on the hypothesis that the student's knowledge does not change during the tutorial session; accordingly, the student model is built without considering the different moments at which data about the student have been collected. This hypothesis makes it possible to simplify the modeling process greatly, but unfortunately it seems too far removed from a realistic view (cf. Huang et al., 1991; Kono et al., 1994; Paiva et al., 1994; Paiva and Self, 1994; Errico, 1996). Let us consider the dialogue excerpt given in Figure 1, taken from the classic paper of Stevens and Collins (1982, p. 18) in the domain of meteorology, where t_7, t_8, etc., refer to different instants in the dialogue.

This dialogue illustrates several points related to time:

1. A student's beliefs may change quickly in a meaningful way because the student learns new concepts, revises previously acquired concepts, or forgets old concepts. For instance, while at t_7 the student is seen to believe that in Washington and Oregon it is cold, the tutor's remark in t_8 causes a change in his knowledge.
2. It is often difficult to identify the persistence of beliefs in student's mind precisely. For instance, before instant t_{28} it is not clear if the student believes the concept "an obstacle represented by mountains or by a cold air mass causes a moving air mass to rise".

... (t_7) *Tutor:* Do you know what the climate is like in Washington and Oregon?

Student: Is it cold?

(t_8) *Tutor:* No, it is rather mild. Can you guess about the rainfall there?

Student: Normal I guess.

(t_9) *Tutor:* Well, the Japan current which starts in the south-eastern Pacific, flows along the coast of Japan and across the North Pacific ending up off the coast of Washington and Oregon. How do you think that current affects the climate there?

Student: It's probably rainy.

(t_{10}) *Tutor:* It is indeed very wet, there are rain forests in both Washington and Oregon. What does that tell you about the temperature of the Japan current?

Student: It's warm.

(t_{11}) *Tutor:* Right. Where do you think the wind blows in that area?

Student: Towards Washington and Oregon.

(t_{12}) *Tutor:* From where?

Student: From the sea.

(t_{13}) *Tutor:* Right again. What do you think happens to the moist air blown over Washington and Oregon by those winds?

Student: It condenses and it rains.

(t_{14}) *Tutor:* Yes, why?

Student: Because the moist air cools and the clouds can't hold the water so it rains.

(t_{15}) *Tutor:* OK, what causes the moist air to cool?

Student: It cools when the wind blows it and it lowers from the sky.

(t_{16}) *Tutor:* What happens to the temperature of moist air when it rises?

Student: It gets warm.

(t_{17}) *Tutor:* No. Warm air rises, but as it rises it cools off. Do you think the mountains in Washington and Oregon have anything to do with cooling the moist air blowing in off the coast?

Student: Yes.

(t_{18}) *Tutor:* How?

Student: As it rises, or even if it doesn't rise, the cold mountains could cool it off.

(t_{19}) *Tutor:* No, contact with a cold object does not provide enough cooling to an air mass to cause

rain. Rainfall is almost always the result of cooling due to rising air. How do you think the mountains might affect the rising of the moist air from over the ocean?

Student: I'm not sure.

(t_{20}) *Tutor:* When the air is blown against the mountains it has to rise to get over them. As it rises it cools and rainfall occurs. Can you guess what the average rainfall is like on the other side of the mountains?

Student: It's probably heavy.

(t_{21}) *Tutor:* No, almost all the moisture condenses out on the ocean side of the mountains, then once the air has passed over the mountains it settles back down in altitude and warms up so there is very little rainfall. In fact the climate east of the Rockies is very dry. Do you see the relationship between the mountains in Washington and Oregon and the cold air mass that sits over Ireland most of the time?

Student: I think so.

(t_{22}) *Tutor:* What do you think it is?

Student: The cold air mass stays low, and warm enough so it doesn't rain.

(t_{23}) *Tutor:* Let's review why it rains in Ireland. Where does the moist air come from there?

Student: From the Gulf Stream.

(t_{24}) *Tutor:* Right. Now what happens when that warm moist air from over the Gulf Stream is blown over Ireland?

Student: It condenses.

(t_{25}) *Tutor:* Right, but why?

Student: Because the air rises and cools.

(t_{26}) *Tutor:* Right again, now can you tell me what causes the air to rise over Ireland?

Student: The wind?

(t_{27}) *Tutor:* The wind moves the air, but that is not what causes it to rise. Do you think the cold air mass that is usually sitting over Ireland might be important?

Student: If it just sits there it is.

(t_{28}) *Tutor:* What happens when the warmer moist air is blown in off the water and hits the stationary cold air mass?

Student: It makes it rise ...

Figure 1. A Socratic dialogue example. (From Stevens and Collins, 1982, p. 18.)

3. A student's beliefs may appear contradictory to an external observer if possible changes are not considered. For instance, at t_{16} the student believes that moist air gets warm when it rises, but this belief is contradictory with what the student is seen to believe at t_{25} if we do not take into account the change that occurred in his knowledge.

In a previous paper (Giangrandi and Tasso, 1996) we have criticized the concept of a *static* student model, i.e., a model which describes the student's knowledge without considering the possible evolution in time; and we have presented and motivated a proposal for a *temporal* student model, i.e. a description of the temporal history of the student's knowledge that includes all the information about the student and makes it possible to explain the student's behaviour for both the past and the current interaction. In the same paper, we introduced a new and original formalism for the representation of a temporal student model.

The goal of this paper is to present an original proposal for managing a temporal student model. The innovative characteristic of our work is a presentation of algorithms that can be used for managing such a temporal student model. In the following section, we review the concept of a temporal student model and we deal with the problem of extending a student model non-monotonically. Section 3 introduces the use of temporal constraints as a way of dealing with uncertainty in the description of temporal knowledge. In Section 4 we analyze the different factors to be considered in an effort to maintain consistency in the student model. Section 5 concludes the paper.

2   The Basic Representation of a Temporal Student Model

The *student model* contains all the information about the student which has been directly observed or derived during the modeling process. More specifically, it describes domain concepts (called *student's beliefs*) which are supposed to mirror what the student knows or does not know about the domain knowledge, including both correct and incorrect concepts.

As was illustrated thoroughly by Giangrandi and Tasso (1996), the basic formalism for representing a temporal student model is consists of temporal formulas. More specifically:

– $B_S(t,\alpha)$, means that at time t the student S believes the concept α, where α refers to a correct (or incorrect) concept of the domain represented by a formula in the propositional calculus;[1]
– $B_S(t_1,t_2,\alpha)$, means that the student S believes the concept α in the time interval spanning from t_1 to t_2.

For instance, referring to the domain of meteorology introduced in Figure 1, the formula $BI_S(t_1,t_2,\text{warm\_moist\_air} \Rightarrow \text{rising\_of\_moist\_air})$ has the intuitive meaning *"The student S believes the concept "warm_moist_air implies rising_of_ moist_air" in the time interval spanning from t_1 to t_2".* In this work we assume a total order for time (i.e., linear time), but in the earlier paper (Giangrandi and Tasso, 1996) we investigated the use of branching time as a way of managing many alternative hypotheses. A *temporal student model* consists of a set of temporal belief formulas.

---

[1] We are currently working on the extension of our representation language to the predicate calculus.

During the tutorial session, it is generally possible to observe the student's use of domain concepts: These are referred to as *explicit beliefs*. The tutorial interaction generally allows a system to observe that the student knows (or does not know) a few domain concepts and, moreover, to observe their application only at specific moments. Concepts which are observed during the tutorial session are called *explicit beliefs*. From explicit beliefs it is possible to hypothesize that the student knows other beliefs by assuming that he behaves logically, following sound inferences: These beliefs are referred to as *implicit beliefs*. For instance, let us assume that we have the following observations in the situation t:

1. $B_S(t, cooling\_of\_moist\_air)$
2. $B_S(t, cooling\_of\_moist\_air \Rightarrow condensed\_moist\_air)$
3. $B_S(t, condensed\_moist\_air \Rightarrow showers\_in\_Washington\_Oregon)$

The student model can be extended with the following implicit beliefs:

4. $BS(t, condensed\_moist\_air)$

derived from 1 and 2; and

5. $BS(t, showers\_in\_Washington\_Oregon)$

derived from 3 and 4.

In the example of the previous section, all the explicit beliefs refer to the same instant of time, and so do the derived implicit beliefs. A different problem concerns the derivation of implicit beliefs across different situations. More precisely, let α be a concept applied by the student during the tutorial interaction and let t be a situation for which no direct observation of the concept α is available: What can be deduced concerning the state of knowledge of α in the situation t from the available observations? A simple and direct solution of this problem is based on *frame axioms* (McCarthy and Hayes, 1969). This solution, however, presents two main drawbacks: (i) it generally needs the introduction of a lot of frame axioms; and (ii) moreover, in our case it is usually very difficult (or even impossible) to know about occurrences of learning and forgetting events, and without this information the frame axioms are not applicable.

An alternative solution to this problem consists in "extending temporally" the observations included in the student model through a nonmonotonic reasoning approach (Ginsberg, 1987). Intuitively, when we observe that the student believes a concept at a given moment then, lacking evidence to the contrary, we hypothesize that the student believes that concept also before and after the specific time of observation. We call this rule the *nonmonotonic temporal inference*, or *NMTI rule*. This idea is formalized in the two following default rules:

1. If the student is seen to know the concept α at the instant t, and it is consistent (with the other available observations and beliefs) to assume he knows this concept in a time interval (a, b) containing t, then assume he knows the concept in that interval.

    $B_S(t, \alpha) \wedge a \leq t \leq b : BI_S(a, b, \alpha) / BI_S(a, b, \alpha)$

2. If the student shows not to know the concept α in the instant t, and it is consistent (with the other available observations and beliefs) to assume he does not know this concept in a time interval (a, b) containing t, then assume he does not know the concept in that interval.

$$\neg B_S(t, \alpha) \wedge a \leq t \leq b : \neg BI_S(a, b, \alpha) / \neg BI_S(a, b, \alpha)$$

An observation which allows the system to derive a belief is called a *supporting observation*.

Example 1. Let us consider the observations shown in Figure 2.

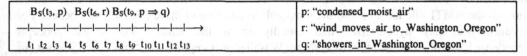

$B_S(t_3, p)$ $B_S(t_6, r)$ $B_S(t_9, p \Rightarrow q)$	p: "condensed_moist_air"
t_1 t_2 t_3 t_4 t_5 t_6 t_7 t_8 t_9 t_{10} t_{11} t_{12} t_{13}	r: "wind_moves_air_to_Washington_Oregon"
	q: "showers_in_Washington_Oregon"

Figure 2. Example 1.

This figure illustrates the case of three concepts observed at different instants. On the basis of these observations we may assume through the NMTI rule, for instance, the following beliefs:

1. $BI_S(t_1, t_{13}$, condensed_moist_air)
2. $BI_S(t_1, t_{13}$, wind_moves_air_to_Washington_Oregon)
3. $BI_S(t_1, t_{13}$, condensed_moist_air $\Rightarrow$ showers_in_Washington_Oregon)

The NMTI rule allows us to derive several beliefs from the same observations, differing only in the width of the respective time intervals, for instance:

1. $BI_S(t_2, t_6$, condensed_moist_air)
2. $BI_S(t_1, t_7$, wind_moves_air_to_Washington_Oregon)
3. $BI_S(t_4, +\infty$, condensed_moist_air $\Rightarrow$ showers_in_Washington_Oregon)
4. $BI_S(t_4, t_6$, showers_in_Washington_Oregon)

(Belief 4 derives from the beliefs 1 and 3, where the time interval (t_4, t_6) is the interval common to the beliefs 1 and 3.) In Section 3, we will consider a more general representation based on the use of temporal constraints in order to capture all of the different possibilities.

The application of the NMTI rule requires specific care in order to avoid the generation of inconsistencies among different beliefs, as is illustrated in the following example.

Example 2. Let us reconsider the previous example and now suppose that a new observation $B_S(t_{12}, \neg q)$ is acquired, as depicted in Figure 3 (where p, q, and r have the same meaning as in the previous example).

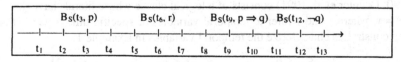

$B_S(t_3, p)$	$B_S(t_6, r)$	$B_S(t_9, p \Rightarrow q)$ $B_S(t_{12}, \neg q)$
t_1 t_2 t_3 t_4	t_5 t_6 t_7	t_8 t_9 t_{10} t_{11} t_{12} t_{13}

Figure 3. Example 2.

In this case, it is not possible to assume

1. $BI_S(t_1, t_{13}, condensed\_moist\_air)$
2. $BI_S(t_1, t_{13}, wind\_moves\_air\_to\_Washington\_Oregon)$
3. $BI_S(t_1, t_{13}, condensed\_moist\_air \Rightarrow showers\_in\_Washington\_Oregon)$
4. $BI_S(t_1, t_{13}, \neg showers\_in\_Washington\_Oregon)$,

since the three beliefs 1, 3 and 4 are inconsistent. A consistent extension of the three observations through the NMTI rule has to avoid the temporal overlapping of these contradictory beliefs. For instance, we may hypothesize[2] that initially in t_1 the student knows the concepts "condensed_moist_air", "wind_moves_air_to_Washington_Oregon" and "condensed_ moist_air $\Rightarrow$ showers_in_Washington_Oregon" and does not know the concept "¬ showers_in_Washington_ Oregon", and that later, at t_8, he removes (or forgets) the concept "condensed_moist_air", and starts to believe the concept "¬ showers_in_Washington_ Oregon":

1. $BI_S(t_1, t_8, condensed\_moist\_air)$
2. $BI_S(t_1, t_{13}, wind\_moves\_air\_to\_Washington\_Oregon)$
3. $BI_S(t_1, t_{13}, condensed\_moist\_air \Rightarrow showers\_in\_Washington\_Oregon)$
4. $BI_S(t_8, t_{13}, \neg showers\_in\_Washington\_Oregon)$

Since the precise points in time at which the student changes his beliefs are usually not known, in the following section we illustrate the use of temporal constraints to manage this kind of uncertainty.

3   Working With Temporal Constraints

The NMTI rule causes two important problems: (i) from a given observation, the rule allows us to derive several beliefs differing in the width of the time interval, and we need to capture all of these different derivations; (ii) we often do not know the precise starting and ending points of beliefs, and we need to deal with this uncertainty. To this end, we generalize the representation of beliefs by introducing *temporal variables* in the specification of the bounds of beliefs. This means replacing the specific time instants t_1, t_2, t_4, etc. (i.e., temporal constants) with the temporal variables a_1, b_1, a_2, etc., whose values may range over time instants. For Example 1 the results are as follows:

1. $BI_S(a_1, b_1, condensed\_moist\_air)$
2. $BI_S(a_2, b_2, wind\_moves\_air\_to\_Washington\_Oregon)$
3. $BI_S(a_3, b_3, condensed\_moist\_air \Rightarrow showers\_in\_Washington\_Oregon)$

The values of temporal variables may range according to *temporal constraints*: Each such (Vilain et al. 1990; Dechter et al. 1991) consists of a logical clause whose literals have the form $x < y$, or $x > y$, or $x = y$, where x and y refer to temporal variables or specific time instants. For instance, the following constraints characterize the temporal variables in Example 1:

$$a_1 \le t_3 \le b_1 \qquad a_2 \le t_6 \le b_2 \qquad a_3 \le t_9 \le b_3$$

---

[2] Obviously, other different evolutionary hypotheses are possible for these concepts.

In this way, the interval of each belief may vary, with the only constraint being that it must contain the instant (or interval) of its supporting observation.

Temporal constraints allow us to specify the width of the student's beliefs with different degrees of precision. At the beginning of an interaction, few data about the student are available and thus temporal variables (delimiting the temporal persistency of beliefs) often range over wide intervals. As further information about the student becomes available, it is possible to add new constraints to the student model, which restrict the range of variability of beliefs. This process allow us to increase the precision in the description of the evolution of the student's knowledge.

Contradictions among student's beliefs are removed through the addition of suitable temporal constraints to the student model. Let us reconsider Example 2 in terms of temporal constraints (with $BI_S(a_4, b_4, \neg showers\_in\_Washington\_Oregon)$ constrained by $a_4 \leq t_{12} \leq b_4$). Since we do not know the specific instant at which the student removes the concept "condensed_moist_air" and learns "$\neg showers\_in\_Washington\_Oregon$", this fact is left uncertain through the general temporal constraint $b_1 < a_4$: The student forgets/removes the concept "condensed_moist_air" before learning the concept "$\neg showers\_in\_Washington\_Oregon$" even though it is not known when these two changes (precisely) occur. The contradiction is avoided because the knowledge of the concept "$\neg showers\_in\_Washington\_Oregon$" does not temporally overlap the knowledge of the concept "showers_in_Washington_Oregon".

The uncertainty about the precise temporal boundaries of the beliefs contained in the student model has the consequence that it is usually not possible to conclude certainly whether the student believes (or does not know) a concept in a given instant but only to consider hypotheses about the student's knowledge. For instance, according to the beliefs and constraints of the (revised) Example 2,

1. $BI_S(a_1, b_1, condensed\_moist\_air)$
2. $BI_S(a_2, b_2, wind\_moves\_air\_to\_Washington\_Oregon)$
3. $BI_S(a_3, b_3, condensed\_moist\_air \Rightarrow showers\_in\_Washington\_Oregon)$
4. $BI_S(a_4, b_4, \neg showers\_in\_Washington\_Oregon)$

with:

$$a_1 \leq t_3 \leq b_1 ; \quad a_2 \leq t_6 \leq b_2 ; \quad a_3 \leq t_9 \leq b_3 ; \quad a_4 \leq t_{12} \leq b_4 ; \quad b_1 < a_4,$$

we can hypothesize that the student believes "condensed_moist_air" in t_1 or in t_5, but not in t_{13}, since $a_1 \leq b_1 < a_4 \leq t_{12} < t_{13}$. Similarly, if we hypothetically assume that the student believes the concept "condensed_moist_air" in t_7 (by hypothesizing $b_1 \geq t_7$), we cannot hypothesize also that the student believes "$\neg showers\_in\_Washington\_Oregon$" in t_7 or in any instant previous to t_7, because $t_7 \leq b_1 < a_4$.

4   Managing a Temporal Student Model

During the tutorial interaction, the modeler analyzes the student's behaviour and, on the basis of the concepts which the student is seen to apply or not to know, it updates the student model. In our work, we assume that at any instant the student believes a consistent set of concepts. This means that the student may have contradictory knowledge over different times, but the knowledge observed at a given time is consistent.

A (temporal) student model consists of a set of beliefs and a set of temporal constraints.[3] The task of the student modeler consists in managing beliefs and temporal constraints contained in the student model, in maintaining consistency, and in updating the student model with new observations. Every time a new observation is collected, a corresponding belief is created through exploitation of the NMTI rule and is added to the student model. In particular, the interval of each belief is constrained to contain the time point (or the time interval) of the supporting observation (we call these constraints related to observations, *observation constraints*), as is indicated in Table 1. These constraints are obviously not sufficient to assure consistency among beliefs. The following sub-sections describe the general procedure applied in order to maintain consistency in the student model.

Table 1. Observation constraints.

Observations	Beliefs	Observation constraints
The student applies α in t	$BI_S(a, b, \alpha)$	$a \le t \le b$
The student applies α in the interval from t_1 to t_2	$BI_S(a, b, \alpha)$	$a \le t_1 \le t_2 \le b$
The student does not know α in t	$\neg BI_S(a, b, \alpha)$	$a \le t \le b$
The student does not know α in the interval from t_1 to t_2	$\neg BI_S(a, b, \alpha)$	$a \le t_1 \le t_2 \le b$

4.1 Restoring Consistency Among Beliefs

Let us consider first the concept of a *minimal conflict set,* (derived from de Kleer and Williams, 1987; Reiter 1987). A *conflict set* is a contradictory set of beliefs. A conflict set is *minimal* if f no proper subset of it is a conflict set. A *conflict region* for a conflict set is the time interval common to all the time intervals of the beliefs included in the minimal conflict set. Conflict sets may be computed through the exploitation of a sound and complete theorem prover which generates all refutations of the beliefs, and which, for each such refutation, records the beliefs entering into the refutation in order to determine the corresponding conflict set. Conflict sets play a fundamental role for modeling the temporal evolution of the student's knowledge, since they make it possible to identify possible changes in the student's knowledge. In this section we consider the problem of how to revise a single conflict set, whereas in Section 4.2 we deal with the problem of managing multiple conflict sets.

Let us consider a conflict set that includes n beliefs $BI_S(a_i, b_i, \alpha_i)$, for $i = 1, ..., n$; let (a_i, b_i) be the time interval for each belief. The conflict region $R = (a_R, b_R)$ is computed as $R = \cap_i (a_i, b_i) = (\max_i a_i, \min_i b_i)$. A contradiction arises when the intersection among beliefs is a non-empty time interval and determines the need to modify some beliefs contained in the student model in order to restore consistency. More specifically, it is necessary to modify the intervals of the beliefs included in the student model by clipping the time intervals of a suitable set of beliefs.[4] For a given

---

[3] In this paper, we focus the attention on the representation of student's beliefs. In general, other kinds of information about the student may be considered in a student model (Giangrandi and Tasso, 1995; Greer and McCalla, 1994).

[4] The idea of clipping time intervals of assertions in order to maintain consistency in a temporal knowledge base was introduced by Dean and McDermott (1987).

belief $BI_S(a, b, \alpha)$ two different kinds of clipping are possible: (i) a *left clipping*, which involves clipping the time interval of the belief on the left-hand side by constraining the lower bound a to a higher value; (ii) a *right clipping*, which involves constraining the upper bound b to a lower value. Before dealing with the general problem, we examine the following simple example.

Example 3. Let us consider the following observations: $B_S(t_1, \text{mild\_in\_Washington\_Oregon})$ and $B_S(t_2, \neg\text{mild\_in\_Washington\_Oregon})$ (with $t_1 < t_2$). From these two observations we obtain the beliefs $BI_S(a_1, b_1, \text{mild\_in\_Washington\_Oregon})$ and $BI_S(a_2, b_2, \neg\text{mild\_in\_Washington\_Oregon})$, with the following constraints: $a_1 \leq t_1 \leq b_1$, $a_2 \leq t_2 \leq b_2$. The contradiction $\{BI_S(a_1, b_1, \text{mild\_in\_Washington\_Oregon}), BI_S(a_2, b_2, \neg\text{mild\_in\_Washington\_Oregon})\}$ is removed if the time interval of the first belief is not allowed to overlap the time interval of the second belief. This fact is expressed by the following disjunction: $a_1 > b_2 \lor a_2 > b_1$—that is, the time interval (a_1, b_1) precedes the interval (a_2, b_2) or, vice versa, the interval (a_2, b_2) precedes the interval (a_1, b_1). Since the literal $a_1 > b_2$ is not consistent with the available observation constraints (because it results in $a_1 \leq t_1 < t_2 \leq b_2$), the previous disjunction simplifies to $a_2 > b_1$. This means that it is appropriate to right clip the belief $BI_S(a_1, b_1, \text{mild\_in\_Washington\_Oregon})$ and to left clip the belief $BI_S(a_2, b_2, \neg\text{mild\_in\_Washington\_Oregon})$. For this reason, we call the constraint $a_2 > b_1$ a *clipping constraint*.

In general, when a conflict set includes more than two beliefs, the revision is accomplished by imposing a *non-overlapping condition* for pairs of time intervals of beliefs in the conflict set. As in the previous example, this non-overlapping condition can be formulated in terms of temporal constraints (clipping constraints) in the following way:

1. $a_1 > b_2 \lor a_1 > b_3 \lor ... \lor a_1 > b_n \lor$
2. $a_2 > b_1 \lor a_2 > b_3 \lor ... \lor a_2 > b_n \lor ... \lor$
3. $a_n > b_1 \lor a_n > b_2 \lor ... \lor a_n > b_{n-1}$.

Each literal $a_i > b_j$ represents a possible pair of clippings: The belief $BI_S(a_i, b_i, \alpha_i)$ is left clipped while the belief $BI_S(a_j, b_j, \alpha_j)$ is right clipped. Furthermore, each literal can also be interpreted as a possible change in the student's knowledge: The student forgets/removes α_i before learning α_j.

As in Example 3, several literals of the previous disjunction can be dropped since they are false given the observational constraints: (i) the literal $a_i > b_j$ when the observation of the concept α_i precedes the observation of the concept α_j; (ii) the literals $a_i > b_j$ and $a_j > b_i$ when the observation of the concept α_i overlaps (totally or partially) the observation of the concept α_j.

Example 4. Let us reconsider Example 2; the (minimal) conflict set is

1. $BI_S(a_1, b_1, \text{condensed\_moist\_air})$
2. $BI_S(a_3, b_3, \text{condensed\_moist\_air}) \Rightarrow \text{showers\_in\_Washington\_Oregon})$
3. $BI_S(a_4, b_4, \neg\text{showers\_in\_Washington\_Oregon})$

with the observation constraints:

$$a_1 \leq t_3 \leq b_1 \; ; \quad a_2 \leq t_6 \leq b_2 \; ; \quad a_3 \leq t_9 \leq b_3 \; ; \quad a_4 \leq t_{12} \leq b_4.$$

By imposing the not-overlapping condition we derive the following clipping constraint:

$$\underline{a_1 > b_3} \lor \underline{a_1 > b_4} \lor a_3 > b_1 \lor \underline{a_3 > b_4} \lor a_4 > b_1 \lor a_4 > b_3$$

Since the underlined literals are false (they are not consistent with the available observations), the disjunction simplifies to $a_3 > b_1 \vee a_4 > b_1 \vee a_4 > b_3$. This constraint describes three possible evolutions:

- before learning the concept "condensed_moist_air $\Rightarrow$ showers_in_Washington_Oregon", the student forgets the concept "condensed_moist_air" (these changes may occur between t_3 and t_9);
- before learning the concept "not showers_in_Washington_Oregon", the student forgets the concept "condensed_moist_air" (these changes may occur between t_3 and t_{12});
- before learning the concept "not showers_in_Washington_Oregon", the student forgets the concept "condensed_moist_air $\Rightarrow$ showers_in_Washington_Oregon" (these changes may occur between t_9 and t_{12}).

4.2 Revising Multiple Conflict Sets

Given a set of beliefs, several conflict sets may occur, and their dependency has to be considered when revising the student model, because the same clippings of beliefs may "adjust" different conflict sets. Intuitively, we aim at explaining the student's behaviour by means of the simplest evolution for his domain knowledge. Therefore, in order to revise the student model we do not proceed with arbitrary clippings but we conform to a principle of minimal change: *We assume that the student changes his beliefs as little as possible consistently with the observed behaviour.* Since each clipping represents a belief change when attempting to restore consistency we aim to perform as few clippings as possible.

Example 5. Let us consider the situation depicted in Figure 4, in which p and q have the same meaning as in Example 1.

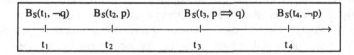

Figure 4. Example 5.

This situation gives rise to the following beliefs:

$$BI_S(a_1, b_1, \neg q), \qquad BI_S(a_2, b_2, p), \qquad BI_S(a_3, b_3, p \Rightarrow q), \qquad BI_S(a_4, b_4, \neg p)$$

(with $a_i \leq t_i \leq b_i$). This student model includes two minimal conflict sets:

1. $C_1 = \{BI_S(a_1, b_1, \neg q), BI_S(a_2, b_2, p), BI_S(a_3, b_3, p \Rightarrow q)\}$
2. $C_2 = \{BI_S(a_2, b_2, p), BI_S(a_4, b_4, \neg p)\}$

When these conflict sets are considered independently, they allow us to derive the following two clipping constraints (according to the process described in Section 4.1):

$$a_2 > b_1 \vee a_3 > b_1 \vee a_3 > b_2 \qquad\qquad a_4 > b_2$$

However, since the belief $BI_S(a_2, b_2, p)$ is common to the two conflict sets, we can notice that a suitable right clipping of the belief $BI_S(a_2, b_2, p)$ (and, correspondingly, the left clipping of other beliefs) can adjust the two conflict sets. This means that we prefer the hypothesis about the student removing/forgetting a single concept instead of the hypotheses about the removal of several concepts.

Example 5 suggests the strategy of considering beliefs common to different (minimal) conflict sets in order to minimize the number of clippings: We look for the (right and left) clippings which "cover" as many conflict sets as possible. More precisely, since each constraint is true when at least one of its literals is true, we look for a "minimal" set of literals which "cover" all the given temporal constraints computed by considering each conflict set independently.[5]

In Example 5, it is possible to identify two minimal set of literals covering both constraints given above:

H_1, 4 clippings: $a_2 > b_1, a_4 > b_2$
H_2, 4 clippings: $a_3 > b_1, a_4 > b_2$
H_3, 3 clippings: $a_3 > b_2, a_4 > b_2$

Each literal $a_j > b_i$ represents a pair of clippings, but when several clippings refer to the same temporal variable, they are counted as a single clipping (because the most restrictive constraint subsumes the others). Following the principle of minimal change, the set H_3 is preferred to the others for revision because it involves fewer clippings.

5 Conclusion

The consideration of time in student modeling appears to be very useful, since it makes it possible to monitor step by step a learning process which is inherently dynamic. A relevant example, also considered in our work, is constituted by intelligent tutoring systems based on Socratic dialogue: These systems could benefit from temporal student modeling so as to represent the evolution of the student knowledge during the dialogue better and in a more fine-grained way. The specific goal of this paper has been the illustration of the algorithms which can be used for managing a temporal student model. Two fundamental features characterize our proposal: 1. We use non-monotonic inferences in order to extend the temporal information available about the student's knowledge. 2. We use temporal constraints in order to deal with uncertainty about the information concerning the student by describing temporal knowledge at different levels of precision. By introducing suitable clipping constraints in the student model, we handle the problem of the existence of possible contradictions among the student's beliefs. Clipping constraints inferred from contradictions (more specifically, from conflict sets) are the basis for identifying plausible changes in the student's knowledge, and the minimization of the number of clippings allows us to explain the student's behaviour in terms of the simplest temporal evolution of the student's knowledge.

Giangrandi and Tasso (1996) deal with two further issues not considered here: branching time for the handling of multiple hypotheses; and nested beliefs for the distinction of the student's beliefs from the tutor's beliefs. We are currently implementing a student model manager based on our new proposal, i.e., a module devoted to the temporal management of all the information re-

---

[5] This idea is similar to the concept of a *hitting set* used in (Reiter, 1987).

sulting from the analysis of the student's behaviour. For this purpose, beliefs are represented and handled through an ATMS (de Kleer, 1986) that is extended to deal with temporal aspects. Furthermore, temporal reasoning over the available temporal information is performed with temporal networks managed by a temporal reasoner that is based on van Beek's (1990) algorithm.

Finally, for the description of domain knowledge we intend to extend our approach from the propositional calculus to the predicate calculus.

References

Dean, T., and McDermott, D. (1987). Temporal data base management. *Artificial Intelligence* 1-55.

Dechter, R., Meiri, I., and Pearl, J. (1991). Temporal constraint networks. *Artificial Intelligence* 49:61-95.

Errico, B. (1996). Student modeling in the situation calculus. In Brna, P., Paiva, A., and Self, J., eds., *Proceedings of the European Conference on Artificial Intelligence in Education*.

de Kleer, J. (1986). An assumption-based TMS. Reprinted in Ginsberg, M. L., ed., *Readings in Nonmonotonic Reasoning*. Morgan Kaufmann, 1987. 280-297.

de Kleer, J., and Williams, B. (1987). Diagnosing multiple faults. *Artificial Intelligence* 32:97-130.

Gärdenfors, P. (1992). Belief revision. In *Handbook of Logic in AI and Logic Programming*.

Giangrandi, P., and Tasso, C. (1995). Truth maintenance techniques for modeling student's behaviour. *Journal of AI and Education* 6(2/3):153-202.

Giangrandi, P., and Tasso, C. (1996). Modeling the temporal evolution of student's knowledge. In Brna, P., Paiva, A., and Self, J., eds., *Proceedings of the European Conference on Artificial Intelligence in Education*. 184-190.

Huang, X. (1994). Modeling a student's inconsistent beliefs and attention. In Greer J. E., and McCalla, G. I., eds. (1994). *Student Modeling: The Key to Individualized Knowledge-Based Instruction*. Springer. 267-279.

Huang, X., McCalla, G. I., Greer J. E., and Neufeld, E. (1991). Revising deductive knowledge and stereotypical knowledge in a student model. *User Modeling and User-Adapted Interaction* 1:87-115.

Kono Y., Ikeda, M. and Mizoguchi, R. (1994). THEMIS: A nonmonotonic inductive student modeling system. *Journal of AI and Education* 5:371-413.

McCarthy, J., and Hayes P. J. (1969). Some philosophical problems from the standpoint of artificial intelligence. Reprinted in Ginsberg, M. L., ed., *Readings in Nonmonotonic Reasoning*. Morgan Kaufmann, 1987. 26-45.

Paiva, A., and Self, J. (1994). A learner model reason maintenance system. In *Proceedings of ECAI '94*.

Paiva, A., Self, J., and Hartley, R. (1994). On the dynamics of learner models. In *Proceedings of ECAI '94*, 163-167.

Reiter, R. (1980). A logic for default reasoning. Ginsberg, M. L., ed., *Readings in Nonmonotonic Reasoning*. Morgan Kaufmann, 1987. 68-93.

Reiter, R., (1987). A theory of diagnosis from first principles. *Artificial Intelligence* 32:57-95.

Van Beek, P., (1990). Reasoning about qualitative temporal information. In *Proceedings of AAAI-90*, 728-734.

Vilain, M., Kautz, H., van Beek, P. (1990). Constraint propagation algorithms for temporal reasoning: A revised report. Reprinted in Weld, D., and de Kleer J., eds., *Readings in Qualitative Reasoning about Physical Systems*. Morgan Kaufmann.

Perspectives

Do We Know What the User Knows, and Does It Matter?
The Epistemics of User Modelling

Michael Ramscar[1,3], Helen Pain[1], and John Lee[2,3]

[1] Department of Artificial Intelligence, University of Edinburgh, Scotland
[2] Human Communication Research Centre, University of Edinburgh, Scotland
[3] Department of Architecture, University of Edinburgh, Scotland

Abstract. Whilst many user models can function perfectly adequately with a behavioural impression of the user, the provision of assistance in some task domains, notably design, requires a richer understanding, incorporating information about the user's knowledge and beliefs. This raises a number of important and difficult questions: How can we know what the user knows, and how can we know that we know? We present evidence that the psychological view of human conceptual knowledge that underpins typical approaches to these questions is flawed. We argue that user knowledge can be modelled, up to a point, but that to ask whether or not we can know what the user knows is to misunderstand the question.

1 What Do We Want to Know?

Many user models can function perfectly adequately with only a behavioural impression of the user: A user's actions can be sufficient input for a system to adapt in order to accommodate the particular needs of a particular user or user type. Even if we include a user's linguistic interaction with a system—in the form of text input—under the heading of "behaviour", then providing that a model can anticipate the form and content of this behaviour, and have some notion of correct versus incorrect manifestations of the behaviour, still there are strategies for modelling such user behaviour in a generalised fashion. Good examples are "buggy" models, such as those developed by Brown and Burton (1978). In some domains (and perhaps in all domains at some times), it is impossible to anticipate the form and content of a user's behaviour. This is especially true of design, where the unpredictability of a designer's behaviour (in the widest possible sense) is perhaps an essential aspect of the activity. Modelling a user's conceptual knowledge raises important questions: How can we know what the user knows; how can we know that we know?

The basic problem facing models of users' conceptual knowledge can be best stated as one of relating the conceptual knowledge of a computer user to corresponding knowledge modelled within the computer (to this extent, modelling a user's concepts deviates little from other user modelling approaches). Since a user's knowledge must be expressed in some kind of external representation for communication with the computer, this is equivalent to the problem of reconciling multiple representations of concepts or objects. Two users might represent an event in their own different ways; the designer of a computer system might represent it a third way.

The weakness of the conceptual models in current techniques in 'knowledge modelling' (ad hoc "generalised" feature decompositions, Ramscar et al., 1996) is unsurprising, given the absence of any convincing psychological model of conceptual categorisation. Development of a psycho-logical model of conceptual categorisation has been fatally hampered by two important, erroneous assumptions: Firstly, categories have often been treated as a rigid, externally imposed phencme-non; secondly, researchers have concentrated upon category representation rather than on the process by which categorisation judgements are made.

This concentration upon category representation is surprising, given Rosch's (1978) theory of prototypical category representations—the basis for much of this work—which argues that: (a) prototypes are best seen metaphorically; what are really referred to are judgements of degrees of prototypicality; and (b) prototypes do not constitute a theory of representation of categories.

We have proposed (Ramscar et al., 1996) an approach to categorisation the focus of which is upon the categorical judgement process rather than on the representation of categories (or category prototypes); focussing on how representations are classified together, rather than specifying the representational form of categories. Research from the study of analogy (which concentrates upon modelling the process whereby two representations are considered analogous) is taken as a starting point for investigating categorical judgements. In doing this we have discarded the distinction between category membership and analogy.

A study by Ramscar and Pain (1996) has shown that where judgements are considered, this distinction does not hold at a cognitive level of description. The study involved giving subjects materials previously used in investigations into analogical similarity (Gentner et al., 1993) and asking them to perform categorisation tasks with them. Subjects' categorisational and analogical judgements utilised the same salient aspects of the representations within the materials, and their judgements of analogical and categorical similarity had a direct congruence, which contradicted previous distinctions between cognitive processes of analogy and categorisation. The removal of this distinction highlighted the parallels to be drawn between models of analogy and categorisa-tion. It is becoming more widely accepted that structure plays a major role in category formation (Goldstone, 1994): Analogical reasoning research addresses a process which reasons amongst structural networks. Forbus et al. (1995) propose the following model of analogical reasoning: (a) Initial selection is dependent upon surface similarity. (b) Analogical similarity is determined by deeper structures.

This is strikingly similar to Medin and Ortony's (1989) proposed knowledge representation scheme for categorisation: (a) The identification procedure is based upon surface features. (b) Classification is determined by deeper structures.

Where research into analogy differs from research into categorisation is in the richness of its process models. A number of detailed, plausible, computationally implementable models of the analogical process exist; the same cannot be said of categorisation. Research in analogy has been far more successful because it has focused upon the analogical process, and the interplay between this process and the representations of analogues (rather than simply determining conditions by which representations might be considered to be analogous). We are now using Gentner's analogy theory to develop an implementable model of the categorisation process.

2   Does It Matter That We May Not Know What We Want to Know?

We have outlined the state of psychological research into categorisation ("conceptualisaticn") and suggested a characterisation of human conceptual judgement that fits the evidence available. Moreover, like Gentner's theory of analogy, it is amenable to computational implementation. Our model makes no distinction between analogical and "literal" conceptual judgements at the cognitive level: Understanding this is essential to understanding human conceptual judgements. Following Wittgenstein (1953), we argue that it is conceptual judgements ("use"), rather than definitive representations which provide the key. Wittgenstein, having demolished the idea of necessary and sufficient conditions for category membership, offers up compelling arguments to believe that "categories" exist insofar as they are used by people, and that they are bounded to the extent to which individuals in a community can agree to boundaries. What is important is not individual representation of "categories", but the alignment, in terms of judgement agreements, between individuals' category representations. It is this alignment between representations that our model aims to capture. According to our model, there is no definitive answer as to whether a given representation is an instance of this or that category. Rather, one must look for an empirical answer: agreements between individuals in a linguistic (conceptual) community. We can show that much of the basis for this agreement stems from structural alignments between individuals' conceptual representations. Our hypothesis is that system representations need not be definitive but rather must function pragmatically. In so far as these representations sufficiently approximate the kind of structure and content representations used by individuals in a given community, they will be able to map and model those human expressions of conceptual knowledge. Such modelling wouldn't enable a system to know what the user knows, nor could it enable it to know that it knew. It might, however, enable it to judge that if some external representations of the user aligned structurally with some of its stored representations, then it could pragmatically attribute certain conceptual knowledge to a user, much as humans do (Wittgenstein, 1953). Having done so, it might then be in a position to respond or adapt to that user knowledge in some useful way.

References

Brown, J. S., and Burton, R. R. (1978). Diagnostic models for procedural bugs in basic mathematical skills. *Cognitive Science* 2:155–192

Forbus K., Gentner, D., and Law, K. (1995). MAC/FAC: A model of similarity based retrieval. *Cognitive Science,* 19:2:141–205

Gentner, D., Ratterman, M., and Forbus, K. (1993). The roles of similarity in transfer. *Cognitive Psychology* 25: 524–575

Goldstone, R. L. (1994). The role of similarity in categorization. *Cognition* 52:125–157.

Medin, D., and Ortony, A. (1989).What is psychological essentialism? In Vosniardou, S., and Ortony, A., eds., *Similarity and Analogical Reasoning*. Cambridge University Press.

Rosch, E. (1978). *Cognition and Categorisation*. Erlbaum.

Ramscar, M., and Pain, H. (1996). Can a real distinction be made between cognitive theories of analogy and categorisation? *Proceedings of the 18th Conference of the Cognitive Science Society*. Erlbaum.

Ramscar, M., Lee, J., and Pain, H. (1996). A cognitively based approach to computer integration for design systems. *Design Studies* 17:4:465–483.

Wittgenstein, L. (1953). *Philosophical Investigations*. Oxford: Blackwell. Translated by Anscombe, G. E. M.

A New View of Interactive Human-Computer Environments

Julita Vassileva

Department of Technical Computer Science, Federal Armed Forces University, Munich, Germany

Abstract. This paper proposes viewing interactive human-computer environments along three orthogonal dimensions: Elements, Processes and Relationships. This view allows us to see in a systematic way some problems of current adaptive systems and to find directions for future development.

1 The EPR View of Interactive Human-Computer Environments

We have recently seen an explosion of adaptive Interactive Human-Computer Environments (IHCE), for example, information retrieval and filtering applications, hypermedia, text and graphic editors, and teaching systems. I feel that there is a need to take a new viewpoint which allows us to integrate most of this work and see it in the light of new theories of learning and cognition and the emerging distributed and networking technologies. I propose viewing IHCE along three orthogonal dimensions: Elements, Processes and Relationships (the *EPR* view). Along each dimension there are categories, which are partially orthogonal. In this way a discrete space is defined in which any system can be classified. Following this view, I define an agent architecture that represents a human or computer system in an IHCE. The main dimensions in the EPR-view are discussed briefly below.

Elements. This dimension refers to the elementary entities about which interaction among the agents takes place. They are: *goals, plans, resources* and *actions*. All agents in an IHCE pursue goals. According to Slade's (1994) goal classification, these can be goals for achievement, preservation, or satisfaction, or crisis-goals, but also duties, tastes and preferences. To achieve goals an agent employs resources, which can be tangible (time, money, credentials, etc.) or cognitive (memory, attention, knowledge and skills). Plans decompose goals into sub-goals which can be achieved by actions and resources. According to Slade's *principle of importance*, an agent will be willing to expend resources to achieve a goal that are proportional to the importance of this goal. We call the motivation of an agent to achieve a goal the *idiosyncratic importance* of this goal for the agent.

Processes. This dimension refers to the processes taking place in an agent. These are: *reaction, reasoning/planning, meta-reasoning/-planning, deciding, meta-deciding, learning* and *meta-learning*. Reaction is achieving a goal with ready (pre-designed or normative) resources or plans. Reasoning is the ability of the agent to generate new plans or to modify existing plans to adapt them for the current goal. Deciding is the ability to choose among conflicting goals. Learning is the ability of the agent to improve its behavior by acquiring new resources, actions, goals, plans. The basic processes (reaction, reasoning, deciding, learning) operate with elements (goals, plans, resources and actions), while the meta-processes operate on basic processes. Meta-reasoning is the ability of the agent to reason about and plan its reasoning process. Meta-decision making is the ability to decide whether to react, reason, or learn. Finally, meta-learning is the ability of the agent to learn how to plan, to decide and to learn (perhaps also meta-reason, meta-decide and meta-learn).

Relationships. This dimension refers to the way the agent interacts with other agents. Agents help each other to achieve their goals, i.e. they adopt each other's goals. An agent can be involved in many relationships with other agents. Each relationship can be classified with respect to several orthogonal sub-dimensions. The *type of agent* shows who is the partner in the relationship: a human user or a computer system. The *type of goal adoption* shows whether the goals that the agent wants to be adopted by the other agent are directly assigned by the agent, inferred by the other agent, or to be developed independently by the other agent (teaching goals). The *symmetry* of the relationship shows the predominant direction of goal-adoptions within this relationship. The *sign* of the relationship shows whether the agents will collaborate (share resources and plans for achieving the same sub-/goals), cooperate (work independently on different sub-goals to achieve the same main goal), compete (for resources in pursuing different goals) or behave adversely (try to block each other's goals).

An agent can apply its processes to influence the inter-agent goal adoption. For example, it can generate a *persuasion* plan for enforcing goal-adoption (teaching strategies in intelligent tutoring systems). It can also reason and infer the goal of the other agent (*diagnosis* of user goals, knowledge state, preferences etc., in adaptive systems).

2   Consequences of the EPR View

From the EPR view of IHCE one can derive the following general architecture of an intelligent communicative agent (see Figure 1). This architecture has the following properties:

- Explicit representation of goals, plans, resources and actions available to the agent.
- Explicit representation of the agent's relationships with other agents and ensuring that all the parameters of the relationship can be manipulated by the agent.
- Internal processes which can be applied to the elements, but also on the parameters of the relationships of the agent and for enforcing inter-agent goal-adoption.

There are several problems of current adaptive IHCEs which could be addressed in a more systematic way in this architecture:

Explicit reasoning about the purpose of adaptation. The system can reason about the importance of the goals adopted from the user directly, the goals inferred from his behavior and the teaching goals which it wants the user to develop. By modifying the parameters "type of goal adoption" and "symmetry" of the relationship between two agents a system can decide whether to adapt, not to adapt, or to teach the user.

Treating users and computer systems as unified agents in a multi-agent environment. Centralized agents called user modeling (UM) brokers can be developed which collect information about normative goals of other agents (applications and users). A UM broker can support cooperation, collaboration, and competition among users and applications. Another type of user model, "UM agents" will learn about their individual users, negotiate with the UM brokers concerning desirable application adaptations, teaching, and possible partners for help or collaboration. UM-agents will collaborate among themselves and compete to get services for their users from the UM broker, while UM brokers will compete among themselves to provide better services.

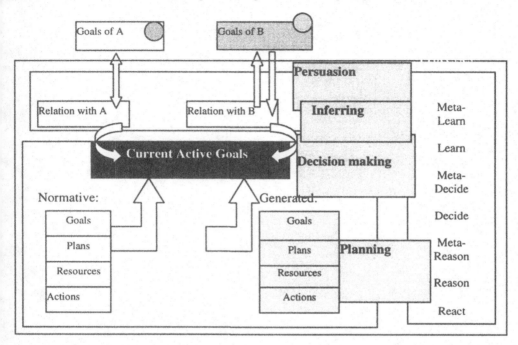

Figure 1. An architecture of an intelligent communicative agent in IHCE.

Taking into account user motivation, emotions, and moods. According to the principle of importance, the motivation can easily be taken into account when reasoning about the relative importance of goals.

Unified model of collaborative, cooperative, competitive, and adverse behavior. A truly adaptive system should be able to modify its type of relationship with the user. The explicit representation of the sign of the relationships will allow the agents to reason and dynamically modify their behavior with respect to other agents.

The EPR view helps to integrate a lot of different research. However, to realize this architecture in a computational framework, one has to find appropriate techniques for reasoning and decision-making, especially with respect to inter-agent relationships.

Reference

Slade, S. (1994) *Goal-Based Decision Making: An Interpersonal Model.* Hillsdale, NJ: Erlbaum.

SPECIAL CONFERENCE SESSIONS

Invited Talks

Agents With Beliefs:
Reflections on Bayesian Methods for User Modeling

Eric Horvitz

Decision Theory and Adaptive Systems Group, Microsoft Research, Redmond, WA, U.S.A.

Uncertainty is inescapable in real-world problem solving, and is particularly salient in attempts to infer the goals and intentions of people. Identifying the goals of users as they interact with computer-based systems, given such evidence as the user's actions and background, and the specific context at hand—and effectively harnessing such information to enhance the quality of human-computer interaction—is typically a challenging problem in decision making under uncertainty.

Significant advances achieved over the last decade in computational methods for learning, representing, and reasoning with uncertain knowledge show promise as a foundation for solving difficult problems in user modeling. The pressure to solve complex, real-world automated reasoning problems has stimulated computer scientists, particularly, those in the Uncertainty in Artificial Intelligence (UAI) subcommunity, to develop approaches to automated inference that build on centuries of achievement in probability theory, and on more recent developments in utility theory. The new methods for encoding knowledge and reasoning under uncertainty have arisen in part from a coupling of methods for assessing and reasoning with probability and utility developed in the Statistics and Decision Analysis (DA) communities with more recent UAI advances in graphical dependency models, including Bayesian networks and influence diagrams.

The relevance of Bayesian networks to user modeling was noticed early on in UAI research. During the mid-1980s, enthusiasm about rule-based production systems led to projects that sensitized many AI researchers to user-modeling concerns. During that time, projects blossomed on the use of production systems for computer-aided instruction, several of which were attempts to transform previously developed diagnostic expert systems into tutoring systems. Interest in user modeling was also stimulated by the goal of extending the capabilities of expert systems to explain complex inference to people with different backgrounds. In addition, a great deal of attention was focused on creating automated "associates" to support complex decision making such as the piloting of fighter planes; many research teams pursued "intent inferencing" systems that could automatically determine the goals and needs of decision makers.

Early work in UAI was framed by pressures to solve problems encountered with attempts to use logical production systems. Moving beyond exploration of how Bayesian models could be used to solve key AI problems with diagnosis of disorders in complex systems, UAI researchers sought to apply Bayesian models to such popular problems of the time as inferring intentions and goals for the computer associate tasks, and pursued such problems as tailoring Bayesian inference and explanation strategies to different classes of users.

In the last five years, interest has been growing steadily in the application of Bayesian representations and inference strategies for modeling the goals and needs of users. These methods are playing an increasingly central role in the User Modeling (UM) community. Bayesian learning and inference hold great promise for use in diagnosing users' goals, recognizing plans, and identifying the best actions to take under uncertainty.

Although methods for automated reasoning under uncertainty have provided investigators interested in user modeling with significant opportunties, they have also brought into focus a spectrum of challenges. I will discuss critical problems and opportunities with developing capabilities for reasoning about a user's intentions and needs under uncertainty. I will touch on technical concerns and issues with implementing and using Bayesian user models that have arisen in the context of several projects over the last decade. I will share experiences gleaned in work on the Pathfinder, Vista, and Lumière projects. All of these projects focused in whole or part on leveraging probabilistic and decision-theoretic user models to enhance human–computer interaction.

Pathfinder was one of the first attempts to demonstrate the ability of rich Bayesian network models to capture complex diagnostic problems. As part of the work on Pathfinder, the core decision-theoretic reasoning methods were extended with user models for tailoring information-gathering and explanation.

The Vista project spawned the creation of the decision-theoretic Vista system that has been used at the NASA Mission Control Center for monitoring the propulsion systems on the Space Shuttle. The work on Vista centered on the modulation of information displayed to users in time-critical, high-stakes decision making. Vista research included the investigation of methods for display management and training based on the concurrent use of distinct Bayesian models of expert and novice beliefs about space shuttle systems.

The Lumière project at Microsoft Research has explored the construction and use of Bayesian user models in software applications. Lumière research has explored methods for identifying the goals of users as they work with software applications. The initial Lumière prototype was completed in 1993 and several generations of systems exploring a variety of extensions have been developed over the last several years. The Lumière protoytpes harness Bayesian inference to generate beliefs about a user's acute and longer-term needs from sequences of a user's actions, program state, and words in a user's query for assistance when such a query is available. Lumière provided the overall architecture and key functionality for the Office Assistant that shipped in Microsoft's Office '97 product line.

I will focus on experiences and technical issues with the development of Lumière and the eventual production of the Office Assistant. I will review the difficulties we faced in building the overall Bayesian Lumière architecture, integrating the Bayesian user modeling with legacy software applications, and transferring the technology to product divisions. I will describe several technical issues including the development and assessment of user models, representation and inference about time-dependent probabilistic relationships, issues with developing and using an event language, and the challenge of innervating software with an event-monitoring system. I will also describe the importance of performing studies with human subjects at different phases of the project and will share video segments of one of our usability studies.

I will conclude by describing several recent efforts to employ probabilistic and decision-theoretic methods for enhancing human-computer interaction and summarize some key long-term opportunities in Bayesian user modeling.

User Interfaces for All:
Developing Interfaces for Diverse User Groups

Constantine Stephanidis

Institute of Computer Science, Foundation for Research and Technology-Hellas (FORTH),
Heraklion, Crete, Greece

Traditionally, adaptive behaviour in human-computer interaction was largely assigned to the human partner, as computer systems did not embody the required sophistication to identify the need for and subsequently implement adaptive behaviour during interaction. As a result, the human operator was required to compensate for the shortcomings of the computer system behaviour and to exhibit the capabilities necessary to accomplish the required tasks. With the emergence of graphical user interfaces, there has been a wide proliferation of lexical technologies incorporating advanced multimedia interaction facilities, novel input/output devices and multi-modal interaction techniques. This has contributed to an ever increasing number of computer users, characterized by their diverse abilities, requirements and preferences. Additionally, the paradigm of usage is progressively shifting from professional/business desktop use to communication-intensive nomadic use. Moreover, the tasks humans have to perform with interactive computer systems have substantially changed in structure and content: They have become more complex and knowledge-demanding.

In the context of the emerging information society, there is a compelling need for comprehensive support for *accessible* and *high-quality* user interfaces. At the core of these two new usability goals is a revised notion of adaptation, according to which user interfaces adapt to different users, different platforms and different styles of interaction. To achieve these goals, the concept of *user interfaces for all* has been proposed following the principles of "design for all" and "universal accessibility". The underlying objective is to ensure accessibility and high quality of interaction by taking into account the individual abilities, requirements and preferences of the user population at large, including disabled and elderly people. In pursuing this goal, it has been necessary to integrate the consolidated results of years of experience and scientific inquiry from various fields of technology. To this end, past experience and recent contributions from the field of user modeling have been particularly useful in driving some relevant development efforts:

Adaptive user interfaces have traditionally been concerned with the coupling of available user interface development systems with tools facilitating the derivation of adaptations based on the monitoring of interaction and assumptions held about the current user. Adaptive user interfaces have been the focal point of concern in a wide variety of research efforts, while several tools have been developed to support adaptive interaction.

- *Adaptable user interfaces* provide tools which allow the user to tailor certain aspects of the interactive system.

- *Model-based interface design* involves the design of user interfaces from a collection of reusable models and knowledge repositories encapsulating a wide variety of details of the user interface design space.
- *Agent-based interaction* entails the use of software agents to delegate responsibility for various aspects of interaction.

Despite the important contributions of the above lines of research on more usable computer-based interactive products, their treatment of accessibility and high quality of interaction has mainly addressed the requirements of the "average" able user. The requirements of disabled and elderly people have been served, until recently, through a reactive *adaptations* approach, whereby dedicated solutions are provided to account for problems introduced by each new generation of technology.

For example, while adaptations had been developed to provide accessibility by blind users to alpha-numerical terminals, the emergence of GUIs and subsequently the WWW caused the same problem of accessibility to appear again, for the same user group. It follows that the adaptations approach, despite the benefits it may bring in the short run, does not serve, either proactively or cost-effectively, the longer-term objectives for user interfaces accessible to *all* users.

Unified user interface development has been defined as a vehicle to serve the goal of user interfaces for all efficiently and effectively. The main objective of this development framework is to support user profile independence, technological platform independence and interaction metaphor independence during the interface development process. In this context, tools supporting the development cycle of unified user interfaces have been developed, collectively constituting the unified user interface development environment.

A *unified interface* comprises a single (i.e. unified) interface implementation, targeted to potentially *all* users. The main properties of a unified interface implementation are: (i) It does not involve any direct "calls" to the target platform(-s) or toolkit(-s); instead, it utilizes specific functionality or tools to connect with the underlying platform(-s) in an independent manner. (ii) It can realise alternative patterns of behaviour, at the lexical, syntactic or semantic levels of interaction, on the basis of externally (to the interface implementation) acquired knowledge (e.g. user abilities, requirements and preferences, task structure) and criteria (e.g. simplicity, error tolerance, direct manipulation, speed). A unified interface implementation can be tailored to the individual user requirements, the interaction facilities of the target platform or toolkit, and to the particular situation of use. A unified interface encompasses alternative dialogue patterns, for different user requirements, while it groups such alternative dialogue patterns together on the basis of an abstraction model. During interaction, abstract dialogues are mapped to physical dialogues on the basis of end-user oriented knowledge; also, knowledge regarding the application domain, design criteria and information about the target platform may be utilized.

The process of developing unified interfaces involves: (i) the realization and incorporation of the necessary run-time physical resources (either knowledge or traditional programming software libraries) for unified interfaces, which are necessary for the transformation of a unified interface into a physical interface instance, given a target user, platform and usage context; and (ii) the utilization of the necessary tools for: (a) the construction of a unified interface as a composition of abstractions at different levels, (b) the manipulation and management of the physical resources, and (c) the establishment of the relationships between the abstractions involved and the available physical resources.

Doctoral Consortium

Plan Processing in User Models

Detlef Küpper

Knowledge-Based Information Systems, University of Konstanz, Germany

Abstract. The goal of this work is a systematic basis for modeling the planned or possible actions taken by the user of a computer system. This type of model should be able to support the recognition of the user's plans as well as the generation of a plan adapted for the user's needs. The paper focuses on the representation of plans and suggests a partition of the user model to separate the user's capabilities from his or her beliefs.

1 Introduction

Within the context of plan processing, *adapted* means that a plan enables a user to reach his goals in the domain, considering the constraints imposed by his specific knowledge and especially his capabilities. Much work has been done in the field of plan recognition (see, e.g., Allen and Perrault, 1980; Carberry, 1990; Kautz, 1991), but the generation of such user-specific plans has been neglected. Nevertheless, plans which enable a user to achieve his goals are essential for online help and assistance systems, and they help make dialog or information systems more cooperative.

This work focuses on the representation of plans in a user model and on the inferences which are needed to generate and present a user-adapted plan. Furthermore it deals with the problem of building and maintaining a user model with respect to plans and how plan recognition will benefit from such a user model. The result of this research will be used to improve the user modeling shell system BGP-MS (Kobsa and Pohl, 1995) with respect to the representation of plans and the inference processes mentioned above. It will be validated by a prototype of an online help system, probably within an office domain comprising a computer network, several operating systems, printers on several floors, and users with various capabilities and needs.

2 Representation of Plans

In this research I follow a terminological approach for the representation of plans: Plan concepts are defined as classes of plans with common features. With respect to the user's knowledge, plan concepts are not distinguished from other concepts in the domain. For example, stereotypes, which represent default knowledge of user groups, may contain such plan concepts. Plan concepts form an abstraction hierarchy which is ordered by subsumption. This is quite common in plan recognition (e.g., Kautz, 1991; Weida and Litman, 1992). Important attributes are preconditions, effects and a decomposition.

To adapt the concepts of plan generation (see, e.g., Fikes and Nilsson, 1971; Penberthy and Weld, 1992) to user-adapted planning, we have to identify actions that the user can carry out. We may use plan concepts if we define the meaning of the attribute's precondition and effect: (1) a user may process an arbitrary instantiation of a plan concept only in situations where all of the plans preconditions are true; (2) a successful execution of a plan instantiation results in an consistent situation containing all specified effects of the plan concept.

Now we may represent the capabilities of a user as set of plan concepts that he is capable of carrying out. Special characteristics of a user that may influence a plan's execution may be represented by constraints (e.g., additional preconditions). As capabilities must be distinguished from knowledge, we must partition the user model (at least) into a belief partition and a capability partition. If a planner uses only plan concepts from a user's capability partition to generate a plan, then the user is capable of processing the complete plan.

3 Decomposition of Plans

A decomposition of a plan concept is a set of (sub)plan concepts with object and time constraints. It describes all possibilities for carrying out an instantiation of the plan concept by processing subplans. In other words, it is a plan description of its plan concept composed of ordered substeps. Such plan descriptions are common in human discourse, and they are convenient for presenting a plan to the user. Note that such a plan description or decomposition also forms a plan concept, one that denotes the set of all instantiations, that fit the description.

Therefore, in general the specification of a decomposition attribute for a plan concept specializes this concept. Alternative executions of a plan concept may be represented by the definition of one specialization of this concept for each alternative with one decomposition each.

This can be exploited to represent a user's knowledge of plan processing. If the belief partition of the user model contains a plan concept without decomposition (neither the plan concept nor one of its specializations has one), this represents the case where the user knows the concept and assumes there is a way of carrying it out, but does not himself know how. If the capability partition contains such a plan concept, this represents the information that the user is capable of processing the plan concept, but it is not known how. This is left to the user whenever the planner generates a plan with such a plan concept.

References

Allen, J. F., Perrault, C. R. (1980). Analyzing intention in utterances. *Artificial Intelligence* 15:143–178.

Carberry, S. (1990). *Plan Recognition in Natural Language Dialogue*. Cambridge, MA: MIT Press.

Fikes, R. E., and Nilsson, N. J. (1971). STRIPS: A new approach to the application of theorem proving to problem solving. *Artificial Intelligence* 2:189–208.

Kautz, H. A. (1991). A formal theory of plan recognition and its implementation. In Allen, Kautz, Pelavin and Tenenberg, eds., *Reasoning about Plans*. San Mateo, CA: Morgan Kaufmann. 69–126.

Kobsa, A., and Pohl, W. (1995). The user modeling shell system BGP-MS. *User Modeling and User-Adapted Interaction* 4: 59–106.

Penberthy, J. S., and Weld, D. S. (1992). UCPOP: A sound, complete, partial order planner for ADL. In *Principles of Knowledge Representation and Reasoning—Proceedings of the 3rd International Conference KR92*, 103–114.

Weida, R., and Litman, D. (1992). Terminological reasoning with constraint networks and an application to plan recognition. In *Principles of Knowledge Representation and Reasoning—Proceedings of the Third International Conference KR92*, 282–293.

Intelligent Help Through Shared Understanding

Gerhard Peter

Research Institute for Applied Knowledge Processing (FAW),
University of Ulm, Germany

Abstract. Modern computer systems are becoming increasingly complex. On the one hand this is a consequence of the extensive functionality needed to execute complex tasks. On the other hand users have various problems in using these systems. This research will investigate how a *shared understanding* between user and system of the task at hand can mitigate these problems.

1 Introduction

Modern computer systems are becoming increasingly complex, often as a consequence of the extensive functionality needed to execute complex tasks. However, users have various problems in using these systems. For example, often users cannot combine, adapt, and modify tools according to their specific needs (Fischer and Reeves, 1992).

The main topic to be addressed over the course of this research is to show how such problems can be mitigated by a *shared understanding* of the task at hand. To develop a shared understanding means that a user and a system come to an agreement about what the task at hand is. On the basis of this understanding the system provides help on what course of action to take, what tools to use, and—if necessary—how to adapt these tools.

The focus will be on environments which offer a user tools that can be combined flexibly ("workbenches" or "suites").

The concepts developed will be validated with examples taken from IPQM, an information system for preventive quality management. IPQM is a workbench comprising of several tools which provide mechanical engineers with quality relevant information during product design.

2 Background

In cooperative problem solving, the user and the system share the problem solving and decision making (Fischer and Reeves, 1992). *Critics* provide situation-specific feedback. However, this feedback often does not take the task at hand into account, i.e. the advice appears to be unspecific, or even worse, redundant.

Wizards in Microsoft programs also provide help on how to proceed. However, they don't take the user's previous experiences into account, and their help is restricted to specific tools, i.e., they cannot advise users on how to combine tools.

3 Methodology

The principal steps to be taken are the development of scenarios, the design of knowledge bases, implementation, and experiments.

Development of scenarios. Scenarios will be developed that demonstrate how a shared understanding between user and system can be achieved. *Activity theory* (for an overview see, e.g., Kaptelinin et al., 1995) provides a suitable background for these scenarios. The main reasons why it is suitable are: Tool mediation is one of its basic principles and the social context of task execution is taken into account.

Design of knowledge bases. It is assumed that the system has to be provided with information concerning the domain, potential tasks a user can perform, methods to cope with these tasks, and available tools and what they can be used for. The latter is called a *tool model* and is an extension to existing approaches, e.g. in Knowledge Level Modeling (Steels, 1993). In order to tailor the advice given to the user's level of experience a user model should be employed.

Ontologies restrict the vocabulary used to describe the models. Not only the designers can access these ontologies but also the users themselves, for example, in order to capture the design rationale of tool adaptations (cf. Luke et al., 1997). Ontologies also provide the foundation for the dialog between the user and the system.

Implementation. The next step is to modify IPQM accordingly, i.e. the appropriate models for tasks, tools, and users have to be implemented. The domain model is already part of IPQM.

User tests. The system will be given to a number of users who will conduct various (predetermined) tasks from preventive quality management which require the combination and/or adaptation of tools. During task execution the users will be asked to think aloud. The experimenter will take notes and provide help if necessary. The measure for the utility of the approach will be the number and the severity of the problems encountered by the users.

4   Conclusion

Modern computer systems are becoming increasingly complex and thus more difficult to use. On the basis of a shared understanding of the task at hand between user and system, the system can provide help on what to do next, what tools to use and how to adapt these tools. The research attempts to give answers to the following questions:

- What are the benefits of achieving a shared understanding?
- Do the benefits of a shared understanding outweigh the efforts?
- Can the results be generalized, i.e. transferred to other domains?

References

Fischer, G., and Reeves, B. N. (1992). Beyond intelligent interfaces: Exploring, analyzing and creating success models of cooperative problem solving. *Applied Intelligence* 1:311–332.

Kaptelinin, V., Kuutti, K., and Bannon, L. (1995). Activity theory: Basic concepts and applications. In Blumenthal, B., Gornostaev, J., and Unger, C., eds. *Proceedings of the 5th East-West Conference on Human-Computer Interaction (EWHCI '95)*, 189–201.

Luke, S., Spector, L., Rager, D., and Hendler, J. (1997). Ontology-based web agents. In *Proceedings of the First International Conference on Autonomous Agents (AA '97)*.

Steels, L. (1993). The componential framework and its role in reusability. In David, J.-M., Krivine, J.-P., and Simmons, R., eds. (1993). *Second Generation Expert Systems*. Berlin: Springer. 273–298.

Global and Analytical Approaches to Variability for the Design of Complex Systems: The Case of Air Traffic Control

Olivier Pierret

CENA, Athis-Mons, France
CNAM, Paris, France

Abstract. The research presented here deals with an ergonomic project concerning the problems of validation in the design of new working aids or systems for air traffic controllers. A differential ergonomic approach based on the study of variability and representativeness in air traffic control is intended to help with the design of more flexible and user-adapted tools.

1 Introduction

1.1 Work Situations Studied

In France, air traffic control (ATC) is ensured by five regional navigation centers (CNRAs), whose role is to provide a safe and efficient air traffic flow. Each of them is divided into specific portions of air space called *sectors* with limits in the horizontal and vertical planes.

At each control position, two controllers—the Executive Controller (EC) and the Planning Controller (PC)—guide flight evolution in a sector according to a theoretical task division which can vary in practice depending on the work situation.

1.2 Research Issues

The current challenges addressed in most of the studies and projects in CENA concern the problem of deciding whether a designed aiding tool corresponds with the characteristics of controllers, work situations and activities and if it will allow controllers to manage air traffic in optimal conditions. An important variability exists in ATC (among controllers, work situations and activity), and there is a need to work out knowledge and formalized methods to facilitate the taking into account of these aspects of variability during the design process. For this reason, two studies are being proposed at the same time (cf. Section 2.2) with the objective of trying to understand and to explain aspects of variability in order to solve the problems of representativeness.

2 Theoretical and Methodological Aspects

2.1 Theoretical Studies of Variability and Design

A bibliographic analysis of studies being conducted which is oriented towards various fields: ergonomics, work psychology, differential psychology and human-machine interface design. Studies referring to variability in operators' activity often concern situations that are far removed from the context of ATC. Therefore, research mentions more variability in terms of inter-individual differences and intra-individual variations than variability of activities depending on factors related to the work situation or to the operators themselves.

For the design of aiding tools, the objective of studying variability is to provide not a model of the operator but models of operators involved in an activity that depends on the characteristics of the situation (for example, changes in the process to be controlled or in the execution of an activity...).

2.2 Methodological Aspects

Two approaches are being adopted in this effort to study variability in ATC :
  – A global approach based on interviews with air traffic controllers in several CNRAs. These interviews are conducted in a working context outside of activity. The aim of this approach is to describe variability and to explain factors from the controllers' point of view.
  – An analytical approach consisting in the analysis of controllers' activity at a position. In this research, the analysis of activity will be centred on task sharing between the EC and the PC on a control position.

3   Variability vs. Stability in the Evolution of Complex Systems

The first data analyses based on the interviews show several things:

  – Studying variability requires a consideration of the stability of the activity as well.
  – The operators' activity evolves. This evolution is caused by human, organisational and technical factors. It has a significant influence on the variability of activity. In fact, the modification of the previous factors leads to the emergence or disappearance of new variability in the activity of the operators.
  – Variability can appear on an individual level or on a collective level, in a specific work situation or a set of work situations, involving the whole control activity or a specific task inside this activity.

4   Long-Term Objectives of This Research

The global model is intended to yield knowledge about variability in ATC. It should orient future studies toward aspects of variability and underline the importance of variability in some aspects of ATC activity and thus the necessity of taking variability into account.

The analytical model is intended to guide the design process. It should yield a representation of what happens in real work situations concerning the dynamic task sharing between the EC and the PC and what variables have to be taken into account during design. It could also bring solutions concerning the important points on which we have to focus when experimenting with or evaluating a new aiding tool (e.g., what types of situation to examine and which controllers).

Security and Privacy Issues in User Modeling

Jörg Schreck

GMD FIT, Human-Computer Interaction Research Department,
St. Augustin, Germany

Abstract. Shared user models and user models maintained through networks pose threats
to system security and the privacy of the user. This work proposes policies of data usage
and models for user-centered control of access to user models which enable user modeling
systems to take into account both heterogeneous user demands and legal constraints.

1 Introduction

Most currently implemented systems that employ a user model work on a local computing base
(e.g., a personal computer). Information gathered about the user of the system resides locally
on this base and is often encoded in the application maintaining the model. By that means,
unintended but effective restrictions to the dissemination of items of the user model have been
established. The trend in the design of new user modeling systems toward (network) connectivity
and standardized content abolishes these immanent borders.

Data about the usage of specific systems that are related to an identifiable person have to
be treated in a special manner, and sometimes legal constraints must be taken into account. The
inclusion of sensitive data usually restricts the treatment to a rigid range of utilization. Accepting
this challenge entails various extensions that have to be made to current user modeling systems.

2 Proposed Research

On the basis of identified user demands, legal constraints, and ethical guidelines, policies for the
use of personal data in user modeling are laid down and proposed for discussion. In accordance
with these policies, access control models are developed, implemented in a prototype, and evaluated. In order to be able to put emphasis on the development of the access control model (cf.
Sandhu, 1996), the employment of existing user modeling (shell) systems is planned.

Basic cryptographic techniques will be incorporated to provide system security. Advanced
techniques (e.g., for authentication and anonymity) will be examined with respect to improvements in privacy and possibly included. The results of research on distributed trusted systems is
considered from the point of view of user modeling, and relevant achievements are integrated into
a user modeling framework. The use of extensive communication facilities, including distributed
objects technology, should provide a maximum of connectivity and flexibility in order to meet
the requirements of networks.

Besides the technical aspects, content-related issues will be addressed. Regarding a multi-
purpose user model, a common terminology and protocol must be established in order to serve
different applications. Arrangements for the collaborative maintenance of such a user model by
different applications have to be made. Means have to be supplied which enable the user to control

and modify the rules of collaboration (e.g., the access control model) and even the content of the user model. Therefore an intelligible user interface has to be developed allowing the inspection and modification of the content as well as the access criteria.

3 Methodology

An investigation of user modeling (shell) systems and user modeling applications is currently being carried out. This investigation centers on privacy and security aspects of design and implementation of these systems and applications. On the basis of an initial requirements specification, induced by literature and standards in familiar fields, strengths and weaknesses are pointed out and discussed. On the basis of these findings, the inclusion of necessary and useful mechanisms into one system is envisaged. A discussion of the proposed means of user influence should clarify users' rights with respect to their models, estimate users' demands and awareness, and show the limits of users' collaboration in the maintenance of the model. An evaluation of the resulting implementation should allow an assessment of the initial requirements specification and summarize the benefits in the form of guidelines.

4 Current Status and Envisaged Implementations

Two implementations are envisaged. The first consists of extensions of the AVANTI system as described by Fink et al. (1997) and enhancement of the user modeling shell system BGP-MS (Kobsa and Pohl, 1995) with mechanisms supporting security and privacy. By putting the privacy policies offered by the AVANTI system at users' disposal, a dialog between users and information providers concerning privacy issues in user modeling should be initiated. The progress of this dialog should continuously foster improvements of the proposed policies.

The results of this implementation are intended to support a second implementation which focuses on the interface between user modeling components and their clients. This implementation should enable the users to specify distinct access constraints on their user model according to their attitude toward privacy and security.

References

Fink, J., Kobsa, A., and Schreck, J. (1997). Personalized hypermedia information provision through adaptive and adaptable system features: User modeling, privacy and security issues. To appear in: *Proceedings of the Fourth International Conference on Intelligence in Services and Networks*. Springer.

Kay, J. (1995). The um toolkit for cooperative user modelling. *User Modeling and User-Adapted Interaction* 3:149-196.

Kobsa, A., and Pohl, W. (1995). The user modeling shell system BGP-MS. *User Modeling and User-Adapted Interaction* 2:59-106.

Orwant, J. (1995). Heterogeneous Learning in the Doppelgänger user modeling system. *User Modeling and User-Adapted Interaction* 2:107-130.

Sandhu, R. (1996). Access control: The neglected frontier. In Pieprzyk, J., and Seberry, J., eds., *Proceedings of the First Australasian Conference on Information Security and Privacy*. Springer. 219-227.

Using a Semantic User Model to Filter the World Wide Web Proactively

Joep Simons*

Nijmegen Institute for Cognition and Information, University of Nijmegen, The Netherlands

Abstract. The research in this paper aims at using world knowledge to aid the user in retrieving information from the World Wide Web. Some issues are identified together with methods to address them.

1 Introduction

Information retrieval systems are consulted to meet an information need. First, users must translate their internal representation of the information need to a query the system understands. Second, the system must match the queries of the users with the stored characterizations of the documents in a fixed archive. An information *filtering* system deals with a user's information need that is relatively stable over time. This is represented by a *user profile*. A profile is used to filter a rapidly changing archive by viewing it as a stream of documents. Finally, a *proactive* filter continually *searches* a rapidly changing archive for documents that match the user profile.

The PROFILE project (`http://www.cogsci.kun.nl/~profile`) develops a proactive information filter for the World Wide Web, which will use linguistic and AI techniques to improve the quality of the document retrieval and the presentation of the document. My PhD research focuses on a component which maintains a model of the user's information need in a specific domain.

2 Issues

Developing an explicit model of a user's information need addresses the following issues:

1. What kind of support should this model give? The research aims at a system which improves the user's satisfaction by two mechanisms: First, by providing an extra filter to remove documents which have undesirable characteristics. For instance, they might be too long, or too technical. Second, by using semantic expansion. By this, we mean inferring concepts that are semantically related to the contents of a query. This can be used to enrich queries made by the user in order to enable the following:

Improving precision. The system can add other terms in a query from the user to cover the context of its meaning. This can improve the percentage of relevant retrieved documents. An example might be the addition of terms like *rails* or *locomotive* after the user queries for *train station*.

---

* This PhD project was initiated and still is inspired by my supervisor Eduard Hoenkamp.

Improving information need coverage. The concepts conveyed by a user query express a vague information need. Expanding these concepts will make it more likely that every aspect of this information need is captured.

Pointing the user to related information. The system may expand and search for these expansions autonomously. For instance, it might retrieve a document about *magnetic trains* if a user shows an interest in *high speed trains*.

2. What aspects of an information need should be represented? A distinction can be made between topics of interest and situational factors. The first term refers to the concepts which are part of the information need. The latter provides a context for a specific information need, for instance, the type of knowledge requested or the background knowledge of the user.

3. How to represent domain information? The system will initially help the user on only one domain (e.g., trains). At the moment we explore the use of the *Stanford Ontology Server* (Rice et al., 1996), which provides collaborative building of knowledge, the option to convert an ontology into a different language, and an interface to let programs access ontologies on the server autonomously.

4. How to infer aspects of an information need? If not provided directly by a user, these aspects should be estimated from other sources. Some considered sources of information are:

Documents read by the user: The system can monitor the user's browsing through World Wide Web. Acceptance of a document by the user can be measured explicitly, by an option in the interface, or implicitly, e.g., by measuring reading time.

Clicking behavior: This can be used, for instance, to estimate the user's browsing strategy or reading capacity.

Information from the group the user belongs to: Information from this group can be used to estimate properties about which the system has no initial information.

5. How to deal with the ambiguity of the actions of the user in regard to the estimation of the information need? Because of this ambiguity, the system should have a way to deal with conflicting hypotheses. As possible formalisms we consider fuzzy logic, Bayesian networks, and Dempster-Shafer theory (cf. Jameson, 1996).

References

Jameson, A. (1996). Numerical uncertainty management in user and student modeling: An overview of systems and issues. *User Modeling and User-Adapted Interaction* 5:193–251.

Rice, J., Farquhar, A., Piernot, P., and Gruber, T. (1996). Using the web instead of a window system. In *Proceedings of CHI'96 Conference on Human Factors in Computing Systems*, 103–110.

Student Modelling for Operational Skill Training in Air Traffic Control

Kalina Yacef

Thomson Radar Australia Corp., Australia, and Laboratoire d'Intelligence Artificielle de Paris 5, France

Abstract. Current student modelling techniques cannot be applied directly to operational training on simulators in complex and dynamic worlds such as Air Traffic Control because of the lack of appropriate expert models and time constraints. The objective of this research is to present a student modelling approach for individualising the simulation training that (1) is specific to operational skill training, (2) can rely on a realistic expert model, and (3) can be used as a basis for a cognitive assessment of the learning.

We are concerned here with the problem of assessing the student for operational skill training in dynamic and highly risky domains, such as Air Traffic Control (ATC) or nuclear plant operations. The aim of this assessment is to derive guidelines for defining the next training exercise in a simulation-based intelligent tutoring system (ITS).

In most ITSs, the student is evaluated on his knowledge (declarative or procedural), not on his operational skills, which are the ability to use these two types of knowledge in a timely, accurate manner, and the ability to cope with dynamic problem solving situations involving multiple activities and goals. Little work has been done in the domain of student modelling for operational skill training. Since a complete model of the domain knowledge is not available for ATC operational training, student modelling techniques are not directly applicable. The training system we are aiming at keeps the human instructor in the loop and assists him in monitoring and evaluating the student and in designing follow-up exercises rather than replacing him totally.

1 Proposed Approach

We propose to use a bi-dimensional student model composed of performance measures and corresponding context, and then to analyse this data using theories of cognitive development to assess the learning and derive the guidelines for the next exercise.

Bi-dimensional student model. This model contains for each task a list of performance indicators captured with their context. The performance measures represent objectively how well the student performed, and the context provides elements to analyse this performance.

Performance measures. These concern the accuracy, speed, and sometimes quality of strategy (economy and efficiency) of each particular task being practiced (Yacef and Alem, 1996).

Context. This is seen here as the pertinent information of the training exercises that can be used for assessing the learning. Interviews with ATC instructors and literature research in ATC training lead us to consider the context as parameters of the traffic situation, fatigue generated by the exercise, and current workload (Regan and Schneider, 1990).

Towards a cognitive assessment of skill acquisition. The concepts introduced by Regian and Schneider (automated and controlled processes), or by Boy (1991), offer a suitable framework for structuring and evaluating the various stages of skill development. To acquire each skill, the student needs to go through the following steps:

1. Practice in a number of situations requiring this particular skill. During this phase the learner constructs situation patterns

2. Exercise this skill under high resource load. Here the student learns to automate the skill by executing other tasks simultaneously and under stress conditions.

We propose here to reason about the set of performance measures according to elements of the context to assess the level of skill acquisition and determine when to move onto a higher level of practice.

Construction of situation patterns. At this stage the idea is to see whether the student has faced and reacted well and quickly to the variety of situations presented. The accuracy measures are related to safety and must be good, whilst the speed performances reflect more on the acquisition process. Once the accuracy and speed general tendencies have been identified, a diagnosis about the construction of situation patterns can be made as well as the decision to move onto a higher level of practice.

Automaticity. The level of automaticity on a particular task can be measured by observing the impact of an increased resource load on the student's performances. When the student's performance on a task is consistent across all the situations (which is given by the previous assessment), the resource load can be raised gradually, up to the threshold indicated by the ATC curriculum (different for each task). If the performance is maintained, it can be assumed that the student has reached an adequate level of automaticity for this particular task. In this case, new topics can be presented to the student according to the curriculum.

2   Evaluation

This approach is currently being implemented and will be evaluated experimentally for validity and reliability using Mark and Greer's (1993) guidelines. The validity will be tested by comparing system output with diagnostic information obtained from human instructors. The reliability will be tested by comparing information obtained from similar sessions. The implications of this work for ATC training will also need to be analysed, particularly for the formalisation of instruction, the productivity of human resources and the quality of the training.

References

Boy, G. A. (1991). *Intelligent Assistant Systems*. Academic Press.

Mark, M. A., and Greer, J. E. (1993). Evaluation methodologies for intelligent tutoring systems. *Journal of AI and Education*, 4:129-153.

Regian, J. W., and Schneider, W. (1990). Assessment procedures for predicting and optimising skill acquisition after extensive practice. In Frederiksen, N., Glaser, R., Lesgold, A., and Shafto, M., eds., *Diagnostic Monitoring of Skill and Knowledge Acquisition*. Hillsdale, NJ: Erlbaum,.

Yacef, K., and Alem, L. (1996). Student and expert modelling for simulation-based training: A cost effective framework. In *Proceedings of the Third International Conference on Intelligent Tutoring Systems*.

AUTHOR INFORMATION

Author Addresses

Irina Akoulchina
LAFORIA-IBP-CNRS
Université Paris VI
4, place Jussieu
75252 Paris Cedex 05
France
akoul@laforia.ibp.fr

David W. Albrecht
Department of Computer Science
Monash University
Clayton, Victoria 3168
Australia
dwa@cs.monash.edu.au

Leonardo Ambrosini
Dipartimento di Informatica e Automazione
Università di Roma Tre
Via della Vasca Navale 84
00146 Roma
Italy
ambrosin@inf.uniroma3.it

John Anderson
Department of Computer Science
University of Manitoba
Winnipeg, MB
Canada R3T 2N2
andersj@cs.umanitoba.ca

David Arnott
Department of Information Systems
Monash University
PO Box 197, Caulfield East, VIC 3145
Australia
david.arnott@is.monash.edu.au

William H. Bares
Multimedia Laboratory
Department of Computer Science
North Carolina State University
Raleigh, NC 27695-8206
U.S.A.
whbares@eos.ncsu.edu

Rob Barrett
IBM Almaden Research Center
650 Harry Rd, NWED-B2
San Jose, CA 95120
U.S.A.
barrett@almaden.ibm.com

Joseph Beck
Center for Knowledge Communication
Department of Computer Science
University of Massachusetts
Amherst, MA 01003-4610
U.S.A.
beck@cs.umass.edu

Eftihia Benaki
Institute of Informatics &
Telecommunications
153 10 Aghia Paraskevi
Athens
Greece

Akshat Bhatnagar
Human Computer Interaction Institute
School of Computer Science
Carnegie Mellon University
Pittsburgh, PA 15213
U.S.A.
ab75+@andrew.cmu.edu

Peter Brusilovsky
Human Computer Interaction Institute
School of Computer Science
Carnegie Mellon University
Pittsburgh, PA 15213
U.S.A.
plb@cs.cmu.edu

Ariel Bud
Department of Computer Science
Monash University
Clayton, Victoria 3168
Australia
bud@cs.monash.edu.au

Susan Bull
The Language Centre
University of Brighton
Falmer, Brighton
East Sussex BN1 9PH
UK
s.bull@brighton.ac.uk

Frada Burstein
Department of Information Systems
Monash University
PO Box 197, Caulfield East, VIC 3145
Australia
frada.burstein@is.monash.edu.au

Sandra Carberry
Department of Computer Science
University of Delaware
Newark, Delaware 19716
U.S.A.
carberry@cis.udel.edu

Paul Chandler
The University of New South Wales
School of Education Studies, UNSW
Sydney
Australia, 2052

Bark Cheung Chiu
School of Computing and Mathematics
Deakin University
Geelong, 3217
Australia
chiu@deakin.edu.au

Vincenzo Cirillo
Dipartimento di Informatica e Automazione
Università di Roma Tre
Via della Vasca Navale 84
00146 Roma
Italy
cirillo@inf.uniroma3.it

John R. Clarke M.D.
Department of Surgery
Allegheny Univ. of the Health Sciences
Philadelphia, PA 19129
U.S.A.
jclarke@gradient.cis.upenn.edu

Jason A. Collins
ARIES Laboratory
Department of Computer Science
University of Saskatchewan
Saskatoon, Saskatchewan S7N 5A9
Canada
jac140@cs.usask.ca

Cristina Conati
University of Pittsburgh
Learning Research and Development Center
3939 O'Hara St.
Pittsburgh, PA 15260
U.S.A.
conati@isp.pitt.edu

Albert T. Corbett
Human Computer Interaction Institute
School of Computer Science
Carnegie Mellon University
Pittsburgh, PA 15213
U.S.A.
corbett+@cmu.edu

Berardina De Carolis
Dipartimento di Informatica
Università di Bari
Via Orabona, 4
70126 Bari
Italy
nadja@aos2.uniba.it

Chrysanne DiMarco
Department of Computer Science
University of Waterloo
Waterloo, Ontario N2L 3G1
Canada
cdimarco@logos.uwaterloo.ca

Gitta Domik
Department of Computer Science
University of Paderborn
Fürstenallee 11
D-33102 Paderborn
Germany
domik@uni-paderborn.de

Anne-Claude Doux
Laboratoires d'Electronique Philips S.A.S.
B.P. 15, 22 avenue Descartes
94453 Limeil-Brevannes
France
doux@lep.research.philips.com

Marek Druzdzel
University of Pittsburgh
Learning Research and Development Center
3939 O'Hara St.
Pittsburgh, PA 15260
U.S.A.
marek@sis.pitt.edu

Alistair D. N. Edwards
Department of Computer Science
University of York
York YO1 5DD
Great Britain
alistair@cs.york.ac.uk

Mark Evans
Department of Computer Science
University of Manitoba
Winnipeg, MB
Canada R3T 2N2
evans@cs.umanitoba.ca

Josef Fink
GMD
Institute for Applied Information
Technology (FIT)
D-53754 Sankt Augustin
Germany
josef.fink@gmd.de

Jean-Gabriel Ganascia
LAFORIA-IBP-CNRS
Université Paris VI
4, place Jussieu
75252 Paris Cedex 05
France
ganascia@laforia.ibp.fr

Abigail Gertner
University of Pittsburgh
Learning Research and Development Center
3939 O'Hara St.
Pittsburgh, PA 15260
U.S.A.
gertner+@pitt.edu

Paolo Giangrandi
Dipartimento di Matematica e Informatica
Università di Udine
via delle Scienze 206
I-33100 Udine
Italy
giangran@dimi.uniud.it

Piotr J. Gmytrasiewicz
Department of Computer Science and
Engineering
University of Texas at Arlington
Box 19015, Arlington, TX 76019
U.S.A.
piotr@cse.uta.edu

Marco Gori
Dipartimento di Ingegneria
dell'Informazione
Università di Siena, Via Roma 56
53100 Siena
Italy
marco@ing.unisi.it

Floriana Grasso
Department of Computing & Electrical
Engineering
Heriot-Watt University – Riccarton
Edinburgh EH14 1AH
UK
floriana@cee.hw.ac.uk

Jim E. Greer
ARIES Laboratory
Department of Computer Science
University of Saskatchewan
Saskatoon, Saskatchewan S7N 5A9
Canada
greer@cs.usask.ca

Jon Atle Gulla
Norwegian University of Science and
Technology (NTNU)
N-7034 Trondheim
Norway
jag@idt.ntnu.no

Bernd Gutkauf
C-Lab, Siemens Nixdorf
University of Paderborn
Fürstenallee 11
D-33094 Paderborn
Germany
gutkauf@c-lab.de

Steve Hanks
Department of Computer Science and
Engineering, Box 352350
University of Washington
Seattle, WA 98195
U.S.A.
hanks@cs.washington.edu

Graeme Hirst
Department of Computer Science
University of Toronto
Toronto, Ontario M5S 3G4
Canada
gh@cs.utoronto.ca

Eric Horvitz
Microsoft Research
9 South
Redmond WA 98052-6399
U.S.A.
horvitz@microsoft.com

Eduard Hovy
USC / Information Sciences Institute
4676 Admiralty Way
Marina del Rey, CA 90292
U.S.A.
hovy@isi.edu

Jörg Höhle
GMD
Institute for Applied Information
Technology (FIT)
D-53754 Sankt Augustin
Germany
joerg.hoehle@gmd.de

Roger I. W. Spooner
Department of Computer Science
University of York
York YO1 5DD
Great Britain
riws@cs.york.ac.uk

Mitsuru Ikeda
ISIR Osaka University
8-1 Mihogaoka
Ibaraki
Osaka 567
Japan
ikeda@ei.sanken.osaka-u.ac.jp

Anthony Jameson
Department of Computer Science
University of Saarbrücken
P.O. Box 151150
66041 Saarbrücken
Germany
jameson@cs.uni-sb.de

Michelle Joab
LAFORIA
Université Paris 6
case courrier 169, 4 place Jussieu
75252 Paris cedex 05
France
joab@laforia.ibp.fr

Osamu Kakusho
Faculty of Economics and Information
Science, Hyogo University
2301, Shin-zaike, Hiraoka-machi
Kakogawa, Hyogo 675-01
Japan
kakusho@humans-kc.hyogo-dai.ac.jp

Slava Kalyuga
The University of New South Wales
School of Education Studies, UNSW
Sydney
Australia, 2052
s.kalyuga@unsw.edu.au

Vangelis A. Karkaletsis
Institute of Informatics &
Telecommunications
153 10 Aghia Paraskevi
Athens
Greece

Alfred Kobsa
GMD
Institute for Applied Information
Technology (FIT)
D-53754 Sankt Augustin
Germany
alfred.kobsa@gmd.de

Vive S. Kumar
ARIES Laboratory
Department of Computer Science
University of Saskatchewan
Saskatoon, Saskatchewan S7N 5A9
Canada

Mark Kuzmycz
School of Computing and Mathematics
Deakin University
Geelong, 3217
Australia
kuzmycz@deakin.edu.au

Detlef Küpper
University of Konstanz
Knowledge Based Information Systems
P.O.Box 55 60 – D92
D-78434 Konstanz
Germany
detlef.kuepper@uni-konstanz.de

Jean-Philippe Laurent
Laboratoires d'Electronique Philips S.A.S.
B.P. 15, 22 avenue Descartes
94453 Limeil-Brevannes
France
laurent@lep.research.philips.com

John Lee
Human Communication Research Centre
University of Edinburgh
Scotland
john@cogsci.ed.ac.uk

Neal Lesh
Department of Computer Science and
Engineering, Box 352350
University of Washington
Seattle, WA 98195
U.S.A.
neal@cs.washington.edu

James C. Lester
Multimedia Laboratory
Department of Computer Science
North Carolina State University
Raleigh, NC 27695-8206
U.S.A.
lester@adm.csc.ncsu.edu

Greg Linden
Department of Computer Science and
Engineering, Box 352350
University of Washington
Seattle, WA 98195
U.S.A.
glinden@cs.washington.edu

José Gabriel Lopes
Departamento de Informática
Universidade Nova de Lisboa
2825 Monte da Caparica
Portugal
@di.fct.unl.pt

Marco Maggini
Dipartimento di Ingegneria
dell'Informazione
Università di Siena, Via Roma 56
53100 Siena
Italy
maggini@ing.unisi.it

Paul P. Maglio
IBM Almaden Research Center
650 Harry Rd, NWED-B2
San Jose, CA 95120
U.S.A.
pmaglio@almaden.ibm.com

Enrico Martinelli
Dipartimento di Ingegneria
dell'Informazione
Università di Siena, Via Roma 56
53100 Siena
Italy
enrico@ing.unisi.it

Gordon I. McCalla
ARIES Laboratory
Department of Computer Science
University of Saskatchewan
Saskatoon, Saskatchewan S7N 5A9
Canada
mccalla@cs.usask.ca

Michael F. McTear
School of Information and Software
Engineering, Univ. of Ulster
Newtownabbey
Co. Antrim BT37 OQB
N. Ireland
mf.mctear@ulst.ac.uk

Paul Meagher
ARIES Laboratory
Department of Computer Science
University of Saskatchewan
Saskatoon, Saskatchewan S7N 5A9
Canada
meagher@cs.usask.ca

Alessandro Micarelli
Dipartimento di Informatica e Automazione
Università di Roma Tre
Via della Vasca Navale 84
00146 Roma
Italy
micarel@inf.uniroma3.it

Maria Milosavljevic
MRI Language Technology Group
Macquarie University
Sydney NSW 2109
Australia
mariam@mpce.mq.edu.au

Riichiro Mizoguchi
ISIR Osaka University
8-1 Mihogaoka
Ibaraki
Osaka 567
Japan
miz@ei.sanken.osaka-u.ac.jp

Claudine Moinard
LAFORIA
Université Paris 6
case courrier 169, 4 place Jussieu
75252 Paris cedex 05
France
moinard@laforia.ibp.fr

Maureen Murphy
School of Information and Software
Engineering, Univ. of Ulster
Newtownabbey
Co. Antrim BT37 OQB
N. Ireland
m.murphy@ulst.ac.uk

Jean-Pierre Nadal
Laboratoire de Physique Statistique
Ecole Normale Superieure
24 rue Lhomond
75231 Paris cedex 05
France
nadal@lep.research.philips.com

Ann E. Nicholson
Department of Computer Science
Monash University
Clayton, Victoria 3168
Australia
annn@cs.monash.edu.au

Andreas Nill
GMD
Institute for Applied Information
Technology (FIT)
D-53754 Sankt Augustin
Germany
andreas.nill@gmd.de

Sanguk Noh
Department of Computer Science and
Engineering
University of Texas at Arlington
Box 19015, Arlington, TX 76019
U.S.A.
noh@cse.uta.edu

Helen Pain
University of Edinburgh
Department of Artificial Intelligence
80 South Bridge
Edinburgh EH1 1HN
Scotland
helen@aisb.ed.ac.uk

Priyanka Paranagama
Department of Information Systems
Monash University
PO Box 197, Caulfield East, VIC 3145
Australia
priyanka@is.monash.edu.au

Cécile Paris
CSIRO Mathematical and Information
Sciences
Locked Bag 17
North Ryde, NSW 2113
Australia
cecile@syd.dit.csiro.au

Kimberley Parsons
Department of Computer Science
University of Waterloo
Waterloo, Ontario N2L 3G1
Canada
kjparsons@neumann.uwaterloo.ca

Gerhard Peter
Research Institute for Applied Knowledge
Processing
P.O.Box 2060
D-89010 Ulm
Germany
gerhard@faw.uni-ulm.de

Olivier Pierret
CENA
Orly Sud 205
94542 Orly Aérogare Cedex
France
pierret@cena.dgac.fr

Sebastiano Pizzutilo
Dipartimento di Informatica
Università di Bari
Via Orabona, 4
70126 Bari
Italy
pizzutil@aos2.uniba.it

Wolfgang Pohl
GMD
Institute for Applied Information
Technology (FIT)
D-53754 Sankt Augustin
Germany
wolfgang.pohl@gmd.de

Paulo Quaresma
Departamento de Informática
Universidade Nova de Lisboa
2825 Monte da Caparica
Portugal
pq@di.fct.unl.pt

Michael Ramscar
Department of Architecture
University of Edinburgh
Scotland
michael@dai.ed.ac.uk

Tefko Saracevic
School of Communication, Information and
Library Studies
Rutgers University
New Brunswick, NJ 08903
U.S.A.
tefko@scils.rutgers.edu

Jörg Schreck
GMD
Institute for Applied Information
Technology (FIT)
D-53754 Sankt Augustin
Germany
joerg.schreck@gmd.de

Elmar Schwarz
Department of Psychology
Carnegie Mellon University
Pittsburgh, PA 15213
U.S.A.
eschwarz@andrew.cmu.edu

Ralph Schäfer
Department of Computer Science
University of Saarbrücken
P.O. Box 151150
66041 Saarbrücken
Germany
ralph@cs.uni-sb.de

Kazuhisa Seta
ISIR Osaka University
8-1 Mihogaoka
Ibaraki
Osaka 567
Japan
seta@ei.sanken.osaka-u.ac.jp

Joep Simons
NICI, University of Nijmegen
Spinoza Building Room B.00.98
P.O. Box 9104
6500 HE Nijmegen
The Netherlands
simons@nici.kun.nl

Matt Smith
School of Computer Science
Middlesex University
Bounds Green Road
London N11
UK
m.r.smith@mdx.ac.uk

Murray Sneesby
Department of Computer Science
University of Manitoba
Winnipeg, MB
Canada R3T 2N2

Marcus Specht
Department of Psychology
University of Trier
D-54286 Trier
Germany
specht@cogpsy.uni-trier.de

Amanda Spink
School of Library and Information Science
University of North Texas
P.O. Box 13796
Denton TX 76203
U.S.A.
spink@lis.admin.unt.edu

Constantine D. Spyropoulos
Institute of Informatics &
Telecommunications
153 10 Aghia Paraskevi
Athens
Greece
costass@iit.nrcps.ariadne-t.gr

Christopher Staff
Department of Computer Science and AI
University of Malta
Tal-Qroqq, Msida MSD 06
Malta
cstaff@cs.um.edu.mt

Adelheit Stein
GMD-IPSI
Dolivostraße 15
D-64293 Darmstadt
Germany
stein@darmstadt.gmd.de

Constantine Stephanidis
Institute of Computer Science, FORTH
Science and Technology Park of Crete
Vassilika Vouton, P.O.Box 1385
GR 711 10 Heraklion, Crete
Greece
cs@csi.forth.gr

Mia Stern
Center for Knowledge Communication
Department of Computer Science
University of Massachusetts
Amherst, MA 01003-4610
U.S.A.
stern@cs.umass.edu

Linda Strachan
Department of Computer Science
University of Manitoba
Winnipeg, MB
Canada R3T 2N2
strachan@cs.umanitoba.ca

John Sweller
The University of New South Wales
School of Education Studies, UNSW
Sydney
Australia, 2052
j.sweller@unsw.edu.au

Carlo Tasso
Dipartimento di Matematica e Informatica
Università di Udine
via delle Scienze 206
I-33100 Udine
Italy
tasso@dimi.uniud.it

Ulrich Thiel
GMD-IPSI
Dolivostraße 15
D-64293 Darmstadt
Germany
thiel@darmstadt.gmd.de

Stefanie Thies
Department of Computer Science
University of Paderborn
Fürstenallee 11
D-33102 Paderborn
Germany
thiesana@uni-paderborn.de

Ray Tkatch
Regional Psychiatric Centre (Prairies)
P.O. Box 9243
Correctional Services Canada
Saskatoon, Saskatchewan S7K 3X5
Canada

Shari Trewin
University of Edinburgh
Department of Artificial Intelligence
80 South Bridge
Edinburgh EH1 1HN
Scotland
shari@aisb.ed.ac.uk

Kurt VanLehn
University of Pittsburgh
Learning Research and Development Center
3939 O'Hara St.
Pittsburgh, PA 15260
U.S.A.
vanlehn+@pitt.edu

Julita Vassileva
Universität der Bundeswehr München
Institut für Technische Informatik
D-85577 Neubiberg
Germany
jiv@informatik.unibw-muenchen.de

Geoffrey I. Webb
School of Computing and Mathematics
Deakin University
Geelong, 3217
Australia
webb@deakin.edu.au

Gerhard Weber
Department of Psychology
University of Trier
D-54286 Trier
Germany
weber@cogpsy.uni-trier.de

Thomas Weyrath
Department of Computer Science
University of Saarbrücken
P.O. Box 151150
66041 Saarbrücken
Germany
tom@cs.uni-sb.de

Beverly Park Woolf
Center for Knowledge Communication
Department of Computer Science
University of Massachusetts
Amherst, MA 01003-4610
U.S.A.
bev@cs.umass.edu

Mei-Mei Wu
Department of Social Education
National Taiwan Normal University
Taipei
Taiwan, R.O.C.

Kalina Yacef
Thomson Radar Australia Corporation
Locked bag 17
North Ryde 2113 NSW
Australia
kalina@syd.dit.csiro.au

Ingrid Zukerman
Department of Computer Science
Monash University
Clayton, Victoria 3168
Australia
ingrid@cs.monash.edu.au

Author Index

Printed in the United States
By Bookmasters